T0201302

SIMULATION AND COMPUTATIONAL RED TEAMING FOR PROBLEM SOLVING

SIMULATION AND COMPUTATIONAL RED TEAMING FOR PROBLEM SOLVING

Jiangjun Tang
School of Engineering and Information Technology
University of New South Wales Canberra

George Leu
School of Engineering and Information Technology
University of New South Wales Canberra

Hussein A. Abbass
School of Engineering and Information Technology
University of New South Wales Canberra

 IEEE Press Series on Computational Intelligence

IEEE PRESS

WILEY

Published by John Wiley & Sons, Inc., Hoboken, New Jersey.
Published simultaneously in Canada.

For general information on our other products and services or for technical support, please contact our Customer Care Department within the United States at (800) 762-2974, outside the United States at (317) 572-3993 or fax (317) 572-4002.

Wiley also publishes its books in a variety of electronic formats. Some content that appears in print may not be available in electronic formats. For more information about Wiley products, visit our web site at www.wiley.com

Library of Congress Cataloging-in-Publication data is available.

Hardback ISBN: 978-1-119-52717-6

Set in 10/12pt TimesLTStd-Roman by SPi Global, Pondicherry, India

Printed in the United States of America

V10014618_102819

CONTENTS

Preface   xi
List of Figures   xv
List of Tables   xxv

PART I   ON PROBLEM SOLVING, COMPUTATIONAL RED
         TEAMING, AND SIMULATION   1

1.   Problem Solving, Simulation, and Computational Red Teaming   3

     1.1   Introduction   3
     1.2   Problem Solving   4
     1.3   Computational Red Teaming and Self-'Verification and
           Validation'   8

2.   Introduction to Fundamentals of Simulation   11

     2.1   Introduction   11
     2.2   System   14
     2.3   Concepts in Simulation   17
     2.4   Simulation Types   21
     2.5   Tools for Simulation   23
     2.6   Conclusion   24

PART II   BEFORE SIMULATION STARTS   25

3.   The Simulation Process   27

     3.1   Introduction   27
     3.2   Define the System and its Environment   27
     3.3   Build a Model   29
     3.4   Encode a Simulator   30
     3.5   Design Sampling Mechanisms   32
     3.6   Run Simulator Under Different Samples   33
     3.7   Summarise Results   33
     3.8   Make a Recommendation   34

3.9 An Evolutionary Approach 35
3.10 A Battle Simulation by Lanchester Square Law 35

4. Simulation Worldview and Conflict Resolution 57

4.1 Simulation Worldview 57
4.2 Simultaneous Events and Conflicts in Simulation 64
4.3 Priority Queue and Binary Heap 68
4.4 Conclusion 72

5. The Language of Abstraction and Representation 73

5.1 Introduction 73
5.2 Informal Representation 75
5.3 Semi-formal Representation 76
5.4 Formal Representation 82
5.5 Finite-state Machine 86
5.6 Ant in Maze Modelled by Finite-state Machine 89
5.7 Conclusion 99

6. Experimental Design 101

6.1 Introduction 101
6.2 Factor Screening 103
6.3 Metamodel and Response Surface 113
6.4 Input Sampling 116
6.5 Output Analysis 117
6.6 Conclusion 120

PART III   SIMULATION METHODOLOGIES 121

7. Discrete Event Simulation 123

7.1 Discrete Event Systems 123
7.2 Discrete Event Simulation 126
7.3 Conclusion 142

8. Discrete Time Simulation 143

8.1 Introduction 143
8.2 Discrete Time System and Modelling 145
8.3 Sample Path 148
8.4 Discrete Time Simulation and Discrete Event Simulation 149
8.5 A Case Study: Car-following Model 151
8.6 Conclusion 154

9. Continuous Simulation   **157**

   9.1   Continuous System   157
   9.2   Continuous Simulation   159
   9.3   Numerical Solution Techniques for Continuous Simulation   164
   9.4   System Dynamics Approach   172
   9.5   Combined Discrete–continuous Simulation   174
   9.6   Conclusion   176

10. Agent-based Simulation   **179**

   10.1   Introduction   179
   10.2   Agent-based Simulation   181
   10.3   Examples of Agent-based Simulation   185
   10.4   Conclusion   194

**PART IV   SIMULATION AND COMPUTATIONAL
            RED TEAMING SYSTEMS**   **197**

11. Knowledge Acquisition   **199**

   11.1   Introduction   199
   11.2   Agent-enabled Knowledge Acquisition: Core Processes   202
   11.3   Human Agents   203
   11.4   Human-inspired Agents   208
   11.5   Machine Agents   211
   11.6   Summary Discussion and Perspectives on Knowledge
            Acquisition   215

12. Computational Intelligence   **219**

   12.1   Introduction   219
   12.2   Evolutionary Computation   223
   12.3   Artificial Neural Networks   232
   12.4   Conclusion   239

13. Computational Red Teaming   **241**

   13.1   Introduction   241
   13.2   Computational Red Teaming: The Challenge Loop   242
   13.3   Computational Red Teaming Objects   243
   13.4   Computational Red Teaming Purposes   244
   13.5   Objectives of Red Teaming Exercises in Computational Red
            Teaming Purposes   245
   13.6   Discovering Biases   246

13.7 Computational Red Teaming Lifecycle: A Systematic Approach
       to Red Teaming Exercises   247
13.8 Conclusion   251

PART V   SIMULATION AND COMPUTATIONAL RED
          TEAMING APPLICATIONS   253

14. **Computational Red Teaming for Battlefield Management**   **255**

    14.1 Introduction   255
    14.2 Battlefield Management Simulation   256
    14.3 Conclusion   261

15. **Computational Red Teaming for Air Traffic Management**   **263**

    15.1 Introduction   263
    15.2 Air Traffic Simulation   263
    15.3 A Human-in-the-loop Application   270
    15.4 Conclusion   271

16. **Computational Red Teaming Application for Skill-based Performance**
    Assessment   **273**

    16.1 Introduction   273
    16.2 Cognitive Task Analysis-based Skill Modelling and Assessment
           Methodology   274
    16.3 Sudoku and Human Players   276
    16.4 Sudoku and Computational Solvers   280
    16.5 The Proposed Skill-based Computational Solver   283
    16.6 Discussion of Simulation Results   293
    16.7 Conclusions   300

17. **Computational Red Teaming for Driver Assessment**   **301**

    17.1 Introduction   301
    17.2 Background on Cognitive Agents   303
    17.3 The Society of Mind Agent   306
    17.4 Society of Mind Agents in an Artificial Environment   312
    17.5 Case Study   325
    17.6 Conclusion   330

18. **Computational Red Teaming for Trusted Autonomous Systems**   **333**

    18.1 Introduction   333
    18.2 Trust for Influence and Shaping   334
    18.3 The Model   335

18.4 Experiment Design and Parameter Settings 342
18.5 Results and Discussion 344
18.6 Conclusion 347

A. Probability and Statistics in Simulation 349

A.1 Foundation of Probability and Statistics 349
A.2 Useful Distributions 369
A.3 Mathematical Characteristics of Random Variables 390
A.4 Conclusion 396

B Sampling and Random Numbers 397

B.1 Introduction 397
B.2 Random Number Generator 400
B.3 Testing Random Number Generators 408
B.4 Approaches to Generating Random Variates 413
B.5 Generating Random Variates 416
B.6 Monte Carlo Method 423
B.7 Conclusion 432

Bibliography 435

Index 459

■■■■ PREFACE

Problem solving is a skill and a process that underpins every aspect of daily life. Problems exist when there is a gap between what we wish to achieve (goal state) and what we currently have (current state). Problem solving bridges this gap by creating the steps, including the processes, algorithms, heuristics, methods, and methodologies, to assist humans and machines to reach their desired goal states. This book presents two core and complementary problem-solving technologies: simulation and computational red teaming (CRT).

Simulation offers a systematic way to understand the system, while CRT creates a powerful environment to understand the interaction space between the system, its environment and its operating contexts. The wide spectrum of opportunities and benefits from using CRT ranges from discovering vulnerabilities to discovering real opportunities to improve the efficiency of the system. Simulation is the reproduction of the behaviour of a system using a model. It transforms our understanding of a system into a model that captures those important elements and relationships in the system and ignores those insignificant factors that could confuse our understanding of the core problem at hand or unnecessarily complicate the model. It mechanises the model into a simulator that could be a software only or a software–hardware environment, parameterises the model with data from the real system or at least from our understanding of it to make it more realistic, samples contexts and scenarios to evaluate the model and explore its behavioural space, and summarises the results into trends to inform decision makers of what to expect. When we loop over this linear sequence many times, we create a powerful tool to understand the system under scrutiny. When augmented with appropriate machine learning to learn trends in the system and optimisation tools to identify appropriate courses of actions, the overall system becomes a living CRT machine capable of thinking with humans, or on its own, to make decisions.

Simulation has been widely used in various areas, including but not limited to engineering, physics, economics, cognitive and behavioural psychology, and social sciences. Today, simulators exist virtually everywhere and for everything. They are used to teach medical students and train pilots, as predictive tools for the mining industry, as a way to understand social influence, as a test and evaluation tool for cyber-security, and as the 'computational brainstorming machine' inside an artificial intelligence agent that needs to think for itself.

Simulation can be achieved using pencil and paper or using a computer. The latter is known as computer-based simulation, and is the context of this book.

This book evolved from the joined experience of the authors gained after many years of teaching different modelling and simulation subjects for undergraduate and postgraduate students, combined with long research activity in computational intelligence, which employed advanced simulation methods and methodologies. This book is the result of the above teaching and research experience, combined with consistent research and practitioner work on CRT.

The book describes simulation in a crescendo that moves from the foundations and the process of building a simulation to computational intelligence aspects that take the simulation topic towards contemporaryuses. The series of CRT examples provides a scene where the fundamentals and advanced topics in simulation meet to solve models of contemporary and complex real-world problems. The multifaceted nature of the book makes it didactic and systematic, yet also creative and enquiring.

For both the novice and the expert in simulation, the book brings the simulation field down to the basics through a systematic presentation of the fundamentals, while steering the interest into questioning how the complexity of this world can be better grasped through using contemporary approaches such as CRT.

The book is structured in five parts, followed by an appendix.

Part I contains two chapters: 'Problem Solving, Simulation, and Computational Red Teaming' and 'Introduction to Fundamentals of Simulation'. The first chapter establishes the motivation and the context of the book, and presents the concept of computer simulation within the larger context of problem solving and concept development. The chapter presents the current issues related to computer simulation and the biases accumulated because of the different evolution of the concept in various fields of activity and applications, emphasising the aspects that are fundamental to computer simulation and common to its application in different domains. The second chapter describes a general framework for the process of building a simulation, and then briefly discusses how real-world phenomena can be modelled and how these models can be investigated through simulation.

Part II provides a detailed treatment of the science underpinning computer imulation, describing the fundamental elements of the process of building and using models and simulations. Thus, this part is organised in four chapters, as follows. The first chapter, 'The Simulation Process' describes the sequence of activities involved in building and using a computer simulation. The remaining three chapters reiterate at a higher level of detail those parts of the simulation process that are paramount for establishing and performing a good quality simulation. The names of these chapters denote those parts:'Simulation Worldview and Conflict Resolution', 'The Language of Abstraction and Representation', and 'Experimental Design'.

Part III describes the main approaches to modelling real-world phenomena and embedding these models into computer simulations – approaches that are based on how these phenomena are viewed by the designers. This part is organised in four chapters, with each chapter describing one fundamental type of simulation, based on the modelling approach: 'Discrete Event Simulation', 'Discrete Time Simulation', 'Continuous Simulation', and 'Agent-based Simulation'.

Part IV takes a step away from the level of simulation methods and presents a service view, which describes a number of advanced artificial intelligence and computational intelligence topics that use simulation as a service to solve real-world problems. These topics, denoted by the names of the chapters, are: 'Knowledge Acquisition', 'Computational Intelligence', and 'Computational Red Teaming'.

Part V is dedicated to examples in which the CRT methodology is instantiated using computer simulation. This part bridges the fundamentals of simulation from Part II and Part III with the advanced topics from Part IV and the motivation of the book presented in Part I, with the purpose of demonstrating how computer simulation and the CRT methodology complement each other to solve complex real-world problems.

To support the reader in the endeavour of understanding both the foundation and the advanced topics in computer simulation, the appendix presents basic materials on probabilities, and then introduces an important set of materials for any simulation course on 'sampling and random numbers'. Only those concepts that are strictly related to the core of the simulation process are presented.

The book targets a broad audience, from the novice to the expert. The book is deliberately structured with consideration of the traditional university semester, where 12 to 14 weeks allow undergraduate students to attend roughly 13 full two-hour lectures per subject. From a teaching perspective, the book is a useful syllabus, with 14 theoretical chapters that suit the lectures during a semester (Parts I, II, III, and IV) and a practical section (Part V) that can provide materials either to complement activities in the laboratory or as the basis for a course on simulation application.

Expert readers can benefit from both the discussions on fundamentals and discussions on advanced topics and applications. The discussion on fundamentals contributes to the disambiguation of the computer simulation concept, and confirms and consolidates best practices, while the discussion on advanced topics – including CRT applications – brings valuable insights and raises opportunities. Finally, when a book is published, it represents the start of another learning journey for the authors when they receive feedback and comments. We welcome comments and look forward to hearing from the readership of the book. We have also created a website populated with slides and examples that we hope will be useful for lecturers and students alike. The website can be found at http://www.husseinabbass.com/SimulationBook/.

Jiangjun Tang, George Leu, and Hussein A. Abbass
Canberra, Australia

Figure 2.1   The system of a vehicle, the sub-system of an engine, and their corresponding boundaries and entities (not all entities are shown here).   16

Figure 2.2   Relationship between resolution, abstraction, and fidelity (adapted from [3]).   20

Figure 2.3   An example of elevator modelling and simulation.   22

Figure 3.1   The steps to develop a simulation.   28

Figure 3.2   Time-advancing mechanism: next-event time advancing and fixed-increment time advancing.   31

Figure 3.3   An example plotting a differential equation and difference equation.   40

Figure 3.4   Blue force level calculated by difference equations with fighting effectiveness in different magnitudes with the same ratio 4 : 1 for blue to red. Fighting effectiveness: $\alpha_b = 0.4$ and $\alpha_r = 0.1$.   41

Figure 3.5   Blue force level calculated by difference equations with fighting effectiveness in different magnitudes with the same ratio 4 : 1 for blue to red. Fighting effectiveness: $\alpha_b = 0.12$ and $\alpha_r = 0.03$.   42

Figure 3.6   The flowchart of a battle simulator – simulator advanced by time.   43

Figure 3.7   The flowchart of a battle simulator – simulator advanced by fire rounds.   44

Figure 3.8   The parameters of LSL declared in a spreadsheet.   45

Figure 3.9   The spreadsheet implementation of LSL based on time.   47

Figure 3.10   The spreadsheet implementation of LSL based on rounds.   47

Figure 3.11   The bell curves of troop sizes: $\mu_B = 1000, \sigma_B = 100$ and $\mu_R = 1200, \sigma_R = 200$.   48

Figure 3.12   The bell curves of fighting effectiveness: $\mu_B = 0.8, \sigma_B = 0.05$ and $\mu_R = 0.6, \sigma_R = 0.1$.   49

Figure 3.13   The CDF of troop sizes: $\mu_B = 1000, \sigma_B = 100$ and $\mu_R = 1200, \sigma_R = 200$.   50

Figure 3.14 The bell curves of fighting effectiveness: $\mu_B = 0.8, \sigma_B = 0.05$ and $\mu_R = 0.6, \sigma_R = 0.1$. 50

Figure 3.15 An implementation of data sampling. 51

Figure 3.16 An implementation of data sampling. 52

Figure 3.17 The force levels of both sides in a battle, where $B_0 = 1034, \alpha_b = 0.749$, $R_0 = 1460$, and $\alpha_r = 0.373$. 54

Figure 4.1 Three traditional simulation worldviews of DES. 59

Figure 4.2 Time advancing in event-scheduling worldview. 59

Figure 4.3 Time advancing in activity-scan worldview. 60

Figure 4.4 The process flow of a grocery shop register. 61

Figure 4.5 Time advancing in process-interaction worldview. 62

Figure 4.6 Time advancing in three-phase worldview. 63

Figure 4.7 Time advancing in agent-oriented worldview. 63

Figure 4.8 Horizontal event list versus vertical event list. 65

Figure 4.9 The effects from FEL data structure and event storing order for the bank account example. 66

Figure 4.10 The binary heap constructed based on the event priorities. 69

Figure 4.11 Obtain and delete the event with the highest priority (lowest key) from the root location of a binary heap, and update node positions accordingly. 70

Figure 4.12 Inserting a new event into a binary heap and reordering the node positions. 71

Figure 5.1 Abstraction – the modelling process. 74

Figure 5.2 An abstract example of a data flow diagram. 76

Figure 5.3 An abstract example of an entity-relationship diagram. 77

Figure 5.4 An abstract example of a class diagram. 77

Figure 5.5 Simple FSM model for a traffic light. 78

Figure 5.6 State transition diagram for traffic light. 78

Figure 5.7 Flowchart building blocks and their meanings. 79

Figure 5.8 Flowchart modelling the determination of a car insurance premium. 80

Figure 5.9 Decision tree modelling for determining a car insurance premium. 82

Figure 5.10 Improved FSM model for a traffic light. 87

Figure 5.11 An ant in a maze. 89

Figure 5.12 'LOST' state – an ant walks forward until hitting a wall. 90

Figure 5.13   'ENCW' (encountering a wall) state – an ant keeps turning left until neither antenna touches a wall.   91

Figure 5.14   An ant walks along the wall by checking if the wall is on its right.   92

Figure 5.15   An ant encountering a wall break or turning corner when walking along the wall on the right side.   93

Figure 5.16   An optimised FSM for modelling ant behaviour to find the way out of a maze.   94

Figure 5.17   A NetLogo implementation of the FSM simulator for modelling an ant's behaviours to find the way out of a maze.   97

Figure 5.18   Simulation results of an ant's behaviours to find the way out of a maze.   98

Figure 6.1   Flowchart of the OFAT process for N factors in a model.   104

Figure 6.2   The main effect calculation by design matrix.   107

Figure 6.3   Calculation of two-factor interaction between Factors 1 and 2 using design matrix.   108

Figure 6.4   Calculation of three-factor interaction between Factors 1, 2, and 3 using design matrix.   109

Figure 6.5   Response surface and contour plot for the metamodel.   115

Figure 6.6   Hypothesis test methods for two or more groups of variables (adapted from [372]).   118

Figure 6.7   Transient and steady-state behaviour of a simulation model.   119

Figure 6.8   A long series of outputs divided into batches.   119

Figure 7.1   A simple queueing system with a single queue and single server.   125

Figure 7.2   Next-event time-advance approach for the single-server queueing system of the mechanical centre.   129

Figure 7.3   Flowchart for a next-event time-advance approach and logical relationships among the components and routines of the simulator for DES.   131

Figure 7.4   FSM of the mechanical support centre driven by client arrival and client departure events.   132

Figure 7.5   Intervals for U and X, inverse transformation for exponential distribution.   135

Figure 7.6   Example of generating U, interval between arrivals (I), and arrival times (a) by Excel.   136

Figure 7.7   Flowchart for arrival event routine.   137

Figure 7.8   Flowchart for departure event routine.   138

Figure 8.1   Discrete time system – input, output, and state.   146

Figure 8.2   Examples of sample path of sheep population.   148

Figure 8.3   A DES approach for the vending machine by FSM.   149

Figure 8.4   A DTS approach for the vending machine represented by flowchart.   150

Figure 8.5   A DTS based on the GM car-following model.   153

Figure 8.6   Speed and acceleration of the following vehicle in the first 50 s produced by DTS based on the GM model.   154

Figure 8.7   Distance between the leading and following vehicles in the first 50 s produced by DTS based on the GM model.   154

Figure 9.1   Velocity of a car starting from rest and speeding up to 20 m/s.   158

Figure 9.2   Velocity of a car that starts from 'stopped' and speeds up to 20 m/s, using a difference equation with $\Delta t = 0.5$.   162

Figure 9.3   Velocity of a car that starts from 'stopped' and speeds up to 20 m/s using a difference equation: $\Delta t = 0.2$.   163

Figure 9.4   Constant acceleration: $a = 2$.   165

Figure 9.5   Variable acceleration described by a Sigmoid function: $a = \frac{2}{1+e^{-t}}$.   166

Figure 9.6   Euler's method for integration of the ordinary differential equation $\frac{dv}{dt}$.   167

Figure 9.7   Euler's method for velocity approximation using different time steps.   169

Figure 9.8   The approximation of velocity using Euler, midpoint and Runge–Kutta 4 methods.   171

Figure 9.9   The approximation of velocity using Euler, midpoint and Runge–Kutta 4 methods – the first five seconds.   171

Figure 9.10   Stock and flow chart for the Lanchester equations.   173

Figure 9.11   The results of a Lanchester battle model using a system dynamics approach in NetLogo ($B(0) = 1034$, $\beta = 0.749$, $R(0) = 1460$ and $\alpha = 0.373$).   174

Figure 9.12   The results of a Lanchester battle model using an Excel spreadsheet ($B(0) = 1034$, $\beta = 0.749$, $R(0) = 1460$, and $\alpha = 0.373$).   175

Figure 10.1   Agent elements and its interactions with other agents and the environment.   182

Figure 10.2   Topologies for agent interaction space.   184

Figure 10.3   ABS of *Life* – the cell states evolve from a random initialisation.   186

Figure 10.4   ABS of *Flocking* – motions of bird flock at different time steps.   188

Figure 10.5   Results from the wolf–sheep predation model with default settings – population size over time.   190

Figure 10.6   Results from the wolf–sheep predation model with slow grass growth rate – population sizes over time.   191

Figure 10.7   The initial state of the social event simulation with 50 agents and a state afterwards.   192

Figure 10.8   Interesting network structures of agent connections.   193

Figure 11.1   KA in relation to various types of systems.   201

Figure 11.2   KA – architectural schema.   204

Figure 11.3   Human agent methods mapped on the KA process: solid line – ample coverage, dashed line – limited coverage.   205

Figure 11.4   Human-inspired agent methods mapped on the KA process: solid line – ample coverage, dashed line – limited coverage.   209

Figure 11.5   Machine agent methods mapped to the KA process: solid line – ample coverage, dashed line – limited coverage.   214

Figure 11.6   The proposed agent perspective: the data size – analysis/representation trade-off.   215

Figure 11.7   A potential three-tier classification: the autonomy – negotiation trade-off.   216

Figure 12.1   Stage 1 – basic steps of modelling and simulation.   220

Figure 12.2   Stage 2 – real system and simulation behaviour data mining.   220

Figure 12.3   Stage 3 – optimisation loop for effects, shaping, and control on the real world.   221

Figure 12.4   Stage 4 – answering questions for the real world.   222

Figure 12.5   Stage 5 – model adaptation to system and environment changes.   222

Figure 12.6   General framework of an EA.   226

Figure 12.7   Examples of chromosomes in various forms of representation.   227

Figure 12.8   Roulette selection in GA.   229

Figure 12.9   Rank selection in GA.   230

Figure 12.10   Single point and two-point crossover in GA.   231

Figure 12.11   Three-stage view of the human brain.   234

Figure 12.12   An artificial neuron.   235

Figure 12.13   The threshold activation function in an artificial neuron.   236

Figure 12.14   The Sigmoid activation function in an artificial neuron.   237

Figure 12.15   Single-layer feed-forward ANN.   238

Figure 12.16   Multi-layer feed-forward ANN.   238

Figure 12.17   Recurrent ANN.   238

Figure 13.1   The CRT loop.   243

Figure 14.1   WISDOM-II. Simulation run example.   259

Figure 14.2   WISDOM-II. Top layer.   260

Figure 14.3   WISDOM-II – overall architecture.   260

Figure 15.1   Agent-based model of an aircraft in ATOMS.   264

Figure 15.2   Visualisation of a simulated scenario using ATOMS – main screen of ATOMS.   265

Figure 15.3   Visualisation of a simulated scenario using ATOMS – ATC.   265

Figure 15.4   Visualisation of a simulated scenario using ATOMS – terminal management area.   266

Figure 15.5   Visualisation of a simulated scenario by ATOMS – pilot cockpit and control. These studies can be undertaken in this simulated environment without touching the real-world system.   266

Figure 15.6   Architecture of TOP-LAT.   267

Figure 15.7   Modules in the core system.   268

Figure 15.8   The situation awareness client of TOP-LAT.   269

Figure 15.9   Client for aviation emissions.   269

Figure 15.10   Client for ATC task load.   270

Figure 15.11   The adaptive logic of the real-time EEG-based augmented cognition system.   271

Figure 16.1   The game knowledge.   277

Figure 16.2   Naked candidates.   278

Figure 16.3   Hidden candidates.   279

Figure 16.4   The skill model.   283

Figure 16.5   The Sudoku solving process.   285

Figure 16.6   The deep neural network for acquisition of skills – architectural schema.   286

Figure 16.7   The same network size for skill acquisition at all levels.   287

Figure 16.8   The deep neural network for acquisition of skills – detailed architecture.   288

Figure 16.9   Training the scanning skill.   290

Figure 16.10   Neural network input.   291

Figure 16.11   Acquisition of scanning skills – various levels of proficiency.   294

Figure 16.12   Acquisition of recognition sub-skills – various levels of proficiency.   295

Figure 16.13   Acquisition of propagation sub-skills – various levels of proficiency.   295

Figure 16.14 Scanning skills training (neural network with 100 differ-ent seeds): 'full' = beginner level $(1 \times BPSP)$; 'dotted' = intermediate level $(2 \times BPSP)$; 'dashed' = advanced level $(5 \times BPSP)$.   296

Figure 16.15 Recognition skills training (neural network with 100 different seeds): 'full' = beginner level $(1 \times BPSP)$; 'dotted' = intermediate level $(2 \times BPSP)$; 'dashed' = advanced level $(5 \times BPSP)$.   297

Figure 16.16 Propagation skills training (neural network with 100 different seeds): 'full' = beginner level $(1 \times BPSP)$; 'dotted' = intermediate level $(2 \times BPSP)$; 'dashed' = advanced level $(5 \times BPSP)$.   297

Figure 16.17 Various levels of Sudoku proficiency for the corresponding levels of primitive-skill proficiency.   299

Figure 16.18 Resultant Sudoku solving proficiency for three levels of aggregated skill proficiency.   299

Figure 17.1   SoM general architectural schema.   309

Figure 17.2   RRA SoM architectural schema with inclusion of innate biases and behavioural propensities.   312

Figure 17.3   Current vehicle c and its possible neighbours.   313

Figure 17.4   Normally distributed values for each personality trait of individuals within a population of drivers.   315

Figure 17.5   Traffic measures for various population sizes: average travel time (t_T), average speed (v_A), travel time index (TTI), total delay (D).   317

Figure 17.6   Decision type (internal agency activation) ratio $< v. >$ population size: □ = affective decision ratio, ∘ = rational decision ratio, Δ = reactive decision ratio.   318

Figure 17.7   Traffic motif ratio per driver population for various population sizes.   319

Figure 17.8   Traffic measures for homogeneous populations with various behavioural patterns: average travel time (t_T), average speed (v_A), travel time index (TTI), total delay (D).   320

Figure 17.9   Decision type for homogeneous populations with various behavioural patterns: □ = affective decision ratio, ∘ = rational decision ratio, Δ = reactive decision ratio.   321

Figure 17.10 Traffic motif ratio per driver population for various population sizes.   321

Figure 17.11 Traffic measures for homogeneous populations with various behavioural patterns: average travel time (t_T), average speed (v_A), travel time Index (TTI), total delay (D).   323

Figure 17.12 Decision type for homogeneous populations with various behavioural patterns: □ = affective decision ratio, ∘ = rational decision ratio, Δ = reactive decision ratio. 324

Figure 17.13 Traffic motif ratio per driver population for various population sizes. 325

Figure 17.14 Spatial distribution of average speed, $\sigma = 0.7$ (realistic Australian population): streets with speed limits of 60, 70 and 80 km/h; darker grey dot colours = higher average speeds (black lines = rail network). 327

Figure 17.15 Spatial distribution of average speed, $\sigma = 0.1$ (homogeneous population): streets with speed limits of 60, 70 and 80 km/h; darker grey dot colours = higher average speeds (black lines = rail network). 327

Figure 17.16 Spatial distribution of average speed, $\sigma = 1.0$ (heterogeneous population): streets with speed limits of 60, 70 and 80 km/h; darker grey dot colours = higher average speeds (black lines = rail network). 328

Figure 17.17 Average speed probability per network for the whole range of heterogeneity: $\sigma \in (0; 1]$. 329

Figure 17.18 Average speed per network for the whole range of heterogeneity: $\sigma \in (0; 1]$. 330

Figure 18.1 Agents' footprints under the red agent's noise (η) impacts on velocity and network with minimum trust effects ($\tau_B = 1$ and $\tau_R = 1$). Scenario 1: $\eta = 0.1$. 340

Figure 18.2 Agents' footprints under the red agent's noise (η) impacts on velocity and network with minimum trust effects ($\tau_B = 1$ and $\tau_R = 1$). Scenario 2: $\eta = 0.1$. 341

Figure 18.3 Agents' footprints under the red agent's noise (η) impacts on velocity and network with minimum trust effects ($\tau_B = 1$ and $\tau_R = 1$). Scenario 3: $\eta = 0.1$. 342

Figure 18.4 Agents' footprints under the red agent's noise (η) impacts on velocity and network with minimum trust effects ($\tau_B = 1$ and $\tau_R = 1$). Scenario 1: $\eta = 0.9$. 343

Figure 18.5 Agents' footprints under the red agent's noise (η) impacts on velocity and network with minimum trust effects ($\tau_B = 1$ and $\tau_R = 1$). Scenario 2: $\eta = 0.9$. 344

Figure 18.6 Agents' footprints under the red agent's noise (η) impacts on velocity and network with minimum trust effects ($\tau_B = 1$ and $\tau_R = 1$). Scenario 3: $\eta = 0.9$. 345

Figure 18.7 Trust effects on agents' behaviours with the red agent noise level at 0.1 in Scenario 3: $\tau_B = 0.2$, $\tau_R = -1$, and $\eta = 0.1$. 346

Figure 18.8   Trust effects on agents' behaviours with the red agent noise level at 0.1 in Scenario 3: $\tau_B = 1, \tau_R = 0.2$, and $\eta = 0.1$.   347

Figure A.1   Venn diagrams – relationships between events for a sample space S.   352

Figure A.2   The relative frequency of event H ($f_n(H)$) when tossing a coin different numbers of times.   354

Figure A.3   Partitions $B_1, B_2, ..., B_7$ in a sample space S.   358

Figure A.4   Probability mass function of X for H occurrences.   363

Figure A.5   CDF of X for H occurrences.   363

Figure A.6   PDF of X for H occurrences.   366

Figure A.7   CDF of X for H occurrences.   366

Figure A.8   Joint probability of $(X \leq x, Y \leq y)$.   367

Figure A.9   Probability of $(x_1 < X \leq x_2, y_1 < y \leq y_2)$.   367

Figure A.10   PDF of uniform distributions.   371

Figure A.11   CDF of uniform distributions.   371

Figure A.12   PDF of exponential distributions.   373

Figure A.13   CDF of exponential distributions.   373

Figure A.14   PDF of gamma distributions.   375

Figure A.15   CDF of gamma distributions.   375

Figure A.16   PDF of Weibull distributions.   376

Figure A.17   CDF of Weibull distributions.   376

Figure A.18   PDF of normal distributions.   378

Figure A.19   CDF of normal distributions.   378

Figure A.20   PDF of lognormal distributions.   380

Figure A.21   CDF of lognormal distributions.   380

Figure A.22   Probability mass function of Bernoulli distribution.   381

Figure A.23   CDF of Bernoulli distribution.   381

Figure A.24   Probability mass function of binomial distribution with $n = 5, p = 0.1$.   383

Figure A.25   Probability mass function of binomial distribution with $n = 10, p = 0.1$.   383

Figure A.26   Probability mass function of binomial distribution with $n = 5, p = 0.5$.   384

Figure A.27   Probability mass function of binomial distribution with $n = 10, p = 0.5$.   384

Figure A.28   Probability mass function of geometric distribution with $p = 0.1$.   385

Figure A.29   Probability mass function of geometric distribution with $p = 0.25$.   386

Figure A.30   Probability mass function of geometric distribution with $p = 0.5$.   386

Figure A.31   Probability mass function of geometric distribution with $p = 0.75$.   387

Figure A.32   Probability mass function of Poisson distribution with $\lambda = 1$.   388

Figure A.33   CDF of Poisson distribution with $\lambda = 1$.   388

Figure A.34   Probability mass function of Poisson distribution with $\lambda = 2$.   389

Figure A.35   CDF of Poisson distribution with $\lambda = 2$.   389

Figure A.36   A target used in a shooting training session.   390

Figure A.37   Mean, median, and mode of gamma distribution.   394

Figure A.38   Mean, median, and mode of lognormal distribution.   394

Figure B.1   Two-dimensional (U_i, U_{i+1}) lattice structure for full period LCGs: $Z_1 = 12Z_{i-1} \mod 101$.   412

Figure B.2   Two-dimensional (U_i, U_{i+1}) lattice structure for full period LCGs ($Z_1 = 3Z_{i-1} \mod 101$).   413

Figure B.3   Three-dimensional (U_i, U_{i+1}, U_{i+2}) lattice structure for $10\,000$ triples from RANDU ($m = 2^{31}$ and $a = 65\,539$).   414

Figure B.4   Acceptance-rejection method for beta $(5, 3)$ with accepted sample size of 50.   417

Figure B.5   Situation of a needle intersected with a line.   425

Figure B.6   The probability of intersections.   426

Figure B.7   Situation of a needle intersecting a line.   427

Figure B.8   The probability of intersection.   427

Figure B.9   The estimated π values by NetLogo and random points (Algorithm 15).   429

LIST OF TABLES

Table 3.1   Questions and Corresponding Equations Encoded in Excel   46

Table 3.2   Some Samples of the Input Datasets to the Simulator   51

Table 3.3   Results Summary of 100 Simulator Runs   53

Table 3.4   Comparison of Battle Results by Different Initial Troop Sizes and Fighting Effectiveness   53

Table 3.5   The Battle Results When Fighting Effectiveness Fixed, but Troop Sizes Varied   54

Table 4.1   The Computational Cost Comparison of Priority Queue Operations for Binary Heap, Ordered Linked List, and Ordered Array   72

Table 5.1   The Most Common Logical Operators   83

Table 5.2   The Truth Table for the Logical Construct Expressed in Eq. (5.1)   84

Table 5.3   Tabular Representation (Truth Table) of Traffic Light FSM   88

Table 5.4   A True Table of the FSM for Modelling an Ant's Behaviours to Find the Way Out of a Maze   95

Table 6.1   Factor Levels and Responses by OFAT   104

Table 6.2   A Tabular Representation of 2^k Factor Design for a Model with Three Factors   105

Table 6.3   Responses of a Model with Two Factors in 2^k Factorial Design   110

Table 6.4   Responses from 10 Replications in a 2^k Factorial Design   112

Table 6.5   Effects and Interactions from 10 Replications in a 2^k Factorial Design   113

Table 6.6   Summary of Useful Distributions Used in Simulation   117

Table 7.1   The Entities and Their Attributes of the DES Model for a Mechanic Support Centre   128

Table 7.2   Event Types in a Single-Server Queueing System and Their Event Routines   137

Table 7.3   Time Period and Number in Queue of the Mechanical Centre   140

Table 8.1   Sheep Population in Each Year ($x_0 = 100$ and $r = 5\%$)   144

Table 8.2   Example of Sheep Population and Farm Asset Growth in Each Year   147

Table 8.3   Difference in Asset Value Because of Growth in Sheep Price   147

Table 9.1   Round-off Errors of the Estimation of Car's Velocity, Using $v_t = \frac{dy}{dt}$ for Different Values of Δt 161

Table 9.2   The True Velocity and the Estimation by Euler's Method for the First 13 s.   168

Table 9.3   Annual interest rate   176

Table 10.1   Agent Attribute Groups and Associated Codes   191

Table 10.2   Group A – Agents and Their Attributes   193

Table 10.3   Group B – Agents and Their Attributes   194

Table 10.4   Group C – Agents and Their Attributes   194

Table 12.1   The First Generation of Chromosomes and Their Fitness for Maximising x^2 228

Table 12.2   Selected Parents and Their Children After Crossover and Mutation Operations   233

Table 16.1   Skill Proficiency – Statistics for Neural Network Training (100 seeds)   298

Table 16.2   Sudoku Proficiency: Statistics for 100 Games Solvable   300

Table 17.1   Traffic Measures for Various Population Sizes   314

Table 17.2   Traffic Measures for Various Population Sizes   318

Table 17.3   Traffic Measures for Various Population Sizes   324

Table 18.1   Results of Red Agent's Noise Effect When $\tau_B = 1$ and $\tau_R = 1$ 338

Table 18.2   Results of Effects from Red Agent's Noise and Trust Factors – Confidence Level is 0.05.   339

Table A.1   Coin-tossing Experiments in History (Rows Are Ordered by the Second Column – the Number of Experiments, n 354

Table A.2   Number of H Occurrences in an Experiment of Tossing a Coin Three Times   362

Table A.3   Probabilities Associated with the Number of H Occurrences in an Experiment of Tossing a Coin Three Times   362

Table A.4   The Probabilities of Scores for Soldiers A and B 391

Table A.5   The Probabilities of Scores for Soldiers A and B by Distances Obeying Exponential Distribution   393

Table B.1   Results from Middle-square Method with Initial $Z_0 = 3404$ 399

Table B.2   Random Numbers Generated by LCG with the Parameters $a = 9, c = 5, m = 8$, and $Z_0 = 7$ 401

Table B.3   A Sequence $\{b\}_1^3 1$ for $x^5 + x^2 + 1$, Using Tausworthe Generator   407

Table B.4   Binary Integers Generated by GFSR for the Polynomial $x^5 + x^2 + 1$ with $l = 5$ and Delay $d = 6$ 408

Table B.5   Results by Monte Carlo Simulation for $I = \int_0^\pi e^x \sin x \, dx = 12.0703$ with Various Values of N 430

Table B.6   Daily Profits of a Cake Shop with Various Numbers of Cakes Baked, Based on an Average Customer Number per Day of 15   432

PART I

On Problem Solving, Computational Red Teaming, and Simulation

Problem Solving, Simulation, and Computational Red Teaming

1.1 INTRODUCTION

Problem solving is present nowadays virtually everywhere, from industry and research-related activities to daily life, and consists of various methods, grouped in a more or less systematic manner, to find solutions to problems. From a very colloquial understanding, problem solving refers to the process in which one attempts to overcome various real-world difficulties using systematic, including trial and error, steps.

The concept of problem solving is used in many disciplines, where practitioners and researchers treat it from different perspectives and describe it using different terminologies. At one extreme, in psychology, problem solving is mainly concerned with the mental processes involved in finding solutions. At the other end of the spectrum, in computer science and related fields (e.g. computational and artificial intelligence, cognitive science, autonomous systems, and robotics), problem solving is mainly associated with computerised processes, in which computer simulation and computational models are employed to find the desired solutions. Between these two extremes, numerous other fields of activity – such as multiple branches of engineering, industrial design, business and economics – employ various combinations of methods for problem solving, where these methods range from introspection and behaviourism, to prototyping and design of experiments, and further to computer modelling and simulation.

Of these, computer modelling and simulation is currently the most preferred working tool in most, if not all, areas mentioned above [35], due to their low cost, speed, and flexibility. However, computer simulation may not be necessary in every real problem-solving situation. Sometimes the real system in which a problem needs to be solved can be accessed as is, and thereby can be studied easily or economically in the physical world, without transferring the problem into conceptual models that are solved through simulation. However, in most cases, the need for evidence-based

Simulation and Computational Red Teaming for Problem Solving, First Edition.
Jiangjun Tang, George Leu, and Hussein A. Abbass.

decision making and the complexity of real-world problems necessitate the use of modelling and simulation. As a result of the unprecedented development of digital computing, we are able to use simulation on a significantly larger scale than ever before. Today's digital computers offer sufficient computational power to run models of real-world problems of virtually any complexity at very low cost and with very little risks involved, thereby rendering the engagement of actual systems less attractive than in the past. Thus, while computer simulation was once reserved for fields such as science and engineering, it is today pertinent in all aspects of our life and has extended to the humanities, social sciences, and psychology.

Thus, it is natural to start our book about simulation by discussing problem solving to: (i) disambiguate the concept of simulation and (ii) position the concept of simulation within the larger problem-solving concept. In addition, another reason for spending some time discussing problem solving before proceeding with the core discussion on simulation is to explain to the reader why and how computational red teaming (CRT) and simulation are related, given that this relationship only becomes meaningful within the context of problem solving.

Thus, in this very first chapter, we take the reader on a brief yet useful journey through the problem-solving process to emphasise the roles in problem solving of the two concepts that create the topic of this book: computer simulation and CRT. To fulfil this purpose, we structure the remainder of the chapter in two parts. The first part describes the problem-solving process and emphasises the role of simulation within this process, while the second part describes the role of CRT in relation to problem solving and simulation.

1.2 PROBLEM SOLVING

Problem solving can be considered the process of finding solutions to difficult or complex issues. According to this relaxed definition, it is acceptable to consider that solving a problem equates with finding a way out, treating a symptom or simply accomplishing a task that is not trivial. This is an accustomed view of problem solving over many fields of activity, which may be accepted in highly informal contexts. However, from a rigorous perspective, solving a problem refers to finding and eliminating the root cause that generated the problem, where a problem is seen as a risk whose time has come – that is, it has a cause that has manifested. According to this view on problem solving, in the following, we briefly present the major steps of the problem-solving process, with the purpose of positioning simulation in the context of this book. These steps are problem recognition, problem definition, and problem solving.

1.2.1 Recognising the Problem

Problem recognition is a matter of proactive diagnosis. In relation to any activity (where we understand an activity to be any combination of concepts, such as products, services, processes, phenomena, and systems), the stakeholders involved in that activity need to devote continuous attention throughout its entire lifecycle to any potential issue that does or may emerge. To ensure this observant behaviour towards the activity, stakeholders need to be in a continuous state of situational awareness, which can be reached only through acquisition of a considerable amount of knowledge about the past, present, and potential future states of the activity. Problem recognition manifests when one or more stakeholders recognise a difference between the desired and actual state of the activity, which has a significant effect on further decision making related to the activity.

Sometimes the problem is created by shaping the goal state to be different from the current state. For example, a chief executive officer (CEO) of a company may recognise that the performance of the company has been steady for a long time, thereby running the risk of becoming too predictable, which makes the company an easy target for its competitors. Thus, the CEO designs new key performance targets with the primary aim of changing the status quo.

Skills and experience, together with the right knowledge-acquisition tools, are needed for stakeholders to be able to recognise problems that need to be solved and/or trends that can lead to problems. To better understand the involvement of knowledge acquisition in this process, a comprehensive view on knowledge-acquisition methods is offered in Chapter 11.

1.2.2 Defining the Problem

Once the stakeholders identify the existence of a problem, the natural step towards solving the problem is to define it. This means that they must structure, state, and represent the problem in an intelligible way, so that the problem can be communicated to peers for further consideration and solving. As with problem recognition, this part of problem solving is also a process that involves acquiring a substantial amount of knowledge about the context, so that it can be properly stated, structured, and represented. In addition, similar to problem recognition, Chapter 11 is a useful reading for understanding how knowledge about problems can be acquired.

It is critical to understand that these three aspects – structure, statement, and representation – are useful for facilitating further actions, such as development and evaluation of potential solutions; thus, problem definition must capture the underlying causes, not (only) the symptoms of the problem. For example, a road management authority observes that roads in a particular area are substantially jammed, and concludes that there is a traffic problem. Thus, when the problem is defined, the traffic jam is not what defines the problem – it is only a symptom. To facilitate solving the problem, it needs to be further quantified in terms of the amount of traffic that exceeds the road capacity. In this way, potential root causes are implied (e.g. insufficient roads, unexpected demand or both), so the problem is defined in a way that can guide analysts to choose appropriate methodologies.

1.2.3 Solving the Problem

1.2.3.1 Establish System Boundary   A problem does not exist in a vacuum. A problem is associated with a certain system (or phenomenon) through its causes,

its effects, interactions with it or a combination of these factors. In turn, this system is situated within an environment. Thus, when solving a problem, it is necessary to establish the boundaries between the system to which the problem is related and the rest of the environment. Whether these boundaries are soft or strong is a matter of the type of problem, the type of system, the type of environment, and ultimately the objectives stated by the system's stakeholders. However, a boundary needs to be considered to ensure further traceability and solvability of the problem.

1.2.3.2 *Formalisation*
After a system boundary is established, the problem can be articulated in a language that is universally understandable by various stakeholders involved in its solving. Thus, the problem, which is real and attached to a real system, can be further abstracted and formalised in a language that allows analysts to discuss it with peers and solve it. To achieve this, the problem is transferred in a model, which is a convenient representation of its real-world version, by using a certain formalism. There are numerous ways to build models that represent real-world problems, such as natural language, prototypes, diagrams, logical constructs or mathematical equations. Each of these has advantages and disadvantages, depending on the purpose of the modeller. A detailed discussion on these is offered later in the book, in Chapter 5. The resultant model is then the foundation on which a computer simulation is designed and performed.

1.2.3.3 *Solve the Model*
Simulation is one of the tools used to both understand the problem and system under consideration, and, when coupled with an appropriate search algorithm, to solve the conceptual model of the problem at hand. An attempt to understand this view is a necessary effort to disambiguate the concept of simulation.

It has become normal across various disciplines for simulation to be viewed as the process of emulating or imitating a real-world phenomenon [35], which is a rather colloquial view that does not sufficiently emphasise the role of a model in a simulation environment. While simulation can indeed be associated with the idea of emulating a real-world phenomenon, it is actually the model representing that phenomenon that is simulated, with the purpose of understanding the model space of behaviours to further understand the phenomenon's space of behaviours.

Thus, depending on how the model represents the real problem, various types of simulation can be considered. For example, let us consider a very simple real-world situation of a boat moving on a river from Point A to Point B. The problem we would like to solve here is to investigate how long it takes to move from A to B, given different speeds of the boat. We need to solve this problem in a way that does not involve the boat itself or the river because finding the solution in this way would not be beneficial for multiple reasons, such as cost, logistics, time, and effort. Thus, we need to solve it in a way that does not involve the real thing, so we build a model to obtain a representation of the real situation, which is good enough to serve our purpose.

Let us consider three cases, where we build three models that represent the boat problem at an increasing level of abstraction: (1) we build a small toy-like wooden boat and place it in a water recipient; (2) on a piece of paper, we draw a line representing the river and a bubble representing the boat; and (3) we represent boat movement using Newton's equations of motion. Each of these three models abstract quite well the real boat problem, and we can use various settings to explore the behaviours of these models. Then, assuming that the models are sufficient representations of the real-world problem, we can infer the behaviours of the boat on the river under different circumstances. Simulation is when we actually run these models under the conditions that we consider relevant to the investigation. In (1), we may move the toy boat by hand along the water recipient at different speeds, conveniently scaled to resemble the spatial/physical constraints present in the real world. In (2), we may add to the drawing several vectors with different directions and amplitudes, representing different velocities of the boat. In (3), we may give different values to variables and parameters that are part of the laws of motion. By using the models to do this, we actually simulate the models, and create the premises for further analysis of their behaviour under different conditions.

1.2.3.4 *Sensitivity Analysis*   After a model is simulated under different conditions of interest, we may perform an analysis on the resultant outputs to infer useful conclusions about its behaviour. In the classic view, where simulation is seen as just an emulation of reality of some kind, the analysis process may not be even relevant or pertinent to the purpose of simulation. However, when we consider simulation from a problem-solving perspective, then we clearly see a motivation, utility, and meaning in performing analysis on the output resulting from simulating the model.

Apart from the analysis of the simulation output, which is needed to infer conclusions on the space of behaviours, sensitivity analysis also needs to be performed, once the model (and its computer implementation, in the case of computer simulation) is in place. Sensitivity analysis investigates how the uncertainty in the output of a model can be related to different sources of uncertainty in its inputs. It usually involves calculating the outcomes under various assumptions to determine the effect of deviations in the inputs on the outputs. Sensitivity analysis is used as part of verification and validation of the model – which we describe in the next paragraph – leading to a number of benefits to the model and the resultant simulation process, such as showing the robustness of the results in the presence of uncertainty, enabling a deeper understanding of the relationship between inputs and outputs, unveiling errors in the model, simplifying the model by fixing those inputs with no or insignificant/irrelevant effect on the output, and identifying redundant parts of the model structure.

1.2.3.5 *Verification and Validation*   However, since simulation refers to running the model, then what we obtain is outputs of the model. Consequently, the analysis of these outputs shows the behaviour space of the model, not of the real-world problem. Thus, only if the model is a valid representation of the real problem, and the simulations were properly run on the model, will we be able to infer and import the simulation conclusions (generated by the model) onto the real problem. These two aspects refer to the validation and verification processes that we need to perform to ensure that the conclusions in the behavioural space of the model apply to the behavioural space of the real problem as well.

In general, verification and validation are the processes that evaluate the answers to the questions *did we build the product correctly?* and *did we build the correct product?*, respectively. In the context of problem solving and simulation, these questions become *did we solve the model correctly?* and *did we solve the correct model?*, respectively. Therefore, through verification we check if the way the simulator was implemented based on the model (and consequently, the way the simulation produces outputs) is correct. Therefore, through verification, we check if the way the simulator was implemented based on the model (and, consequently, the way the simulation produces outputs) is correct. Further, through validation, we check if the conceptual model we created actually represents the real problem in a necessary and sufficient manner, so that it can serve our purpose.

1.3   COMPUTATIONAL RED TEAMING AND SELF-'VERIFICATION AND VALIDATION'

While this is the introductory chapter of this book and should be accessible to all readers, we do recommend a brief consultation of Chapter 13 before continuing reading this section for those readers who are not at all familiar with red teaming concepts. This will help understand the involvement of red teaming in the topic of simulation.

In brief, red teaming is a practice in which an entity, denoted the blue team, employs another entity, denoted the red team, to act as its hypothetical opponent. By employing a red team that emulates the opponent's intentions and challenging actions towards the blue team's system, the blue entity can test and evaluate its own course of actions in relation to specific objectives. There may be many types of blue, which we call red teaming objects, to illustrate the object to which the red teaming process is applied. For example, we can apply red teaming to plans, decisions, ideas, strategies, models, simulations, systems, the operation of systems, and the performance of tasks. In addition, red teaming may be used by blue for a variety of reasons, which we call red teaming purposes. Some examples of these purposes can be unveiling vulnerabilities, discovering blind spots, verifying and validating assumptions, and exploring the space of possibilities.

Let us now emphasise a certain combination of these objects and purposes. Let us assume a situation in which the red teaming objects are a model of a real system and the resultant simulation, and the red teaming purposes are verification and validation of assumptions. Now, we start seeing a certain connection between simulation and red teaming in the context of problem solving. If we express the above situation in other words, we obtain the following.

We have a real-world problem that we need to solve. We transfer the real problem into a conceptual model that represents the real problem at an assumed necessary and sufficient degree of fidelity, and hope they are equivalent with respect to our purpose of finding the solution. Further, we transfer the conceptual model into a computer (numeric) simulator, and then simulate the model under different conditions, and reach conclusions about the behaviour of the model – that is, we find the solution to the model. Then, assuming that (1) the simulation reflects the conceptual model and (2) the model reflects the real-world problem, we infer that the solution for the model can also be applied to the real-world problem. Thus, we solve the problem using simulation. However, we can never be sure whether (1) and (2) are true – we can only hope that our assumptions were correct. We may have made an implementation mistake, and the simulation did not run the model correctly. Also, we may have made incorrect assumptions when creating the conceptual model, so the model did not suit the real-world problem. By employing a red teaming exercise to test these two aspects, we use red teaming as a verification and validation mechanism for our simulation and problem solving, respectively.

CHAPTER 2

Introduction to Fundamentals of Simulation

2.1 INTRODUCTION

Simulation has been widely used in industry and research in various areas, including, but not limited to, engineering, economics, chemistry, and medical sciences. Simulation, as a concept and a field of activity, can be studied from multiple points of view, such as theory and principles, methodologies and methods, and practical applications and tools. In this chapter, we provide an introduction to simulation from a broad perspective. We first describe the fundamental theoretical aspects related to simulation and highlight the benefits of it. We then briefly discuss from a methodological perspective the most important simulation paradigms: discrete event simulation, continuous simulation, agent-based simulation, parallel simulation, and distributed simulation. This is followed by a practical perspective in which we present some successful applications of the simulation paradigm, and describe some of the most popular tools, such as NetLogo programming language.

As explained in Chapter 1, simulation can be viewed from a broad perspective as the process of solving the model of a real-world problem to further solve that problem. Simulation is present nowadays virtually everywhere, from industry and research-related activities to our day-to-day life. For example, if we plan to go to a new restaurant for dinner and try to find a route to it, we may search the restaurant's address on a map and then determine a path to travel there. Frequently in real life, several candidate routes will exist to the restaurant; thus, we consider each of them and imagine ourselves driving or walking on the map and estimate the time spent on the road. Finally, a preferred route is found based on some basis, such as the shortest distance or ease of driving. This process occurring in the mind is a simulation. In this process, we model ourselves as moving objects capable of exhibiting driving and navigation behaviours to find a path in a road network. Given that this example is simple and straightforward, it does not require any computational aids for the simulation. However, many complex processes and systems exist in the real world – for

Simulation and Computational Red Teaming for Problem Solving, First Edition.
Jiangjun Tang, George Leu, and Hussein A. Abbass.
© 2020 by The Institute of Electrical and Electronics Engineers, Inc. Published 2020 by John Wiley & Sons, Inc.

example, a road traffic system of a city consists of both physical entities (e.g. road networks, vehicles, traffic lights, and passengers) and intangible items (e.g. traffic rules). Modelling and simulating such complex systems requires many mathematical and logical models to be built, many interactions between entities to be considered, and possibly a large amount of data to be analysed. Such an endeavour is beyond the limited capability of human beings; therefore, computer-based techniques become essential. Computers are used to implement and evaluate a model numerically in a simulation, and then the expected characteristics of the model are estimated by using the gathered output. In this book, we focus on computer-based simulation, which nowadays covers a vast majority of the topics related to simulation and modelling.

To simulate and study a system, we must make some assumptions about it. Typically, these assumptions are refined as mathematical or logical relationships that become models in a simulation to represent the real-world system. After the system is modelled, simulation applies some mechanisms to describe or imitate the behaviours of the modelled system. In addition, we must gather and analyse the output from the experiments conducted by the simulation so that we can verify and validate the simulation, and then gain understanding of how the corresponding real system works. Meanwhile, a visualisation of the simulation may make the system more understandable. Obviously, designing and developing a proper simulation is not an easy job. However, once developed, the simulation becomes an extremely powerful tool for studying the real system of interest because it allows the replication in vitro, without risks, of a wide range of behaviours that the system may exhibit in real life. Thus, simulation is currently the preferred working tool in many areas [35], such as:

- problem solving
- understanding systems
- model and data validation
- new system testing and evaluation
- data analysis support
- control real-time processes (compressing or expanding time frames)
- potential outcome prediction
- answering 'what-if' questions
- training and educating humans
- computer automation.

Simulation is not necessary in every case of studying or problem solving. Sometimes, the actual system can be accessed and studied easily or in an economically efficient manner. No validation is needed when studying the actual system and, in simple cases, the results are more accurate than a model in most cases. However, in other cases, it is infeasible or even impossible to engage the real system because:

- it may not be accessible (e.g. human evolutionary history)
- it may be costly to engage the system (e.g. launching a space shuttle)

- it may be dangerous to engage the system (e.g. battlefield)
- the system may simply not exist (e.g. an authentic quantum computer).

In the above cases, simulation can help users to study a system and solve some problems without touching the real system. By using simulation, a model that represents an equivalent surrogate of the real system is studied. As a result of this, validation of the model must be undertaken and questions about whether the model correctly reflects the actual system must be asked during validation. For example, when designing a car, it is much cheaper to build a full-scale car clay model than to build a real car because of the alterations that may be suffered by the model until finalising the design. Physical models can usually be found in design (e.g. the example of a car clay model) or training (e.g. aircraft simulators for pilots). However, physical models are rarely of interest in operations research or analysis (e.g. logistics), where mathematical models are commonly used. Mathematical models refer to manipulating logical and quantitative relationships to see how the model reacts to/answers the inputs/questions of interest. In some cases, mathematical models are simple enough to be represented using some close-form equations that can be solved using various analytical techniques. However, when mathematical models become complex, so do the analytical representation and manipulation, and simulation becomes a better option for studying the real system. The main advantages of modelling and simulation can be highlighted as follows. The main advantages of modelling and simulation can be highlighted as follows.

- **Cost-effective:** Designing, building, and testing real systems (such as a rocket) can be expensive. Simulation can provide practical feedback on the correctness and efficiency of the design when designing real-world systems before the system is actually constructed. Simulation allows users to manipulate the design and make changes to the system to obtain more information and then optimise the design. All this occurs without committing any additional resources.
- **Flexible levels of abstraction:** Simulation provides the possibility to study a system at different abstraction levels. This enables users to study both micro-systems (such as atoms and quantum phenomena) and macro-systems (such as global economics or planetary-level environmental phenomena). Given that systems are composed of multiple entities and their actions/interactions, they can be studied at different levels of detail through simulation. We can focus only on the system-level behaviours of a system without considering the details of the individual entities, or we can study the behaviour and interactions of individual entities to understand the behaviour of the system.
- **Compress and expand time:** Simulation time is different from the wall clock time (real time); thus, when needed, users can speed up or slow down the behaviours or processes under investigation to improve understanding of the phenomena. When compressing a simulation time, users can attain outputs from a simulation much faster than from a real system. Therefore, more simulation runs can be performed and more results can be analysed and studied in a given

real-time period. In contrast, slowing down a simulation allows users to study the details of each state change for systems that evolve rapidly in reality, such as chemical reactions.

- **Ease of answering 'what-if' questions:** A simulation can be run in different contexts, allowing users to answer 'what-if' questions. By manipulating the scenarios and inputs of a simulation, different outputs can be generated to understand the effect of the changes on the system.

- **Better training and education:** Simulation is an effective tool for training and education. Using multi-media means (including visuals and sound), simulation can demonstrate a system to users to enable a better understanding of real phenomena. Simulation can also immerse users in a virtual environment through advanced virtual-reality techniques, where users can interact with artificial objects or other users within the simulation to gain better experiences from the training.

However, simulation entails a number of disadvantages. First, designing and building a simulation can be a complex task that requires theoretical knowledge and practical expertise in relation to the phenomenon of interest; thus, designers and developers need special training. Second, it is difficult to interpret the results of a simulation because of the inherent uncertainty yielding from the fact that the model is an approximate surrogate of the real system, which can introduce unknown or unexpected artefacts to the analysis. Thus, inappropriate use of a simulation can be time consuming and cost ineffective, thereby potentially leading to unexpected outcomes. Yet, despite these inherent disadvantages, simulation is a powerful tool, and is often the only tool available to both researchers and practitioners for understanding real-world systems.

In the following sections, we will discuss several concepts that are essential to simulation, such as the concepts of system and model.

2.2 SYSTEM

Simulation is used to recreate in vitro the behaviour of real-world systems. Thus, the concept of 'system' is important for both the real world and the simulated environment. Systems can be seen in many forms. A system can refer to a physical entity with a certain functionality, such as a vehicle, a mining machine, or a building. A system can be also an organisation, a society, a stock market, an ecosystem, or other similar constructs that operate at a more conceptual level, yet still in the real world. A classical definition found in the literature states that a system is 'a collection of entities acting and interacting together towards the accomplishment of some logical end' [348]. While clear and concise, this definition is not adequate in the context of modelling and simulation, where systems require deeper insight and a more comprehensive approach. Hence, in this book, we refer to systems using a more elaborate definition borrowed from [2].

Definition 2.2.1. *A system is a set of entities: each could possess a capacity to receive inputs, perform tasks, generate effects and complement some other entities towards achieving goals defined by a common purpose.*

The above definition extends the classical definition of a 'system' towards a higher level of detail. This definition includes the keywords *entities, inputs, tasks, effects, goals,* and *purpose.* Multiple interacting, interrelated or interdependent entities compose the system and must be clearly mapped within a boundary that encapsulates them. An entity can receive inputs from other entities or from the environment in which the system operates. After some particular tasks are performed by an entity, the entity generates effects on other entities, on the system or on the environment while moving towards its goals. The tasks, effects, and goals of an entity reflect the purpose of this entity within the system boundaries. All entities work together to serve the common purpose of the system.

Definition 2.2.2. *The purpose of a system is the reason for being from the perspective of an external observer.*

The definition of 'the purpose of a system' used here implies that the purpose of a system is an external judgement that is made by an external stakeholder or observer [2]. Thus, it can be said that the purpose of a system is defined by an entity that is external to the system boundaries, including the owner of the system. Even if the system is self-consciousness, the way it sees its own purpose remains its own perception of its purpose, which could differ from how its purpose is seen by others. Therefore, different purposes of a system can be defined by different external entities, derived from their own different external views of this system.

For example, a vehicle is a system that consists of many different components that work together, including the engine, gearbox, brakes, wheels, suspension, vehicle body, safety equipment, and trip computer. From its own perspective, the purpose of a vehicle is to move on the road. However, for a driver or a passenger, the purpose of a vehicle is to take them from one location to other. From a courier company view, the purpose of a vehicle is to generate a profit from delivering goods. For a public transportation company, a vehicle is a means of serving the local population. For a government agency (e.g. road authority), the purpose of a vehicle is only for registration, taxation, and management.

As discussed before, modelling and simulation is used to solve some particular problems in a given context. The different views on the purposes of a system are reflected in the way the system is modelled and simulated. The same system can be modelled in different ways because of the different purposes of the system from different modeller views. Therefore, it is important to identify the purpose of a system according to the context in which modelling and simulation are used as study tools. Let us refer again to the vehicle example. In a logistic simulation that a courier uses to solve some scheduling problems, the vehicle can be simply modelled as an object with the capacity of moving and loading goods, while consuming fuel. The details of the engine, gearbox, and other components inside the vehicle do not need to be

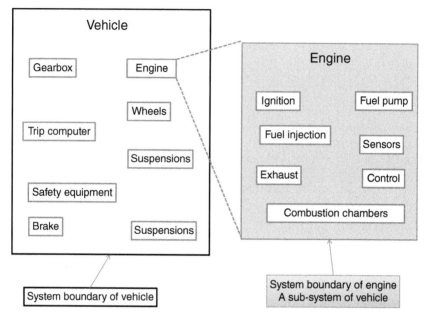

FIGURE 2.1   The system of a vehicle, the sub-system of an engine, and their corresponding boundaries and entities (not all entities are shown here).

considered. This is because the purpose of the vehicle in this logistic simulation is to deliver goods from one place to another in a given time. In contrast, when modelling a vehicle for a design department of an automotive manufacturer, all the components in the vehicle must be modelled in fine detail because the purpose is to design a working vehicle built from all necessary and operative components.

An entity can be a system on its own, which can be seen as a sub-system of the whole. In the vehicle design example, components such as the engine or gearbox can be taken into account as subsystems within the vehicle as a whole. A sub-system can be studied independently within its own boundary, and, as a consequence, can be further decomposed into smaller systems. For example, the vehicle engine as a system has combustion chambers, ignition, fuel pump and injection, control, exhaust and others. These subsystems may be decomposed into even smaller components. Figure 2.1 illustrates that a vehicle is a system, the engine is a sub-system of the vehicle, and the boundaries of these systems encapsulate the corresponding entities. The boundary of a system introduces another concept: the 'environment' of a system.

Definition 2.2.3. *The environment of a system S consists of all entities that reside outside S, including their properties and actions.*

As illustrated in Figure 2.1, all entities within the vehicle, except the engine, and their properties and actions become the environment of the engine system. Without the 'vehicle' environment, the engine can be a boat engine, a plane engine, or a mower engine. Therefore, the environment of a system defines the inputs and constraints applied to the system and it is affected by the output from the system. The environment also constitutes the space where uncertainties and unknowns reside. These uncertainties and unknowns must be considered when studying a system, and are usually associated with risks.

As stated in Definition 2.2.1, all the entities or subsystems of a system work together for an overall purpose. The purpose of the system is realised by the effects generated by the entities' actions. The engine produces power to drive other components so that the car can move, and the brakes provide braking force to stop the car. The definition of 'effect' from [2] is presented below.

Definition 2.2.4. *An effect is a measurable outcome generated by an action or caused by a change in a system state.*

First, the definition emphasises that the effect must be measurable for a simulation, especially in computer-based simulations. If the effect cannot be measured, we must use some indicators for the effect to represent them in a simulation. Therefore, it is necessary to quantify the outputs of a system and then transform them into measurable effects before starting modelling and simulation. For example, the power of an engine can be measured in horse power. Second, the definition states that the effects are generated by an action or caused by a system state change. A stopped engine cannot provide power until it starts running (the state of an engine changes from stopped to running). A brake provides braking force only when it is applied (the action of applying the brake occurs). We also note that an entity requires inputs to take actions or perform tasks (i.e. to produce effects); for example, an engine needs fuel as input to start running. Thus, effects do not occur in a vacuum – they are always associated with some causes.

Thus, the starting point of modelling and simulation must be understanding the system to be modelled from every aspect, including its purpose, the entities inside its boundaries, the inputs to the system and to each entity, the causes for producing effects from an entity, and the respective effects.

2.3   CONCEPTS IN SIMULATION

Typically, a model is a static representation of the real system, while a simulator encodes the model, and a simulation is an overall process that uses the simulator with sampled inputs to reproduce the behaviour of the real system. The formal definitions of the concepts in simulation discussed in this book also follow the book [3].

2.3.1   Model, Simulator, and Simulation

To simulate a real system, we first need to transfer this system into a model. Thus, we make some assumptions of the real system, based on which we generate mathematical, logical, and other relationships to constitute a model that is then used to understand the comprehensive behaviour of the system. The model is the funda-mental constituent of a simulation. The definition of the concept of 'model' is given as below.

Definition 2.3.1. *A model is a representation of a real system in some form.*

'A model is a representation of a system' means that entities and their relation-ships within the real system are mapped into a corresponding equivalent model. The model must capture the system's capability to receive inputs, behaviours, and effects. A model can take various forms. In the example at the beginning of this chapter, the thoughts about selecting a route to a restaurant are a model. A model can be a linguis-tic description, such as the script used in drama. A model can be a diagram, such as the structure, behaviour, or interaction diagrams used in the Unified Modelling Lan-guage (UML). Further, a model can consist of mathematical or logical expressions, such as Newton's laws of motion.

However, while various forms of models exist, that does not mean we can choose any form for a model at will. We must use an appropriate form that represents the sys-tem best in the context of study. Looking at the previous vehicle examples, a vehicle system is modelled as a moving object in a logistic simulation because the objective of the simulation is to solve a scheduling problem, instead of designing a vehicle. In contrast, the model becomes an accurate replica of a vehicle system when it is used in a simulation for designing a new car because the goal is to design a workable vehicle. As demonstrated in this example, a model represents a system in a form that is not the form of the system itself. However, both vehicle models are valid in the given contexts. These contexts are actually what generate the model assumptions.

Definition 2.3.2. *Model assumptions represent the conditions under which the model is assumed to be valid.*

For example, we can use the following equations as a model of the motion of a falling object, where the model assumptions are that the object motion follows Newton's laws and there are no other external forces on the falling object:

$$v(t + \Delta t) = v(t) + \Delta t \times g \qquad (2.1)$$

where $v(t)$ is the velocity at time t, and $v(t + \Delta t)$ is the velocity at time $t + \Delta t$. $v(t + \Delta t)$ is derived from both $v(t)$ and the acceleration g. g is equal to the gravitational acceleration only if there are no other forces affecting the falling object.

If we remove the condition 'no other external forces on the falling object' from the assumption and introduce the resistance of air, Eq. (2.1) is no longer valid for modelling this falling object. The equation must be modified under the assumption that the falling object follows Newton's laws and air resistance affects the object:

$$v(t + \Delta t) = v(t) + \Delta t \times (g + d) \qquad (2.2)$$

where *d* is the deceleration caused by the air resistance, which is in the reverse direction of gravitational acceleration *g*. Further, the equation will be more complex when introducing more conditions, such as wind effects. Thus, model assumptions should be carefully considered and defined at the beginning of modelling a system. Otherwise, the resultant model may not be valid.

Once a model of a system is built for computer-based simulation, it can be transformed into a piece of code.

Definition 2.3.3. *A simulator is an encoding of the model in a suitable software system.*

For example, a driving simulator may look like a driver's cab, yet this vehicle is moving in the virtual world using a driving model.

Definition 2.3.4. *Simulation is the ability to reproduce the behaviour of a system through a model.*

Simulation is an overall process whereby we manipulate a simulator with different input samples to generate outputs, and then analyse the outputs to understand how the modelled system behaves on those inputs. The behaviours of a simulator observed from a simulation are not necessarily exactly the same as the behaviours of the real system. The relationship between them is captured by three concepts: resolution, abstraction, and fidelity.

2.3.2 Resolution, Abstraction, and Fidelity

Resolution is the level of detail at which we see a system. Abstraction is the level of detail at which we represent a system through a model, according to the resolution. Fidelity is the level of detail at which a model or simulation actually reflects a system according to the abstraction. Fidelity also affects the level of detail of the outputs generated by a simulation. Figure 2.2 depicts the interdependency among these concepts.

Definition 2.3.5. *Resolution is what the modeller intends to model about the problem.*

Definition 2.3.6. *Abstraction is what the modeller decides to include in or exclude from the model.*

From the definitions given above, we conclude that resolution is a function of the system, while abstraction is a function of the model. Now, let us return to the falling object example. The acceleration is a key contributor to the motion of the falling object and is affected by many factors. This is the level that the modeller decides to consider. The modeller needs to decide whether to use the gravitational acceleration only, or the gravitational acceleration combined with other small factors, such as air

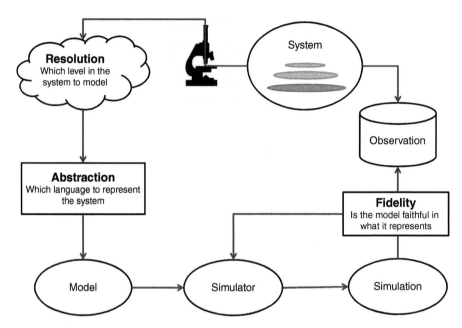

FIGURE 2.2   Relationship between resolution, abstraction, and fidelity (adapted from [3]).

resistance. The decision of an appropriate resolution level is the key decision that modellers must make at the beginning of building a simulation for a system.

Thus, we keep in mind that modellers map the system to a model at the appropriate (desired or imposed by modelling purpose) resolution level. Abstraction in modelling assumes identifying and including the causes and principles that truly govern the behaviour of the system, yet ignoring unessential details that do not contribute to this behaviour. (Do we consider the objective/scope of the study when ignoring system-level details?) In the falling object example, if the modeller includes air resistance in the model, then a decision should be also made about whether the air resistance is a constant or a variable affected by the spatial variation of air density. This is an example of how to abstract a system. Now, let us consider the fidelity.

Definition 2.3.7. *Fidelity is a measure of model coverage of the space defined by the level of resolution.*

Fidelity is about faithfulness and completeness. If only the gravitational acceleration is considered for the falling object based on the resolution decision, the corresponding model can accurately reproduce the behaviour of a falling object only in vacuum. This model may generate some close approximation of the behaviour of a falling object in other environments. In this case, the level of fidelity is low.

2.4 SIMULATION TYPES

In this section, we discuss simulations according to several classifications. In the first classification, a simulation can be static or dynamic. Static simulation models represent a system at a particular time or a system where time plays no role, such as Monte Carlo models. Dynamic simulation models are representations of systems that evolve over time, such as for manufacturing or transportation. From a different point of view, simulations can be classified as deterministic or stochastic, according to whether random variables are involved or not. Deterministic simulation models do not contain any probabilistic features, while stochastic simulation models have at least one random input. A chemical reaction is an example of a deterministic model, where all relations and interactions are clearly determined by a set of equations. Stochastic simulations are more commonly found in real-world applications. In addition, based on how simulations advance over time, they can be classified as discrete event or continuous. In discrete event simulation, the state of the system changes instantaneously at separate time points. Continuous simulation is a simulation where the state of the system changes continuously with respect to time. Using continuous or discrete model depends on the objectives of the study. In addition to the classifications mentioned above, two other types of simulation are briefly discussed in this section: parallel and distributed.

2.4.1 Discrete Event Simulation

Discrete event simulation (DES) transforms the model from one state to another by the instantaneous occurrence of special events over time. An event is an instantaneous occurrence that causes state changes in a system. The state of the system is represented by a set of variables that completely describes the system at a given time. These variables are called state variables. Events are usually stored in an event list in a DES and are trigged by simulation time. Once an event is trigged, the system state changes.

Let us consider an example in which the operation of an elevator needs to be simulated. An elevator has several buttons: one to close the door, one to open the door, and a number for different levels. Elevator's doors are opened after the 'open door' button is pressed. Thus, the event ('open door' button being pressed) makes the elevator change the state from door closed to door opened. The door of the elevator is closed and the button for level selection is enabled when the 'close door' button is pressed. Once one of the buttons for a level is pressed, the elevator will go up or down, from the current level to the selected level. When an elevator simulation is built based on the above descriptions, this is a DES.

Figure 2.3 illustrates the events of door open/close and the button for Level 1 being pressed in an elevator simulation. In this elevator example, the event is generated by pressing a button, and the state variables of an elevator include the door status (opened or closed) and the current level.

Another typical DES example is a queueing system, which will be discussed in Chapter 7.

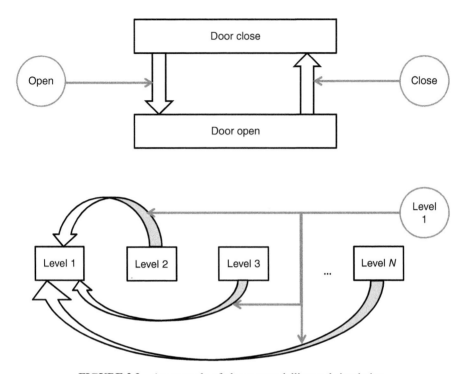

FIGURE 2.3   An example of elevator modelling and simulation.

The strong point of DES is that systems can be easily simulated using digital computers, since these are themselves discrete systems. This aspect will be also discussed in Chapter 7.

2.4.2   Continuous Simulation

In continuous simulation, the evolution of a system is processed continuously with respect to time advances. In such a way, the states of the system (state variables) are continuously changed along time advancing. Continuous simulation is often used to simulate physical systems (e.g. the motion of an object) and other continuous time-varying systems, including electrical, hydraulic, and mechanical systems, to continuously track the changes or response. Differential equations are the most precise mathematical models used for continuous simulation. Despite computers being discrete systems, continuous simulation can be easily implemented by porting the continuous differential equations to numeric difference equations. Other numerical approximation methods, such as Euler method, are also useful to solve differential equations on digital computers.

One example of continuous simulation is the simulation of a moving vehicle on the road. Once the vehicle's engine starts, the vehicle keeps moving on the road, depending on its velocity and acceleration. The position and velocity of the vehicle change continuously over time. To model it, we can use the following equations to represent the changes of the vehicle position:

$$v(t + \Delta t) = v(t) + \Delta t \times a \qquad (2.3)$$

where $v(t)$ is the velocity at time t, and $v(t + \Delta t)$ is the velocity at time $t + \Delta t$. $v(t + \Delta t)$ is derived from both $v(t)$ and the acceleration a only if there are no other effects:

$$p(t + \Delta t) = p(t) + v(t + \Delta t) \qquad (2.4)$$

Then the position $p(t + \Delta t)$ is calculated using the previous position $p(t)$ and the current velocity $(v(t + \Delta t)$. By both Eqs. (2.3) and (2.4), a moving vehicle can be modelled.

Sometimes we may find that the characteristics of both DES and continuous simulation exist simultaneously in a system. If we introduce a traffic light in the above example, then the vehicle must stop when it encounters a red traffic light at a road junction. Here, the event 'encountering a red traffic light' changes the vehicle state from moving to stopped. Therefore, DES and continuous simulation are not incompatible. However, one type – either discrete event or continuous simulation – can be dominant in a simulation according to the problem studied. In the given example, it will be a DES if we would like to study the individual vehicle behaviours.

2.4.3 Agent-based Simulation

In agent-based simulation [258], entities in a real system are modelled as a number of autonomous actors, called agents. Then the aggregate behaviours that emerge from the interaction among agents can be observed from the simulation for further study. Agent-based simulation can be found in many research areas, typically social studies.

2.4.4 Parallel and Distributed Simulation

Following advances in distributed computing, parallel and distributed simulation [150] became popular during the last two decades. A single simulation model of several simulation programs can be executed on multiple computers to reduce the execution time, to gather information from geographic distributed locations, and for fault tolerance. One famous example of parallel and distributed simulation is High Level Architecture (HLA) [105], which was proposed by the US Defence Department. High Level Architecture is equipped with a runtime infrastructure to manage different computer simulations' interactions with each other. It has been applied in various domains, including defence, space, and manufacturing.

2.5 TOOLS FOR SIMULATION

Object-oriented programming languages, such as Java and C++, are powerful tools for modelling and simulation. The models of individual entities in a system can be encapsulated as objects, and the actions and interactions can be programmed as functions of those objects. However, using these programming languages may require certain levels of skills and experience in programming that are not accessible to modellers.

Fortunately, some high-level modelling and simulation tools are now available, including NetLogo, Powersim, AnyLogic, and DESMO-J, which are viable and simpler alternatives to programming. NetLogo is a programmable modelling environment for simulating natural and social phenomena [402]. AnyLogic is a Java-based simulation tool providing multiple modelling and simulation methods [22]. Powersim covers various areas for modelling and simulation, such as electronic circuit and digital control [321]. DESMO-J provides a framework for discrete event modelling and simulation [114]. Simulink, as a module of MATLAB, is also a powerful simulation tool to use.

2.6 CONCLUSION

In this chapter, we have introduced the basic concepts of modelling and simulation. We briefly described different types of simulation, including DES and continuous simulation, and provided some application examples. In the following chapters, we will study the details of the methodologies and techniques for the different simulation types mentioned in this chapter.

PART II

Before Simulation Starts

CHAPTER 3

The Simulation Process

This chapter describes in detail the modelling and simulation process. Usually, a modelling and simulation process is an evolutionary approach in which a model may be refined several times. However, it is easier to understand if the modelling and simulation process is first described in a logic sequence, and then addressed in an evolutionary manner. At the end of the chapter, a battle simulation that implements the Lanchester combat model is used as an example to demonstrate the whole modelling and simulation process.

3.1 INTRODUCTION

This chapter focuses on how to develop and use a simulation. A modelling and simulation exercise involves several development stages and is usually an evolutionary approach. This means that the modeller may revisit the model because of various changes in the modelled system and/or its environment, new study objectives or other reasons. To describe the process clearly, we will employ a logic sequence to investigate each stage first. Therefore, the following sections are organised based on the logic sequence to develop a simulation, as illustrated in Figure 3.1. Then the simulation lifecycle is discussed in a recursive manner.

3.2 DEFINE THE SYSTEM AND ITS ENVIRONMENT

The first step to start building a simulation is to study the relevant system and its environment, and then define them. Studying a system can be seen as a process to gather an insight view of the system. The insight view of the system can be obtained in many ways. It can be gained from the knowledge and experience of the system owners – for example, a factory manager can provide details of a production line in his or her factory. It can be gained from observations of a system – for example, the solar system. It may be better to use scientific methods to gain the insight view – that is, gather the input and output data of the system, and then summarise them using analytic methods. In some cases, the traditional statistic methods are sufficient

Simulation and Computational Red Teaming for Problem Solving, First Edition.
Jiangjun Tang, George Leu, and Hussein A. Abbass.

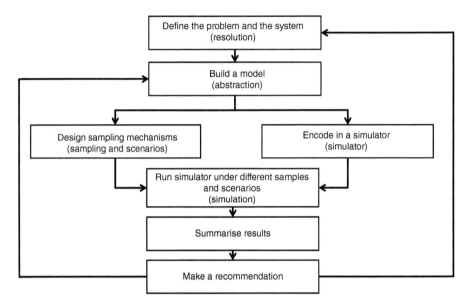

FIGURE 3.1   The steps to develop a simulation.

for processing the data from the system and providing understanding of the system. However, in other cases, when the amount of data resulting from the system becomes very high, advanced methodologies, such as data mining, may be required to discover the underpinnings of the system operation. However, some systems are too complex to be understood by the above methods.

In this case, the insight view is usually obtained and refined through the whole cycle of developing a simulation. This will be discussed at the end of this section. Gaining the insight view involves studying and defining a number of aspects related to the system of interest: the system itself and its component entities, the relations and interactions among entities, the inputs and outputs, the effects from entities, and the system boundary. It is also necessary to identify and define the environment where the system operates, as part of the attempt to define the system. The environment shapes the space of constraints and uncertainties affecting the system; hence, the behaviours of a system may vary in different environments. For example, temperature may affect a chemical reaction. All environmental factors that could potentially affect the behaviour of the system should be defined. In addition, all necessary quantitative measures of the system (e.g. effects and variations) should be clearly defined.

Apart from the implicit fundamental purpose of a simulation – that is, to understand the system of interest – a simulation is usually employed to solve a problem. As discussed in Section 2.2, different stakeholders may have different viewpoints of the same system. This leads to different problems of interest in the view of different stakeholders. Therefore, it is necessary to define the problem when intending to use a simulation to solve a problem. A well-defined problem specifies the appropriate objectives, constraints, assumptions, relationships between the relevant system and the environment, effects, and so on. For instance, when the problem is to study the trajectory of a falling object, some assumptions must be made before using Eq. (2.1) to describe its motion – such as assuming that the falling object is placed in a vacuum.

Both system and problem definitions decide how the proposed simulation will occur. Formal requirements of a simulation can be produced as the result of both exercises. According to the requirements for the proposed simulation, a modeller makes the first critical decision on the resolution level of the system. For example, a vehicle can be seen as an object moving from one location to another in a logistic simulation, and it is not necessary to know the details of how the vehicle moves, such as engine operation, transmission, and steering. In this case, the resolution level of the simulated vehicle is low.

In summary, the tasks required by this stage include:

- identifying the objective of the simulation
- formalising the problems
- understanding the relevant system
- deciding the resolution
- defining the system to model.

A good understanding of the system and a well-defined problem ensure the correct answer to the correct problem by the correct simulation.

3.3   BUILD A MODEL

Once the system and problem are defined, the modeller can start building a model. Given that a model is a representation of a system in some form, it is essential to select an appropriate representation form for the system according to the simulation requirements. For a computer-based simulation, a model commonly consists of mathematical or logical expressions, such as Newton's laws of motion for a moving object. This mathematical and logical model describes the essence of a system because it constructs a comprehensible structure for the system and reveals the cause-effect relations. The data of a system are also quantified by modelling the system through mathematical or logical expressions. Mathematical or logical expressions are not limited to sets of equations and formulas. The graphical notions, such as Petri net and finite-state machine, are also useful mathematical modelling tools. These graphical modelling techniques provide the stepwise process notation for a system. Modelling a system through mathematics facilitates further implementation of the model into computer programs.

Building a model for a system is the process that transfers the understanding about the system (the system definition) into a representation. This transformation involves the process of abstraction. Therefore, the abstraction level should be decided by modeller as well. It is necessary for a model to capture the concepts about a system based on the simulation requirements, but the unimportant details should be excluded. This abstraction process corresponds to the resolution decision made in the previous step.

For example, the mechanical parts of a vehicle need not be considered in a vehicle model used by a logistic simulation. After the abstraction, the model should remain valid under the defined assumptions (model validation and verification will be discussed at the end of this section). Building a model is also an evolutionary approach. It starts with a simple model to capture the core concepts of a system and then the model is enriched towards an elaborate representation of the system. This process of enrichment may continue alongside the growth of the modeller's confidence in the consistency between the model and the system during the whole simulation lifetime (this will be addressed in detail later in this book).

Another critical challenge in building a model is deciding which values to assign to various parameters used by the model. A model can produce different results if its parameters are initialised differently. Assigning appropriate values to parameters requires gathering relevant data from the system and then performing analysis on these data. For example, when using a Poisson distribution to represent customers' arrival patterns in a queueing system, the value for the arrival rate must be assigned. The arrival rate can be obtained from the historical data gathered by observation or other means from the real queueing system.

However, uncertainty exists in almost every system, and this challenges the accuracy/correctness of the values assigned to the parameters. Therefore, it is important to identify and address the uncertainty when building a model. Two types of uncertainties are the most important in the context of modelling and simulation: aleatory and epistemic. Aleatory uncertainties assume pure random variations that cannot be characterised rigorously, yet can be represented only through probabilistic methods. In the previous example, Poisson distribution is used to present the probability of a given number of events occurring in a fixed interval of time. Epistemic uncertainties are structured uncertainties that may be learnt from observations or study of the system. Epistemic uncertainties can be transferred into aleatory uncertainties if confidence about the epistemic can be established by the study. However, it is difficult in cases where we must make an educated guess to handle the epistemic uncertainties. If an epistemic uncertainty is known in a system, this uncertainty must be addressed in the simulation, typically in two possible ways: (1) identify the epistemic uncertainty and reduce it or (2) accept the risks associated with it. The choice of these options depends on the objectives of the simulation. If the objective of a simulation is to gain deep knowledge about a system, we must identify and reduce the epistemic uncertainties. In contrast, we may decide to accept the risks associated with the uncertainty when it costs too much to reduce/eliminate it. Techniques to handle uncertainties include: (1) pseudo-random number generators and (2) probabilities and statistics, which are discussed in detail in Chapter 6 and Appendix B.

For many complex systems, many different models constitute a whole-system model.

3.4   ENCODE A SIMULATOR

In the previous step, the system definition was transformed into a model. Encoding the model as a simulator is the second transformation when developing a simulation. A simulator implemented in a computer-based program allows us to run the model as many times as we want and to mimic the system in different ways. Simple models can be implemented by some spreadsheet software, such as Microsoft Excel. However, in most cases, we are facing a complex model. Encoding such kinds of simulators relies on programming languages or advanced simulation software packages, which were briefly introduced in Section 2.5. Besides the tools for building a simulator, some relevant techniques are also addressed here.

Simulation time is produced by the clock used in a simulation, which is different from a wall clock (real time). Therefore, simulation provides the ability to control the time (compressing or expanding) within a simulation.

Two time-advance mechanisms are used in simulation: next-event time advance and fixed-increment time advance. Next-event time advance involves the simulation time ticking based on the occurrence of certain events. Each event is associated with an occurring time, and simulation time jumps to the next event time once the current event finished. As shown at the top of Figure 3.2, after Event 1 occurs, simulation time jumps from T_1 to T_2 directly. Fixed-increment time advance involves the simulation time advancing in a fixed interval, regardless of the events. Some special methods have to be introduced to handle situations in which an event occurs in the middle of the time interval, as for Event 2 and Event 3 shown at the bottom of Figure 3.2. Therefore, fixed-increment time advance is more complicated than next-event time advance. For this reason, next-event time-advance techniques are more commonly used in simulation. Both time-advance mechanisms will be discussed in Chapter 7.

Next-event time advancing

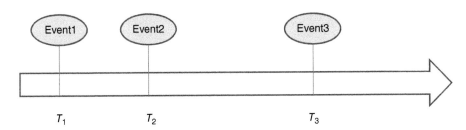

Fixed-increment time advancing

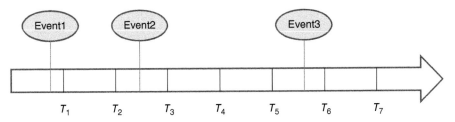

FIGURE 3.2   Time-advancing mechanism: next-event time advancing and fixed-increment time advancing.

For a continuous simulation, differential equations are the most accurate tool to describe the behaviour of a system. However, it is not an easy job to code the differential equations by programming languages. Alternatively, difference equations are commonly used in the simulator encoding.

Given that uncertainties exist in most systems, uncertainty handling must be addressed during the encoding of the model in the simulator. This usually involves various techniques for implementing random number generators, probability distributions and so on.

Visualisation is a useful tool to provide users with an intuitive feeling about a system, especially in training and education. Visualisation of a simulation helps users to better understand the underpinnings of the real system. Hence, providing a simulator with visualisation capability is a good way to demonstrate how a system works.

3.5 DESIGN SAMPLING MECHANISMS

It is obvious from the above discussion that data are needed to both define a system and build a model. Data are also necessary to generate inputs for the simulator. Given that the data volume may be huge for some systems, it is costly or even impossible to enumerate every possible input for the resultant simulation. In addition, even if all data are somehow acquired, there is no guarantee of the completeness of the data because of inherent imperfections in the observation or data acquisition processes. Thus, uncertainty exists in the data about the real system, which may affect the behaviour of the simulated system. Therefore, we need to apply some sampling methods to produce the best possible input dataset for the intended simulator.

To design a sampling mechanism, the population and sampling frame must first be decided. Both are the source from which the samples are drawn. The population covers all available data. For some simple cases, such as the products from a production line, we can draw the samples directly from the population. However, sometimes it is costly or impossible to draw samples from the whole population, yet can be done within a sampling frame. A sampling frame is a list within the population for drawing samples. When multiple sampling frames are extracted form a population, care must be taken so that the frames do not overlap with each other. For example, it may be too difficult to include the whole population of people in a social network. In this case, we can draw samples from sampling frames, such as people from the same location or people who are married.

Sampling methods can be classified as probabilistic and non-probabilistic. In probabilistic sampling, each individual in a population has a chance to be drawn as a sample. Probabilistic sampling includes simple random sampling, systematic sampling, stratified sampling, and others. The probability of an individual being selected can be accurately determined in this method – for example, all individuals have the same chance of being selected in simple random sampling, which coincides with uniform distribution. The main advantage of probabilistic sampling is that it can produce unbiased samples. In non-probabilistic sampling, a certain deterministic or quasi-deterministic selection criteria/method is used to choose samples. By doing so, it is possible that some individuals in a population have no chance of being selected as a sample because of the inherent biases introduced by the designer-generated selection criteria. Methods in this category include, but are not limited to, accidental sampling, quota sampling, and purposive sampling. The sampling methods will be discussed again in detail in Chapter 6.

3.6 RUN SIMULATOR UNDER DIFFERENT SAMPLES

After the model is validated and the simulator is tested, we can start the experimental design and then run the simulator with different sampled inputs. Running the simulator facilitates answering the questions stemming from the system and problem definition, together with the subsequent hypotheses derived from these questions. Below we offer two definitions for the 'hypothesis' concept, taken from [3]. The first definition refers to testing whether the simulator is consistent with the relevant system. The second definition refers to testing whether the simulator is able to demonstrate the cause-effect relationships within a system, and whether it is able to solve the questions asked.

Definition 3.6.1. *A hypothesis is a statement of a prior belief formed about the outcome of an experiment.*

Definition 3.6.2. *A hypothesis is a prior belief of the existence of a cause-effect relationship.*

Experiments are designed to prove or dismiss the hypotheses. The definition of the 'experiment' concept is given as below.

Definition 3.6.3. *An experiment is a situation that is conditioned by the designer to exclude unwanted factors, while carefully including wanted factors, to examine a cause-effect relationship [3].*

As the definition suggests, we need to exclude the unwanted factors in experiments, since systems work in an environment that may contain some unnecessary factors not relevant to the purpose of the simulation. The unwanted factors within a system should be reduced during the model-building stage of the simulation process. If only the 'wanted' factors are included in an experiment, it is easier to focus on the key elements, identify the cause-effect relationships between them, and subsequently solve the problem initially posed, provided that the hypothesis is proven to be correct.

3.7 SUMMARISE RESULTS

Following the experiments stage, the results from the simulation need to be collected and stored for further analysis. Many techniques can be used to analyse and summarise the results from the experiments. Traditional statistic methods can be used for some straightforward studies. However, as discussed at the beginning of this chapter, sometimes the results yielding from a simulation cannot easily be interpreted and presented. In these cases, some advanced approaches, such as data mining, are required to facilitate users to deal with these complex results. Whichever approach is used for results analysis, it should serve the purpose of problem solving or system understanding, as defined in the first step. Tables or graphical charts are often useful to present findings to users.

In the summarising stage, sensitive analysis can be conducted to identify the key entities within a system and to determine the parameter value assignments, which can contribute to refining the model. The aggregate findings of the experiments should answer the question, and a conclusion must be drawn at the end of this exercise.

3.8 MAKE A RECOMMENDATION

The recommendation can be derived from the results analysis. It may include the possible solutions for the problem initially posed. It may also suggest model modifications or further experiments to increase precision. In some cases, it may lead to proposing a new simulation because the current understanding of the system is insufficient, the model of the system is incorrect, the proposed simulation cannot solve the problem or other reasons.

3.8.1 Verification and Validation

As you may notice, one important aspect – verification and validation – is not included in the above steps for developing a simulation, nor included in Figure 3.1. In fact, verification and validation are coupled with many steps, including building a model and encoding a simulator, because each of them involves some kind transformation. Hence, we discuss verification and validation separately.

Verification is a procedure to check the transformational accuracy for the transformations from both a system definition to a model and a model to a simulator. Verification checks whether the implemented model and the simulator are consistent with the requirement specifications and satisfy the intended purpose of the model. Validation is a testing process to determine the extent to which the model and the simulator actually represent the real system. Ideally, a model and its subsequent simulator should be equivalent to the real system they intend to simulate. In reality, a valid model or a simulator means that they are the closest representations possible for the relevant real system under the established assumptions.

The nature of the simulation makes the verification and validation difficult. Some useful software engineering techniques for verifying and validating a simulation development are suggested in [396] and include:

- Unit tests: aim to test a specific module or group of modules against some detailed design. Useful for entity functions testing (checking the effects from an entity).

- Integration tests: test an integrated piece of subsystems. The relationships between entities of a system can be tested with this method.
- System tests: compare the software system against the software requirements. Help validate the transformation from a model to a simulator.
- Acceptance tests: ensure that the system meets the user requirements, which means verifying that the simulator is equivalent to the real system.
- Regression testing: verifies that the modifications of a system do not cause unintended effects. Given that simulation developing is usually an evolutionary approach, modifications of models or simulators may occur frequently. This test is needed each time after changes occur.

In addition to verification and validation, accreditation is often used. Verification and validation focus on the technical aspects of the model and simulator testing, while accreditation is a formal decision process to determine whether the simulation is the appropriate one for the planned job.

3.9   AN EVOLUTIONARY APPROACH

The logic sequence to build a simulation was introduced in the previous sections. However, simulation development is an evolutionary approach, as aforementioned. Some steps may be recursively invoked during a simulation development. For example, a modeller may gather more insight view when validating a model and then it is necessary to go back and redefine the system. Running a simulator with different sampling inputs may show that values of some parameters are not accurate enough, so the model must be revisited to reassign the parameter vales, and, further, the simulator must be modified accordingly. As explained earlier in the model-building stage, the modeller may start with a simple version of the model and then enrich it as more understanding of the system is gained.

To demonstrate the full process of building a simulation, in the next section, we describe in detail a step-by-step example to build a battle simulation.

3.10   A BATTLE SIMULATION BY LANCHESTER SQUARE LAW

In this section, a step-by-step process is described to show how to model a battle between two forces and how to simulate with very basic information. First, the problem is introduced as follows.

Two forces, blue and red, engage with each other in an open terrain. Each side is composed of only infantry equipped with rifles. The actual troop sizes of blue and red are unknown, but the gathered information shows that the troop sizes of both sides follow the Gaussian distribution. The mean of the troop size for blue is 1000 with a standard deviation of 100. The red force has a mean value of the troop size equal to 1200 and a large standard deviation of 200. Both sides place all people in the battle at the beginning, without keeping any reserve troops. The different training on each side results in different fighting effectiveness. The values of the fighting effectiveness of blue and red are also unknown, but they follow the same Gaussian distributions. The mean of blue effectiveness is 0.8 with a 0.05 standard deviation, while red has effectiveness of 0.6 with a standard deviation of 0.1. Each side is visible to the other; therefore, both sides are able to aim and fire on the selected targets, with the fire distributed evenly over targets. Once a target is eliminated, fire can be shifted to other targets immediately. Reinforcement troops are not available for either side. The objective of each side is to destroy all enemies in the battle.

We need build a simulation for the battle as described, and use it to answer the following questions when the troop size and fighting effectiveness of each side are known:

- Who will win?
- How long will the battle last?
- How many survivors will the winner have?
- How will the casualties happen over time?
- Which factor is the most important to win a battle – troop size or fighting power?

3.10.1 Define a System

In the problem stated above, the system to be modelled contains two entities: blue force and red force. The open terrain enables both sides to see their opponent. Each force is composed of homogeneous troops (only infantry) with direct fire weapons (rifles). The behaviours of both sides involve selecting a target, aiming and firing on the target, and shifting fire to another target once a target is eliminated. The effects yielded from these behaviours are casualties in the opponent's force. The definitions of the system and its environment are summarised as follows:

- Entities: blue and red forces.
  - Homogeneous troop: infantry.
  - Direct fire weapon: rifles.
  - Troop size: both sides place all their people in the battle at the beginning.
  - Fighting effectiveness: is decided by their training.
- Behaviours:
  - aim and select a target
  - fire on the target
  - shift to another target once the selected target is eliminated.
- Effects: opponent casualties.
- Relationship between entities: warring sides.
- Environment: an open terrain where each side is visible to the other side.

In this case, there is no way to zoom in the system from the force level to a smaller unit level (e.g. platoon or individual soldier) because only the basic information is available in the problem description. Therefore, the resolution level is decided as the force level for the system. The force level resolution is sufficient to answer the posed questions.

3.10.2   Build a Model

According to the given definitions of the system and problem, let $B(t)$ and $R(t)$ denote the troop size for blue and red at time t, respectively. Let us assume that time can be measured in minutes, hours or days from the beginning of the battle. $B(0)$ and $R(0)$ are the initial troop sizes at the time when $t = 0$. The casualties on one side are mainly caused by direct fire from the other side. Given that both sides contain only homogeneous infantry force with rifles, the attrition level of one side depends on the fire power of the other side. The fire power can be seen as the force strength and depends on the number of infantry firing rifles, quality of the rifles, training and skills of the individuals, and so on. At first, we assume that both sides have everything identical except troop size. Therefore, the number of infantries (troop size) of a force at time t gives the strength of this force, and affects the attrition level of the opponent at time t. It is obvious that 10 infantries can cause more damage than 5 infantries when other factors are identical because 10 infantries can fire double the amount of bullets as 5 infantries.

In reality, both $B(t)$ and $R(t)$ are non-negative integers. However, it is convenient to investigate their changes in an idealised situation where we assume that both $B(t)$ and $R(t)$ are continuous functions over time. For example, the blue force has 1000 infantries and red has 1100 infantries when a battle starts at 1000 hours. At 1100 hours, blue has 800 infantries and red has 950 infantries. If a linear interpolation is used, there are 966.6 in blue and 1075 in red at 1010 hours. This means that the blue force lost 33.4 infantries and red lost 25 infantries in the first 10 minutes. Assuming that $B(t)$ and $R(t)$ are differentiable of t, we can use these to model the force strength (the troop size) as smooth functions through differential equations over time. In reality, many factors affect the force strength during a battle, such as reinforcements, weapon failures, non-combat casualties, and others. For our case, these factors must be ignored because we are planning to build a high-level model for the battle based on the limited available information. In summary, we assume that the casualty rate of the blue force is proportional to the force strength of the red force, and vice versa. Therefore, the differential equations for the attrition can be:

$$\frac{dB}{dt} = -\alpha_r R(t), \quad B(0) = B_0 \text{ and } \alpha_r > 0 \tag{3.1}$$

$$\frac{dR}{dt} = -\alpha_b B(t), \quad R(0) = R_0 \text{ and } \alpha_b > 0 \tag{3.2}$$

where $\frac{dB}{dt}$ is the attrition rate of the blue force over time, and $\frac{dR}{dt}$ is the attrition rate of the red force over time, α_b is the effectiveness of the blue force's fire on red, and α_r is the effectiveness of the red force's fire on blue. Both Eqs. (3.1) and (3.2) form a mathematical model known in the literature as the 'Lanchester-type combat model' [231]. As described by the above equations, the attrition rate of one force is proportional to the troop size and fighting effectiveness of the opposing force in a very short timeframe.

In this model, the fight effectiveness is uniform for a force over time because it assumes that the force contains homogeneous troop type. B and R are always greater than or equal to zero, as negative numbers have no physical meaning for a troop size. Therefore, we assume that the force with survivors wins the battle when it ends, and the battle ends only at the time when the troop size of one or both forces reaches zero. Neither side wins the battle for the latter case.

There are two common forms of the Lanchester combat model: (1) Lanchester linear law and (2) Lanchester square law (LSL). Lanchester assumed that the linear model is primarily applied to ancient combat, where usually one-to-one fight happens because of the weapon capabilities. The Lanchester linear law can also be used in the case of indirect fire, such as artillery, in contemporary warfare [246]. The Lanchester linear law applies equal weight to troop size and fighting effectiveness for force strength. However, the linear law is not suitable for our case because both sides are capable of direct fire. The LSL is more applicable to contemporary battles where the one-to-one fighting mode has changed to one-to-many or many-to-many because of using direct fire. From Eqs. (3.1) and (3.2), the chain rule from calculus can be used to derive a single equation as follows, if we are interested in B as a function of R, instead of B and R as functions of t:

$$\frac{dB}{dR} = \frac{\alpha_r R}{\alpha_b B}. \tag{3.3}$$

The above equation represents the differential casualty ratio of blue and red. This differential equation can be solved by separating variables and integration of both sides, from which we attain the following equation:

$$\alpha_b B^2 - \alpha_r R^2 = C. \tag{3.4}$$

The equation expresses the relative force strength as a constant (C) and measures the force strength by the fighting effectiveness of a force multiplied by the square of its troop size in the square law. This relationship between the force strength is called the LSL. As indicated in the above equation, the outcome of a battle modelled by the LSL is more sensitive to the troop size than the fight effectiveness, which leads to a common debate of quantity versus quality in the literature. We will discuss this later in the analysis section.

We also note again that fighting effectiveness (α) is not a probability of annihilating a certain number of enemies at one fire, but rather a proportional force strength. In the basic Lanchester combat model, the fighting effectiveness is determined at the beginning and does not change over time. This assumption makes Eq. (3.4) true. Therefore, the basic Lanchester model is a deterministic model that can be solved by any analytical solution. For example, the sign of the constant (C) indicates which side wins if there is no reinforcement for either side during the battle. If $C > 0$, the blue force wins, while the red force wins if $C < 0$. However, $C \equiv 0$ means that both sides have equal force strength and the result of the battle is a 'draw'. The battle modelled by LSL will last forever based on the differential equations, according to which the number of survivors of both sides becomes closer and closer to zero, yet never reaches zero. In this situation, we consider that neither side has survivors simply because B and R must be non-negative integers in reality. The last case gives the LSL equality condition:

$$\alpha_b B^2 = \alpha_r R^2. \tag{3.5}$$

It is straightforward to determine which side wins by the constant C, once the initial troop size and fighting effectiveness are given for both blue and red forces. Given that C is unknown, it can be solved with some initial conditions, including the troop size and fighting effectiveness. It is usually easy to attain the initial number of infantries in a force. However, it is challenging to gain an accurate value for a force's fight effectiveness because there are many factors contributing to fighting effectiveness, including the training and skills of individuals, quality of weapons, and morale of soldiers. Luckily, in our case, the range of the possible fighting effectiveness for each side is given in the problem definition, so this can be used directly in this model.

In light of all the above discussion, we decide to use the LSL as the model for the battle described in the problem introduction because all assumptions of the LSL are applicable to the system and problem definitions. These assumptions are: (1) homogeneous troops using direct fire, (2) fire uniformly distributed on the enemy targets, and (3) no reinforcement for either side during the battle. The outcome from the LSL is the attrition level of the two forces, which is in agreement with the resolution of the system decided in the previous step. Therefore, the abstraction level of the model is appropriate for the system.

3.10.3   Encode a Simulator

Thus far, we have used differential equations to represent the model of LSL, as shown in the previous section. It is not easy to encode these in a computer system. Many common programming languages support operations such as addition, subtraction, multiplication, division, and other basic numerical calculus. However, handling the derivatives in differential equations is difficult and usually not supported natively by most programming languages. Therefore, we need to use some numerical approximation techniques, such as the Euler method, to solve differential equations before encoding the model into the simulator. Alternatively, we can convert the differential equations into difference equations to make them suitable for discrete computer programs. For example, the attrition rate of LSL described by Eqs. (3.1) and (3.2) can be converted into difference equations as follows:

$$B_{n+1} = B_t - \alpha_r R_n \tag{3.6a}$$

$$R_{n+1} = R_t - \alpha_b B_n. \tag{3.6b}$$

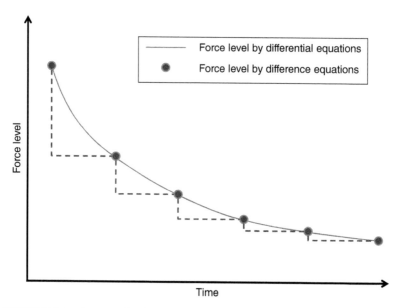

FIGURE 3.3   An example plotting a differential equation and difference equation.

In the differential equations, the attrition continuously occurs over time – a fact that corresponds to reality (both sides exchange fire continuously in a battle). However, in the difference equations shown above, we assume that the battle is divided into several stages, and both sides exchange fire only at a time point of every stage. During this very short time, all fires from one side are evenly targeted at the opponent, and vice versa. The casualties of both sides then occur immediately after exchanging fire. Thus, the subscript n means that exchanging fire occurred n rounds, but was not equal to the time in the battle (simulation time). Equation (3.6) expresses that the force levels of blue and red are B_{n+1} and R_{n+1}, respectively, after $n + 1$ rounds of fire exchanging. Let us now consider an example for the blue force level calculated by differential and difference equations, respectively, as illustrated in Figure 3.3.

The force level of blue continuously reduces over time when calculated using differential equations, and is visualised as a smooth descending line in the chart. However, the stepped reduction is found in the results from the difference equations as a set of points shown in the figure. This indicates that the force level changes instantaneously as a result of a round of fire exchange. Therefore, it is a discrete representation of the LSL. If the intervals between each update can be reduced and are small enough, we can generate a huge number of points and then connect them with lines that can approximate the smooth line produced by differential equations. From this example, we can conclude that differential equations reflect the continuous dynamics of a system, while difference equations reflect the discrete states of a system. In the LSL, reducing the magnitude of fighting effectiveness is the only way to achieve this objective. As stated in Eq. (3.4), the LSL indicates the relative fighting strength. As long as the ratio of fighting effectiveness remains the same, we can adjust

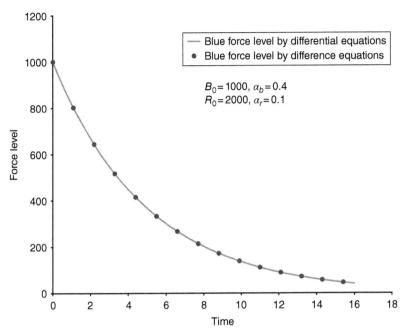

FIGURE 3.4   Blue force level calculated by difference equations with fighting effectiveness in different magnitudes with the same ratio 4 : 1 for blue to red. Fighting effectiveness: $\alpha_b = 0.4$ and $\alpha_r = 0.1$.

the magnitude for the purpose of reducing the fighting strength in a round, and so the intervals between force levels can be decreased. As shown in Figures 3.4 and 3.5, there are more points along the line in Figure 3.5 than in Figure 3.4 when the fighting effectiveness of both sides reduces. The ratio of the fighting effectiveness is still 4 : 1 for blue to red after the magnitude changes.

   Although the time axes are presented in both Figures 3.4 and 3.5, the difference equations do not explicitly express the time concept, but rather the firing rounds. Instead, the differential equations are coupled with the simulation (battle) time shown by time axis. We can use the difference questions to answer many questions, such as who wins the battle and the casualties after a round of fire. However, using the proposed difference equations, it is difficult to answer questions related to battle time, such as when the battle will end. We can provide the number of rounds after which the battle ends, yet that does not indicate the actual ending time. To solve such time-related questions, we must return to the differential equations and find a way to solve them and encode the LSL into a simulator.

   As a closed-form mathematical model, the differential equations of the LSL can be solved by analytic solutions once the initial troop sizes and fighting effectiveness of both sides are known. After extensive derivations from the above differential equations (details can be found in [376]), the relationship between force level and time in the LSL can be represented by the following parametric equations:

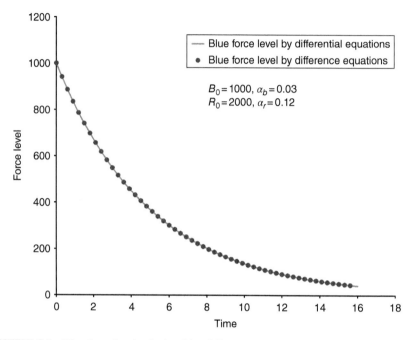

FIGURE 3.5   Blue force level calculated by difference equations with fighting effectiveness in different magnitudes with the same ratio 4 : 1 for blue to red. Fighting effectiveness: $\alpha_b = 0.12$ and $\alpha_r = 0.03$.

$$B(t) = B_0 \cosh(\sqrt{\alpha_r \alpha_b}\, t) - R_0 \sqrt{\frac{\alpha_r}{\alpha_b}} \sinh(\sqrt{\alpha_r \alpha_b}\, t) \qquad (3.7\text{a})$$

$$R(t) = R_0 \cosh(\sqrt{\alpha_r \alpha_b}\, t) - B_0 \sqrt{\frac{\alpha_b}{\alpha_r}} \sinh(\sqrt{\alpha_r \alpha_b}\, t). \qquad (3.7\text{b})$$

Given that there is no way to present a continuous number in a discrete computer system, the time unit in the above equations must be small enough to gain a close approximation for the LSL in differential equation form. From this point of view, the above equations are another set of difference equations in terms of discrete simulation (battle) time. We can also derive the equations for the battle ending time and the remaining force level of the winner from the above equations. According to the LSL, blue wins when it has more force strength than red, and the calculations for the battle ending time and number of survivors for blue are as follows:

$$\begin{cases} t_{end} = \dfrac{1}{2\sqrt{\alpha_r \alpha_b}} \ln\left(\dfrac{\sqrt{\alpha_r} R_0 + \sqrt{\alpha_b} B_0}{\sqrt{\alpha_b} B_0 - \sqrt{\alpha_r} R_0} \right) \\[4mm] B_{end} = B_0 \sqrt{1 - \dfrac{\alpha_r R_0^2}{\alpha_b B_0^2}} \end{cases} \quad \text{if} \quad \alpha_b B_0^2 > \alpha_r R_0^2 \qquad (3.8)$$

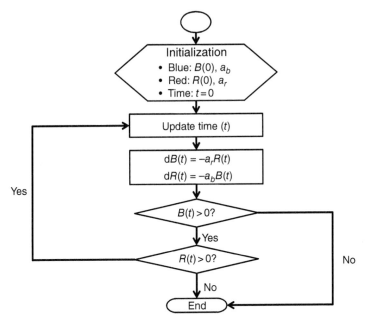

FIGURE 3.6   The flowchart of a battle simulator – simulator advanced by time.

Otherwise, the ending time and number of survivors for red are calculated as follows:

$$
\begin{cases}
t_{end} = \dfrac{1}{2\sqrt{\alpha_r \alpha_b}} \ln\left(\dfrac{\sqrt{\alpha_r}R_0 + \sqrt{\alpha_b}B_0}{\sqrt{\alpha_r}R_0 - \sqrt{\alpha_b}B_0}\right) \\[2ex]
R_{end} = R_0 \sqrt{1 - \dfrac{\alpha_b B_0^2}{\alpha_r R_0^2}}.
\end{cases}
\qquad \text{if} \quad \alpha_b B_0^2 > \alpha_r R_0^2 \qquad (3.9)
$$

Now we have all the necessary equations allowing us to encode the model into a simulator, as the equations are able to answer the questions about the final states of the battle. However, we would alsolike to use them to investigate how the battle proceeds over time. Therefore, the logic of how the simulator runs in terms of time needs to be designed to investigate time-related problems before starting encoding. Figure 3.6 displays a flowchart describing how the proposed simulator runs in terms of time advancing. It starts with initialising the parameters of the simulator, which include troop size, fighting effectiveness, and time. The force levels are updated in time according to the LSL. If neither force's number reaches zero, the time advances and force strength level are updated by LSL again. These steps repeat until one side has no infantry left, and then the simulation ends by exiting the simulator. Following the logic illustrated in Figure 3.6, we can investigate the dynamics of the force levels over time during a battle. A similar logic can be found in Figure 3.7, where the simulator is advanced by fire rounds instead of time advancing. This is a simulator updating force levels according to the difference equations (Eq. (3.6)). Both simulators should give the same results, despite the different representations encoded in the simulator. As the sets of equations suggested, encoding a simulator based on

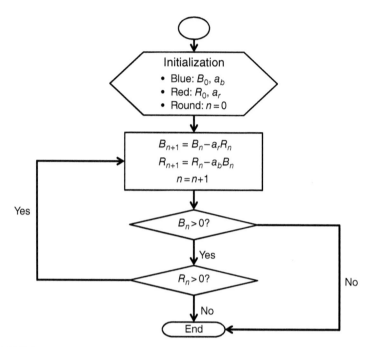

FIGURE 3.7   The flowchart of a battle simulator – simulator advanced by fire rounds.

fire rounds is much easier than encoding it based on time advancing. However, the time-based simulator is still necessary to investigate casualties over time.

For this simulator, spreadsheet software (e.g. Microsoft Excel) is used and an Excel spreadsheet called 'LanchesterSquareLaw.xlsx' is created. At first, the parameters used in the LSL must be declared in the sheet 'Lanchester', which is shown on the left side of Figure 3.8. A number of scroll bars are implemented to adjust these inputs easily when running simulations.

The equations answering the questions related to force strength and the final state of the battle can also be encoded in a spreadsheet. This type of question and the corresponding equations are listed in Table 3.1.

As seen in the equations presented in the table, many common variables exist in many places that only depend on the initial parameters. Therefore, a list of temporal variables that are created and calculated in advance is shown on the right side of Figure 3.8. This technique will help us later, when coding long equations for the simulator. It also reduces the unnecessary computational cost of calculating these variables repeatedly during simulation, despite their values being unchanged once the initial parameters are decided.

Now we need to start writing the function to evaluate the changes in the force level over time. Based on the last two equations in the above table, it is straightforward to generate a series of data to describe the force level changes in a spreadsheet. Given that it is still a discrete representation of the force level changes over time, the time interval must be set first. As shown in Figure 3.8, there is a parameter called

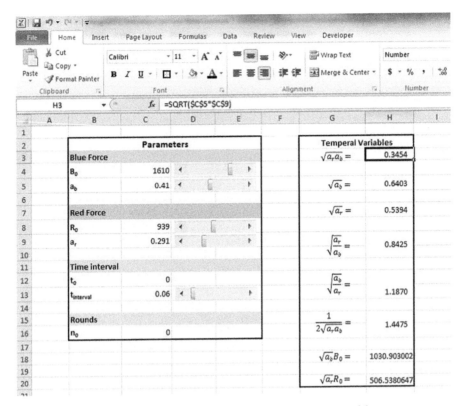

FIGURE 3.8   The parameters of LSL declared in a spreadsheet.

$t_{interval}$ that decides how much the time advances in every step. As discussed before, smaller values result in a more accurate approximation of the continuous differential function. Therefore, this parameter is always smaller than one. We then type Equation 3.7 into a spreadsheet with the parameters and temporal variables declared before. Similarly, we can gain from Excel another set of data about force level changes based on the rounds of fire, according to the difference equations. These are implemented in two separate sheets – one called 'TimeBasedSimulator' and the other called 'RoundBasedSimulator' – in 'LanchesterSquareLaw.xlsx'. In addition to the numerical values produced by equations, graphical charts are also added to visualise the force level changes. Figures 3.9 and 3.10 show the implementations based on time and rounds.

Thus far, our battle simulator has been implemented in Excel based on the LSL. After carefully checking all equations typed in the spreadsheets, we move to the next step: sampling data for simulation.

3.10.4 Sampling Data

As stated by the problem description, we cannot attain the actual numbers for the initial troop size and fighting effectiveness of both sides. This leads to uncertainty of

TABLE 3.1   Questions and Corresponding Equations Encoded in Excel

Questions	Answer and equations
Force strength	Blue: $\alpha_b B^2$ Red: $\alpha_r R^2$
Who wins?	If $\alpha_b B^2 - \alpha_r R^2 = C > 0$, blue wins If $\alpha_b B^2 - \alpha_r R^2 = C < 0$, red wins If $\alpha_b B^2 - \alpha_r R^2 = C \equiv 0$, DRAW
How long will the battle last?	If blue wins, $t_{end} = \dfrac{1}{2\sqrt{\alpha_r \alpha_b}} \ln\left(\dfrac{\sqrt{\alpha_r} R_0 + \sqrt{\alpha_b} B_0}{\sqrt{\alpha_b} B_0 - \sqrt{\alpha_r} R_0} \right)$ If red wins, $t_{end} = \dfrac{1}{2\sqrt{\alpha_r \alpha_b}} \ln\left(\dfrac{\sqrt{\alpha_r} R_0 + \sqrt{\alpha_b} B_0}{\sqrt{\alpha_r} R_0 - \sqrt{\alpha_b} B_0} \right)$ if DRAW, the battle lasts forever, based on the above equations. However, in reality, it should end when the number of troops on either or both sides is less than 1.
How many survivors will the winner have?	If blue wins, $B_{end} = B_0 \sqrt{1 - \dfrac{\alpha_r R_0^2}{\alpha_b B_0^2}}$ If red wins, $R_{end} = R_0 \sqrt{1 - \dfrac{\alpha_b B_0^2}{\alpha_r R_0^2}}$ If DRAW, zeros for both sides.
How will the casualties happen over time?	$B(t) = B_0 \cosh(\sqrt{\alpha_r \alpha_b}\, t) - R_0 \sqrt{\dfrac{\alpha_r}{\alpha_b}} \sinh(\sqrt{\alpha_r \alpha_b}\, t)$ $R(t) = R_0 \cosh(\sqrt{\alpha_r \alpha_b}\, t) - B_0 \sqrt{\dfrac{\alpha_b}{\alpha_r}} \sinh(\sqrt{\alpha_r \alpha_b}\, t)$

the battle results, although the LSL is a deterministic model with given parameters. Therefore, we need to decide the initial values for the parameters used in our simulator. Given that we use a computer-based simulator, we can run simulations as many times as we wish; thus, we can take a brute-force approach in which we simulate every possible value of the two parameters. However, it is obviously not feasible to enumerate every possible situation. There are in total 100 million combinations of blue–red battles if both blue and red forces have only 100 different possible troop sizes and 100 different outcomes for fighting effectiveness. Running such a huge number of experiments is very costly and time consuming, even if they are run on a computer. Therefore, we need to design a sampling method to select some data as input to the simulator and then deduce the actual behaviour of the system from the results obtained from the sampling data.

Let us imagine that both blue and red commanders independently make decisions about the number of infantries for a battle without knowing any information about the other side. Both troop sizes can be seen as the outcomes generated from Gaussian distributions under the given mean and standard deviation with random probabilities. Also, the fighting effectiveness of both sides depends on many factors (e.g. soldier

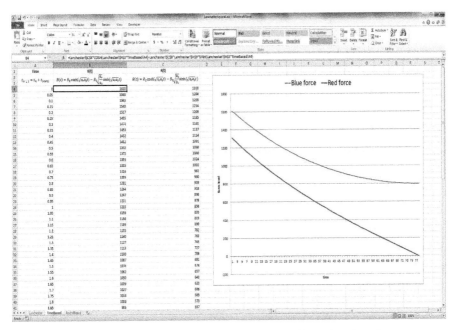

FIGURE 3.9   The spreadsheet implementation of LSL based on time.

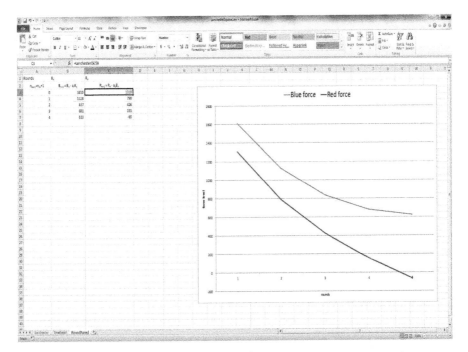

FIGURE 3.10   The spreadsheet implementation of LSL based on rounds.

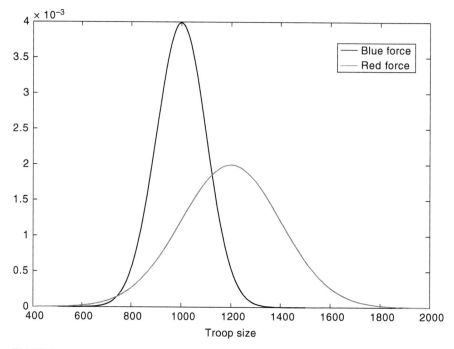

FIGURE 3.11   The bell curves of troop sizes: $\mu_B = 1000, \sigma_B = 100$ and $\mu_R = 1200$, $\sigma_R = 200$.

morale), yet is determined before the battle begins. The factors affecting the fighting effectiveness of the opponents are unknown, yet their effects (i.e. the fight effectiveness) follow the Gaussian distributions as well. With the given information, the troop size and fighting effectiveness can be visualised as bell curves using probability density function (PDF).

As shown in Figures 3.11 and 3.12, the bell curves of the blue force's troop size and fighting effectiveness are spread smaller than those of the red force because the blue force has smaller standard deviations of both troop size and fighting effectiveness. This means that the blue force has more chances to attain a troop size and fighting effectiveness close to their means. Several methods can be used to gain a number from a normal distribution, including Box–Muller method [51] and Marsaglia polar method [268]. Here, we will use a straightforward method to generate the initial troop size and fighting effectiveness by a given probability based on cumulative distribution function (CDF). Figures 3.13 and 3.14 visualise the CDFs for the force levels and fighting effectiveness of both sides. The y axis in the figure shows the cumulative distribution of the probabilities. The sum of all probabilities is 1. If we can randomly generate a random number between 0 and 1, we can find a value from the normal distribution. Let us consider the troop size of blue force as an example. If a number is generated randomly and its value is 0.5, we locate this value on the **Y** axis in Figure 3.13 draw a horizontal line intersected with the blue curve. A vertical line

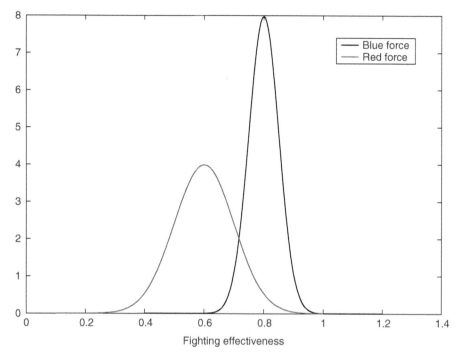

FIGURE 3.12   The bell curves of fighting effectiveness: $\mu_B = 0.8, \sigma_B = 0.05$ and $\mu_R = 0.6$, $\sigma_R = 0.1$.

can be drawn from the intersection towards the **X** axis. The intersection between the vertical line and **X** axis will give us the value of the blue force's troop size – that is, 1000. Similarly, we can use the same method to attain the fighting effectiveness of the blue force. Therefore, the inverse function of the normal CDF can be used to generate numbers that belong to a normal distribution.

Given that we are using Excel as the tool for implementation, we can use the **RAND** function as the random number generator. Excel also provides an inverse function of normal CDF called **NORMINV** to generate numbers from a Gaussian distribution by a given probability. The steps to obtain troop size and fighting effectiveness are as follows:

1. Generate a random number by a uniform distribution as the probability (p), and $0 < p < 1$ (using **RAND()** in Excel).
2. Obtain the troop size from the given Gaussian distribution with mean (μ) and standard deviation (σ) by the probability p [using **NORMINV**(p, μ, σ) in Excel].
3. Save the generated number of troop size in a candidate list.

The above methods are implemented in the sheet of 'Data Sampling' in 'LanchesterSquare- Lar.xls', as shown in Figure 3.15. One hundred sets of input data

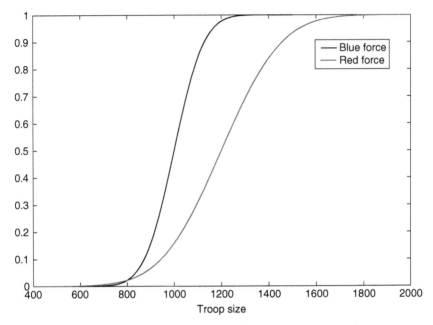

FIGURE 3.13   The CDF of troop sizes: $\mu_B = 1000, \sigma_B = 100$ and $\mu_R = 1200, \sigma_R = 200$.

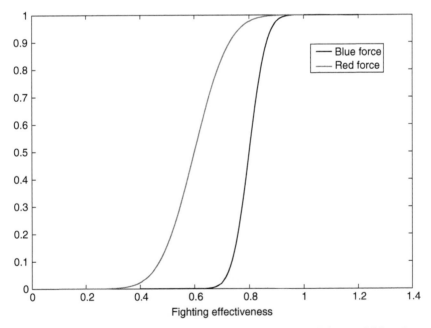

FIGURE 3.14   The bell curves of fighting effectiveness: $\mu_B = 0.8, \sigma_B = 0.05$ and $\mu_R = 0.6, \sigma_R = 0.1$.

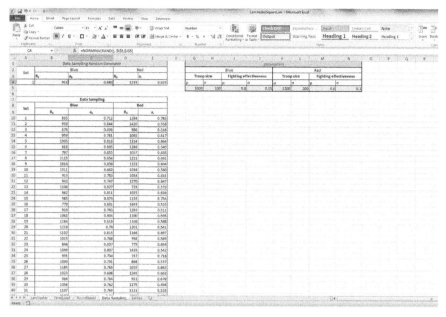

FIGURE 3.15   An implementation of data sampling.

TABLE 3.2   Some Samples of the Input Datasets to the Simulator

	Blue		Red	
Set	Troop size	Fighting effectiveness	Troop size	Fighting effectiveness
1	935	0.712	1284	0.783
2	938	0.844	1420	0.558
3	874	0.806	986	0.518
4	959	0.781	1065	0.617
5	1005	0.816	1314	0.664
6	818	0.895	1286	0.540
7	797	0.855	1057	0.435
8	1115	0.854	1221	0.691
9	1016	0.806	1323	0.804
10	1011	0.662	1034	0.580

are generated using the above method. Each set includes four values, corresponding to the initial troop sizes and the fighting effectiveness of both sides. Some sample inputs are listed in Table 3.2.

3.10.5   Simulation and Results

Now, we start the simulation with the implemented model and sampling data. It is not a time-consuming job to enter each input set into the spreadsheet to run the simulator.

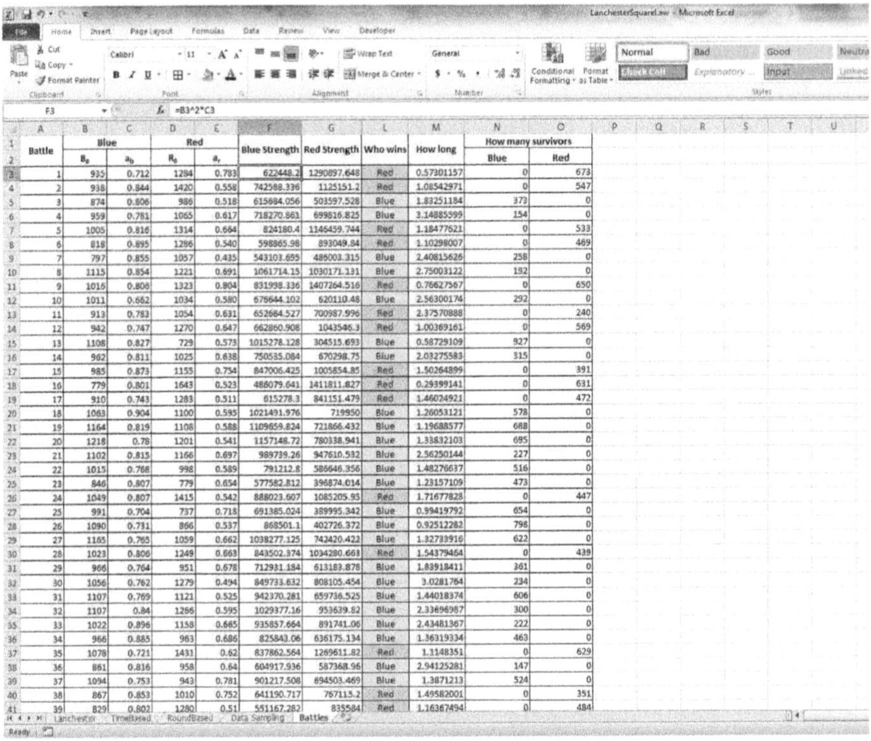

Battle	Blue		Red		Blue Strength	Red Strength	Who wins	How long	How many survivors	
	B_0	a_b	R_0	a_r					Blue	Red
1	935	0.712	1284	0.783	622448.2	1290897.648	Red	0.57301157	0	673
2	938	0.844	1420	0.558	742588.336	1125151.2	Red	1.08542971	0	547
3	874	0.806	986	0.518	615684.056	503597.528	Blue	1.83251184	373	0
4	959	0.781	1065	0.617	718270.861	699816.825	Blue	3.14885599	154	0
5	1005	0.816	1314	0.664	824180.4	1146459.744	Red	1.18477621	0	533
6	818	0.895	1286	0.540	598865.98	893049.84	Red	1.10298007	0	469
7	797	0.855	1057	0.435	543103.695	486003.315	Blue	2.40815626	258	0
8	1115	0.854	1221	0.691	1061714.15	1030171.131	Blue	2.75003122	192	0
9	1016	0.806	1323	0.804	831998.336	1407264.516	Red	0.76627567	0	650
10	1011	0.662	1034	0.580	676644.102	620110.48	Blue	2.56300174	292	0
11	913	0.783	1054	0.631	652684.527	700987.996	Red	2.37570888	0	240
12	942	0.747	1270	0.647	662860.908	1043546.3	Red	1.00369161	0	569
13	1108	0.827	729	0.573	1015278.128	304515.693	Blue	0.58729109	927	0
14	962	0.811	1025	0.638	750535.084	670298.75	Blue	2.03275583	315	0
15	985	0.873	1155	0.754	847006.425	1005854.85	Red	1.50264899	0	391
16	779	0.801	1643	0.523	486079.641	1411811.827	Red	0.29399141	0	631
17	910	0.743	1283	0.511	615278.3	841151.479	Red	1.46024921	0	472
18	1063	0.904	1100	0.595	1021491.976	719950	Blue	1.26053121	578	0
19	1164	0.819	1108	0.588	1109659.824	721866.432	Blue	1.19688577	688	0
20	1218	0.78	1201	0.541	1157148.72	780338.941	Blue	1.33832103	695	0
21	1102	0.815	1166	0.697	989739.26	947610.532	Blue	2.56250144	227	0
22	1015	0.768	998	0.589	791212.8	586646.356	Blue	1.48276637	516	0
23	846	0.807	779	0.654	577582.812	396874.014	Blue	1.23157109	473	0
24	1049	0.807	1415	0.542	888023.607	1085205.95	Red	1.71677828	0	447
25	991	0.704	737	0.718	691385.024	389995.342	Blue	0.99419792	654	0
26	1090	0.731	866	0.537	868501.1	402726.372	Blue	0.92512282	798	0
27	1165	0.765	1059	0.662	1038277.125	742420.422	Blue	1.32733916	622	0
28	1023	0.806	1249	0.663	843502.374	1034280.663	Red	1.54379464	0	439
29	966	0.764	951	0.678	712931.184	613183.878	Blue	1.83918411	361	0
30	1056	0.762	1279	0.494	849733.632	808105.454	Blue	3.0281764	234	0
31	1107	0.769	1121	0.525	942370.281	659736.525	Blue	1.44018374	606	0
32	1107	0.84	1266	0.595	1029377.16	953639.82	Blue	2.33696987	300	0
33	1022	0.896	1158	0.665	935857.664	891741.06	Blue	2.43481367	222	0
34	966	0.885	963	0.686	825843.06	636175.134	Blue	1.36319334	463	0
35	1078	0.721	1431	0.62	837862.564	1269611.82	Red	1.1148351	0	629
36	861	0.816	958	0.64	604917.936	587368.96	Blue	2.94125281	147	0
37	1094	0.753	943	0.781	901217.508	694503.469	Blue	1.3871213	524	0
38	867	0.853	1010	0.752	641190.717	767115.2	Red	1.49582001	0	351
39	829	0.802	1280	0.51	551167.282	835584	Red	1.16367494	0	484

FIGURE 3.16 An implementation of data sampling.

Hence, a sheet called 'Battles' is created and the sampling data are copied to this sheet. In this sheet, we calculate all results related to the final state of the battle. The implementation is shown in Figure 3.16. Now, in the spreadsheet 'TimeBasedSimulator', we can choose some interesting cases for further analysis of the casualties.

At first, the results – such as who won, the number of survivors and the battle duration – are summarised in Table 3.3. The blue force won 45 battles, while the red force won 55 battles. The average number of survivors of the red force when they won was greater than the average number of the blue force. In addition, the blue force took a longer time on average to win a battle than did the red force. The overall results suggest that the red force has slightly more chances (55 : 45) to win a battle in the given conditions.

Now, let us compare the conditions (initial troop size and fighting effectiveness) under which the blue or red force can win a battle. There are 55 battles won by a force with quantitative superiority, yet no advantages in fight effectiveness. However, only 25 battles are won by a force with a lower number of infantries, yet greater fighting effectiveness. The other 20 battles are won by a force with advantages in both numbers and fighting effectiveness. Therefore, Table 3.4 implies that troop size is the key factor for a force to win a battle, which conforms to the LSL.

TABLE 3.3   Results Summary of 100 Simulator Runs

	Number of wins	Average number of survivors if won	Average time to win a battle
Blue	45	461	2.3678
Red	55	488	1.3315
Draw	0	NA	NA

TABLE 3.4   Comparison of Battle Results by Different Initial Troop Sizes and Fighting Effectiveness

Troop size	Fighting effectiveness	Blue won	Red won	Draw
$B_0 > R_0$	$\alpha_b > \alpha_r$	18	0	0
	$\alpha_b < \alpha_r$	2	0	0
	$\alpha_b \equiv \alpha_r$	0	0	0
$B_0 < R_0$	$\alpha_b > \alpha_r$	25	53	0
	$\alpha_b < \alpha_r$	0	2	0
	$\alpha_b \equiv \alpha_r$	0	0	0
$B_0 \equiv R_0$	$\alpha_b > \alpha_r$	0	0	0
	$\alpha_b < \alpha_r$	0	0	0
	$\alpha_b \equiv \alpha_r$	0	0	0
Total		45	55	0

We use the longest battle from the above results as the example to investigate the casualties of both sides over time in a battle. The parameters of the longest battle ($B_0 = 1034$, $\alpha_b = 0.749$, $R_0 = 1460$, and $\alpha_r = 0.373$) are set in the 'Lanchester' sheet at first, and the corresponding results are automatically produced in 'TimeBasedSimulator'. Figure 3.17 shows the force level changing over time during this battle. The force levels of both sides decreased quickly at the beginning of the battle. Blue caused casualties in red by its higher fighting effectiveness, while red caused damage to blue by numbers. As the battle progresses, the reduction rates of both force levels grow smaller because of the reduction of the force level of both sides. In this example, blue wins the battle because there is a small difference in the numbers, yet blue had double the fighting effectiveness compared with red.

We can also use this simulator to answer some 'what-if' questions. For example, what is the result if both sides take the average troop size and fighting effectiveness into a battle? Simply type the average values for both sides in the 'Lanchester' sheet and simulate again. We see that the red force wins and has 327 survivors, with the battle ending at time 2.8513. Table 3.5 summarises the results when we fix the fighting effectiveness for both sides as their mean values, yet vary their troop size from the $\mu - 3\sigma$ to $\mu + 3\sigma$ with the step equal to the standard deviation (σ). The table also shows that the force with advantage in numbers wins most battles. Similarly, we can fix the troop size and vary the fighting effectiveness to see the results.

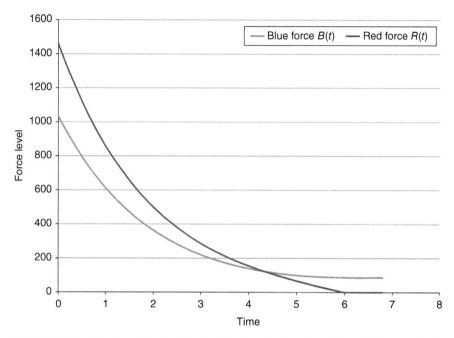

FIGURE 3.17 The force levels of both sides in a battle, where $B_0 = 1034$, $\alpha_b = 0.749$, $R_0 = 1460$, and $\alpha_r = 0.373$.

TABLE 3.5 **The Battle Results When Fighting Effectiveness Fixed, but Troop Sizes Varied**

		Blue force with fighting effectiveness $\alpha_b = 0.8$						
		$B_0 = $ 700	$B_0 = $ 800	$B_0 = $ 900	$B_0 = $ 1,000	$B_0 = $ 1,100	$B_0 = $ 1,200	$B_0 = $ 1,300
Red force with	$R_0 = 600$	Blue	Blue	Blue	Blue	Blue	Blue	Blue
fighting	$R_0 = 800$	Blue	Blue	Blue	Blue	Blue	Blue	Blue
effectiveness	$R_0 = 1000$	Red	Red	Blue	Blue	Blue	Blue	Blue
$\alpha_r = 0.6$	$R_0 = 1200$	Red	Red	Red	Red	Blue	Blue	Blue
	$R_0 = 1400$	Red	Red	Red	Red	Red	Red	Blue
	$R_0 = 1600$	Red	Red	Red	Red	Red	Red	Red
	$R_0 = 1800$	Red	Red	Red	Red	Red	Red	Red

3.10.6 Draw a Conclusion

As the results suggested, the troop size is more important than the fighting effectiveness if we use the LSL. This means that we should place all available troops into the battle at the beginning. The side with the larger troop size most likely wins the battle if the difference between the two forces' fighting effectiveness is not too large.

This further leads to the quality–quantity debate in the literature, which is beyond our scope.

From the above exercises, it can be seen that we can build a model for a real system, encode the model into a simulator, and then run the simulation on it to solve some problems. Some methods and techniques, such as distributions, were briefly introduced in the description of the step-by-step process; more details on these can be found in Appendix A.

CHAPTER 4

Simulation Worldview and Conflict Resolution

A simulation has both static and dynamic structures to describe a system. There are several different approaches to structuring a model, including event-scheduling, activity-scanning, process-interaction, and so forth. These approaches represent what is called 'simulation worldview'. Simulation worldviews are often subject to various conflicts because of unavoidable situations in which multiple events occur simultaneously. This renders it necessary for modellers to employ various conflict-resolution methods. While many of these methods are available in the literature, there is no generalised approach that can resolve all kind of conflicts; thus, modellers must develop the resolutions based on the actual cases. In this chapter, we discuss in detail the concept of worldview, and describe the most relevant approaches. Along with the worldview presentation, we also provide several examples to address the conflict-resolution development. We conclude the chapter by discussing in detail the priority queue – one of the most popular methods for rescheduling simultaneous events.

4.1   SIMULATION WORLDVIEW

As discussed in the previous chapters, a simulation model contains not only static, but also dynamic structures. The static structure of a model includes the possible system states, the collection of system entities and their attributes. For example, a traffic light has three states: red light on, green light on, and yellow light on. The dynamic structure describes when and how the model changes over time. The static structure of a traffic light model may be shared by various traffic light models, which have common entities, attributes, and states. However, the dynamic structure may vary from one model to another, depending on the purpose. For example, the dynamic structure of a model representing a timer-controlled traffic light is that the timer signal triggers the change of the traffic light states at predefined time intervals. For a model representing a sensor-controlled traffic light, the sensors detect the traffic flow and,

Simulation and Computational Red Teaming for Problem Solving, First Edition.
Jiangjun Tang, George Leu, and Hussein A. Abbass.

based on this flow, trigger the change of the traffic light states. Therefore, different mechanisms that enable the operation of a system may lead to different approaches for representing the dynamic structure of a model. The way the dynamic structure of a model is described is the 'simulation worldview'. In this section, we focus on a number of popular simulation worldviews, including:

- three classic simulation worldviews for DES:
  - event scheduling,
  - activity scanning,
  - process interaction
- a three-phase worldview for discrete time/event simulation
- an agent-oriented worldview for agent – ased simulation.

4.1.1 Simulation Worldview of Discrete Event Simulation

Event scheduling, activity scanning, and process interaction are three traditional simulation worldviews of DES that have been widely adopted in many simulation software packages [352]. All three simulation worldviews were developed in the 1960s and have been continuously refined since then. As their names suggest, they focus on events, activities, and processes when evolving model dynamics over time [74]. As defined in Chapter 7, an event in a DES is an instantaneous occurrence that may change the state of a system. Two definitions for a DES – activity and process – need to be introduced before discussing the three simulation worldviews.

Definition 4.1.1. *An **activity** is the state of an entity of a system over a time interval.*

Definition 4.1.2. *A **process** is the succession of entity states over a time span when it goes through a system.*

Example 4.1.1. *There is only one register in a grocery shop. The register serves one customer at each time. If the register is busy, customers have to wait in a queue.*

Figure 4.1 depicts the three worldviews from a customer perspective for the above example, which is a typical single-server queueing system.

As shown in the figure, there are two major types of events: 'customer arrival' and 'customer departure'. Both affect the register states and queue length. From an event-scheduling worldview perspective, the modeller must define these events in the system, the sequence of events according to the time line, and the event effects on the system state. Therefore, the register of the grocery shop is viewed as a series of instantaneous events (customer arrivals and departures) that changes the register state over time. The new system state can be determined by the current state and the occurring event. For example, the register changes from idle to busy when the first customer arrives, and the simulation time advances to the time instant of the first customer arrival. Usually, time advancing in event-scheduling worldview is next-event

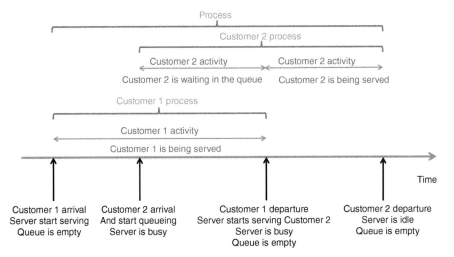

FIGURE 4.1   Three traditional simulation worldviews of DES.

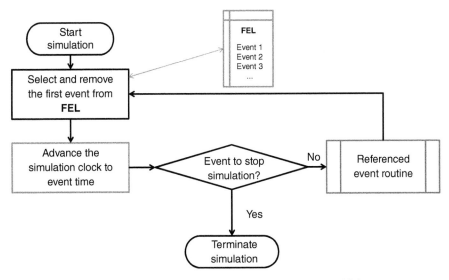

FIGURE 4.2   Time advancing in event-scheduling worldview.

time advancing, which is achieved by using a future event list (FEL) that stores all scheduled events. Therefore, the simulation time cannot advance within an event. The details of the time advancing in the event-scheduling worldview are graphically represented in Figure 4.2.

There are two major steps involved in event-scheduling time advancing. First, the simulation advances the time to the value of the first event time in the FEL. Second, a corresponding event routine is invoked to handle the event and change the system state. For example, if the first event in FEL is a customer departure event, then a departure routine is invoked. The details on different event routines can be found in Chapter 7.

The activity-scanning worldview focuses on the activities in a system and the conditions that allow these activities to start. The conditions are usually defined by the availability of resources. For the grocery register example, the resource of the system is the register. When the register is available, an arriving customer can be served immediately; otherwise, this customer has to wait in the queue. Thus, the status of the service decides the activity (either being served or waiting) that can be taken by an arriving customer. Resource status is changed by various events – for example, the register state changes from idle to busy when a customer arrives. In addition, an activity can last for a certain amount of time – for example, the waiting activity of the second customer shown in Figure 4.1. In the activity-scanning worldview, the conditions of each activity are checked at every simulation time advancing. If all conditions of an activity are satisfied, this activity is executed. Hence, simulation with activity-scanning worldview has a list storing all possible activities and associated conditions. The modeller usually needs to construct an activity list based on FEL to adopt the activity-scanning worldview in the simulation. A simple fixed time-advancing mechanism for this simulation worldview is illustrated in Figure 4.3.

In the process-interaction worldview, the system is viewed as the movement of a set of passive entities going through the system. Therefore, a process of one entity is a sequence of all associated entities, activities and other time delays associated with the entity flowing through the system. The time delays are caused by the limited resources available to the entities. As illustrated in Figure 4.1, the process of the first customer includes arriving at the register, being served by the register (delay) and leaving the shop. The sequence of the second customer includes arriving at the shop, waiting in the queue (delay), being served (delay), and leaving. The flow of entities moving through the system is called 'process flow'.

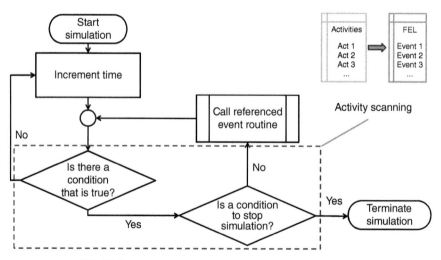

FIGURE 4.3   Time advancing in activity-scan worldview.

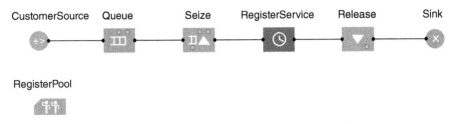

FIGURE 4.4 The process flow of a grocery shop register.

To model a DES with the process-interaction worldview, the modellers need to identify the entities flowing in the system, which usually consume resources. They then need to construct the process that moves the entity from one place to another in a flow. Many simulation software packages (e.g. AnyLogic) adopt process flow as a modelling tool for DES. An example of process flow built with AnyLogic for the grocery shop register is displayed in Figure 4.4.

The basic blocks of a process flow include the resource, queue, delay, seize, release, and sink blocks, as shown in the figure. The resource block generates the customer arrivals. The resource or the service in a system is usually modelled as a delay block. Seize blocks can hold a reserved resource or service when it is occupied by a customer. Once the service is finished, a release block frees the resource and makes it available for the first customer in the queue block. As shown in the figure, there is a resource pool representing the register, which is associated with the seize and release blocks. Thus, the seize and release blocks know which resource and how many resources to handle. The sink blocks absorb the leaving customers and discard them in the computer memory. Although the time-advancing mechanism of the simulation with the process-interaction view is implemented and handled by simulation software packages, it is worth discussing here to enable a good understanding.

As illustrated in Figure 4.5, a FEL still exists in the simulation, but it holds the scheduled processes. There is also a current event list (CEL) that stores the current processes at the current simulation clock time. The processes move from FEL to CEL before the simulation clock ticks. Then the simulation clock moves to the first process time in the CEL and checks the conditions to execute this process. The conditions are usually related to resource availability. If resources are available, the process is executed. Otherwise, the execution time of this process has to be rescheduled and the process has to be moved back to FEL. These steps are repeated in a simulation until the termination conditions are reached.

Thus far, we have introduced the three classic simulation worldview approaches. A more in-depth discussion can be found in [35] and [139].

4.1.2 Three-Phase Worldview

The three-phase worldview is another popular simulation worldview. It combines activity-scanning and event-scheduling to avoid the inefficiency caused by the activity scanning occurring at fixed time intervals. In the three-phase worldview, there are

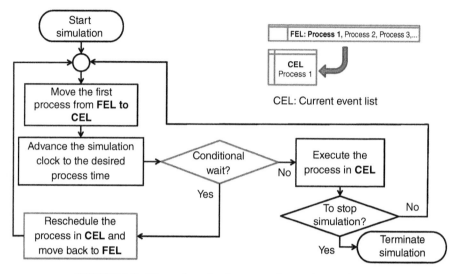

FIGURE 4.5   Time advancing in process-interaction worldview.

three types of activities, named **A**, **B**, and **C**. **A** type activities are called for scanning time. **B** type activities are the activities that have starting and finishing times that can be predicted in advance. Thus, **B**s are bound to occurring activities and can be scheduled using classic event-scheduling methods. **B**s can be stored in FEL. **C** type activities are conditional activities. In the grocery shop example, customer arrivals are unconditional activities of type **B**, which can be scheduled and stored in an event list. However, the activity of a customer waiting or being served is conditioned by the state of the register; thus, they are type **C**.

Figure 4.6 summarises in a visual manner the three phases that occur at every simulation time step in the three-phase worldview:

- A phase: simulation clock advances to the next event time by checking **B**s
- B phase: events in **B**s with the same time value of the simulation clock are executed
- C phase: any activities in **C**s that meet the execution conditions are executed.

4.1.3   Agent-Oriented Worldview

As a result of the increased popularity of agent-based simulation, the agent-oriented worldview was proposed. The agent-oriented worldview focuses on agents in a system. An agent has its own attributes and behaviour, and also interacts with other agents within or outside the system. In the agent-oriented worldview, the system dynamics evolve through the agents' interactions. This is closely related to the object-oriented worldview because agents in a system are commonly implemented by classes, and the interactions between agents are modelled by interfaces.

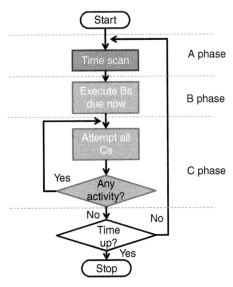

FIGURE 4.6   Time advancing in three-phase worldview.

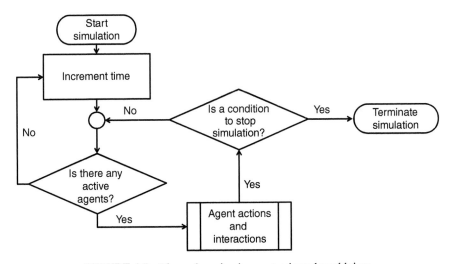

FIGURE 4.7   Time advancing in agent-oriented worldview.

Time advancing in the agent-oriented worldview is illustrated in Figure 4.7. The actions and interactions of active agents are executed at each simulation time step. These result in changes in the agent states and consequently affect the system states.

Here, the agent-oriented worldview is mainly applied for agent-based simulation, which is discussed in Chapter 10.

4.2 SIMULTANEOUS EVENTS AND CONFLICTS IN SIMULATION

As discussed earlier in the chapter, every simulation worldview evolves model dynamics by focusing on a particular aspect of the simulation. In the event-scheduling worldview, the event scheduling is the core of the simulation. The activity-scanning worldview focuses on the activities and their occurring conditions in a simulation. The time sequence of processes of a simulation is the centre of the process-interaction worldview. The three-phase worldview considers the events and activities to improve efficiency. The agent-oriented worldview concentrates on scheduling agents' activities and interactions. All simulation worldviews require some data structures (e.g. FEL and CEL) to store the scheduled events, activities, processes, interactions, and so on. With this also comes the need to have efficient and effective methods to access these scheduled items.

4.2.1 Simultaneous Events and Priorities

One common implementation for the scheduled items is a 'List'. Usually, FEL or CEL can be seen as a horizontal event list, where all events are arranged horizontally according to their occurrence time. This is efficient enough for most cases, unless some simultaneous events exist in the simulation.

Definition 4.2.1. *Simultaneous events are two or more events that have identical occurrence timestamps and an unspecified execution order/priority.*

By using horizontal event lists, simultaneous events can be fetched together, but their execution order is unknown. Given that events are stored horizontally in the list, as shown in Figure 4.8, this also increases the event scanning time for accessing all simultaneous events. Therefore, vertical event lists are used to improve accessing efficiency [386]. Vertical event lists group the simultaneous events into sub-lists vertically, as illustrated in Figure 4.8, and then treat them as one event in the horizontal time line. In this way, it becomes possible and efficient to scan and access all simultaneous events at one time point.

However, the execution order of simultaneous events is still unknown in this data structure. In some cases, simultaneous events cause conflicts in a simulation. A different execution order for the same set of simultaneous events may lead to different simulation results. Moreover, some execution sequences may cause abnormal system behaviours that are not intended by modellers. The following example of a bank account explains why the execution order is important.

Example 4.2.1. *A couple, Tom and Mary, hold a bank account that has an available balance of $500. We assume that there are two transactions occurring simultaneously:*

- *Tom deposits $500 at time point t*
- *Mary withdraws $600 at the same time point t.*

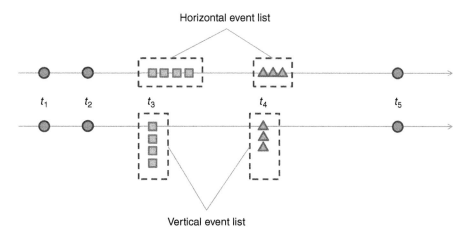

FIGURE 4.8   Horizontal event list versus vertical event list.

A bank system handles all transactions operated on this account. However, it does not have any particular sequence to deal with simultaneous transactions. Given that the sequence of these two transactions is unknown, there are two possible outcomes from the bank system:

1. *If the system processes the deposit event first, then everything runs well.*
2. *However, if the system processes the withdrawal event first, then there are insufficient funds for Mary and the second transaction cannot be operated at all.*

From the above example, it is clear how different outputs from a system can be caused by the order in which different events are executed. Sometimes the results are not expected, while other times they are not even possible. Of the many methods that have been proposed for handling simultaneous events in a simulation, tie-breaking rules is perhaps the most common approach.

Tie-breaking simply executes the simultaneous events in the order that they are returned by the data structure implemented for the scheduled event list. In this manner, the execution order follows the positions at which the events were recorded in the event lists. The data structure of scheduled events can be a list, a stack or others. The order of events in a list is first-in-first-out (FIFO), while for a stack is last-in-first-out (LIFO), so that the last arriving event is always popped out first. The tie-breaking rule is sufficient to guarantee that DES is reproducible when deterministic event scheduling is used for a single thread of execution in a sequential simulation. The reason for this is that the sequence of simultaneous events is decided based on a predefined data structure. However, being reproducible is not enough to guarantee that the output from the simulation fits the modeller's intention, unless the modeller builds the data structure and the storing sequence of events accordingly. Let us return to the bank account example to examine the effects generated by FEL data structure and events storing order when using tie-breaking rules.

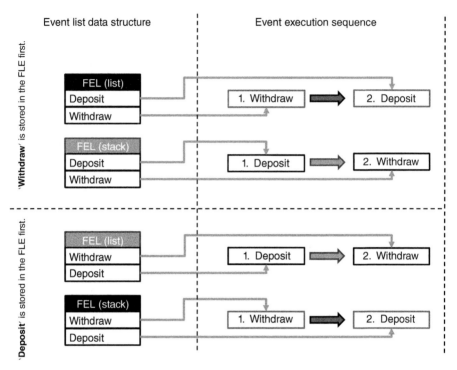

FIGURE 4.9 The effects from FEL data structure and event storing order for the bank account example.

If we want to allow Tom and Mary to operate their account without any issues, the expected transaction order should be deposit $500 first and then withdraw $600. As shown in Figure 4.9, the execution sequence of simultaneous events is what we want only when the FEL is a list and the 'deposit' event is stored in the list before the 'withdraw' event, or when the FEL is a stack and the 'withdraw' event is saved into FEL before the 'deposit' event. Therefore, only the two cases in the middle of Figure 4.9 are usually what a modeller wants to achieve to simulate the bank account. These examples show that tie-break can handle the simultaneous events to meet the modeller's intention, but there is no guarantee of it. It is highly dependable on the data structure used to store the events.

Another way is to rely on tie-breaking with unique identifications (IDs) for enforcing the desired event execution order. The event IDs can be generated by a global counter in the simulator. They are automatically assigned to an event when this is initialised. In this way, the execution order of simultaneous events purely depends on the order of the event IDs, regardless of the event list data structure. For example, if the event 'deposit' has the ID '1', and the event 'withdraw' has the ID '2', then the order in which they are executed is 'deposit' before 'withdraw', regardless of how the event list is implemented (i.e. FIFO or LIFO). Tie-breaking with event IDs may save the effort on the data structure design, but the logic of event initialisation is critical.

For example, the output from the system is not expected at all if the 'withdraw' event has a smaller ID than the 'deposit' event.

A more flexible way to avoid unintended event execution order is to assign priorities to simultaneous events. The priorities of events should be established when initialising them in a simulation. For the bank account example, we can always give higher priority to 'deposit' events. Thus, the event 'deposit' can be executed before 'withdraw' events, even if they occur simultaneously.

Sometimes, event priorities in a system can be derived from the existing rules/constraints of that system, such as urgency (patients at an emergency centre), common sense and courtesy (boarding order at a bus stop), event context (deposit and withdraw to or from a bank account) or others. These user- defined priorities should be stored in a simulator library and assigned to events before simulation starts. Another user-defined event priority example is discussed below.

Example 4.2.2. *An elevator is going down from Level 8 to the ground floor. Two simultaneous events occur when the elevator is between Level 4 and 3:*

- *Event A: someone presses the 'down' button at Level 5*
- *Event B: someone presses the 'up' button at the ground floor.*

For safety, the elevator should respond to Event B first, and then to Event A. Thus, the elevator keeps going down, which is safe for the passengers in the elevator, even though it may not be efficient for the elevator to go down to the ground floor and then go up to Level 5 from an operational cost perspective.

Establishing the appropriate priorities for events is a difficult task in many systems and, in addition, there is no universal way to achieve this. As discussed in the elevator example, many factors affect user-defined priorities, including the context of the system, the operational context, the objective of the study, and many others. A set of proper event priorities can resolve the conflicts in DES caused by simultaneous events and can lead the simulation to produce the expected outcomes

4.2.2 Conflict and Resolution in Agent-Based Simulation

Agent-based simulation (ABS) can be subject to conflicts as well. Conflicts in ABS can emerge in various situations – for example, multiple agents compete for the same resource and space or interact with the same agent simultaneously. Similar to DES, limited resources and space is the main reason for conflicts in ABS. The conflicts in ABS can be resolved in a simple manner by using random order or in more elaborate ways by establishing user-defined priorities [258].

In random order, simultaneous agent actions and interactions are randomly reordered at each time step. This can remove any bias in the simulation results caused by some arbitrary ordering of agents' activities. However, because of the random nature of this approach, a degree of randomness will exist in the agents' actions and interactions; hence, the simulation has to be run many times to obtain statistically significant results. This creates a disadvantage, in that the high number of runs results in high computational cost.

Another way of solving the conflicts is to assign priorities to agents so that some agents have high priority to take actions and interact with others, while others have low priority for their activities. Similar to event priorities in DES, user-defined priorities have to be established before running simulations. Again, designing agent priorities depends on many factors, including the existing rules and constraints, system context, and so on. The output from ABS is affected by user-defined priorities, as can be seen in the following example.

Example 4.2.3. *In an ABS, two agents are competing for the same resource at time t. At that time, only one resource unit is available. Agent A consumes one unit of resource, but Agent B needs three units of resource. This conflict for resource can be resolved in three different ways based on agents' priority:*

1. *Both agents have the same priority, and no one can obtain the resource.*
2. *Agent A has higher priority and attains the resource.*
3. *Agent B has higher priority and attains the resource.*

Consequently, these three resolutions produce three different results in the simulation:

- *If the first resolution is employed in the simulation, then neither agent can survive.*
- *If the second resolution is adopted in the simulation, Agent A can survive to the next time step, but Agent B may die if the resource shortage is fatal at this time step.*
- *Agent B gains the available resource unit and still waits for another two if it does not die at this time step because of the shortage. Agent A may die if it needs this resource to survive at this time step.*

As seen in the example, the priorities are critical to the simulation outcomes. It is also possible for us to run all the above three resolutions with simulation replications, and then analyse and summarise the results for the final conclusions. However, this may require a large amount of extra computational cost to enumerate all possible resolutions when many agents have simultaneous activities in a simulation. Therefore, establishing agent priorities can ease the computational effort, but potential biases are introduced to the simulation results.

4.3 PRIORITY QUEUE AND BINARY HEAP

As discussed in the previous section, user-defined priority for events, activities, and processes is a common approach to handle conflicts in a simulation. The events scheduled based on their priorities form a priority queue. However, the dynamics of a

Event	a	b	c	d	e	f	g
Key (lower is higher priority)	2	3	1	4	12	8	9

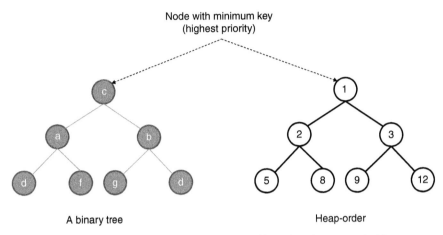

FIGURE 4.10 The binary heap constructed based on the event priorities.

model may require frequent rescheduling of events, activities, and processes during a simulation. The operations on the priority queue – such as creation, insertion and deletion – may often occur. To manipulate the priority queue efficiently, many algorithms have been proposed over time [101], out of which we describe in the following the most relevant algorithm: the 'binary heap operations' method.

A binary heap has a binary tree structure. Each node in a binary tree has a maximum of two children. In a binary heap, an event is represented as a node in the tree. Each node of the binary heap has a key that represents its priority. As the name suggests, a binary heap also has the so-called heap order property – that is, the key of every node, except the root, is always less than or equal to its children's keys. Therefore, a node with lower key is a node with higher priority, while the root is always the node with the minimum key (highest priority event) in the binary heap. During a simulation, the root of a binary heap can be easily obtained and executed before all other nodes (events).

A binary heap of the events can be easily constructed based on binary heap properties and events priorities. Figure 4.10 shows a binary heap for a given set of events. The left side of the figure lists the event name for each node and the right side shows the associated key values (priorities) to represent each node. As seen in the figure, event 'c' is the root node in the binary tree and has the highest priority. Then, the keys of the parent nodes are less than or equal to their children's keys. Therefore, the tree presented in the figure satisfies the heap order property.

During a simulation, it happens very frequently to operate on a queue for extracting certain events, such as the highest priority event. Example 4.3.1 shows the process of obtaining and removing the root from a binary heap.

Example 4.3.1. *Suppose we wish to attain the highest priority event from a binary heap, as shown in the top left of Figure 4.11.*

The first step is to remove this event from the root of the binary heap so that the root position is empty. Then the rightmost leaf node at the bottom level is moved to the root location. In this case, the event with the priority value of 29 is shifted there, so that the binary heap becomes a new binary tree, shown in Step 2. Obviously, this binary tree does not satisfy the heap order requirements. It is necessary to reorder the nodes based on their key values and make it a binary heap again. To do this, we compare the key value of the root with the key values of its children. If the key value of the root is greater than the minimum key value of its children, then the event at the root position is swapped with the child whose key value is the smallest. After Step 3, the child node with a key value of 15 moves to the root position. Then, we repeat the above steps until all parent nodes have key values smaller than or equal to those of their children. The final binary heap after deletion is presented in the bottom right corner of Figure 4.11.

During a simulation, as a result of the dynamics of the model, it may also occur that new events and activities are created. In this case, insertion operations are needed.

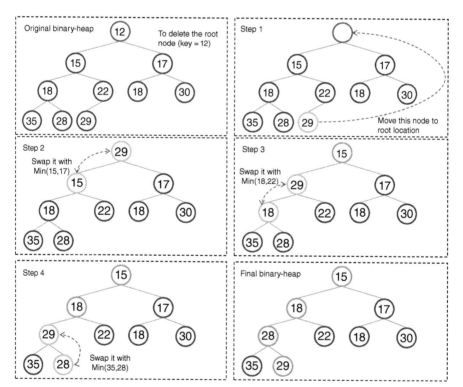

FIGURE 4.11 Obtain and delete the event with the highest priority (lowest key) from the root location of a binary heap, and update node positions accordingly.

In this case, insertion operations are needed. Example 4.3.2 shows the process of inserting a new event and updating the nodes based on the resultant event priorities.

Example 4.3.2. *The original binary heap is shown in the top left corner of Figure 4.12. Now, we need to insert a new event with the priority of 13.*

First, the location of a 'hole' is identified in the binary heap, where a hole is an empty position in the bottom layer. Then, the new node is added to this position, as shown in Step 1. If the key value of this new node is higher than the parent's key value, this new node position is swapped with its parent's position. In this example, the new node moves to the position of its parent, whose key value is 22, while the parent goes to the new node position and becomes a child of the new node. This process is repeated until the key value of the new node's parent is lower than its key value. The final binary heap is illustrated in the bottom right of Figure 4.12.

The binary heap is an efficient data structure compared with other methods for manipulating the priority queue in simulation, such as the 'ordered linked list' or the 'ordered array'. In Table 4.1, we present the computational cost for the worst-case comparisons among them, with regard to the deletion and insertion operations discussed above.

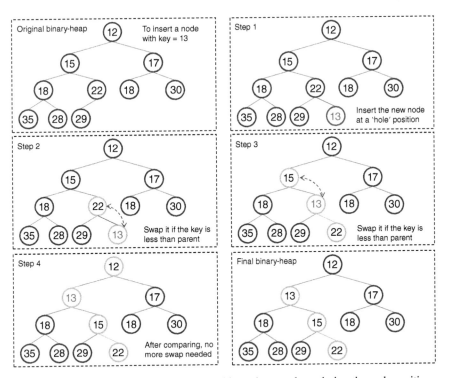

FIGURE 4.12   Inserting a new event into a binary heap and reordering the node positions.

TABLE 4.1   The Computational Cost Comparison of Priority Queue Operations for Binary Heap, Ordered Linked List, and Ordered Array

Operations	Construction	Delete the node with min key	Insert a node
Binary heap	$O(N)$	$O(\lg N)$	$O(\lg N)$
Ordered linked list	$O(N)$	$O(1)$	$O(N)$
Ordered array	$O(N)$	$O(N)$	$O(N + \lg N)$

4.4   CONCLUSION

In this chapter, we discussed in detail the concept of simulation worldview, along with the most important approaches. It is important for modellers to know and understand which worldviews are adopted in a simulation software package, so they can focus on the particular aspects of the real system and identify the key elements to be used for modelling – that is, events, activities, processes, agent interaction, and so on. Although a simulation worldview provides the mechanism to evolve a model's dynamics, sometimes conflicts occur because of simultaneous events or activities. In such cases, conflict-resolution mechanisms must be designed and implemented in simulation. The tie-breaking rule is a simple and straightforward way to handle conflicts, but user-defined priorities for arranging the execution order of simultaneous events or activities is a more powerful approach. However, it is difficult to develop appropriate user-defined priority mechanisms, since they depend on the system context and constraints, study objectives, common sense, and many other factors. The conflicts in ABS and their resolving mechanisms were also addressed in this chapter, while more details of ABS can be found in Chapter 10.

Given that priority events or activities are usually represented as priority queues, an efficient data structure – the binary heap – was discussed at the end of this chapter. Although most simulation software packages have built-in data structures for priority events, it is important for modellers to understand how they work before taking them for granted. Through the binary heap example, we provided a useful and insightful view of how a priority data structure works.

In summary, there are many ways to resolve conflicts in simulation and no general guidelines for doing this. Thus, modellers should handle this issue according to the relevant circumstances.

CHAPTER 5

The Language of Abstraction and Representation

This chapter focuses on the representation side of the process of building a simulation. Selecting how to represent the real system in a model is essential for the resultant simulation. There are various ways to represent a real system in a model – a diagram, an equation, a text script or others. In any of the cases, representation should be formal so that it can be translated into a simulator that a computer can understand. In this chapter, we discuss the most important methods for representation, insisting on those that have high relevance to computer simulation. We then use the example of finite-state machine – one of the most popular modelling approaches – to demonstrate the process of creating a model of a real system.

5.1 INTRODUCTION

The word 'modelling' reflects the process that transforms a real system into an abstract representation of it. A system might be too complex to include every feature of it in the representation. Therefore, a representation should focus on the important information and relationships. As discussed in Chapter 2, modellers need to consider resolution, abstraction, and fidelity when modelling and simulating a system. Modelling requires the modeller to decide on an appropriate level of abstraction to ensure that the representation suits the purpose. A suitable representation for a system allows us to further transform it into some form that a computer can understand (e.g., code). Further, we could apply many formal methods to solve problems by simulation. As shown in Figure 5.1, the red box encapsulates the process of transforming the modeller's understanding of a system into a model by abstraction.

Abstraction is the mapping, at a decided level of resolution, of the system into a suitable representation. Thus, abstraction in modelling can be viewed as a process of identifying the causes and principles in a system that truly govern the behaviour

Simulation and Computational Red Teaming for Problem Solving, First Edition.
Jiangjun Tang, George Leu, and Hussein A. Abbass.
© 2020 by The Institute of Electrical and Electronics Engineers, Inc. Published 2020 by John Wiley & Sons, Inc.

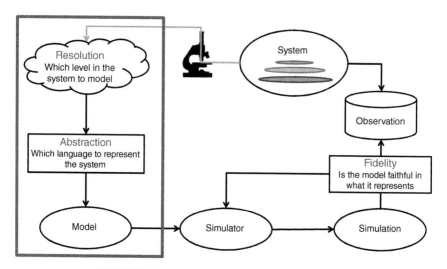

FIGURE 5.1 Abstraction – the modelling process.

in which the modeller is interested, while ignoring details that do not contribute to this behaviour. A model is valid only under certain assumptions. For example, a mass point following Newton's laws is a valid model for a moving car in a traffic system, yet is not a valid model in the context of car designing. A model should meet the modeller's needs and the simulation's requirements and objectives. Sometimes, the cost of the model and simulator development, along with other factors, also play a critical role in abstraction.

A system can be represented in various forms. A form of representation can be natural language description, such as a story book or a script given to actors to perform in a film. A diagram can also be a representation form, such as the blueprint of a building. Of course, the representations should be formal so they can be used for computer-based simulation, since they need to be ported into a simulator. Therefore, analytic representations, certain types of diagrams or logical representations are more appropriate for use in computer-based simulation models.

After a decision is made on the resolution and abstraction levels of a representation form, we can say that the resultant model becomes a representation of the real-world system in a form that is not the form of that system itself. However, regardless of what representation is selected to create a model, that representation should reproduce the system behaviour with a certain fidelity level corresponding to the decided resolution.

In this chapter, we discuss the most important representation paradigms, and use finite-state machine as an example to show how to abstract a system into a model under certain assumptions. We note that, to provide the reader a complete view on representation, we start by describing all major approaches to representation, including informal methods. Later in the chapter, we focus the discussion on formal methods for representation, which are especially relevant to computer simulation.

5.2 INFORMAL REPRESENTATION

5.2.1 Prototyping and Analogy

Humans can use representation at any moment in time, during any step we take during our lifetime. Without realising, we store and manipulate representations of the real world to make decisions about virtually anything. These representations are usually not highly abstract or highly specialised, but rather informal or casual.

Let us consider the following example, in which we see a boat moving on a river between two wharfs, and we wish to describe this situation to a young child who has not yet mastered the language of diagrams, mathematics or even natural spoken language. One immediate way to do so is to employ objects that are analogues of the real ones to describe the situation. For example, we could use a small model of a boat that we move along a blue winding line on the floor, between two small models of a deck or wharf. This is a good enough representation of the boat moving problem, which suits the purpose of describing the situation to a child. It is a representation situated at a very low level of abstraction; however, through analogy, we managed to represent the real-world system.

Of course, this example is very naive, but we can always think of more complex ones, in which the simple analogy can involve a prototyping work, such as in the case of testing the design of a vehicle by producing a fully working prototype. While simple analogy and prototyping (which involves analogy as well) may seem detached from each other through the scale of the representation activity, they reflect the same type of informal abstraction, and consequently the same very intuitive way of reflecting the behaviour of a real system.

5.2.2 Natural Language

Natural language is already an ontological construct that is at a higher level of abstraction than the simple analogy or prototyping. However, it is still an informal representation, in which the system is described using a list of statements that describe its functionality, the applicable constraints, and its behaviour overall.

With the help of natural language, we can now use words to explain to the young child that the boat navigates on the river between two wharfs. The child will not need to see the physical objects symbolising the components of the system, but will need to master the ontological construct that we use to explain the facts (i.e., the language) so that he or she understands what we say.

Neither analogy nor natural language have an immediate role in computer simulation; however, we still mention them because they are ways of representing and describing real systems that are inherent to human thinking, and cannot be entirely disregarded even when the focus is on computer simulation. They are indirectly related to simulation by being the immediate means of describing any real-world facts, and facilitating the further representation of these facts at higher levels of abstraction, such as diagram-based, rule-based, logic-based, or mathematics-based ontological constructs.

5.3 SEMI-FORMAL REPRESENTATION

While numerous semi-formal methods are available for representing real-world systems, in this chapter, we only present diagramming and rule-based representation, which are most relevant to computer simulation.

5.3.1 Diagrams

Diagrams can capture a certain system of interest from different points of view, such as the static structure, the processes running as part of its operation, the data flow that it generates, or the relations between component entities. Typically, they are the result of an analysis of the system that enables the modeller to use a certain diagramming language to represent the system of interest. While there are a large variety of approaches to analysis, we only present below three types, which are typically used for a wide range of problems: structured analysis, data-centric analysis, and object-oriented analysis. Each of them can use various types of diagrams or combinations of diagrams.

Structured analysis views the system as a collection of processes that transform input data into output data; thus, it focuses on the processes involved in the operation of a system and is used mainly in processing intensive applications. The typical forms of representation in this case are data flow diagrams, which offer a functional view on the system behaviour that is intuitive and natural to most people and is consistent with the way system engineers think. However, structured analysis does not give much insight into the structure of data. Figure 5.2 shows a general view of a data flow diagram.

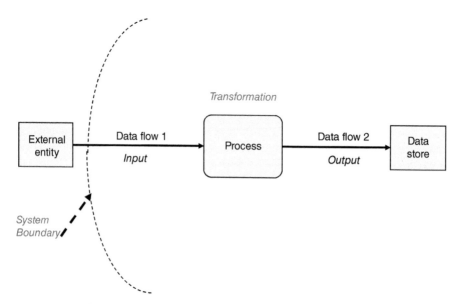

FIGURE 5.2   An abstract example of a data flow diagram.

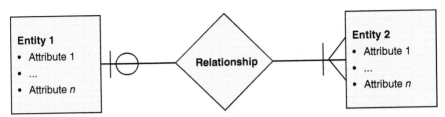

FIGURE 5.3   An abstract example of an entity-relationship diagram.

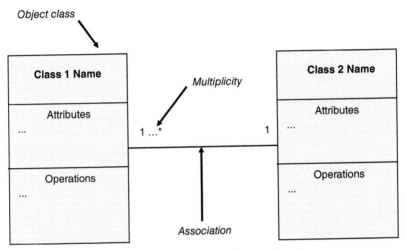

FIGURE 5.4   An abstract example of a class diagram.

Data-centric analysis views the system as a collection of related data entities; thus, it focuses on data structures and relationships and is used mainly in data-intensive contexts. Entity-relationship diagrams are typically used to represent the systems of interest, as shown in Figure 5.3.

Object-oriented analysis combines the two perspectives described above – processes and data – and views the system as a collection of interacting objects. Object-oriented analysis identifies the objects (or object classes) that exist in the problem domain and specifies their attributes, operation, and associations with other objects. Class diagrams (Figure 5.4) are one of the most popular methods used to represent the systems in the object-oriented paradigm.

5.3.2   Diagramming Examples

5.3.2.1   *State Transition Diagrams*   State transition diagrams are perhaps the most appropriate ways of describing the behaviour of a system (Figure 5.5). The finite-state machine (FSM) example we provide later in the chapter actually shows that FSM is one of the classic forms of state transition diagram.

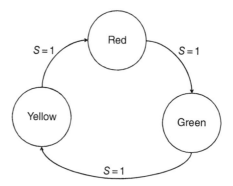

FIGURE 5.5   Simple FSM model for a traffic light.

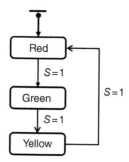

FIGURE 5.6   State transition diagram for traffic light.

To illustrate the application of state transition diagrams in simulation, we use Example 5.3.1. The situation presented in this example can be modelled as a state transition diagram, as in Figure 5.6. As shown in Figure 5.6, the rounded rectangles represent the states and the arrows represent the transitions from one state to another.

Example 5.3.1. *In this example, a traffic light is controlled by a timer and has three coloured lights: red, green, and yellow. This traffic light changes the colours from one to another when it receives triggering signals from a timer. The timer sends triggering signals at two fixed intervals: it sends a signal after 5 minutes if the light is red or green, and sends a signal after 20 seconds if the light is yellow. The order of the colour change is: red to green, green to yellow, and yellow to red. The traffic light keeps the same colour if no triggering signal is received.*

The transitions in a state transition diagram can be triggered in various ways, including:

- Timeout: a transition occurs after a specified time has passed. For example, the traffic light is controlled by a timer, and the timer can trigger the light state changes.

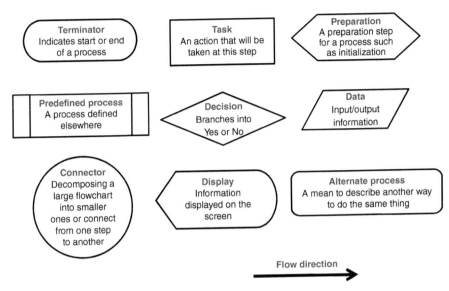

FIGURE 5.7   Flowchart building blocks and their meanings.

- Rate: a transition is triggered based on probability. For example, a machine has a probability of failure.
- Condition: a transition occurs under certain conditions. For example, flooding occurs when the river level exceeds the riverbank height.
- Message: a transition is caused by the communications between agents. This is commonly seen in ABS, where agents exchange information about the system or environment.
- Arrival: a transition occurs when an agent arrives at its destination. For example, a bus arrives at a terminal so that passengers start boarding.

State transition diagrams have been adopted by many simulation software packages (e.g. AnyLogic). They can be used to model the behaviours of an agent at a microscopic level.

5.3.2.2 Flowcharts
A flowchart is another form of diagramming, mainly associated with (but not limited to) structured analysis. It consists of a visual representation of the logic that models a work flow, a process or an algorithm. Flowcharts offer a sufficient level of detail to transform the process into the code that computers can understand. There are a set of shapes available in flowcharts depicting different meanings, as shown in Figure 5.7.

The following example demonstrates how to use a flowchart to model a process when an insurance company determines the premium for car insurance.

Example 5.3.2. *We assume that an insurance company calculates the car insurance premium based on the following information from the applicants: age, parking location, and accident history. The premium is adjusted based on the above information as follows:*

- *If applicant's age is less than 25, then the base premium is $500. Otherwise, the base is $400.*
- *If the car is not parked in a garage, then the premium increases by $50.*
- *If there was any accident claimed in the last five years, the premium increases by $100. Otherwise, the premium is deducted by $50.*

The logic of the insurance company to determine the premium is modelled as a flowchart shown in Figure 5.8.

As this example indicates, a flowchart can be used to study and model a system – especially the processes in the system. In addition, flowcharts are also useful for documenting a model because they can clearly depict the logic inside a system.

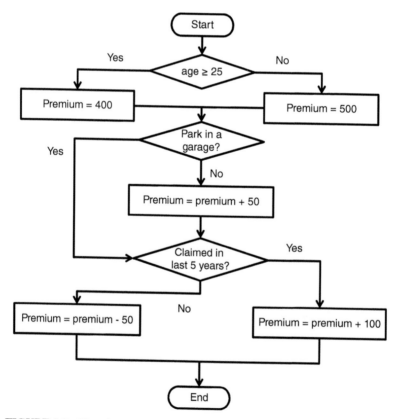

FIGURE 5.8 Flowchart modelling the determination of a car insurance premium.

5.3.3 Rule-Based Representation

Rule-based representation is an approach to representation in which knowledge about the system of interest is captured in lists of 'if-then' rules showing the behaviour of the system under different conditions. Depending on the type of system and the purpose of the modeller, two types of rules can be used as part of these rule sets: forward chaining rules or deductive approach, and backward chaining rules or inductive approach. The limitation of these sets of simple if-then statements is that they cannot treat situations where more complex decision making needs to be embedded in the representation, such as when a robot must be able to carry an object from Location A to Location B and must decide on the best route, yet also needs to take care and avoid the obstacles present on whichever route it chooses. To handle this type of behaviour, subsumption rule-based architectures are typically employed. Subsumption architectures were initially related to artificial intelligence (AI) and AI-related applications, such as intelligent agent simulations. They assume a decomposition of the behaviour into smaller blocks placed on several layers, and representation of these blocks in a hierarchy in which higher levels subsume the lower ones. In the robot example, the robot first needs to be able to avoid obstacles to successfully follow a certain route from A to B. Thus, the output of the simple if-then rules describing obstacle avoidance are used as input for the higher-level decision related to following the route. Thus, subsumption architectures are actually derived into rule-based language as nested if-then statements.

Decision trees are a good example of rule-based representations, where simple if-then statements and potential subsequent nested if-then statements are ported into diagram formulations, in the form of tree structure graphs. In the following section, we present an application of decision tree representation for a practical example.

5.3.3.1 *Decision Trees* Another way to model the insurance premium example is by using a decision tree [324]. A decision tree represents the choice between a number of alternatives through a tree structure. Hence, a decision tree consists of nodes and branches. In a decision tree, each internal node is a test on an attribute ('if'), such as the age of an applicant, while each branch encodes the outcome of the attribute test ('then'), such as an insurance premium increasing or reduction. At the bottom of a decision tree, each leaf node is a classification. Thus, a decision can be made after traversing the tree.

Figure 5.9 displays how the insurance premium calculation can be completed by using a decision tree.

As shown in the figure, the decision nodes are represented by squares and the leaf nodes are represented by triangles. There is also another type of node, called a 'chance node', which is not presented in the above example. Chance nodes are for random events and are represented by triangles in a decision tree. Given that everything in this insurance calculation is deterministic, no chance nodes are included in the above example. However, if a prize given to applicants by chance is introduced in the model,

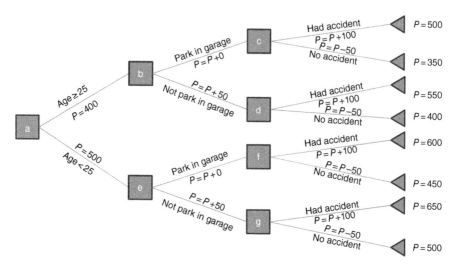

FIGURE 5.9 Decision tree modelling for determining a car insurance premium.

the insurance premium can be reduced for some randomly chosen applicants. In such a case, chance nodes are needed.

In summary, decision trees can be used in modelling the decision processes of a system, and can also be used in operations research, specifically in decision analysis. In addition, decision trees have been used successfully in machine learning, for tasks such as classification.

5.4 FORMAL REPRESENTATION

5.4.1 Logical Representation

5.4.1.1 *Propositional Logic* Propositional logic, or 0th order logic is focused on the truth value (true or false) of whole statements, without being concerned with their internal structure. Thus, a proposition is seen as an atomic construct, which can be coupled with other propositions using logical connectives (or operators) to build larger constructs that in turn will have a resultant truth value. The value of the resultant propositional constructs depends on the truth value of their components.

Propositional logic represents knowledge using formal logical languages built on the following components, which can be expressed in natural language or in mathematical symbols:

1. a set of propositions (or formulas, or constants)
2. a set of operators
3. a set of axioms (or inference rules)
4. a logical consequence of the propositional construct

TABLE 5.1 The Most Common Logical Operators

Operator	Natural language	Math. symbol	Type
Negation	not	~	Unary
Conjunction	and	&	Binary
Inclusive disjunction	or	—	Binary
Implication	if-then	=>	Binary
Equivalence	if and only if	<=>	Binary
Exclusive disjunction	exclusive or	<~>	Binary

Let as assume the following propositional logic construct expressed in natural language:

- Set of axioms (A):
  - If it is cloudy, then it is raining.
  - If it is raining, then it is cloudy.
  - Either it is raining or it is cloudy.
- Logical consequence (C):
  - It is cloudy and it is raining.

In this propositional construct, the logical consequence C is inferred from the set of axioms A. The logical conclusion and each of the axioms are made of formulas (or propositions), such as 'it is cloudy' or 'it is raining', and operators, such as the words 'if-then', 'or', and 'and'.

To transfer this propositional construct into a mathematical symbol representation, alphabetic symbols are typically used for propositions, and symbols from Table 5.1 are used for operators, where Table 5.1 describes the most common mathematical symbols used in propositional logic. The representation of the logical construct then becomes like in Eq. (5.1), where p symbolises 'it is cloudy' and q symbolises 'it is raining'. We note that formulas or propositions from natural language are called 'constants' in mathematical representation; thus, p and q in Eq. (5.1) are called constants.

$$A = \{p => q, q => p, p|q\}; \quad C = \{p\&q\} \tag{5.1}$$

As stated above, in propositional logic, formulas or propositions, as well as the resultant logical constructs, are considered based on their truth value: either true or false. Thus, typically, the knowledge represented using propositional logic constructs is interpreted based on the truth table's various formulas (propositions), operators and axioms, and the logical consequences of them. Table 5.2 shows the truth value interpretation of the logical construct expressed in Eq. (5.1), which in turn is a representation with mathematical symbols of the natural language example discussed above.

TABLE 5.2   The Truth Table for the Logical Construct Expressed in Eq. (5.1)

Constants		Set of axioms (A)			Consequence (C)
p	p	$p \Rightarrow q$	$q \Rightarrow p$	$p \| q$	$p \& q$
T	T	T	T	T	T
T	F	F	T	T	F
F	T	T	F	T	F
F	F	T	T	F	F

Propositional logic has the main advantage of simplicity because it focuses on whole propositions, and not on their structure; thus, interpreting the logical consequence of the axioms is relatively straightforward. However, this also makes it unsuitable for representing real-world situations that depend on the elements constituting the propositions. In other words, the constituents of the propositions, and consequently the propositions, are not constant, but variable. Thus, a more expressive approach to representing these situations is needed – that is, a different formalism and semantic of axioms and conclusions. In the next section, we briefly introduce one of these approaches: the predicate logic.

5.4.1.2   *Predicate Logic*   Predicate logic, also known as first-order logic, is a formal logical language/system that uses sentences containing quantifiable variables, rather than whole constant propositions. A simple and intuitive example showing this difference is the following sentence: 'John is a male'. In propositional logic, this sentence is fixed and refers to John only. Its truth value depends on John, and no one else, being a male and no one else. In predicate logic, we are able to generalise this statement to apply to any person (i.e. 'X is a man') and further to any gender (i.e., 'X is a Y'). Thus, we are able to introduce variability by introducing quantifiers, or variables. Essential to first-order logic languages are two key aspects: the syntax, which determines which collections of symbols are legal expressions, and the semantics, which determine the meanings of these expressions.

In addition to the concept of first order, the predicate logic representations can be extended to higher-order constructs (i.e. '*n*th-order logic'), in which predicates are not simple variables, but instead have predicates or functions as arguments. In other words, predicates themselves can be further quantified, thereby providing further means to encode more complex knowledge about real phenomena, such as the behaviour of real systems of interest for simulation.

However, the richer language provided by predicate logic comes at the cost of loss of decidability for logical consequence. First-order logic, as well as higher-order predicate logic, are not entirely decidable (and are termed 'semi-decidable'), which means it is possible to show that a formula *is*, but it may not be possible to show that *is not* – a logical consequence of a set of axioms. Thus, more complex ways of interpreting the logical consequence are generally needed when employing predicate logic representation.

5.4.2 Analytic Representation

Mathematical analytic language can also be used to create models that represent how real systems work. As we know, many systems are abstracted as sets of equations, such as Newton's laws for object motion, or Maxwell's equations describing the electro-magnetic field. An analytic model uses mathematics language to describe a system based on mathematical concepts. It is the most precise representation for many systems. Therefore, mathematical models should be the first choice for modelling a system, whenever possible.

Mathematical representations usually take the form of equations or systems of equations, and consist of two components: variables describing the state of a system, and operators describing the relationships between system variables. Newton's laws and Maxwell's equations are examples of equation-based models. Apart from pure equations, a mathematical model can also be embedded in diagram formulations, such as the FSM, which will be discussed later in this chapter.

A system may have different mathematical representations based on the study requirements and assumptions.

Example 5.4.1. *A study on aircraft fuel consumption requires the building of a detailed aircraft model to estimate the amount of fuel burned during aircraft operation. In this example, a high-resolution model is required; thus, the total-energy model [78] can be chosen as a suitable representation for modelling the aerodynamics of the aircraft.*

$$(T - D)V_{TAS} = mg\frac{\mathrm{d}h}{\mathrm{d}t} + mV_{TAS}\frac{\mathrm{d}V_{TAS}}{\mathrm{d}t} \qquad (5.2)$$

where,

- *T: thrust acting parallel to the aircraft velocity vector [newton]*
- *D: aerodynamic drag [newton]*
- *m: aircraft mass [kilogram]*
- *h: altitude [m]*
- *g: gravitational acceleration [9.81 m/s^2]*
- *V_{TAS}: true airspeed [m/s]*
- *$\frac{\mathrm{d}}{\mathrm{d}t}$ time derivative.*

Using Eq. (5.2), the thrust of an aircraft can be obtained so that the fuel consumption can be further calculated.

However, if the study intends to perform a simulation on the aircraft landing sequence, it is not necessary to go into such detail, although having an aircraft aerodynamic model to represent aircraft moments would still be a valid choice. To study the landing sequence, each landing aircraft can be represented by a simple differential equation:

$$\frac{\mathrm{d}p}{\mathrm{d}t} = v \qquad (5.3)$$

where p is the 3-D position of an aircraft – including latitude, longitude, and altitude – and v is the velocity of an aircraft. This equation is enough to obtain the positions of aircraft when they are in the air and to study their landing behaviours. Using this simple mathematical form can save significant computational cost in simulation runs, compared with that from Eq. (5.2), while still achieving the objective of the study.

Example 5.4.1 shows that the decision on model representation depends on the study requirements and objectives.

5.4.3 Flexibility of Representation

Many other representation methods are applicable for modelling. The modeller has the flexibility to select an appropriate representation based on its own knowledge and understanding of the system. Therefore, the choice of a representation method is flexible, as long as the representation: (1) meets the objectives and requirements of the intended simulation, (2) can describe the system behaviours at the abstraction level that matches the decided resolution level, and (3) is valid under certain assumptions.

5.5 FINITE-STATE MACHINE

From here, and throughout the rest of the chapter, we use the FSM concept to demonstrate the process of creating a representation of a real system. A FSM [159] is a mathematical representation formulated under a diagramming framework. FSM is a traditional approach used to model the behaviour of a system, which gained large popularity over the years and is usually studied under the broader field of automata theory [187]. A FSM abstracts a system that can go through a finite number of states. This system can be only in one state at a particular time point, and the behaviour of the system is characterised by that state. The state of the machine at any given time point is called the 'current state', and this state changes into another state trigged by an event or condition that is called 'transition'. Therefore, a FSM is defined by a set of finite states and triggering events. A FSM is a restricted Turing machine [382, 383]. A Turing machine is a machine with an unlimited memory capacity that has a movable read/write head on an infinity storage tape, and the read/write head can move forward and backward. However, a FSM can only work on a sequence of inputs in one direction. In other words, if the FSM has a read/write head, this head can only move in one direction. Also, a FSM has limited memory because of the finite number of states.

The behaviours that can be modelled using FSMs can be found in many devices that can perform sets of predefined actions in a sequence that depends on the sequence of the triggering event occurrences. Examples include an elevator, an automatic vending machine, and a turnstile. FSMs also facilitate solving problems in various domains, such as behavioural modelling in simulating autonomous entities [117], machine learning [289], pattern recognition [389], and evolutionary computation [142].

To better explain how FSMs operate, we use Example 5.3.1, which we presented earlier in the chapter. From a FSM perspective, the traffic light in this example has

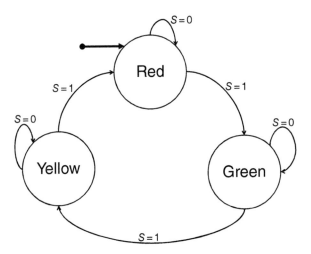

FIGURE 5.10   Improved FSM model for a traffic light.

three states (red, green, and yellow) and a transition (the timer signal). Let us denote the time signal by s, and assign it two possible values: 1 for a signal sent, and 0 for no signal. Once the traffic light receives a timer signal, it changes the colour. We can model the system graphically, as shown in Figure 5.5. The circles represent the three possible states of the traffic light: red, green, and yellow. As shown in the figure, the traffic light changes the colour from red to green, from green to yellow, or from yellow to red once it receives the timer signals, illustrated as $s = 1$ on the transition arrows. By using this model, we can only partially reproduce the traffic light behaviour because the situations where the traffic light does not receive any signal are not included in this state machine model. In these situations, the traffic light should keep the current light colour. Therefore, we use the 'loop' transitions ($s = 0$) to represent this behaviour in Figure 5.10. Moreover, we have not defined an initial state of this traffic light. As shown in Figure 5.10, we refine the model by adding an indication of the initial state of the traffic light as a solid circle and an arrow pointing to the red state.

Thus far, we have modelled a traffic light using a FSM. Although the FSM described in Figure 5.10 may not be perfect, it conceptually represents all behaviours of a simple traffic light system. A FSM truth table can be built based on the current state and inputs. As shown in Table 5.3, the next state of the system is determined by the current state and input.

From this example, we conclude that systems that can be modelled using a FSM have some key characteristics, as follows:

- The system can be described by a finite set of states.
- The system must have a finite set of inputs/events that can trigger system state changes.

TABLE 5.3   Tabular Representation (Truth Table) of Traffic Light FSM

Input (s)	Current state	Next state
1	Red	Green
1	Green	Yellow
1	Yellow	Red
0	Red	Red
0	Green	Green
0	Yellow	Yellow

- The behaviour of the system at a given time point is decided by the current state and the input or event that occurs at that time.
- The behaviour of the system is predefined for each possible input or event in each state.
- The system has a particular initial state.

A formal mathematical definition of a FSM can allow us to understand systems and help us to communicate with others about the system modelling. A FSM (A) can be defined as a tuple $A = (\Sigma, Q, q_0, \delta, F)$, where

- Σ is a finite input alphabet of A
- Q is a finite set of states of A
- q_0 is the initial state of A
- $\delta: Q \times \Sigma \rightarrow Q$ is a set of transitions
- $F \subseteq Q_A$ is a set of final states of A.

For the traffic light example, we can transform the graphical representation of the FSM presented in Figure 5.10 into a mathematical definition: $M = (\Sigma, Q, q_0, \delta, F)$, where

$\Sigma = \{0, 1\}$
$Q = \{R, G, Y\}$
$q_0 = \{R\}$
$F = \{R, G, Y\}$
$\delta = \{\delta(R, 0, R), \delta(R, 1, G), \delta(G, 0, G), \delta(G, 1, Y), \delta(Y, 0, Y), \delta(Y, 1, R)\}$

R, G, and Y indicate red, green, and yellow lights, respectively. $\delta(q, x, p)$ is equivalent to $\delta(q, x) = p$, which means the current state q is changed to the next state p ($p \subseteq Q$) by the input x.

An example of using FSM for simulating an ant's behaviour in a maze is discussed in Section 5.6.

5.6   ANT IN MAZE MODELLED BY FINITE-STATE MACHINE

In this section, we consider an example that demonstrates how to use a FSM for simulating the behaviours of an ant in a maze [395].

Example 5.6.1. *As shown in Figure 5.11, an ant is trapped in a maze and must find its way out. The ant has two antennae, left and right, that sense the environment. When the antennae touch a wall, the ant receives a signal. The ant can go forwards and turn left and right. Let us assume that the ant is a wall follower and uses the right-hand rule – that is, walking along the wall and keeping its right antenna to the wall.*

5.6.1   Finite-State Machine Modelling

In this example, the essential aspect to be modelled is how the ant moves around the maze to find the way out; thus, the model is not required to consider how the ant crawls using its legs. The resolution of the resultant model only goes to the basic movements that an ant can perform. Let us suppose that the actions taken by the ant are only 'going forward' (*FD*), 'turning left' (*TL*), and 'turning right' (*TR*). We also assume that the ant moves at a constant speed, and turns left or right at a constant angular speed as well. Hence, the ant travels fixed distances and turns a fixed amount of angular degrees at each time step. The responses of the ant to the environment are trigged by its antennae sensing. Let us denote L for the signal from the left antenna, and R for the one from the right. The possible values of both L and R are 0 for nothing

FIGURE 5.11   An ant in a maze.

sensed and 1 for touching a wall. The possible actions taken by an ant when sensing a wall are the three actions listed previously.

We now abstract the ant behaviours in the maze by using a FSM model. At first, we define a FSM for the ant as a five-element tuple $A = (\Sigma, Q, q_0, \delta, F)$. The input to the FSM is the information sensed by the antennae of the ant. As a result, the input alphabet for the machine is the combination of all possible values of L and R – that is $\Sigma = \{\{0, 0\}, \{1, 0\}, \{1, 1\}, \{0, 1\} \{1, *\}, \{*, 1\}\}$. The wildcard '*' used in the last two means that we only consider the signal from one antenna, either left or right, regardless of the sensing result from the other one. As discussed before, the resolution of the model decides the abstraction of the model. Therefore, the intended FSM only considers three actions (going forward, turning left, and turning right) and the related states of an ant in a maze.

We now try to enumerate the possible states in which an ant can be as it moves through the maze. Clearly, the initial state of the ant is 'LOST' ($q_0 = LOST$) because it has no idea where it is at the beginning. Given that the ant is a wall follower, it must find a wall first. Hence, we let it walk forward until its antennae hit a wall. As shown in Figure 5.12, the ant keeps walking forward when it is in a 'lost' state ($L = 0$ and $R = 0$). The ant possibly hits a wall with both antennae or with one of its antennae. Therefore, any one of the inputs $\{\{1, 0\}, \{0, 1\}, \{1, 1\}\}$ triggers a state change in the ant from 'LOST' to other. Consequently, we can build the first state of our FSM, as in the bottom left corner of Figure 5.12. An action forward is associated with this state and is depicted as '*FD*' inside the state circle. A 'loop' transition back to the 'LOST' state also exists for the situation where neither of the antennae touches a wall. The second transition of states is when at least one antenna touches a wall. We use 'ENCW' to denote the state to which the ant transits from 'LOST' when it encounters a wall.

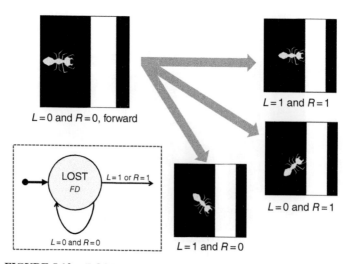

FIGURE 5.12 'LOST' state – an ant walks forward until hitting a wall.

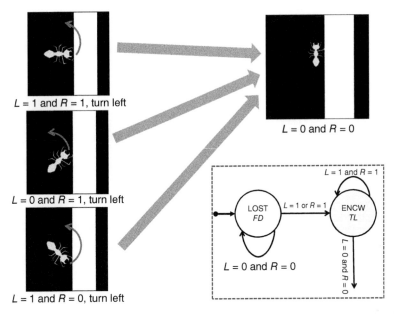

FIGURE 5.13 'ENCW' (encountering a wall) state – an ant keeps turning left until neither antenna touches a wall.

In summary, the state transitions are as follows: an initial transition that points to 'LOST' state, two transitions from state 'LOST' to 'ENCW'

- $\delta(LOST, \{1, *\}, ENCW)$
- $\delta(LOST, \{*, 1\}, ENCW)$

and a loop back transition: $\delta(LOST, \{0, 0\}, LOST)$. The transition $\delta(LOST, \{1, 1\}, LOST)$ is covered by the first two transitions by using the wildcard '*', which can be either 0 or 1.

In the 'ENCW' state, the ant must keep turning left until neither antenna touches the wall any more. After the turn, the wall is on the right side of the ant and the ant can start following the wall. This procedure and the state corresponding with the action 'turn left' of the FSM are illustrated in Figure 5.13. Once a wall is touched/found by the ant, the ant starts walking forward along the wall. Therefore, the state of the ant is not 'ENCW' anymore, and the arrow points down to a new state.

In the new state, the ant starts walking forward. As a wall follower using the right-hand rule, the ant must keep checking whether there is a wall there when walking forward. This can be done by turning the ant a little to the right at every step forward. If the ant's right antenna touches a wall, this means the ant is on the correct track. Thus, we define a new state and a new transition. We name the new state 'WALKR', as shown in Figure 5.14. This state is reached by transition from 'ENCW' state:

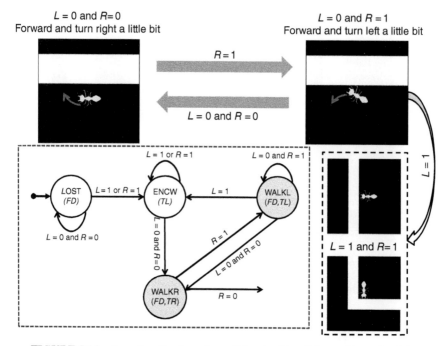

FIGURE 5.14 An ant walks along the wall by checking if the wall is on its right.

- $\delta(ENCW, \{1, *\}, ENCW)$
- $\delta(ENCW, \{*, 1\}, ENCW)$
- $\delta(ENCW, \{0, 0\}, WALKR)$

The wildcards in the first two transitions mean that the ant is staying in the same state of 'ENCW' when any one of the two antennae touches a wall.

Once the ant ensures a wall is on its right side, it must turn slightly left until there is no contact between its right antenna and the wall. This makes the ant move back to the desired direction. This becomes a new state of the ant called 'WALKL'. Both 'WALKR' and 'WALKL' occur alternately, as illustrated in Figure 5.14 to correct the ant's direction and ensure that there is a wall on the ant's right side. Thus, the transitions involved in both states are:

- $\delta(WLAKR, \{*, 1\}, WALKL)$
- $\delta(WALKL, \{0, 0\}, WALKR)$
- $\delta(WALKL, \{0, 1\}, WALKL)$

For the first transition, the ant needs to know the value of its right antenna only, because it has to check only whether there is a wall on its right side.

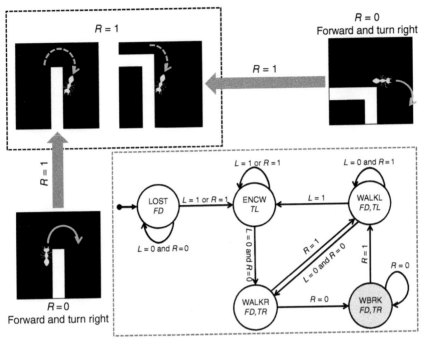

FIGURE 5.15   An ant encountering a wall break or turning corner when walking along the wall on the right side.

In summary, 'WALKR' allows the ant to be sure that it is following a wall on its right side, while 'WALKL' keeps correcting the direction of the ant once the wall checking is done.

There is also the possibility that the ant's left antenna touches a wall when the ant is in the 'WALKL' state. This means that the ant's path is blocked by another wall or that the ant encountered an inner wall corner because the right antenna has already touched a wall. In this case, we could apply the same strategy as in the 'ENCW' state to let the ant keep turning left until there is no wall in front of it. Thus, there is a transition from the 'WALKL' state back to the 'ENCW' state, triggered by the left antenna touching a wall ($L = 1$). This is defined by:

- $\delta(WALKL, \{1, *\}, ENCW)$

Given that we do not need to care about the left antenna, a wildcard is used to represent this transition.

Then there is the possibility that the ant does not sense a wall with its right antenna when in the 'WALKR' state. This is illustrated as a transition at the bottom of Figure 5.14. This situation could be caused by either a wall break or a turning corner, as shown in Figure 5.15. We use 'WBRK' to denote this state, and define the corresponding transition from 'WALKR' to 'WBRK' as follows:

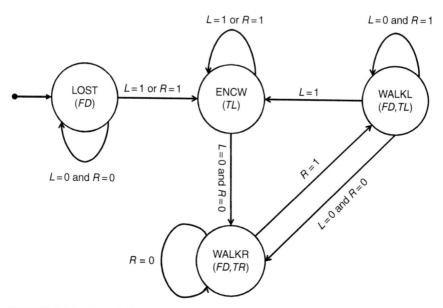

FIGURE 5.16   An optimised FSM for modelling ant behaviour to find the way out of a maze.

- $\delta(WALKR, \{*, 0\}, WBRK)$

During the 'WBRK' state, the ant makes a right turn until its right antenna hits a wall. Once a wall is found on the right side of the ant, the ant's state becomes 'WALKL'. The two possible transitions from the 'WBRK' state can be defined as follows:

- $\delta(WBRK, \{*, 0\}, WBRK)$
- $\delta(WBRK, \{*, 1\}, WALKL)$

Now, a complete FSM modelling of the ant's movement to find the way out of the maze is constructed and visualised at the bottom left of Figure 5.15. However, if we inspect the FSM carefully, there are some equivalent transitions and states. Both 'WALKR' and 'WBRK' have transitions trigged by the same event $\{1, *\}$ and go to the same destination state 'WALKL'. Further, both 'WALKR' and 'WBRK' have another transition caused by $\{*, 0\}$ that leads to the same actions: going forward and turning right. Therefore, we could eliminate the state 'WBRK' in the proposed FSM, which gives us a new optimised FSM with the minimum required states and transitions, as illustrated in Figure 5.16. The optimisation of the FSM allows us to implement the FSM model easily and efficiently.

Based on the graphical representation of the FSM and the transitions discussed before, a complete truth table can be built (Table 5.4).

TABLE 5.4   A True Table of the FSM for Modelling an Ant's Behaviours to Find the Way Out of a Maze

State	Actions	L	R	Next state
LOST	FD	0	0	LOST
LOST	FD	1	*	ENCW
LOST	FD	*	1	ENCW
ENCW	TL	1	*	ENCW
ENCW	TL	*	1	ENCW
ENCW	TL	0	0	WALKR
WALKR	FD,TR	*	0	WALKR
WALKR	FD,TR	*	1	WALKL
WALKL	FD,TL	1	*	ENCW
WALKL	FD,TL	0	1	WALKL
WALKL	FD,TL	0	0	WALKR

Thus far, we have constructed a FSM model for an ant's behaviour to find the way out of a maze. In the next section, we will discuss the implementation of a simulator for this model.

5.6.2   A Simulator for Finite-State Machine

To implement a simulator for a FSM, the **while-switch** instruction is typically used by most of the programming languages (e.g. Java). Here, we will use a pseudo-code to present the idea of implementing a FSM by **while-switch** for the above ant example.

The logic is simple: we keep the ant moving in the maze and change its states according to the information sensed until it finds the exit point of the maze. This is why we use a **while** loop with the condition $Loc \neq OUT$, where Loc is the variable representing the current location of the ant, and OUT the variable representing the current location of the ant, and OUT is a constant for the exit point of the maze. Once the ant's location is at the exit point, the **while** terminates, as shown in Algorithm 1. As we discussed in the previous section, the speed of the ant is a constant denoted by $step$ in the algorithm. The turning rate of the ant is also predefined as a constant called deg. The ant moves in the maze by taking actions according to its current state, as described in the FSM model. The actions include:

- FORWARD by $step$ when it is 'LOST'
- TURN LEFT by deg when it is 'ENCW'
- FORWARD by $step$ and TURN RIGHT by deg when it is 'WALKR'
- FORWARD by $step$ TURN LEFT by deg when it is 'WALKL'.

Therefore, we need keep checking the ant's states when the simulator is running. We could use nested **if** statements to complete these checks. However, a **switch** statement may be the better option for a FSM because it is easy and clear for us to identify each state and map it to the cases enumerated in a **switch** statement. Thus, the **while-switch** instruction is a popular paradigm for FSM implementation. Based on the FSM diagram and the truth table listed in the previous section, a possible solution is depicted in Algorithm 1.

Algorithm 1 Implementation of FSM for an Ant in Maze

Require: *IN*, *OUT* {locations of start and exit}
Require: *step*, *deg* {forward speed and turning rate}
 1: *Loc = IN* {the location of an ant}
 2: *state = LOST* {the state of an ant}
 3: $L = 0$, $R = 0$ {the signal sensed by an ant's left antenna and right antenna respectively}
 4: **while** *Loc* $\neq$ *OUT* **do**
 5:    **switch** (*state*)
 6:    **case** *LOST*
 7:       FORWARD by *step* {forward a *step* at one iteration}
 8:       Sense by left and right antenna
 9:       **if** $L \equiv 1$ or $R \equiv 1$ **then**
10:          *state = ENCW*
11:       **end if**
12:    **case** *ENCW*:
13:       TURN LEFT by *deg* {turn left by a *deg* at one iteration}
14:       Sense by left and right antenna
15:       **if** $L \equiv 0$ and $R \equiv 0$ **then**
16:          *state = WALKR*
17:       **end if**
18:    **case** *WALKR*:
19:       FORWARD by *step* and TURN RIGHT by *deg* {forward a *step* and turn right by a *deg* at one iteration}
20:       Sense by left and right antenna
21:       **if** $R \equiv 1$ **then**
22:          *state = WALKL*
23:       **endif**
24:    **case** *WALKL*:
25:       FORWARD by *step* and TURN LEFT by *deg*
26:       Sense by left and right antenna
27:       **if** $L \equiv 1$ **then**
28:          *state = ENCW*
29:       **else if** $L \equiv 0$ and $R \equiv 0$ **then**
30:          *state = WALKR*
31:       **end if**
32:    **end switch**
33:    Update *Loc*
34: **end while**

In Algorithm 1, we did not explicitly implement the 'loop' transition for each state of the ant because it is not necessary to introduce more **if** checks for something that

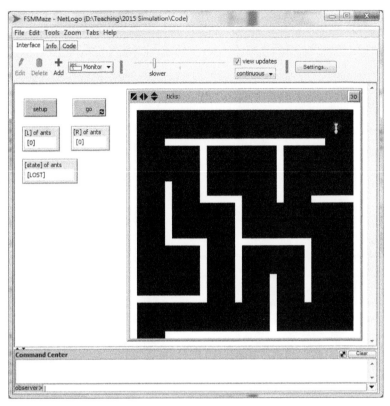

FIGURE 5.17 A NetLogo implementation of the FSM simulator for modelling an ant's behaviours to find the way out of a maze.

does not affect the ant state, but instead reduces the algorithm's efficiency for state machines more complex than the ant example.

Of course, this is one possible way to implement a FSM. We also could use other methods to complete this. For example, we may use the object-oriented paradigm to implement a FSM. In this case, the ant (or the FSM of the ant) and its attributes (states, actions, and sensors) can be wrapped in a class, and then we could implement functions for each state of the ant from which the corresponding effects are produced.

We use NetLogo to implement the simulator for the ant behaviours in a maze following the implementation detailed in Algorithm 1. However, the above algorithm focuses only on the FSM implementation with the assumption that the function of the sensing works. In the actual implementation by NetLogo, we suppose that the ant can sense two areas: one is its 10 o'clock position (front-left), and another is 2 o'clock position (front-right), and the corresponding functions are implemented. Another addition necessary for the above algorithm is to construct a maze. A maze can be designed and built by hand or other methods; however, it is beyond the scope of this book and left for readers to investigate. The simulator implemented by NetLogo is shown in Figure 5.17.

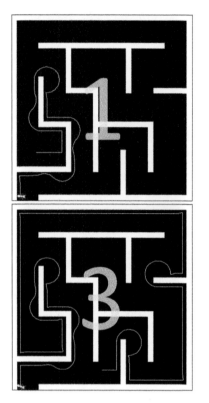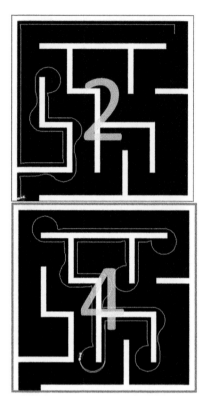

FIGURE 5.18   Simulation results of an ant's behaviours to find the way out of a maze.

This simulator has a predefined maze displayed on the right side of the GUI. The ant is illustrated in yellow and the initial location of the ant can be any place within the maze. On the left side, there are some variable monitors for displaying the value of the sensing signals from both antennae, as well as the state of the ant. The values of these variables may change at each iteration, which offers us some intuitive views on how ants are driven by the FSM.

5.6.3   Simulating the Ant in a Maze

We initialise the ant's location at four different positions within the same maze and then run the simulator. In all runs, we use the following parameters for the ant's actions:

- the forward step: $step = 0.2$
- the turning rate: $deg = 5$, for both left and right turns.

Figure 5.18 shows the ant's tracks produced by these four runs. The results of the first three runs show how the ant found the exit point of the maze by using the strategy of wall following and the right-hand rule. These three tracks clearly show that the ant followed the right side wall when looking for the exit. The initial tracks are straight, meaning that the ant kept going forward when the state was 'LOST'. As soon as it touched a wall, it started making a left turn until neither antenna was in contact with a wall. Although the tracks cannot clearly show the state transitions between 'WALKR' and 'WALKL', the ant kept changing to its left and then to its right to check walls. In addition, the big turning curves demonstrate that the ant made large right turns when it encountered wall breaks or wall corners. As demonstrated in the first three runs, the FSM of the ant seems to work perfectly and can allow the ant to find its way out from the maze.

However, what happened in the last run? As the figure shows, the ant seemed to be trapped. It went along a track that was obviously an endless loop. Does this mean that our FSM is wrong? The answer is no. This run was caused by the strategy adopted by our FSM model, not by our FSM model itself. Given that the ant follows the right-hand rule, there is no opportunity for it to jump out from the middle section of the maze. The only path that the ant can follow is exactly as illustrated by the ant's track in the fourth figure. FSM is a deterministic model and can only exist in predefined states and perform predefined actions. Therefore, the only way to let the ant out of the maze is to introduce other strategies (actions) and new states to the FSM ant model.

5.7 CONCLUSION

In this chapter, we have discussed a number of representation methods. As the examples indicated, there is high flexibility in choosing the representation for modelling a system. Many different approaches can achieve the same modelling objective for the same system. For example, the traffic light can be modelled as a FSM, flowchart, or state transition diagram, and all of them are capable of reproducing the traffic light behaviours. We also used an example that successfully modelled an ant's behaviour in a maze by using a FSM. Although the use of FSMs has some drawbacks and limitations, as explained in the ant example, they provide a simple and efficient way to model the dynamic behaviour of a system with finite states and transitions. Moreover, FSMs can be used in other types of modelling and simulation. For example, FSMs can be used to model agent behaviours in ABSs.

███████ **CHAPTER 6**

Experimental Design

Both experimentation and output analysis are critical to the success of a simulation. Good experimental design leads to good simulation results. Appropriate output analysis can satisfy the study requirements and meet the objectives. In this chapter, we introduce common experimental design methods for simulation, with a focus on the 2^k factorial screening. Through this method, the key factors in a system can be identified and further investigated via simulation. Another technique, the response surface, can be used to predict some basic behaviours of a system in response to changes in the values of different factors. In addition, given the potential randomness involved in the simulation, hypothesis tests are needed to conclude that the findings obtained via the experimental design are statistically meaningful. Finally, some basic ideas for performing analysis on simulation outputs are discussed to conclude the chapter.

6.1 INTRODUCTION

Once a model is built, experimentation and output analysis are needed to satisfy study requirements and meet the simulation objectives. Therefore, good experimentation and output analysis are critical to successful modelling and simulation. Through experimentation we can examine the correctness of the modelling process as part of the verification and validation process. In addition, we can perform goal-directed experiments as the result of good experimental design. Through experimental design, the key factors affecting the system of interest can be identified and studied further. In addition, these key factors contribute to our simulation goals and objectives. It is also essential to apply analysis methods on the simulation results to extract meaningful information from the gathered data. Therefore, experimentation and output analysis are critical parts of the simulation lifecycle.

In general, a model usually takes inputs and generates outputs under certain assumptions. The input parameters and assumptions composing a model are called **factors**, while the measures on output performance are called **responses**. Factors and

Simulation and Computational Red Teaming for Problem Solving, First Edition.
Jiangjun Tang, George Leu, and Hussein A. Abbass.
© 2020 by The Institute of Electrical and Electronics Engineers, Inc. Published 2020 by John Wiley & Sons, Inc.

responses take different values grouped into different levels. The decisions on factors must be made before conducting a simulation. Generally, there are two options: the first is to use the fixed parameters and assumptions of a model for all simulations, while the second is to experimentally change the factor values depending on the study objective. For the grocery shop example discussed in Chapter 4, the factors associated with the model include the client arrival rate, efficiency of the register, number of registers, and so on. We can fix the client arrival rate and register efficiency to perform some deterministic simulations and analyse client queue length. However, we can also manipulate them by probability distributions with various parameter settings to understand the dynamics of the queue length in different situations. Here, the queue length is the response from the model in which we are interested.

The model factors can be seen as part of two categories: **quantitative** and **qualitative** factors. The quantitative factors are those that can hold numerical values, such as the number of registers in the grocery shop. However, the qualitative factors represent structural assumptions that are not naturally quantified. For example, the client queue in a grocery shop is a FIFO queue, while the patients in the emergency room of a hospital are organised in a priority queue. These rules for queues are qualitative factors. Factors in experiments can also be seen as **controllable** and **uncontrollable**. The difference between them involves whether the factors represent action options to owners of the system. In experiments, we usually focus on the controllable factors because they are most relevant to decision makers. In the grocery shop example, the number of registers is a controllable factor; we can adjust it in experiments to see how it affects the queue length, so that we can provide advice to decision makers. However, we are also interested in some uncontrollable factors in the experiments, such as whether the shop register can handle a situation in which the client number increases by 10%. Although the client number is not controllable in the real world, we can still manipulate it in the experiments to answer some interesting what-if questions. It is clear from the above discussion that variation of factors may affect the response level. However, the magnitude of the effects on the model response may be different from one factor to another. To determine the most effective factors of a model, experimental design is needed.

If there is only one factor, experimentation is generally a relatively easy task. We just need to try different values of a factor to see how the model responds. Of course, we still need an appropriate sampling method to generate the input values of the factor (sampling methods are discussed in detail in Section 6.4). However, in practice, models with a single factor are very rare; usually, multiple factors coexist and interact in a model. In this case, enumerating all possible combinations of factors' values requires a large amount of simulations to identify which factors have the greatest effect on the response. Thus, finding efficient methods that determine the key factors of a model with the least amount of simulations is the primary objective of experimental design. It is more efficient to carefully design experiments than use brute-force approaches (i.e., all combinations of factor values) or a hit-or-miss sequence of runs. In the following section, we describe 'factor screening' – one of the most popular methods for systematic design of experiments, which allows efficient identification of key factors.

6.2 FACTOR SCREENING

Factor screening, also known as sensitivity analysis, is an experimental design approach that searches for the most important factors in a model. These most important factors can cause large response variations in the experiments. There are many factor screening methods in literature, including the one-factor-at-a-time method [137], 2^k factorial design, 2^{k-p} factorial design [50], and sequential bifuraction [45]. In this section, we focus on the first two methods.

6.2.1 One-factor-at-a-time Method

The one-factor-at-a-time (OFAT) method is a simple and intuitive method; however, it comes with certain drawbacks, as we will see in the following discussion. Suppose there are k ($k \geq 2$) factors in a model and we need to estimate their effects on the response. OFAT considers one factor as the factor of interest, fixes the other $k - 1$ factors at base levels, and then runs simulations with different values of the factor of interest to evaluate how this influences the response. The process is applied k times, considering at each iteration another factor as the factor of interest. This is a simple way of determining which factors have the most significant effect on the model response. The whole process of OFAT is illustrated in the flowchart below.

Example 6.2.1. *Assume there are two factors, A and B, in a model. The base levels for them are A^- and B^-, respectively, and their proposed levels are A^+ and B^+, respectively. According to OFAT (from the model based on the flowchart in Figure 6.1), there are three possible combinations of A, B, and the corresponding response (R). These are presented in Table 6.1.*

The effect of factor A from A^- to A^+ when factor B remains at base level can be calculated by

$$R(A^+, B^-) - R(A^-, B^-)$$

As seen in this example, OFAT is simple, yet it is not efficient because it requires a large number of simulation runs (different combinations of factor values) to obtain a specified precision. For a model with two factors, each with two desired levels, it requires three simulation runs. The number of required simulation runs increases dramatically when the number of factors and the number of proposed levels increase. Further, OFAT does not measure any interactions between factors. In the above example, the combined effect of both factors A and B (when they change from the base level to the proposed level) is not estimated because A is fixed at the base level when evaluating the effect of factor B based on the OFAT approach, and the vice-versa.

As a result of the limitations of OFAT, an advanced method called 2^k factorial design was proposed, as follows.

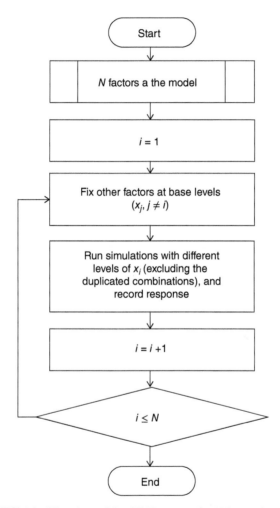

FIGURE 6.1 Flowchart of the OFAT process for N factors in a model.

TABLE 6.1 Factor Levels and Responses by OFAT

i	A	B	R
1	A^-	B^-	$R(A^-, B^-)$
1	A^+	B^-	$R(A^+, B^-)$
2	A^-	B^+	$R(A^-, B^+)$

TABLE 6.2   A Tabular Representation of 2^k Factor Design for a Model with Three Factors

Design points (i)	Factor 1	Factor 2	Factor 3	Response (R_i)
1	−	−	−	R_1
2	+	−	−	R_2
3	−	+	−	R_3
4	+	+	−	R_4
5	−	−	+	R_5
6	+	−	+	R_6
7	−	+	+	R_7
8	+	+	+	R_8

6.2.2 2^k Factorial Design

2^k factorial design is a more economical strategy for identifying factor effects on the response and interactions between factors. This method assumes that each factor has two levels only – one is low and the other is high. All combinations of factor levels become the design points. Therefore, the effect on response is investigated by running simulations at each design point. If a model has k factors, then there are 2^k combinations available – hence the name of the method: 2^k factorial design.

6.2.2.1   Factor Main Effect
To perform the 2^k factorial design, we assume that the response is approximately linear or at least monotonic over the range of factors. In this case, we can estimate factors' effects on the response based on only the low and high values. Generally, a minus sign '−' is used for the low level of a factor, and a plus sign '+' is used for the high level. The actual values of these levels need to be consulted with system experts before a decision is made. Based on the '−' and '+' notation, we can use a compact tabular representation of the 2^k factor design, as in Example 6.2.2.

Example 6.2.2. *A model contains three factors. A tabular 2^k factor design for the model can be represented as in Table 6.2.*

As shown in the table, there are in total eight design points (all possible factor level combinations) and correspondingly a total of eight responses from these design points. Table 6.2 is also called a 'design matrix', and facilitates the calculation of effects and interactions.

The main effect of a factor is the average change in the response caused by the change of this factor level from '−' to '+', while all other factor levels are fixed. Taking the first factor in Table 6.2 as an example, $R_2 - R_1$, $R_4 - R_3$, $R_6 - R_5$, and $R_8 - R_7$ are the differences in response caused by only the changes in Factor 1 level because the levels of the other two remain either '−' or '+'. Then, the main effect of the factor can be derived from the average of these changes. Let j denote a factor and e_j represent the main effect of factor j; then, the main effect of all three factors in the previous example can be formalised as a set of equations as below:

$$e_1 = \frac{(R_2 - R_1) + (R_4 - R_3) + (R_6 - R_5) + (R_8 - R_7)}{4} \tag{6.1a}$$

$$e_2 = \frac{(R_3 - R_1) + (R_4 - R_2) + (R_7 - R_5) + (R_8 - R_6)}{4} \tag{6.1b}$$

$$e_3 = \frac{(R_3 - R_1) + (R_6 - R_2) + (R_7 - R_3) + (R_8 - R_4)}{4}. \tag{6.1c}$$

Another easy way to calculate the main effect of a factor is to use the design matrix. If the notations '−' and '+' for the low and high levels can be seen as '−1', and '+1', then the dot product between the factor column and the response column in the design matrix is actually the sum of the all response changes caused by this factor. This is further averaged by 2^{k-1} 1 to obtain the main effect. For example, Factor 2 in Table 6.2 can be calculated following the process shown in Figure 6.2.

The dot product between the Factor 2 column and the response column is:

$$-R_1 - R_2 + R_3 + R_4 - R_5 - R_6 + R_7 + R_8.$$

If we rearrange conveniently the terms in the above expression, we can obtain the same form of the numerator as in Eq. (6.1), from which we can easily attain the main effect. Further, the main effects of other factors can be obtained in a similar manner using this method.

6.2.2.2 *Factor Interaction*   Apart from the main effect, we are also interested in the interactions between factors. If the effect of a factor j_p depends on another factor j_q, then we say that factors j_p and j_q interact with each other. The interaction between two factors is measured by the difference between the average effect of factor j_p when the level of factor j_q is '+' and the average effect of factor j_p when the level of factor j_q is '−'. This difference is the two-factor interaction effect denoted by $e_{j_p j_q}$ which is also called $j_p \times j_q$ interaction. Based on the definition, the two-factor interaction effects for Example 6.2.2 can be formed into the following equations:

$$e_{12} = \frac{1}{2}\left[\frac{(R_4 - R_3) + (R_8 - R_7)}{2} - \frac{(R_2 - R_1) + (R_6 - R_5)}{2} \right] \tag{6.2a}$$

$$e_{13} = \frac{1}{2}\left[\frac{(R_6 - R_5) + (R_8 - R_7)}{2} - \frac{(R_2 - R_1) + (R_4 - R_3)}{2} \right] \tag{6.2b}$$

$$e_{23} = \frac{1}{2}\left[\frac{(R_7 - R_5) + (R_8 - R_6)}{2} - \frac{(R_3 - R_1) + (R_4 - R_2)}{2} \right]. \tag{6.2c}$$

In Eq. (6.2), the average effect of Factor 1 when Factor 2 level is '+' is modelled as the first part in the square brackets, while its average effect when Factor 2 level is

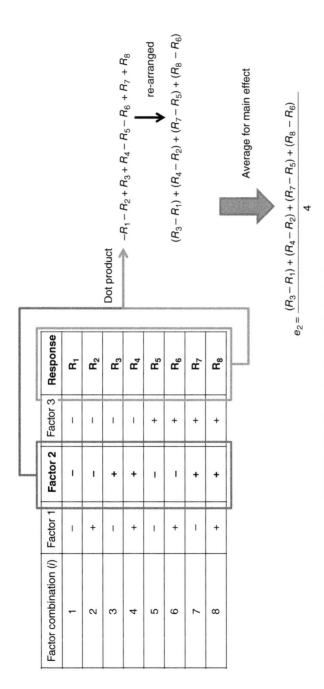

Factor combination (*i*)	Factor 1	Factor 2	Factor 3	Response
1	–	–	–	R_1
2	+	–	–	R_2
3	–	+	–	R_3
4	+	+	–	R_4
5	–	–	+	R_5
6	+	–	+	R_6
7	–	+	+	R_7
8	+	+	+	R_8

Dot product

$$-R_1 - R_2 + R_3 + R_4 - R_5 - R_6 + R_7 + R_8$$

re-arranged

$$(R_3 - R_1) + (R_4 - R_2) + (R_7 - R_5) + (R_8 - R_6)$$

Average for main effect

$$e_2 = \frac{(R_3 - R_1) + (R_4 - R_2) + (R_7 - R_5) + (R_8 - R_6)}{4}$$

FIGURE 6.2 The main effect calculation by design matrix.

Factor combination (/)	Factor 1	Factor 2	Factor 3	Response	Factor 1 × Factor 2 × Response
1	–	–	–	R_1	$+R_1$
2	+	–	–	R_2	$-R_2$
3	–	+	–	R_3	$-R_3$
4	+	+	–	R_4	$+R_4$
5	–	–	+	R_5	$+R_5$
6	+	–	+	R_6	$-R_6$
7	–	+	+	R_7	$-R_7$
8	+	+	+	R_8	$+R_8$

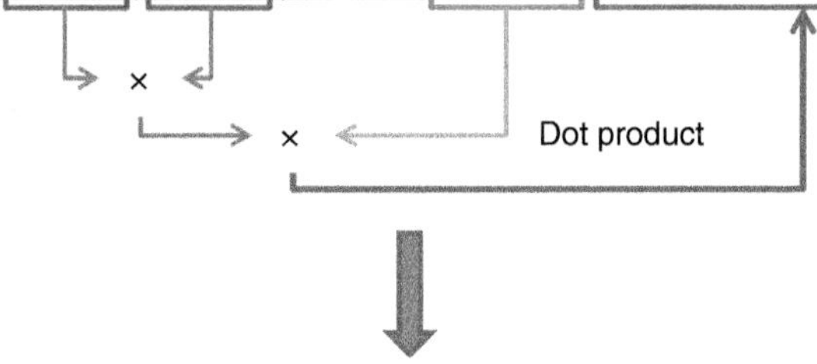

Dot product

$$e_{12} = \frac{R_1 - R_2 - R_3 + R_4 + R_5 - R_6 - R_7 + R_8}{4}$$

FIGURE 6.3 Calculation of two-factor interaction between Factors 1 and 2 using design matrix.

'–' is the second part in the square brackets. Then, the difference between them is calculated and further divided by 2 because the interaction involves two factors.

The interaction can also be easily calculated using the design matrix as the example shown in Figure 6.3. Clearly, the equation derived from the design matrix in the figure is an equivalent form of Eq. (6.2). The two-factor interaction effect is completely symmetric; therefore, $e_12 = e_21$, $e_13 = e_31$, and $e_23 = e_32$.

The three-factor interaction in a model can be viewed as the one-half difference between the two-factor interaction effect $e_{j_p j_q}$ when the third factor j_r changes its level from '–' to '+'. Figure 6.4 illustrates the logic behind it and the corresponding calculations. The Factors 1 and 2 interaction effect when the third factor level is '–' can be calculated from the first four rows. Similarly, their interaction effect when Factor 3 is at '+' level can be obtained from the last four rows. Then, the one-half difference between them can be derived. Thus, the equation of the three-factor interaction effect for Example 6.2.2 is

$$e_{123} = \frac{1}{2} \left[\frac{(R_8 - R_7) - (R_6 - R_5)}{2} - \frac{(R_4 - R_3) - (R_2 - R_1)}{2} \right]. \qquad (6.3)$$

Figure 6.4 illustrates a simple way to calculate the three-factor interaction effect using a design matrix. The interaction of the three factors can be derived from the dot

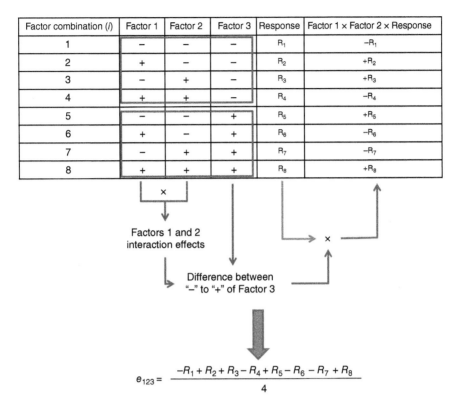

Factor combination (i)	Factor 1	Factor 2	Factor 3	Response	Factor 1 × Factor 2 × Response
1	−	−	−	R_1	$-R_1$
2	+	−	−	R_2	$+R_2$
3	−	+	−	R_3	$+R_3$
4	+	+	−	R_4	$-R_4$
5	−	−	+	R_5	$+R_5$
6	+	−	+	R_6	$-R_6$
7	−	+	+	R_7	$-R_7$
8	+	+	+	R_8	$+R_8$

Factors 1 and 2
interaction effects

Difference between
"−" to "+" of Factor 3

$$e_{123} = \frac{-R_1 + R_2 + R_3 - R_4 + R_5 - R_6 - R_7 + R_8}{4}$$

FIGURE 6.4   Calculation of three-factor interaction between Factors 1, 2, and 3 using design matrix.

product between all factor level columns and the corresponding response column. The equation at the bottom of the figure is another equivalent form of Eq. (6.3).

As shown in the above examples, the design matrix is an efficient and effective way to calculate the interaction between factors. It is also easy to extend the method for estimating the interactions between more than three factors.

It is important to note that, sometimes, one factor in a model may seem less important to the response from the main effect estimations, yet it can have a large influence on the response when interacting with other factors.

Example 6.2.3.   *A model has two factors, A and B. After applying 2^k factorial design, the corresponding responses are produced, and listed in Table 6.3*
Based on the above table, the main effects of Factors A and B are

$$e_A = \frac{(79 - 38) + (22 - 62)}{2} = 0.5$$

and

$$e_B = \frac{(62 - 38) + (22 - 79)}{2} = -16.5.$$

TABLE 6.3   Responses of a Model with Two Factors in 2^k Factorial Design

Design point i	A	B	R_i
1	−	−	38
1	+	−	79
1	−	+	62
1	+	+	22

The above calculation shows that Factor B has a more significant effect than Factor A on this model. The main effect of Factor B on the response is −16.5 when it changes its level from '−' to '+', while Factor A only affects the response by 0.5. Thus far, it seems that Factor A does not strongly affect the model response. Now, let us look at the interaction between these two factors.

$$e_{AB} = \frac{38 - 79 - 62 + 22}{2} = -40.5.$$

Surprisingly, the two-factor interaction effect (A × B) is much higher than any individual main effect. In fact, Factor A seems to have a significant effect on the response when it works together with Factor B. Is this truly significant? It looks much higher than all others, but without conducting an appropriate test of hypothesis, this conclusion is not scientifically sound.

Example 6.2.3 shows a case in which an important factor is hidden in the presence of a significant interaction. Therefore, it is necessary to estimate both the main factor effects and factor interaction effects to determine the most important factor in a model.

6.2.2.3   Hypothesis Test on Effects

Given that virtually any model involves a certain amount of randomness, the responses from a model are usually random variables. A random variable is not an ad-hoc variable. A random variable is a variable, the values it takes follow a probabilistic distribution. This probability distribution captures the patterns in the behaviour of the variable. For example, consider a random variable that produces values according to a normal distribution with zero mean and a unit standard deviation. The values this variable will have 99% of the time will fall in the range [−3, 3] due to the properties of a normal distribution.

Consequently, the effects derived from the responses are also random and in effect, will follow a probability distribution that is a mixture of the distributions of the factors. It is necessary to conclude that the effects from factors are statistically significant to determine the most important factor in a model. This can be achieved by hypothesis tests, such as the 't-test', on the calculated effects.

Before we show an example below on how t-test is used, it is important to understand that each test of significance has its own assumptions. Therefore, the choice of a test of significance is not arbitrarily. The analyst must understand the acceptable assumptions in the particular experiment and the appropriate test of significance suitable for these assumptions. For example, t-test assumes that the data follows a normal distribution and the number of cases to be tested is small. With a large number of cases increases, a z-test would be more appropriate. How large is large? As a rule of thumb, when the number of cases exceeds 30, a z-test could be used.

A hypothesis tested with the t-test considers the following steps:

1. Replicate the whole design n times to obtain n independent values of each effect.

2. Let e_j^i be the observed main effect of factor j on replication i, for $i = 1, 2, ..., n$. Then the average of the effect from all replications is:

$$\bar{e}_j(n) = \frac{\sum\limits_{i=1}^{n} e_j^i}{n} \qquad (6.4)$$

3. The standard deviation of effects is:

$$S_j^2(n) = \frac{\sum\limits_{i=1}^{n} (e_j^i - \bar{e}_j(n))^2}{n-1} \qquad (6.5)$$

4. Then, perform the t-test on the average effects to check the confidence intervals of all effects.

Given that detailed discussions on the t-test can be found in many statistics textbooks, only a brief introduction is given here. To perform the t-test on an effect, we need to calculate the expected main effect $E(e_j)$ first, as in Eq. (6.6):

$$E(e_j) = \bar{e}_j(n) \pm t_{n-1,1-\alpha/2} \sqrt{\frac{S_j^2(n)}{n}} \qquad (6.6)$$

where $t_{n-1,1-\alpha/2}$ can be obtained from the t-test table. Here, $100(1 - \alpha)\%$ is the confidence interval for the expected main effect $E(e_j)$. For example, the percentage of the confidence interval is 95% for an effect when $\alpha = 0.05$. If $E(e_j)$ does not contain zero, this effect is statistically meaningful. Otherwise, there is no statistical evidence for it. The following example demonstrates how a t-test is performed on the factor effects.

Example 6.2.4. *Suppose there are two factors, A and B, in a model. We consider a 2^k factorial design where $A^- = 15$, $A^+ = 55$, $B^- = 10$, and $B^+ = 40$. After running 10 replications ($n = 10$) for each design point, the responses are obtained as in Table 6.4.*

TABLE 6.4 Responses from 10 Replications in a 2^k Factorial Design

Design point	1	2	3	4	5	6	7	8	9	10	Average	Sample variance
A = 15, B = 10	123.55	116.09	114.54	128.20	114.14	119.37	114.79	113.77	116.86	121.67	118.30	23.27
A = 55, B = 10	145.78	143.54	147.94	141.37	147.18	145.47	147.87	148.97	143.74	146.07	145.79	5.55
A = 15, B = 40	114.43	121.30	114.63	117.91	115.69	112.57	112.76	124.37	117.88	118.53	117.01	14.26
A = 55, B = 40	151.02	148.98	149.01	150.21	150.73	153.34	151.09	149.83	151.95	149.58	150.57	1.86

TABLE 6.5   Effects and Interactions from 10 Replications in a 2^k Factorial Design

Effect	1	2	3	4	5	6	7	8	9	10	$e_j(10)$	$S_j^2(10)$
e_A	29.41	27.56	33.89	22.74	34.04	33.43	35.71	30.33	30.47	27.72	30.53	15.29
e_B	−1.94	5.33	0.58	−0.73	2.55	0.54	0.59	5.74	4.62	0.19	1.75	7.10
$e_A B$	7.18	0.12	0.49	9.56	1.00	7.34	2.62	−4.87	3.59	3.33	3.04	17.83

The main effects and interactions are calculated and listed in Table 6.5. Given that $t_{9,0.95} = 1.83$ from a t-test table, the expected effects and interaction for Factors A and B are:

$$E(e_j) = \bar{e}_j(10) \pm 1.83 \sqrt{\frac{S_j^2(10)}{10}}$$

$$E(e_A) = 30.53 \pm 2.267$$

$$E(e_A) = 1.746 \pm 1.544$$

and

$$E(e_A) = 3.305 \pm 2.448$$

Thus, all effects appear to be significant because their confidence intervals do not include zeros.

Thus far, we have discussed relevant methodologies for determining the important factors in a model. Many other techniques for factor screening exist, such as 2^{k-p} or sequential bifuration; however, we do not present them in this book. Interested readers are encouraged to read Montgomery's book [292].

The results from 2^k factorial design can also be used to build a metamodel for the prediction of behaviours of a model. In the next section, we discuss this possibility.

6.3   METAMODEL AND RESPONSE SURFACE

Once the most important factors of a model are identified, modellers may be able to predict the response changes by these factors without running the actual simulations. Thus, a metamodel of the simulation model can be built to see how the simulation transforms a particular set of input factor values into the output response [52].

In the beginning of the last section, we mentioned that the 2^k factorial design is used in cases where there is an approximately linear or at least a monotonic relationship between the factor ranges and response. Therefore, the usual way to construct a metamodel is to use a first-order or second-order regression model based on the results found in the 2^k factorial design. The resultant regression model can predict the response for other factor level combinations and can also be used to optimise the response roughly by adjusting the factor level combinations.

The results from Example 6.2.4 are used here to build a metamodel by first-order regression. For the two factors, A and B, existing in the model, let us assume that the expected combined effect from A and B, $E[R(A,B)]$, can be represented by the following linear regression equation:

$$E[R(A,B)] = \beta_0 + \beta_A x_A + \beta_B x_B + \beta_{AB} x_a x_b \tag{6.7}$$

where β_0, β_A, β_B, and $\beta_A B$ are coded variables. In the beginning, the coded variables can be derived from the 2^k factorial design; then, all coefficients can be calculated. Once all the coefficients are decided for the model, we can try different factor level combinations to see the response changes.

To obtain the coded variable values, the average of the factor level is calculated first. For Example 6.2.4, the average factor levels of A and B are $\overline{A} = 35$ and $\overline{B} = 25$ respectively. Let ΔA and ΔB be the differences between '$-$' and '$+$' levels for Factors A and B, so that $\Delta A = 40$ and $\Delta B = 30$. Then the coded variables can be calculated as follows:

$$x_A = \frac{2(A - \overline{A})}{\Delta A} \tag{6.8a}$$

$$x_B = \frac{2(B - \overline{B})}{\Delta B}. \tag{6.8b}$$

Using the above equations, we can compress the factor level range into a range from -1 to $+1$. For example, $x_A = -1$ when $A = 15$ and $x_A = +1$ when $A = 55$. Coded variables are commonly used in experimental design because the effect on the response of a change in factor is always measured relatively to the range -1 to $+1$.

Now, let $\overline{e}_A(10)$, $\overline{e}_B(10)$, and $\overline{e}_{AB}(10)$ be the estimated average effects from 10 replications of Example (6.7) for the main effect of Factor A, the main effect of Factor B, and the effect of A and B interaction. Then, $\overline{R}_F(10)$ is the average of response over all factorial design points and over all 10 replications. The least-square estimations of coefficients can be obtained as follows:

$$\hat{\beta}_0 = \overline{R}_F(10), \ \hat{\beta}_A = \frac{\overline{e}_A(10)}{2}, \ \hat{\beta}_B = \frac{\overline{e}_B(10)}{2}, \ \hat{\beta}_{AB} = \frac{\overline{e}_{AB}(10)}{2}.$$

Therefore, the expected response can be formulated by replacing the least-square estimator of coefficients in Eq. (6.7) as follows:

$$E[R(A,B)] = 139.917 + 15.265 x_A + 0.837 x_B + 1.517 x_{AB}.$$

If we replace the coded variables with the factor levels, the fitted regression model for Example 6.2.4 can be obtained.

$$E[R(A,B)] = 109.1735 + 0.6368A - 0.1188B + 0.0051AB$$

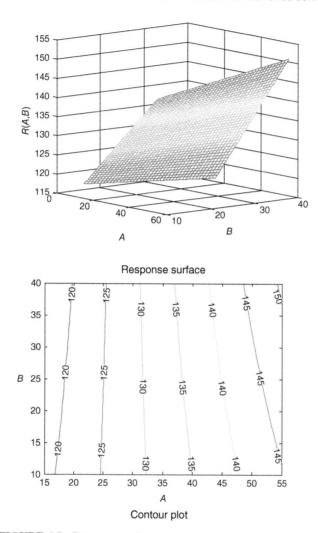

FIGURE 6.5   Response surface and contour plot for the metamodel.

The metamodel can be graphically represented as the response surface of the simulation model, as shown in Figure 6.5.

From the contour between '−' and '+' levels of Factors A and B (shown in the figure), the response surface can be seen for the full model's response to factor level changes. This visual representation can give modellers important insights into how the simulation model behaves, driven by different factor level combinations. In addition, it enables modellers or decision makers to fine-tune the important factors for some particular objectives before the actual experiments start. However, response surface is an approximation of the actual simulation and may be inaccurate.

6.4 INPUT SAMPLING

Thus far, we have shown how the 2^k factorial design allows us to determine the most important factors in a simulation model, and the response surface offers the possibility to generate some predictions of the simulation model response to factor level changes. Based on the findings from both, we can use combinations of more levels of the important factors as the input to perform experiments. In addition, the randomness in a model must be captured and sometimes must be embedded in the input. There are many examples in the real world that have at least one random component. Below, we list some of these examples:

- Transportation: interval between bus arrivals, loading time, and customer travel times.
- Manufacturing: processing time, number of machine failures, and machine repair time.
- Communication: message types, packet lengths, and interval times between packets.
- Economics: exchange rates, share trading volume, and gross domestic product.
- Defence-related: outcomes from an engagement, payloads of missile, and hit rates of artillery.

Therefore, the input to a model can sometimes be a set of random variables. To obtain combinations of different levels of input factors with some kind of randomness, appropriate sampling techniques are needed. Usually, the values of input variables can be sampled from historical data, empirical distributions, and theoretical distributions.

When using historical data as a sampling source, the data values themselves collected from the real system are used directly in the simulation. Given that this is actually an exact replication of the data gathered from the real system, the simulation can only reproduce what happened historically if the model is correctly built. For this reason, historical data can be used for verification and validation of a simulation model. However, there may not be enough data for the desired simulation runs if the historical data are only available for a short period or are not collected completely.

The second approach is to define an empirical distribution function from the data values collected from the real system, and then sample the data from this empirical distribution for simulation runs. This process involves an additional transformation from raw data to a high-level empirical distribution. One issue resulting from this transformation is that it is not possible for an empirical distribution to produce results outside the range of the observed data. Consequently, there is no possibility for 'extreme' events to occur in any simulation run. However, for some studies, we may be interested in the response from the model when some extreme cases occur. For example, an empirical distribution does not capture an abnormal event in which all machines are broken in a factory, but the decision maker would like to know the outcomes of such a situation by a simulation.

The final method is to use theoretical distributions as the sampling source. In this case, the theoretical distribution that fits the actual data values from the real system

TABLE 6.6   Summary of Useful Distributions Used in Simulation

	Distribution	Usage
Continuous	Uniform	$U(0, 1)$ is essential in generating random values from all other distributions
	Exponential	Interval times of 'customers'; time to failure of an equipment.
	Gamma	Time to complete some tasks
	Weibull	Time to complete some task, time to failure of an equipment; Used as a rough model in the absence of data
	Normal	Errors of various types
	Lognormal	Time to complete some task; or used as a rough model in the absence of data
	Triangular	Used as a rough model in the absence of data
Discrete	Bernoulli	Used to generate other discrete random varieties
	Discrete Uniform	Used as a 'first' model for a quantity that is varying between two integers
	Geometric	Number of 'defective' items in a batch, or number of items demanded from an inventory.
	Poisson	Number of events that occur in a time interval

must first be determined, such as the Gaussian distribution. Then, the input values from this distribution are sampled for simulation runs. A theoretical distribution is a compact way of representing a set of data values. It is easier to change than historical data and empirical distribution because adjusting some parameter values results in a different sampling dataset. For example, the bell shape of a Gaussian distribution can be changed by increasing or decreasing the standard deviation value. Theoretical distributions also allow us to produce some results that are outside the range of the observed data. Therefore, 'extreme' events may occur with a certain probability in the simulation runs. Given that theoretical distributions have many advantages over others, they are the most common way to implement the data sampling source in simulation. Table 6.6 lists the theoretical distributions that are most common for modelling and simulation.

A detailed discussion on the above distributions can be found in Appendix A. In addition, some important methods for generating random variables from theoretical distributions are discussed in Appendix B.

6.5   OUTPUT ANALYSIS

Based on the findings from factor screening and using the appropriate sampling methods, a set of input variables can be generated for simulation experiments. Once the output from the experiments is collected, the related analysis can be undertaken. Traditional statistical analysis can be used for output analysis, such as estimation of means and variances. The ways the analysis is performed depends on the simulation

	Two groups		n groups ($n > 2$)	
Data distributions	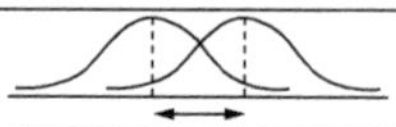		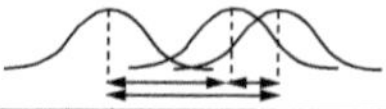	
Parametric test (normality) — Unpaired (independent)	• Unpaired t-test	**Analysis of variance (ANOVA)**	• One-way ANOVA	
Paired (related)	• Paired t-test		• Two-way ANOVA	
Non-parametric test (non-normality) — Unpaired (independent)	• Menn–Whitney U-test	One-way data	Kruskal–Wallis test	
Paired (related)	• Sign test • Wilcoxon signed-ranks test	Two-way data	Friedman test	

FIGURE 6.6 Hypothesis test methods for two or more groups of variables (adapted from [372]).

objectives. For example, if we wish to investigate the usage of a register in a grocery shop, we may estimate the mean usage and its standard deviation to determine how busy the register is over time. Aside from the traditional methods, it is also possible to use some advanced techniques, such as data mining, to extract meaningful information from the output. Regardless of the analysis methods used, the findings need to be tested to demonstrate their statistical significance. If the experiments have only one output, then methods similar to those discussed in Section 6.2.2 can be used for a hypothesis test on single output. However, in most cases, there are two or more output variables from simulation experiments, which may or may not be related to each other. For these cases, more complex test methods are needed. Takagi summarised several hypothesis test methods for multiple output simulation experiments. We present this summary in Figure 6.6.

Sometimes, transient and steady-state behaviours are observed in a simulation model. As depicted in Figure 6.7, the transient behaviour usually occurs at the beginning of a simulation run, and then the simulation behaviour tends to be steady over time. One example is the queue length of a queueing system, which may vary largely in the first few minutes and then become stable if the client arrival rate and the server efficiency remain unchanged during the simulation.

In many cases, we may be interested in the output from the steady state of a simulation to study the long-term behaviour of a system. However, as shown in Figure 6.7, the transient behaviour introduces noise that affects the long-term behaviour. This obviously affects the output analysis and findings. The easiest way to eliminate this problem is to divide the output in two groups: one group from the transient phase and one group from the stable phase. Then individual analysis can be conducted on each of them. Aside from this simple fix, a number of methodologies have been proposed to perform a steady-state output analysis, including batch means, independent replications, standardised time series, and others [35]. An extensive presentation of

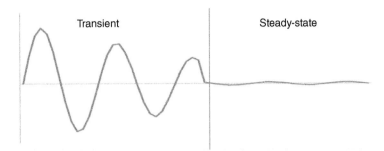

FIGURE 6.7   Transient and steady-state behaviour of a simulation model.

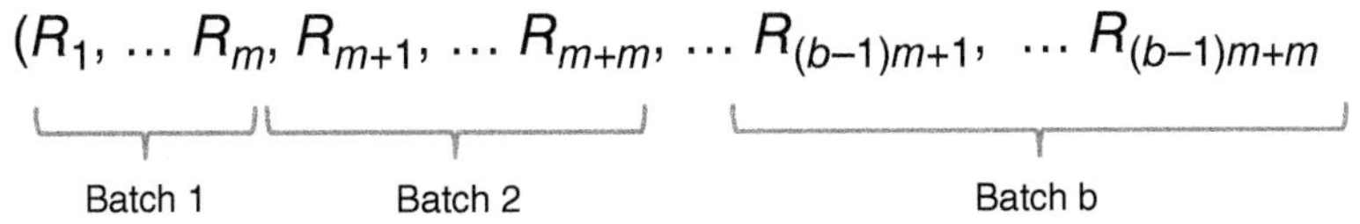

$$(R_1, \ \dots \ R_m, \ R_{m+1}, \ \dots \ R_{m+m}, \ \dots \ R_{(b-1)m+1}, \ \dots \ R_{(b-1)m+m}$$

Batch 1   Batch 2   Batch b

FIGURE 6.8   A long series of outputs divided into batches.

these methods is beyond the scope of this book; however, to create a clear view of the experimentation in simulation, we briefly describe in the following the most popular of these methods: the method of batch means.

Assume that we attain a number of responses (R) from a simulation. We can divide this long output series into a number of contiguous batches, as shown in Figure 6.8. Then, the central limit theorem can be applied if we assume that the means of the resultant batches can be approximated as independent and identical normal distribution. Therefore, the mean of the ith batch can be calculated as in Eq. (6.9).

$$B_i = \frac{1}{m} \sum_{j-1}^{m} R_{(i-1)m+j} \tag{6.9}$$

Then, the average of the all batches' means is:

$$\overline{B} = \frac{1}{b} \sum_{i=1}^{b} B_i \tag{6.10}$$

Further, the variance of all batches' means can be obtained:

$$S_B = \frac{1}{b-1} \sum_{i-1}^{b} (B_i - \overline{B})^2 \tag{6.11}$$

Finally, we can attain the $100(1 - \alpha)\%$ confidence interval of the expected mean as follows:

$$E(B) = \overline{B} \pm t_{n-1,1-\alpha/2} \sqrt{\frac{S_B}{b}} \tag{6.12}$$

Through the above exercise, we can determine whether the steady-state analysis on the output is statistically meaningful.

In summary of the above discussion, we again emphasise that, while numerous analysis methods exist, the modeller needs to consider the simulation objective when deciding the actual method to be used to analyse a simulation output.

6.6 CONCLUSION

In this chapter, we first introduced a number of methods for determining the most important factors of a model in a systematic manner. We then discussed a number of methods for constructing metamodels and the associated response surface. These two parts of the chapter offered the foundation of the experimental design for simulation. The experimental design exercises offer modellers some goal-directed guidelines for conducting experiments. An appropriate experimental design saves modellers time and effort for the actual experimentation and satisfies the study requirements.

We also showed later in the chapter that the decision on the sampling methods and sampling source is critical to the simulation experiment. Historical data are useful for validating the model by comparing the outputs from a simulation with the historical records from a real system. Empirical distributions allow some flexibility to generate input variables when historical data are insufficient for simulation runs. However, extreme cases cannot be observed during simulation runs. Theoretical distributions are a compact and flexible way to represent a set of input variables. They can produce abnormal events so that potential hidden problems are exposed by the simulation. Thus, we summarised the most common theoretical distributions and their application areas.

Finally, we briefly discussed some output analysis methods, and indicated that the actual ways to analyse the results of a simulation depend on the simulation requirements and objectives. We finalised the chapter by presenting one technique for steady-state analysis – batch means – with the purpose of giving the reader an idea of how to handle situations in which models demonstrate both transient and steady-state behaviours in simulation runs.

PART III

Simulation Methodologies

CHAPTER 7

Discrete Event Simulation

This chapter describes in detail discrete event systems and DES, from both a theoretical and practical perspective. The theoretical part focuses on the concepts, definitions and methods used in DES. The practical part offers details on how to build a simulation for a single-server queueing system.

7.1 DISCRETE EVENT SYSTEMS

In many cases, we use simulation to study a system that has a set of discrete states and is driven by a number of discrete events. The state transitions of this system only occur at discrete time points at which some events happen. We can find many examples of this type of system in daily life. The example of the elevator in Chapter 2 is one of them. Another example is an online ordering system, such as eBay or Amazon, where several states of buyers' orders exist, including 'order placed', 'payment fulfilled', 'order dispatched', 'order delivered', and 'order finalised'. The evolution of the order states depends entirely on a number of occurrences of discrete events. For example, the state of an order changes from 'order dispatched' to 'order delivered' at the occurrence of the event: *goods of an order are received by buyer and delivery document is signed*. These types of systems are called discrete event systems.

Definition 7.1.1. *A discrete event system is a discrete-state and event-driven system – that is, its state evolution depends entirely on the occurrence of asynchronous discrete events over time [75].*

As the definition states, there are two common features shared by discrete event systems. First, the state space is a discrete set. Second, the state transitions mechanism is event driven. These features involve two important concepts: **state** and **event**.

Definition 7.1.2. *The **state** of a system is the measurable information describing the system's behaviours and status at a snapshot of time at t.*

Simulation and Computational Red Teaming for Problem Solving, First Edition.
Jiangjun Tang, George Leu, and Hussein A. Abbass.

The information describing a system state must be measurable; otherwise, it cannot be mathematically modelled. The state of a system is typically a vector, denoted here by $x(t)$. The components of $x(t)$, $x_1(t), x_2(t), ..., x_n(t)$, are called **state variables**. Given that the state of a system includes the behaviour and status at a time point t, the system output at another time point t', for all $t' \geq t$, can be determined by the system state and the inputs to the system at the time point t. A system can have many states that, taken together, form its state space.

Definition 7.1.3. *The **state space** of a system, denoted by X, is the set of all possible values that the system's state could take.*

For example, the state of a machine can be selected from a state space {ON, OFF}, or from another state space {BUSY, IDLE, DOWN}, depending on the actual study. An inventory of a product can be a state from a natural state space, in which the actual stock levels are indicated through non-negative integers $\{0, 1, 2, ..., n\}$.

In discrete event systems, state transitions are driven by events. The concept of 'event' is a complex issue in system theory. Here, an event can be thought of as an instantaneous occurrence that causes the transition of a system from one state to another. An event may be:

- an action that is taken: for example, an online order placed by a buyer
- a spontaneous occurrence dictated by nature: for example, a car experiences an engine breakdown for a reason that is too complicated to be determined
- the result of several conditions suddenly being met: for example, the river water level exceeds the river bank.

We use e to denote an event and E to denote a set of events. Clearly, E is a discrete set in a discrete event system and the events in the set can be enumerated. Let us consider a service facility with a single server, such as a bank teller. The events affecting the bank teller state ($X = \{BUSY, IDLE\}$) are 'customer arrival' and 'customer departure'. Hence, we can define an event set for the bank teller as:

$$E = \{A, D\}$$

where A denotes the event of 'customer arrival', and D denotes the event of 'customer departure'. When A occurs, the bank teller state is 'BUSY'. The bank teller state becomes 'IDLE' when D occurs. This example also illustrates that a discrete event system is driven by discrete event.

In theory, the bank teller in the above example is actually a queueing system, where a customer needs to wait to be served by the bank teller if other customers arrived earlier. Formally, a queueing system consists of three elements:

- entities: usually referred to as clients that are waiting for some resources, such as customers to a bank teller, vehicles waiting for service or orders waiting to be processed

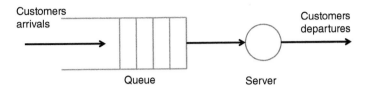

FIGURE 7.1   A simple queueing system with a single queue and single server.

- resources: servers that provide some service to client; they hold the objectives for which the waiting is done by clients
- queue: the space where clients are waiting for resources.

Figure 7.1 shows a simple queueing system where only a single queue and single server exist. Each arriving client is either immediately served by the server or joins a queue to wait for the service. After being served, the clients leave the system immediately. The motivation of the queueing system study is that the resources are limited; otherwise, waiting is unnecessary. This leads to researches determining how to adequately satisfy clients' needs, how to provide resources fairly and efficiently for different clients, and how to balance the cost of running the system. In the real world, many complex discrete event systems are composed of many small queueing systems working together.

A typical computer system consists of a number of service providers (servers), such as processors, memories, and storages. Jobs, processes, and transactions running on a computer system as clients compete for these resources. If a server (e.g. a central processing unit [CPU]) is busy when a process requires it, this process has to wait in a queue. There are many queues in a computer system, such as a queue for a CPU or a queue for I/O peripheral devices (e.g. storage disks). Therefore, we can easily use the queueing model to represent this kind of system.

Communication systems (e.g. a computer network) constitute another example of a queueing system. A typical example is the network hub that connects several computers. These computers share one channel on a hub to communicate with each other. If the hub is being used by a computer, then other computers need to wait until it becomes free (or idle). When two computers try to send messages through the hub simultaneously, a collision occurs and both have to wait for a certain period (decided according to various algorithms specialised in multiple access and collision detection) and then try to transmit packets again. Although communication systems (e.g. the internet or a telephone network) are complex, they can be represented using fairly simple queueing systems.

In a traffic system, vehicles can be considered clients that use services offered by traffic lights, toll booths, parking areas, roads, and so on. In the traffic light example discussed in the first chapter, traffic systems can be viewed as discrete event systems. Queueing models can also provide a convenient framework to describe a manufacturing process, where production parts are clients and the machines are servers providing specific operations on these parts. Given that the resource of manufacturing systems is physically limited, parts are stored in buffers where they wait to be processed.

All the above examples contain some types of queueing models; however, the rules for selecting the next client from a queue may vary from one to another. Some systems may apply simple rules of the FIFO type or similar (such as the bank teller), while others may employ more complex algorithms, such as the carrier-sense multiple access with collision detection (CSMA/CD) algorithm. In essence, queueing systems can be seen as basic building blocks of a more complex discrete event system; therefore, we will use a queueing system as the supporting example for discussing the DES in this chapter.

7.2 DISCRETE EVENT SIMULATION

To model and study a discrete system, many methods can be used. Some methods (e.g. FSM and Markov chain) can very successfully handle simple discrete event systems, such as single-server queueing systems, yet are not appropriate for more complex systems that employ, for example, multiple queues or multiple servers. In such cases, simulation, especially the DES, becomes a powerful tool.

DES models are discrete event systems that change at only a countable number of time points, where the time points correspond to the occurrence of events. In DES, an event can be defined as follows.

Definition 7.2.1. *An **event** in a DES is an instantaneous occurrence that may change the state variables of a system.*

There are some differences between an event in a discrete event system and an event in a DES. In the simulation case, events may or may not change the system state. Sometimes, an event in a simulation occurs, yet does not affect the system state. For example, an event may be used to determine the end of a simulation at a particular time. We use the same notation, e and E, for an event and a set of events, respectively, in the simulation. In addition, the state and state space in DES share the same definitions as those of discrete event systems.

Example 7.2.1. *A mechanical support centre (a single server) in a military base provides maintenance services for all types of motor vehicles, including motorbikes, four-wheel drives, trucks, armoured vehicles, and other military transportation means. We would like to estimate the average delay in queue of arriving vehicles (clients). The delay in queue is the length of the time interval from the moment of a vehicle arriving at the centre to the moment it starts being served. In this case, we can use DES to study the average delay of vehicles because the centre's state transition (from idle to busy or from busy to idle) is driven by discrete events, such as vehicle arrivals. To build a model to represent the centre, the state variables need to be defined – that is, the number of vehicles waiting in queue to be served, the arrival time of each vehicle waiting in queue, and whether the centre is **idle** or **busy**. A vehicle waits in the queue or is served immediately on arrival depending on the* *state of the centre (busy or idle). The number of vehicles in the queue determines whether the centre is idle or busy when the centre completes serving a vehicle. The arrival time of vehicles is needed to calculate their delay in the queue as the difference between serving start time and arrival time, given that the service start time will be known during the simulation. Apart from the states, there are also two events associated with the mechanical support centre: the arrival of a vehicle and the completion of service for the vehicle, with the latter event resulting in the vehicle's departure. Arrival of a vehicle causes a change in the centre state from idle to busy, or an increase by one of the waiting queue. Similarly, a vehicle departure changes the system status from busy to idle, or decreases the number of vehicles in the waiting queue by one. Both events (arrival and departure) affect the system state.*

7.2.1 Models of a Discrete Event Simulation

The mechanical support centre in the above example is a typical single server queueing system. We can use DES to study this system to estimate, for example, the average delay. First, we need to design a model for this system that includes the following entities:

- server: the mechanical support centre
- clients: the vehicles to be served by the centre
- queue: the queue of vehicles waiting for service
- events: the instantaneous occurrences in the system, such as vehicle arrivals and departures
- process: the actual service provided by the centre to clients, such as vehicle maintenance and repairs.

Given that the objective of using simulation is to estimate the average delay of vehicles in the queue, we consider only the intervals between the time point of a vehicle arrival and the time point of a vehicle beginning being served. Therefore, the details of actual processes (such as how to repair a vehicle) are not taken into account. In this case, the resolution of the model is low because we only consider the time-related information. Based on this, an abstraction level can be decided as well: everything related to the time of the entities – such as the arrival time of a client, time spent on service and departure time of a client – is included in the model, while other information is not included. Thus, the basic attributes of the entities are summarised in Table 7.1.

The system variables defined in the above table are sufficient to represent the system operation and to build the model for a single-server queueing system, given the established study objective.

7.2.2 Time-advance Mechanism of a Discrete Event Simulation

Given the dynamic nature of DES models, it is necessary to decide the time-advance mechanism when building a simulator. This involves implementing a simulation

TABLE 7.1   The Entities and Their Attributes of the DES Model for a Mechanic Support Centre

Entities	Attributes	Variable
Mechanical support centre	Centre status at time t, either *IDLE* or *BUSY*	$S(t)$
Process	Time that centre spends serving ith vehicle	s_i
Vehicle	Arrival time of ith vehicle	a_i
	Delay in queue of ith vehicle	D_i
	Time at which ith vehicle completes services and departs	$c_i = a_i + D_i + s_i$
Queue	Number of vehicles in the queue	n
	Time interval between arrival of $i-1$st and ith vehicle	$I_i = a_i - a_{i-1}$
Events	Time of occurrence of jth event of any type	e_j

clock and describing how this clock ticks. As discussed in the first chapter, a simulation clock does not need to be exactly the same as a wall clock (a real-world clock) – a fact that allows the simulated system to be run and evaluated faster than the real system. We remind the reader that, in Section 3.4, we mentioned two approaches for time advancing: the next-event and fixed-increment methods. Clearly, the next-event time-advance mechanism is more suitable for a DES than the fixed-increment time-advance mechanism (although fixed-increment time advance is still applicable for a DES). In the example of a mechanical support centre, the simulation clock starts at $e_0 = 0$ and is advanced from one event to another as depicted in Figure 7.2.

An event of any type can trigger the advance of the simulation time, as shown by the curves with arrows in the figure. At time $e_0 = 0$, the centre is idle because no clients arrive. When the event of the first vehicle arrival (e_1) occurs, the simulation time is advanced to that time. Given that there is no vehicle waiting in the queue, the first vehicle is served immediately after its arrival (so the delay of D_1 is 0) and the status of the centre becomes busy at time e_1 (a_1). When the second event, e_2 (a_2), occurs (arrival of the second vehicle), the vehicle has to wait in the queue until the centre spends s_1 time completing the service for the first client, at time c_1. The number of vehicles in the queue is one at this time. The number of vehicles in the queue is one at this time. The interval between the first and second vehicle is $I_2 = a_2 - a_1$ and the delay of the second vehicle is $D_2 = c_1 - a_2$. The total time for the second vehicle from arrival to departure (after being served) is $a_2 + D_2 + s_2$, which is the completing time of c_2. During the waiting period of the second vehicle and the service time of the first vehicle, another event (arrival of the third vehicle) occurs and the simulation time is advanced to t_3. The number of vehicles in the queue is two from e_3 (t_3) to e_4 (c_1) because the first vehicle leaves the centre and the centre starts serving the second vehicle. The status of the centre is always busy starting with time point e_1 when the first vehicle arrives, as shown in Figure 7.2.

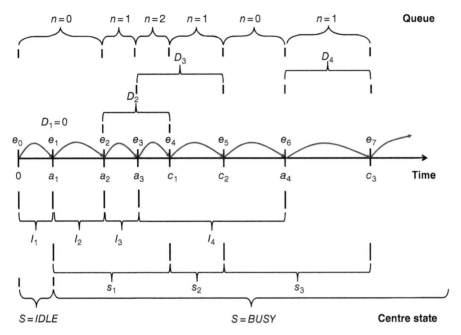

FIGURE 7.2   Next-event time-advance approach for the single-server queueing system of the mechanical centre.

7.2.3   Simulator of a Discrete Event Simulation

Thus far, we have decided the model and the time-advance mechanism of the simulation for this mechanical support centre. It is now time for us to build a simulator, for which we will consider the following elements:

- System state: the state variables describing the system at a particular time.
- Simulation clock: a variable that keeps track of the current value of the simulation time. The initial value of the simulation clock is usually 0 for a simulation. The value of this variable 'hops' with each event, as illustrated in Figure 7.2, because we use the next-event time-advance mechanism.
- Event list: at least one list of events exists in the simulator to store the pending events that have not yet been treated, and their time of occurrence.
- Statistical variables: a set of variables that keeps track of the system's statistics. For example, the delay of each vehicle is recorded to obtain the average delay of the whole system in the above example. These variables provide the quantitative measures for the performance of a system and are used to generate statistical reports.

In addition to the above components, the simulator also contains the following routines and processes that control the simulator and evolve the model:

- Initialisation routine: a sub-program that initialises the simulation model, including state variables, simulation clock and event list at time 0. It also resets the statistical variables
- Timing routine: a sub-program that determines the time of the next event in the event list and advances the simulation time to that time when the next event occurs.
- Event routine: a sub-program that updates the system state variables when a particular event occurs. Given that different event types cause different states of the system, one event routine corresponds to one event type.
- Library routines: a set of programs that generates random numbers and variates from the probability distributions used by the simulation model. For the above example, they are used to generate the times of arrival events and other inputs to the model.
- Report generator: a utility program that generates statistical reports about system performance using the statistical variables recorded in a simulation.

The logical relationships among the above components and routines are depicted in Figure 7.3. The solid lines with arrows describe the control flow of the simulator, while the dashed lines with arrows illustrate how the routines or processes access the components of the simulator.

When using the simulator shown in Figure 7.3 for DES, the simulation starts at time 0 with the initialising routine. This sets the simulation clock to zero and the system state to *IDLE*, clears all statistical variables, and creates an empty event list. Then the time routine is invoked by the simulator to determine the most imminent event and its type. If the ith event is the next to occur, time routine advances the simulation clock to the time (e_i) when this event will happen. This triggers the simulator to invoke a particular event routine that is responsible for the type of ith event. Usually, there are three types of activities conducted by the event routine:

1. Update the system state according to the event type and the current system state – for example, if the system state is *IDLE* and the ith event is a client arrival event, then the system state is updated to *BUSY*.
2. Update statistical variables according to system performance measures.
3. Generate future events and their occurring time by invoking library routines.

The future events and their occurring time are usually generated from probability distributions, which will be discussed in detail later in this book. After all routines are completed, the simulator checks whether the termination condition is met – that is, whether a special event marking the end occurs. If not, the simulator repeatedly invokes time and event routines to keep running the simulation. Otherwise, the simulator stops the simulation and invokes the report generator to produce statistical results on the system performance. For the mechanical support centre example, we can use FSM as the engine to update the system state changes induced by different event types.

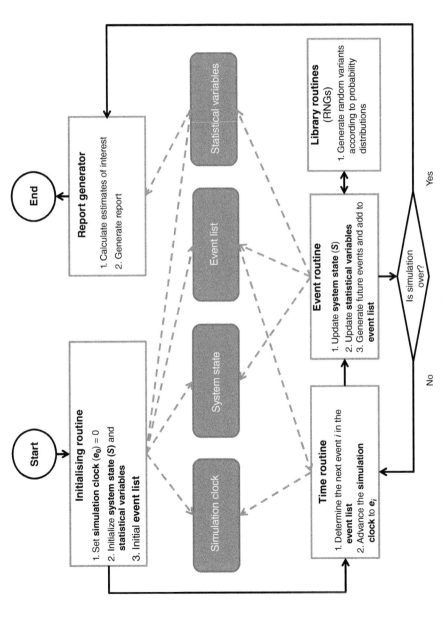

FIGURE 7.3 Flowchart for a next-event time-advance approach and logical relationships among the components and routines of the simulator for DES.

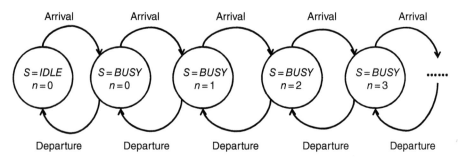

FIGURE 7.4 FSM of the mechanical support centre driven by client arrival and client departure events.

As shown in Figure 7.4, the centre is *IDLE* when no client arrival occurs, and becomes *BUSY* once a client arrives in the centre. When a new client arrives and the centre is *BUSY*, the number of clients in the waiting queue increases by one. If no service is completed by the centre, the length of the queue continues growing as more clients arrive. Once the centre completes a service for a client and the client leaves, the centre state becomes *IDLE* if no client is in the queue, or the centre serves another client and the length of the queue decreases by one. The values of entity attributes at each time point when an event occurs (e.g. delay, D and service time, s) are stored in the statistical variables.

Figure 7.4 presents an attempt to use a FSM to represent the queueing system from the mechanical centre example. It can be seen that it may not be possible to enumerate all states for a complicated queueing system, such as multi-server queueing systems. Therefore, a DES becomes a suitable and powerful tool to simulate the dynamics of complex queueing systems.

7.2.4 Input to a Discrete Event Simulation

The input to the simulator for the above example includes vehicle (client) arrival and completing the service for a vehicle (client departure). There are three possible ways to collect the data used as input for a DES [234]:

1. Historical data collected from the real system are used directly as input for the simulation. For example, we could collect all the actual data from the mechanical centre in the past, such as the intervals between client arrivals, or the time for completing a service.

2. Data sampled from the collected system data using empirical distribution functions. For example, we can sample a client arrival interval from the distribution representing arrival intervals when we need this in the simulation.

3. Artificial data sampled from theoretical distributions that fit the data collected from the system. If a particular theoretical distribution (e.g. exponential) with some parameters is good for approximating the intervals between client arrivals in a system, we can sample the arrival intervals from this distribution when the arrival interval is needed in the simulation.

A simulation using the first type of data as input can only reproduce what happened historically. It may be useful for validating a simulation by comparing the outputs from the simulation with the outputs from the real system, but it is not good for investigating new problems. In addition, historical data are sometimes insufficient to run the simulation as expected. The second type of input avoids some of the shortcomings of the first type of input. This is usually the preferred input to a simulation, yet still has some drawbacks. First, empirical distributions may have some 'irregularities', especially when only a small number of samples are available. Second, since the empirical distributions are derived from the system data, they cannot explore situations outside the range of the data collected from the system. The third type of input, theoretical distributions, is a compact way of representing a set of data values; therefore, it can provide a sufficiently large quantity of sample data for a simulation. Consequently, theoretical distribution smooths out the data to avoid 'irregularities'. When using theoretical distributions, it is also possible to obtain some extreme values that have not yet or cannot be acquired from the real system. We could easily adjust the parameters of a theoretical distribution to generate datasets with different characteristics from the original dataset to answer some what-if questions. For example, we can investigate the effect on the delay when the service rate is reduced by 10% simply by reducing the mean of the exponential distribution by 10%. Given that the third type of input – theoretical distribution – has many advantages, we use this method to generate the input for the mechanical support centre example.

To sample the data from a theoretical distribution, we need a random number generator that generates random numbers of IID $U(0, 1)$, and then produces the random variates from a certain probability distribution. All these are included in the library routine. For the mechanical centre example, we assume that a vehicle departs from the centre immediately after the service is completed, although in reality some delay may exist. Therefore, only two inputs have to be decided: the intervals between vehicle arrivals and the times for completing a service. Given that both are time intervals, we can use exponential distribution to model them, provided that exponential distribution with certain parameters fits the historical data well. The fitness level is determined by performing hypothesis tests for the distribution and the data. Thus (from Appendix A),the PDF exponential distribution with mean θ is:

$$f(x) = \begin{cases} \frac{1}{\theta}e^{-x/\theta} & x \geq 0 \\ 0 & \text{otherwise} \end{cases} . \qquad (7.1)$$

We remember that, in the mechanical centre example, clients are served in a FIFO manner. In queueing theory, a single-server queue with exponential intervals between arrivals and service times and FIFO queueing discipline is usually called a '$M/M/1$ queue' [170]. It is necessary to generate random variates from an exponential distribution to manipulate the simulator. First, we need a random number generator to generate IID $U(0, 1)$ random numbers that have the PDF:

$$f(x) = \begin{cases} 1 & 0 \leq x \leq 1 \\ 0 & \text{otherwise} \end{cases} . \qquad (7.2)$$

After obtaining a random number U from IDD $U(0, 1)$, we need to apply some kind of transformation of the exponential distribution to generate the random variates by U. There are a number of techniques to generate random variates from a particular probability distribution, including inverse-transform (the inverse of the distribution function), composition (a convex combination of other distributions), convolutions, and acceptance-rejection. Here, we use the inverse-transform algorithm to generate random variates from an exponential distribution. The CDF of a random variable, X, obeying an exponential distribution with the mean θ can be defined as:

$$F(x) = P(X \leq x) = \int_0^x \frac{1}{\theta} e^{-\frac{t}{\theta}} \, dt$$

$$= 1 - e^{\frac{x}{\theta}} \qquad x \geq 0 \tag{7.3}$$

The inverse function of the above CDF can be easily derived when letting the obtained uniformly distributed random number $U = F(x)$:

$$F^{-1}(U) = -\beta \ln(1 - U). \tag{7.4}$$

Given that U uniformly distributed in the interval $[0, 1]$, $1 - U$ is also uniformly distributed in the interval of $[0, 1]$. We could replace $1 - U$ with U to simplify the above equation and let X be $F^{-1}(U)$, therefore, the above equation can be defined as below:

$$X = -\beta \ln(U). \tag{7.5}$$

Note that replacing $1 - U$ with U causes negative correlation of the X's with the U's, however, it gains some efficiency by eliminating the subtraction. Figure 7.5 shows the intervals for U and X when using the inverse transformation for exponential distribution. The black line is the CDF of an exponential distribution with $\theta = 3$, while the blue line is the corresponding PDF. The interval between $U_1 = 0.15$ and $U_2 = 0.2$ is 5%, which leads to a very small range of X falling in the interval $[0.48755, 0.66943]$. However, another interval of U's ($[0.9, 0.95]$) that also occupies 5% of U leads to a larger range of X falling in the interval $[6.9078, 8.9872]$. This means that we will have a higher chance of X falling in the interval $[0.48755, 0.66943]$ than in the interval $[6.9078, 8.9872]$, which is explained by the PDF curve. Therefore, the inverse transformation should work for the purpose of obtaining random variates from a certain distribution.

Once we select a suitable distribution for input data sampling, the associated parameters must be determined according to the fitness to the collected data. For an exponential distribution, only the mean θ is required. If we know the average number of client arrivals in a given period, we can calculate the average interval between arrivals. Poisson distribution can be used here to model the arrivals in a given period as follows:

$$P(x) = \frac{\lambda^x e^{-\lambda}}{x!} \tag{7.6}$$

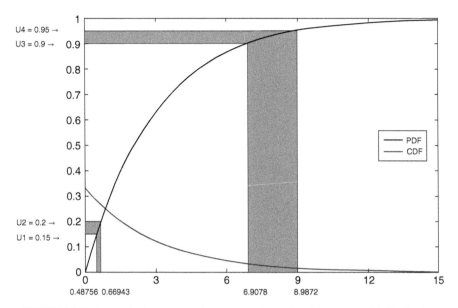

FIGURE 7.5 Intervals for U and X, inverse transformation for exponential distribution.

where λ is the average arrival rate. In general, this distribution will give us the number of clients arriving at the server in any given period. For the example of the mechanical centre, we are interested in the time interval between arrivals, rather than the number of client arrivals. Therefore, we can calculate the average time interval between arrivals (θ) as the reciprocal of the average arrival rate (λ), though both may be calculated from the historical data as well.

Example 7.2.2. *From the historical data of the mechanical centre, we know that the average rate of vehicle arrivals in an hour is five. We would like to use exponential distribution to generate the arrival intervals between vehicles and the corresponding times of arrivals. The following steps are performed for this purpose:*

1. *Calculate θ: given that the average arrival rate per hour is five, the average interval between arrivals is $\frac{60}{5} = 12$ minutes, that is, the mean θ of an exponential distribution.*
2. *Generate random IID $U(0, 1)$ random numbers U.*
3. *Generate random variates $t \sim expo(\theta)$ by U.*

Many simulation software packages are able to generate both U and I. Here, we use Excel for this example, although the random number generator implemented in Excel has poor quality in terms of randomness.

Figure 7.6 shows the implementation for generating U, I and the arrival times a in Excel. Column A shows the IDs of the vehicles determined by their arrival sequence.

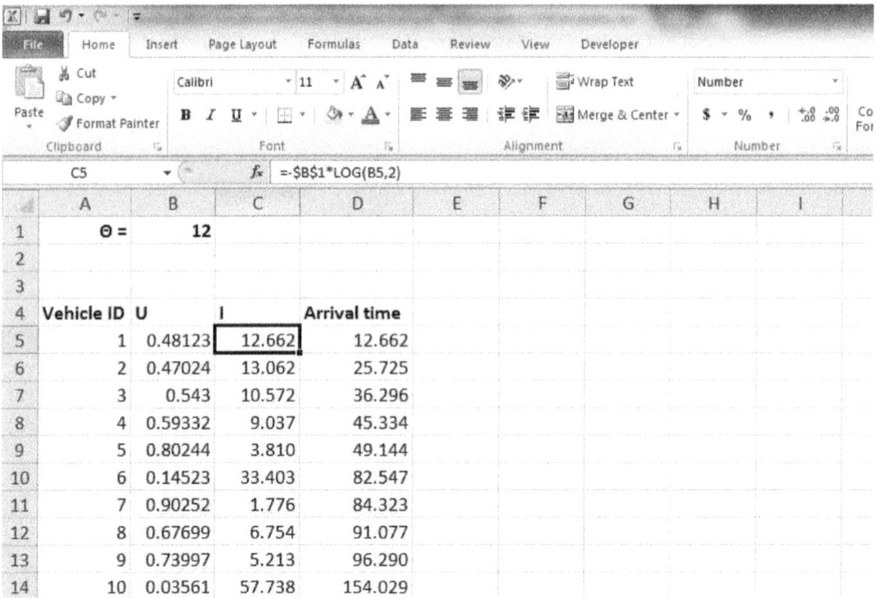

	A	B	C	D
1	Θ =	12		
2				
3				
4	Vehicle ID	U	I	Arrival time
5	1	0.48123	12.662	12.662
6	2	0.47024	13.062	25.725
7	3	0.543	10.572	36.296
8	4	0.59332	9.037	45.334
9	5	0.80244	3.810	49.144
10	6	0.14523	33.403	82.547
11	7	0.90252	1.776	84.323
12	8	0.67699	6.754	91.077
13	9	0.73997	5.213	96.290
14	10	0.03561	57.738	154.029

FIGURE 7.6 Example of generating U, interval between arrivals (I), and arrival times (a) by Excel.

Column B shows the random numbers generated by the inbuilt function Rand(), and is used as input to Eq. (7.5). Then, the intervals between arrivals (I) are listed in Column C. Given that $e_0 = 0$, *the first vehicle arrives at the time point 12.662. The arrival time of the second vehicle is* $a_2 = a_1 + I_2 = 25.725$. *The following vehicle arrival times are calculated in the same manner, and eventually we can obtain all arrival times for all vehicles.*

7.2.5 Event Routines

For a single-server queueing system, such as the mechanical centre, there are two types of events – client arrivals and client departures (service completed) – affecting the system state, as shown in Figure 7.4. To differentiate them, each event type is given an ID and associated with an independent random variates generator. The occurrences of different event types are handled by different event routines in the simulator, as summarised in Table 7.2.

Figure 7.7 illustrates the flowchart for arrival event routine, while Figure 7.8 shows the flowchart for departure event routine. When an arrival event occurs, the arrival routine schedules the next arrival event ($a_i + 1$) using the library routine (randomly generates the time of this event). If the server is busy, the size of the queue increases by one. Otherwise, the server becomes busy and the routine determines the service time (s_i) for this client, also using the library routine. Based on this information, the

TABLE 7.2   Event Types in a Single-Server Queueing System and Their Event Routines

Type of event	Type ID	Event routine
Customer arrival to the system	1	Arrival event routine
Customer departure from the system after completing service	2	Departure event routine

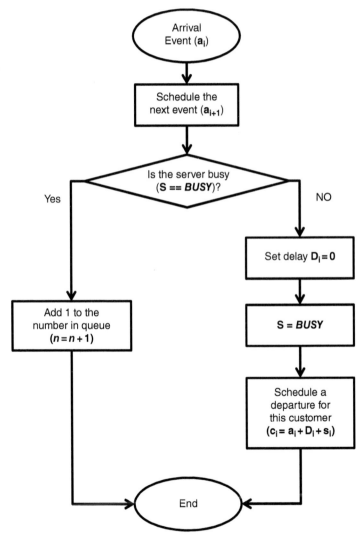

FIGURE 7.7   Flowchart for arrival event routine.

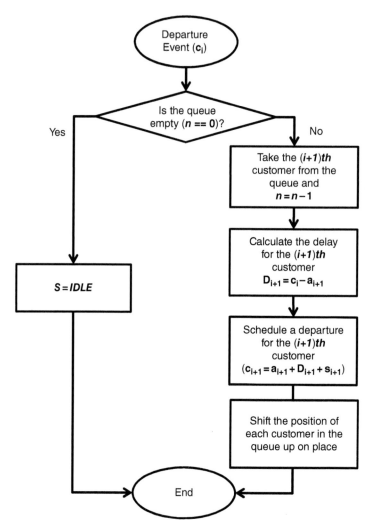

FIGURE 7.8   Flowchart for departure event routine.

routine sets the time of the departure event for this client (c_i). This departure event is added to the departure event list. In addition, the departure event routine checks whether the queue is empty ($n = 0$) when a departure event occurs (c_i). If the queue is empty, the system state becomes *IDLE* immediately. Otherwise, the departure event routine attains the first ($i + 1$th) client in the queue and schedules the service time (s_i) for it. The delay of this customer (D_{i+1}) is also calculated using its arrival time (a_i) and the service start time (i.e. the time when the previous client departs from the system [c_i]), so $D_{i+1} = c_i - a_{i+1}$. The time when service is completed for this client can be obtained by $c_{i+1} = a_i + D_{i+1} + s_{i+1}$ as well. Of course, some statistical variables (such as delays and service time) must be stored during both event routines to generate the system performance report. Although these are not included in the flowcharts shown in the above figures, they can be easily plugged into the processes of both event routines.

As shown in Figure 7.3, both event routines are invoked by the time routine according to the simulation clock that is advanced by the events.

7.2.6 Statistical Variables and Report Generator

One of the objectives of simulating a discrete event system is to investigate system performance, such as the expected average delay in a queue, which was of interest in the example of the mechanical support centre. The decision about which statistical variables to be recorded in a simulator depends on the requirements for the simulation. In the following, we discuss three common performance measures for single-sever queueing systems in the context of DES.

7.2.6.1 *Expected Average Delay*   Calculating the expected average delay in a queue of N customers in a simulation requires the simulator to store the delay of each customer $(D_1, D_2, ..., D_N)$. The expected average delay is denoted $d(N)$, and is easily obtained, as follows:

$$\overline{d}(N) = \frac{\sum_{i=1}^{N} D_i}{N}. \tag{7.7}$$

In theory, the average delay should be a measure of a large (in fact, infinite) number of clients. However, we estimate it from a given run of the simulation that only contains a finite number of customers. We use 'expected' here because the average delay observed from a simulation run depends on random variables, such as arrival intervals or service time. Different simulation runs with different random variables may generate different average delays. Hence, we call it expected average delay. The delays of each client, including those with delay zero (system is idle when they arrive), are considered in the above equation, as depicted in Figure 7.7. The expected average delay provides the performance indicator from the clients' point of view. The smaller expected average delay implies that clients can expect a shorter waiting time for a service.

7.2.6.2 *Expected Average Number in Queue*   This measure indicates that the average number is taken over a period during which N clients are observed in a simulation. The measure is taken over time (continuous), rather than per customer (discrete). Therefore, we need a method to define the time-average number of customers in a queue. First, let $Q(t)$ be the number of clients in the queue at time t, for any real number $t \geq 0$, and denote $T(N)$ as the time required to observe N clients in the simulation. Thus, $Q(t)$ is a non-negative number for any t between zero and $T(N)$. Second, we can define a variable, p_i, for a proportion of time that $Q(t)$ is equal

TABLE 7.3   Time Period and Number in Queue of the Mechanical Centre

Time period	0–1.1	1.1–1.4	1.4–3	3–3.5	3.5–4.5	4.5–5.8	5.8–7.1	7.1–7.9
Number in queue	0	1	0	1	2	3	2	1
State	IDLE	BUSY	BUSY	BUSY	BUSY	BUSY	BUSY	BUSY

to i, and $0 \le p_i \le 1$. Therefore, there may be many p_i, with $\sum p_i = 1$. The expected average number in a queue is denoted $q(N)$ and can be calculated using p_i as follows:

$$q(N) = \sum_{i=0}^{\infty} i p_i. \tag{7.8}$$

Hence, $q(N)$ is a weighted average of all possible queue lengths, i (the weight is the time proportion, p_i). The time proportion p_i is calculated using the actual period (T_i) when the queue length is i with the total time $T(N)$ as below:

$$p_i = \frac{T_i}{T}.$$

Therefore, we can use the absolute time period (T_i) instead of the time proportion p_i to calculate the average number in the queue by:

$$q(N) = \frac{\sum_{i=0}^{\infty} i T_i}{T(N)}. \tag{7.9}$$

Example 7.2.3. *From a simulation of the mechanical centre, we observed the number in the queue and the associated time period as listed in Table 7.3 for the case when N = 6.*

Based on the available data, we can obtain the T_i for $i = 0, 1, 2, 3$ first. For example, the queue is empty during two periods: from 0 to 1.1 and from 1.4 to 3. Therefore, $T_0 = 1.1 + 1.6 = 2.7$. In a similar manner, we can calculate all other T_i.

$$T_0 = 1.1 + 1.6 = 2.7$$

$$T_1 = 0.3 + 0.5 + 0.8 = 1.6$$

$$T_2 = 1 + 1.3 = 2.3$$

$$T_3 = 1.3$$

Then, $q(N)$ can be obtained using Eq. (7.9).

$$q(6) = \frac{0 \times 2.7 + 1 \times 1.6 + 2 \times 2.3 + 3 \times 1.3}{7.9} = 1.28$$

The expected average number in the queue is 1.28 for the observed data in Table 7.3.

7.2.6.3 *Busyness of the Server*   This measure shows the proportion of time that the server is in a 'busy' state. The information about the period during which a server is busy can also be recorded during the simulation. Similar to the average number in the queue, the time proportion can be calculated using the following equation:

$$U(N) = \frac{T(S = BUSY)}{T(N)} \tag{7.10}$$

where $U(N)$ is used to denote the proportion of time in which the server is busy, $T(S = BUSY)$ is the cumulated amount of time in which the server is busy, and $T(N)$ is the total time for a simulation with N observed clients.

Example 7.2.4. *We now calculate the proportion of time in which the server is busy for the example presented in Table 7.3,.*
The time in which the server is busy is obtained by

$$T(S = BUSY) = 0.3 + 1.6 + 0.5 + 1 + 1.3 + 1.3 + 0.8 = 6.8.$$

Then the proportion of time in which server is busy becomes:

$$U(6) = \frac{6.8}{7.9} = 0.86.$$

For the data considered in Table 7.3, the server is busy for 86% of the total time.

Thus far, we have discussed three common measures for a single-queueing system. However, in practice, we may find many other aspects that need to be measured, depending on the real system to be studied, and the requirements of the study.

7.2.7 Summary of Discrete Event Simulation

The components and logic of a DES have been discussed in the previous sections. The logic and steps to perform a DES for a discrete event system include:

1. understand the system being studied and identify the objective of the study;
2. build a model for the system, taking into account entities, attributes and so on;
3. construct and implement a simulator for the system, including events, time-advance mechanism, random variates generators and so on;
4. define the statistical variables according to the objectives of the study; and
5. run the simulation and generate the appropriate reports.

7.3 CONCLUSION

This chapter has described in detail the concepts of discrete event system and DES. A single-server queueing system was used as an example to show how to build the model and the simulator for a DES. The components of the discrete event simulator are discussed in detail, including entities and their attributes, time-advancing mechanisms, and so on. A logic relationship between simulator components and their corresponding working flow was illustrated. Then, the methods to determine the inputs to the simulator and ways to generate random variates from a given distribution were discussed. We also introduced three common performance measures on queueing systems as an example for generating reports. Therefore, the reader of this chapter should be able to build a DES for any single-server queueing system and adopt it for more complex discrete event systems.

CHAPTER 8

Discrete Time Simulation

Discrete time systems can be found in many real-world contexts, such as operation of digital computers, economics, and road traffic. In this chapter, we define discrete time systems and describe the methodology for modelling and simulating them. The theoretical discussion is then instantiated in several examples that cover the essential aspects of discrete time simulation.

8.1 INTRODUCTION

In the real world, many systems operate inherently in discrete time. For example, a digital computer is a typical discrete time system. A digital computer has an internal discrete time clock and instructions are executed when the clock 'ticks'. For example, a CPU clocked at 1 GHz, which represents one billion cycles per second, theoretically executes one billion instructions in one second. Other examples of discrete time systems can be found in many other domains, such as in micro-economics, where data are reported at regular time intervals; digital control systems, such as computer numerical control machines; and others.

To better explain the operation of such systems, we start by looking at a simple real-world example.

Example 8.1.1. *We assume a sheep farm that currently operates with 100 sheep. The sheep population growth rate is 5% per year. The objective of the study is to understand how the sheep population of the farm changes over time.*

Given that only the yearly growth rate of the sheep population is known, what we can study in this case is the change of stock population in each year, which is actually a discrete time process. First, some variables can be defined based on the above problem statement:

- *A variable representing time t, $t \in \{0, 1, 2, ...\}$.*
- *A system state variable (x_t), which is the sheep population size in year t.*

Simulation and Computational Red Teaming for Problem Solving, First Edition.
Jiangjun Tang, George Leu, and Hussein A. Abbass.

TABLE 8.1 Sheep Population in Each Year ($x_0 = 100$ and $r = 5\%$)

Year (t)	Sheep population (x_t)
0	100
1	105
2	110.25
3	115.76
...	
8	147.75
9	155.13
10	162.89
...	

- *For year 0, the initial sheep population size is 100, which can be denoted by $x_0 = 100$.*
- *x_t is the population size of year t, then the population size of the next year is x_{t+1}*
- *The yearly population growth rate (r), which equals 5%.*

The relationship between the population size in the current year and the next year can be easily constructed using the growth rate, r, as below:

$$x_{t+1} = x_t + r \times x_t \tag{8.1}$$

Equation (8.1) describes how the system state x changes occur at discrete time steps. Considering the initial population ($x_0 = 100$) and the growth rate ($r = 5\%$) in the equations, we can obtain the yearly sheep population size, as illustrated in Table 8.1.

We can clearly see in this example how variables – the sheep population (x_t), the input (yearly growth rate r) and the output (yearly increment of sheep population $x_t \times r$) – are defined only for discrete time points, t. Therefore, the sheep population of the farm in this example can be viewed as a discrete time system [307]. Based on this example, the definition of a discrete time system can be given as follows:

Definition 8.1.1. *A discrete time system is a system for which the state, input, and output variables are defined only for discrete moments in time.*

In the next sections, the state, input, and output variables of discrete time systems will be discussed in detail, along with the methods for building discrete time simulations. Then, a comparison of discrete time simulation and DES is presented. Finally, we conclude this chapter with an example that simulates microscopic traffic – a car-following model.

8.2 DISCRETE TIME SYSTEM AND MODELLING

As suggested by the definition, the time domain of a discrete time system is discrete. This means that the spacing between successive time points may be arbitrary or uniform. In the sheep farm example, the time space, t, was divided uniformly into years: $t \in \{0, 1, 2, ...\}$. However, time can also be partitioned using arbitrary intervals, as in the case of discrete event systems, where the system clock ticks at the time point when a particular event happens. Hence, from this point of view, a discrete event system is a special case of a discrete time system (the relationship between discrete time and discrete event systems will be discussed later in this chapter).

To model and simulate a discrete time system, a particular type of simulation – called discrete time simulation (DTS) – is typically employed. The resultant DTS will use a time-advancing mechanism that can be either a fixed-increment time-advancing mechanism (uniform spacing) or a next-event time-advancing mechanism (arbitrary) due to the discrete nature of the real-world system to be simulated.

At each simulation clock tick, the state of a discrete time system may be changed by its input and may produce some output, with a subsequent effect. The system state, input, and output are measurable variables of the system; thus, we can collect the data by taking measurements at specific time points over a period, such as the share prices in a stock market each day, the sheep population of a farm at the beginning of a year and the voltage and currents of an electric circuit.

Let us consider that the input variable, u, is a function of time:

$$u(t_k) = \{u_1(t_k), u_2(t_k), ..., u_p(t_k)\}, \ k \in \{0, 1, 2, ..., n\}. \tag{8.2}$$

The initial state can be represented as in the following equation:

$$x(t_0) = x_0. \tag{8.3}$$

We note that the initial state does not depend on the input variable, while all other states do. The state of the system at time (t_{k+1}) is a time function of the input variables and the system state at the previous time point (t_k):

$$x(t_{k+1}) = f(x(t_k), u(t_k), t_k), \ k \in \{0, 1, 2, ..., n\} \tag{8.4}$$

where $f(\cdot)$ is a time function that can change the system state based on the system state and input at the time instant (t_k). Similarly, the system output variable y can be defined as a time function as well:

$$y(t_k) = \{y_1(t_k), y_2(t_k), ..., y_q(t_k)\} \tag{8.5}$$

The output at arbitrary time points $y(t_k)$, is determined by the input and system state variables and can be expressed as:

$$y(t_k) = g(x(t_k), u(t_k), t_k), \ k \in \{0, 1, 2, ..., n\} \tag{8.6}$$

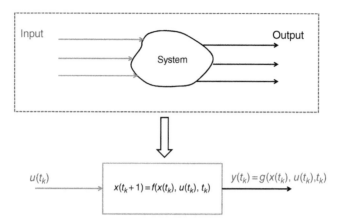

FIGURE 8.1   Discrete time system – input, output, and state.

where $g(\cdot)$ is the function that produces the output from a system, using the system state and input to the system at time point t_k.

The output can be further classified into internal and external. The internal output is a transition of the system state, such as the increment of sheep population in each year. The external output creates effects in the environment – for example, sheep are an asset of the farm; thus, changes in the sheep population may increase or decrease the total asset of the farm. Figure 8.1 describes in a visual manner the relationship between the input, state, and output variables of a discrete time system.

Example 8.2.1. *We continue the sheep farm example by assuming that each sheep is worth $300. Based on this, we can formalise a model for estimating the total farm assets in each year, as follows:*

- *Input (u):*
  - *The first input is the yearly sheep growth rate, $u_1(t_k) = r = 5\%$.*
  - *The second input is the price of each sheep, $u_2(t_k) = 300$.*
- *State (x):*
  - *The initial sheep population size is $x_0 = 100$.*
  - *$x(t_k)$ is the sheep population size of year t_k. Therefore, the size of the sheep population can be modelled by:*

$$x(t_{k+1}) = f(x(t_k), u_1(t_k), t_k) = x(t_k) + x(t_k) \times u_1(t_k)$$

- *Output (y):*
  - *The internal output $y_1(t_k) = x(t_k) \times u_1(t_k)$ is the increment of the sheep population.*

TABLE 8.2 Example of Sheep Population and Farm Asset Growth in Each Year

Year (k)	Input (u_{t_k})	State ($x(t_k)$)	Output 2 ($y_1(t_k)$)	Output 2 ($y_2(t_k)$)
0	{0.05, 300}	100	5	$30 000
1	{0.05, 300}	105	5.25	$31 500
2	{0.05, 300}	110.25	5.51	$33 075
3	{0.05, 300}	115.76	5.78	$34 728.75
		...		

TABLE 8.3 Difference in Asset Value Because of Growth in Sheep Price

Year (k)	Input (u_{t_k})	State ($x(t_k)$)	$y_2(t_k)$, $u_2 = 320$	$y_2'(t_k)$, $u_2' = 300$	Asset difference
		...			
7	{0.05, 300}	140.71		$42 213.01	$0
8	{0.05, 350}	147.75	$47 278.57	$44 323.66	$2954.91
9	{0.05, 350}	155.13	$49 642.50	$46 539.85	$3102.66
10	{0.05, 350}	162.89	$52 124.63	$48 866.84	$3257.79

- *The external output $y_2(t_k)$, is the total farm assets, which takes into account the sheep value, and can be represented by:*

$$y(t_k) = g(x(t_k), u(t_k), t_k) = x(t_k) \times u_2(t_k).$$

Based on the above model, the sheep population and farm assets can be easily calculated. Table 8.2 shows the results of this calculation.

Sometimes, the input variables of a system may change in time, affecting the system state variables and outputs. If the sheep population growth rate remains unchanged, but the sheep price increases to $320 from Year 8, the farm's assets will be affected by the sheep price growth. Table 8.3 shows the difference in the farm assets resulting from the sheep price growth.

Through the above examples, we introduced the basic methods to construct a DTS for a discrete time system, considering the very simple objectives assumed in these examples. However, DTS may be employed for a variety of purposes; hence, various objectives need to be taken into account. Sometimes, we are interested in the behaviours of a discrete time system. On some other occasions, we would like to evaluate the effects on the environment of a discrete time system over a period, or solve some problems. To achieve these objectives, it is important to collect data about input, system state and output variables, and then conduct relevant analysis of these data.

The time series of input, system state, and output data generally contain a large amount of values. However, depending on the purpose of simulation, only parts or segments of these data may be of interest. Specialised methods are required to extract the useful segments from the whole volume of recorded data. In the following section, we describe the 'sample path' – also known as 'trajectory' – a useful technique to extract the relevant dataset and conduct analysis.

8.3 SAMPLE PATH

Time points in discrete time system belong to the set T of natural numbers. Correspondingly, the input sample path is a function from the set T of time points to the set of input variables u. The output and system state sample paths are also functions from the set T of time points to the set of output variables y and state variables x, respectively. The sample path allows us to study the system dynamics in any given period.

The value of a sample path at a specific time t is defined by $z(t)$. z can be a state, an input, or an output sample path. Similarly, the values of a sample path over an interval from t_m to t_n can be denoted $z < t_m, t_n >$. The endpoints of a time interval can open or close, depending on the situation. Thus, we can scope the time interval by inclusion using '[' and ']', or by exclusion using '(' and ')'. Figure 8.2 illustrates some examples of sample paths in different time intervals that are defined by inclusion or exclusion symbols. In the sheep farm example, if we are interested in the sheep

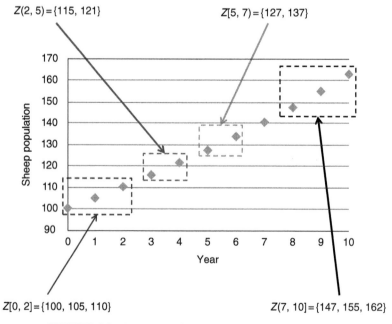

FIGURE 8.2 Examples of sample path of sheep population.

population growth in the first three years (year count starts from zero), we could extract the values ($z[0, 2]$) of the state sample path to use them for the investigation.

The above notation provides an easy way to represent the whole or any segment of the sample path for system variables. Based on this, we can use the extracted segments according to the intended simulation objectives.

8.4   DISCRETE TIME SIMULATION AND DISCRETE EVENT SIMULATION

DES is a special case of DTS, as mentioned earlier in this chapter. The dynamics of DES are driven by a set of discrete events that occur at specific time instants. Therefore, DES can be seen as a special case of DTS, in which the intervals between time points are defined by the event occurrence times. In the following, we use another example – the simulation of a vending machine – to describe the differences between a DES approach and a DTS approach.

Example 8.4.1. *A vending machine is used for selling various soft drinks to customers. To keep this example intuitive, we include the following simplifying assumptions: all drinks are priced at one dollar, the vending machine accepts only one-dollar coins, and the machine provides a soft drink once a customer inserts a coin and makes selection.*

It is obvious that a DES approach is perfectly fine for this vending machine because its states are driven by a set of discrete events {COIN INSERTED, SELECTION MADE, DRINK TAKEN}. Further, a FSM can be used for modelling the operation of this DES.

As shown in Figure 8.3, there are three system states of the vending machine: 'waiting coins', 'waiting selection', and 'vending drink'. The events of 'coin

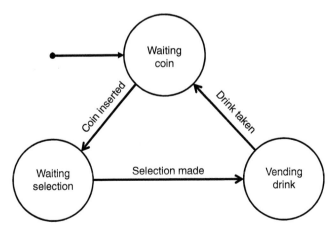

FIGURE 8.3   A DES approach for the vending machine by FSM.

inserted', 'selection made', and 'drink taken' trigger the vending machine state to change from one to another. For example, the state of the machine changes from 'waiting coin' to 'waiting selection' when the event 'coin inserted' occurs, and changes to 'vending drink' once a selection is made by the customer. The machine then moves again to 'waiting coin' state after the chosen drink is taken by the customer.

In the above FSM model, the time points when the machine changes its state depend on the times when events are happening. Hence, the time points of the state changes are not uniformly distributed in the time domain. However, let us assume that there is an internal digital clock ticking every second in the machine. At each clock tick, the machine checks whether any event has occurred. If there is no event occurring, the vending machine maintains the current state. Otherwise, it changes to a specific state triggered by the respective event. In such a case, the vending machine is driven by time, so we can try to re-model it using DTS.

To apply a DTS approach, we could use a flowchart to model the system behaviour with consideration of an internal clock ticking. Unlike the FSM (DES) approach, the time concept is explicitly introduced in the DTS approach. A 'null' event is also introduced to represent the situation in which there is no event happening when the clock ticks. The clock in the vending machine keeps ticking. If any event except the 'null' event occurs before each clock tick, the vending machine's state changes. Figure 8.4 displays a flowchart representation of a DTS approach for the vending machine.

The differences between DES and DTS can now be clearly seen from their visual representations, in Figures 8.3 and 8.4, respectively. In DES, system state transitions are caused by asynchronous events and the system state is expected to change at every

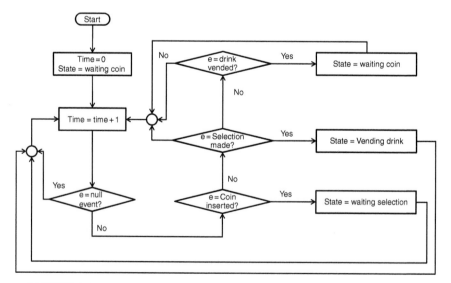

FIGURE 8.4 A DTS approach for the vending machine represented by flowchart.

occurrence of an event. In contrast, in DTS, system state transitions are synchronous, guided by the system clock. At each clock tick, an event is selected and, if it is not a 'null' event, the system state changes. We say that the time information is explicit in DTS, yet implicit in DES.

In the vending machine example, DES has certain advantages over DTS. This is mainly due to the nature of the vending machine system, which is driven by events. However, DTS has advantages over DES in some cases where the system time space is discrete and the time intervals between state changes are uniform. The sheep farm example presented earlier in this chapter is a good case in which DTS should be used instead of DES.

Keeping in mind the above discussion, in the next section, we describe in detail the steps taken to build in a DTS approach a microscopic road traffic model for a car-following simulation.

8.5 A CASE STUDY: CAR-FOLLOWING MODEL

In microscopic traffic modelling and simulation, many car-following models have been developed [53] over time. These include safety distance or collision-avoidance models, linear (Helly) models, psychophysical or action-point models, fuzzy logic-based models, and others. These models aim to describe the behaviours of drivers when they accelerate or decelerate while driving, based on the traffic conditions surrounding them. In this section, a well-known car-following model – the non-linear General Motors (GM) model [154] – is used as an example.

The GM model was one of the first safety distance and collision-avoidance models, and was developed by GM researchers. The GM model has evolved over time and now has many versions in which various parameters are tuned differently in line with the context in which the models are used. The most popular GM model has the following mathematical form:

$$a_{n+1}(t + \Delta t) = \left[\frac{(\alpha(l, m)v_{n+1}(t))^m}{(x_n(t - \delta T) - x_{n+1}(t - \delta T))^l} \right] [v_n(t - \delta T) - v_{n+1}(t - \delta T)] \quad (8.7)$$

where,

- n is the leading vehicle
- $n + 1$ is the following vehicle
- t represents the time in seconds
- Δt is the time interval for each update
- δT is the response time of driver(s)
- x is the position of a vehicle at a particular time relative to an origin (metres)
- v is the speed of a vehicle (metres per second)
- a is the acceleration or deceleration rate of a vehicle (metres per second^2)

- $\alpha(l, m)$ is a constant whose dimensions are dependent on the exponents l and m, where l is the distance headway exponent and m is the speed exponent. These parameters need to be calibrated with field data to reproduce realistic car following behaviours.

Equation (8.7) predicts the acceleration of a following vehicle based on the relative distance to the leading vehicle $(x_n(t - \delta T) - x_{n+1}(t - \delta T))$ and to the speed difference of leading and following vehicles $(v_n(t - \delta T) - v_{n+1}(t - \delta T))$. The GM model also considers the reaction time, δT of the drivers. Speeding up or slowing down is decided by the driver of the following vehicle at time $t + \Delta t$ according to the surrounding traffic flow conditions at time $t - \delta T$. Therefore, there is a response time window, δT, for a driver to react to a stimulus from the leading vehicle.

The sensitivity to the distances between leading and following vehicles is modelled as a denominator of a fraction. Therefore, long distances between vehicles will introduce more gradual acceleration/deceleration profiles. In contrast, short distances will result in more rapid changes in speed to avoid collisions. As seen in the last part of Eq. (8.7), sensitivity to speed is also taken into account. High speed differences between leading and following vehicles will lead to high acceleration/deceleration rates, so that the following vehicle can catch up with the leading vehicle's speed.

Equation (8.7) an appropriate discrete time representation for a DTS approach to build a microscopic traffic simulation. First, the leading vehicle motion can be modelled using Newton's laws if its initial position, speed, and acceleration rate at each time step are known:

$$v_1(t + \Delta t) = v_1(t) + a_1(t)\Delta t \tag{8.8a}$$

$$x_1(t + \Delta t) = x_1(t) + \frac{1}{2}a_1(t)\Delta t^2. \tag{8.8b}$$

Based on Eq. (8.7), the acceleration rate of the following vehicles can be decided at each time step based on: (i) the leading vehicle's characteristics and (ii) its own characteristics at time $t - \delta T$. Then Newton's law of motion is applied to update the speed and position of the following vehicle. The logic of this DTS is illustrated by a flowchart in Figure 8.5.

We now continue the above discussion with a concrete example to investigate the car-following behaviours produced by the above DTS approach.

Example 8.5.1. *Two cars are moving on a road. The leading vehicle has an initial speed of 13 m/s, while the following vehicle's initial speed is 10 m/s, without any acceleration or deceleration applied at the beginning. The distance between the two vehicles is 16 m. The target speed for the leading vehicle is 60 km/h (16.67 m/s), which is the speed limit of the road. The acceleration rates of the leading vehicle during the first few seconds are listed below:*

- $t = 0$, $a_1(0) = 0.5$
- $t = 1$, $a_1(1) = 1$

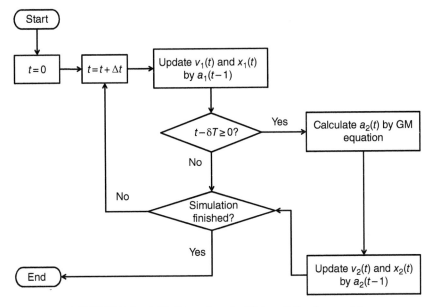

FIGURE 8.5 A DTS based on the GM car-following model.

- $t = 2,\ a_1(2) = 1.5$
- $t = 3,\ a_1(3) = 0.5$
- $t = 4,\ a_1(4) = -0.5.$

The reaction time of the driver in the following vehicle is two seconds, so $\delta T = 2.$ We also consider that the time step, Δt, of the simulation is one second, and we assume that $l = 1$, $m = 0$, and $\alpha(l, m) = 13$. Using these assumptions, the behaviour of the following vehicle can now be simulated by using the DTS approach described earlier. The speeds and accelerations of the following vehicle in the first 50 seconds of the simulation are plotted in Figure 8.6. As shown in the figure, the acceleration rate of the following vehicle changes over time, but becomes more stable later in the simulation. Correspondingly, the following vehicle's speed fluctuates at the beginning, but later tends to stay around 16 m/s, which is the target speed of the leading vehicle. The distance between the two vehicles is illustrated in Figure 8.7.

The distance between the two vehicles converges towards values around 25 m in the last 20 s because the following vehicle tries to synchronise its speed with the leading vehicle.

In summary, we note that the car-following example clearly indicates that DTS is more suitable than a DES approach in this case because the updates of the vehicle states occur synchronously at every second. We also note that this example is very simple, yet very useful and intuitive for understanding how a DTS simulation works,

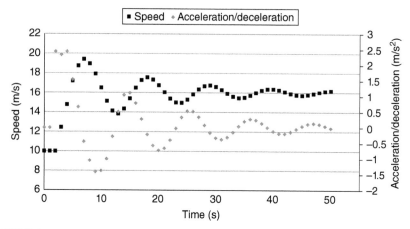

FIGURE 8.6   Speed and acceleration of the following vehicle in the first 50 s produced by DTS based on the GM model.

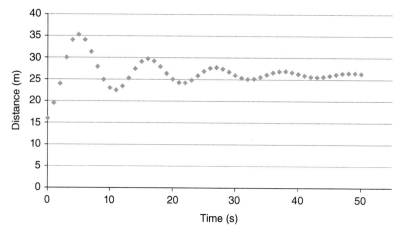

FIGURE 8.7   Distance between the leading and following vehicles in the first 50 s produced by DTS based on the GM model.

and how it can be built. However, DTS can be applied in many other applications that are much more complex than simple car following, where simulation of discrete time systems is needed for various reasons.

8.6   CONCLUSION

In this chapter, we introduced the concept of a discrete time system and explained through several examples how a DTS can be built. We also used a vending machine example to demonstrate that DTS is a general case of DES, being able to model and simulate a discrete event system. However, DES can simplify the modelling process for a discrete event system, and is easy to understand. DTS is more suitable for systems in which the states change at uniformly distributed time points, as in the car-following example. In conclusion, if the system is event driven, DES is better, whereas if the system is time driven, DTS is better. Later, in Chapter 9, we will see that DTS can also be used for continuous time systems if the appropriate conversion methods are used.

Continuous Simulation

Earlier in this book, we discussed discrete systems and the two types of simulation associated with them: discrete time and discrete event. However, there are numerous real-world systems whose states do not evolve in a discrete manner; instead, they change continuously over time. Consequently, they are called continuous systems, and the corresponding tool for investigating them is called continuous simulation. In this chapter, we introduce the most relevant methods for building models and simulators for continuous simulation. Differential equations are the most precise tools for describing the operation of a continuous system. To use them in a discrete digital computer system, we need to apply some numerical techniques that solve the continuous differential equations, such as Runge–Kutta method. In this chapter, we revisit the Lanchester models discussed for discrete systems, with the purpose of introducing the fundamental concepts of system dynamics for a continuous system. Given that many real-world systems combine both discrete and continuous dynamics, we also present an example that describes a combined discrete–continuous simulation.

9.1 CONTINUOUS SYSTEM

Earlier in the book, we discussed discrete systems, in which system states are evolved by discrete events or by discrete time steps. However, there are many systems in the real world, such as the physical systems involving mechanical, electrical, thermal, or hydraulic operation, whose dynamics are continuous in nature. For example, a car starts from a 'stopped' state and speeds up to 20 m/s with constant acceleration. Before the car starts, its velocity is zero. The state variables of the car, such as velocity and position, change once it starts. The velocity of the car increases continuously without a discernible pause until it reaches the target velocity (20 m/s). In addition, a car's position keeps changing unless the car fully stops. As illustrated in Figure 9.1, a car's velocity changes from 0 at Time 0 to 20 m/s at Time 10 with a

Simulation and Computational Red Teaming for Problem Solving, First Edition.
Jiangjun Tang, George Leu, and Hussein A. Abbass.
© 2020 by The Institute of Electrical and Electronics Engineers, Inc. Published 2020 by John Wiley & Sons, Inc.

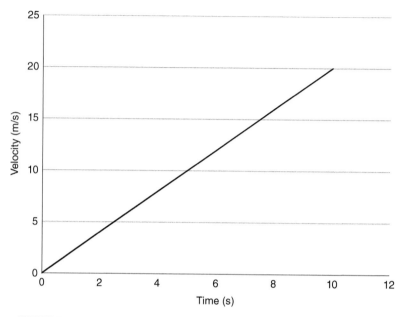

FIGURE 9.1   Velocity of a car starting from rest and speeding up to 20 m/s.

constant acceleration of 2 m/s^2, generating a continuous curve (a straight line in this case because of the constant acceleration).

Figure 9.1 also demonstrates that the system variables associated with a continuous system evolve continuously with no interruptions. From the above example, the definition of a continuous system can be given as follows.

Definition 9.1.1.   *A continuous system is a system in which the state variables change continuously with respect to time.*

In addition to the physical systems, there are many other types of continuous systems operating in different domains, which include, but are not limited to, business, social systems, and ecosystems. A stock market can be viewed as a continuous system in which the price of shares changes continuously over time under the influence of numerous factors. Another example is a predator–prey system in which the populations of two or more species (such as wolves and sheep) are closely dependent on each other. A population can be counted in general using discrete numbers; however, if the numbers are large enough, we can treat them as continuous real numbers (we will address this aspect in detail later in the chapter, using an example).

Clearly, discrete system concepts and the associated discrete simulation versions are not suitable tools to describe continuous systems, where the system state variables are not driven by discrete elements. Thus, in the following, we describe in detail the concepts related to continuous simulation.

9.2 CONTINUOUS SIMULATION

Continuous simulation is relevant to the modelling over time of a continuous system. The models of a continuous simulation describe the system state variables and their changes continuously with respect to time. Thus, continuous simulations can be used to represent any continuous time-varying systems.

A continuous simulation starts from understanding the physics of the continuous system, and then constructs the appropriate differential equations for both system state variables and system outputs. The differential equations are the foundation of a continuous simulation model because they are the most accurate mathematical model for describing the continuous evolution of system states. Some differential equations may be simple enough to be solved by analytical methods; however, most of the continuous systems involve complicated differential equations that are difficult to implement on digital computers. In such cases, the differential equations can be transformed into difference equations and solved using certain numerical methods. Difference equations are more suitable when a digital computer system has to discretise the continuous system, and can be implemented on digital computers much easier than continuous differential ones. When building a continuous simulator, the appropriate numerical implementation of the continuous mathematical model must be chosen, according to the actual problem. The appropriate numerical implementation means that the selected method must precisely represent the original differential equations. The numerical implementations involve a variety of numerical analysis techniques, such as Euler's method and Runge–Kutta methods. These techniques are discussed in detail later in the chapter, in Section 9.3. For now, let us consider the following example.

Example 9.2.1. *A car starts from a 'stopped' state and speeds up to 20 m/s with a constant acceleration of 2 m/s². Build a simulation to describe the change over time of the velocity of the car.*

In the following, we use this example to describe how to build a continuous simulation.

9.2.1 Model of a Continuous System

In the above example, the changes of the car's velocity are the result of a continuous function that describes the states of the system at any point in time. Therefore, differential equations are the best way to model these continuous functions. The velocity of the car at a time point t can be obtained by calculating the derivative of the position of the car with respect to time, as below:

$$v = \frac{dy}{dt} \tag{9.1}$$

where $y = y(t)$ is the instantaneous position at time point t. Similarly, we can also evaluate the derivative of the velocity with respect to time to represent the acceleration, as follows:

$$a = \frac{dv}{dt} = \frac{dy}{dt^2}. \tag{9.2}$$

The mathematical model including both the above equations is able to describe in a continuous manner the variation over time of the car's velocity and acceleration. Thus, a continuous simulation usually involves the differential equations that state the relationship between the rate of change of the system variables and the time.

In this example, the differential equations are simple enough and can be solved using classic analytical methods. We can obtain the values of the car's state variables (velocity and acceleration) for all time points from the functions (Eqs. (9.1) and (9.2)) of the initial values of these state variables at Time 0.

9.2.2   Continuous Simulator Implementation

Once the mathematical model is decided, we start implementing the simulator. First, the differential equation of velocity in the above car model needs to be coded in the simulator. Based on Eq. (9.1), we can approximate the velocity at time t by the concept of limit, as below:

$$v_t = \frac{dy}{dt} = \lim_{\Delta t \to 0} \frac{y_{t+\Delta t} - y_t}{\Delta t}.$$

The position of the car at time t (i.e. y_t) can be obtained from the classic equation of motion:

$$y_t = v_0 t + \frac{1}{2} a t^2$$

in which $v_0 = 0$. Therefore, the equation becomes:

$$y_t = \frac{1}{2} a t^2.$$

Further, the velocity can be estimated by plugging the last equation into the first one, as shown in the following equation:

$$v_t = \lim_{\Delta t \to 0} \frac{a((t + \Delta t)^2 - t^2)}{2\Delta t}. \tag{9.3}$$

The above equation can be easily coded in any software, such as Microsoft Excel or Java. However, one variable, Δt, in the above equation must be decided in advance. As the equation suggests, a smaller Δt will generate a more accurate approximation of the car's velocity at time t. To prove this, let us try different values of Δt to see the estimation of the car's velocity at time $t = 1$. Table 9.1 shows the velocity approximation at time $t = 1$ for different values of Δt, based on Eq. (9.3). The implementation was made in Microsoft Excel 2010.

Interestingly, the error reduces significantly as Δt decreases from 1 to 10^{-8}, yet grows if Δt continues to decrease. The smallest $\Delta t = 10^{-16}$ even gives the largest error of -2 among all estimations. Clearly, Eq. (9.3) does not have any mathematical or logical errors, yet does not work as expected. The only issue with Eq. (9.3) is that

TABLE 9.1 Round-off Errors of the Estimation of Car's Velocity, Using $v_t = \frac{dy}{dt}$ for Different Values of Δt

Δt	t	$t + \Delta t$	t^2	$(t + \Delta t)^2$	Approximate by Eq. (9.3)	$v_t = at$	Error
1	1	2	1	4	3	2	1
0.01	1	1.01	1	1.0201	2.01	2	0.01
0.0001	1	1.0001	1	1.00020001	2.0001	2	1E − 04
0.000001	1	1.000001	1	1.000002	2.000001	2	9.99924E − 07
1.00E − 08	1	1.00000001	1	1.00000002	1.999999988	2	−1.21549E − 08
1.00E − 10	1	1	1	1	2.000000165	2	1.65481E − 07
1.00E − 12	1	1	1	1	2.000177801	2	0.000177801
1.00E − 14	1	1	1	1	1.998401444	2	−0.001598556
1.00E − 16	1	1	1	1	0	2	−2

it intends to divide a very small number by another very small number, and both are very close to zero when $\Delta t \rightarrow 0$. The operations on small numbers lead to a particular type of error, called round-off error (or rounding error) [385] which is caused by the binary representations of the floating-point numbers either on the computer system or in software packages. Round-off errors usually occur when numerical operations involve extremely small or large real numbers [327]. Any computer system or software package (including simulation tools) has a certain designed precision level for floating-point numbers. Anything on a digital computer is binary; thus, any real number is stored in binary formats as compact as possible to save storage space. In other words, a floating-point number is represented by a limited number of binary bits on a digital computer system. For example, the floating-point numbers in Microsoft Excel are designed based on IEEE 754 [194]. The results of the operations on small real numbers are usually very long (e.g. 100 bits or infinity), and cannot be stored in a finite amount of space (e.g, 32 or 64 bits). Therefore, the results must be rounded down to fit this finite amount of space. This applies to any computer system. For this reason, round-off errors may appear in computer simulations, as we demonstrated above.

In the car example, although the continuous system of a moving vehicle can be accurately modelled using Eq. (9.3), this representation cannot be accurately handled by a digital computer system because of round-off errors. Thus, if we wish to use the above approach and model the variation of velocity using the derivative of positions with respect to time, we need to carefully select an appropriate value for Δt when implementing the model on a digital computer. This value cannot be too large, since it disobeys the concept of limit (e.g. $\Delta = 1$). Further, it cannot be too small, since it leads to round-off errors. The round-off errors are cumulative, causing fundamental limitations on the stability and quality of the intended continuous simulation. For the car velocity example, $\Delta t = 10^{-8}$ is a good choice when the simulator is implemented in Excel.

Most continuous systems are not as simple as this example; thus, finding the solutions for the resultant set of differential equations in an analytical manner may

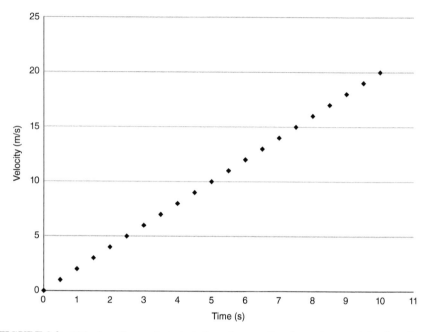

FIGURE 9.2   Velocity of a car that starts from 'stopped' and speeds up to 20 m/s, using a difference equation with $\Delta t = 0.5$.

become extremely difficult, if not impossible. In addition, as we mentioned earlier, implementing the continuous differential equations for a continuous simulation on a digital computer may not be possible because of the discrete operation of the latter. In such cases, difference equations become useful for a digital computer system to simulate a continuous system. For the car example, the velocity equation can be represented by a difference equation if the acceleration, a, is a constant variable, as follows:

$$v_{t+\Delta t} = v_t + a\Delta t \qquad (9.4)$$

where Δt is a fixed time increment, and is usually a small value (e.g. 1 s or 10 ms). Given that the acceleration of the car is constant, Eq. (9.4) is valid for describing in a discrete manner the changes of the car's velocity.

The changes in velocity – with velocity implemented based on the above equation – are visualised in Figure 9.2, where the time increment Δt is set to 0.5 s (500 ms). Given that the calculations occur at discrete time points, the velocities of the car are illustrated as square marks distributed evenly along a straight line (not shown in the figure). If the time increment (Δt) becomes smaller, the density of these marks increases. If the time increment (Δt) is very close to zero, all these points can virtually make a (visual perception of a) continuous line, as shown in Figure 9.3, although the calculations occur at discrete time points. Of course,

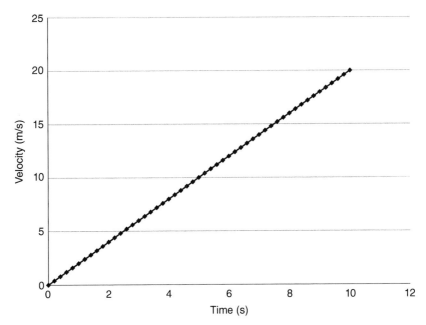

FIGURE 9.3   Velocity of a car that starts from 'stopped' and speeds up to 20 m/s using a difference equation: $\Delta t = 0.2$.

because of the potential round-off errors, an appropriate value must be decided for Δt. As demonstrated in the example, the difference equation is an alternative method to implement the simulator for the car velocity model. However, it is not always easy to transform differential equations into difference equations for some continuous systems. Therefore, other numerical methods are required, which we will discuss later in the chapter, in Section 9.3.

As described in the car example, the fixed-increment time-advancing mechanism is typically used for implementing continuous simulators. The challenge here is to determine an appropriate time interval that is small enough to ensure accuracy. As seen in the example, the outputs (the values of system state variables over time) from the simulator are smoother when a smaller time interval is selected. However, this interval also cannot be too small because of the round-off errors. Although larger time intervals can save some computational cost when simulating a continuous system (less iterations are required to complete a simulation), some significant errors may be introduced because of the discretisation of the continuous system. These issues will also be discussed in detail in Section 9.3.

9.2.3   Run a Continuous Simulation

Up to this point, the car example discussed above did not involve any degree of randomness in either the continuous model or the associated simulator. The car motion was described completely and precisely by the differential equations. Thus, once the initial state variables of the car are known, the outputs from the differential equations or difference equations are fully determined. From this perspective, continuous systems are called deterministic, and the associated continuous simulation becomes a deterministic simulation. However, it is possible to include random aspects in a continuous simulation.

9.3 NUMERICAL SOLUTION TECHNIQUES FOR CONTINUOUS SIMULATION

The differential equations yielded from many continuous systems are not integrable. In such cases, we must use some numerical integration methods when implementing the simulator for a continuous system. However, we have already seen earlier in this chapter that it is a difficult task to transfer a continuous system onto a discrete computer system because this causes potential problems, such as round-off errors, truncation errors, and others. In this section, we focus on the most relevant numerical techniques that discretise a continuous system in time and control these potential errors.

9.3.1 Euler's Method

In the previous example, we discussed the simple case of a moving car solved by the difference equations. The acceleration of the car was constant, so the velocity of the car over time could be easily obtained using Eq. (9.4). However, in practice, the acceleration of a car is variable, with the variation being typically non-linear in nature. Thus, in the following we will treat this more general case.

Example 9.3.1. *Assume that a car starts from a 'stopped' state and accelerates to 20 m/s with a variable acceleration a, as described by the the following Sigmoid function of time (t) for all t ≥ 0:*

$$a = \frac{2}{1 + e^{-2(t-2.5)}}$$

Simulate the car motion and estimate its velocity over time until it reaches the target speed.

For the above example, the velocity of the car can be estimated by Eq. (9.4), Section 9.2.2, but some significant errors may be introduced by Δt. First, we consider the velocity of a car when it accelerates at a constant rate, as shown in Figure 9.4. The change of car velocity over time is displayed as the blue area in the image, which is mathematically represented by Eq. (9.4). For example, the change in velocity from $t_3 = 3$ to $t_4 = 4$ is the product of the time interval $\Delta t = 1$ and the acceleration rate a. Thus, $a \times \Delta t$ represents the area, and $v_2 = v_1 + a\Delta t$. For the constant acceleration rate, this is an accurate method for computing the car's velocity at any time point.

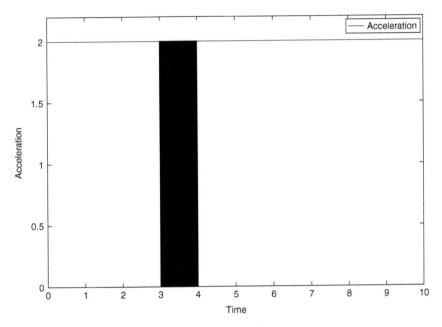

FIGURE 9.4   Constant acceleration: $a = 2$.

However, when we consider that the acceleration varies by time, shown by the curve in Figure 9.5, the method used above generates the errors illustrated as the space above the blue rectangle and below the acceleration curve. Clearly, the method used for the constant acceleration example is unable to obtain an accurate value of the change in velocity; thus, it is impossible for us to compute the exact value of the car's velocity at any time point. However, the error (space between the rectangle and curve) becomes smaller when the time step, Δt, is smaller. Therefore, if we follow the approach used for constant acceleration, Δt must have an appropriate small value to control the errors. The acceleration, a, in Eq. (9.4) is an instantaneous acceleration; therefore, an approximation of the car's velocity can be achieved only based on some instantaneous values at the previous step. This process is called **Euler's method**. Euler's method is the most common and simplest numerical method that can be used on a digital computer for implementation of continuous simulation.

Now, we invert Eq. (9.2) to estimate the velocity, v, at the next time step, $v_{t+\Delta t}$, based on the value of v_t and dv/dt, as below:

$$\frac{dv}{dt} \approx \frac{v_{t+\Delta t} - v_t}{\Delta t}$$

$$v_{t+\Delta t} \approx v_t + \frac{dv}{dt}\bigg|_{v,t} \Delta t \tag{9.5}$$

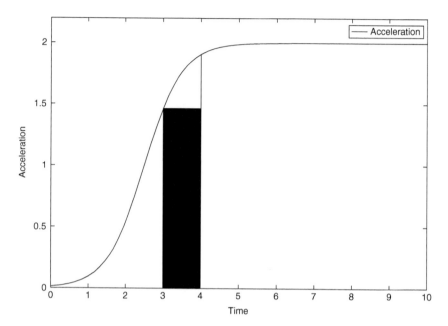

FIGURE 9.5   Variable acceleration described by a Sigmoid function: $a = \frac{2}{1+e^{-t}}$.

The derivatives of ordinary differential equations also take the form of a certain function, $f(v, t)$. Thus, we can use Euler's method to obtain the velocity as follows:

$$v_{t+\Delta t} \approx v_t + f(v, t)\Delta t \tag{9.6}$$

The above equation is quite similar to Eq. (9.4), yet we use the function $f(v, t) = \frac{dv}{dt}$ instead of a constant value of a. In addition, Eq. (9.6) can be seen as a linear function $y = c + km$, where the slope k is $\frac{dv}{dt}$. In fact, $\frac{dv}{dt}$ is the slope of the tangent to the velocity curve, depicted by an arrow in Figure 9.6. The tangent is pointing to an estimation for time $t = 3$ obtained using Euler's method (Eq. (9.6)) and the instantaneous values of velocity and acceleration at time $t = 2$, yet the real value sits on the curve, illustrated by the circle. Clearly, Euler's method is limited by the fact that the derivative is always approximated as the tangent of the velocity curve. If the velocity function is a straight line, as in Figure 9.3, Euler's method has no problem at all because the tangents at any point are always aligned with the function curve. However, Euler's method always produces estimations that deviate from the actual track when a certain curvature exists because it follows the direction of the tangent. Thus, in this example, the velocity of the car is always under-estimated.

Table 9.2 presents the results obtained using Euler's method with the time step $\Delta t = 1$, and the comparison against the true values. The error at each step is propagated as indicated in the table. This error can be reduced by choosing a smaller time step when estimating the velocity. As shown in Figure 9.7, the curves of the velocity

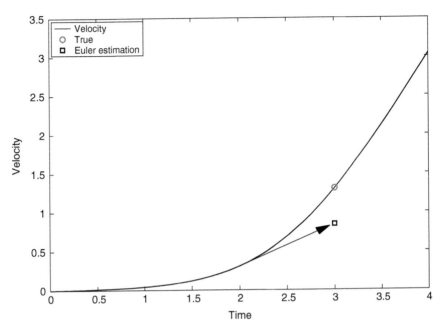

FIGURE 9.6   Euler's method for integration of the ordinary differential equation $\frac{dv}{dt}$.

estimated by Euler methods are closer to the curve of the true solution function when Δt is smaller. In theory, the error from Euler's method is scaling with Δt which can be revealed by expanding Eq. (9.5) into Taylor series.

Euler's method is the first-order numerical procedure for solving ordinary differential equations with a given initial value. It is a basic method for solving differential equations in a continuous system, and, as discussed above, it has some problems with estimation accuracy. Therefore, the method is rarely recommended for practical situations. However, Euler's method is important for the fact that it stands at the foundation of numerical integration and is essential for other numerical techniques, including the Runge–Kutta methods.

9.3.2   Runge–Kutta Methods

To overcome the limitations of Euler's method, a number of techniques have been proposed over the years. One straightforward implementation is the range of Runge–Kutta methods. The Euler integration equation can be reformulated for general-purpose use as follows:

$$x_{t+\Delta t} = x_t + f(x, t)\Delta t. \tag{9.7}$$

The equation evaluates the derivative only once at time t and then advances a solution to the next time step, $t + \Delta t$, by the derivative $f(x, t)$ at the beginning of that interval.

TABLE 9.2 The True Velocity and the Estimation by Euler's Method for the First 13 s.

Time	True velocity	Euler's velocity	Error	Time	True velocity	Euler's velocity	Error
0	0	0	0	7	8.993408054	7.998177898	0.995230156
1	0.041872003	0.013385702	0.028486301	8	10.99330135	9.997931108	0.995370245
2	0.306546339	0.108237448	0.198308891	9	12.99328691	11.99789771	0.995389206
3	1.306546339	0.646120291	0.660426048	10	14.99328496	13.99789318	0.995391772
4	3.041872003	2.108237448	0.933634555	11	16.99328469	15.99789257	0.99539212
5	5	4.013385702	0.986614298	12	18.99328466	17.99789249	0.995392167
6	6.994196118	6	0.994196118	13	20.99328465	19.99789248	0.995392173

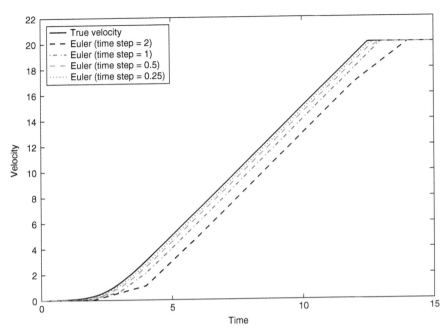

FIGURE 9.7 Euler's method for velocity approximation using different time steps.

Hence, the error cannot be avoided when any curvature exists in the solution function. RungeKutta methods evaluate the derivative at multiple sub-steps within one interval before advancing to the next full time step to cancel the first-order error term [322].

The standard Runge–Kutta method is called the midpoint method. There are two evaluations of the derivative within one time step. Similar to Euler's method, the first derivative is evaluated at the beginning of the interval (t), but we then advance only half of the time step ($\Delta t/2$) to obtain the midpoint, $x_{t+\Delta t/2}$. The derivative at this intermediate point ($t + \Delta t/2, x_{t+\Delta t/2}$) is evaluated again, and then this derivative $f(t + \Delta t/2, x_{t+\Delta t/2})$ is used to advance the solution towards the full time step. This process can be summarised as below:

$$x_{t+\Delta t/2} = x_t + f(t, x_t)\frac{1}{2}\Delta t$$

$$x_{t+\Delta t} = x + f\left(t + \frac{1}{2}\Delta t, x_{t+\Delta t/2}\right)\Delta t. \tag{9.8}$$

To implement the above equations, it is useful to change the notation we used in Eq. (9.7) as follows:

$$k_1 = f(t, x_t)\Delta t$$

$$x_{t+\Delta t} = x_t + k_1. \tag{9.9}$$

Then, the midpoint integration Eq. (9.8) can be formulated as:

$$k_1 = f(t, x_t)\Delta t$$

$$k_2 = f\left(t + \frac{1}{2}\Delta t, x_t + \frac{1}{2}k_1\right)\Delta t \qquad (9.10)$$

$$x_{t+\Delta t} = x_t + k_2.$$

Through this process, the first-order Euler formula is transformed into the second-order formula presented above. The midpoint method is the standard version in the Runge–Kutta range of methods. Starting from this idea, more advanced methods involving higher degrees of complexity have been derived. The most common method is the fourth-order Runge–Kutta method (Runge–Kutta 4), which, instead of estimating the middle point and evaluating the derivative by the midpoint method, evaluates the derivative four times in each time step: once at the beginning of the time step, twice at the midpoints, and once at the end of the time step. The fourth-order method can be summarised as follows:

$$k_1 = f(t, x_t)\Delta t$$

$$k_2 = f\left(t + \frac{1}{2}\Delta t, x_t + \frac{1}{2}k_1\right)\Delta t$$

$$k_3 = f\left(t + \frac{1}{2}\Delta t, x_t + \frac{1}{2}k_2\right)\Delta t \qquad (9.11)$$

$$k_4 = f\left(t + \frac{1}{2}\Delta t, x_t + \frac{1}{2}k_3\right)\Delta t$$

$$x_{t+\Delta t} = x_t + \frac{k_1}{6} + \frac{k_2}{3} + \frac{k_3}{3} + \frac{k_4}{6}.$$

Let us now use the car example to investigate both the midpoint and fourth-order Runge–Kutta methods. Given that the time points of evaluating the derivative in each time step are different, we use different time steps for the three methods to ensure a fair comparison. There are 24 estimations displayed as triangles in Figure 9.8 within the 12 s produced by Euler, where the time step $\Delta t = 0.5$. The midpoint method evaluates the derivative twice in each time step, so $\Delta t = 1$, and a total 12 asterisks are shown. For the fourth-order Runge–Kutta method, only six approximations are made because $\Delta t = 2$; these are shown using cross marks. Overall, we can see from Figure 9.8 that both the midpoint and Runge–Kutta 4 methods are much better than Euler's method. If we zoom in and investigate only the first five seconds (shown in Figure 9.9), Runge–Kutta 4 has better performance than midpoint before $t = 3$, even though it uses a larger time step, Δt. The acceleration becomes stable after $t = 3$ because of the behaviour of the sigmoid function; thus, both midpoint and Runge–Kutta 4 have similar performance after this time point. We understand from this example that using higher-order formulas (midpoint and Runge–Kutta 4) provides a significant improvement in terms of accuracy compared with lower-order formulas (Euler's method), while keeping a fairly similar computational efficiency.

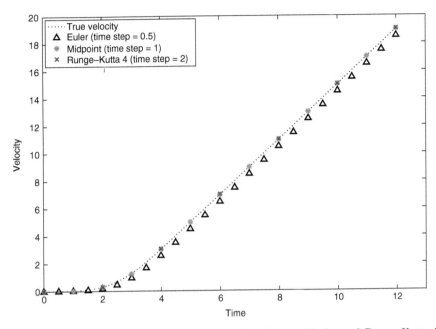

FIGURE 9.8   The approximation of velocity using Euler, midpoint and Runge–Kutta 4 methods.

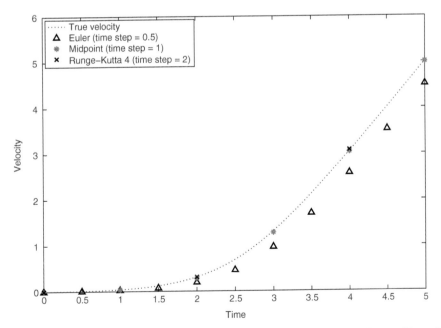

FIGURE 9.9   The approximation of velocity using Euler, midpoint and Runge–Kutta 4 methods – the first five seconds.

Euler's method based on the initial derivative introduces a first error term up to term of order Δt^2, while the error term for the second-order formula (the midpoint method) is introduced up to order Δt^3. With the fourth-order RungeKutta method, the error term is introduced until the term of order Δt^5. Clearly, a higher-order formula can outperform the lower-order ones in most cases, but not always. As shown in the example, there is not much difference in the approximation made by midpoint and Runge–Kutta 4 after $t = 3$ because of the mathematical characteristics of the sigmoid function, which make the acceleration stable and consequently cause a linear increase of the velocity.

In summary, we have thus far discussed two numerical techniques for solving differential equations. In many situations, Runge–Kutta methods are the appropriate techniques and are good enough to implement continuous simulations. However, there are many other advanced techniques for achieving higher accuracy, such as the adaptive time-step method. Extensive discussions on these advanced methods can be found in Press's book [322].

9.4 SYSTEM DYNAMICS APPROACH

There are other methods for building a continuous simulation. System dynamics [365] is one type of continuous simulation, which is largely used for strategic planning, policy analysis and improvement, and other purposes in business, government, and military domains. With the aid of a stock and flow chart and other diagrams, this approach provides users an intuitive insight into the non-linear behaviour of a complex system over time. Here, we use the Lanchester model [231] to introduce some basic concepts of system dynamics. The Lanchester model was introduced in Chapter 3, where we discussed an example for modelling process that used a set of difference equations and an analytical solution. In the following, we provide a short review of this model.

Example 9.4.1. *Two forces (blue and red) engage on a battle field. The blue force has an initial force level of b and a fighting effectiveness of β, while the red force has an initial force level of r and a fighting effectiveness of α. During the battle, the attrition of one force level over time can be estimated using the Lanchester model. The attrition of the blue force caused by the red force level and fighting effectiveness can be formulated using a differential equation as follows:*

$$\frac{db}{dt} = -\alpha r(t) \quad \alpha > 0.$$

Similarly, the attrition of the red force can be formulated as follows:

$$\frac{dr}{dt} = -\beta b(t) \quad \beta > 0$$

where both b(0) and r(0) are the initial force levels of the blue and red forces, respectively, and have non-negative values.

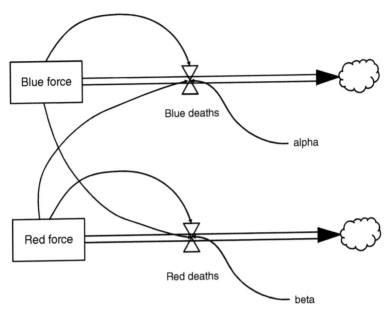

FIGURE 9.10   Stock and flow chart for the Lanchester equations.

The following key components of the system dynamics concept are used for the Lanchester model example presented above:

- A **stock** represents the accumulation of a 'resource'. In this example, the stock represents the initial force levels of both blue and red forces, and is illustrated using rectangles in the stock and flow chart. A stock can be the population of a species, the water level in a dam, the inventory of a product or others.
- A **flow** is a stream going in or out of the stock. A double-line arrow is used to represent a flow, and a valve with a butterfly shape on the pipe symbolises the ability to control the rate of the flow passing through. In the example, the control valve represents the death of both the blue and red forces at each time step.
- Variables are necessary for parametrising the valve (e.g. the fighting effectiveness, β and α).
- A link (illustrated using a single-line arrow) passes the information – such as the values of variables and stocks – to the valve.

The above components are visualised as a stock and flow chart in Figure 9.10.

This model can be easily implemented using NetLogo. The built-in 'system dynamics modeller' provides a graphical user interface for constructing stock and flow charts following the approach described above. The interface also allows the user to provide the equations for the valves controlling the flow. For example, the death of the blue force can be defined by

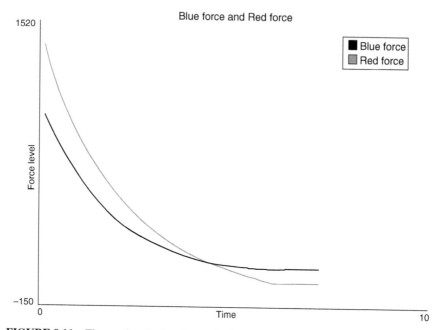

FIGURE 9.11 The results of a Lanchester battle model using a system dynamics approach in NetLogo ($B(0) = 1034$, $\beta = 0.749$, $R(0) = 1460$ and $\alpha = 0.373$).

$$\text{blue death} = \begin{cases} \text{red force} \times \alpha & \text{blue force} \geq 0 \\ 0 & \text{otherwise} \end{cases}.$$

Figure 9.11 shows the results from the system dynamics approach implemented in NetLogo, and Figure 9.12 shows the results from the implementation in Excel (the latter was presented in detail in Chapter 3). The results from both approaches are exactly the same; thus, the same trends of blue and red force levels are illustrated in both figures.

9.5 COMBINED DISCRETE–CONTINUOUS SIMULATION

Some systems may contain both continuous and discrete components in the real world. This generates the need for a combined discretecontinuous simulation that considers both the continuous and discrete aspects. In a combined discretecontinuous simulation, the system state variables can change discretely or continuously. The interactions among the discrete and continuous changes fall into three major categories (Pritsker [323]), as follows:

- A continuous state variable may be discretely changed by a discrete event.
- The relationship governing the continuous state variables (e.g. differential equations) may be changed at a particular time by a discrete event.

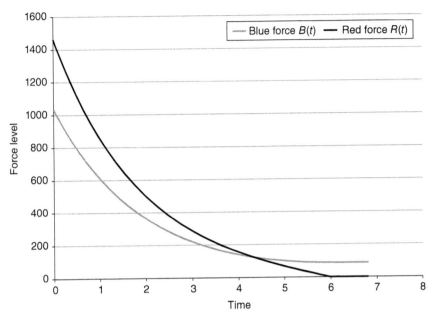

FIGURE 9.12   The results of a Lanchester battle model using an Excel spreadsheet ($B(0) =$ 1034, $\beta = 0.749, R(0) = 1460$, and $\alpha = 0.373$).

- A discrete event may be triggered or scheduled once a continuous state variable achieves a threshold value.

We briefly describe a combined discrete–continuous simulation using the example of a bank account system.

Example 9.5.1. *Assume that a savings account is established, and an initialised deposit noted P0 is made. Deposits to or withdrawals from this account can be made at any time point. Compound interest is applied to this account, and the variable annual interest rate listed in Table 9.3. is applied depending on the account balance to attract more deposits.*

The interest is added to the account every day, so the balance of the account continues increasing if there are no withdrawals. From a long-term perspective, the balance changes continuously. In addition, any change in the account balance – by deposit, withdrawal or interest gained – takes immediate effect, on which the interest rate is applied.

As described above, the simulation for such a system is a combined discrete–continuous simulation. The model for this account contains both discrete events and continuous system state variables. The discrete events include three types of events: deposit to the account, withdrawal from the account and interest rate adjustment. The continuous system variable is the balance available in this account

TABLE 9.3   Annual interest rate

Amount	Annual interest rate (%)
$\leq$\$1 000	2
$\leq$\$5 000	3
$\geq$\$10 000	3.5

P_t. First, the compound interest can be modelled using the following differential equation:

$$\frac{dP}{dt} = Pr. \tag{9.12}$$

This equation can be solved analytically, allowing us to obtain the account balance, P, at a time point t as follows (therefore, no numerical methods are required here):

$$P_t = P_0 e^{rt}. \tag{9.13}$$

As mentioned before, three discrete events may occur in the system and the occurrences may affect the system state variables and the relationship governing the continuous state variables.

- If a 'deposit' event occurs at a time point t, it immediately increases the account balance, p_t, and may trigger the 'interest rate adjustment' event if p_t is above a certain threshold value.
- If a 'withdrawal' event occurs, it immediately decreases the account balance, p_t, and may trigger the 'interest rate adjustment' event if p_t is below a certain threshold value.
- The 'interest rate adjustment' event affects the compound interest calculation according to Eq. (9.13).

In addition, the 'interest rate adjustment' event can also be trigged by the continuous increment of the account balance generated by gaining interest. In this case, in Eq. (9.13), we need to replace the parameter P_0 with the current available balance, P_t, and the interest rate, r, with the new interest rate. At the same time, we need to reset the parameter t as well.

9.6 CONCLUSION

In this chapter, we discussed in detail continuous systems and continuous simulation. We demonstrated that differential equations are the fundamental tool in continuous simulation, and we introduced a number of relevant numerical techniques for implementing these continuous equations in digital computing systems. We also showed that the discretisation of a continuous system comes with a number of issues, such as round-off errors, and we described in detail how the numerical techniques should be chosen and tuned to mitigate these issues. The examples we used throughout the chapter showed that, in general, higher-order formulas (e.g. Runge–Kutta methods) are better than lower-order formulas (e.g. Euler's method), but not always. Thus, we emphasise that it is important to select an appropriate numerical method and an appropriate time step for the discretisation, according to the mathematical characteristics residing in the models when implementing a continuous simulator because both contribute to controlling errors. In addition to the classic computational approaches to building a simulation, we also briefly discussed the system dynamics concept, in which stock and flow diagrams are employed for modelling various continuous systems. Finally, we used a relevant example – the savings account – to introduce combined discrete–continuous simulations, since many systems in the real world are neither completely discrete nor completely continuous.

CHAPTER 10

Agent-based Simulation

ABSs have been widely used in various disciplines over the last decades. As the literature shows, ABS has many advantages when modelling systems that involve many individual behaviours, such as social systems or ecological systems. In this chapter, we introduce and describe in detail the concept of ABS, and discuss some of the most popular methodologies and tools for designing and developing an ABS. In addition, we demonstrate through a number of relevant examples how to build and use an ABS.

10.1 INTRODUCTION

ABS has become a popular simulation approach in the last decades. ABS is a computational framework for simulating dynamic processes involving a population of autonomous and heterogeneous agents that interact extensively with each other [260]. ABS can be traced back to complex adaptive systems (CASs) [184], which study how autonomous agents can self-organise using their limited cognitive and perceptual abilities to better fit the environment, in the context of a complex system (usually a natural system). Agent-based modelling has been largely used for investigating various aspects of artificial life [232], such as the cellular automaton [61]. It appears that the term 'agent' was introduced by Holland and Miller in 1991 [185]. ABS also has a close relationship with the concept of a multi-agent system (MAS) [134], which is a sub-field of distributed AI. A MAS consists of a number of intelligent agents interacting in an environment to solve a given problem. In some disciplines, ABS is known under other names, such as individual-based modelling in ecology [110].

ABS is different from other approaches in terms of the process and activities, such as DES or system dynamics, which are mainly driven by equation-based modelling. The need for ABS comes from the modelling of individual behaviours and interactions in the real world. ABS focuses on the behaviours of individual agents, which are difficult to model using equations, as in DES or system dynamics. For example, human behaviours and their interactions are usually non-linear functions, and are too complex to be formalised in any mathematical equations. In this case, an ABS

Simulation and Computational Red Teaming for Problem Solving, First Edition.
Jiangjun Tang, George Leu, and Hussein A. Abbass.
© 2020 by The Institute of Electrical and Electronics Engineers, Inc. Published 2020 by John Wiley & Sons, Inc.

becomes a suitable approach to model and simulate human behaviours and interactions [47, 127]. The use of agents allows us to relax assumptions when modelling and simulating some systems. For example, the traditional method of modelling an economics system relies on many assumptions, including perfect markets, long-term equilibrium and others. However, because of advances in data sciences and technologies, we can now take a more realistic view of economic systems by using heterogeneous agents as entities in that system, while making fewer assumptions [377]. The availability of micro-level data about a variety of real systems allows us to better understand individual behaviour and facilitates the modelling of individual entities of a system as agents by using ABS [85]. Further, the advent of computational power makes it possible to perform large-scale ABS with thousands of agents, such as studies on disease spread networks and criminal or terrorist networks [387]. As a result of the benefits mentioned above, applications of ABS can now be found virtually everywhere, in domains such as ecology [167], finance [325], traffic systems [11], supply chains [371], and many others.

In ABS, agents may represent people, groups of people, organisations, countries, animals, or other individuals operating in a system. There is no universal definition of an agent in the literature; rather, researchers define agents from their own perspectives, usually limited to particular fields of application or even applications. For example, in a social theory view, an agent is an independent component of a system [33]; in AI, an agent is a system component exhibiting adaptive behaviour [201]; and, in general computer science, an agent is an autonomous component of a system [77]. Macal and North summarised a set of fundamental features that agents should possess [258, 259], as follows:

- An agent is an autonomous entity that senses its environment and other agents. The behaviours of agents, including making decisions and taking actions, are based on the perceived information.
- An agent is self-contained. An agent is identifiable and has a boundary that encapsulates its own attributes, characteristics, and behaviours, although some characteristics may be shared among agents.
- An agent is social. Agents interact with others by following some protocols or mechanisms. Various interactions among agents may occur in a system, including agent recognition, information exchange, collaboration, cooperation, negotiation, influence, and others.

In addition to these fundamental features, agents usually have some resource attributes, such as energy and inventory. In an ABS, agents may consume these resources and seek ways to replenish them. Thus, an agent may have explicit goals guiding its behaviours, such as reducing resource consumption. It is not necessary for an agent to perform certain behaviours to maximise its goals. However, the goals could be the benchmarks that the agent uses to assess the outcome of its behaviour to improve it if needed. This leads to another feature of agents – that is, the capability to learn and adapt their behaviours based on their own experiences or those of other agents. In such cases, the agents must embed base rules to generate the usual behaviour and advanced rules for changing the base rules. Further, the existence of a learning and adapting mechanism/behaviour requires agents to have memory, which is usually in the form of dynamic attributes. In contrast to the dynamic attributes, the basic attributes of an agent are low-level attributes that cannot be inferred from other basic attributes. For example, the age, height, and weight of an agent representing a human are low-level irreducible attributes, while memory is a dynamic attribute that can be aggregated or inferred from other attributes and/or experiences. Usually, an agent lives in and interacts with an environment, so the resultant behaviour is subject to its current position in relation to that environment.

The rest of this chapter is organised as follows. In the next section, we discuss some basic concepts of an ABS. We then introduce some popular methodologies for designing and developing an ABS. This is followed by the demonstration of a number of concrete applications that use ABS. Finally, we present some conclusions on agents and ABS.

10.2   AGENT-BASED SIMULATION

As stated earlier in this chapter, there is no universal definition of an agent in ABS; however, agents usually exhibit a number of fundamental features. Figure 10.1 illustrates the most common elements of an agent in an ABS, along with its interactions with the environment and other agents.

Based on this figure, the concept of ABS [260] can formalised as follows:

$$ABS = \{A, I, E, T\} \tag{10.1}$$

where A is a set of agents, I is the interaction space, E is the environment where agents live, and T is the time-advance mechanism. Further, an agent can be formalised in a similar manner, as a five-tuple:

$$a = \{B, S, D, N, M\} \quad a \in A \tag{10.2}$$

where B is a set of behaviours, S is a set of static attributes, D is a set of dynamic attributes, N is the set of neighbouring agents with which the agent interacts in I, and M is the mechanism for updating the agent's states.

10.2.1   Agent Behaviours

Agent behaviours consist of a set of rules that guide the agent to sense the environment and its neighbours, to make decisions and to take actions. Modelling agents' behaviours is the essential component of ABS. The modelling focuses on the behaviours and interactions at individual level, and does not necessarily include the explicit modelling of the emergent system behaviours (i.e. the ones that can be observed by an external observer).

The foundation of modelling agent behaviours is the behavioural theories from social and cognitive sciences sciences [20, 175]. Typically, data from surveys or

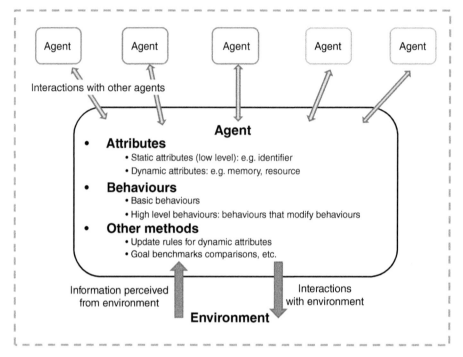

FIGURE 10.1   Agent elements and its interactions with other agents and the environment.

empirical observations are the basis for abstracting the agent behaviour representations under some reasonable assumptions.

The agent behaviour model based on rational choice [358] is one of the most used models in ABS. The assumption of a rational-choice agent model is that the agent is able to make decisions about the optimal way to act based on its perceived information. One example of rational agent implementation is the belief–desire–intention model [328]. This model provides practical reasoning for rational agents [56] based on a structure consisting of three essential components:

- **Belief**: the informational state of an agent, which represents the agent's belief about its world based on the perceived information (where perceived information includes information about its surrounding environment and other agents).
- **Desire**: the motivational state of an agent, which represents the goals or situations that the agent would like to achieve.
- **Intention**: the deliberative state of the agent, in which an agent chooses to execute plans for the future based on its beliefs and desires.

Although differences exist between equation-based models and agent-based models, it is possible for an agent-based model to combine with other models. Thus, various mathematical expressions can be used for modelling agent behaviours, such as Petri net [220], Markov chain [309], and FSM [370].

Agent behaviours can be described in many ways in a model. For example, one usual way is to represent agent behaviours through a set of **if–then** rules. Some more advanced representations can also be found in the literature, such as neural networks [311] and evolutionary programming [264].

10.2.2   Interaction Space and Neighbours

Given that agents are social entities, their behaviours are influenced by interactions with other agents. Thus, an interaction protocol must be established for the agents in an ABS, such as communication, movement, competition for resources, and so on. Therefore, we need to specify with whom an agent can interact, and where the interactions between agents can occur. This is related to the interaction space or social space, I, and is usually represented as a network. Various topologies can be used in ABS, including, but not limited to, the following.

10.2.2.1 Aspatial Model   In this model, agents reside in a pool and do not have specific spatial locations. Agents are usually randomly paired for their interactions. Therefore, the neighbours, N, of an agent are randomly selected.

10.2.2.2 Grid Space   The interaction space is structured as a grid, consisting of a number of cells. One cell can be occupied by one or more agents. Agents interact only with the agents, N, residing in the immediate neighbouring cells. For example, an agent may interact with its four neighbours in four directions – north, south, east, and west – or an agent may interact with all eight neighbours that surround it. This approach is typically used in cellular automata, such as Game of Life [153].

10.2.2.3 Euclidean Space   Agents live and roam in a 2-D or higher dimensional space. Interactions occur among the agents who are close enough to each other. The close agents or neighbours, N, are determined by Euclidean distance. One example of agent simulation that uses the Euclidean space is Boids [335].

10.2.2.4 Geographic Information System   Agents are distributed in the environment based on their geographic positioning information, and interact with their neighbours based on their realistic locations. Thus, a geographic information system (GIS) is a common approach for applications where physical location on Earth plays an important role.

10.2.2.5 Network Topology   The network topology is a popular implementation of interaction space for ABS, especially in social sciences. The neighbours of an agent, N, in a network are the agents directly connected through network links, and the interactions occur among them. This is a more general way to specify the neighbours of an agent and sometimes is more accurate (e.g. a virtual social network). A network can be static, where the links are defined in advance and the topology remains

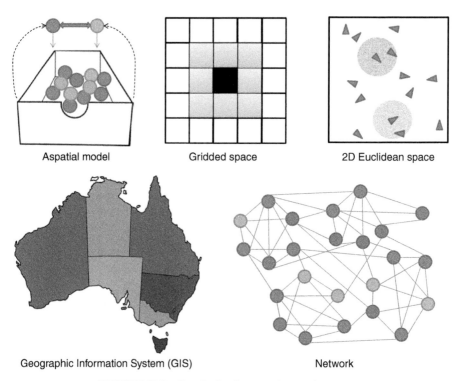

Aspatial model   Gridded space   2D Euclidean space

Geographic Information System (GIS)   Network

FIGURE 10.2 Topologies for agent interaction space.

constant during the lifecycle of the simulation, or can be dynamic, where nodes and links may change over time, requiring additional mechanisms to be designed and implemented in the model.

Figure 10.2 shows in a visual manner the topologies discussed above. The decision of what topology to use to model the interaction space depends on the characteristics of the system to be simulated. We will discuss some of these topologies with Examples 10.3.

10.2.3 State-update and Time-advance in Agent-based Simulation

In an ABS, agents have well-defined states that vary over time. The state of an agent at a time point is defined by the values of its attributes, while the state of the whole system is represented by the aggregation of all agent states. As a result, in ABS, the system state-updating mechanism is closely related to the time-advance mechanism.

Although both discrete and continuous time-advance mechanisms can be used in ABS, the discrete time-advance mechanism is more commonly implemented.

In discrete implementation, we can consider the behaviours of an agent and the interactions among agents as a set of discrete events. The system states change at particular time points when these events occur. In this manner, an ABS is similar to a DES. Therefore, the time-advance mechanisms (next-event time advancing and fixed-increment time advancing) used by DES can be adopted in ABS. However, next-event time advancing requires a complex event-scheduling mechanism because an ABS usually involves a large number of agents, behaviours, and interactions. Thus, fixed-increment time advancing is more popular for most ABSs, such as cellular automata. By using fixed-increment time advancing in ABS, agents take action and interact with each other at each time step. In an ABS with fixed-increment time advancing, conflicts may arise when all agents interact simultaneously at a time step because agents may compete with each other for the same space or resources. To overcome this problem, the sequence of agent interactions is randomly reordered at each time step. This can remove any bias in the simulation results caused by some arbitrary ordering of agent interactions. However, because of the randomness residing in this method, the ABS must be run many times to obtain statistically significant results. As a result, one issue with this conflict-resolution mechanism is that it leads to a large amount of computation.

10.2.4 Agent-based Simulation Development

ABS is a bottom-up approach that emphasises individual agent modelling. Some guidelines for ABS design and development have been proposed, such as the ODD (Overview, Design concepts, Details) protocol [168]. The basic principle for ABS design and development is to start from the individual agent design and modelling, and then consider the aggregation of agent behaviours to obtain an emergent behaviour of the whole system. At the stage of individual agent modelling, we take into account the purpose of the model, and the low-level attributes and basic behaviours of an agent. We then consider the interaction protocols for agent interactions, the topology of interaction space, the environment representation and other system-level aspects. Finally, we need to validate the models and results.

As a result of the nature of ABS, object-oriented programming languages, such as Java, are the most suitable tools that can be used for implementation, while high-level approaches, such as the UML, can facilitate developers to build the conceptual models [38]. In addition, a number of off-the-shelf agent-based modelling and simulation software packages are available, such as NetLogo [402], AnyLogic [22], and Repast Simphony [333].

10.3 EXAMPLES OF AGENT-BASED SIMULATION

In this section, we discuss some ABS applications. We start with two simple models and then introduce other more complex models.

10.3.1 Life and Flocking

A cellular automata is usually a grid space consisting of a number of cells, in which each cell has a finite set of states, with one state at a given time point. The cellular automata operates using a set of simple rules that determine a cell's state at the next time point based on the value of this cell and the values of the neighbouring cells. **Life** [153] is an example of cellular automata.

Example 10.3.1. *Let us consider a 2-D grid space in which each cell can have two states: ON or OFF. The initial states of cells are randomly initialised at the beginning ($t = 0$). There are three rules in **Life** to update cells' states at the next time step:*

- *If there are exactly two neighbours of a cell being ON at time step t_i, then this cell will retain the same state at the next time step t_{i+1}.*
- *If there are exactly three neighbours of a cell being ON at time step t_i, then the next state of this cell will be ON at t_{i+1}.*
- *Otherwise, the cell's state will be OFF at t_{i+1}.*

We consider each cell in this 2-D grid space to be an agent that has a state variable with two possible values ($\{ON, OFF\}$) and predefined behaviours based on the three rules. The environment in *Life* is only the grid space that provides position references to an agent for identifying its neighbours (usually eight agents surrounding it in a 2-D grid space, as shown in Figure 10.2). The agent retrieves the information from its neighbouring agent states and then decides how to update its own state at the next time step. The system state is represented by the states of all agents taken together at a particular time.

Figure 10.3 shows snapshots from a simulation of *Life* that starts with random initialisation of cell states and evolves over time. Some distinctive patterns can be observed after several generations, as shown in the figure. The interaction space is scoped by the surrounding cells, and an agent updates its states based on the local

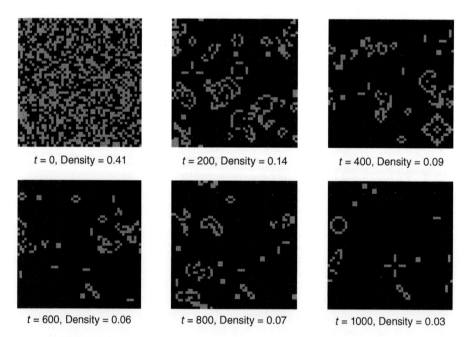

| $t = 0$, Density = 0.41 | $t = 200$, Density = 0.14 | $t = 400$, Density = 0.09 |
| $t = 600$, Density = 0.06 | $t = 800$, Density = 0.07 | $t = 1000$, Density = 0.03 |

FIGURE 10.3 ABS of *Life* – the cell states evolve from a random initialisation.

information only. The outcome from the *Life* simulation is sensitive to initial agent states. Various initial states of cells combined with the three simple rules and local information can produce different patterns through the *Life* simulation. Therefore, this simulation can create a virtually infinite number of diverse virtual worlds. In addition, the observed patterns demonstrate the 'emergence' of a system behaviour as the result of aggregating individual agent behaviours. For a better understanding of the concept of 'emergent behaviour' of a system, we continue by presenting another example: *Flocking* [401].

Example 10.3.2. *Emergent behaviours can be clearly observed in nature, in the motion of bird flocks, fish schools, or stock herds. For example, a flock of birds flies in one direction, while each bird maintains separation with the other birds. Each bird aligns its direction with the birds that are close to it, instead of following a leading bird. In addition, some separate flocks may merge into one large flock. Here, we will apply the following three rules for guiding individual behaviours to mimic the emergent flocking behaviour by using an ABS:*

- *Cohesion: each bird moves towards the average position of its neighbouring birds, but avoids collision.*
- *Alignment: each bird turns to the average heading of its neighbouring birds.*
- *Separation: each bird steers to avoid collisions with its neighbouring birds.*

For the above *Flocking* example, we model each bird as an agent in the ABS. The interaction space is a Euclidean distance space, meaning that the neighbours of a bird are determined by the Euclidean distance to it. The headings and positions of all birds are initialised randomly at the very beginning. All birds move at a constant speed. The behaviour of a bird is guided by the above three rules, applied to the information perceived from its nearby birds – that is, their headings and positions. Figure 10.4 shows a simulation of emergent *Flocking* behaviour at different time steps with 100 birds that are randomly assigned locations and headings at the beginning. The emergent behaviours of the birds can be clearly observed during the simulation.

The rules for behaviours in both *Life* and *Flocking* are very simple and intuitive; however, they result in a complex behaviour at system level through agent interactions. Therefore, this implies that complex real-world phenomena can be represented by agent-based models, even when individual agents only embed simple behaviours.

10.3.2 An Ecosystem: Predator–Prey Model

ABS is widely used in ecosystem studies. One example is the predatorprey paradigm, which we demonstrate here using the wolfsheep predation model [403] found in NegLogo model libraries.

Example 10.3.3. *In the wolfsheep predation model, wolves and sheep live in a 51 × 51 grid space (called patch) where grass can grow. From a food chain perspective,*

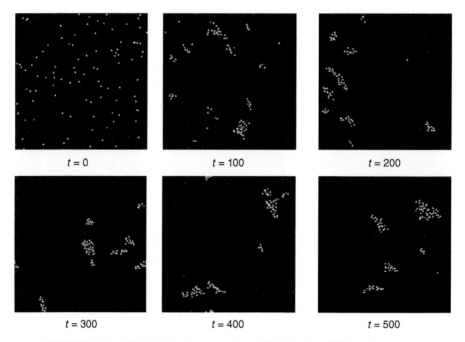

$t = 0$ $t = 100$ $t = 200$

$t = 300$ $t = 400$ $t = 500$

FIGURE 10.4 ABS of *Flocking* – motions of bird flock at different time steps.

wolves eat sheep, while sheep eat grass. Wolves and sheep randomly roam within the grid space seeking food to replenish their energy, which is in turn consumed by the movement. Both wolves and sheep die once they run out of energy. To assure the survival of their species, both wolves and sheep can reproduce and create offspring by consuming energy. However, there are reproduction rates associated with these two species, respectively. In addition, once the grass of a grid is eaten, it will only regrow after a fixed amount of time.

The default set up of this model is as follows:

- Initially, 100 sheep and 50 wolves are randomly located in the 51×51 grid:
  - The heading of each animal is randomly assigned.
  - Each animal is allocated an amount of energy:
    - A sheep has initial energy that is a uniform random number in the set $[0, 1, ..., 7]$.
    - A wolf has initial energy that is a uniform random number in the set $[0, 1, ..., 39]$.
- The time mechanism in this model is fixed-increment time advancing. At each time step:

- The heading on an animal is its previous heading plus a random value from a symmetric triangular distribution, in the interval $[-50, 50]$.
- Each animal moves forward one unit and consumes one unit of energy.
- Each animal will have offspring with a given reproduction rate:

  • A sheep will have offspring with a reproduction rate of 0.04, and half of its energy is passed to the offspring if reproduction occurs.
  • A wolf will have offspring with a reproduction rate of 0.05, and half of its energy is passed to the offspring if reproduction occurs.
  • A new offspring has an initial heading uniformly distributed in the range [0,360].

- A sheep gains four units of energy once when eating the grass in one grid.
- A wolf gains 20 units of energy when eating a sheep. A wolf randomly catches a sheep in its grid to eat.
- An animal dies when its energy is less than zero.
• It takes a certain number of time units for grass to regrow after it is eaten by sheep. The time for grass to grow in a grid is uniformly distributed from 0 to 29. Therefore, grass has different growth rates in different grids, but rates are less than 30 time units.

Figure 10.5 plots the population size of wolves and sheep, and the amount of grass over 1,000 iterations (the grass amount is on the secondary vertical axis). The equilibrium of populations is illustrated in this scenario. However, the stability of this ecosystem can be easily broken. For example, if we adjust the time for grass regrowth from 30 to 50 time units, Figure 10.6 shows that the wolves became extinct because of the reduction of sheep population caused by the slow growth rate of grass. While this is just an example using the default settings, many other interesting ecology problems can be investigated using this model.

10.3.3 Social Behaviours

In this section, we will build an ABS to simulate human behaviours at a social event, such as a party or conference. At a social event, people may or may not know each other; however, they will try to make new friends to extend their social network. We use ABS to mimic the way people make friends at a social event, as follows.

Example 10.3.4. *A number of people attend a social event. We assume that they do not know each other before the social event. Each person has the following four attributes:*

• *Age: the age of a person*
• *Occupation: the occupation of a person*

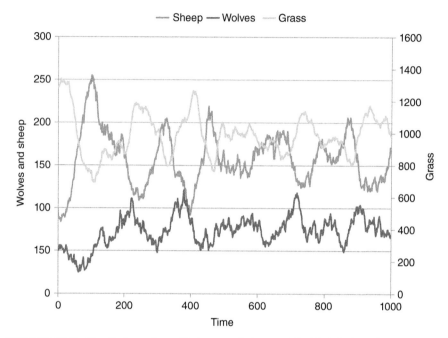

FIGURE 10.5   Results from the wolf–sheep predation model with default settings – population size over time.

- *Hobby: the hobby of a person*
- *Topic: a discussion topic that a person enjoys.*

At the social event, people wander around seeking someone to talk to. From a common sense point of view, each person tries to know and make friends with someone who has similar attributes because they are most likely to have common interests. Once a connection among two or more people is established, they will move towards each other and then stop moving and hold a conversation.

At first, people attending the social event are modelled as agents with the four attributes: age, occupation, hobby, and topic. Then, we classify the people's attributes into groups and allocate a corresponding group code as the attribute value, instead of directly using their actual values. Suppose there are five different age groups, five different occupations, five different hobbies, and five different topics found within the population of participants. Table 10.1 lists the possible codes for each attribute group. For example, the value of age is 1 for an agent who is 25 years old.

The simulator is implemented according to the following design considerations:

- The environment of the social event is a 81 × 81 square space. The environment in this simulator serves only to define the boundary of agents' moving area.
- Initially, all agents are randomly located in this space.

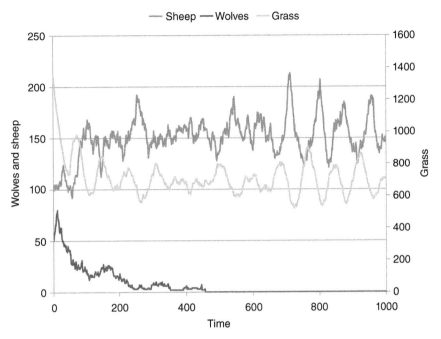

FIGURE 10.6 Results from the wolf–sheep predation model with slow grass growth rate – population sizes over time.

TABLE 10.1   Agent Attribute Groups and Associated Codes

Attribute	Codes	Meaning
Age	$\{1, 2, 3, 4, 5\}$	Five different age groups, e.g. 20s, 30s, 40s, 50s, and 60s
Occupation	$\{1, 2, 3, 4, 5\}$	Five different occupations
Hobby	$\{1, 2, 3, 4, 5\}$	Five different hobbies
Topic	$\{1, 2, 3, 4, 5\}$	Five different topics

- Each agent has four attributes that are randomly initialised:
  - Age: a code corresponds to an age range. The code is a uniform random number in the set $\{1, 2, 3, 4, 5\}$.
  - Occupation: a code corresponds to an occupation group. The code is a uniform random number in the set $\{1, 2, 3, 4, 5\}$.
  - Hobby: a code corresponds to a hobby group. The code is a uniform random number in the set $\{1, 2, 3, 4, 5\}$.
  - Topic: a code corresponds to a topic group. The code is a uniform random number in the set $\{1, 2, 3, 4, 5\}$.

- The simulator uses fixed-increment time advance. At each time step:
  - Each agent interacts with the closest agent, and makes connecting decisions. If they share at least three common attributes, they connect with each other. Otherwise, they do not connect.
  - If an agent has not been connected with others, this agent selects a random heading in the interval [0,360] for north and [0,180] for south), and moves on that heading a random number of units in the set {0, 1, 2, ..., 10}.
  - If an agent is connected with others, this agent moves towards the others. If connected agents are close enough (i.e. when the distance from the agent to the centroid of all connected agents is less than or equal to two units), they stop moving and start a conversation.

Figure 10.7 illustrates the initial state and the state at time 1800 of a simulation run initialised with 50 agents. At the beginning, all agents randomly wander around the interaction space and try to make connections with other agents who have similar attributes. As time passes, some agents connect and move towards each other. The right side picture in Figure 10.7 shows that many small groups are established, while some agents are still isolated from groups. This outcome is a common phenomenon that can be observed in any social event; thus, this example is able to replicate with certain plausibility the emergence of group-level behaviour in this context.

In addition to the above observations, there are some interesting network structures of agent connections resulting from this simulation. Let us zoom in to observe in detail three groups of participants at the party, as shown in Figure 10.8. We would like to investigate further what causes the emergence of these structures and how are different from each other.

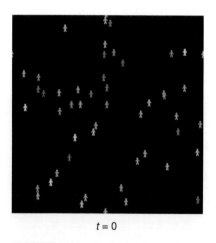 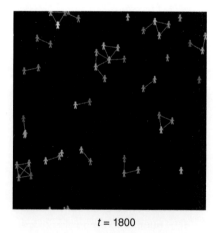

$t = 0$ $t = 1800$

FIGURE 10.7   The initial state of the social event simulation with 50 agents and a state afterwards.

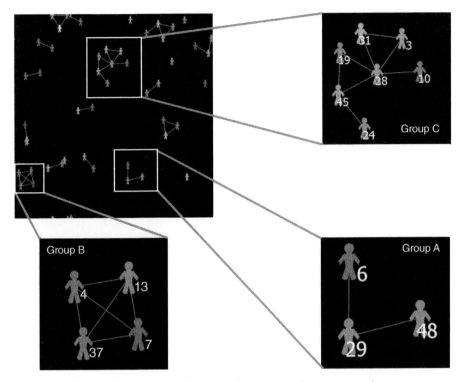

FIGURE 10.8   Interesting network structures of agent connections.

TABLE 10.2   Group A – Agents and Their Attributes

Group A	Age	Occupation	Hobby	Topic
Agent 6	1	3	1	1
Agent 29	1	3	1	2
Agent 48	3	3	1	2

For Group A, both Agent 6 and 48 are connected to Agent 29; however, interestingly, there is no connection between Agents 6 and 48. Looking closely at their attributes, listed in Table 10.2, Agent 6 shares only two common attributes with Agent 48 – occupation and hobby; therefore, it is not possible for them to connect directly. However, Agent 29 has three common attributes shared with Agents 6 and 48, and can be viewed as the intermediator for Agents 6 and 48. Therefore, Agent 6 can talk with Agent 48 through Agent 29. This is a plausible behaviour in the real world as well, when, for example, someone may know other people through a common friend.

Group B contains four agents that are fully connected with each other. Through studying their attributes, described in Table 10.3, we see that all four agents have

TABLE 10.3   Group B – Agents and Their Attributes

Group B	Age	Occupation	Hobby	Topic
Agent 4	1	3	3	3
Agent 7	3	3	3	3
Agent 13	4	3	3	3
Agent 37	2	3	3	3

TABLE 10.4   Group C – Agents and Their Attributes

Group C		Age	Occupation	Hobby	Topic
Subnet C1	Agent 3	3	2	2	1
	Agent 31	3	3	2	1
	Agent 10	2	1	2	1
Hub	Agent 28	3	1	2	1
Subnet C2	Agent 19	3	1	1	1
	Agent 45	3	1	3	1
	Agent 24	3	1	3	4

common values for occupation, hobby, and topic, while their ages are different. Hence, they are linked directly with each other in this group, and should have some exciting conversation.

Group C is the largest group observed from this scenario so far. The structure of the agent connections in this group is also complex. It contains two sub-networks that are both connected with Agent 28. Therefore, Agent 28 is the key person who acts as a hub. As Table 10.4 shows, the first sub-network includes Agents 3 and 31, who have common ages, hobbies, and topics with Agent 28, while the second sub-network contains Agents 19 and 45, who share common occupations, hobbies, and topics with Agent 28. There are also two agents (Agents 10 and 24) connected with Agents 28 and 45 individually because they do not have more than three common attributes shared with any of the two sub-networks.

As the results suggest, some interesting behaviours of the participants were exhibited at this social event, simulated through an ABS. It is possible for us to extend this simulation by applying various network topologies to the interaction to investigate how they influence the emergence of connections. For example, Agent 24 may be convinced by Agent 45 to change its itopic of interest from four to one. In such a case, the network structure will change completely.

10.4   CONCLUSION

In this chapter, we have introduced the concept of ABS and covered the most relevant ABS aspects, which include agent behaviour modelling, interaction space, and time-advancing mechanism. We also provided brief references to the topics related to ABS, such as CASs and MASs. Further, we demonstrated through two examples – *Life* and *Flocking* – that emergent complex behaviours can be obtained by aggregation of simple agent behaviours and their interactions, thereby implying that we could model and mimic complex phenomena in the real world by using simple agents in the appropriate ABS settings. We then demonstrated through other examples – the predator–prey paradigm and social event simulation – the capability of ABS to be used in various fields for both scientific research and real-world applications.

PART IV

Simulation and Computational Red Teaming Systems

CHAPTER 11

Knowledge Acquisition

11.1 INTRODUCTION

The design and development of a simulation model rely on transforming the knowledge that exists in human understanding of a system or that is already encoded in an artificial system into formal representations that could be used in a computational environment. Knowledge acquisition techniques are pertinent in this process. The remainder of this chapter stems from our previous work published in [248].

In this chapter, we structure the discussion by classifying the knowledge-acquisition methods in three categories: human, human-inspired, and autonomous machine agents. For the first two categories, the investigation is typically focused on classic cognitive task analysis. The third category treats knowledge acquisition from the perspective of autonomous knowledge discovery. Finally, we discuss an emergent fourth category of methods that are related to knowledge acquisition via red teaming and coevolution.

Knowledge acquisition (KA) attempts to understand the underpinnings of an observable phenomenon. The KA process has knowledge as the primary output, where knowledge is an abstract representation of the real phenomenon at a certain (desired) level of detail. This representation is essentially an ontological construct, which can be seen as a set of necessary and sufficient concepts that capture the underpinnings of the real phenomenon. The construct should allow one to replicate the phenomenon in a different context, alter the phenomenon or communicate the phenomenon to others. A KA process can be employed in a very broad range of situations: it can be used for learning, to create computational models that improve the behaviours of the entities under investigation, or for general problem solving.

In the context of computer simulation, acquiring knowledge about a certain real system is a prerequisite for the representation stage in the process of building a simulation. In Chapter 5, we discussed in detail the most important aspects related to representation, yet we presented a narrow view, which was necessary and sufficient for the novice reader to understand the process of building a simulation. In this

Simulation and Computational Red Teaming for Problem Solving, First Edition.
Jiangjun Tang, George Leu, and Hussein A. Abbass.

chapter, we enhance the discussion on representation by including it in the broader concept of knowledge representation, which in turn is the final stage of the much broader KA process.

In general, KA can be employed for extracting understanding about three types of entities (or systems): natural, technical, and human activity systems. The weather can be used as an example of a natural system. If one operates an aircraft fleet, then gaining understanding about the weather is paramount for purposes such as flight safety or fuel efficiency. Based on observations and/or measurements of parameters – such as temperature, pressure, or humidity – further analysis can be performed to generate a representation of the weather cycle that can be communicated to aircraft pilots. Human-made technical systems can be investigated from a KA perspective using the same tools: observations and measurements. An example from the same domain is the lifecycle of an aircraft. An aircraft is usually under permanent observation from its conception up to its decommissioning. During its lifecycle, continuous detailed measurements are performed to understand what may lead to both normal and abnormal flight behaviours. The knowledge yielding from this permanent KA process is then employed for various purposes, such as design improvement if flaws are discovered in the initial design, or communicating operational aspects to pilots and engineers.

Human activity is different from the other two categories because the tools available for the KA process are not only in the passive domain (observations and measurements). In this context, KA can be active, where the KA process involves asking or even challenging humans to obtain an understanding of their behaviour. The weather or an aircraft cannot be asked why it behaves the way it does, but humans can. Representations of humans' behaviours (i.e. knowledge) can be elicited using numerous techniques. An example is the activity of an aircraft pilot. This can be categorised as a human activity system because it encompasses all types of entities, weather, aircraft and pilot, corresponding to natural, technical, and human activity systems, respectively. These entities have their own behaviours and interact continuously; however, the pilot, through his or her skills and decision-making capabilities, is the entity responsible for steering the overall system. From a KA perspective, one may be interested in understanding the pilot's decisions and actions, and their effect on the natural and technical components of the system. The knowledge gained can be further used to improve the pilot's skills or teach those skills to other pilots. It is therefore paramount to generate a consistent representation of the behaviour of interest, and commit to this representation.

Figure 11.1 summarises the above discussion in a visual manner, presenting at a very high level the main sources of knowledge (natural, technical, and human systems), the main ways of acquiring that knowledge (observe, measure, and ask), and the acquiring agency. We note that acquisition from human activity systems involves all methods of acquiring knowledge. In addition, human activity systems embed to a great extent the knowledge underpinning the other two major types of systems (as we explained above, in the aircraft pilot example). For these two reasons, we discuss KA: (i) based on the type of acquiring agency and (ii) through the lens of human activity,

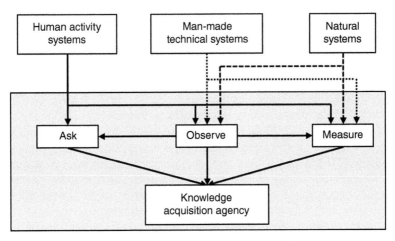

FIGURE 11.1   KA in relation to various types of systems.

considering that the methods we present cover the most general cases, yet can always be filtered and reduced to particular ones. For example, if a KA method involves asking, observation, and measuring when dealing with humans, then the same method can be adjusted to support only measuring when applied to natural phenomena.

Thus, in this chapter, we discuss KA in relation to human activity systems, and we consider three types of agencies, accounting for three categories of KA methods: human, human-inspired, and machine agents. Typically, a KA process involves interaction between one or more elicitors and one or more subject matter experts (SMEs). Human agents in a KA context mean that both the elicitors and the SMEs are humans; this is typically treated with cognitive task analysis (CTA) approaches. In the category of human-inspired agents, CTA methods are still used, but the human elicitors are substituted with computer programs that replicate their actions. Methods in the machine agents category assume that both the elicitor and the SME are computational entities. These entities have standalone behaviour, which means that the eliciting agents do not emulate known behaviours of the human elicitors, but rather autonomously extract knowledge from the SMEs. In addition, the SMEs are not human experts or their recorded behaviour; instead, they consist of artefactual data generated by the system of interest. With respect to this category of methods, the KA process can be seen as a knowledge discovery process, where the machine agents try to extract causal relations and meaning from artefactual data that are typically unstructured and/or unsorted.

The chapter is organised as follows. In Section 11.2, the core stages of the KA process are discussed and an architectural schema of this process is sketched. Sections 11.3–11.5 discuss the most important methods in each category: human, human-inspired, and machine agents. Then, Section 11.6 briefly discusses the link between KA and the CRT concept. Finally, Section 11.7 concludes the chapter.

11.2   AGENT-ENABLED KNOWLEDGE ACQUISITION: CORE PROCESSES

The KA literature typically focuses on the internal mechanism of the acquisition, and devotes less attention to describing the overall KA process, which includes the relationship between the acquisition method and the purpose of the KA exercise [98, 102, 398, 406, 407]. The decision of how to perform KA depends greatly on the purpose of the exercise. Roth et al. [338] followed a CTA perspective, and noted that KA is a task-related activity, 'with no best practice, or general methodology in place'. Kurgan and Musilek [226] adopted a knowledge discovery perspective, and identified a number of KA process models, with various numbers of stages. The authors commented on the lack of formalisation of the knowledge discovery process, since the models they identified varied from three to as many as nine stage processes.

However, some agreement exists on the major components of the KA process, regardless of its purpose, with many studies acknowledging a 'big 3 model'. In [48], the three stages are 'data elicitation' from the SMEs; 'data interpretation', which infers the knowledge from the elicited data; and 'knowledge modelling', which represents the inferred knowledge using a (computational) model. Similarly, in [98], Cooke considered the three stages to be 'knowledge elicitation', 'knowledge explication', and 'knowledge formalisation'. Cooke also noted that the goal of KA is 'to externalise the knowledge into a form that can be later implemented in a computer'. This promotes the idea that the resultant representation should be computational in nature. This idea is also mentioned in other studies, such as [48, 165], and [217]. In relation to the elicitation stage, a distinction is made in the literature [104, 131] between the knowledge elicited from humans and other sources, such as task documentation or historical data. However, Cooke noted that the knowledge resultant from this extraction process should be verified and enriched with that from elicitation of human SMEs. Later, in a study by Crandall et al. [102], KA was presented in a similar manner, with the stages called 'knowledge elicitation', 'data analysis', and 'knowledge representation'. Elicitation was seen as the activity of collecting information about 'judgements, strategies, knowledge, and skills that underlie performance', with no concern about the source of data (human SME or otherwise). The data analysis stage was described as consisting of actions taken for 'structuring data, identifying findings, and discovering meaning'. The difference from the earlier view of Cooke is in the knowledge representation stage, which in Crandall et al. focused on externalising and presenting the data. In Cooke's study, this was the goal of the whole KA exercise. In addition, Cooke explicitly associated the formalisation stage with the formulation of a computational model, while Crandall et al. noted that representation is 'displaying data, presenting findings, and communicating meaning', with an emphasis on communicating the outcome of the data analysis. An approach different from those discussed above was presented in two studies by Yates and Feldon [406, 407], where the authors agreed on the three-stage KA process, yet emphasised that the last two stages – analysis and representation – are typically handled together. They noted that these cannot be easily separated when modelling the elicited knowledge. The literature on knowledge discovery also acknowledges the three-stage approach. In this research direction, the three stages are called 'data pre-processing', 'data mining', and 'knowledge interpretation and evaluation' [64, 297, 298, 303].

Following the above discussion, it became apparent that there is a need for a universal process model to support KA. The discussion showed that there is sufficient work in the literature in this direction, yet not sufficient consensus. Therefore, we need to summarise the existing literature and commit to a KA process model that illustrates the relationship between the KA agencies and the KA process. To achieve this, we first give an intuitive example. Consider that one intends to extract knowledge about the behaviour of aircraft pilots to communicate this knowledge to pilot schools to improve pilot training curricula. In this case, the first question is whether the pilots are available in person for the KA exercise, or whether the exercise will be run on artefacts of their activity (these can be, for example, flight data from onboard computers). If the pilots are available, one would need to know how many of them participate in the KA process. If only a few pilots are available, then one or several human elicitors (i.e. human agency) would be enough. If the number of pilots is very large (e.g. the pilot cohort of an airline), then automated/computerised versions of the human elicitors (i.e. human-inspired agency) will be needed to handle them. If no pilot is available and only artefactual data of their activity are available, then, again, the amount of available data leads to various options. If a low amount of data is available, the analysis can be performed by humans; this would apply to simple data, such as the change of course. If large amounts of data are available (i.e. detailed records of all manoeuvres), then machine agents should be employed to mine these data. Figure 11.2 shows a generalisation of the above example. The figure proposes a decision tree to support the modeller in identifying the appropriate methods throughout the KA process, and also shows how the three types of KA agents can contribute to KA.

11.3 HUMAN AGENTS

The literature on human-based KA is vast, with numerous approaches adopted in recent decades [94, 98]. Very thorough and well documented surveys of the classic KA approaches have been published in the past, mainly during the 1990s and early 2000s [48, 98, 351, 398]. More recently, in the last decade, several important reviews discussed modern human-based KA methods [94, 181, 380, 406]. In this section, we briefly describe the most relevant categories of methods belonging to human-based KA, and summarise the most important methods belonging to each of them. To guide the discussion, we illustrate in Figure 11.3 how human agent methods map onto the KA process.

11.3.1 Informal Methods

Observations and interviews are the most popular techniques in this category, being typically used in direct acquisition. In these, a human elicitor tries to extract knowledge about task performance from a human SME from their observed (observations)

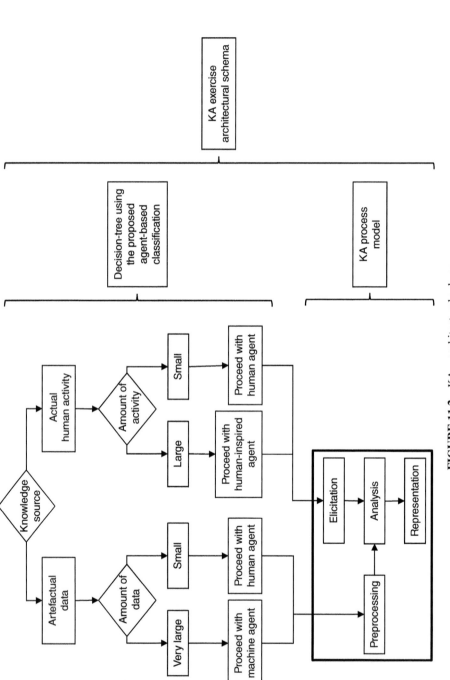

FIGURE 11.2 KA – architectural schema.

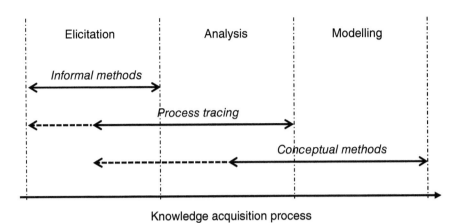

FIGURE 11.3   Human agent methods mapped on the KA process: solid line – ample coverage, dashed line – limited coverage.

actions and/or from their active response to task-related enquiries (interviews). The methods are highly informal, verbal and descriptive, and usually require that the elicitor has substantial domain knowledge. Alternatively, the elicitor may not have domain knowledge, but in this case should be highly qualified and experienced in interviewing techniques. The methods in this category are useful in the initial stage of KA (see Figure 11.3) when there is a need to form an initial view on the task or problem domain.

Observation methods try to extract meaningful information from the observed human behaviour that occurs during the performance of a task. They can be applied either directly, when the human performs the actual task, or indirectly to records of that performance [121, 180]. Meyer [282] noted that observation is typically used in 'manual' KA, when the knowledge engineer needs to become familiar with the domain. This familiarisation should occur before other techniques are employed, such as interviews or more formal methods. Observations gather details about the conscious and unconscious behaviour of the human SMEs and investigate how the development of their expertise occurs. Cooke [98] described three fundamental observation techniques: 'active participation', 'focused observation', and 'structured observation'. We note that observation is largely perceived as a passive activity. However, in some cases, the elicitor participates in the task together with the SMEs; this is known as active observation, since the elicitor observes while doing. Hoffman [180] provided six categories of tasks to which observations can be applied: familiar tasks, simulated familiar tasks, limited information tasks, constraint processing tasks, combined constraints tasks, and tough cases.

Interviews are another important approach to informal human agent KA. Interviews can be structured or unstructured, can be direct or indirect, and may include explicit or implied questions [98, 180, 398]. Unlike observations, interviews are typically retrospective in nature – that is, the SMEs are asked to recall details about tasks performed in the past. The structured interviews are predefined to various extents in terms of their content and sequencing [98]. In relation to how strictly they follow the predetermined format, interviews can be structured, semi-structured, or prompted. The structured interviews provide systematic and fairly complete insights into the domain of interest, and have relatively short duration in general. However, they require increased preparation effort in advance before the interview actually occurs. The literature [94, 98, 282] identifies nine major techniques for performing structured interviews: focused discussions, teach-back, role play, twenty-questions, Cloze experiment, Likert scale items, question-answering protocols, question-naires, and group interview techniques. Unlike structured interviews, unstructured interviews do not follow a predetermined format. The elicitor proceeds freely and adapts to the SME's behaviour, uncovering as much information as the subject can retrieve. Unstructured interviews are typically employed, and well suited, to the early stages of eliciting [98]. They do not require that the elicitor possesses any domain knowledge, but require highly qualified and experienced interviewers, which in turn requires great effort in training the elicitors on how to guide interviews. Another drawback of unstructured interviews is that the data they output may be 'copious and unwieldy' [398].

11.3.2 Semi-formal Methods

Semi-formal approaches are usually known as process tracing methods. These methods use think-aloud protocols to extract information about the performance of a SME on a task or set of tasks. They can occur either while the tasks are performed or via subsequent recalls of that performance. Process tracing methods are highly dependent on the tasks performed, similar to informal methods. They require that the elicitor has expertise in the problem domain. The difference from informal methods is that direct interaction with the SME is not essential, and the data that need to be captured from the SME are predefined. The process tracing approach is generally considered more formal than observations and interviews, and is applied in the elicitation and analysis stages of KA (see Figure 11.3). This facilitates understanding of the cognitive structure of task performance. The literature on semi-formal methods categorises the methods into four large groups: verbal reports, non-verbal reports, cognitive walk-through, and decision analysis [98, 398]. These will be briefly described in the following paragraphs. For more comprehensive discussions, several detailed reviews can be consulted [41, 98, 181, 398].

Methods in the verbal report category [148, 172, 245] consider that the elicitors capture information based on how the SMEs verbally describe their reasoning for performing the task in a certain way. Verbal reports can be self-reported if the SME comments on his or her own experience, or shadowed if another SME comments on the way the subject performs the task. The communication can be online, when the SME speaks while performing the task, or offline, when the SME explains things retrospectively. These methods are typically used in the initial stage of knowledge elicitation, and provide the raw data that can be further used for more formal analysis.

Methods in the non-verbal report category [98, 148, 163, 342] collect the data of interest through means other than verbal. These means can be inputs for

computer-based tasks, such as mouse or keystrokes; body movement communication, such as facial expressions or gait; or psycho-physiological data, such as
electroencephalography, galvanic skin response, and heart rate. Similar to the verbal
reports, the non-verbal reports are employed in the initial stage of knowledge
elicitation.

In cognitive walk-through [108, 228, 263, 398], the elicitor goes through the task of
interest and asks questions from the perspective of the user. This involves establishing
a sequence of actions that a subject must take to perform the task, and a set of system
responses to these actions. Then the actual questioning sequence follows, when the
elicitor goes through the task asking questions to themselves. Typically, the cognitive
walk-through operates through verbal protocols, having the advantage that is easy to
implement and cost-effective.

Decision analysis [54, 98, 398] is used to analyse quantitatively the decision points
within a task. This requires that the decision points have already been identified
using other early stage methods, such as verbal and non-verbal reports or cognitive
walk-through. Therefore, decision analysis is mainly employed in the analysis stage
of KA, after the initial elicitation has been performed. Methods in the decision analysis category use statistical techniques to generate quantitative information related to
the decision points of interest. For comprehensive discussions on decision analysis,
several detailed reviews can be consulted in [122, 191, 211].

11.3.3 Conceptual Methods

Conceptual methods generate structured, interrelated representations of concepts
of interest within a problem domain. Typically, these methods are indirect, using
multiple sources of domain expertise. These sources can be humans or artefacts of
humans' activity, such as task documentation, logs, and practitioners' guides. The
aggregated output of these sources is used to form a composite structural representation of the acquired knowledge (see Figure 11.3). Several broad families of methods
are described in the literature in relation to conceptual methods [98, 362]: diagramming, conceptual graph analysis, error analysis, repertory grids, and sensory-motor
process charts. These are briefly described in the following paragraphs.

Diagramming methods are perhaps the most commonly used approaches to general knowledge representation. They illustrate intuitively the key concepts that subsume all the other aspects of the task or domain of interest [332, 398]. Apart from
being very intuitive, they also require low effort to generate. Simple diagrams can
represent very complex tasks with little time and cost required to produce them. A
drawback is that if the task complexity is about a certain level, the resultant diagrams
may also need to be complex to be able to properly represent the tasks. In this case,
diagrams alone are insufficient, and other complementary methods usually need to
be used to produce more consistent representations.

Methods grouped under conceptual graph analysis [162] produce conceptual
maps of the tasks of interest by using graph theoretical representations. In these
graphs, the nodes represent events, goals, states or actions, and the links (directional
or non-directional) indicate the relationships between the elements represented in

nodes. The graphs can describe various structures of the concepts, such as spatial, causal, or taxonomic. In essence, these methods can be seen as a structured way to transfer knowledge from an implicit to an explicit form.

Error analysis [398] attempts to identify the sources of errors and categorise these errors. The methods capture all errors made by SMEs during the performance of the task, and then analyse them to establish relationships with the cognitive processes involved. This means that they map the errors onto the corresponding cognitive processing failures. The advantage of using error analysis methods is that they offer in-depth insight into the intimate cognitive processes and functions, which further leads to realistic representations of thought processes. However, their use is usually limited to those tasks that are prone to errors, such as safety critical domains or investigation of incidents [215].

A repertory grid [55, 398] is a category of methods that rate the task-related concepts along so-called 'dichotomous dimensions', also known as 'constructs' [98]. The constructs are organised hierarchically to separate various domain concepts. The SMEs give the elicitor ratings for the various constructs identified, and these are placed into grids, on rows and columns, according to the rating. Distance metrics, such as relatedness or proximity, are then extracted from the grid by calculating the correlation between the rated constructs. The output of repertory grid techniques cannot be used as a representation, and needs further efforts to properly model the knowledge. Applicable methods are hierarchical clustering or similar.

Another important category of formal methods is sensory-motor process charts. These methods focus on the mental activity [204, 398] of SMEs, taking into account sensing and sensory information and their relationship to the task of interest. The output of these methods is in the form of skill charts yielding from the patterns observed during the task performance. Typically, these methods apply a set of predefined steps, which account for the key mental activities involved in psycho-motor tasks – that is, planning, initiating, controlling, ending, and checking [398].

11.4 HUMAN-INSPIRED AGENTS

Methods in the category of human-inspired agent are essentially automated versions of human agent methods. They are used to speed up the KA process when the amount of data exceeds the capabilities of human elicitors, or when these elicitors are not available. The human-inspired KA agents provide a substantial contribution to the KA literature by advancing KA-related activities from entirely human-based efforts towards entirely human-independent efforts. Human-inspired KA agents do not bring new approaches to the intrinsic mechanisms of the acquisition; instead, they propose new ways of implementing the human-based methods in computer programs. Therefore, these methods contribute to the body of research and literature with their capabilities in emulating and automating human agent actions, with the purpose of enhancing the speed and increasing the convenience of the KA process.

The literature on human-inspired KA agents can be seen from two perspectives, which will be discussed in the following subsections. The first perspective

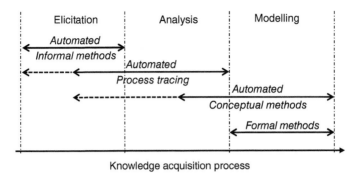

FIGURE 11.4   Human-inspired agent methods mapped on the KA process: solid line – ample coverage, dashed line – limited coverage.

captures work on automating classic human-based KA, especially informal and semi-formal methods, such as automated interviews and automated analysis of verbal and non-verbal protocols [98, 152]. The second perspective captures standalone implementations of models of human activity and thought as part of formal KA techniques [94, 398]. Figure 11.4 provides an illustration of how the human-inspired agent methods map on the KA process.

11.4.1 Automated Human Agent Methods

Work on automation of the informal methods consists of computer programs that provide either fully automated or semi-automated interviews. The most popular classic tools described in the literature are Cognosys [404], MORE [206] and its enhanced version MOLE [130], SALT [266], and ASK [171].

Work on the automation of semi-formal methods (i.e. process tracing) has focused on computer programs automating the verbal protocol analysis methods. These were used to record and analyse automatically the thinking aloud about tasks which SMEs provided. The most popular classic tools reported by the literature in this direction were programs such as Cognosys [404], KRITON [116], LAPS [182], MACAO [29], and MEDKAT [199].

Work on the automation of conceptual methods concentrated on two directions. In the first direction, the computer programs were used for structuring knowledge. The tools reported in the literature were related to psychological scaling, such as AQUINAS, KRITON, IRA-Grid, and FLEXIGrid [48, 81]. In the second direction, the efforts were focused on various personal-construct psychology-related methods, with the purpose of eliciting and analysing knowledge. Most of the tools reported in the literature concentrated on repertory grids, such as AQUINAS, ETS and IRA-Grid, FLEXIGrid, KRITON, KITTEN, and SMEE [145, 300].

The above methods have been also applied in domains that are less explored by classic KA. The literature reported work in directions such as virtual environments, worlds and societies, or computer games [31, 176, 313, 319], where the knowledge is extracted from artificial, computer-generated entities, instead of humans, and the resultant artefactual data of their activity. In [313], for example, the online artificial society game *Second Life* is used for automated data collection. The study proposes artificial elicitors that extract knowledge from the avatars populating the *Second Life* environment. *Second Life* is also used in [176], where human-inspired KA is implemented as software-controlled 'bot' avatars to collect data automatically. The framework proposed in [176] compares the KA results of a human elicitor controlling an avatar with those of a 'bot' controlling the avatar, where the two interview characters (both human-controlled and computer-generated avatars) are from *Second Life*. Yee and Bailenson [408] sought to collect longitudinal behavioural data from virtual worlds, and proposed a KA framework that allows the extraction of avatar-related data for several weeks in real time, with a temporal resolution below one minute.

11.4.2   Formal Knowledge Acquisition Methods

Formal methods are used only for the knowledge representation stages (see Figure 11.4). In these methods, the KA process is implemented using computer simulations that model human activity. Thus, the acquisition process is not based on the actual performance of the tasks or records of it, but on models of humans built on various assumptions [398]. The literature considers that these methods are inspired from assumed understanding of the human mind and cognition, and are formalised into computational models that attempt to replicate human behaviour [94, 102, 181, 398]. Most of the work in this direction is based on cognitive architectures for general intelligence, which aim to recreate computationally various human problem-solving and decision-making processes. The most important approaches to this category of methods are discussed in the following paragraphs.

The Human Processor is a model inspired from the human information processor theory [68, 69], and was intended to be a framework for humancomputer interaction. It consists of three interconnected processors – perceptual, cognitive and motor – and several memory stores that serve general storage and/or processing purposes [254]. In KA, the methods in the Human Processor framework can be employed to model various parameters that participate in breaking down complex tasks into detailed components, while also considering temporal aspects. The task decomposition in relation to the corresponding cognitive processes and skills is typically very detailed, up to an 'atomistic' [398] level. This leads to very accurate results, especially when the tasks to be modelled are simple enough to allow easy decomposition.

Goals, Operators, Methods, and Selection rules (GOMS) was also presented initially as a humancomputer interaction framework, starting from human information processor [25, 73, 125, 166, 214], but with the task modelling and decomposition focused on higher-level cognitive processes. In KA, GOMS can be applied to error-free tasks, where the sequence of actions that must be taken is known. Depending on this sequence, GOMS provides understanding of the interaction between the system and its user(s). This makes the model highly task specific, which means that major rework is needed to apply it to new tasks. Several GOMS versions have been reported in the literature, including Basic GOMS, Natural GOMS Language, and Cognitive-Perceptual-Motor GOMS [363, 398].

The Adaptive Character of Thought (ACT) framework was inspired by the 'ACT*' introduced by Anderson in the 1980s [18]. Its implementation takes the form of a cognitive agent architecture [19, 62, 344]. In ACT, the authors start with the assumption that cognition emerges from the interaction between procedural and declarative knowledge. In the proposed framework, procedural knowledge is represented by units called 'production rules', which encode various changes in the environment. The declarative knowledge is represented using another type of units, called 'chunks'. These encode objects that exist or operate in the environment. In KA, the ACT framework is concerned with skill acquisition, and is typically employed in the problem-solving domain, assuming a problem-solving structure of the 'means-ends' type [398]. In essence, ACT is a way to understand how complex problem-solving skills are learned, and, in doing so, it can represent both declarative and procedural knowledge. The ACT-based representation of knowledge (ARK) model [98, 155, 274, 398] is an extension of the ACT framework in which goal decomposition is used as the main tool. ARK employs a procedure that divides goals into sub-goals and/or actions. Further, it uses ACT production rules to model goal–sub-goal, and goal–action relationships as a network of objects and their interactions. The ARK framework is able to represent consistently the network-based representation of the domain knowledge, as well as the corresponding procedures applied to that knowledge.

Another important framework is that of the standalone cognitive simulation methods [339, 398]. The methods in this category use inputs from scenarios in the domain of interest to generate realistic cognitive computational models that can then be investigated against the actual observed human behaviour. The models gradually evolved to become cognitive agent architectures for general intelligence, which aimed to produce behaviour not limited to the same scenarios used to build them. In KA, the scope of cognitive simulation is reduced to replicating through simulation behaviours related to the tasks of interest. The purpose of this is to allow further analysis and decomposition in increasingly high levels of detail. Examples of cognitive simulation frameworks are Cognitive Environment Simulation (CES) [339], SOAR [229], CLARION [369], CogAff [95], and Society of Mind [251]. All these frameworks were proposed during the 1980s and have been continuously updated and maintained over the years, up to the present. They have eventuated in complex cognitive architectures that are largely used currently for modelling knowledge and behaviour in a wide range of application fields [251].

11.5 MACHINE AGENTS

The way that machine agents acquire knowledge no longer resembles or depends on the way humans perform tasks. On the one hand, they implement KA processes that are not intended to be plausible from the human elicitor's point of view. On the other hand, they acquire data from unattended artefactual data resulting from human activity systems, instead of humans or their recorded behaviour. As such, the machine agents employ a variety of computational intelligence technologies to perform a human-independent KA process, known as autonomous knowledge discovery. Through this, they aim to generate useful models of the knowledge hidden in the artefactual data.

11.5.1 Technologies that Enable Agents for Knowledge Acquisition

Before discussing the KA methods that use machine agents, it is necessary to understand the major technologies that allow the existence of these agents. When summarising the relevant literature, it became apparent that statistical analysis, machine learning, and evolutionary computation are the three main enabling technologies for machine agent KA. Techniques in these three categories can be employed separately or combined to implement agents capable of performing the autonomous KA process. In essence, these techniques are based on the foundations of learning and optimisation discussed in Chapter 12. Thus, for the novice reader, Chapter 12 is important for gaining better understanding of how KA through machine agents operates.

11.5.1.1 Statistical Analysis   In autonomous knowledge discovery contexts, statistical analysis methods are mainly employed to extract the structure [203] and/or causal relations [186] hidden in artefactual data. From the KA process point of view, statistical analysis captures and disseminates data mathematically to define models for prediction. Some of the most important approaches reported in the literature are Bayesian networks [301], rule-based methods [200], k-means techniques [209], regression analysis [120], and decision tree analysis [336]. While this list is not exhaustive, these approaches have generated a substantial amount of research, not only in general KA, but also in the KA related to human activity systems, which is the focus of this chapter. Detailed discussions on the formalism and theoretical grounds of these methods can be found in [8]. In addition, thorough descriptions of their application in KA can be found in [43, 208].

The main benefit of using statistical analysis methods is that they have a strong mathematical foundation; hence, they can offer well-defined and reliable insights into the mechanisms underpinning the artefactual data of interest. The drawback is that they can only handle well-structured data [42]. The typical use of the statistical analysis methods is in the inference modules [84, 205], which are employed for tasks such as data pre-processing, rule mining, and clustering/classification.

11.5.1.2 Machine Learning   Machine learning attempts to give artificial agents the ability to autonomously learn facts about various phenomena. From the KA point of view, this equates with the ability to uncover and understand the structure and causal relations hidden in the artefactual data. The two main types of machine learning are supervised and unsupervised. In supervised learning, the existence of prior domain knowledge is assumed, whereas, in unsupervised learning, the machine agents operate independently in the knowledge discovery process.

Examples of the most important paradigms in machine learning are inductive logic programming [100, 304], support vector machines [312, 330], reinforcement learning [219, 243], and artificial meural networks [72, 82, 200]. These paradigms have generated perhaps the most significant body of research in the KA field. For more detailed discussions on machine learning, the following reviews can be consulted [208, 269, 291].

It is common in knowledge discovery exercises that machine learning is used together with statistical methods to extract information from non-linear and multidimensional datasets, which cannot be handled by statistical methods alone. Examples include the use of neural networks supported by symbolic production systems in the form of rule sets (crisp, rough, or fuzzy). As a consequence, usually, the machine agent KA employs various combinations of machine learning methods, which in turn use subsequent statistical analysis. This leads to complex integrated machine agents that typically cover more than one stage in the KA process.

11.5.1.3 Evolutionary Computation Evolutionary computation (EC) provides robust search techniques that perform a convenient mix of global and local search in the solution space. This makes them versatile methods in the KA context. However, EC is not used as a standalone method to implement acquisition tasks, such as feature selection, rule mining, clustering, or classification. Instead, it evolves the parameters of other methods with the purpose of improving the quality of knowledge captured by those methods. EC has been used successfully in the processing of large quantities of raw noisy data, where large numbers of parameters used by other standalone KA methods needed to be optimised so that the respective methods could perform optimally [135, 303].

Most of the EC techniques applied in KA belong to the category of standard genetic algorithms (GAs), both the single and multi-objective versions. Thorough reviews of the applications of these can be found in [34, 113, 216, 225, 296]. Some non-standard EC techniques have also been used in KA tasks, such as the non-dominated sorting GA [14, 196], niched Pareto GA [126], evolutionary multi-objective algorithm for feature selection [388], and evolutionary local search algorithm [216, 411]. For the interested reader, [298] and [297] offer very comprehensive reviews of the EC techniques used in various KA applications for tasks such as feature selection, classification, clustering, and association rule mining.

Machine agents can use one or several EC techniques, which can further use statistical analysis and/or machine learning methods. The resultant machine agents may cover more than one stage of the KA process.

11.5.2   Mining Agents

Autonomous knowledge discovery extensively uses machine agents. In [65, 66], it is noted that autonomous agents and knowledge discovery emerged as separate standalone research fields; however, later, some of the methods merged into a new field of research – 'agent mining'. The agent mining concept has been intensely

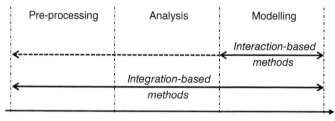

FIGURE 11.5   Machine agent methods mapped to the KA process: solid line – ample coverage, dashed line – limited coverage.

discussed in many studies [32, 67, 84, 205, 293]. Mining agents have been proposed under different names, such as knowledge-driven agents [32], knowledge collector agents [293], and miner agents [13, 84]. In a study by Cao et al. [65], three major approaches were identified in relation to KA/knowledge discovery: data mining-driven agents, agent-driven data mining, and their successor – agent mining. In the data mining-driven agents approach, the data mining and knowledge discovery methods enhance the capabilities of the agents. For the agent-driven data mining approach, the opposite occurs – agent technologies are employed to improve data mining. The agent mining approach combines the two approaches – agent and multi-agent technologies with data mining and knowledge discovery methods.

The above discussion is important to illustrate how research interest converged towards autonomous knowledge discovery powered by machine agents. Two major categories of agents play an important role in autonomous knowledge discovery, and are discussed further in this chapter: interaction-based and integration-based agents. Figure 11.5 displays how these two machine agent paradigms relate to the KA process.

The interaction-based methods pertain to the multi-agent paradigm, where the learning mechanism underlying the KA process is implemented using various interactions and behaviours, such as collaboration, cooperation, negotiation, competition, and imitation [173, 326, 341, 412]. While many types of social interactions exist, the literature only reports significant amounts of work for collaboration, cooperation, and negotiation, in relation to knowledge discovery. Detailed discussions on interaction-based agents can be found in [9, 83, 173, 251, 326, 353] for collaborative approaches and in [13, 87, 118, 235] for cooperation and negotiation (including cooperative negotiation approaches).

The integration-based methods are mostly concerned with single agents. They usually employ complex autonomous agents that perform the mining individually. These agents integrate one or more of the enabling technologies to perform the knowledge discovery tasks of interest [86, 205, 293], such as rule extraction clustering and classification. Chemchem and Drias [84] categorised the integration approaches into three major streams: agents based on expert systems, agents based on machine learning, and agents based on data mining. Most of the existing literature acknowledges that all frameworks proposed over time integrate to various extents these three major types of agents under different names, such as sub-agents, modules, components, units, and processes. The interested reader can find more detailed discussions, as well as a number of relevant instantiations of integration agents, in the following studies [32, 84, 86, 135, 205, 293, 355].

11.6 SUMMARY DISCUSSION AND PERSPECTIVES ON KNOWLEDGE ACQUISITION

The previous sections of this chapter discussed KA in human activity systems from an agent point of view. A summary of this point of view was illustrated in Figure 11.2, which can also act as a roadmap – a decision tree – associated with the KA process model. A refinement of this illustration, which considers the discussion provided thus far in the chapter is now shown in Figure 11.6. In addition to providing decision support, the agent view on KA can also indicate the performance level that can be achieved by each type of agent, based on the trade-off between the size of the knowledge source and the level of detail for analysis and representation. This idea is summarised in Figure 11.6, where a trade-off curve is displayed for each type of agent.

In the following, we discuss two possible directions that are candidates for significant work in KA: co-evolutionary KA and challenge-based KA.

The work discussed in this chapter does not take into account the change in the knowledge-acquiring agent generated by the interaction with the knowledge-sourcing agent. Thus, the agents discussed thus far do not employ mechanisms to handle the

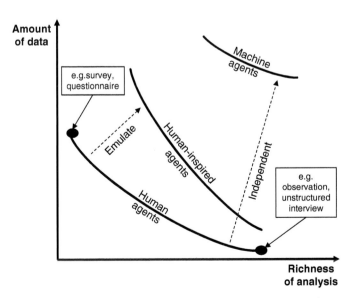

FIGURE 11.6 The proposed agent perspective: the data size – analysis/representation trade-off.

change in their own level of knowledge. For example, if their perception about the acquired knowledge changes during the KA process, this may significantly influence the ontological construct they generate to represent the knowledge. From this point of view, the KA process can be considered a coevolution process in which both parties interact and gradually improve their understanding of the problem. The literature reports a very small number of studies that relate coevolution to KA [255, 394], but an explicit classification of the work is not yet available.

Challenging is another aspect that is not present in the literature discussed thus far. KA methods usually focus on extracting knowledge from a source. Depending on the types of eliciting and sourcing entities, some amount of interaction may be considered; however, this interaction is not at the level where the eliciting entity challenges the sourcing entity towards knowledge improvement. An example illustrating this idea is an elicitor that intends to acquire knowledge about a problem, yet the sourcing entity is not sufficiently knowledgeable to satisfy the elicitor's needs. In this case, the elicitor can choose to challenge the sourcing entity towards learning about the domain, which later can lead to capturing knowledge of better quality. This was recently described as part of the CRT paradigm [4, 12, 318]; however, literature related to KA is still in its infancy.

Coevolution and CRT can complement the agent view on KA with two more perspectives: (i) the level of autonomy present in the interaction between eliciting and sourcing agents and (ii) the ability of the KA techniques to support this interaction. The first aspect is concerned with the ability of a KA agent to autonomously search

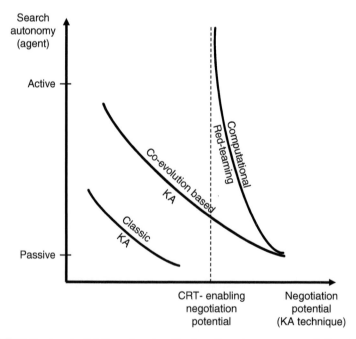

FIGURE 11.7   A potential three-tier classification: the autonomy – negotiation trade-off.

for a relevant ontological construct and further fill it with the appropriate elements. At one end of the spectrum, a passive agent can only handle the data made available to it, and fill the agreed ontological construct using those data. At the other end of the spectrum, an active agent should search autonomously for data that contribute to filling the ontological construct. An example is a human agent who interviews an SME. Here, the human elicitor can actively seek for clarifications if the SME's answers are not filling the ontological construct as required. The second aspect considers the ability of the KA agents to negotiate the ontological construct such that they achieve the agreed KA goals.

It becomes apparent from the above discussion that a trade-off exists between the two aspects, which is the basis of a potential three-tier classification using coevolution and CRT. Figure 11.7 illustrates this classification as three trade-off curves. The curve with the lowest performance essentially accounts for the classic views on KA. The other two curves, in increasing order of performance, are the co-evolutionary and CRT-based views.

CHAPTER 12

Computational Intelligence

This chapter reviews the modelling and simulation process by considering some additional steps. There are five stages when evolving the modelling and simulation process towards an adaptive solution to a real-world problem. To apply this process, advanced computational intelligence approaches involving optimisation and/or data mining techniques are required. Thus, this chapter also introduces some of these techniques, such as EC and artificial neural networks, which were inspired by natural phenomena and imitate the behaviour of evolution and the brain, respectively. Both techniques are widely used in optimisation, machine learning, and many other areas. They can also be combined with modelling and simulation for particular studies.

12.1 INTRODUCTION

Most discussions in the previous chapters concentrated on how to model and simulate a real system with regard to some objectives. These discussions were based on a process adapted from [3]. The initial steps of this process are depicted in Figure 12.1, where a modeller builds a model and implements a simulator based on some level of problem understanding, their own perception and the tasks at hand, including the purpose of the model and their individual biases.

Once the model is built and a simulator is implemented, validation and verification must be undertaken to check whether the model reproduces the behaviour of the real system and whether the simulator was implemented properly. Both questions are answered by the components added in Figure 12.2.

Further, the behaviours observed from both the real system and the simulation are recorded, and then some analysis or data mining methods can be applied to them for comparison. This comparison offers a simple way to validate the model against the real system. Verification is an internal process that compares the model specification to the simulator's implementation. The data recorded from the simulation allow the modeller to apply verification techniques. The system illustrated in Figure 12.2 can imitate the real system faithfully, and then creates opportunities for us to investigate problems that can be tested on a simulation, but not on the real system, such as

Simulation and Computational Red Teaming for Problem Solving, First Edition.
Jiangjun Tang, George Leu, and Hussein A. Abbass.

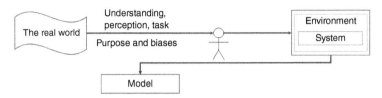

FIGURE 12.1   Stage 1 – basic steps of modelling and simulation.

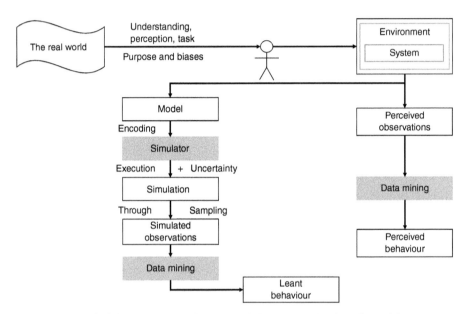

FIGURE 12.2   Stage 2 – real system and simulation behaviour data mining.

optimising the road traffic flow at an intersection by changing the traffic light control sequences and timing.

If we add an optimisation loop that connects the simulation and the real world, as shown in Figure 12.3, we can use the simulation to find the optimal solution for an objective function. For the traffic light example, the optimisation component takes the output from the simulation (i.e. the traffic flow) and then tries to manipulate the control sequences or the timing, which are fed back to simulation to maximise the flow. Here, the optimisation component is called 'behavioural optimisation' because it mainly focuses on reproducing the behaviour of the system without necessarily considering the differences between the model's internal mechanism and the real system's internal working mechanism. For the traffic light example, we only need to know that the traffic light changes colours in a particular sequence, without necessarily knowing how these colours are actually changing (i.e. the electrical hardware operation). There are many ways to design and implement the optimisation components, such as the EC techniques, which will be introduced in Section 12.2.

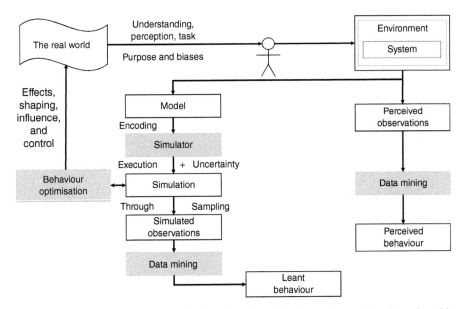

FIGURE 12.3 Stage 3 – optimisation loop for effects, shaping, and control on the real world.

As shown in Figure 12.4, we can also add another component to ask the simulation questions that reveal patterns that we cannot reveal in the real world. The simplest case is to ask simulation 'what–if' questions. Data mining techniques can be applied here to extract indirect patterns and generalisations on the real system. By using the system illustrated in Figure 12.4, we can perform in the simulated environment experiments that cannot be performed in the real world, extract information from the simulation without touching the real system, and predict the effect of changing something in the system.

The system discussed thus far presents a static view of a model and the associated simulator. However, in many cases, the real systems may exhibit internal changes that occur late, after the model has been created. This leads to the model drifting away from the real system – an issue that requires a lot of effort and time to modify the existing model according to the real-world changes. Sometimes, an entirely new model must be built because the patches applied to the existing model cannot catch up with the changes the real system experiences. Figure 12.5 shows how this issue can be addressed by introducing an error calculation component to calculate the differences between the model and the real system. Then, an optimisation component can be applied to make adjustments to the model, so that the errors are minimised. Further, the whole process can be automated by closing the appropriate feedback loops.

The above five stages for modelling and simulation require optimisation and data mining techniques, as seen in the figures. There are many ways to perform optimisation and data mining. In this chapter, we will focus on two techniques: EC and artificial neural networks (ANNs). Both are inspired by nature and simulate biological

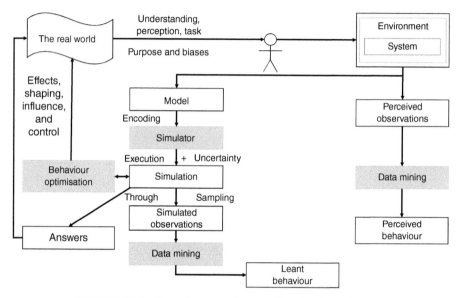

FIGURE 12.4   Stage 4 – answering questions for the real world.

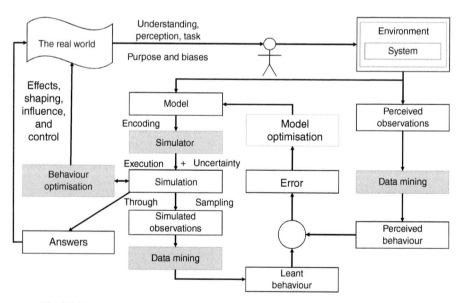

FIGURE 12.5   Stage 5 – model adaptation to system and environment changes.

phenomena. EC employs some of the biological mechanisms of genetic evolution and works with populations of solutions to solve optimisation or machine learning tasks. ANNs emulate to various extents the operation of the brain and imitate behaviours such as perception, pattern recognition, and feature extraction. Both of them are discussed in the following sections.

12.2 EVOLUTIONARY COMPUTATION

12.2.1 Evolutionary Computation Background

EC refers to employing computational models inspired from natural evolution to solve various problems of interest. The subsequent techniques and methods used under the EC paradigm are typically referred to as evolutionary algorithms (EAs). These build to various extents on Darwinian and neo-Darwinian views on evolution by employing abstractions of paradigms such as *natural selection* and *survival of the fittest* to perform stochastic searches for the optimal solutions to the problems of interest.

A colloquial view of evolution that serves well to introduce EC to the novice is as follows. Consider a population of individuals operating in its environmental niche. An environmental pressure applies to the current generation of individuals, leading to a mechanism that selects those individuals that fit best in the environment. In this process, the individuals with the best fit have more chances of reproducing than those with a lower fit; thus, favourable traits are likely to be passed to the next generations. The fitting individuals reproduce to generate offspring by mixing their traits by means of gene recombination (crossover). During the reproduction process, or as part of an individual's existence within its generation, small random variations may occur in the genes (mutation), which lead to the emergence of new traits. The new individuals obtained via recombination and/or mutation become part of the population (arguably, as a new generation), and allow the selection mechanism to act again. As this process iteratively continues, the populations evolve towards better adapted individuals in relation to the respective environmental niche.

In essence, EC techniques mimic the process described above to search for and/or create better quality solutions to a problem of interest. Algorithm 2, adapted from [124], presents the generic steps employed by EC techniques, which summarise a highly abstract view on biological evolution. The individuals in the initial population are generated either randomly or using problem-specific heuristics [124]; these individuals represent imperfect candidate solutions to the problem of interest. After initialisation, each candidate solution in the population is evaluated for its fitness based on the objective function that needs to be optimised. *Selection* is then applied to choose the individuals for recombination, and genetic operators, such as *crossover* and *mutation*, are applied to give 'birth' to offspring. The offspring are evaluated for their fitness based on the objective function, and then the population is replaced/updated with a selection of individuals for the next generation. This selection can be from both parent and offspring populations or from offspring only.

Repeating this process is the equivalent of a guided random search in which the initial imperfect solutions to the problem evolve towards (quasi) optimal ones.

Algorithm 2 Pseudo-code for a Generic EC Technique

1: *initialise(Population p)*
2: *Evaluate* each candidate p_i in p
3: **while** ! termination condition satisfied **do**
4:   *select* parents
5:   *crossover* parents
6:   *mutate* offspring
7:   *evaluate* offspring
8:   *select* individuals for new generation
9: **end while**

The endeavour of transferring the complex biological evolution processes into their abstract computational counterparts used in EC dates back to as early as the 1940s. The idea that evolution can be used in computational models preceded even the actual computer technology. In his seminal paper on computers and intelligence, incepted late in the 1940s and published in 1950 [384], Turing, among other ideas, speculated on a way to achieve machine intelligence in a non-deterministic manner, without employing either logic or knowledge [224]. This is the education and learning way – that is, growing the intelligence – which was seen by Turing as a form of genetic search, where a combination of genes is sought via a survival value criterion [224]. Turing stated that 'there is an obvious connection between this process and evolution', and further identified the required elements of such endeavour, which resemble those of Darwinian natural evolution theories: 'hereditary material', 'mutations', and 'natural selection'. Turing's view found echoes in the early work on EC, which was fuelled by the desire to achieve AI. In modern days, the common understanding of the purpose of EC is rather that of a problem-solving tool, even though the domain is still seen as a sub-field of the larger AI field.

Historically, one of the first reported studies employing actual computers to simulate evolution was published in 1957 by Fraser [149], anticipating some of the important methods that appeared later (i.e. evolution strategies and GAs [143]). Later, the field grew substantially into four main directions of research. In chronological order of their inception, these are evolutionary programming, evolution strategies, GAs, and genetic programming. In each of these directions, the methods focus on different aspects of the natural evolution and/or different forms of representing the problems of interest. Evolutionary programming was introduced in the early 1960s by Fogel et al. [144] as a learning process aiming to generate AI, focusing on behaviour changes at species level [142] (i.e. members of the population are seen as part of specific species, rather than members of the same species). Around the same period, though slightly later, evolution strategies were proposed by Rechenberg [331] and Schwefel [354], and focused on behaviour changes at individual level [142]. GAs were reported by Holland [183] in the early 1970s, with a focus on the genetic (chromosomal) operators employed by evolution [142]. The latest addition, genetic programming, emerged in the early 1990s following the pioneering work of Koza [222, 223]. The four areas were initially investigated separately; however, they gradually diffused and mixed to become 'dialects' of one large umbrella known as EC [124]. Currently, the terminology refers to the whole field as EC, while the subsequent techniques used are typically termed EAs. Discussing this broad literature is beyond the scope of this chapter, which has the purpose of introducing the key technical and historical concepts to the novice. However, the interested reader can find comprehensive discussions of the field in [143], focused on historical aspects and the biological substrates of EC, and in [124], focused on the technicalities of the methods and more recent achievements of the field.

In light of the introduction of the field presented above, we offer in the following an introduction to the technicalities of EAs by discussing a set of generic aspects likely to be seen in a broad range of applications.

12.2.2   The Structure of Evolutionary Algorithms

Before proceeding to a description of the main elements of an EA, it worth noting that, while presenting it as a generic view, the elements are most suitable to the class of GAs. We chose this approach because GAs have known the widest use since their inception, and employ the most diverse set of evolutionary/genetic principles. Thus, we will continue to use the term EAs in this section, which is sufficient for the reader who is novice in computational intelligence.

As discussed earlier in this chapter, an EA is a guided search algorithm that relies on a population of solutions. Many problems, especially NP-hard problems, have a huge search space in which the feasible solutions reside. Finding a solution to some instances of NP-hard problems requires significant resources. An exhaustive search is not a feasible option in this case and smart search methods can assist in finding better quality solutions in a feasible time. These smart methods mostly rely on heuristics. EAs fall into this class of randomised heuristics, where the search process relies on stochastic operators that are guided by probability distributions.

An EA starts with a set/population of solutions. Each individual in the population is represented by its chromosome, which encodes a potential solution to the problem. Chromosomes are the substrate on which various genetic operators – such as selection, crossover, and mutation – can operate. Each solution is evaluated, and then solutions are compared against each other and/or against an objective function based on their fitness. Similar to natural selection in biological evolution, individuals with better fitness have more chances to reproduce. The selected individuals produce a new population called offspring. The reproduction process usually involves crossover and mutation processes, which introduce variation in the population. The process of selection and reproduction repeats until some conditions are satisfied – for example, the maximum generation is reached or an acceptable solution is found. Figure 12.6 describes the general framework of an EA. Figure 12.6 describes the general framework of an EA.

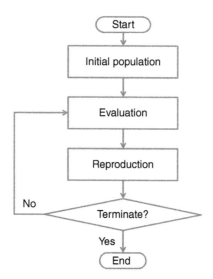

FIGURE 12.6   General framework of an EA.

As seen above, some biological evolution terms are borrowed by EAs, including chromosome, fitness, selection, and others. These terms map concepts from biological evolution into the EA context. A chromosome encodes the parameters of a solution, where the parameters can be viewed as genes. The fitness of a chromosome indicates how well an individual performs for a specific problem to achieve the objectives. Therefore, selection of better individuals is based on fitness evaluations, similar to natural selection in biology. There are two common operators involved in reproduction: crossover and mutation. Both borrow the mechanisms of descent with modifications and mutation from biological evolution. Offspring are the children produced by selected individuals, which are supposed to be better than their parents.

12.2.2.1 *Chromosome*   A chromosome is used to encode a set of parameters of a solution. These parameters must be encoded into some format in which the EA can operate. In the early days of EAs, binary encoding was very popular; this operated by converting the decimal values that a variable can take in a problem into binary numbers. However, many other different representation schemes have been reported in the literature, including integer, real valued, permutation, tree representation [124] and text, as well as mixtures of these. Figure 12.7 shows some examples of encoding solutions of problems into several representations.

In summary, the way to encode a chromosome is flexible, depending strongly on the problem of interest. As shown in the figure, a set of chromosomes (which represent the individuals) forms the population on which an EA operates.

12.2.2.2 *Fitness Evaluation*   AA fitness function is needed to evaluate an individual's fitness. The fitness function represents the performance metric of the individuals in the population using the objective we wish to achieve. While the objective

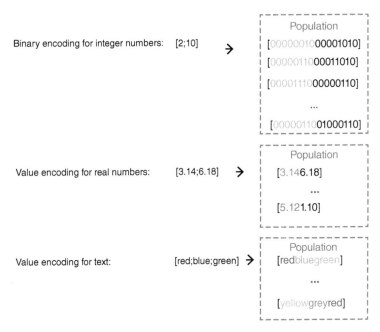

FIGURE 12.7   Examples of chromosomes in various forms of representation.

function evaluates the success of a solution, a fitness function normally refers to how one solution compares with another in the population in terms of its objective value. For example, the fitness function could be the rank of solutions in a population based on their objective value, or the percentage that a solution is better or worse than the average objective values in a population. As such, an objective function is a measure of a solution performance independent of any other solution. A fitness function is a measure of a solution performance relative to other solutions in a population. For simplicity, we will use both words to mean the same thing for this chapter. Example 12.2.1 shows how to define a fitness function for a given problem and how to encode the parameters into a chromosome for evaluation.

Example 12.2.1. *We wish to find a solution x that maximises the value of x^2, where x can be any non-negative integer. Assuming that the fitness function is the objective function, the function used in this example is:*

$$f(x) = x^2$$

Let us assume that the population size is four, and let us randomly initialise the values of x, as listed in the first column of Table 12.1. After encoding x into an 8-bit binary representation, the initial population can be formed as shown in the second column of Table 12.1. Then the fitness of each individual is evaluated by the above fitness function, as listed in the table. Based on individuals' fitness, selection can be performed.

TABLE 12.1   The First Generation of Chromosomes and Their Fitness for Maximising x^2

x	Chromosome	Fitness
13	00001101	169
24	00011000	576
8	00001000	64
19	00010011	361

12.2.2.3 Selection   Inspired by natural evolution, the selection refers to the process in which the better individuals should survive and create new offspring. Thus, the parents are selected for reproduction based on their fitness. Many approaches for parent selection are available in the literature, with the most popular being roulette wheel selection, rank selection and tournament selection [160].

In roulette wheel selection, individuals with better fitness have more chance to be selected for reproduction than individuals with inferior fitness. At first, each individual's fitness is converted into a probability of selection. Then, the resultant probabilities occupy slots on a roulette wheel in proportion to their probability. Each time the roulette wheel spins, an individual is selected. Those occupying larger slots because of their higher fitness are selected more than those occupying smaller slots.

Figure 12.8 shows the roulette wheel selection process for Example 12.2.1. As seen at the bottom left, the expected selection times of each individual depend on its fitness. The strong ones, such as Individuals 2 and 4, have higher probability of being selected (larger sectors on the roulette wheel). Algorithm 3 the pseudo-code for roulette wheel selection for implementation on a computer.

Algorithm 3 Roulette Selection in GA

1: $s = \sum_{i=1}^{popsize} fitness_{chrom_i}$
2: $sc = 0$
3: $rc = RANDOM\ (0, s)$
4: **for** $i = 1$ **to** *popsize* **do**
5:    $sc = xd + fitness_{chrom_i}$
6:    **if** $sc > rc$ **then**
7:       **return** $chrom_i$
8:    **end if**
9: **end for**

However, when the individual fitness differs significantly, then the weakest individuals have a very slim chance of being selected. This may cause the whole population to evolve towards one direction quickly, and lose diversity in the population. When this style of evolution is not desired, other methods of selection can be chosen. One of these methods is rank selection. Instead of directly using individual fitness as a probability, individuals are ranked based on their fitness first. Hence, the worst

Ind. no.	Value	Chromosome	Fitness $f(x) = x^2$	Probability of selection (f/sum)
1	13	01101	169	**0.14**
2	24	11000	576	**0.49**
3	8	01000	64	**0.06**
4	19	10011	361	**0.31**
sum			1170	**1**
favg			293	**0.25**

Roulette wheel

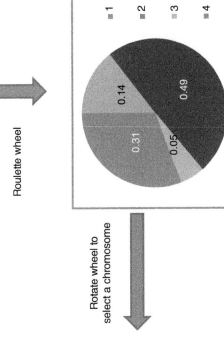

Rotate wheel to select a chromosome

Ind. no.	Value	Chromosome	Expected selection times (f/favg)
1	13	01101	0.58
2	24	11000	1.97
3	8	01000	0.22
4	19	10011	1.23
sum			4
favg			1

FIGURE 12.8 Roulette selection in GA.

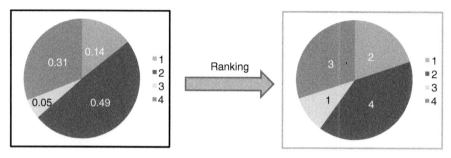

FIGURE 12.9 Rank selection in GA.

individual receives the lowest rank and the best individual receives the highest rank. Selection is based on these ranks.

As shown in Figure 12.9, the individual selection probability for Example 12.2.1 is converted into ranks. The third individual, which is the worst in the population, has an increased probability of selection.

Both the probability calculation in roulette selection and the individual ranks in rank selection could become computationally expensive in some applications, especially as the population size increases. A more computationally efficient selection strategy is tournament selection [286].

In tournament selection, two individuals i and j ($i \neq j$) from a population are randomly selected and then compete with each other based on their fitness. If chromosome i is better than chromosome j, then chromosome i is selected as a parent. Otherwise, chromosome j is selected as a parent. Then, another pair of chromosomes p and q ($p \neq q$) are selected and compared, with the better individual becoming the second parent. Once two parents are decided, they reproduce and create offspring. We note that there is no process for calculating probabilities or individual ranking in tournament selection; thus, computational costs associated with sorting-like operations are eliminated.

In some selection methods, the best chromosome is kept to the next generation, with other children generated by the selected parents. This selection strategy is called 'elitism'. After storing the best chromosomes, the parents can be selected for reproduction as usual, using any of the selection methods discussed above. Elitism can improve the speed of convergence for GA. In Example 12.2.1, the second individual, $x_2 = 24$, should be kept if an elitist strategy is applied.

12.2.2.4 *Crossover and Mutation*

In a generic EA, two operators are applied on selected parents to reproduce and create offspring. One is crossover and the other is mutation. The actual performance of the EA depends on both. The crossover is an operator that produces children based on selected genes from both parents. There are many ways to perform crossover, with single-point and two-point crossover being the most common. In single-point crossover, a random crossover position, k, is selected in the chromosome, where k is less than the length of the chromosome. For the 8-bit binary encoded chromosome, $k \leq 8$. Then, two selected parents exchange all genes

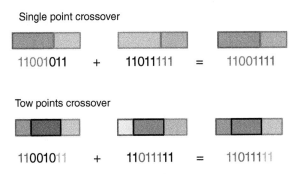

FIGURE 12.10   Single point and two-point crossover in GA.

beyond that position to generate two children. Similarly, in two-point crossover, two exchanging positions are chosen in the chromosome, and then two parents swap the genes between these two positions to produce children. These two crossover methods are illustrated in Figure 12.10. Many other crossover operators can be found in the literature, including ones that apply to real-value representations by imitating binary representations, such as simulated binary crossover (SBX) [111].

Many types of mutation operators are available for EAs, of which we only describe the most common two. The first is the bit inversion method – a method suitable for binary encoded chromosomes, in which a sequence of bits in the chromosome is selected and the value of the bits is inverted. For example, after the second bit in the binary chromosome [10000010] is selected and inverted, a new chromosome [11000010] is generated. The second operator is real-value mutation, and is suitable for chromosomes that encode solutions using real numbers. In this mutation operator, a real number in a chromosome is randomly selected and then randomly changed in a specified range. Let us assume that there is a chromosome [1.295.684.115.32] in which each value (gene) can be in the interval [0, 10]. If the third position of this chromosome is selected for mutation and the new randomly generated value from the given range is 3.66, the new chromosome is [1.295.683.665.32]. Typically, the probability of mutating a chromosome in a population is kept at low levels by design; otherwise, the EA becomes a random search method.

We revisit the population used in Example 12.2.1 demonstrate how roulette wheel selection and reproduction work.

We assume that, after evaluating the first generation, the fitness of each individual and its selection probability are obtained as shown in Figure 12.8. To produce four children, two pairs of parents are selected by roulette selection as follows:

1. [00001101] (13) and [00011000](24)
2. [00011000](24) and [00010011](19)

After applying single-point crossover at the randomly selected bit position $k = 8$, the first pair generates two children: [00001100] (12) and [00011001] (25). Similarly, the second pair generates two children, [00011011] (27) and [00010000] (16), for crossover at bit position $k = 5$. The fourth child is selected to mutate. Its sixth bit is inverted, so that the fourth child becomes [00010100] (20). After all children are generated, their fitness levels are evaluated. The selected parents and their children generated by crossover and mutation are listed in Table 12.2.

Table 12.2 also lists the entire process of crossover and mutation for generating offspring. It shows that the new generation is better than the first generation in terms of the average fitness. If the evolution continues, better solutions will continue to be generated.

12.3 ARTIFICIAL NEURAL NETWORKS

12.3.1 Artificial Neural Networks Background

ANNs solve problems by emulating the way in which the brain performs particular tasks or functions. ANNs have been widely used as function approximators for prediction and pattern recognition, memories, and compression techniques.

The brain is a highly complex, non-linear, and parallel computer with structural constituents called neurons. Different clusters of neurons sit underneath different cognitive tasks and functions, including perception, pattern recognition, and motor control. They are able to build their own behavioural rules over time through 'experience'. A widely accepted three-stage view on the human nervous system [24] is illustrated in Figure 12.11.

The brain is presented as the 'neural net' in the middle of the diagram. On its left, there is a block called 'receptors', which transform the stimuli from the human body or external environment into electrical impulse and send them to the brain. On the right side, the 'effectors' block converts the electrical impulse from the brain into discernible responses to the human body or external environment. As seen in the figure, there are two sets of arrows. The arrows from left to right represent the forward transmission of information, while the arrows from right to left represent feedback. In this way, the brain acts on both stimulus and internal feedbacks. A human brain has approximately 10 billion neurons and 60 trillion synapses. Synapses or nerve endings are the elementary structures and functional units that mediate the interaction between neurons. Neurons encode their outputs as a series of voltage pulses called spikes or action potentials. From this point of view, a human brain is a huge neural network connected by synapses. It takes stimuli as input and generates responses as output.

ANNs are inspired by the operation of the brain, and attempt to model and simulate its behaviours. Most of the work in AI and related fields has focused on two major directions: electrical (spiking) and mathematical (punctual) models of neurons. For completeness reasons, we provide below a brief set of notes related to both categories. However, only the mathematical approach will be described in detail in this chapter, since this is the one that pertains to simulation topics.

12.3.1.1 *The Electric (Spiking) Neurons* Electric neuron models are based on the concept of action potential to represent and model the functions of the nervous

TABLE 12.2 Selected Parents and Their Children After Crossover and Mutation Operations

Ind. no.	Selected value	Selected chromosome	Mate with (random)	Crossover site(random)	Chromosome after crossover	Mutation point (random)	Chromosome after mutation	New value	Fitness $f = x^2$
1	13	00001101	2	4	00011000	N/A	00001100	12	144
2	24	00011000	1	4	00011001	N/A	00011001	25	625
3	24	00011000	4	2	00011011	N/A	00011011	27	729
4	19	00010011	3	2	00010000	3	00010100	20	400
sum									1898
favg									474

FIGURE 12.11   Three-stage view of the human brain.

cell. They are inspired by the fundamental electrical processes considered not only as the foundation of information transmission through the nervous system, but also the fundamental mechanisms for response and adaptation to environmental conditions in both animal and vegetable reigns. In particular, for neurons, the action potential is the substrate for intercellular communication, known as 'neural impulse' or 'spike' [169, 290]. Sequences of action potentials received and generated by neurons are called spike trains, and implement an information-processing effect that can be used for modelling and solving a broad range of problems, typically related to embodied entities (e.g. vision and motor processing in robotics, brain-machine interaction, and prosthetics).

Electric models propose simplified representations, which offer various extents of consistence with the natural operation of the biological neurons [158]. One of the most studied formal electric models that generated a vast body of neural computation literature for more than a century [59, 60] is the Integrate-and-Fire (IF) model, which builds on the mechanism of temporal summation of potentials present in the biophysical neurons. The IF concept dates from as early as 1907, and numerous variations have since been proposed until the present day. One of the first descriptions of the IF concept from a neural computation perspective is the leaky IF (LIF) model introduced by Stein [364]. Later, major iterations of the IF/LIF approach included the quadratic IF models [129], the time-varying IF models [366], the IF or burst models [76, 361], the exponential IF models [57, 147], the Izhikevich neuron [198] and the generalised IF models [202, 283], each of which generate significant amounts of both applied and theoretical studies. In addition, a number of other approaches generated a significant body of research, building on different features of the biophysical neurons, such as the spike response models, which simplify the spike generation to a single-variable threshold model [157], and the resonate-and-fire model, which concentrates on the operation of the neurons in a resonant regime [197].

12.3.1.2 *The Mathematical Neurons*   Mathematical models adopt a punctual representation of the neuron, where the focus is only on the relationship between inputs and outputs. These models assume that a neuron state, and hence its output, is based on a threshold function that takes as input the weighted sum of the connections entering it from other neurons. The pioneer work of McCulloch and Pitts [277] proposed the simplest mathematical model – a binary punctual neuron acting as a basic threshold gate and producing binary output based on the simple weighted sum of the inputs. The simple approach of McCulloch and Pitts further evolved towards the more versatile perceptron [337], which in turn generated advanced models that included various linear and non-linear threshold functions [227, 315] and non-binary, discrete, and continuous valued outputs [315].

The classic connectionist approach on ANNs has its roots in the mathematical neuron models. The resultant ANNs are used in the vast majority for computing in machine learning, data mining, pattern recognition, and other related fields that are part of contemporary computational intelligence research, under the umbrella of neural information processing [99]. Computation based on punctual neuron models has been employed by all major connectionist approaches, such as the feed-forward multi-layer networks with back-propagation, radial basis function networks [190], adaptive resonance theory [70, 71], self-organising maps [221], the Hopfield associative networks [188], and the more general concept of deep (learning) neural networks [347].

For the interested reader, we provide a number of references from different historical periods that discuss both single neuron models and the resultant ANNs in relation to the mathematical underpinnings of their operation. These advanced readings can be found in [227, 279, 367, 400].

12.3.2 A Closer Look at Mathematical Artificial Neural Networks

A mathematical artificial neuron is typically modelled using a structure like that shown in Figure 12.12, where x_i are the inputs to the neuron and y_k is the output from the neuron.

As seen in the figure, the neuron has a set of synapses responsible for perceiving the input signals. Each synapse is characterised by a weight (w_{ki}) or strength of its own. Unlike real neurons, in the artificial ones, the weight of synapses can take negative values. There is also an external bias, b_k as an input to the neuron, which can increase or decrease the signal. A sum operator sits in the middle, producing a weighted sum between the input signals and the weights of synapses; thus, it acts as a linear combiner. An activation function behind the sum operator limits the amplitude of the output from the neuron. According to this model, a neuron k can be described by the pair of equations:

$$v_k = \sum_{j}^{m} w_{kj} x_j \tag{12.1a}$$

$$y_k = \phi(v_k) \tag{12.1b}$$

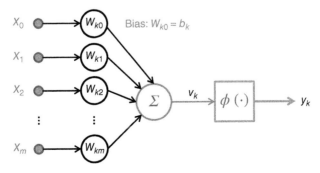

FIGURE 12.12   An artificial neuron.

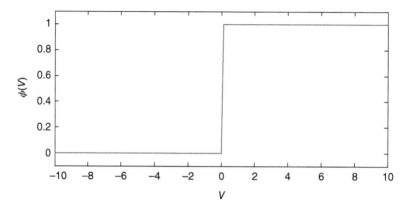

FIGURE 12.13 The threshold activation function in an artificial neuron.

The activation function can take many forms. One straightforward implementation is called the 'threshold' function, for which the output is either 0 or 1 depending on whether the weighted sum is negative or not. Thus, the mathematical representation for a threshold activation can be described as follows:

$$y_k = \begin{cases} 0 & v_k < 0 \\ 1 & v_k \geq 0 \end{cases} \tag{12.2}$$

As seen in Figure 12.13, the activation by threshold is a step function. It produces only two possible values as neural outputs. If a smoother output is desired, then the sigmoid function can be used for activation. A sigmoid function has an 's'-shape graph and assumes that the output is continuous in the interval [01]. We usually use the logistic function to define a sigmoid function, as shown in Eq. (12.3):

$$\phi(v) = \frac{1}{(1 + \exp{-\alpha v})} \tag{12.3}$$

where α is the slope parameter of the sigmoid function. As seen in Figure 12.14, the slope of the curve changes according to the values of α. By using sigmoid functions, the artificial neuron can produce many more different values along the interval [0,1], not only 0 and 1.

Although the sum operator produces linear combinations of the synapse weights and input signals, the activation function, such as sigmoid function, generates a non-linear relationship between the input signals and the response. This shows more resemblance to the real neuron operation than the simple threshold function case.

In summary, the artificial neurons used to build ANNs are slim in biological plausibility and do not resemble real biological neurons. However, they were still inspired by some fundamental behavioural building blocks of a biological neuron, such as stimuli perception and aggregation, input processing and output generation. At the same time, they are capable of solving a large variety of complex and very complex tasks.

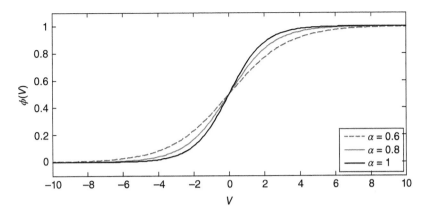

FIGURE 12.14   The Sigmoid activation function in an artificial neuron.

12.3.2.1 *Typical Mathematical Neural Networks*   An ANN consists of many artificial neurons, connected together conveniently to perform certain computational tasks. Thus, a neural network can be seen as a directed graph consisting of nodes with interconnected synaptic and activation links. The synaptic links provide weighted sums that are linear input–output relations, as discussed before. The activation links provide non-linear input–output relations through the activation function. To represent a neural network as a directed graph, we need a set of source nodes that supply input signals to a neuron (computational node), and a number of communication links that interconnect a source and the computational nodes. As illustrated in Figure 12.12, the small nodes in the first layer are the source nodes, the computational node consists of a sum operator and an activation function, and all the communication links are represented by arrows showing the information flow. From a single neuron to a whole network, the architecture of the neurons in a neural network needs to be designed. Two basic topological architectures are feed-forward networks and recurrent networks.

Feed-forward networks are directed acyclic graphs with no loops; therefore, they do not have internal memories that could help them use their previous actions to decide on new ones. They can take different forms that range from a single-layer feed-forward network to multi-layer feed-forward networks. As the names suggest, single-layer feed-forward networks have only an input layer of source nodes that links directly to an output layer of neurons. As shown in Figure 12.15, this is the simplest network structure and is strictly a feed-forward network. Multi-layer feed-forward networks have one or more hidden layers. The simplest multi-layer network is shown in Figure 12.16 with a single hidden layer between source nodes and output nodes. The hidden layer acts as intermediate transformations from the input space to the desired output space. This structure enables ANNs to extract high-order statistics from their inputs.

Recurrent ANNs have at least one loop in the network, as shown in Figure 12.17. The feedback loop allows the network to develop some form of a memory to

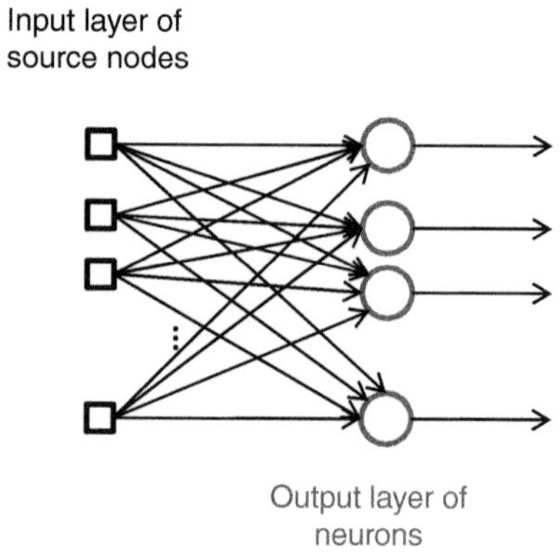

Input layer of
source nodes

Output layer of
neurons

FIGURE 12.15   Single-layer feed-forward ANN.

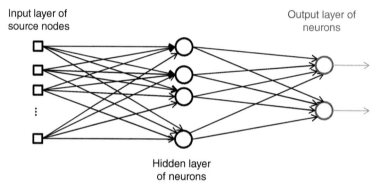

Input layer of
source nodes

Output layer of
neurons

Hidden layer
of neurons

FIGURE 12.16   Multi-layer feed-forward ANN.

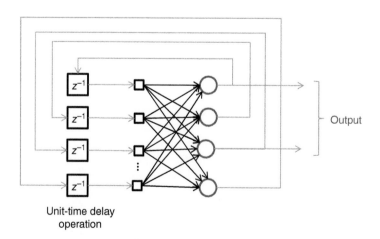

Unit-time delay
operation

Output

FIGURE 12.17   Recurrent ANN.

approximate a dynamical system. The unit-time delay unit z^{-1} produces non-linear dynamic behaviours if the ANN contains non-linear units.

More information on mathematical ANNs can be found in numerous books, such as Haykin's book [177]. Next, we discuss briefly how a network learns.

12.3.2.2 Learning via Mathematical Artificial Neural Networks   Learning in an ANN involves two forms of decisions. The first is design decisions related to the architecture and activation functions. The second is to optimise the parameters of the network, including the weights and the hyper parameters that derive the rate and nature of weight updates.

The adjustment process for the network weights is usually what is meant when discussing basic forms of learning in ANN. There are three generic forms of learning strategies:

- Supervised learning: provides the training examples and correct answers for the ANN. The weights of the ANN connections are adjusted to make the output match the given correct answers.
- Unsupervised learning: the correct answers are not provided to the ANN. Therefore, the ANN must explore the hidden structure of the data or the correlations between patterns in the data.
- Reinforcement learning: gives rewards to ANN according to the interaction between ANN and its working environment. The rewards are usually embedded in the environment. ANN weights are updated to obtain high levels of reward.

The learning rules refer to the algorithms that adjust ANN connection weights. These algorithms can be error-correction rules, Boltzman learning, Hebbian learning, competitive learning, and others.

A special type of learning, which combines EC and neural networks, is neuro-evolution. In neuro-evolution, EAs are mainly used to optimise the ANN weights. In this case, the weights can be encoded as chromosomes, and the learning errors can represent the fitness. Thus, the objective of the EA is to minimise the errors. While this is the typical use of EAs in neuro-evolutionary approaches, their use can be extended to optimise other aspects of the neural networks, such as the architecture itself (i.e. the hyper-parameters).

12.4 CONCLUSION

In this chapter, we have offered a gentle introduction to EC and ANNs, which targets readers who are novices in computational intelligence. EC and ANNs both model and simulate natural phenomena at very high abstraction levels, and have been successfully used in a wide range of applications. EC can be used to optimise the parameters of a simulation model or generate scenarios for the simulation model. ANNs can be used to make decisions within a simulation model or learn and approximate the behaviour of a simulation model. At the start of the chapter, we discussed how optimisation and learning can play various roles in transforming the simulation from a simple reproduction of the behaviour of a system to a thinking machine. In the next chapter, we will see how this thinking machine can challenge and discover vulnerabilities and risks in systems, in plans and equally in other simulation models.

CHAPTER 13

Computational Red Teaming

13.1 INTRODUCTION

In this chapter, we offer a brief view of the red teaming (RT) and CRT concepts to provide to the reader the necessary knowledge to understand their role in modelling and simulation. While, in this book, we are particularly interested in the self-verification role, which is the most relevant in the context of modelling and simulation, this chapter provides a broader view that includes other major purposes, together with aspects that we consider necessary and sufficient to grasp the CRT concept.

CRT is a concept that evolved rapidly in the last decade, bridging the classic RT practice for military organisations and socio-technical systems with intelligent systems and AI [5], and gaining substantial weight as a scientific endeavour. From a colloquial understanding, yielding from military planning and decision making, RT is a practice that involves a blue team representing its own forces and a hypothetical red team representing the opponent. By employing a red team that emulates the opponent's intentions and actions towards the blue team's forces, the blue team can test and evaluate its own course of actions in relation to specific objectives.

CRT is the way to render the RT process computable, where computable means not only bringing computers and computational intelligence into the RT world, but also ensuring a structured, systematic, consistent, and scientific treatment for any RT exercise. The way that the word 'computational' adds to RT must be emphasised before continuing the discussion on CRT. Traditionally, there is a RT practice that involves a process inherent to human thinking, in which the devil's advocate is played by a certain entity to increase situation awareness and unveil potential risks related to its own actions. This practice guided the RT field for several decades, during which the process was entirely problem-related, typically considered from an organisational perspective and performed by humans or teams of human experts. A later addition to the concept involved various degrees of automation, where human RT experts were replaced by computer versions – hence the name of 'automated red teaming'. However, this new addition did not contribute sufficiently to the concept to make the RT process itself structured, systematic, and scientifically grounded. CRT

Simulation and Computational Red Teaming for Problem Solving, First Edition.
Jiangjun Tang, George Leu, and Hussein A. Abbass.
© 2020 by The Institute of Electrical and Electronics Engineers, Inc. Published 2020 by John Wiley & Sons, Inc.

is the scientific approach to RT, which takes the RT process from the practitioner's world, dominated by human expert and problem-related decisions, to become universally applicable (i.e. computable). We could say that, if RT is the phenomenon, then CRT is the science that 'grasps' the phenomenon, not just a computerised version of RT.

Over time, several formal definitions have been proposed in the literature for CRT, in line with the evolution of the RT concept. In [5], the authors stated that "CRT is concerned with the computational side of RT, be it to carry out the whole activity in silico or be it to augment a human-based RT exercise with computational models and methods", which describes rather a computerisation of classic RT. However, a more recent definition, and perhaps the most comprehensive and structured definition, is presented in [4], where the author described CRT as:

a structured approach for modelling and executing exercises by deliberately challenging the competitive reciprocal interaction among two or more players and monitoring how concepts, plans, technologies, human behavior, or any events related to the system or situation under study is unfolding from a risk lens, with the objective of understanding the space of possibilities, sometimes exploring non-conventional behaviors, testing strategies, and mitigating risk.

The definition is structured because it captures the essential aspects of an RT exercise – the challenge-centred process, the object and the purpose – and is comprehensive through the broad range of objects and purposes enumerated.

CRT may be used for a variety of purposes, as stated above. In relation to this book, we are particularly interested in the self-verification role, which is the most relevant in the context of modelling and simulation. However, in this chapter, we provide a broad view that includes all other major purposes, so that the reader can capture a necessary wide view on the CRT concept to understand its role in simulation. Thus, the rest of the chapter is organised as follows. First, we briefly describe the CRT cycle to give the reader an initial view of the RT concept. Second, we describe the most relevant objects and purposes of RT exercises, and discuss the objectives to be achieved by RT exercises within these purposes. Finally, we provide a brief view of how an RT exercise can be designed and performed in a systematic and scientific manner.

13.2 COMPUTATIONAL RED TEAMING: THE CHALLENGE LOOP

The RT process is focused on deliberately challenging the system of interest (the blue). The red agent cannot think in isolation; instead, it strongly depends on the existence and actions of the blue, which in turn depend on the actions of the red. To take these challenging actions, the red must first assess the blue to find its weaknesses, and subsequently determine potential directions to launch challenges. Further, to be able to assess the blue, the red must achieve a proper representation of the blue's decision making, and understand how its capabilities (for CRT applied to socio-technical

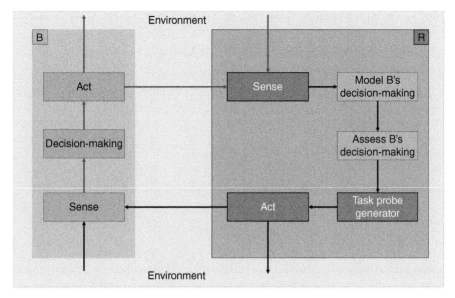

FIGURE 13.1   The CRT loop.

systems) or skills (for CRT applied to human cognition) develop. Only after properly modelling the blue's decision making and capability/skill-acquisition process will the red be able to generate challenging actions directed towards the blue's weaknesses, that is the 'task probing'. In Figure 13.1, we illustrate this loop in which the interaction between the red and blue agents occurs.

13.3   COMPUTATIONAL RED TEAMING OBJECTS

The CRT literature is diverse in terms of the combination of objects (entities to which CRT is applied) and purpose (reason why CRT is applied), covering a wide range of socio-technical and human activity systems. Alongside the classical studies in the military domain, which emphasised challenging concepts and plans with the purpose of testing strategies [21, 92, 133, 236], CRT is used in virtually every context, from vulnerability assessment and penetration tests [46, 119, 329] to data mining and farming [93, 132], air traffic control [6, 410], and strategy games [112, 179].

While the main body of research has concentrated on using various CRT frameworks for objects (and subsequent purposes) related to socio-technical systems, recent studies used CRT in the cognitive domain, where the CRT object was cognition of human individuals or groups, for purposes such as augmentation of human performance and cognitive skills [1, 16]. In the cognitive domain, the only object of the CRT process consists of the relevant set of cognitive skills of a human individual/group; hence, the colloquial understanding of CRT would be that a red entity takes challenging actions towards a human individual/group (the blue entity) to augment the cognitive skills of the latter in relation to certain tasks of interest.

13.4   COMPUTATIONAL RED TEAMING PURPOSES

13.4.1   Understanding the Space of Possibilities

An RT exercise is not about the red defeating the blue. Perhaps the most common aim is to simply help the blue gain a greater understanding of what is possible within the context of its actions. Arguably, any entity, such as the blue agent in our case, has its own inherent biases generated by the culture in which it operates. The red attempts to help the blue overcome these biases by exposing the blue to possibilities that the blue may not have previously considered. Helping the blue discover and appreciate this space of possibilities can further lead the blue to designing more robust strategies and taking advantage of new opportunities with regard to its operational context.

13.4.2   Exploring Non-Conventional Behaviours

Another purpose for performing RT exercises, which derives from the one described above, is to explore non-conventional behaviours. By belonging to a certain environment, and adapting to this environment, the blue will tend to develop certain ways of action that become modus operandi. These actions will be considered norms and taken as granted, becoming the thought-baseline (bias) that steers the blue's perception, ability to understand the environment, and reasoning process used for decision making. Thus, anything that falls outside these norms will be inherently considered non-conventional. RT can change this status quo and help the blue to discover those behaviours that are perceived as non-conventional to its culture and environment, and to understand the advantages and disadvantages of both conventional and non-conventional behaviours in its operation.

13.4.3   Testing Strategies

A strategy usually refers to the set of methods that are able to transform the resources available to an entity into the goals of that entity. Strategies must be tested and continuously refined, from their inception through to the moment that they are implemented, as well as after implementation. In fast-changing environments, indicators for assessing the performance of strategies are vital because the environment may reach states that were not considered during the design stage. An RT exercise can transform the process of designing a strategy from a one-off product into a lifelong learning endeavour. In this case, the testing process is seen as a strategy in itself, which works hand-in-hand with any strategy. Through RT, a strategy is consistently assessed, challenged, and tested against alternate strategies and plausible counter-strategies.

13.4.4   Mitigating Risk

Risk mitigation is another purpose of RT exercises. Under the broad concept of risk, an RT exercise can be seen as a facilitator that assures the blue's continuous consciousness and self-awareness of the risks involved in its operation. As a result of this consciousness and self-awareness, risk-mitigation strategies emerge as the process of RT discovers and challenges different risks within a situation. Thus, through challenge, various risks are mitigated by steering away their negative effects on the blue, or by changing the blue's courses of action to transform negative effects into positive ones. In [4], the author stated that 'RT is about being smart and strategic in every move'.

13.4.5 Self-Verification

Another purpose of RT exercises, and the most important in the context of this book, is 'self-verification'. By employing RT, a blue team or agent can verify the quality of its work products, where quality means the consistency of these products with their intended use and with the business cases that created the need for them. Within the framework of this book, which we explained in Chapter 1, RT plays the role of the self-verification mechanism over the whole lifecycle of solving a problem. Specifically to computer simulation, which solves the model that represents the problem of interest, RT is the fundamental means for verification and validation of this model against the real problem. Later, in the final part of this book, which is dedicated to CRT applications, we will see clearly how the CRT concept governs these applications to ensure the success of various simulations.

13.5 OBJECTIVES OF RED TEAMING EXERCISES IN COMPUTATIONAL RED TEAMING PURPOSES

As an exercise, RT focuses on forming deliberate challenges to achieve various objectives, within the purpose of the exercise. In the following, we describe the most important of these objectives.

13.5.1 Discovering Vulnerabilities

A vulnerability is typically seen as the exposure of a low robust (and potentially critical) component of a system to a hazard or a threat. Finding vulnerabilities pertains to any type of system or application; however, it became most popular and relevant in cyber-security contexts, where RT has been used extensively for penetration tests on computer networks and various types of client–server systems. In these cases, RT has the objective of finding effective strategies to penetrate these networks/systems. As a result of these penetration attempts, vulnerabilities within the tested system are revealed and the blue has the opportunity to fix them.

13.5.2 Discovering Opportunities

Discovering opportunities is an immediate effect of discovering vulnerabilities, complementing the latter. A vulnerability discovered when the red follows the reciprocal interaction in the RT process inherently creates a potential opportunity for the blue.

It is a 'potential' opportunity because there is no guarantee that, if the blue team attempts to exploit a vulnerability of the red, it will not create a vulnerability in its own system. In addition, we note that creating an opportunity should not be seen as a potential to create damage in the red through exploiting the red's vulnerabilities. In contrast, an opportunity may exist through helping the red to close its own vulnerability, which in turn will lead to a better red agent, which will better discover the blue's vulnerabilities. This is where we emphasise the importance of the concept of 'reciprocal interaction' in the challenging process. By fixing a red's vulnerability, the blue can actually facilitate the fixing of more of its own vulnerabilities.

13.6   DISCOVERING BIASES

It is known in general that, without a bias, one cannot make a decision; thus, every decision carries a certain bias. In conclusion, biases are not necessarily bad, but they may become bad when they have negative effects on the decision. However, a good approach is to be aware of both types of biases to learn how to deal with them. If the RT exercise reveals these biases, the blue becomes more conscious of their existence in advance, and thus is able to investigate their effect on its own activity and establish ways of improvement. Revealing biases can open doors for opportunities.

13.6.1   Training

RT is a very effective training technique. In a normal training exercise (non-RT), training scenarios are standardised for all participants; however, in RT training, the training evolves differently for each participant. If we consider that the blue is the trainee and the red is the trainer, then every time something about the blue changes (such as additional capabilities, skills, and/or new knowledge) it becomes necessary for the red to evaluate the need to change its own training strategy. Through interaction with the trainee, the trainer discovers areas that require more attention, and the training exercise is tailored to place greater weight on these areas. Equally, the trainee learns both from its own mistakes and from the designed and/or unintentional mistakes of the trainer. In effect, RT not only trains the blue to be efficient in the task, but also trains the blue's ability to adapt when the task changes. In summary, RT trains the blue 'to think', not just 'to do'. This differentiates RT from non-RT training.

13.6.2   Creating Thinking Tools

As explained earlier in this chapter, an RT exercise assists players to gain understanding and appreciation of the complexity of a situation – situation awareness. In this case, at a conceptual level, RT mimics a person performing self-talking. In general, the dynamics of this back-and-forth interaction teaches participants and observers about the richness and depth of the situation and opens their judgement towards more strategic thinking. In the RT context, the reciprocal interaction between the red and blue creates an environment of self-consciousness of the existence of an opponent.

RT transforms the thinking process of both teams, and teaches each of them to be always aware of the existence of the other and its intentions and readiness to engage.

13.6.3 Creating Future Memories and Contingency Plans

One aspect that needs to be clear in relation to RT is that an RT exercise is realistic, but not the real thing. If the RT exercise is genuine, then there is no difference from the blue living the real life and accumulating experience from day-to-day life situations. The RT exercise happens *in vitro* and adds to the blue's memory experiences that it cannot afford to acquire in real life. If lessons from the RT exercise are properly learnt by the blue, the experiences created *in vitro* can be engraved in its memory and retrieved when needed (e.g. when similar real-world situations are encountered).

13.6.4 Washing Memory

As stated above, RT can be used to learn about situations that may not yet have been encountered in real life. However, in a similar manner, RT can be used to 'unlearn' situations that have been encountered in real life, so that the blue is prepared for new ways of thinking in situations to be encountered in the future. Memory washing is important because, whenever an entity is trained for a purpose and becomes skilled in a certain type of task, it may also de-skill in other types of tasks that are not as much exercised. Thus, employing RT exercises for appropriate skilling and de-skilling is an important objective within the framework of CRT purposes.

13.7 COMPUTATIONAL RED TEAMING LIFECYCLE: A SYSTEMATIC APPROACH TO RED TEAMING EXERCISES

As explained earlier in this chapter, the true value of the word 'computational' and meaning of CRT is to design and implement an RT exercise in a systematic way, according to a clear and structured process. In the following, we briefly describe the main steps involved in the lifecycle of an RT exercise.

13.7.1 Setting the Purpose, Scope, and Success Criteria

While RT is exploratory in nature, it is essential to have a clear understanding of the purpose, scope, and criteria of success for the exercise before moving forward – that is, to clarify the answers to questions of 'why', 'what', and 'so what'. The purpose of the RT exercise defines the subsequent objectives, and acts as a reminder of why the exercise is being conducted. It influences all the steps further taken for designing the exercise.

The scope of an RT exercise is a list of soft constraints defining the context of the exercise. Given that these constraints are soft, they can be broken, so they can be ambiguous in nature and their only purpose is to ensure that the exercise is not entirely unbounded. A scope defines what is essential, what is useful to have, and what is irrelevant in the context of an RT exercise. However, unlike in contexts such as project management or system engineering, in CRT, the scope should not be fixed in order to support the interactive nature of the RT exercise, which may necessitate a change in scope.

The criteria of success are measures of utility to indicate how the success of the RT exercise will be judged. Their values can be used to demonstrate the added value of the exercise, and will define whether the exercise was successful in fulfilling its purpose or not. If success criteria are not known, it is difficult to define which data to collect, which factors should be measured, how to measure the factors, and on what basis the effectiveness of the exercise can be justified.

In summary, the purpose, scope, and criteria of success establish a set of guidelines to measure the appropriateness and cost benefit of each decision to be made in the remaining steps of an RT exercise.

13.7.2 Designing the Exercise

An RT exercise is no different from any other type of experimentation exercise we may conduct. Experimentation is a general concept with its own guidelines and principles, and an RT exercise is one type of experimentation. An RT experiment needs to focus on the design of the red and blue, along with the interaction between them. In RT, the experiment needs to focus on designing the deliberate challenge – that is, how each side will challenge the other side. In addition, the objective is not simply to win or play the game, but to learn how to stretch each side's boundaries to the limit.

Thus, as part of the design stage, the following steps should be considered to ensure the success of the exercise:

Designing the scenario: A scenario for an RT exercise can be considered like the storyline in a movie. It should not tell exactly what every actor will do, but rather describe the role and character each actor will play. Thus, the RT scenario is similar to a storyline, not to a script. This storyline defines the context, players, and players' roles, while the dynamics of the interaction generate the script – that is, the RT exercise as a whole. A scenario only defines the contextual information for the starting point of the story, but, in RT, should never define how the story will evolve and what the conclusions will be. These are the responsibilities of the whole RT exercise.

Designing data collection plan: We recall here that an RT exercise is not about who wins or loses, but about the thinking process that each side experiences to make their decisions, and the deliberate challenges that each side imposes on the other side. Thus, an effective data-collection plan is an essential part of the RT exercise. A data-collection plan details the data to be collected by asking a number of questions: Which data will be collected? What are the objectives of collecting these data? What is the intended analysis? Who is the owner of each piece of data? Where will the data be collected? How will the data be collected and by whom? What access control will each data user have? How will the raw and processed data be stored and where?

Selecting the players: Selecting the appropriate players for each team is also essential for the success of an RT exercise. Decisions on the structure and capabilities of the red team are more difficult than those for the blue team. The red team in an RT exercise needs to be skilled in red behaviour, not in blue behaviour. If it is skilled in blue behaviour, it may be necessary to de-skill the red players.

Briefs and training: Briefs given to both red and blue need to be designed, scrutinised and analysed carefully. These briefs contain information of the 'known-known' – or what each entity knows about the other – and affect the level of creativity that each entity will exhibit in attempting to deliberately challenge the other. An issue related to providing briefs is training. Sometimes, is not sufficient to use entities that 'can' act as red without proper training before conducting the exercise. Training can provide the extra skills/capabilities necessary to create the red.

13.7.3 Conducting the Exercise

An RT exercise begins the moment the need for RT is announced – that is, before the purpose, scope, and criteria of success are designed. This is important because this moment dictates the constraints about which information should be communicated and to whom. Conducting the exercise is the stage when the experiment and game begin. This is the moment in which both red and blue prepare for engagement and interaction, and the moment in which the scenarios previously established are executed.

The RT exercise typically involves more actors, not only the red and blue. In addition to the red and blue, there are other teams that facilitate the exercise, including the team of designers who design the exercise; the team of observers who watch the exercise unfolding; the team of analysts who specialise in analysing the RT exercise qualitatively and quantitatively; and the technical team responsible for all technical aspects of the exercise, including monitoring the automated data-collection tools. Sometimes other colours may be used to designate other teams. For example, designers, analysts, and observers are grouped into a white team, while a green colour denotes a special team who supports and acts as a coalition of the blue team. More colours can be introduced to define other groups with interest in the exercise. It is important that each entity does not interfere with the tasks and purpose of other entities. The technical team should be invisible to both the red and blue so that they do not distract them when performing their tasks, while observers should be separated from the analysts so they are not influenced by analysts' discussions, and so on.

13.7.4 Monitoring the Exercise

During the RT exercise, it is also important to ensure that the exercise is unfolding as expected, and is meeting its intended objectives. This is achieved by real-time monitoring and analysis of the RT exercise. Given that RT exercises involve significant amounts of effort, it is unwise to conduct the exercise, collect the data for analysis, and then discover, for example, that there is a problem in the data. Thus, it is very important that appropriate tools are in place to continuously monitor the exercise in real time and analyse the data as they are generated. This real-time analysis will focus on indicators related to whether the RT exercise is meeting its objectives, and will be used to ascertain and analyse potential problems in the experiment.

13.7.5   Performing Post-Exercise Analysis

While certain analysis occurs as the exercise is unfolding, most of the analysis required to extract trends and patterns (i.e. lessons) will be offline and will occur after the RT exercise is conducted. This is sometimes because of the need to have the complete dataset of the exercise before a pattern can be extracted. Sometimes, the analysis may need to propagate information forward and backward in the data to establish the reasons and rationale for the extracted pattern; thus, it is important to bring both the red and blue back to the analysis room after the exercise is completed. In this situation, the events can be played back, while reflecting on why certain sequences of events occurred the way they did during the exercise. This process of reflection may be designed as part of the training process for both the red and blue, as it may be necessary later, during the analysis, to understand the results and outcomes of the exercise.

13.7.6   Documenting the Exercise

An RT exercise can be seen as any other project that we may manage; hence, the experience needs to be documented thoroughly. Documenting the exercise allows the owners of the RT exercise or third-party entities to consult the documents if situations similar to those experimented in the exercise happen in real life. The documentation of the RT exercise needs to go beyond the basic level of documentation of the experiment to include the decisions made, their rationale, their expected consequences, and the findings of the post-exercise analysis. The documentation should include how the decisions affected the situation experimented in the exercise, how they were perceived by the various actors involved, what went right, what went wrong, and how they could have been amended.

13.7.7   Lessons Learnt and Process Improvement

RT exercises are a capability that an organisation should see as a lifelong continuous capability. Every exercise teaches the organisation how to perform the next exercise in an improved manner. Therefore, lessons learnt on RT should be captured, documented, and stored as a source of knowledge for future exercises. There is low likelihood that the first RT exercise will be conducted perfectly by an organisation. In addition, even if one exercise is perfect, there is no guarantee that the next ones will be. RT exercises are complex and the chance of something going wrong is very high, as is the chance that something going right in one exercise will go wrong in a future exercise. Overconfidence, human bias and the complex nature of the situations and decisions encountered during RT exercises are inherent contributors to the potential failure of these. Thus, lessons learnt from an RT exercise should become part of the organisation's memory and culture.

13.8 CONCLUSION

In this chapter, we have offered a brief view on the RT and CRT concepts, so that the reader can better understand their relationship to modelling and simulation. While, in this book, we are particularly interested in the self-verification role, which is relevant in the context of modelling and simulation, this chapter provides a broader view that includes other major purposes, together with the necessary aspects required to grasp the CRT concept.

PART V

Simulation and Computational Red Teaming Applications

Computational Red Teaming for Battlefield Management

14.1 INTRODUCTION

In this chapter, we describe an application in which the CRT concept is applied at both strategic and tactical level to model the reciprocal interaction and learning (co-evolution) between two forces, in the context of command and control in battlefield management. While this application, Warfare Intelligent System for Dynamic Optimisation of Missions (WISDOM)/WISDOM-II, is complex and can be used for multiple purposes, we only describe its architecture at a general level to illustrate the potential of the two concepts described in this book – CRT and simulation – if used together. The work on WISDOM spanned a few papers that form the basis of the materials in this chapter [21, 405].

Earlier in the book, in Chapter 13, we provided an overview of the concepts of RT and CRT, and how they can have broad understanding and implications in various fields of activity and applications, depending on the perspective applied to them. The perspective adopted in this chapter views RT as the process of studying a problem by anticipating adversary behaviours. When seen in the context of simulation, behaviour space is divided into two groups: one controlled by red, which represents the set of adversary (bad) behaviours, and one controlled by blue, which represents the set of defender (good) behaviours. Through RT, an analyst can learn about the future through forward prediction of scenarios. Defence organisations have been the traditional users of RT techniques; however, these techniques were mainly in the range of classic human-based RT. Recently, more defence and defence-related decision makers have started to employ – with the support of simulation – various computational approaches to RT, such as machine learning and EC (these two important computational intelligence techniques were discussed in Chapter 12). Optimisation of operational, tactical, and strategic decisions can be made based on the findings of the computational methods in use. Traditionally, optimisation of defence operations relied on the findings of human-based war gaming, which was expensive and provided insufficient capabilities for problem space exploration.

Simulation and Computational Red Teaming for Problem Solving, First Edition.
Jiangjun Tang, George Leu, and Hussein A. Abbass.
© 2020 by The Institute of Electrical and Electronics Engineers, Inc. Published 2020 by John Wiley & Sons, Inc.

Recently, computer simulations of MASs have become valuable tools for optimising defence operations. Potential strategic and tactical decisions are generated within and evaluated by multi-agent simulation modules to investigate system behaviours.

In this chapter, we provide an application in which RT principles are used in conjunction with computational techniques and MASs for understanding the characteristics and properties of the search space of complex adaptive combat systems. Thus, in the next section, we provide an overview of WISDOM [405] – a simulation environment for exploring network-centric warfare using ABS.

14.2 BATTLEFIELD MANAGEMENT SIMULATION

The history of using simulation in the military domain can be traced back to antiquity. However, computer-based simulation for military purposes emerged in recent decades. Traditionally, defence simulation has adopted what is known as Lanchester equations to model and further investigate combat issues, such as force attrition. Lanchester equations are a set of linear dynamic equations that treat attrition as a continuous function over time; thus, combat is modelled as a deterministic process in which an attrition rate coefficient is assumed. The advantage of this approach is that equations are intuitive and easy to apply. However, the resultant models can only provide an ideal model of military operations that is too abstract and far from realistic. In general, equation-based models suffer from two major drawbacks in relation to battlefield modelling and simulation. The first is that they are unable to deal with the dynamics of non-linear interaction between opponents. The non-linearity of warfare means that small changes in certain critical conditions can profoundly change the outcomes. The second drawback is that they are unable to handle spatial variations of forces – that is, there is no link between movement and attrition. Another set of important aspects that cannot be investigated using equation-based models is related to individual human factors (such as personality, motivation, and affect) and group human factors (such as team cohesion and trust). This renders it difficult to anticipate the behaviours of individuals and groups. Moreover, the nature of the terrain is usually neglected and it is not possible to model the suppressive effects of weapons.

In light of the above discussion, it is more appropriate to view combat as a CAS, in which the relevant entities are modelled from a MAS perspective. Further, we can describe several essential aspects that bring together CAS and combat:

Non-linear interaction: Combat forces consist of a significant number of components interacting with each other non-linearly.

Hierarchical structure: By nature, forces are organised in a command and control hierarchy that is actually a complex system in its own right.

Decentralised control: In military operations, each combatant is an autonomous agent that acts reactively based on its sensor information within the overall objective or plan.

Self-organisation: Despite the local actions of a combatant appearing to be chaotic, when seen over time, a long-term order emerges.

Non-equilibrium order: By nature, equilibrium is not a characteristic of military conflicts.

Adaptation: It is not possible for combat forces to succeed in their designated missions without being able to adapt to changes in the environment.

Collectivist dynamics: The hierarchical structure of forces dictates a command chain, where low-level combatants and high-level command structures continuously communicate and feedback their states and actions.

The concept of MAS is a natural platform for studying CAS. Combat entities are modelled as agents, usually with a set of predefined characteristics. These agents adapt, evolve, and co-evolve with and within their environment. By modelling an individual constituent of a CAS as an agent, we are able to simulate a real-world system using an artificial world populated by interacting agents and processes. In particular, MASs are effective for representing real-world systems composed of non-linear interacting parts that have a large space of complex decisions and/or behaviours to choose from, such as those situations in combat.

Several MASs designed specifically for combat have been developed over the years by various research groups associated with the defence organisations of different countries, such as US defence (e.g. Irreducible Semi-Autonomous Adaptive Combat [ISAAC] and Enhanced ISAAC Neural Simulation Toolkit [EINSTein]), New Zealand defence (e.g. Map Aware Non-uniform Automata [MANA]), and Australian defence (e.g. the Conceptual Research Oriented Combat Agent Distillation Implemented in the Littoral Environment [CROCADILE] and WISDOM and WISDOM-II developed by the University of New South Wales at the Australian Defence Force Academy [405]). In this chapter, the CRT application uses WISDOM and WISDOM-II as the simulation engine.

14.2.1 WISDOM

WISDOM and its enhanced version, WISDOM-II, are complex adaptive combat systems developed by the Artificial Life and Adaptive Robotics Laboratory, School of Engineering and Information Technology, University of New South Wales Canberra, at the Australian Defence Force Academy. WISDOM is a multi-agent simulation combat system that facilitates the analysis and understanding of land combat. By using this system, analysts are able to gain an understanding of the overall shape and dynamics of a battle, and whether some factors are more influential than others in determining the outcome of an operation.

The WISDOM environment employs a low-resolution abstract model in which the detailed physics of combat are ignored, while only the characteristics of combatant, defence operation, and behaviours are modelled. An agent in WISDOM consists of four components: sensors, capabilities, movements, and communications. Each agent is driven by five types of personality features: desire to move towards a healthy friend, injured friend, healthy opponent, injured opponent, and the flag (a target position in the environment) based on information gleaned from the sensors. The first four types of personality features can be different for each sensor. At each simulation time step, an agent can decide to move, fire, or communicate with other agents. Although, in real-life systems, an agent can fire while moving, WISDOM assumes that only one action can be performed because the time step of the simulator is too small. This assumption helps understand the trade-offs between these decisions. The movements of agents in WISDOM are determined by an attraction–repulsion weighting system based on agents' personalities. The weights are aggregated using a penalty function, as in (14.1). The movement equations are variations of equations of motion for different types of mobility, in which the direction of agent movement is selected according to the maximum weights (minimum penalty). Four modes of mobility are available: leg walking, wheel movements, swimming, and flying.

$$W_{\text{new}} = \sum_{i=1}^{n} \frac{P^v}{D_{\text{new}}^i} + \sum_{j=1}^{m} \left(\frac{P^c}{D_{\text{new}}^j} \right) + \frac{P_{\text{new}}^t}{D_{\text{new}}^t} \qquad (14.1)$$

In addition to movement, agents can also communicate by exchanging words or signals. The communication framework (who is allowed to communicate to whom, how, when, and where) is defined using graph structures. The health defines the level of energy for an agent. Initially, all agents start with a maximum level of energy, where the maximum level, as defined by users, is different for different agent types. When an agent is hit by opponents' fire, the degradation of its health depends on the strength of the firing weapon.

Users can choose from four terrain types by selecting one of four different colours when plotting the map of the terrain. These types are urban land, water, pasture, and rough terrain. The type of terrain affects the nature of agent movement. Similar to other systems, agents have a number of parameters defining their personalities. Figure 14.1 depicts a screen dump for one part of the interface defining the parameters for scenarios. The probability to hit weight is a measure of the agent's firing skills. No cell in the environment can be occupied by more than one agent at any particular moment of time.

At each simulation time step, an agent can either decide to move, fire, or communicate with other agents. The decision-making mechanism used by each agent to decide on the appropriate direction to move is based on the agent's personalities. Overall, there are 10 personality weights for each agent. The value of each personality is a continuous number between -1 and $+1$. A positive weight implies the level of desire to move in the direction associated with the characteristics, while a negative weight implies the level of desire to avoid this direction. Calculations are done synchronously, as well as the moves. This process is repeated for each time step in the simulation.

14.2.2 WISDOM-II

WISDOM-II [405] is an enhancement of WISDOM, and concentrates on a network perspective of warfare (network-centric warfare) to explore decision space in battlefield environments using ABS.

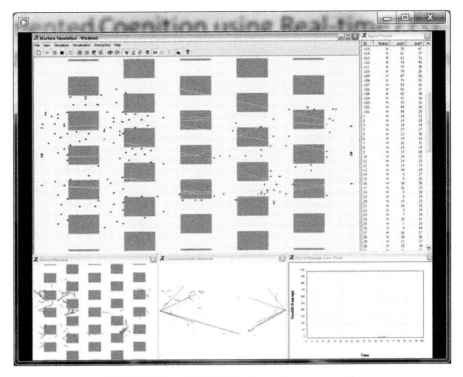

FIGURE 14.1   WISDOM-II. Simulation run example.

WISDOM-II uses WISDOM as a substrate, yet was developed on the Network Centric Multi-Agent Architecture, which adopts a two-layer architecture. The top layer is an influence network based on the influence diagram. As shown in Figure 14.2, it defines the relationship types and how one type of relationship influences other types. For example, the communication network is influenced by the command and control network and vision network, and has an effect on the situation awareness network.

The bottom layer is a set of agents that reflect these relationship types in the influence network. The agents interact using these relationships. For example, agents that can see each other and communicate with each other are connected in the lower layer, so that the influence of vision on communication would form a connection in the top layer. Integrating these two layers, the big picture of WISDOM-II can be seen in Figure 14.3.

A clear command and control hierarchy can be seen in this architecture. At the general commander level, strategic decisions – such as defend, occupy, and survey – can be made and passed to the lower level. At the group level, tactical decisions – such as agent movements and attack of enemy units – can be made and executed. A simulation run of WIDSOM-II is shown in Figure 14.1.

WISDOM-II is able to conduct real-time reasoning on the network (group) level based on network theory. A rule-based algorithm is used to make strategic decisions,

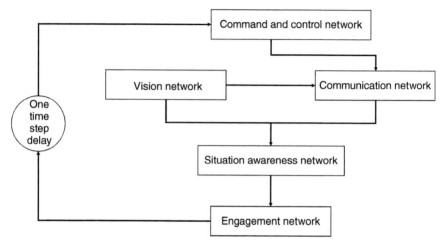

FIGURE 14.2 WISDOM-II. Top layer.

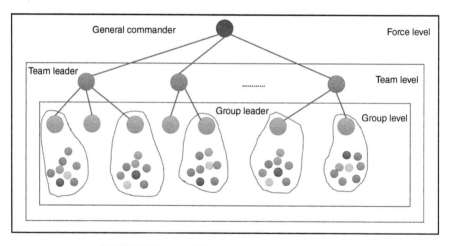

FIGURE 14.3 WISDOM-II – overall architecture.

which guides a semi-reactive agent to make tactical decisions through the network structure. Therefore, the interaction between tactics and strategies can be easily captured.

Other simulations following a similar architecture to that embedded in WISDOM-II have recently become available for training purposes. One Semi-Automated Forces (OneSAFs) [310] is one example. OOneSAFAQ: Colud we change term 'OOneSAF' to 'OneSAF'. Please check and suggest. is an entity-level simulation that supports both computer-generated forces (CGFs) and semi-automated forces (SAFs). CGFs model and simulate combat entities and systems that are actors. A SAF is a CGF in which the entities have some level of autonomy. A SAF usually requires a human to undertake holistic planning, provide goals for goal-directed behaviours and so on. OneSAF was built to represent modular and future forces, and provides entities, units, and behaviours across a large spectrum of military operations. In OneSAF, unit behaviours are modelled and represented at different levels, such as from fire team to company. OneSAF is also able to simulate operations in urban or terrain. Many countries, including Australia, have used OneSAF successfully for training purposes [96].

14.3 CONCLUSION

There are many simulation environments available for investigation of warfare and decision making in defence-related contexts. In this chapter, we have briefly described WISDOM and WISDOM-II – two ABS environments emphasising the network perspective on the battlefield. These environments provide support for RT exercises and, through that, can model the co-evolutionary aspect of combatants' interaction, as well as the co-evolutionary aspect of the combatant–environment interaction. Both environments have been part of our modelling and simulation over the years, and have provided substantial results for practitioners in the field of RT (military organisations), as well scientific evidence for the theoretical foundation of CRT.

CHAPTER 15

Computational Red Teaming for Air Traffic Management

15.1 INTRODUCTION

Modelling and simulation have been successfully used in numerous applications in many different areas. In this chapter, we present a CRT application in the context of air traffic management, which includes an air traffic simulation and a hybrid human-in-the-loop application that combines simulation, optimisation and data mining techniques, and human–computer interaction.

We describe a CRT application in which CRT is used with the purpose of improving the operation of a system by observing the system, assessing its status, and providing advice to actors based on this assessment.

Thus, we first describe an air traffic simulator called Air Traffic Operations and Management Simulator (ATOMS), which is coupled with a real-time tactical advisory system for air traffic management called Trajectory Optimisation and Prediction of Live Air Traffic (TOP-LAT), in which aircraft are modelled in ATOMS. Both systems provide the capability to evaluate advanced air traffic management concepts in a simulated environment that can handle both artificially generated situations and accurate replicas of real-world situations. We then describe a human-in-the-loop application that investigates the cognitive aspects of air traffic controllers (ATCs) based on the CRT concept.

15.2 AIR TRAFFIC SIMULATION

15.2.1 Air Traffic Operations and Management Simulator (ATOMS)

ATOMS [11] is an air traffic and airspace modelling and simulation system for the analysis of advanced air traffic management concepts, such as free flight. ATOMS uses a multi-agent-based modelling paradigm for modular design and easy integration

Simulation and Computational Red Teaming for Problem Solving, First Edition.
Jiangjun Tang, George Leu, and Hussein A. Abbass.
© 2020 by The Institute of Electrical and Electronics Engineers, Inc. Published 2020 by John Wiley & Sons, Inc.

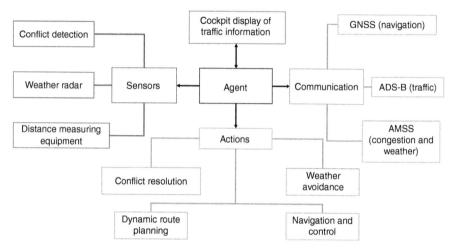

FIGURE 15.1 Agent-based model of an aircraft in ATOMS.

of various air traffic subsystems. It can simulate end-to-end airspace operations and air navigation procedures for conventional air traffic, as well as for free flight. Atmospheric and wind data that are modelled in ATOMS result in accurate trajectory predictions.

In ATOMS, each aircraft is modelled as an agent, as depicted in Figure 15.1. This aircraft agent senses the environment (such as neighbouring aircraft, weather conditions, and route deviations), communicates with other agents, makes decisions, and takes action.

To make aircraft agents fly in the simulation, the total energy model from BADA 3.6 [78] is used as the base model for aircraft aerodynamics. This aerodynamics model enables the simulation to reproduce the aircraft behaviours – such as climb/descent and acceleration/deceleration – at a very high level of detail. It can also generate the fuel consumption according to the applied aircraft thrust. Thus, ATOMS can estimate the aircraft pollution level by fuel consumption based on some of the existing aviation emission models, such as the NASA-Boeing Emission Model (*BEM2*) [39].

The input to ATOMS consists of script-based flight plans that indicate the aircraft type, origin, destination, departure time, and route. ATOMS constructs aircraft agents based on their flight plans and simulates them in a discrete time manner. At each time step in a simulation, aircraft agents sense the environment, take action, and interact with each other. Figure 15.2 presents an example in which ATOMS is simulating an artificial scenario in the Australian airspace.

As shown in Figure 15.2, ATOMS also models geographical and airspace objects, such as maps, flight information regions, airways, and the atmosphere. These consist of the environment in which aircraft fly.

ATOMS adopts a client–server architecture so that there are several light-clients available, including an ATC client, a pilot cockpit display and control client, and an

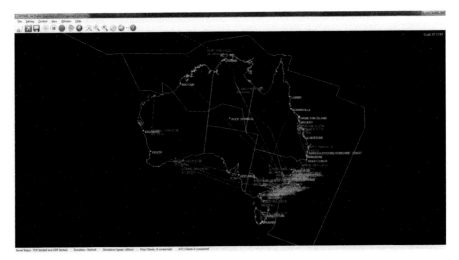

FIGURE 15.2 Visualisation of a simulated scenario using ATOMS – main screen of ATOMS.

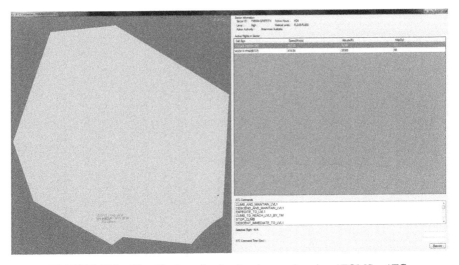

FIGURE 15.3 Visualisation of a simulated scenario using ATOMS – ATC.

airport runway client. Each client communicates with ATOMS through networks; therefore, they can be deployed remotely.

Figure 15.3 shows the interface of an ATC client. Given that airspace is sectorised into many sectors for easy air traffic management, an ATC is usually responsible for the safety of air traffic within one sector. The ATC client has a visualisation for the air traffic within a particular sector, and a list of commands that can be sent to pilots for execution.

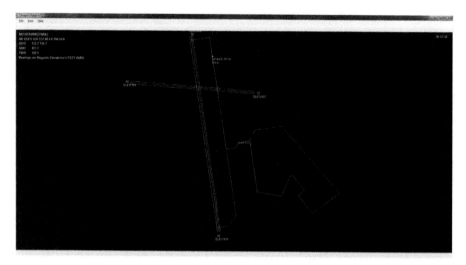

FIGURE 15.4 Visualisation of a simulated scenario using ATOMS – terminal management area.

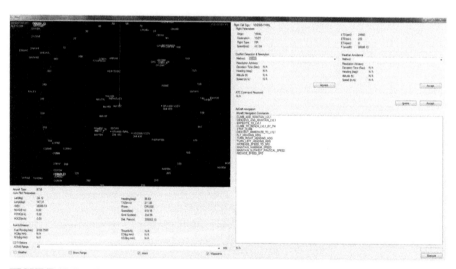

FIGURE 15.5 Visualisation of a simulated scenario by ATOMS – pilot cockpit and control. These studies can be undertaken in this simulated environment without touching the real-world system.

An airport runway client is shown in Figure 15.4, which presents the layout of the runway and situation awareness of aircraft taking off and landing.

The pilot client allows users to monitor an aircraft through the cockpit display, and control it with a set of commands, such as climb and descent, as shown in Figure 15.5.

15.2.2 Trajectory Optimisation and Prediction of Live Air Traffic (TOP-LAT)

Based on the aircraft model used in ATOMS, we developed another set of software packages called Trajectory Optimization and Prediction of Live Air Traffic (TOP-LAT), which has the capability to provide real-time air traffic situation awareness and safety advice, monitor environmental impact, and make suggestions on airspace sectorisation and optimal tactical flight trajectory. The system architecture of TOP-LAT is described in Figure 15.6.

TOP-LAT takes real-time data, such as flight positions and weather information, and combines them with geographic data. It relies on data cleaning and data fusion techniques to aggregate all sources of information, and then uses the aggregation to produce a desired output. Given that real-time traffic data are a set of discrete time series datasets, the gap between two datasets must be filled; otherwise, aircraft will be hopping from one discrete location to another. We also expect this system to provide real-time estimation of fuel consumption and emissions; therefore, a detailed aircraft aerodynamics model is required, such as the one used in ATOMS. Following a divide-and-conquer philosophy, the 'core' component of TOP-LAT is designed to embed several modules, as shown Figure 15.7.

Each module in the core system has its own functionalities. For example, the flight aerodynamic module uses the BADA 3.6 aerodynamics equations to simulate an aircraft flying, and the airspace complexity module measures the real-time ATC task load based on dynamic density metrics [271]. The kernel manages the interaction and

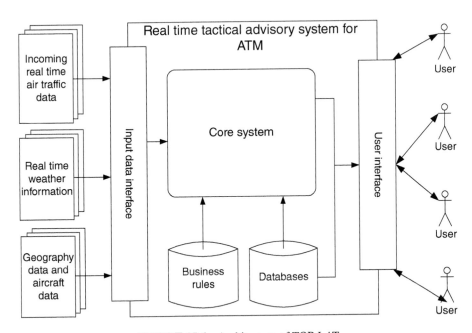

FIGURE 15.6 Architecture of TOP-LAT.

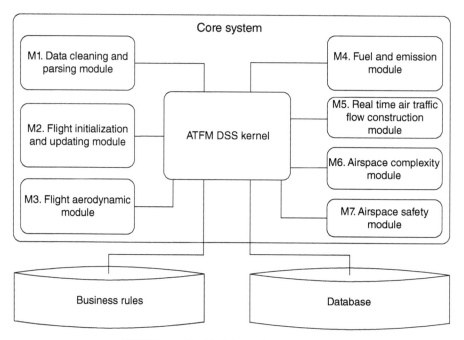

FIGURE 15.7 Modules in the core system.

data management among these modules, and forwards intermediate results to target modules for further processing, to the databases for storing, or to the user interface (we do not provide a detailed description of each module because of space limitations). Consequently, several clients are developed.

As shown in Figure 15.8, the first client provides real-time air traffic situation awareness to users. Users can use this to monitor the real-time air traffic in a given region. The information reinterpreted in this client includes the flight positions within Australian flight information regions, weather information, particular sector configurations, and the terminal area.

The second client allows users to investigate the aviation environment impact on the airspace. As aforementioned, the pollution emitted by aircraft is estimated from the aircraft aerodynamic and aviation emission models. To store the emission data, the airspace is divided into small grids ($1°/1°/1000$ ft). Each grid holds the emissions from any aircraft that goes through it. Each grid also records the time stamp of the moment when pollution was emitted by the aircraft. Figure 15.9 illustrates the carbon dioxide emissions within Australia's flight information regions. Given that the grid is in a 3-D space, the left picture shows the lateral view of how carbon dioxide is distributed, while the right picture illustrates the vertical view of how carbon dioxide is spread along the altitude.

A client to monitor ATC task load based on the airspace complexity is shown in Figure 15.10. This client provides the visualisation of ATC workload indicators to supervisors. It maps the real-time airspace complexity of each sector onto a colour

(a)

(b)

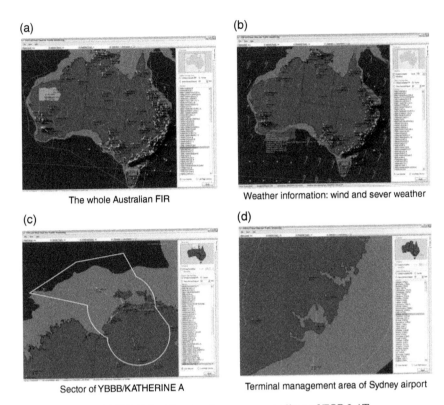

The whole Australian FIR

Weather information: wind and sever weather

(c)

(d)

Sector of YBBB/KATHERINE A

Terminal management area of Sydney airport

FIGURE 15.8   The situation awareness client of TOP-LAT.

(a)

(b)

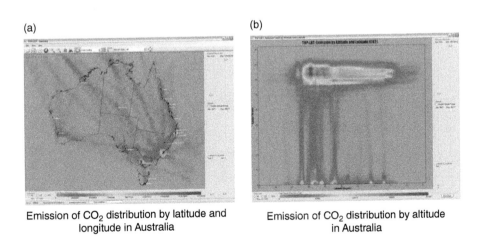

Emission of CO_2 distribution by latitude and longitude in Australia

Emission of CO_2 distribution by altitude in Australia

FIGURE 15.9   Client for aviation emissions.

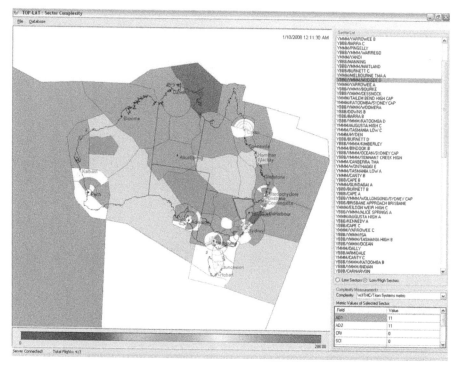

FIGURE 15.10   Client for ATC task load.

map so that it is intuitive to supervisors. TOP-LAT also has other advisory clients providing safety monitoring, trajectory optimisation, and dynamic airspace vectorisation suggestions to users.

TOP-LAT can also work in tandem with ATOMS. For example, the real traffic data can be extracted from TOP-LAT and fed into ATOMS to evaluate how advanced air traffic management concepts (such as free flight) work in a real-world situation. In contrast, ATOMS can simulate a flight itself and feed the live data of this flight into TOP-LAT to evaluate its effect in reality.

15.3   A HUMAN-IN-THE-LOOP APPLICATION

As discussed earlier in this book, we can use a simulation to shape reality. Taking air traffic management as an example, we would like to change the airspace complexity to manage the ATC workload based on objective measurements (airspace dynamic density) and subjective measurements (ATC's cognitive state). To achieve this objective, we need a shadow simulation to reproduce the reality on a computer, and an optimisation method to find a way to adjust the airspace complexity in real time. Figure 15.11 depicts the architecture of a real-time electroencephalography (EEG)-based augmented cognition system [7].

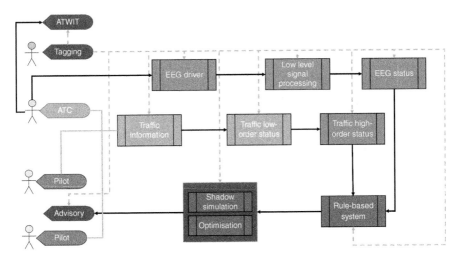

FIGURE 15.11   The adaptive logic of the real-time EEG-based augmented cognition system.

As the ATC interacts with the traffic scenario, his or her EEG data are captured, recorded, and analysed, and high-order engagement indicators are calculated in real time. Simultaneously, the traffic is analysed to extract traffic-related complexity metrics in real time. Both EEG and traffic indicators are used in a rule-based system that decides if there is a need for adaptation. Once such a need is established, an adaptive control mechanism is triggered. The adaptive control mechanism is undertaken by the shadow simulation and optimisation components. The shadow simulations must be fast enough for a real-time environment; thus, they operate at low resolution, abstraction, and fidelity levels, yet can produce acceptable outputs in a short timeframe. The traffic conditions are predicted by this shadow simulation. These predictions, along with the ATC cognitive measures, are forwarded into the optimisation component to generate an adaptive strategy over a look-ahead time. These strategies can be requests for climbing to certain flight levels, or for deviating routes. These requests are then executed by the pilot if approved by the ATC. In such a way, the real situation is affected by the outputs from shadow simulation and optimisation.

15.4 CONCLUSION

There are numerous modelling and simulation applications in the literature, which use a variety of principles, theories, and methods employed in modelling and simulation, such as ABS, DTS, human-in-the-loop, and so on.

In this chapter, we have presented a CRT application in which CRT is used in the cognitive domain for improving system performance based on improvement of the ATCs' and pilots' efficiency.

To describe the CRT application in the air traffic context, we first described the simulation environment that enabled the CRT exercise: the ATOMS air traffic simulator and the TOP-LAT real-time tactical advisory system for air traffic management. These two simulators provided the capability to evaluate advanced air traffic management concepts in a simulated environment, and made possible the application that investigated the cognitive aspects of ATC based on the CRT concept.

CHAPTER 16

Computational Red Teaming Application for Skill-based Performance Assessment

16.1 INTRODUCTION

In this chapter, we present a CRT application that focuses on skill representation, where skill representation is part of the skill assessment stage in the CRT process. The work is based on our previous publication [247].

Skill representation is demonstrated using a Sudoku puzzle. We implement computationally real human skills used in Sudoku solving, and their acquisition, in a cognitively plausible manner by using feed-forward neural networks with back-propagation, and supervised learning. The skills are attached to a hard-coded constraint propagation computational Sudoku solver, where the solving procedure is fixed, and the needed skills are represented through neural networks. The chapter shows how the skill-based solver achieves proficiency in Sudoku, depending on the amount of skills acquired through the neural networks. The application presented in this chapter serves as the foundation for developing more complex skill and skill-acquisition models usable in general simulation frameworks related to the skill assessment aspect of CRT.

CRT assumes that a red agent takes action to challenge a blue agent, with a variety of purposes. From a cognitive perspective, one of these purposes is to push blue human agents to improve their skills. The process involves two major phases. First, the red must find proper ways of action to challenge the blue – the *task probing*. Second, to find those ways of action, the red must first assess the blue's skills to find its weaknesses and seek potential directions of improvement. This represents the *skill assessment* required before the blue can improve their skills. The representation of the blue's skills plays an essential role.

While the main body of research has concentrated on using various CRT frameworks for objects and purposes related to socio-technical systems, only few and very

Simulation and Computational Red Teaming for Problem Solving, First Edition.
Jiangjun Tang, George Leu, and Hussein A. Abbass.

recent studies tried to use CRT in the cognitive domain, where the CRT object is cognition of human individuals, for purposes such as augmentation of human performance and cognitive skills [1, 16]. In the cognitive domain, the only object of the CRT process consists of the cognitive skills of a human individual; hence, the colloquial understanding of CRT is that a red entity takes challenging actions towards a human (the blue entity) to augment the cognitive skills of the latter in relation to certain tasks of interest. However, to undertake the challenging actions, the red must first assess the blue's skills to find its weaknesses and subsequent potential directions for improvement. Further, to be able to assess the blue's skills, the red must achieve proper representation of these skills and understand how they develop. Only after properly modelling the skills, skill-acquisition process and assessment process will the red be able to generate challenging actions directed towards the blue's weaknesses. Thus, skill modelling and assessment (SMA) is paramount in creating the challenge capability of the red entity, and is subsequently an essential component of the overall CRT exercise. However, a structured approach for this essential component of the CRT has not yet been reported in the literature.

This chapter builds on the cognitive domain of the CRT by presenting a methodology for the SMA component. The methodology is based on CTA, and enhances the classic general CTA sequence with a CRT-specific component that models cognitive skill acquisition. The proposed CTA-based methodology is instantiated and demonstrated in a practical context using the Sudoku puzzle. The Sudoku puzzle is used as a vehicle for testing the methodology and demonstrating the computability of the SMA component of CRT. At the same time, the puzzle implicitly becomes a tool for demonstrating the skill acquisition, the learning process and the resultant task/skill proficiency.

The chapter is organised as follows. Section 16.2 briefly describes the SMA methodology and its rationale in the CRT context. Sections 16.3 and 16.4 describe the path from the human player Sudoku solvers to computational solvers as follows: Section 16.3 shows how we choose from the range of human skills used in Sudoku solving, and Section 16.4 investigates the computational Sudoku solvers for facilitating the transfer of human skills into a skill representation and acquisition model. Section 16.5 describes the methodology used for modelling the skills and a neural network-based skill-acquisition process. Section 16.6 presents and discusses the results of the resultant simulation. The final section concludes the discussion and summarises the lessons learnt.

16.2 COGNITIVE TASK ANALYSIS-BASED SKILL MODELLING AND ASSESSMENT METHODOLOGY

CTA provides a very diverse range of techniques to extract and/or describe the knowledge required for performance of a task. It is a valuable approach used to capture the cognitive skills used by experts to accomplish a target task at a desired standard of performance [285, 338]. The outcome is typically a description of the performance objectives, equipment, conceptual knowledge, procedural knowledge, and performance standards used by experts as they perform a task. The descriptions are formatted so they can be used as records of task performance and to inform novices in a way that helps them achieve the performance goals in any context. The descriptions are then used to develop expert systems, as tests to certify job or task competence, and for training to acquire new or more complex knowledge.

The reason for using a CTA-based methodology in a CRT context is the very nature of the CTA, whose purpose is to identify and explain the mental processes and skills involved in performing a certain task. This approach is pertinent in the context of the SMA stage of the CRT process, where skill knowledge about the blue agent can be achieved through a detailed investigation of the cognitive skills involved in a task by performing a realistic and comprehensive decomposition of the solving process into sub-tasks, along with the associated skills and sub-skills needed to perform them. After establishing the primitive skills, their interaction and interdependency, and the intimate nature of the task-solving process, one can further create a realistic computational task solver that holds high resemblance with the human solving process. If such a solver models and implements in a cognitively plausible manner the architecture of skills and the subsequent skill acquisition process, along with a plausible solving process, then it can be used to reveal those skills that are insufficiently developed or completely missing in humans, as facilitators for development of targeted, microscopically-enabled, individually-customised challenge models. A scenario explaining the above statement is a computational solver of a task 'A' that runs in parallel with a human player solving the task 'A', and monitors if the human moves correctly through the solving process and if the human correctly applies the corresponding skills. The challenging process could then consist of either suggesting actions to the human in real time, or proposing customised tasks that would expose the player to situations involving the missing skills – that is, acquire skills by thinking or doing, respectively [308].

We conjecture that a realistic computational solver should start from the concepts of skill acquisition through experience [17], skill re-utilisation and integration [344], and skill heterarchy (scaffold) [350] – concepts that are present in most major classical cognitive theories, such as the unified theories of cognition [302], the SoM [287], and the ACT-R [19], as well as in the resultant cognitive computational architectures that instantiate them [229, 251, 343]. The proficiency of a human player in solving a task is nevertheless given by the proficiency in each of the skills required for solving that task. When the human fails to apply one of the skills or applies a skill incorrectly because of lack of training/experience in using that skill, the resultant overall ability to solve the task is influenced by that particular skill in itself, and also by the inability to apply other skills that depend on it in the overall solving process.

16.2.1 Instantiation of Skill Modelling and Assessment Methodology on Sudoku Puzzle

The CTA-based methodology described above is instantiated and demonstrated in a practical context using the Sudoku puzzle. First, Sudoku solving is a task that can easily fit into the CTA paradigm because the solving process is well structured and highly traceable, thus being suitable for task/skill decomposition. Second, the puzzle is very popular and largely available for use in both printed and digital formats online and offline. Moreover, in addition to the puzzle itself, a large amount of practitioner documentation is also available. The third reason is the existence of a consistent body of research that associates Sudoku solving with various cognitive abilities, such as associative memory [189, 409], logical thinking and reasoning [30, 256], lateral thinking [320], and working memory [80, 164]. Some studies have proposed Sudoku-based training programs for improving various cognitive abilities in students [30], while others used Sudoku puzzles as remedial methods for patients with various mental illnesses [80, 123, 305] or to alleviate age-related cognitive degeneration [164, 174]. In addition, studies in cognitive neuroscience used Sudoku in conjunction with various physiological sensors, such as EEG, to measure the cognitive load [294, 295] or establish relations between various steps in the solving process and specific neural activity patterns [381, 392, 393].

Thus, based on the CTA-based SMA methodology, we implement a human-like skill-based computational Sudoku solver that emulates in a cognitively plausible manner the steps followed by human players to solve the puzzle. The solver uses a heterarchical model [17, 287] of primitive Sudoku skills, a human-like algorithm to apply the skills, and a deep architecture of neural networks to represent and learn these skills from scratch. For each of the primitive skills considered in the skill model we assign a primitive neural network in the deep neural network architecture, and we simulate various levels of proficiency by varying the amount of 'exposure' of that network to situations containing the skill. We then test the overall Sudoku proficiency of the solver in a set of Sudoku games, using several setups in which we set different levels of proficiency for the primitive skills in the skill heterarchy.

16.3 SUDOKU AND HUMAN PLAYERS

Sudoku is a number puzzle that, in its most popular form, consists of 81 cells contained in a 9×9 square grid, which is further divided into nine boxes of 3×3 cells. The goal of the player is to fill all cells in the grid with single digits between 1 and 9, so that a given number appears only once in the unit it belongs to (the unit can be a row, a column, or a box). These are the Sudoku rules or constraints. In general, the Sudoku puzzle can be structured as a $n \times n$ grid with n subsequent boxes of $\sqrt{n} \times \sqrt{n}$ cells. The constraints for a grid G can then be expressed in general as follows:

1. **Cell:** A cell $C_{ij} \in G$ must be filled with exactly one number v_{ij} with value between 1 and n.
2. **Row:** All values in a row i must be unique: $v_{ij} \neq v_{ik}$, $\forall i = 1, n$ and $\forall j, k = 1, n$ with $j \neq k$.
3. **Column:** All values in a column j must be unique: $v_{ij} \neq v_{kj}$, $\forall j = 1, n$ and $\forall i, k = 1, n$ with $i \neq k$.
4. **Box:** All values in a box $B_i \in G$ must be unique: $v_{jk} \neq v_{pq}$, $\forall d \in B_i$, with $i = 1, n$.

The skills needed to solve Sudoku grids of various levels of difficulty have been described over time by many enthusiastic practitioners in puzzle-solving communities around the world. As a result, an impressive documentation on Sudoku has been published in the last few decades, since the puzzle gained tremendous popularity worldwide [26, 320]. Human players learn these skills gradually as they gain experience with the game, or in an accelerated manner by studying the existing documentation. Subsequently, the difficulty of Sudoku puzzles has been defined by practitioners based on the complexity of the skills required to solve them. Some of the Sudoku documentation [26, 79, 109] assumed that players choose which skills to use based on the perceived difficulty of the game and the current grid state. Using this approach, some authors consider that the difficulty of a Sudoku puzzle is proportional to the number of times a skill is used [270].

16.3.1 Playing a Game

In this chapter the 9×9 Sudoku board is used. A player visits the empty cells, applies the Sudoku constraints, and generates the lists of candidates for them. This process is displayed in Figure 16.1, where Figure 16.1a shows the application of Sudoku constraints to cell C_{G4}, and Figure 16.1b shows the lists of candidates for all empty cells in the grid.

The player applies various Sudoku skills and propagates the Sudoku constraints to reduce the lists of candidates to unique candidates [359] for all empty cells in the grid, which leads to filling the grid and solving the puzzle.

16.3.1.1 The Scanning Skill   To be able to solve an empty cell, the players first need to be able to locate and direct their attention towards the whole unit of which the cell is a part in the grid. Finding the relevant unit (row, column, or box) for a particular cell is an acquired skill, without which a player cannot proceed to any other action in a Sudoku game. While this skill may seem trivial from a human perspective, it is nevertheless one of the cognitive skills that remains at the foundation of Sudoku

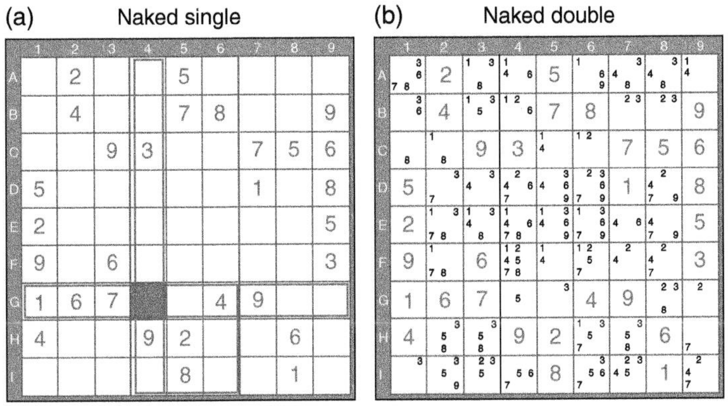

FIGURE 16.1   The game knowledge.

solving, and one of the essential skills that needs to be modelled in the case of a skill-based cognitive solver that learns the game from the scratch.

16.3.1.2 The Domain Propagation Skills

Once the players are able to find the proper unit for one or more cells of interest, they can proceed to propagating the domain to reduce the lists of candidates – also known as *degrees of freedom* – of empty cells. The skills considered in this study belong to two categories – the *naked* and the *hidden* candidates. While this is not a complete list of skills, these actually allow the solving of a significant number of Sudoku games. More complex skills can be adopted for solving very difficult games [320], yet it is beyond the scope of this study to investigate an exhaustive list of skills. Thus, we concentrate on four domain propagation skills, as follows.

The set of naked candidate skills consists of finding and propagating naked singles and doubles (Figure 16.2). Recognising and propagating a naked single is the most basic skill, where, after the application of Sudoku constraints, a cell has only one possible candidate. The value of this unique candidate solves the empty cell, and is propagated by removing the candidate value from the candidate lists of all other cells situated in the same unit(s). A naked single is illustrated in Figure 16.2a in cell C_{A1}.

For naked doubles, the lists of candidates are checked for a pair of cells in a Sudoku unit containing only the same two candidates. These candidates can only go in these cells; thus, the propagation is done by removing them from the candidate lists of all other unsolved cells in that unit. In Figure 16.2b, the cells situated in Column 3 at C_{F3} and C_{I3} show a naked double containing the candidate values (2, 3).

The set of hidden candidate skills consists of finding and propagating hidden singles and doubles (Figure 16.3). For the hidden single, if a candidate value appears in only one cell in a Sudoku unit (row, column, or box), the value becomes the unique candidate for that cell, and the rest is removed. Then, the candidate becomes a naked

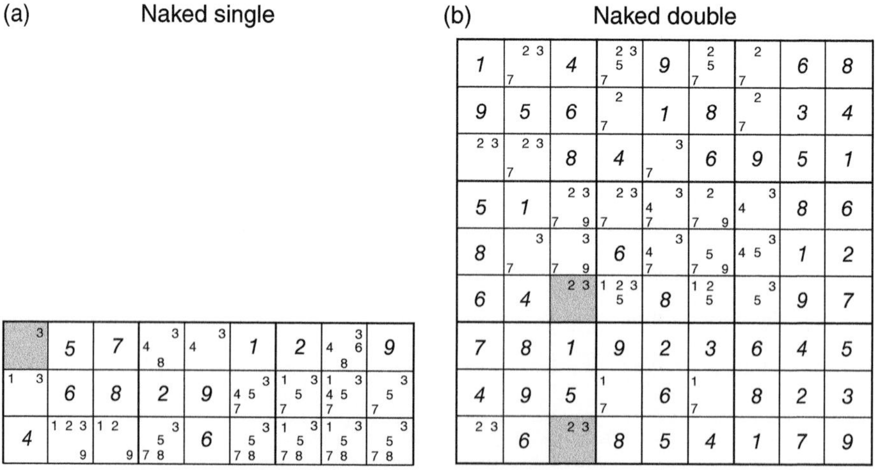

FIGURE 16.2   Naked candidates.

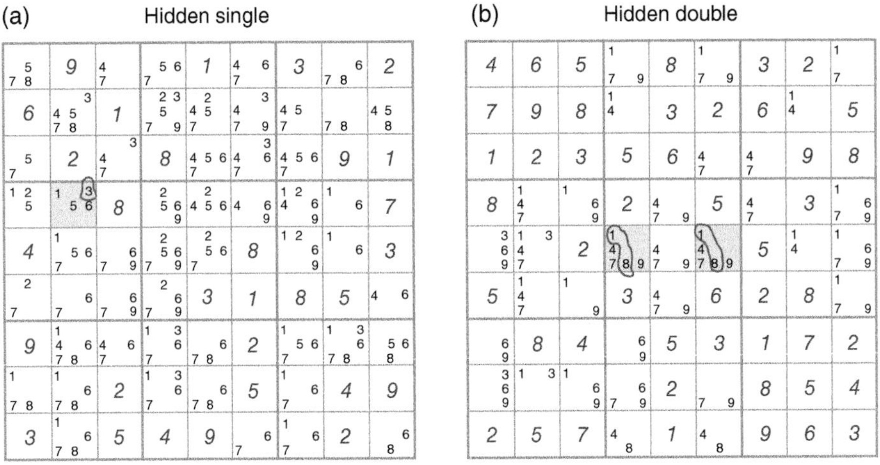

(a)   Hidden single   (b)   Hidden double

FIGURE 16.3   Hidden candidates.

single and propagates the domain as a naked single. Figure 16.3a shows value 3 as a hidden single in cell C_{D2}. For the hidden double, if a given pair of candidates appears in only two empty cells in a unit, then only these candidates must remain in these cells, and all other candidates are removed. Then, the hidden double becomes a naked double and propagates the domain as a naked double. Figure 16.3b shows the hidden pair $(1, 8)$ in cells C_{E4} and C_{E6}.

It can be observed from the above description that the domain propagation skills consist of two stages, in which two sub-skills are applied. In the first stage, there is a pattern recognition skill in which the player checks the pattern of the lists of candidates in a unit to see if a particular skill can be applied. After the pattern is found to be part of the valid ones, the actual propagation of domain is executed. We note that this decomposition of the domain propagation skills into sub-skills is of extreme cognitive importance to the proposed computational skill-based solver.

16.3.1.3 The 'Skill Selection' Skill

In Sudoku documentation [26, 79, 109], authors usually consider that players choose the domain propagation skills based on the perceived context at the current move. Thus, the propagation of domains can be very different depending on which of the domain propagation skills are performed, when they are performed, and to which cells/units. Proficiency in Sudoku depends nevertheless on mastering the domain propagation skills; however, two players with the same propagation skillset can generate different propagation patterns. This is because the selection of the appropriate domain propagation skills is itself a skill acquired and continuously improved through experience.

A discussion on skill selection based on the available practitioners' literature [26, 79, 109] reveals two main approaches to solving the puzzle. It is considered that most Sudoku players adopt an exhaustive use of the propagation skills. In this case, the player performs the skills in a predefined order for any game, starting with the simple ones and gradually progressing towards the more complex ones. This is an exhaustive search method; however, it is not similar to the brute-force computational method of solving Sudoku (discussed in the next section), which is not plausible from a human player perspective, and not related to realistic Sudoku skills. The exhaustive performance of skills is plausible from a human player perspective, and we could computationally model a player that masters domain propagation skills, but has not yet accumulated comprehensive experience/exposure to Sudoku games, and hence has less developed skill-selection skills.

More advanced users tend to adopt a recursive use of the propagation skills. In this case, if the player performs a skill i at a moment in time and the propagation unveils clue patterns immediately usable with other skills, then the player follows that propagation branch until the propagation is not possible any more. Following this, the player returns to where it was and continues with skill i. This method provides a wiser use of skills, and the propagation of domain towards the completion of the game is potentially faster.

Both the recursive and the exhaustive selection of skills are identical in terms of the ability of the player to complete a game; they only create different propagation patterns that allow more experienced users to complete games in fewer steps and thus with less effort. From a computational perspective, the exhaustive selection provides a propagation pattern constant over the space of Sudoku games, while the recursive selection generates a game-dependant propagation pattern. In this study, we will use exhaustive selection because it is more trackable and consistent over multiple games, compared with recursive selection.

16.4 SUDOKU AND COMPUTATIONAL SOLVERS

Research on computational Sudoku solvers is rich, given the relatively short history of the game. However, most of the existing approaches focus on designing efficient solvers, without necessarily considering the plausibility of the solving process (what to do) or the cognitive skills (how to do it) involved in solving. In relation to these two key aspects – the solving process and the cognitive skills – we identified in the existing literature two categories of approaches: pure search-based solvers and cognitively plausible solvers.

16.4.1 Search-based Computational Sudoku Solvers

In this category, the solvers are based purely on search or optimisation and are not concerned with the process or the skills adopted by a human player. They mainly aim to reduce the implementation and computational complexity and to solve the puzzle through holistic search, without Sudoku-specific expertise and skills.

The simplest in this category, which is the least effective, is the exhaustive solver. This is a brute-force method that uses the full space of possible grids to perform a backtracked depth-first search through the resultant solution tree [44]. Another simple solver is the 'pencil and paper' algorithm [103], which visits cells in the grid and generates a search tree on the fly.

Another class of computational solvers in this category is based on stochastic techniques. Several studies tried to develop nature-inspired heuristics to find the unique Sudoku solutions. For example, a swarm robotics solver was proposed in [314]. This uses an artificial bee colony (ABC) to perform a guided exploration of the Sudoku grid search space. The algorithm mimics the behaviour of foraging bees, which is used for building (partial/local) solutions in the problem domain. The algorithm aims to minimise the number of duplicate digits on each row and column. The authors compared the ABC algorithm with a Sudoku solver based on a classic GA proposed by Mantere and Koljonen [265], and showed that the ABC solver significantly outperformed the GA solver (i.e. on average, 6 243 processing cycles for ABC versus 1 238 749 cycles for GA). Perez and Marwala [317] proposed and compared four stochastic optimisation solvers: a cultural GA (CGA), a repulsive particle swarm optimisation (RPSO) algorithm, a quantum simulated annealing (QSA) algorithm, and a hybrid method combining a GA with simulated annealing (HGASA). The authors found that the CGA, QSA, and HGASA were successful, with runtimes of 28, 65, and 1.447, seconds, respectively, while the RPSO failed to solve any puzzle.

Mathematically, the general $n \times n$ formulation of Sudoku is considered [128, 373, 397] an NP- complete problem belonging to the set of 21 NP-complete problems defined in [210]. Takayuki and Takahiro [373] provided the first computational Sudoku solver that used this assumption and demonstrated that the problem can be solved in finite time. Later, another approach [128] converted through reduction a Sudoku problem into a 'Boolean satisfiability' problem, also known as SAT. The approach allowed not only the solving, but also the analysis of a Sudoku puzzle difficulty from a polynomial computation time perspective. A similar SAT-based solver was also proposed in [397], where the author described a straightforward translation of a Sudoku grid into a propositional formula. The translation, combined with a general-purpose SAT solver, was able to solve 9×9 puzzles within milliseconds.

16.4.2   Cognitively Plausible Computational Solvers

In this second category, the solvers could be plausible from a cognitive perspective, and could have the potential of resembling the underpinnings of general human thinking. However, they still aim to solve, rather than to design human-like solvers, and do not attempt to recreate the solving process and skills adopted by human players.

One class of solvers in this category is based on neural networks and consists of classic connectionist approaches [189, 409]. The neural network-based solvers are still holistic search approaches that solve the puzzles without Sudoku knowledge and skills; however, their neural-based implementation in itself implies a certain cognitive plausibility. In [409], the authors introduced a Sudoku solver that used the Qtron energy-driven neural network model. First, they mapped the Sudoku rules in the energy function of the Qtron. Then, they minimised the energy function, while using a noise-injection mechanism to ensure that local minima were avoided. The authors showed that the algorithm was not successful in the absence of noise; however, with the noise injected, the success rate was 100% and the runtime was within one second. In addition, they demonstrated that the algorithm could be used not only for solving, but also for generating puzzles with unique solutions. In a different approach, Hopfield [189] considered that neural networks do not work well when applied to Sudoku because they tend to make errors on the way. While [409] treated this problem by injecting noise in the Qtron, Hopfield assumed that the search space during a Sudoku game can be mapped into an associative memory. This is then used to recognise the inherent errors and reposition the neural network representation of the Sudoku grid on the proper search path.

Another major approach in this category is represented by constraint propagation solvers. Several studies considered that Sudoku puzzles can be treated as constraint satisfaction problems [306, 359], and solved using constraint programming techniques. Constraint propagation solvers are purely computational methods, and the studies proposing them follow the same purpose as the rest of the computational approaches – that is, to produce proficient Sudoku solvers with minimal computational complexity and no domain knowledge. However, the constraint propagation processes described in both [359] and [306] follow the sequence of steps taken by human Sudoku solvers. They describe the algorithm followed by human players to reduce the degree of freedom of empty cells and propagate the domain. Norvig [306] noted that the major task performed by humans when playing Sudoku is not to fill an empty cell, but to eliminate the multiple candidates for it, as a result of applying and propagating the Sudoku constraints. Yet the author did not mention in which way the propagation of constraints resembles human thinking. This was explained in [359] where Simonis stated that the skills used by human players when trying to eliminate redundant candidates from cells are actually propagation schemes that participate in a constraint propagation process that eventually solves the constraint satisfaction problem. Simonis stated that 'they [human players] apply complex propagation schemes with names like **X-Wing** and **Swordfish** to find solutions of a rather simple looking puzzle called Sudoku. Unfortunately, they are not aware that this is constraint programming'. An even more advanced step towards demonstrating this concept was taken in [44], where the authors implemented the constraint propagation based on a set of actual Sudoku skills (e.g. naked candidates, hidden candidates, and Nishio-guess). The authors did not relate their algorithm to the constraint propagation formalism or to the concept of cognitive skills, and referred to it as 'rule-based', yet emphasised that it 'consists of testing a puzzle for certain rules that … eliminate candidate numbers. This algorithm is similar to the one human solver uses'.

16.4.3   Towards a Human-like Skill-based Computational Solver

It is clear that the existing approaches do not qualify for a hypothetical third category of human-like skill-based Sudoku solvers, which should take into account the steps taken by human players, human players' realistic skills, and a cognitively plausible acquisition of these skills, all in an architecture that is itself cognitively plausible. In this chapter, we build on the concepts proposed by the constraint propagation solvers. We support the idea that solving Sudoku is fundamentally a constraint propagation problem [306, 359]. A human player applies the Sudoku constraints (rules) and gradually finds unique candidates for the empty cells in the Sudoku grid. Each time an empty cell is solved, the grid status changes, and application of the Sudoku constraints in the new conditions unveils new clues that lead to solving other cells. Thus, the player unveils clue after clue until the last empty cell is solved. This actually describes a constraint propagation process that is undertaken by the human player. However, the constraint propagation solvers are ideal computational implementations of the constraint propagation process performed by humans. From a human player perspective, the constraint propagation solvers implement perfect/ideal human players that have infinite Sudoku skills and flawless cognitive abilities, so that they produce the propagation of constraints in an optimal manner. In reality though, a human player may have limited skills, such as the learned ability to recognise and apply Sudoku-specific clue patterns or the learned ability to choose between several simultaneously available clue patterns. Thus, the resultant propagation of constraints occurs in an imperfect manner.

The proposed skill-based solver embeds the model of a number of skills required for a certain level of Sudoku proficiency, the model of learning the skills from the scratch, and the model of the solving process.

16.5   THE PROPOSED SKILL-BASED COMPUTATIONAL SOLVER

Earlier in the chapter, we presented in detail the Sudoku solving process from a human player's perspective, starting from practitioners' experience and the literature. Based on the descriptive presentation of the skills involved in Sudoku solving, and taking into account the discussion on computational Sudoku solvers, we propose a skill model as the foundation of the skill-based computational solver, as shown in Figure 16.4. The skill model consists of three levels: a lower level consisting of

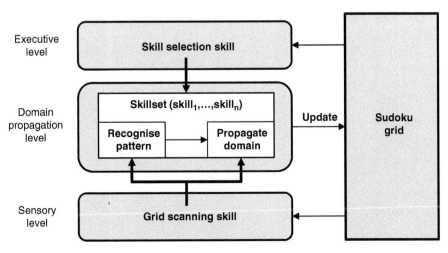

FIGURE 16.4   The skill model.

the visual grid-scanning skill, a middle level containing a set of two-stage domain propagation skills, and a higher level consisting of the skill selection (executive) skill.

We note that the domain propagation level relies directly on the sensory level, without which the cells could not be accessed to be used for recognition and propagation. The executive level relies on the domain propagation level, without which there would be no existing skills to choose from. Thus, the executive level depends indirectly on the sensory level, only through the need to access cells when needed. For this reason, only the skills in the domain propagation level are considered for skill selection.

16.5.1 The Solving Algorithm

Figure 16.5 shows the process flow that stands at the core of the proposed Sudoku solver. The process is human-like, following the same steps described in Sudoku practitioners' literature. It embeds the skills used by human players and describes how the skills in each level of the proposed skill model are used throughout the game. We emphasise that the solver captures and models, in a realistic manner, the interaction of the human player with the Sudoku grid during the puzzle solving – that is, the scanning skill is performed at each step, in support of the domain propagation skills, when the need to consult the grid arises.

The executive level is the backbone of the computational solver, and is implemented based on the exhaustive selection described earlier in the chapter. Algorithm 4 presents the resultant computational algorithm, which in words can be described as follows. The agent starts with the simplest skill checking for the naked singles on all empty cells in the grid. After finding and propagating them, it searches again through the grid until no other naked single is found. In a similar manner, it then checks for and propagates the hidden singles, naked doubles and hidden doubles, and repeats the process if the game is not over.

Of all the skills considered in the skill model, the executive level is the only one that is hard-coded in the solver; subsequently, the skill selection skill is not subject to a skill acquisition process, like the other skills. All other skills are subject to a learning process that we model using an architecture of neural networks, as described in the following section.

16.5.2 The Deep Neural Network Architecture for Skill Acquisition

Figure 16.6 presents the skill model as a deep neural network architecture. The executive level of skills, the skill selection, is hard coded and not subject to a learning process. This was explained in detail in the previous section and described in Algorithm 4. For the other two levels, scanning and domain propagation, the skills and subsequent skill-acquisition process are modelled through feed-forward neural networks with a back-propagation mechanism.

In general, we could use feed-forward networks with different sizes for the different skills they train. Figure 16.6 shows this general case, where the indexes s, r, and

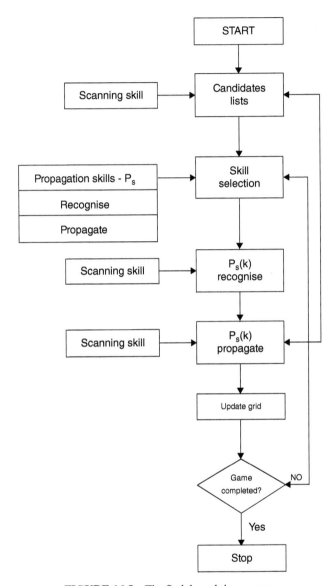

FIGURE 16.5   The Sudoku solving process.

p denote the size of input, hidden and output layers for scanning skill, recognition sub-skills, and propagation sub-skills, respectively. However, in this study, we use networks with the same size, with 81 units in the input layer, 10 units in the hidden layer and 9 units in the output layer, as shown in Figure 16.7. The detailed architecture of neural networks, customised to the Sudoku skills considered in this chapter, is presented in Figure 16.8, where all networks have identical structure and size.

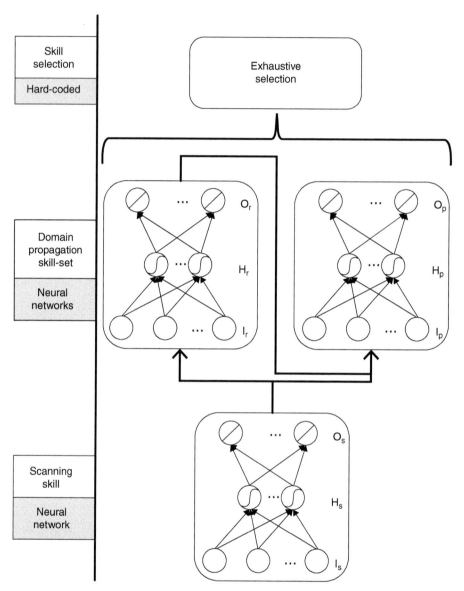

FIGURE 16.6   The deep neural network for acquisition of skills – architectural schema.

We use the standard tanh function for modelling the activation function of nodes in the networks and the mean square root error function for the subsequent gradient minimisation. We use artificially generated training sets (explained in detail in the following subsections) that are split in ratios of 0.7, 0.15, and 0.15 for training, internal cross-validation, and generalisation testing, respectively.

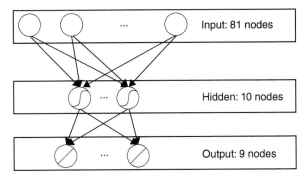

FIGURE 16.7   The same network size for skill acquisition at all levels.

Algorithm 4 Exhaustive Selection

1: {Input: initial Sudoku grid (G)}
2: sort propagation skill-set P_s in ascending order of skill complexity
3: {generate initial candidates list for each cell}
4: **for all** *cells* $C_{ij} \in G$ **do**
5:     perform scan skill S_s
6:     apply Sudoku constraints
7: **end for**
8: {reduce candidates lists to unique candidates}
9: **while** !*EndOf Game* **do**
10:     **for** i = 1 **to** $size(P_s)$ **do**
11:         **while** $P_s(i)$ is still applicable **do**
12:             **for all** *emptycells* **do**
13:                 perform scan skill S_s
14:                 perform $P_s(i).recognition$
15:                 perform scan skill S_s
16:                 perform $P_s(i).propagation$
17:                 update candidate lists
18:                 update grid
19:             **end for**
20:             check $P_s(i)$ applicability
21:         **end while**
22:     **end for**
23:     Check *EndOf Game*
24: **end while**

16.5.3   The Experience-based Skill Acquisition

To ensure the cognitive plausibility of the proposed Sudoku solver, we adopt an understanding of training neural networks that reflects the skill acquisition in humans, as opposed to the general machine learning understanding of neural networks. From a

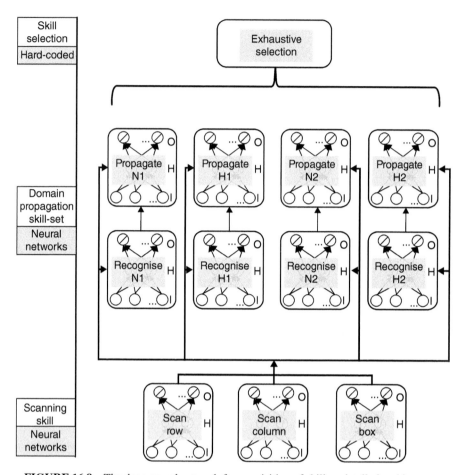

FIGURE 16.8   The deep neural network for acquisition of skills – detailed architecture.

purely computational intelligence perspective (machine learning), supervised training of standard feed-forward neural networks can easily produce 100% success rates
in recognising the patterns considered for learning, given that the appropriate training datasets are used. Given that generating the proper training datasets for the skills
considered in this study is possible, we can assume that delivering perfectly trained
networks for Sudoku skills is achievable as well. However, our purpose is not to train
the networks to perfection, but to reveal the skill-acquisition process – that is, to produce various levels of proficiency for primitive skills as a result of the amount of
exposure of the solver to tasks requiring the usage of those skills [49, 344]. Thus,
we generate various levels of skill proficiency by training the primitive skills used in
this study with training datasets of different sizes. In this way, we emulate the human
process of gaining proficiency in a skill by repeatedly performing the tasks related to
that skill. We associate the number of samples in a training dataset with the amount

of times the solver used that skill. The richer the datasets, the higher the success rate of the trained neural networks in recognising the skill-related patterns.

16.5.3.1 *Basic Primitive-skill Proficiency*

We further explain the skill proficiency idea discussed above by using a practical Sudoku example. We consider that the skill to be trained is the recognition sub-skill corresponding to the naked single pattern. This means that the solver must recognise in a Sudoku unit the cell(s) with only one candidate. Given that there are 9 cells in a Sudoku unit, and the unique candidate can be a digit from 1 to 9, there are 81 possibilities of a naked single in any unit, if we assume that only a maximum of one naked single can exist in a unit. Thus, we can artificially generate 81 data samples, with each sample representing a unit that contains a single candidate in one of the cells, and random lists of candidates in the other eight cells. From the skill-acquisition perspective, this represents a solver that has been exposed only once to each of the 81 possible appearances of a naked single in a unit. We consider this the basic expertise that the Sudoku solver can achieve in this primitive skill, similar to a beginner level, and we will refer to this throughout this chapter as *basic primitive-skill proficiency* (BPSP) for a primitive skill, i.

We expect that a neural network associated with one of the primitive skills that is trained with a BPSP dataset will have a fairly low success rate in recognising the pattern of that skill. We also expect that higher success rates will be obtained by using larger training datasets that account for multiple exposures to each possible appearance of a skill pattern in a Sudoku unit. This equals using datasets of sizes multiple times the BPSP dataset size (e.g. $5 \times BPSP$, $10 \times BPSP$, etc.). Thus, when aggregating the primitive skills into the proposed solver architecture, we expect that, with the same set of primitive skills, we can generate solvers of different overall Sudoku proficiency, depending on the level of primitive skill proficiency for which the deep neural networks were trained.

In the following subsection, we describe in detail the BPSP training datasets for each primitive skill considered in this study.

16.5.4 Training Datasets for Basic Primitive-skill Proficiency

16.5.4.1 *Scanning Skills*

The role of the scanning skill is to retrieve the unit to which the current cell belongs, where a unit can be a row, column or box, depending on the situation. Thus, training the scanning skill involves training three neural networks to recognise/locate the three types of units, with one network for each type. The input encoding and output interpretation for each type of unit are shown in Figure 16.9.

The training dataset is a binary matrix consisting of 81 samples ($X_{ij}, i = 1 : 81, j = 1 : 81$). In the arbitrary sample shown in Figure 16.9, the 81 inputs encode the position of a cell in the Sudoku grid, where the cells in the grid are numbered by row and then by column, starting from the top-left corner. For each of the three networks, the output shows the unit to which the cell belongs. In the current example, the current target set $t_k = t_k(1 : 9)$ will have the elements corresponding to Row 4, Column 7 and Box 6 set to 1, and all other elements set to -1.

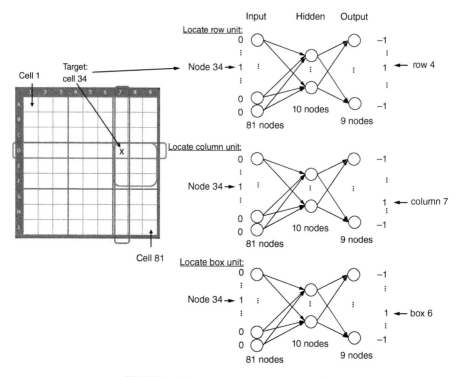

FIGURE 16.9   Training the scanning skill.

16.5.4.2 *Domain Recognition Sub-skills*   When performing the recognition sub-skill, the solver must recognise the pattern of a propagation skill in the lists of candidates in a unit. To do so, the output of scanning skill is used – that is, the unit provided by the scanning skill is where the pattern is searched. We model the skills and the skill-acquisition process using neural networks with the same structure presented in Figure 16.7.

Figure 16.10 shows how the information about the candidate list is encoded into the input layer of neural networks. In a Sudoku unit, each of the nine cells can have a maximum of nine potential candidates – that is, the digits from 1 to 9. However, at a certain step in the game, the current candidate lists usually contain fewer than nine digits; the lists can be depicted as in the third row of the table. We encode the decimal values of the candidates into binary values, as presented in the third row. The total length of the binary encoded lists of candidates is 81; thus, we use neural networks with 81 neurons in the input layer. The nine nodes in the output layer correspond to the nine cells in a Sudoku unit. Depending on which skill is subject to recognition, the cells where the skill pattern exists will fire.

For each skill, artificially generated training and target sets are used, as shown in Algorithm 5. Thus, we implement four networks that train the naked single, hidden single, naked, double and hidden double, candidate skills, each of them with its own training and target datasets.

Sudoku unit (row/col/box)	Cell 1	...	Cell 9
All possible candidates	123456789	...	123456789
Current candidate list	2 4 7 9	...	3 5 89
Encoding	010100101	...	001010011

NN input: 81 neurons

FIGURE 16.10   Neural network input.

Algorithm 5 Recognition Stage: Training and Target Sets for a Skill $S_i \in SkillSet$

1: {Input: Skill S_i }
2: **for** i = 1 **to** No. of S_i patterns in a Sudoku unit **do**
3:    **for all** cells in the Sudoku unit **do**
4:       trainingSet: $x(i, allcells) = S_i$ pattern
5:       targetSet: $t(i, allOutputN odes) = 1$
6:    **end for**
7: **end for**
8: **for** j = 1 **to** No. of S_i patterns in a Sudoku unit **do**
9:    **for all** cells in the Sudoku unit **do**
10:      trainingSet: $x(i + j, allcells) = randompattern$
11:      targetSet: $t(i, allOutputNodes) = -1$
12:    **end for**
13: **end for**

For the single candidate skills, naked and hidden, the training dataset contains 81 samples of length 81 bits ($X_{ij}, i = 1 : 81, j = 1 : 81$). The 81 samples correspond to all possible appearances of a naked or hidden single in a unit (i.e. there can be 81 naked/hidden single situations in a Sudoku column, row or box).

For the double candidate skills, naked and hidden, the training dataset contains 1296 samples of length 81 bits ($X_{ij}, i = 1 : 1296, j = 1 : 81$), corresponding to all possible appearances of a double candidate in a unit (i.e. there can be 1296 naked double situations in a Sudoku column, row or box).

The target set is a matrix $T(i, k)$ with ($i = 1 : TrainSetSize, k = 1 : 9$), defined as in Eq. (16.1). For the single candidates, the output will consist of a single node with a value of 1, corresponding to the cell in the unit where the candidate is located. For the double candidates, two of the output units will fire, showing the cell where the candidates are located.

$$T(i, k) = \begin{cases} 1 & \text{if } X(i, 1 : 81) \text{ contains the skill pattern} \\ -1 & \text{otherwise} \end{cases} \tag{16.1}$$

16.5.4.3 Domain Propagation Sub-skills For the propagation sub-skills, the solver must reduce the candidate lists of all cells in the unit or units eligible for change in relation to the candidate pattern recognised by the recognition sub-skill. This is also modelled using the same neural network structure as with the other levels of skills (Figure 16.7).

The input layer uses the same encoding as in the propagation sub-skill case (Figure 16.10) – that is, the lists of candidates for all 9 cells in the unit of interest generate an 81 binary array for the 81 nodes. The nine nodes in the output layer correspond to the nine candidates of the current cell to be updated. Depending on which skill is subject to propagation, the nodes corresponding to the candidates that need to be removed from the cell will fire. We note that the cells in a unit that is eligible for propagation are updated one by one; thus, the propagation sub-skills are performed on cells, not on whole units.

The artificially generated training datasets for the four training processes (four skills) are similar to the recognition sub-skills case. However, the target sets are different, since the outputs encode the list of nine candidates of a cell, instead of the nine cells of a Sudoku unit. For the naked candidates, the propagation process updates the cell of interest by removing the recognised candidates from the candidates list; thus, the target set is a matrix $T_{naked}(i, k)$ ($i = 1 : TrainSetSize, k = 1 : 9$), defined as in Eq. (16.2). For the hidden candidates, the propagation process updates the cell of interest by removing all other candidates, except the recognised ones. Thus, the target set is a matrix $T_{hidden}(i, k)$ ($i = 1 : TrainSetSize, k = 1 : 9$), defined as in Eq. (16.3). The generation of both the training and target sets is described in Algorithm 6.

$$T_{naked}(i, k) = \begin{cases} 1 & \text{if } X(i, 1 : 81) \text{ contains the skill pattern} \\ -1 & \text{otherwise} \end{cases} \tag{16.2}$$

$$T_{hidden}(i, k) = \begin{cases} -1 & \text{if } X(i, 1 : 81) \text{ contains the skill pattern} \\ 1 & \text{otherwise} \end{cases} \tag{16.3}$$

Algorithm 6 Propagation Stage: Training and Target Sets for a Skill $S_i \in SkillSet$

1: {Input: Skill S_i }
2: **for** i = 1 **to** No. of S_i patterns in a Sudoku unit **do**
3:     **for all** cells in the current Sudoku unit **do**
4:         trainingSet: $x(i, allcells) = S_i$ *pattern*
5:     **end for**
6: **end for**
7: **for all** cells in the current Sudoku unit **do**
8:     auxiliarVector=output(S_i-related candidates in the cell)
9:     targetSet: $t(i, auxiliarVector) = -1$
10: **end for**

16.6 DISCUSSION OF SIMULATION RESULTS

We test the proposed solver in two sets of experiments. In the first set, we test the acquisition of primitive skills and investigate how the proficiency in each skill is determined by the exposure of the solving entity to certain amounts of situations requiring the use of that skill. This is achieved by training the corresponding neural networks separately, with artificially generated training sets of various sizes, as explained earlier in the chapter. In the second set of experiments, we investigate the overall Sudoku proficiency generated by the aggregate use of primitive skills with various levels of proficiency. The primitive skills trained in advance with artificial data are aggregated in the proposed solver, and then the solver is tested in 100 real Sudoku games selected from sudoku-solutions.com. The *Sudoku-Solutions* website is one of the many websites that offer free Sudoku games. Of the 785 games of various difficulty levels, we selected a set of 100 games so that each game can be solved with exactly the set of four domain propagation skills considered in this study: single candidates – naked and hidden, and double candidates – naked and hidden. The reason for this choice is that easier games do not use all four skills, and hence the testing of the proposed solver would be incomplete, while more difficult games require other skills not considered in this chapter, and hence the solver would be unable to finish the games. Further, to measure the levels of proficiency for the primitive skills and for the Sudoku solver, we define the *primitive-skill proficiency* and *overall Sudoku proficiency* as follows.

The proficiency in a primitive skill is the success rate in recognising/using the clue-pattern associated with a particular skill, which, in other words, is the success rate of the corresponding neural network when tested with samples from the test dataset. Equation (16.4) shows the proficiency of a primitive skill i, where t_S is the number of successful samples and t_D is the size of the test data-set:

$$P_{skill_i} = \frac{t_S}{t_D}. \tag{16.4}$$

The overall proficiency in solving Sudoku games is defined using the remaining degrees of freedom of empty cells in the grid after exhausting all possible ways of advancing in the game-solving process. The degree of freedom for an empty cell, f_c, is the number of possible candidates found after propagation of domains. If the Sudoku grid is complete, there is no degree of freedom left. If the grid still has empty cells, the degrees of freedom in each empty cell are added, generating $f = \sum f_c$ – the total degree of freedom for the grid. The performance of the solver is inversely proportional to f: the fewer degrees of freedom remaining in the Sudoku grid, the better the solver performed. Thus, the overall Sudoku proficiency, P_{Sudoku}, is defined as in Eq. (16.5), where f_{final} is the remaining total degree of freedom, and $f_{initial}$ is the total degree of freedom at the beginning of the game:

$$P_{Sudoku} = 1 - \frac{f_{final}}{f_{initial}}. \tag{16.5}$$

16.6.1   Primitive Skills Proficiency

We first test the acquisition process for each of the primitive skills by training the corresponding neural networks with artificially generated training sets of various sizes s, with $s = k \times BPSP$, where $k = 1 : 10$. To ensure the statistical validity of the results, for each skill and for each size of the training set, we run 100 simulations corresponding to 100 random initialisations of weights in the neural networks. Figures 16.11–16.13 show, for the scanning, recognition and propagation skills, respectively, the mean value of the proficiency calculated for each skill over the set of 100 simulations, for datasets with size from $1 \times BPSP$ to $10 \times BPSP$. It can be seen that, when trained with small datasets, the neural networks have low success rates, which translates into low proficiency for the corresponding skill. It can also be seen that the proficiency grows rapidly with the dataset size and reaches a maximum for all skills at $5 \times BPSP$. Based on this fact, we consider three levels of proficiency that we use for further investigations: beginner, intermediate, and advanced, corresponding to $1 \times BPSP$, $2 \times BPSP$, and $5 \times BPSP$, respectively.

Figures 16.14–16.16 show the success rates of the neural networks trained with the datasets corresponding to the three skill proficiency levels. The figures display the actual success rates for each skill in each category of skills considered in this study over the set of 100 simulations. It can be seen that the $1 \times BPSP$ case shows low and unstable success rates, which resembles a human player who does not master

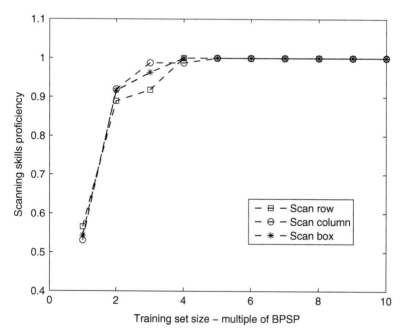

FIGURE 16.11   Acquisition of scanning skills – various levels of proficiency.

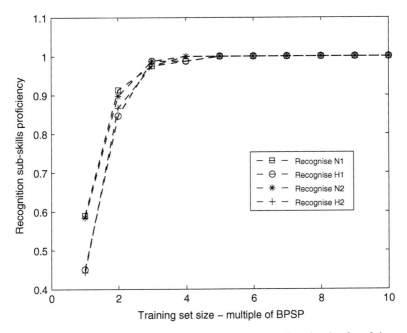

FIGURE 16.12   Acquisition of recognition sub-skills – various levels of proficiency.

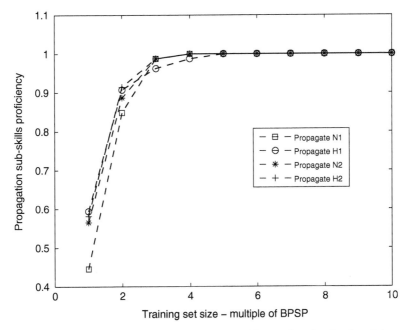

FIGURE 16.13   Acquisition of propagation sub-skills – various levels of proficiency.

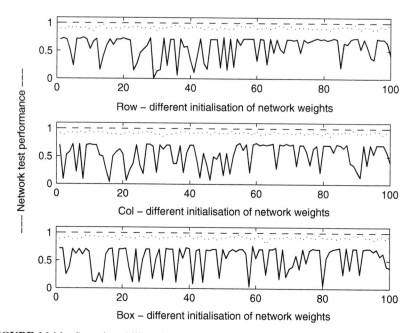

FIGURE 16.14   Scanning skills training (neural network with 100 different seeds): 'full' = beginner level ($1 \times BPSP$); 'dotted' = intermediate level ($2 \times BPSP$); 'dashed' = advanced level ($5 \times BPSP$).

the skill properly. In contrast, at the advanced level of proficiency, the recognition is flawless, regardless of the situation.

In addition, for a more detailed view, Table 16.1 shows the statistical measures, mean and standard deviation of the data presented visually in Figures 16.14–16.16.

16.6.2   Overall Sudoku Solving Proficiency

When aggregating the primitive skills into the solver, the overall Sudoku proficiency shows a similar behaviour to that of the primitive skills, as shown in Figure 16.17. When all primitive skills are trained with $1 \times BPSP$ datasets, the solver shows very low proficiency – the resultant mean value over the set of 100 Sudoku games is very low. Then, the proficiency grows rapidly as the solver aggregates better trained primitive skills. This is consistent with the variation of proficiency in the case of primitive skills, showing the consistency of the aggregation of primitive skills into the skill model and the validity of the proposed solving architecture. For a more detailed view, we further investigate the behaviour of the solver for three cases: a beginner solver that aggregates only beginner-level primitive skills (trained with $1 \times BPSp$), an intermediate solver that aggregates only intermediate primitive skills ($2 \times BPSp$), and an advanced solver that aggregates advanced primitive skills ($5 \times BPSP$).

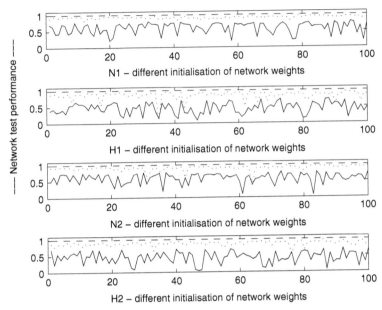

FIGURE 16.15 Recognition skills training (neural network with 100 different seeds): 'full' = beginner level $(1 \times BPSP)$; 'dotted' = intermediate level $(2 \times BPSP)$; 'dashed' = advanced level $(5 \times BPSP)$.

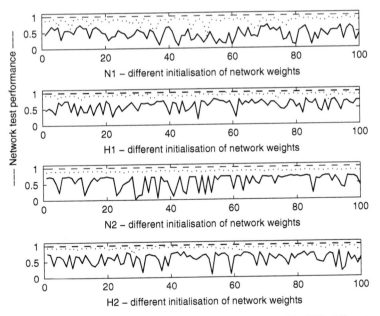

FIGURE 16.16 Propagation skills training (neural network with 100 different seeds): 'full' = beginner level $(1 \times BPSP)$; 'dotted' = intermediate level $(2 \times BPSP)$; 'dashed' = advanced level $(5 \times BPSP)$.

TABLE 16.1   Skill Proficiency – Statistics for Neural Network Training (100 seeds)

Skill	Measure	Proficiency level		
		Beginner	Interm	Advanced
Scan	Mean	0.5656	0.9177	1.0000
Row	Std dev	0.2055	0.0260	0
Scan	Mean	0.5310	0.9194	1.0000
Column	Std dev	0.2128	0.0234	0
Scan	Mean	0.5428	0.9154	1.0000
Box	Std dev	0.2260	0.0261	0
Recognise	Mean	0.5899	0.9131	1.0000
N1	Std dev	0.1615	0.0356	0
Recognise	Mean	0.4507	0.8469	1.0000
H1	Std dev	0.1636	0.1286	0
Recognise	Mean	0.5849	0.8975	1.0000
N2	Std dev	0.1499	0.0778	0
Recognise	Mean	0.4430	0.8670	1.0000
H2	Std dev	0.1755	0.0668	0
Propagate	Mean	0.4462	0.8486	1.0000
N1	Std dev	0.1714	0.0983	0
Propagate	Mean	0.5942	0.9075	1.0000
H1	Std dev	0.1453	0.0421	0
Propagate	Mean	0.5656	0.8866	1.0000
N2	Std dev	0.2055	0.0158	0
Propagate	Mean	0.5817	0.9140	1.0000
H2	Std dev	0.1678	0.0380	0

Figure 16.18 visually presents the actual proficiency of the solver over the 100 Sudoku games for the three solvers. A difference in performance can be seen between the three cases, from the low and unstable performance of the beginner solver to the maximum and stable performance of the advanced solver. In addition, Table 16.2 shows the mean and standard deviation of the data presented visually in Figure 16.18.

Overall, the results presented in this section demonstrate that the proficiency of the proposed solver to solve Sudoku games depends on the proficiency acquired in each of the primitive skills used in the solving process. This further verifies the consistency of the proposed skill model and the consistency of the aggregation of these skills into the solving process. From a different point of view, this also resembles the solving behaviour of a human player, and supports our assumption that the proposed skill-based solver can be used in various scenarios for the training and development of certain human cognitive abilities.

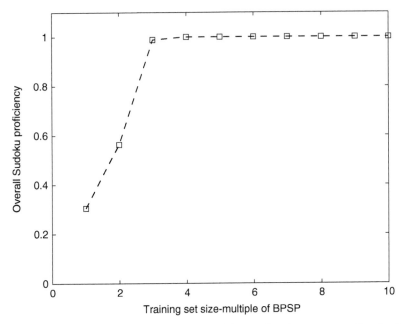

FIGURE 16.17   Various levels of Sudoku proficiency for the corresponding levels of primitive-skill proficiency.

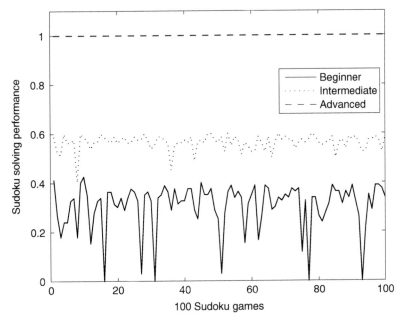

FIGURE 16.18   Resultant Sudoku solving proficiency for three levels of aggregated skill proficiency.

TABLE 16.2   Sudoku Proficiency: Statistics for 100 Games Solvable

Aggregated skill level	Sudoku solving proficiency, S_p	
	Mean	Std dev.
Beginner	0.3053	0.9600
Interm.	0.5637	0.0315
Advanced	1.000	0

16.7 CONCLUSIONS

In this chapter, we have introduced a novel computational Sudoku solver that takes into account the human skills involved in puzzle solving. To emulate in a cognitively plausible manner the steps followed by human players to solve the puzzle, we created a model of skills starting from the existing practitioners' experience and literature. We then used the proposed skill model in a deep architecture of feed-forward neural networks with back-propagation to implement the acquisition of the human-like Sudoku skills from scratch.

The experiments demonstrated the plausibility of using human-like skills in computational Sudoku solvers, and demonstrated the concept of skill acquisition in relation to the proficiency of this solver. We first demonstrated the skill-acquisition process for the primitive skills by training the corresponding neural networks with datasets of different sizes to emulate the exposure of a human player to various amounts of situations involving the respective skills. Further, we demonstrated that the proposed skill-based computational Sudoku solver can achieve certain levels of proficiency by aggregating primitive skills through the deep architecture of feed-forward neural networks.

In conclusion, this study instantiates computationally the solving behaviour of a human player, illustrating that proficiency in solving Sudoku games depends on the proficiency acquired in each of the primitive skills used in the solving process. Even though a limited set of skills was considered, we believe that the concept presented in the chapter is a pertinent addition to the work undertaken on Sudoku in the cognitive psychology and cognitive neuroscience fields, for education or medical purposes. The results shown in the chapter support our assumption that the proposed skill-based solver can be used in various scenarios for the training and development of certain human cognitive abilities using Sudoku-like puzzles, either separately or in conjunction with other methods.

Further, we consider that the results we obtained are a solid base for developing more complex skill models and skill-acquisition architectures usable in more general decision-making frameworks, outside the field of puzzle solving.

CHAPTER 17

Computational Red Teaming for Driver Assessment

17.1 INTRODUCTION

In this chapter, we present an application that couples CRT and ABS to assess the performance level of road traffic systems. A cognitive driver agent built in the *Society of Mind* paradigm is used to investigate how individual behaviours of car drivers aggregate, and how the resultant collective behaviour influences the road traffic overall. The *Society of Mind* driver agent assumes reactive, rational and affective internal agencies that compete to impose their own decision in traffic. Internal agency competition is based on real-time variable inputs from the traffic environment and constant personal preferences from innate personality traits. Populations of drivers with various personality mixes are used to compute various traffic performance metrics and to study the agent interactions in a multi-agent situation. These populations are first used on an artificially generated road network, and then a case study is performed on the real road maps of the city of Melbourne. Overall, this application demonstrates through computer simulation the importance of behavioural mix of driver populations for traffic performance. The remainder of the chapter is based on [249, 250].

Knowing the influence of driver behaviour on traffic performance is a key issue in transportation because of the virtually infinite range of non-rational types of actions generated by the variety of human behavioural patterns. Thus, traffic modelling and the assessment of traffic performance should consider not only the motion of the vehicles and the resultant observable traffic pattern, but also the complex behavioural aspects that generate them [23, 88]. Decisions in traffic conditions are obviously the result of processing the inputs from the instantaneous traffic context. In general, a human driver can be considered to make three major types of decision when in traffic. First, drivers can make rational decisions to drive safely, avoid annoying other drivers, and obey traffic regulations. Second, they can make affective decisions based on their current emotional state, regardless of safety, annoying other drivers, and traffic regulations. Third, they can display reactive behaviour when they must perform

Simulation and Computational Red Teaming for Problem Solving, First Edition.
Jiangjun Tang, George Leu, and Hussein A. Abbass.
© 2020 by The Institute of Electrical and Electronics Engineers, Inc. Published 2020 by John Wiley & Sons, Inc.

avoiding actions to escape from an immediate danger, such as a collision. Thus, it can be said that the driver is always in the position of choosing between several internal voices that try to impose their view on the current situation.

However, constant personal preferences from innate personality traits are also important, as they affect the way that contextual inputs are perceived and processed in real time by the internal voices. It cannot be neglected that the personality of an individual makes an important contribution to moderating and influencing instantaneous decisions. Arguably, an agent with these characteristics allows the creation of populations of drivers with various mixes of individual personalities. The resultant populations will show different behavioural patterns, depending on the mix of individual personalities. Further, they can be used in various traffic contexts to study their influence on traffic performance.

Thus, in this chapter a *Society of Mind* (SoM) [287] cognitive agent is used for modelling artificial drivers with a variety of driving behaviours. The agent is used to investigate the influence of collective driver behaviour on road traffic performance. The SoM driver agent assumes reactive, rational, and affective internal agencies that compete to impose their own decision in traffic. Internal agency competition is based on real-time variable inputs from the traffic environment and constant personal preferences from innate personality traits. Populations of drivers with various personality mixes are used to investigate a set of relevant traffic performance metrics and to study the agent interactions in a multi-agent situation. First, these populations are used on an artificially generated map to create insight into the potential of the SoM driver agent. Second, a case study is performed on a real road map of the city of Melbourne to demonstrate the usability of the SoM approach in a real-life context.

The involvement of CRT in this application is twofold. First, through the use of SoM, a plausible cognitive model of drivers' decision making is generated. The components of this decision-making model account for the most detailed level of task decomposition in a road traffic system. Thus, modelling the driver agents in the traffic system context accounts for the task decomposition component of the CRT process in a similar manner to skill modelling in the Sudoku solving context (Chapter 16). Second, the agent-based application aims to assess the level of performance of a system (road traffic system in this case) with the purpose of unveiling its vulnerabilities, which is the very purpose of a CRT exercise in general.

The chapter is organised as follows. Section 17.2 provides a brief discussion of cognitive agents to introduce the novice reader to the world of cognitive agent modelling. Section 17.3 describes in detail the SoM theory on the human mind and cognition, and explains the rationale for using this concept in the context of CRT and driver/traffic modelling. Sections 17.4 and 17.5 show how the resultant driver agents are actually used in road traffic simulations placed in artificial and real traffic contexts, respectively. The final section concludes the discussion and summarises the lessons learnt from this application.

17.2   BACKGROUND ON COGNITIVE AGENTS

From the point of view of the cognitive capabilities involved in agents' operation, three fundamental approaches have been intensely studied as part of the agent paradigm: reactive, rational, and affective agents.

Reactive agents are mainly capable of reacting rapidly to changes in their immediate environment, and have no or very simple internal representation of this environment. They are built in a behaviour-based paradigm [340], providing very tight coupling between perception and action. For this reason, it is considered that reactive agents fall into a so-called *sense–react cycle*. Autonomous decision making (intelligence) is not an intrinsic attribute, but rather the result of the interaction between the agent and its environment. Existing reactive agents are mainly based on three major designs: standard stimulus-response (or condition-action) agent systems [284], subsumption architectures [58], and agent network architectures [262].

The tight coupling between the *perception* and *action* stages in the sense–react paradigm and the lack of complex decision-making mechanisms have some advantages. Reactive agents are ideal in very dynamic environments, and their implementation is simple, leading to low computational complexity. In addition, reactive agents do not have a central planning component. This allows a high degree of adaptability and flexibility, making possible their usage in massive simulations. However, their simplicity also has unavoidable limitations. Given that they do not possess an internal representation of the world, decision (reaction) is based on local information only. Consequently, they need sufficient information available from the local environment. As a result, reactive agents have a so-called short-term view. They do not possess long-term planning capabilities, and are unable to make decisions based on the global state of the environment.

From a cognitive perspective, reactive agents are not intelligent per se [340]. They do not make use of real cognitive capabilities; rather, the MASs of which they are a part indicate an emergent collective intelligence. Thus, implementations of reactive agents are limited to simple robots or reactive entities in individual setups, and to ant colonies, swarms, or bird flocks in multi-agent setups.

Rational agents assume long-term planning of actions centred on a set of basic goals. They belong to the category of intelligent agents, being able to decide and act in more than just a reactive manner. Decision making is based on their internal reasoning and view of the surrounding world, considering a set of alternative courses of action. The environment is represented internally as an explicit symbolic model of the world, and decisions are made through logical reasoning based on pattern matching and symbolic manipulation. Given this architectural approach, deliberative agents fall into the sense–decide–act paradigm when viewed from the perception-action perspective.

Rational agents have the advantage that they can cover more real-world problems because decision-making mechanisms are closer to the human reasoning processes. However, for this reason, they are more computationally complex than reactive agents because generation of plans and processing of choice require more complex implementation and higher computational effort. In addition, they can only model rational cognitive processes and hence rational behaviour, since decision making is based on choice and usually involves a certain profit function. The most important architectural approaches for designing rational agents are *believe-desire-intention* [328] and *procedural reasoning system* [195], with popular agent implementations such as IRMA, GRATE, and PRS/dMARS.

Affective agents emerged as the result of a shift in AI and the emergence of cognitive sciences. Researchers realised that designing complex agents without affect may not be possible for the simple reason that there are no entities without affect in nature at all [345], let alone the humans. Damasio [106] showed in the theory of somatic markers that normal operation of human decision making requires an emotional mechanism that regulates the rational reasoning. This mechanism creates biased affective forecasts of the potential consequences of an action. If this emotional signal is eliminated, the brain only uses rational reasoning, which slows down or even jeopardises decision making because of the many possible conflicting options. The assumption was demonstrated through studies with disordered patients without emotional capabilities. These patients became lost in endless rational-choice problems, being incapable of making even the simplest decision, such as which outfit to wear for a certain event [107].

However, not only humans, but even simple organisms with no rational capabilities have been found to have certain affective underpinnings that generate various behavioural patterns, such as attraction and aversion. Scheutz and Logan [348] considered that any agent of a certain cognitive complexity possesses affective states that act below or above (or at) a rational layer [345].

Affective agents have components that, in connection with other internal or external components, can instantiate affective states. Thus, affective agents contain explicit or implicit representations of various affective states (i.e. desires, emotions, and moods). From a perception–action point of view, affective agents are similar to rational ones. They fall into the same sense–decide–act paradigm, except that the internal decision-making mechanisms in the decisional stage are different from deliberative agents. Affective agents appeared as a response to rational agents' inability to deal with cognitive contexts situated outside the usability range of rational decision theory tools [37].

17.2.1 Complex Cognitive (Hybrid) Agents

The primary goal of complex cognitive agents is to identify and replicate or computationally represent the cognitive processes underlying human behaviour. With a tremendous variety of such processes studied by various sciences or fields of activity, very little can be achieved by trying to work on them separately. Thus, none of the fundamental architectural approaches are suitable for building complex cognitive agents. Thus, it becomes evident that the discussion should continue around various ways of unifying these three fundamental cognitive processes: reactive, rational, and affective.

Perhaps the most relevant example supporting this inference is Newell's *unified theory of cognition*, which unifies in a single view some of the theories explaining human activity and thinking [302]. Arguably, all existing cognitive agent architectures align with this approach, more or less, in either a formally acknowledged way or a de facto manner. From an architectural point of view, hybrid approaches have been suggested to combine multiple types of cognitive capabilities (SOAR [229], ACT-R [19], CLARION [368, 369], and CoggAff [360]). The obvious and commonly used approach is to use some or all fundamental architectural approaches as subsystems in an overall complex architecture in a layered manner, as a hierarchy of cognitive capabilities. In such an architecture, agents' control subsystems are arranged into a hierarchy, with higher layers dealing with information at increasing levels of abstraction. Most of the hybrid architectures consider the reactive component as representing lower-level cognitive processes and providing fast response to events without complex reasoning. This is controlled by either (or both) a rational or an affective component situated at a higher abstraction level, which contains a model of the world and makes decisions according to rational or affective reasoning. A problem in such architectures is how to model the interactions and the control between hierarchical layers.

Such architectures were mainly classified into horizontal and vertical layers [136]. In horizontally layered architectures, each layer has access to sensing and acting, thereby making possible a potential decomposition into sub-agents. Each layer is connected to sensorial input and action output, and so produces suggestions about what actions should be taken. These suggestions are processed by the higher hierarchical layers. A disadvantage of the approach is the informational bottleneck that can appear in the central control system. In vertically layered architectures, sensorial input and action output are connected to the lowest layer. Thus, only the lowest layer is involved in sensing and actuating, while higher layers are involved in complex cognitive processing and decision making. A sub-agent decomposition becomes difficult in this case, and an architecture of this type is intolerant to layer failure.

In another study, Sloman [360] discussed the same control frameworks in different terms. He mentioned a concurrently active design similar to horizontal layering, and a pipelined design similar to vertical layering. In addition, the hierarchical aspect of layered designs was addressed in the same study. Sloman considered a dominance dimension of architectures that consists of the amount of control exercised by higher-level cognitive processes onto the lower levels. The dominance is higher when higher levels exercise a stricter control on lower levels. In the opposite direction, the dominance decreases when lower levels are allowed other types of interactions apart from the subordination ones.

The idea of hierarchy and dominance also triggers a discussion about the type of control within the hierarchy. Sloman noted that higher cognitive processes could directly turn on and off various inferior processes. In addition, they can indirectly influence their operation by acting as modulators, or, in the less direct type of control, can facilitate their training and/or evolution.

Yet most of the existing hierarchical approaches have been criticised for a number of drawbacks. Perhaps the most important is the hierarchical approach in itself, which requires rigid control frameworks. Arguably, this limits the range of cognitive skills that designs can handle, and makes changes in design very difficult. In addition, scientific communities grouped around fields such as cognitive science, decision theory,

AI and others have not yet found a consensus regarding which cognitive processes are positioned at which abstraction level. As a result, the existing architectures and the way they describe the interactions between various agencies (i.e. reactive, rational, and affective) are not entirely supported by formal theories.

As opposed to the hierarchical view, non-hierarchical architectural approaches can also be taken into account. The core of a non-hierarchical view of agents is that reactive, rational, and affective components coexist at the same cognitive capability level, yet are active in different contexts. They participate in the overall decision-making process by trying to impose their own decision in a given situation. As a result, their importance rises and falls according to the instantaneous context the individual is experiencing. Such a view was proposed by Marvin Minsky in the SoM cognitive theory published in the mid-1980s [287]. Central to SoM is the idea that human actions emerge from a so-called *heterarchy* of interacting and competing internal entities. These entities can be ideas, sensorial perceptions, memories of past actions, or the effect of those. In the application presented in this chapter, Minsky's approach is considered relevant for modelling the internal mental states of an agent driver because it explains the internal voices (choices) to which the driver must listen when making decisions in various traffic conditions.

17.3 THE SOCIETY OF MIND AGENT

17.3.1 Relevant Elements of the Society of Mind Paradigm

Among the many concepts and assumptions upon which Minsky's theory is built, several aspects are relevant for this application: the principle of non-compromise, the K-line theory of memory and the agent heterarchy. They hold an important role for both the SoM theory and the SoM driver agent that we present in this chapter.

17.3.1.1 Conflict and Compromise: the Principle of Non-compromise
The human mind is viewed as containing numerous agencies that compete at any moment in time to impose their own view/decision about the action to be taken. These agencies rise and fall in terms of their strength in the competing process, based on instantaneous internal and external contextual factors. This permanent conflict-like process always has a single winner, as a compromise between two or more agencies is impossible – hence the name *principle of non-compromise*. This is a view that opposes the usual approaches in the agent paradigm. In all major cognitive agent architectures, regardless of the cognitive theory they follow, decisions are modelled through conflict resolution mechanisms. These mechanisms are implemented based on certain profit or utility functions to generate a convenient compromise outcome, given a set of possible courses of action. The principle of non-compromise was not formally validated from an agent paradigm point of view. However, the existence of internal agencies within the mind of human individuals and the non-compromising competition between them have been studied in psychology under the name of *dialogical self*. The dialogical self considers the human mind as a collection of voices trying to be

heard and to impose their own way of action, similar to SoM. Dysfunctions observed by psychiatric practitioners in patients with multiple personality, dissociative disorders, or decision-making disabilities are generated by a *collapse of the dialogical self*, as stated in [257]. Also, Hermans [178] viewed this as an *organisational problem* of the self. He considered that if voices are unable to non-compromise, they start to overlap in the decision-making process, thereby generating ambiguous or improper courses of action.

17.3.1.2 The K-line Theory of Memory The *K-line theory of memory* is also a metaphor in which the memory of past actions is seen as the knowledge base from which component entities of the agencies in the society (of mind) are made. Perhaps there is no better way of explaining this than citing Minsky's words:

> *You want to repair a bicycle. Before you start, smear your hands with red paint. Then every tool you need to use will end up with red marks on it. When you're done, just remember that red means* good *for fixing bicycles. Next time you fix a bicycle, you can save time by taking out all the red-marked tools in advance.*
> *If you use different colours for different jobs, some tools will end up marked with several colours. That is, each agent can become attached to many different K-lines. Later, when there's a job to do, just activate the proper K-line for that kind of job, and all the tools used in the past for similar jobs will automatically become available.*

In the same way as stated in the bicycle tools story, decisions about choosing a certain course of action are based on recalling and re-composing past experiences, facts, actions, or images of the world. These are stocked in the long – term memory as the result of encountering various life situations [287, 288]. K-line selection *remembers* only those bits of information available in the long-term memory which are relevant for the current life context to which the individual is exposed. A similar concept was used in some cognitive agent architectures under the name of *chunking* [19, 230]. However, its computational instantiations were limited to implementations built on symbolic production rules. Examples are the rule-based chunking mechanism used to implement the long-term knowledge base in SOAR [229] and the long-term declarative memory included in the meta-cognitive control layer in ACT-R [343]. Yet decision making in both SOAR and ACT-R relies almost exclusively on recalling and selecting facts from the long-term knowledge base. In other words, the chunking mechanism is the decision making. In Minksy's approach K-line selection is viewed only as a step within the decision-making process. The *remembering* mechanism feeds multiple agents and agencies of the mind to support their state update and their position in the sub-agent competition process.

17.3.1.3 Agent Heterarchy The principle of non-compromise, together with K-line selection of past events, are the main constituents for creating what Minksy called a *heterarchy* of agents within the internal society of the mind. The idea of heterarchy is proposed as opposite to *heterarchy*, which, in Minsky's opinion, is a simple yet rather inaccurate and insufficient way of dividing work into simple tasks to solve complex problems. Within the human mind, an agent hierarchy can be organised as a tree, with each agent having simple things to do: *look up* for instructions from the supervisor and *look down* to exercise control over the subordinates. However, Minsky claimed that *hierarchies do not always work*, and argued that, in most complex cognitive tasks, internal sub-agents must use each other's skills. Thus, none of them can be above or below (i.e. a supervisor or subordinate) in a hypothetical hierarchy, but rather are part of a heterarchy. In this heterarchy, not only a tree-like structure exists, but also loops and cross-connected rings, depending on the context. Minsky suggested that such heterarchical structures must use memory to regulate their activity. In addition, as a result of lacking a strict hierarchy, they need a certain mechanism to establish which agent is the dominant voice at a certain moment in time. Consequently, instead of a fixed-control framework that governs a hierarchy, a dynamic regulatory process is suggested. In this process, the K-line memory selection and the principle of non-compromise are dynamically governing the heterarchy.

17.3.2 Society of Mind Architectural Schema

It could be argued that an agent architecture starting from Minsky's approach can offer the desired representation of the variety of cognitive capabilities with a logically and computationally slender design. However, there is a huge variety of human cognitive capabilities, and, accordingly, a huge range of resultant behavioural patterns. Hence, an eventual driver agent implementation of an agent architecture based on Minsky's view should handle this variety by taking into account two major types of mental features: the real-time context-generated affective states and the non-contextual innate personality traits.

A problem that appears in the process of transferring the narrative description into an architectural schema is the K-line theory of memory. If the principle of non-compromise can be represented as it is when following Minsky's narrative description step-by-step, the K-line theory must be slightly altered. The reason for this alteration is that implementation of the K-line theory as it is in a potential application equals recreating the whole long-term knowledge base – that is, the evolution of an individual from the moment of birth to the present time of the simulation. The K-line theory of memory in Minsky's view is essentially a narrative way of explaining the process of formation of the human mind (the *self*). It actually describes the emergence of intelligence and cognitive capabilities throughout the evolution of an individual. An artificial agent with this type of K-line representation should be the subject of tremendous training in advance, before the simulation starts, to build in it the desired knowledge base – the cognitive capabilities of interest.

Arguably, another way of creating the long-term knowledge base is through the agent structure itself. The internal structure of an agent and the interactions between its components show what and how the agent processes input information to generate output, which actually accounts for the knowledge base. In this case, decisions are

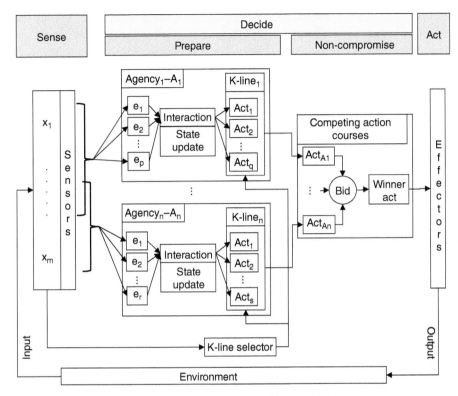

FIGURE 17.1   SoM general architectural schema.

built around the agent's structure: if the agent's structure is flexible, then the decisional process becomes versatile. Starting with this idea, the K-line memory can be understood and implemented as follows. K-line selection is seen as a set of potential actions that an agency of the SoM agent proposes at the current step for the next step, given its internal state and the current state of the environment. Hence, the K-line selector does not select from a set of past actions and tools to generate an action for the present time, as in the chunking mechanism. Rather, from a set of 'ready to do' actions of a sub-agency, it selects only the action that is applicable to the current environmental state. As an example, assume a driver agent in an affective state of advanced anger. Anger is known to generate actions such as speeding, tailgating, and cutting off other drivers. If there is no other vehicle on the street in that specific moment, then cutting off and tailgating other drivers are not applicable to the context. The only valid anger-related action to be proposed for actuation is speeding.

Figure 17.1 shows the proposed architectural framework of a potential SoM agent, and describes its potential internal dynamics. It includes the modified form of K-line selection, the non-compromise principle, and the heterarchy of agents.

The SoM agent consists of a number n of sub-agencies A $(A_i; i = 1, n)$, each of which contain a set of internal entities (called basic agents) e. An agency A_i senses the environment by gathering from the larger input dataset x ($x_i; i = 1, m$) only the information that is relevant to it (to A_i). Then, its internal entities interact and update their states, and through that the state of the entire agency. Thus, the agency A_i is able to propose a set $K\text{-}line_i$, of actions that are usually the result of that particular interaction of internal entities e. However, not all these potential actions are relevant to the current context – that is, the state of the environment and state of the overall SoM agent within the environment. A K-line selector identifies and selects from the $K\text{-}line_i$ set of potential actions only the action act_{Ai} which is relevant to the current context. This action further participates in a bid (the non-compromising competition) with the actions proposed by the other sub-agencies. According to a certain bidding rule/strategy, only one course of action will win and be transferred to effectors to actuate the action in the environment.

The SoM agent architecture falls in a classic sense–decide–act cycle. The SoM agent senses the environment through its agencies, decides on a course of action, and acts on the environment through effectors. However, the internal design of the decisional stage suggests an approach such as sense–prepare–non-compromise–act (SPNA). This approach is more relevant for the SoM paradigm by showing in a more appropriate way the real dynamics in the perception-action cycle. All the internal processing occurring inside each agency before the competition stage reflects the path from sensing to a state of preparedness. In this state, the overall SoM agent becomes aware and prepared for multiple courses of action and their effects. Thus, the *prepare* stage can be considered a first step in the decisional process. Then, when the agent is aware of the multiple courses of action, the next stage of the decisional process starts: the competition. Following Minsky's principle of non-compromise, this stage is named the 'non-compromise' step.

From an architectural point of view, the SoM architecture can be treated as a non-hierarchical hybrid architecture in which numerous competing cognitive processes can be simultaneously considered. Arguably, the resultant SoM agent is extremely versatile to begin with because of its very design.

First, the SoM agent is able to cope with complex problems that combine all n types of cognitive processes corresponding to the n agencies (A_1 to A_n). Hence, the range of cognitive capabilities supported by a SoM agent is given by the number and types of agencies implemented in a potential instantiation. Second, a complex SoM agent consisting of n agencies can reduce its capabilities when needed by inhibiting one or more of its agencies when the current tasks do not involve certain cognitive processes. This can be implemented by suppressing the whole cognitive processing branch for the unused capability (e.g. suppress one agency from the SPNA loop). Even simpler, this can be achieved by obstructing the participation in the bidding process through enforcement of a disqualifying value. It can then be assumed that an agent of this type has high portability over various fields of activity. At the same time, it offers a certain theoretical support, despite being based on a metaphorical understanding of the human mind, rather than on a well-established cognitive theory.

17.3.3   The Society of Mind Driver Agent

17.3.3.1 Architectural Schema   The previous section presented a general architectural schema that transferred Minsky's narrative approach on the human mind and cognition into a potential architectural instantiation. The general architectural schema emphasises the ability to insert in a SoM agent as many cognitive functions are needed for a specific task, in the form of agencies, to obtain the desired behaviour. However, in this application, the agencies of interest are those relevant in a traffic context: reactive, rational, and affective. Arguably, a driver agent containing these three agencies would cover a very wide range of cognitive processes, allowing high versatility and high representation power of driving behaviour.

Hence, the driver agent instantiation proposes a three-tier reactive–rational–affective (RRA) SoM architectural approach. The approach starts from the assumption that a human driver can be in most driving situations in the position of choosing between the following three major types of decisions:

- **Reactive decision**: an agent (human) must react to sudden, unexpected changes in the environment/context by taking rapid avoiding actions to escape from an immediate danger.
- **Rational decision**: an agent (human) makes rational decisions to fulfil goals related to his or her own (or others' or environmental) safety, abide by social/legal norms and regulations, or follow a certain prescribed and generally accepted profit or utility function.
- **Affective decision**: an agent (human) makes affective decisions based on the current emotional state, regardless of social norms and regulations, safety, annoyance caused to others, or unwanted effects on the environment.

Figure 17.2 shows the three-tier RRA SoM schema that implements the driver agent. The internal dynamics of the RRA SoM agent are similar to those explained for the general case, and for this reason only a generic representation of the three agencies is shown in this figure. Given that the RRA SoM agent is a particular case of the more general SoM schema, it is assumed that it retains the same features as the general SoM agent: versatility, power of representation of a wide range of human behaviours, and high portability.

17.3.3.2 Individual Biases and Behavioural Propensities   In addition to the RRA assumption made above, another addition must be made to Minsky's SoM paradigm to obtain a more versatile agent: the innate individual biases and behavioural propensities. Figure 17.2 shows how non-contextual mental factors, either innate or acquired, can be added to the contextual data acquired from sensors to update the current state of an agent. However, while the figure shows both innate and acquired behavioural propensities, only the innate behavioural features are considered in this application, in the form of personality.

Implementation of personality, as the expression of innate behavioural propensities, is based on Goldberg's model of personality [161]. The model assumes the

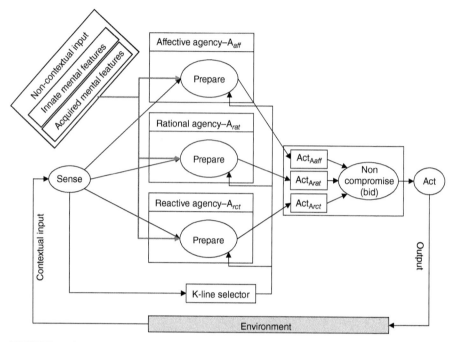

FIGURE 17.2 RRA SoM architectural schema with inclusion of innate biases and behavioural propensities.

existence of five fundamental bipolar dimensions of the human personality, and places the humans in a continuous range between two extremes (low and high traits) for each of the five factors. The five bipolar personality factors are openness, conscientiousness, extraversion, agreeableness, and neuroticism (OCEAN); and are represented as a five-dimensional tuple: $P(P_O, P_C, P_E, P_A, P_N)$, with $P_i \in (-\infty; \infty)$, where P_i are the personality factors. To obtain a computationally usable representation, values of personality factors P_i limited to the finite real interval $P_i \in [-P_{max}; P_{max}]$, where $P_{max} = 1$. The values of personality traits/factors are considered system constants and are assigned to the agent at the beginning of simulation. They are fed to internal agencies during the simulation, together with variable contextual information from sensors, and they participate in the state update process implemented in each agency.

17.4 SOCIETY OF MIND AGENTS IN AN ARTIFICIAL ENVIRONMENT

17.4.1 Experimental Setup

A simplified traffic simulator is created following the design principles used in some of the most popular traffic simulators, such as VISSIM [146] and AIMSUN [36]. The road segments are defined through the spatial (geographical) coordinates, and the vehicle motion uses a continuous representation of the physical space. Vehicles

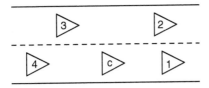

FIGURE 17.3 Current vehicle c and its possible neighbours.

adjust their position at each time step of the simulation according to the instantaneous speed resultant from the SoM agent's internal dynamics. Hence, the simulator allows the import and usage of real global positioning system (GPS)/GIS maps data, in which road segments are defined by geographical waypoints. However, in this section, only an artificially generated simplified map is used, as it is more relevant to the proposed traffic behaviour investigation.

17.4.1.1 *Street Map, Vehicles, and Traffic Regulations* The artificially generated map implements a road network consisting of roads with two lanes per direction in the shape of a rectangular grid with 16 (4 × 4) road junctions modelled as four-way uncontrolled intersections. Priority, passing, and lane usage rules are as in the Australian formulation of the general asymmetric traffic regulations in use worldwide [213]:

- the left lane is the default lane; the right lane should only be used for overtaking or entering road junctions if the direction of movement requests it
- passing through a road junction follows the 'left-hand side' priority rule
- the maximum *legal* speed is 60 km/h (also used below to describe free-flow traffic to calculate some of the traffic performance measures)
- the maximum deceleration used to compute the ideal minimum following distance and the ideal minimum gap acceptance for lane changing is -9 m/s^2.

In traffic, at any moment in time, a vehicle can be in one of the traffic situations described in Figure 17.3 and Table 17.1 – in this study, called *traffic motifs*.

17.4.1.2 *Traffic Demand, Origin–Destination Matrix, and Routes* Given that the street map is a regular network, the inhabitants are considered uniformly distributed in space; hence, the traffic demand follows the same type of distribution. Thus, the population of drivers used in simulations is spatially assigned uniformly to the existing map, and subsequently the origin-destination matrix is also generated following uniform distribution. Then, for each individual, the route from origin to destination is calculated using the shortest-path approach, with a random choice where multiple paths of the same length exist. In the next step, the behavioural propensities (personality traits) are assigned to individuals in the population of drivers according to a certain statistical distribution to investigate the resultant traffic behaviour. The traffic simulator is run for populations with various sizes and statistical personality

TABLE 17.1 Traffic Measures for Various Population Sizes

Motif no.	Neighbouring	Description
1	C	Current vehicle
2	C1	Current vehicle and neighbour 1
3	C4	Current vehicle and neighbour 4
4	C14	Current vehicle and neighbour 4
5	C12	Current vehicle and neighbours 1, 2
6	C34	Current vehicle and neighbours 3, 4
7	C124	Current vehicle and neighbours 1, 2, 4
8	C134	Current vehicle and neighbours 1, 3, 4
9	C1234	Current vehicle with all neighbours

inputs, and the appropriate traffic behaviour measures are calculated, as explained in the following sections.

17.4.1.3 Driver Populations

In relation to the map and traffic assignment explained above, driver populations can be investigated in two directions: the size and the personality (behavioural pattern) mix.

Size. Population size has an obvious influence on system performance because it creates either relaxed or busy traffic. In this study, the artificially generated map is used with populations of sizes in multiples of 100 between 100 and 1000 drivers.

Personality mix. The behavioural pattern of an individual driver is implemented using personality traits as the expression of innate behavioural propensities. As a reminder, for each SoM driver agent, personality is implemented using the *big five* personality model as a five-dimensional tuple $P(P_O, P_C, P_E, P_A, P_N)$, with $P_i \in (-\infty; \infty)$, where the infinite interval is computationally represented by limiting the values of personality factors to a finite real interval $P_i \in [-P_{max}; P_{max}]$, with $P_{max} = 1$.

Individually, different personality traits generate different behavioural patterns for individual agents. If the discussion is extended to more individuals, the resultant population of drivers is expected to show different collective behavioural patterns, depending on the mix of individual personalities. These mixes can be generated as simply as multiplying an individual driver agent and obtaining a purely homogeneous population made of individual drivers with identical personalities. Further, for a more realistic view, personalities of individuals can follow certain statistical distributions, resulting in populations with various degrees of heterogeneity. Figure 17.4 shows an example of how the personality traits of individuals are initialised within the population of drivers, according to a certain statistical distribution. In this figure, a generic normal distribution is presented. The process is similar for normal distribution or other distributions. In this study, both homogeneous and heterogeneous mixes

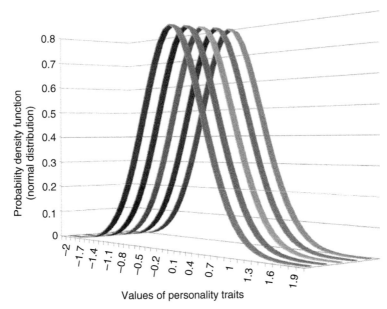

FIGURE 17.4 Normally distributed values for each personality trait of individuals within a population of drivers.

are treated: homogeneous populations of identical driver agents, and heterogeneous populations with uniform and normal distribution of individual personality traits.

17.4.1.4 Traffic Performance Measures

Through using various populations of drivers, such as those described in the previous paragraphs, the traffic performance is assessed and discussed using a set of system-level traffic measures. These measures have been found by several studies to be of critical importance [63]: average travel time, average travel speed, travel time index, and total delay. These are briefly explained below.

Average travel time (t_T). Average travel time is defined as the average over the whole population of drivers of the individual travel time, where individual travel time is the time for a vehicle to travel between two points (origin and destination in this study).

Average travel speed (v_a). Average travel speed is defined as the average over the whole population of drivers of the individual travel speed, where individual travel speed is the average speed for a vehicle to travel between two points (origin and destination in this study).

Travel time index (*TTI*). Travel time index is defined as $TTI = tTa \times tTi$, where tTa is the actual average travel time of the population, and tTi is the average travel time in ideal free-flow conditions (constant speed of 60 km/h in this study).

Total delay (D). Total delay is defined as the total time spent in traffic above the ideal time recorded in free-flow conditions (constant speed of 60 km/h in this study).

17.4.2 Performance Investigation

17.4.2.1 *Influence of Population Size*   In a first step, it is important to investigate how the performance-related traffic measures are influenced by the population size. It is also important to establish how this influence is related to the expected behaviour of SoM driver agents in a multi-agent setup.

From a traffic performance perspective, it is expected that traffic quality decreases when the number of vehicles on the road increases. This fact is confirmed by the simulation results shown in Figure 17.5, where all the traffic measures considered in this study deteriorate when the population size increases. Additionally, Table 17.2 presents the exact values for the trends displayed in Figure 17.5.

However, from the SoM driver agent perspective, it is important to understand how the decisions of individual agents are affected by traffic density, and how the dynamics of driver population change as a result. It can be inferred that, in the current multi-agent setup, deterioration of traffic performance with the population size appears as a result of increasing pressure on individual drivers when roads become busier. This fact potentially generates an increased amount of affective decisions at the driver population level.

The results shown in Figures 17.6 and 17.7 confirm the above statement. Figure 17.7 shows what was expected from a traffic point of view: as the population grows, individual drivers are increasingly involved in higher density traffic motifs. For populations of 100–300 drivers, most of the driver agents are involved in traffic motifs 1, 2, and 3 (zero or one neighbour). As the population size grows, the number of drivers involved in high-density traffic motifs increases as a result of increased vehicle density. Thus, populations of 700–1000 individuals have a high ratio of drivers involved in motif 9 (all four neighbours). From the SoM driver agent point of view, Figure 17.6 shows how the ratio of affective decisions grows with the population size, similar to the ratio of involvement in higher density traffic motifs. Consequently, it can be concluded that the activation ratio of individual internal agencies is dependent on the ratio of involvement in traffic motifs. The affective decision increases with traffic density, as does the reactive decision as a result of riskier behaviour generated by affective decisions, while the rational decision decreases accordingly.

However, this issue needs to be further studied using more types of population in a high-density traffic context to determine how traffic performance alters when the behavioural pattern of the population changes. Until now, the investigation was focused on the influence of population size on traffic performance using homogeneous populations of different sizes. These populations consisted of identical SoM driver agents with balanced personality traits ($P_i = 0$). However, the results suggested that not only density itself, but also interaction between drivers, has an influence on traffic performance. Thus, a more detailed view of the composition of driver populations is needed to understand more clearly how individual behaviour contributes to collective behavioural patterns of driver populations.

The investigation is performed for the case of high density, with populations of 1000 SoM driver agents. First, the ideal case of perfectly homogeneous populations

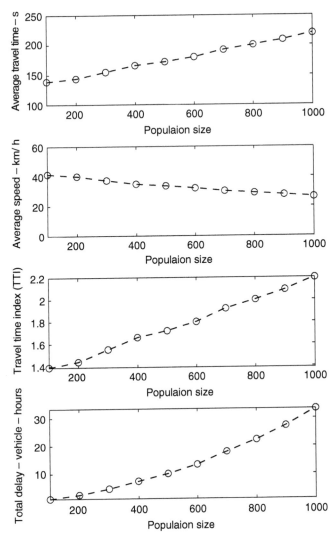

FIGURE 17.5 Traffic measures for various population sizes: average travel time (t_T), average speed (v_A), travel time index (*TTI*), total delay (*D*).

is analysed (drivers with identical personality features). This shows how populations with certain deviations from the balance point of personality – either towards negative or positive sides of personality – change the individual behaviour and, through this, the traffic behaviour. Second, a similar investigation is performed for the case of heterogeneous populations. This should provide insight into a more realistic scenario, in which the personalities of individual drivers in a population follow a certain statistical distribution.

TABLE 17.2   Traffic Measures for Various Population Sizes

PopulationSize	t_T	v_A	TTI	D
100	139	41.44	1.39	1.08
200	144	40.00	1.44	2.44
300	155	37.16	1.55	4.58
400	166	34.70	1.66	7.33
500	172	33.49	1.72	10.00
600	180	32.00	1.80	13.33
700	192	30.00	1.92	17.89
800	200	28.80	2.00	22.22
900	209	27.56	2.09	27.25
1000	220	26.18	2.20	33.33

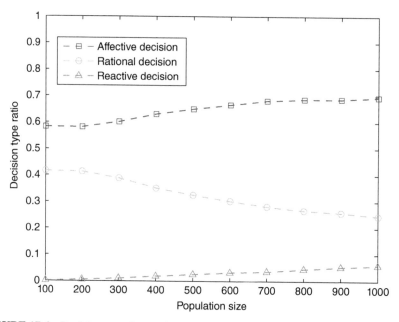

FIGURE 17.6   Decision type (internal agency activation) ratio < v. > population size: □ = affective decision ratio, ∘ = rational decision ratio, △ = reactive decision ratio.

17.4.2.2 Dynamics of Homogeneous Populations of Drivers   Simulations
are run for a set of populations with 1000 identical SoM driver agents with individual personality traits P_i sweeping the interval $[-1; 1]$ with a step of 0.1, where -1 represents negative and 1 represents positive personalities.

From the agent perspective, it is expected that the amount of non-rational decisions in traffic increases as the personality traits deviate towards the negative side of the personality space. In addition, a directly proportional variation of non-rational

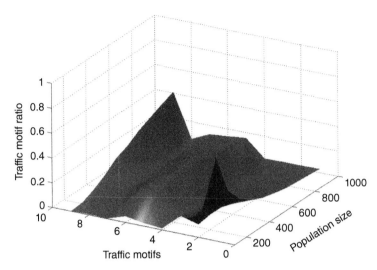

FIGURE 17.7   Traffic motif ratio per driver population for various population sizes.

decision rate with the traffic motif density is expected. The hypothesis is confirmed by the current multi-agent setup investigation. Figure 17.8 shows how all traffic measures considered in this study deteriorate as the population personality pattern moves towards negativity.

The pattern of traffic performance deterioration is consistent with variation in the collective activation (decision type) ratio for the internal agencies of individual SoM driver agents (Figure 17.9). The decision type ratio is calculated based on the total amount of decisions of a certain type (affective, rational, or reactive) made throughout the simulation for all SoM driver agents in the population. The results show how populations situated towards the negative end of personality display an increased affective decision ratio – that is, higher deviations from rationality. It is confirmed that populations consisting of driver agents with negative personality traits tend to generate an increased overall behavioural pattern that deviates from rationality. This results in deterioration of traffic performance.

In addition to this dependency, Figure 17.10 shows that better traffic performance is obtained in the case of populations of positive individuals, even though the amount of traffic motifs of high density (motif 9) is higher. This suggests that populations of individuals with a positive personality can provide high traffic performance even in high-density traffic. In contrast, the populations situated on the negative side generate low traffic performance despite the traffic density being lower.

Overall, the investigation on homogeneous populations confirms that traffic performance decreases when density increases not only because of the density in itself. There is also the influence of drivers' decisions when facing dense situations (traffic motifs). The analysis showed that, in the same density conditions, homogeneous populations of drivers with positive personality traits allow better traffic outcomes than those consisting of negative drivers.

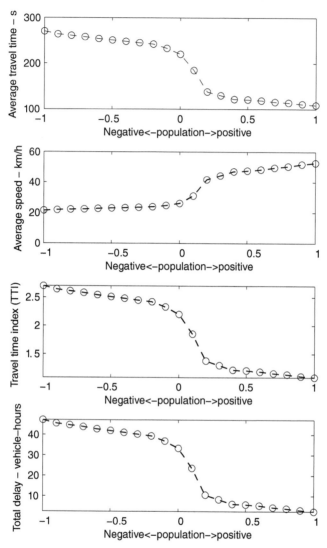

FIGURE 17.8   Traffic measures for homogeneous populations with various behavioural patterns: average travel time (t_T), average speed (v_A), travel time index (*TTI*), total delay (*D*).

Yet, the fact of having a homogeneous population of drivers – situated towards the positive or negative side of the personality spectrum – is itself an ideal situation. Indeed, this serves to offer convincing proof that differences in drivers' individual behavioural propensities generate differences in the overall traffic performance of the resultant population of drivers. However, no population in real life has identical individuals. Hence, a more realistic investigation is needed to create a complete picture of the influence of collective behaviour on traffic performance. This analysis is provided in the next subsection.

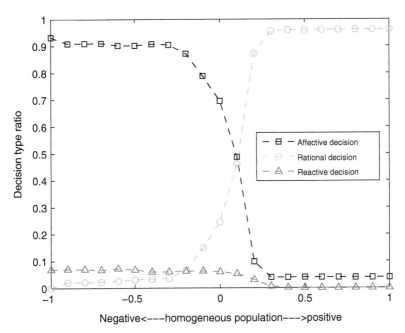

FIGURE 17.9 Decision type for homogeneous populations with various behavioural patterns: □ = affective decision ratio, ∘ = rational decision ratio, △ = reactive decision ratio.

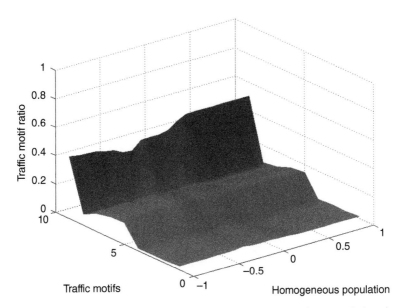

FIGURE 17.10   Traffic motif ratio per driver population for various population sizes.

17.4.2.3 *Dynamics of Heterogeneous Populations of Drivers* In the previous subsection, the investigation focused on ideal homogeneous populations to show that driver populations with different personality patterns have different behaviours in traffic conditions. However, real populations show various degrees of heterogeneity of personality features, particularly (but not solely) depending on geographical factors.

This generates certain patterns in the statistical distribution of personality traits – an aspect that was intensely studied by the theory of personality and individual difference [349]. Allik and McCrae [17] found that people living in the same country or region show similar or identical means of personality traits, whereas those geographically separated or historically isolated from each other have less similar means of personality traits [15]. Standard deviation was also found to depend on geographical aspects [275]. McCrae found that Asian and African nations had lower standard deviations from the established means when compared with European and American populations.

From a traffic behaviour perspective, it becomes obvious that an accurate investigation of a real geographical area must take into account the personality distribution of the local population of drivers. In this section, the artificially generated map is used without a specific geographical localisation. The investigation is performed using driver populations with various degrees of heterogeneity (standard deviation) of personality traits to observe the effect of personality distribution on both traffic performance and the dynamics of the agent population.

Thus, the study is performed for populations of 1000 drivers, in which the majority of individuals have a balanced personality and only a reduced amount are situated towards the extremes of personality space. From a statistical distribution point of view, it is assumed that personalities of drivers in populations follow normal distributions, with $\mu = 0$ and $\sigma > 0$. From a heterogeneity point of view, variation of σ from 0 towards ∞ equals populations ranging from purely homogeneous when $\sigma = 0$ to purely heterogeneous (uniform distribution) when $\sigma \to \infty$.

Given that the personality representation is computationally limited to the real interval $[-1; 1]$, the investigation is performed for values of between 0 and 1 $\sigma \in (0; 1]$. It is considered that $\sigma = 0$ represents the balanced homogeneous population investigated earlier in this paper, and any value of $\sigma > 1$ can approximate a uniform distribution.

From a traffic performance point of view, the results depicted in Figure 17.11 show that all traffic measures deteriorate strongly as the heterogeneity (represented by σ) increases. Additionally, Table 17.3 presents the exact values for the trends presented in Figure 17.11. This finding is important because it shows that the dynamics of a heterogeneous population actually jeopardise the fluency of traffic as the heterogeneity increases. In other words, the more diverse the interacting drivers, the more impediment they create for traffic flow, resulting in an overall inefficient collective behavioural pattern. This aspect is also supported by data recorded in Figure 17.12, with the ratio of affective decision per population growing on behalf of the rational decision as the heterogeneity (σ) increases. The traffic motif ratios per population

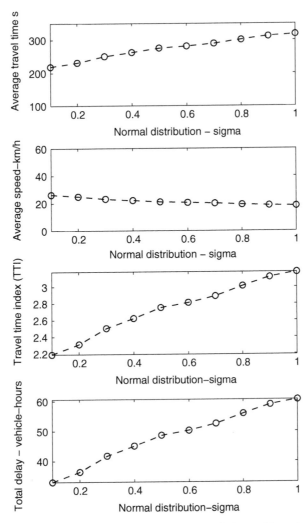

FIGURE 17.11 Traffic measures for homogeneous populations with various behavioural patterns: average travel time (t_T), average speed (v_A), travel time Index (*TTI*), total delay (*D*).

(Figure 17.13) also show that, for similar involvement in dense traffic motifs, populations with lower heterogeneity cope better. These populations generate an overall collective behavioural pattern that allows higher traffic performance.

From a different point of view, the above results also show that deterioration of traffic performance is significantly more important than in the previously discussed case of homogeneous populations. It can be seen that the travel times recorded for heterogeneous populations are generally higher than those recorded for homogeneous populations.

TABLE 17.3   Traffic Measures for Various Population Sizes

σ	t_T	v_A	TTI	D
0.1	219	26.30	2.19	33.06
0.2	231	24.94	2.31	36.39
0.3	250	23.04	2.50	41.67
0.4	262	21.98	2.62	45.00
0.5	275	20.95	2.75	48.61
0.6	281	20.50	2.81	50.28
0.7	289	19.93	2.89	52.5
0.8	301	19.14	3.01	55.83
0.9	312	18.46	3.12	58.89
1	318	18.11	31.8	60.56

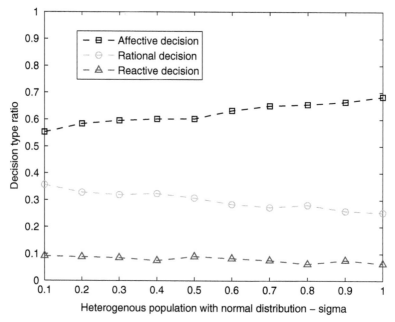

FIGURE 17.12   Decision type for homogeneous populations with various behavioural patterns: □ = affective decision ratio, ∘ = rational decision ratio, △ = reactive decision ratio.

The worst case of homogeneous population, corresponding to extreme negative personalities, generates an average travel time $t_T = 275$ s (Figure 17.8). In comparison, the worse scenario for normal distributed populations has an average travel time $t_T = 318$ s (Figure 17.11). It can be seen from the two cases that the common point from a traffic performance perspective corresponds to populations with $P_i = -0.5$ (middle of negative personality space) on the homogeneous side, and to populations with $\sigma = 0.3$ on the heterogeneous side.

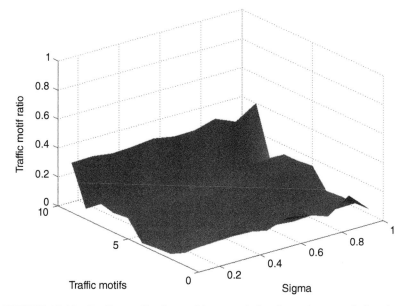

FIGURE 17.13   Traffic motif ratio per driver population for various population sizes.

17.5   CASE STUDY

The previous section demonstrated how the mix of individual personalities in a population of drivers can dramatically influence road traffic performance. However, the investigation was performed on an artificially generated road map. In this section, the investigation is performed on a real road map of the city of Melbourne.

17.5.1   Experimental Setup

To perform the proposed investigation, real data extracted from GPS navigation maps of the Melbourne area are used. The GPS data come with an extra feature. A node in a transportation network is defined by a change in the network, rather than the traditional definition of being a station or a road junction. Hence, the graphs used in this investigation are built as follows. Any node in the network is a waypoint defined by waypoint ID and position (latitude and longitude), while links are directed pairs of waypoints, which means a waypoint is not necessarily a road junction. Thus, the resultant graphs do not follow the layout of station-based models currently used for planning and operation (e.g. Melbourne public transport system – *www.metlinkmelbourne.com.au*). It is expected that a network defined as in the GPS-based approach can represent the system in a more detailed manner, allowing a more effective investigation.

The real data necessary for network analysis were obtained from the Open Street Map system by accessing the Open Street Map website (*www.openstreetmap.org*) and exporting the area of interest (Melbourne area) in XML format. In addition, data about the spatial distribution of the population were taken from the Victorian Government population report [391].

In addition to the infrastructure representation, road traffic is added to the above GIS structure. To perform the traffic behaviour assessment, populations of car drivers implemented using SoM driver agents are considered in a similar manner as in the artificially generated context. Populations of SoM agent drivers with various degrees of heterogeneity are used to compute traffic/resilience measures over the express roads of Melbourne – streets with speed limits of 100, 80, 70, and 60 km/h. Personality traits within the driver population are considered normally distributed, with $\mu = 0$ and various values of σ, with $\sigma \in (0; 1]$. The distribution of personality traits for Melbourne drivers is considered normal, with $\mu = 0$ and $\sigma = 0.7$ based on previous findings in personality theory [15, 275, 276, 349]. In these studies, the authors found that personality traits for the Australian population have a standard deviation situated towards the higher end (higher heterogeneity) of the standard deviation interval from a number of 56 countries around the world.

The methodology described above allows a system-level investigation of traffic behaviour in the Melbourne area. The approach can be generalised to any geographical area covered by a GPS navigation map, and is a cost-effective, systemic, and structured approach to quantify and manage road traffic performance, in line with CRT principles.

17.5.2 Results

The investigation performed in this subsection uses populations of SoM driver agents with various heterogeneity degrees. For all cases, the traffic performance is assessed with regard to the average speed in different locations of the physical express road networks.

17.5.2.1 Spatial Distribution of Average Speed (S_v).
This measure shows the average speed of vehicles passing through various road segments situated in different locations across the city. Speed sensors placed at each waypoint of GPS maps record instantaneous speeds of the vehicles passing by. The spatially located average speed is then calculated for each sensor over the duration of the whole traffic simulation. However, this measure only has a visual effect, placing coloured dots on the city map. The average speeds are displayed with different colours for each express road network. For each network, lighter nuances show lower speeds and darker nuances show higher speeds. Figure 17.14 displays the distribution over the city of average speeds for the realistic population ($\sigma = 0.7$). Figures 17.15 and 17.16 display the same measure for two extremes: highly homogeneous population ($\sigma = 0.1$) and highly heterogeneous population ($\sigma = 1$), respectively.

Visually, it can be concluded that, overall, the images show higher average speeds for homogeneous populations and lower average speeds for heterogeneous populations. The realistic population is situated in between, closer to the heterogeneous end of the spectrum. However, such a conclusion could be subjective because of the visual

FIGURE 17.14   Spatial distribution of average speed, $\sigma = 0.7$ (realistic Australian population): streets with speed limits of 60, 70 and 80 km/h; darker grey dot colours = higher average speeds (black lines = rail network).

FIGURE 17.15   Spatial distribution of average speed, $\sigma = 0.1$ (homogeneous population): streets with speed limits of 60, 70 and 80 km/h; darker grey dot colours = higher average speeds (black lines = rail network).

FIGURE 17.16   Spatial distribution of average speed, $\sigma = 1.0$ (heterogeneous population): streets with speed limits of 60, 70 and 80 km/h; darker grey dot colours = higher average speeds (black lines = rail network).

nature of the observation. Thus, this aspect is further investigated by displaying the probability that average speeds fall in certain speed intervals, conveniently chosen for each express network. To attain a clearer view of this finding, average speed probability is computed for all ranges of heterogeneity: $\sigma \in (0; 1]$. Figure 17.17 shows how the probability for high speed decreases strongly with higher heterogeneity, while medium speed increases strongly and low speed is fairly steady or decreases slightly. This demonstrates that traffic performance decreases with population heterogeneity – a finding consistent with the results obtained for the artificial road network investigated earlier in the chapter.

17.5.2.2   *Average Speed Per Network (N$_v$).*   The average speed per network indicates, for each express road network (100, 80, 70, and 60 km/h), the overall average speed recorded by all speed sensors for all vehicles throughout the simulation.

Figure 17.18 confirms that the average speed over each network decreases when population heterogeneity increases. On one side, this fact is consistent with the results discussed for the artificially generated environment. However, from a different point of view, this demonstrates a dramatic under-use of system resources when driver behaviour is taken into account.

As an example, it can be clearly seen that, on roads with a speed limit of 100 km/h, the actual average speed for the realistic population is only 66 km/h, while, for the

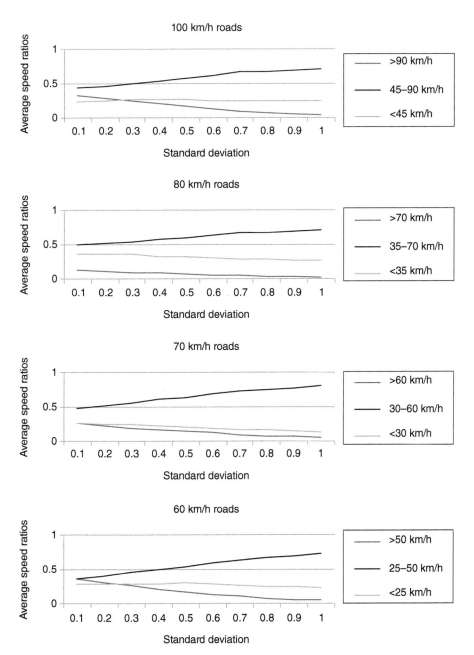

FIGURE 17.17 Average speed probability per network for the whole range of heterogeneity: $\sigma \in (0; 1]$.

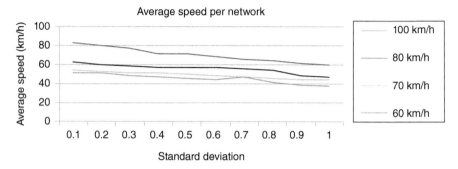

FIGURE 17.18   Average speed per network for the whole range of heterogeneity: $\sigma \in (0; 1]$.

best case of a highly homogeneous population, the average speed is 82 km/h. Thus, despite the infrastructure existing and high speeds being legally and physically possible, system use remains very low, depending dramatically on the behavioural pattern of the local population of drivers.

17.6 CONCLUSION

In this chapter, a SoM driver agent was used in a multi-agent setup to demonstrate the importance of population behaviour for traffic performance. The investigation was first performed on an artificially generated road map, and then on a real map of the city of Melbourne.

For the artificial road map, first, the influence of the size of driver populations on traffic performance was investigated using populations of identical drivers with balanced personalities. An immediate and obvious conclusion was that larger populations of drivers generate increased vehicle density that deteriorates the overall traffic performance. However, investigation of population dynamics indicated that the behavioural pattern is also important for the overall traffic performance, not only the number of drivers. This finding was further explored using ideal homogeneous populations situated at various distances in the personality space from the balance point ($P_i = 0$) on both negative and positive sides. The investigation confirmed that traffic performance is significantly altered when the population personality pattern deviates from the balance point towards the extremes of the behavioural/personality space. It was shown that traffic performance decreases as the population deviates towards the negative side. The investigation was then extended to heterogeneous populations of drivers in which the personalities of individual drivers were not identical, but followed certain statistical distributions. It was shown that traffic performance decreases significantly when the heterogeneity increases. The overall deterioration of traffic performance for heterogeneous populations was significantly more important than that for the homogeneous ones. This demonstrated that interactions between drivers with different personalities lead to lower traffic quality than do interactions between identical drivers.

For the case study on the city of Melbourne, it was demonstrated that the driver agent instantiation of SoM agent architecture, previously tested in an artificial environment, can be successfully used in real-world contexts for investigating complex issues. One such issue is the behavioural aspect involved in the performance of road transport systems of real geographical areas. From a transportation perspective, it can be said that infrastructure is what is offered to the local population – an aspect in which system users are passive entities that do not influence the system. In contrast, a behavioural approach treats system users as active entities that influence the system through their behaviour. Hence, an investigation in this direction should clearly focus on the traffic performance generated by individual car drivers, and the resultant population-level behavioural pattern. The results demonstrated that investigation of behavioural aspects is a *sine qua non* condition for performing pertinent and complete assessments of road transport systems. It was shown that the behaviour of populations of drivers can lead to a dramatic under-use of the resources offered by the infrastructure.

On one side, from a traffic perspective, the main insight gained from this study is as follows. The use of behaviour-enabled artificial populations of driver agents could significantly improve planning, assessment, and design outcomes. This could have broad implications in both day-to-day urban activity approaches and artificial life autonomous systems approaches in transportation.

From a different point of view, the study also demonstrated the usability of the SoM agent architecture through its implementation as a SoM driver agent in a multi-agent setup. The investigation performed on SoM driver populations with various personality mixes showed that the resultant collective behaviour was plausible. It was consistent with possible real-life traffic behaviour expectations.

CHAPTER 18

Computational Red Teaming for Trusted Autonomous Systems

18.1 INTRODUCTION

In large-scale socio-technical systems, the existing causal relationships between components may be hidden by the complexity of their non-linear interaction. Without appropriate mechanisms to facilitate understanding of how various effects are generated, it is difficult to manage these systems. Effects can be designed in such systems via social operators, such as influencing and shaping. These two operators are typically treated in an ad-hoc manner, without proper models and metrics. Both rely on how well the trust concept is grasped. If it is not well understood, these operators cannot generate the desired effects in the direction of interest. This chapter presents a model for influencing and shaping that employs CRT. The model is demonstrated and validated computationally using a simulation environment where social influencing and shaping are applied to an artificial society. The remainder of the discussion in this chapter is based on our previously published work [374].

Influencing and shaping have received increased interest in recent years. Influencing requires exertion of a certain form of social power. Servi and Elson [356] investigated influence in online social media contexts, where they defined it as 'the capacity to shift the patterns of emotion levels expressed by social media users'. The authors considered that measuring influence involves first identifying deviations in users' emotion levels, and then examining how much these deviations can be related to a user. The process of influence creates short-term deviations in emotional patterns; however, the question that arises is whether a persistent application of influencing operators can create long-term deviations – that is, the shaping operator.

In another study [357], Shmueli et al. commented on several computational tools that measure the shaping process and the way this affects human behaviour in real-life scenarios. One of the means identified as essential for influencing humans in a social system is trust. In the literature, trust is considered a complex socio-psychological concept that has a significant effect on aspects such as social persuasion. A detailed discussion on the trust concept can be found in [318].

Simulation and Computational Red Teaming for Problem Solving, First Edition.
Jiangjun Tang, George Leu, and Hussein A. Abbass.
© 2020 by The Institute of Electrical and Electronics Engineers, Inc. Published 2020 by John Wiley & Sons, Inc.

The research in [233] is one of the few studies that suggests a distinction between influence and shaping. The authors noted that influence is related to changing attitudes, behaviours or decisions of individuals and groups, whereas shaping is a change to an organisation or the environment. In relation to this, most of the literature tends to agree that social influencing leads to shaping.

This chapter builds on this difference between influence and shaping. First, this distinction is important because it implies that influencing is a sufficient condition for shaping. Second, it is important in computational social sciences to facilitate the creation of models that are not ambiguous about the socio-psychological phenomena under investigation. Third, the distinction is important because it clarifies that influencing and shaping work on different time scales – influencing is effective in the short term, whereas shaping is more effective in the long term.

To investigate these social operators, a CRT model is used in this chapter. In this model, a red agent acts on a blue team to influence, shape and sometimes distract the blue team from its goals. We note that the model should not be considered from a competition or conflict point of view. The model has general applicability – for example, the red agent may be a leader who promotes a positive attitude within a team, or a social worker who adjusts the social behaviour of the members of a group of people.

18.2   TRUST FOR INFLUENCE AND SHAPING

In the following, we further explain the concepts discussed above to offer the reader a good foundation for understanding the CRT application presented in this chapter.

Definition 18.2.1. *An influence process is an operation that causes a short-term effect in the attitude or behaviour of an individual, group, or a system.*

Definition 18.2.2. *A shaping process is an operation that causes a long-term effect in the attitude or behaviour of an individual, group, or a system.*

We note that the term 'effect' is used instead of 'change' because sometimes social influence and shaping need to operate to maintain the status quo. For example, if an agent A tries to influence another agent B by changing B's behaviour, then an agent C can try to mitigate agent A's influence by influencing B to maintain its behaviour unchanged. Thus, influence does not necessarily require a change. From a mathematical perspective, social influence would alter the parameters of a model, whereas social shaping would alter the constraint system.

The above could be illustrated using the following scenario, which is used as a demonstrator in this chapter. A group of blue agents tries to follow a blue leader. A red agent tries to influence or shape the blue team. All agents are connected through a network. Each agent, excluding the blue leader and the red, tries to align its behaviours with its neighbours, where the neighbours of the current agent are all other agents directly connected to it. The blue leader tries to reach a position in space, which is the goal of the blue team. If all agents fully trust each other, and there is no effect from the red agent, it is expected that the blue's intention will propagate throughout the network, and, over time, the blue follower agents will move towards the blue goal.

The red agent also aligns with the neighbouring agents (the ones to which it is directly connected), yet tries to influence and/or shape their behaviour to suit its own goal (e.g. its goal could be to turn the blue agents away from the blue's goal). The social influence exercised by the red agent is represented by its movement, which in turn affects the movement of its neighbours. The social shaping exercised by the red agent is represented by a network rewiring mechanism. Given that connections in a network are constraints on the network topology, this translates into constraints on the behaviour of the agents. If the network is rewired (by the red agent), this changes the neighbourhood of the system and the subsequent behaviours. Trust is considered on a scale between -1 and 1, where '1' denotes the maximum trust and '-1' denotes the maximum distrust. In this scenario, distrust and mistrust are not considered. In addition, the value '0' is a neutral indicator denoting that no information exist about an agent (agent's trustworthiness cannot be decided).

18.3   THE MODEL

The scenario described above uses the Boids [334] agent-based model. Here, all agents are initialised with random headings and positions in space, and are connected through a network structure that allows information exchange. The neighbourhood is defined most of the time using the Hamming distance between two agents in the network; however, in certain contexts, it is also defined using the spatial proximity of the agents (the latter definition pertains to the classic Boids model described in [334]).

The rules used in the model are the classic rules of the Boids model: cohesion, alignment, and separation. The difference from the classic Boids model is that the first two rules are applied to neighbourhoods defined by network connections, while the separation rule is applied using the Euclidean distance in the physical space.

Further, a trust factor is considered for each agent, whose value decides how much the respective agent trusts the information perceived from others. The first two rules (cohesion and alignment) are scaled using the trust factor before agents' velocities are updated. When the trust factor is 1, an agent fully trusts, and therefore considers useful, the cohesion and alignment information from its neighbours. When the trust factor is -1, the agent distrusts the information received, and therefore takes the reverse/opposite action.

The model contains three types of agents: the blue leader (A_B), the regular (following) blue agent, and the red agent (A_R). The blue leader moves towards the location of the established goal, and tries to make the other blue agents follow it. The regular blue agents operate based on rules and neighbourhood. They sense their neighbours through network connections for cohesion and alignment, and through Euclidean distance for separation. These are then used to decide on their velocities/movement. The red agent controls the level of noise (η) in the velocity and network connections, with the purpose of influencing and shaping.

The set of agents A operates in a space (S) defined by width (*spaceW*) and (*spaceL*). All agents are connected based on a 'random network' topology, where the probability of connection is p. If n agents are considered in the set A, one of these is the blue leader, one is the red agent, and $n - 2$ are the regular blue agents. Then, the network can be denoted as $N(n, p)$. The goal (G) is a 2-D position situated in one of the corners of the space S. The blue leader always tries to move towards G. A small area surrounding the goal G is denoted by δ. When the blue leader reaches this area, the position of the goal G changes. The following common attributes are defined for all agents:

- position (p), $p \in S$, is a 2-D coordinate
- velocity (v) is a 2-D vector representing the agent's movement (heading and speed) in a time unit
- cohesion velocity (*cohesionV*) of an agent is the velocity calculated based on the mass of all agents that are connected to this agent
- alignment velocity (*alignmentV*) of an agent is the velocity calculated based on the average velocity of all agents that are connected to this agent
- separation velocity (*separationV*) of an agent is the velocity that forces this agent to keep a certain small distance from its neighbours and is based on the Euclidean distance
- velocity weights:
  - cohesion weight (w_c): a scaling factor for the cohesion velocity
  - alignment weight (w_a): a scaling factor for the alignment velocity
  - separation weight (w_s): a scaling factor for the separation velocity
- trust factor (τ) defines how much an agent trusts its neighbours; it has an effect on cohesion and alignment, but not on separation.

All agents except the blue leader move towards their neighbours' location guided by the cohesion vector. The cohesion vector, *cohesionV$_i$* of an agent A_i is:

$$cohesionV_i = \frac{\sum_{j=0}^{|N|} p_j}{|N|} - p_i \qquad (18.1)$$

where $|N|$ is the cardinality of the neighbourhood N.
The alignment velocity of an agent with its neighbours is:

$$alignmentV_i = \frac{\sum_{j=0}^{|N|} v_j}{|N|} - v_i. \qquad (18.2)$$

The separation velocity of an agent is calculated using neighbours N_d in the spatial proximity of other agents as follows:

$$separation V_i = -\sum_{j=0}^{|N_d|} (p_j - p_i). \qquad (18.3)$$

The trust factor of a blue agent is updated by the average trust factors of all its neighbours (N) as follows (note that the trust factors of the blue leader and red agent are not updated):

$$\tau_i = 0.5 \times \left(\tau_i + \frac{\sum_{j=0}^{|N|} \tau_j}{|N|} \right). \qquad (18.4)$$

Given that the blue leader always tries to reach the goal G, its velocity at each step is not affected by any factor. The velocities of all other agents are updated according to Eq. (18.5):

$$v = v + \tau \times (w_c \times cohesion V + w_a \times alignment V) + w_s \times separation V \qquad (18.5)$$

where $cohesion V$, $Alignment V$, and $separation V$ are normalised vectors. Then, based on the updated velocity vectors, the position at time t of each agent can be updated by:

$$p = p + v_t. \qquad (18.6)$$

If the updated position of an agent falls outside of the space S, a reflection rule is applied. If trust has a positive value, then the corresponding agent adjusts its velocity according to $cohesion V$ and $alignment V$, as shown in Eq. (18.5). If the trust has negative value, the same equation is used, but opposite directions are considered for the $cohesion V$ and $alignment V$. If $\tau = 0$, this means the agent 'does not know' anyone, thus, only the separation vector is considered in the velocity update.

At each time step, the red agent has the ability to introduce heading noise, changes in the network structure or both. The heading noise propagates to the regular blue agents through the network connections, and leads to deviations in the movement direction of some blue agents. This occurs at each time step. The changes in the network structure lead to long-term effects on blue agents.

The red agent updates its velocity ($v_{RedAgent}$) using the same mechanism as the regular blue agents (see Eq. (18.5)), to which some noise is added. Equation (18.7) shows how noise generated using a normal distribution ($N(0, \eta)$) is added to the updated velocity of the red agent. Then, based on the noisy velocity, the position is updated using Eq. (18.6):

$$v_{RedAgent} = v_{RedAgent} + N(0, \eta) \qquad (18.7)$$

TABLE 18.1 Results of Red Agent's Noise Effect When $\tau_B = 1$ and $\tau_R = 1$

	R1	R2	R3	R4	R5	R6	R7	R8	R9	R10	Avg	STD	Conf.
Scenario1: Velocity noise													
$\eta = 0.1$	47.64	46.78	39.26	56.63	47.09	67.29	60.65	38.76	42.99	44.86	49.19	8.90	6.36
$\eta = 0.9$	145.90	155.75	168.04	199.94	171.94	243.61	162.15	144.08	103.82	117.94	161.32	37.65	26.93
e_η	98.27	108.97	128.78	143.31	124.85	176.33	101.50	105.33	60.83	73.08	112.12	31.70	22.68
Scenario 2: Network changes													
$\eta = 0.1$	45.71	59.28	47.39	54.31	58.14	69.65	50.27	44.35	43.90	48.83	52.18	7.78	5.56
$\eta = 0.9$	61.23	57.63	56.30	81.25	53.65	74.69	55.76	40.86	47.74	52.03	58.11	11.36	8.13
e_η	15.52	-1.65	8.91	26.94	-4.49	5.04	5.49	-3.49	3.85	3.20	5.93	9.00	6.44
Scenario 3: Velocity noise and network changes													
$\eta = 0.1$	45.34	47.09	65.90	54.05	51.93	84.91	54.66	41.11	43.88	52.21	54.11	12.23	8.75
$\eta = 0.9$	213.49	168.69	197.52	188.80	171.62	236.93	174.46	183.98	84.95	122.82	174.32	41.20	29.47
e_η	168.15	121.59	131.62	134.75	119.69	152.02	119.80	142.87	41.07	70.61	120.22	35.90	25.68

TABLE 18.2   Results of Effects from Red Agent's Noise and Trust Factors – Confidence Level is 0.05

Effect	R1	R2	R3	R4	R5	R6	R7	R8	R9	R10	Avg	STD	Conf.
Scenario 1: Velocity noise													
e_{τ_B}	-170.40	-146.54	-83.92	-55.00	-131.83	-6.05	-128.09	-110.66	-184.81	-152.86	-117.02	55.01	39.35
e_{τ_R}	165.32	160.08	95.83	71.21	149.41	8.11	133.20	111.97	167.79	160.23	122.31	51.75	37.02
e_N	1.78	15.84	-9.18	6.22	6.74	3.40	-13.50	0.35	-14.64	-17.58	-2.06	11.04	7.90
Scenario 2: Network changes													
e_{τ_B}	-122.99	-165.55	-144.34	-64.94	-168.15	-8.09	-154.27	-170.61	-189.59	-187.66	-137.62	58.31	41.71
e_{τ_R}	142.72	177.17	154.10	77.45	186.62	24.03	164.25	172.02	171.13	172.02	144.17	52.25	37.38
e_N	42.90	1.75	12.81	19.08	8.50	-1.08	-0.29	-12.17	25.41	-15.03	8.19	17.62	12.61
Scenario 3: Velocity noise and network changes													
e_{τ_B}	-151.65	-140.59	-132.44	-35.97	-166.98	-7.63	-159.37	-171.89	-194.38	-163.85	-132.47	61.12	43.72
e_{τ_R}	157.63	152.23	147.97	38.06	176.90	16.03	175.96	163.48	171.95	174.82	137.50	59.31	42.43
e_N	2.27	22.60	15.16	14.70	21.23	4.64	5.73	10.22	20.50	8.15	12.52	7.38	5.28

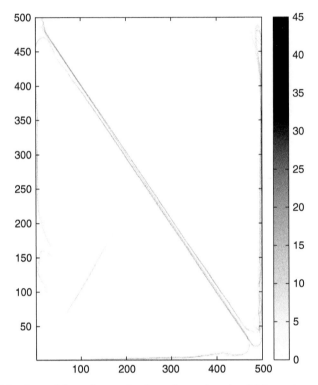

FIGURE 18.1 Agents' footprints under the red agent's noise (η) impacts on velocity and network with minimum trust effects ($\tau_B = 1$ and $\tau_R = 1$). Scenario 1: $\eta = 0.1$.

The changes in the network are performed by the red agent using the noise level, η as a probability of the following steps:

1. Randomly pick up a blue agent (A_i) connected to the red agent.
2. Randomly pick up another blue agent (A_j) connected with A_i.
3. Break the connection between A_i and A_j.
4. Connect the red agent with a randomly chosen blue agent A_j.

Following the above steps, the connections between the red agent and the blue agents change, while keeping constant the number of edges in the network. These topological updates are expected to produce effects in the long-term because: (i) the path along which the information propagates changes and (ii) agents' neighbourhoods change – that is, some blue agents may receive inconsistent updates from their neighbours.

Given the antagonist goals of the blue leader and red agent, the 'effect' implemented in the model can be seen as 'how well the regular blue agents follow the blue leader given the influence and shaping induced by the red agent'. A straightforward

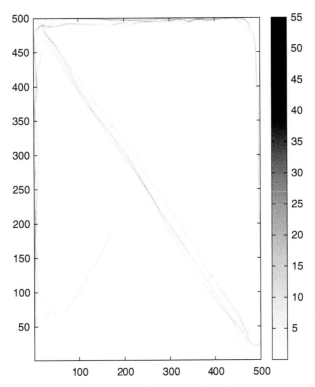

FIGURE 18.2 Agents' footprints under the red agent's noise (η) impacts on velocity and network with minimum trust effects ($\tau_B = 1$ and $\tau_R = 1$). Scenario 2: $\eta = 0.1$.

measure of this effect is the average distance between blue agents and the goal when the blue leader reaches the goal. If this distance is small, then the blue agents followed the blue leader well. If this distance is large, then the red agent was effective in distracting the blue agents.

In a simulation run, the blue leader must reach the goal multiple times. Reaching the goal once is considered an iteration. Each time the goal is reached and the effect is measured, the location of the goal changes. The overall effect of a simulation run is measured as the average effect of all iterations, except the first one. This is excluded to eliminate the warm-up period resulting from the random initialisation of agents. Overall, the effect is calculated as in Eq. (18.8):

$$\bar{d} = \frac{1}{M}\left(\sum_{m=1}^{M}\frac{1}{n}\sum_{i=1}^{n}d_{m,i}\right) \tag{18.8}$$

where M is the number of iterations (except the first one), n is the number of blue agents, and $d_{m,i}$ is the distance between agent i and the goal at the mth iteration.

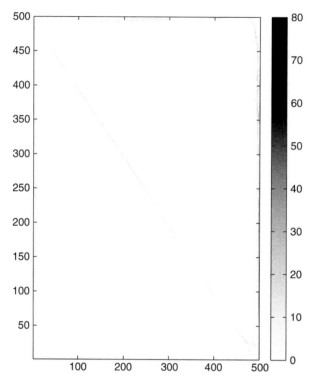

FIGURE 18.3   Agents' footprints under the red agent's noise (η) impacts on velocity and network with minimum trust effects ($\tau_B = 1$ and $\tau_R = 1$). Scenario 3: $\eta = 0.1$.

18.4   EXPERIMENT DESIGN AND PARAMETER SETTINGS

To evaluate the 'effects' of the short-term influence and long-term shaping induced by the red agent, two experimental stages are used. The first is focused on the amount of noise the red agent introduces, while the effect of the trust factor is minimised. The second takes into account both the noise and the trust factor.

The number of blue agents in the simulation is set to 25, which means a total of 27 agents. The simulation space S is a 500×500 square. For all agents, the initial position and heading are randomly generated using a uniform distribution. Agents' speed is constant and equals 1 unit of space per time step. The velocity weights for all agents except the blue leader are: $w_c = 0.4$, $w_a = 0.4$, and $w_s = 0.2$. The values of the trust factor for all regular blue agents are randomly assigned in the interval $[-1, 1]$, following a uniform distribution. The connections between agents are given by a random network $N(n, 0.1)$ with $n = 27$.

Two levels of noise are used in the experiments, as follows: $\eta^- = 0.1$ and $\eta^+ = 0.9$. In the first experimental stage, the effect of the trust factor needs to be reduced. This is obtained by assuming the trust value is 1 for all agents. This means that all blue agents trust all perceived information, including the information given by the red agent. In

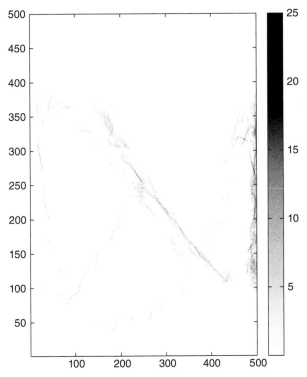

FIGURE 18.4   Agents' footprints under the red agent's noise (η) impacts on velocity and network with minimum trust effects ($\tau_B = 1$ and $\tau_R = 1$). Scenario 1: $\eta = 0.9$.

the second experimental stage, the blue leader and the red agent have two levels of trust each. For the blue leader, the levels are $\tau_B^- = 0.2$ and $\tau_B^+ = 1$, while, for the red agent, these are $\tau_R^- = -0.2$ and $\tau_R^+ = -1$.

To evaluate the effect of the red agent's behaviour, three scenarios are considered. In Scenario 1, the red agent introduces noise to its heading at each time step. This noise influences all its neighbours immediately, and propagates through the network. In Scenario 2, the red agent alters the network structure at each time step. This reshapes the environment in which the blue agents operate. In Scenario 3, the red agent applies both behaviours: introduces noises to its heading and changes network structures. This introduces both influencing and shaping in the model.

Using the 2^k factorial design described in [292], a total of two factor combinations are available for the first stage and eight for the second stage, where each combination can be studied in three scenarios. In addition, because of the random initialisation of the model parameters, a minimum of 10 simulation runs for each factor combination and effect is desired to ensure statistically significant/consistent results. To summarise, 60 ($3 \times 2 \times 10$) simulation runs are performed for the first experimental stage and 240 ($3 \times 8 \times 10$) are performed for the second one.

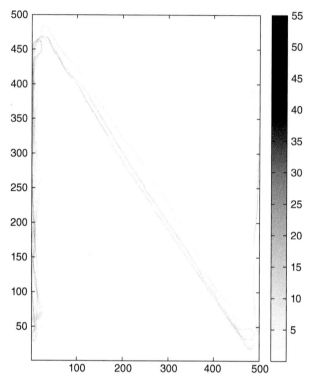

FIGURE 18.5 Agents' footprints under the red agent's noise (η) impacts on velocity and network with minimum trust effects ($\tau_B = 1$ and $\tau_R = 1$). Scenario 2: $\eta = 0.9$.

18.5   RESULTS AND DISCUSSION

Table 18.1 presents the results of the first-stage experiments. The distance $(\overline{d})$ between the blue agents and the goal is listed in Columns 2–11 for each of the 10 simulation runs. The last three columns show the average over the 10 runs, the standard deviations and the confidence intervals obtained at $\alpha = 0.05$.

The results indicate that the deviation from the goal experienced by the blue agents is proportional to the amount of noise induced by the red agent. It can also be seen that the changes in the network structure decrease the blue agents' performance, but the magnitude of this decrease is not significant. This is an expected result because the shaping operator works on a longer time scale than influence. When both influence and shaping are applied, the effect is more profound than when either of them operates in isolation.

Table 18.2 presents the results of the second stage of experiments. In this case, the trust factors of the blue leader and red agent seem to be critical, while the noise induced by the red agent is not. The response of the model to the trust factor is expected because, when the blue leader has a higher level of trust, all blue agents

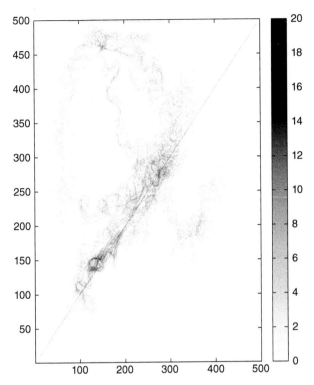

FIGURE 18.6   Agents' footprints under the red agent's noise (η) impacts on velocity and network with minimum trust effects ($\tau_B = 1$ and $\tau_R = 1$). Scenario 3: $\eta = 0.9$.

follow it better (lower values of the effect can be observed for e_{τ_B}). In contrast, the blue agents exhibit disordered behaviours (larger value of e_{τ_R}) if the red agent has low negative trust value. This situation is found in all three scenarios, and the effects of trust factors are all statistically significant. On the noise side, this has some effect on the blue agents; however, this is negligible when compared with the effect of the trust factor. Negative trust values taken by the blue agents counteract the influence generated by both the blue and red agents.

The noise induced by the red agent can still affect the blue agents via both short-term influence (velocity) and long-term shaping (network structures) if the values (and the subsequent effects) of trust are low. When the trust factors are high, the situation changes – trust significantly affects the behaviours of the blue agents.

In Figures 18.1–18.6 the agents' footprints are displayed for the case when the red agent affects velocity, network structure or both, and the trust effects are minimal. The footprints are obtained from the first runs of all three scenarios in the first experimental stage, and the results are listed in Column R1 of Table 18.1.

Figures 18.1–18.3 demonstrate that the blue leader successfully guides the other agents towards the goal. When noise increases, the blue agents' trajectories are

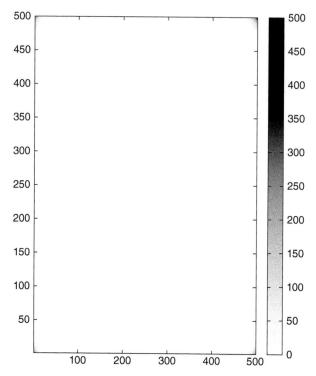

FIGURE 18.7   Trust effects on agents' behaviours with the red agent noise level at 0.1 in Scenario 3: $\tau_B = 0.2$, $\tau_R = -1$, and $\eta = 0.1$.

disturbed, as shown in Figure 18.4. Figure 18.5 shows that changes in the network structure do not generate much effect on the blue agents' behaviours. However, the blue agents' behaviours are more random when the red affects both velocity and network structure. This is a disordered behaviour, as more scattered blue agents' footprints can be observed in the last figure.

In Figures 18.7 and 18.8, two examples of agent footprints can be seen. These are affected by trust with small noise values ($\eta = 0.1$). The footprints presented in Figure 18.7 are extracted from the first run of the third scenario in the second stage, with $\tau_B = 0.2$ and $\tau_R = -1$. When the value of the red agent's trust is -1, the negative effect on the blue agents' trust is continuously broadcast throughout the network. In the end, all blue agents will have a negative trust value close to -1 because the blue leader does not have many resources ($\tau_B = 0.2$) to counteract the red agent. The result is that all blue agents distrust each other, and gradually spread out towards the boundaries of the simulation space. With a reflection rule in place, they are forced back into the space S, which causes the blue agents to move around the corners after several time steps, as shown in Figure 18.7.

Figure 18.8 shows the agents' footprints obtained from the third scenario in the second stage, where $\tau_B = 1$, $\tau_R = -0.2$, and $\eta = 0.1$. Some trajectory patterns can be

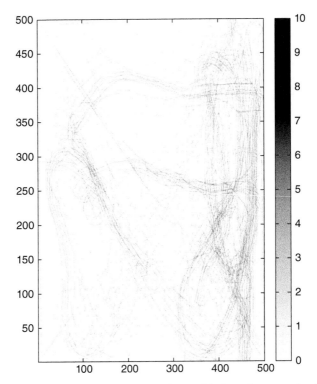

FIGURE 18.8   Trust effects on agents' behaviours with the red agent noise level at 0.1 in Scenario 3: $\tau_B = 1$, $\tau_R = 0.2$, and $\eta = 0.1$.

observed from Figure 18.8. It can be seen that the blue leader has enough resources, in terms of trust values, to counteract the red agent's behaviour. In the end, all blue agents will have positive trust values passed from the blue leader. Even if the red agent influences their velocity and connections, the blue agents can still follow the blue leader to reach the goal locations, as demonstrated by the trajectory patterns.

In summary, based on the results presented above, it can be concluded that trust has a more significant effect on the blue agents' behaviours than does the noise induced by the red agent.

18.6   CONCLUSION

This chapter has presented a CRT scenario that demonstrated the concepts of trust, influence, and shaping using multi-agent simulation, where the agent model was an extension of the classic Boids model. Network topology for situation awareness and a trust factor on perceived information were added to the classic Boids model to enable the investigation of influence and shaping.

Several experiments were designed and conducted to differentiate between the effects of influence and shaping on a system. The results showed that short-term influence can have an immediate effect on the system, which was very easy to observe. The long-term shaping also had an effect on the system, but this effect was not easily observable, especially when influence was also present. Overall, the most critical role was played by the trust between agents. Based on these experimental results, it can be concluded that trust dominates agents' behaviours, regardless of the noise induced by the red agent.

Probability and Statistics in Simulation

A.1 FOUNDATION OF PROBABILITY AND STATISTICS

In this chapter, we discuss the fundamentals of probabilities and statistics, and cover a number of distributions that are most relevant in the context of modelling and simulation. We then discuss a number of probability distributions that are commonly applied in modelling and simulation.

A.1.1 Experiments, Sample Space, and Random Event

We encounter many phenomena and systems with uncertainties in our daily life. These phenomena and systems are prone to producing unknown or unexpected outcomes. In statistics, these systems, together with the processes of generating such outcomes, are generally viewed under the umbrella of 'experiments', which from a very general perspective can be defined as follows:

Definition A.1.1. *An **experiment** is any deliberate run/observation of a process with unknown outcome, which results in a collection of data to be used for further study.*

Some examples of experiments are listed below:

E_1 Observing the result of flipping a coin once.
E_2 Observing the result of flipping a coin twice.
E_3 Observing the results from rolling a dice.
E_4 Recording the number of incoming calls to an emergency department every hour.
E_5 Recording the minimum and maximum daily temperatures of a city.
E_6 Recording the intervals (minutes) between the departure time of buses from a terminal.

We note that all the above experiments have something in common: their results are unknown. For example, the result from tossing a coin will be heads or tails, but we do not know exactly which one will appear before tossing it. We can repeat the

Simulation and Computational Red Teaming for Problem Solving, First Edition.
Jiangjun Tang, George Leu, and Hussein A. Abbass.

experiment under the same conditions as many times as we wish, and observe the results thousands of times. Based on the above examples, we can summarise by saying that the characteristics of an experiment are as follows:

- The experiment can be repeated indefinitely under the same conditions.
- The experiment can have more than one possible outcome, and each possible outcome can be specified in advance.
- The outcome of the experiment is unknown before it runs, and the outcome depends on chance.

In statistics, an experiment with the above characteristics is called a 'random experiment'. Although the actual result is unknown, the possible outcomes from an experiment can be specified as a set of occurrences, which is called a 'sample space'.

Definition A.1.2. *A sample space (S) is the collection of all possible outcomes of an experiment.*

The sample space of an experiment is normally denoted as a set containing multiple elements. The sample space for the examples listed above can be expressed as follows:

$$S_1 = \{H, T\} \tag{A.1a}$$
$$S_2 = \{HH, HT, TH, TT\} \tag{A.1b}$$
$$S_3 = \{1, 2, 3, 4, 5, 6\} \tag{A.1c}$$
$$S_4 = \{0, 1, 2, 3, ...\} \tag{A.1d}$$
$$S_5 = \{(x, y) | T_0 \le x \le y \le T_1\} \tag{A.1e}$$
$$S_6 = \{t | t \ge 0\} \tag{A.1f}$$

H is for head and T is for tail for the experiments of tossing a coin (E_1 and E_2). There are six possible results from rolling a dice; hence, the sample space S_3. The number of incoming calls to an emergency department every hour can be zero or many as shown in the sample space S_4. x and y are the minimum and maximum daily temperature of a city, with the assumption that the temperature range of this city is from T_0 to T_1. The interval time between two bus departures is always equal to or greater than zero.

The elements in a sample space of an experiment are decided according to the objective of the experiment. For example, the sample spaces of the first and second experiment are different, even if the same coin is used in both, because the first is to toss the coin once, while the second is to toss the coin twice.

In reality, we are usually interested in some particular outcome collections from an experiment. For example, in the experiment E_6, we could be interested in the intervals between two bus departures that are not greater than five minutes. All samples satisfying this condition become a subset of S_6: $A = \{t | 0 \le t \le 5\}$. This subset A is called a random event of E_6. Obviously, the situation of $0 \leq t \leq 5$ occurs only when a sample point is from A.

Definition A.1.3. *A* **statistical event** *is any collection of outcomes from an experiment.*

Any member element of the sample space is an event. Any event that consists of a single outcome in the sample space is called a **simple event**. For example, there are two simple events $\{H\}$ and $\{T\}$ for E_1. Rolling a dice in E_3 has six simple events that are $\{1\}$, $\{2\}$, $\{3\}$, $\{4\}$, $\{5\}$, and $\{6\}$. The sample space S contains every possible sample point. The results from an experiment can always be found in the sample space S of this experiment. Therefore, S is a **certain event** that definitely occurs. In contrast, an empty set (ϕ) cannot occur in any experiment because no element exists in it; therefore, it is called an **impossible event**. Let us now consider the following examples.

Example A.1.1. *For E_2, we consider an event $A_{2,1}$ in which H occurs at the first coin toss. We can then express this as:*

$$A_{2,1} = \{HH, HT\}$$

In addition, we consider an event $A_{2,2}$, in which H appears both times when the coin is tossed. This can be expressed as:

$$A_{2,2} = \{HH\}$$

Example A.1.2. *For E_5, we consider an event $A_{5,1}$, in which the difference between the minimum and maximum temperatures is greater than 10 degrees. This can be expressed as: $A_{5,1} = \{(x,y) | y - x > 10, T_0 \leq x \leq y \leq T_1\}$.*

Given that any event of an experiment can be seen as a set, set theory is used to represent relations between events. If events A and B are in the same sample space S of an experiment, then:

1. $A \subset B$ means that event B contains event A. In other words, B must occur if A occurs. Further, if $A \subset B$ and $B \subset A$, then $A = B$.
2. $A \cup B = \{x | x \in A \text{ or } x \in B\}$ means that either A or B occurs, or both occur.
3. $A \cap B = \{x | x \in A \text{ and } x \in B\}$ is the intersection of A and B. It means that both A and B occur.
4. $A - B = \{x | x \in A \text{ and } x \notin B\}$ is used to show that only A occurs but B does not occur.
5. $A \cap B = \phi$ is a mutually exclusive event. It is impossible for A and B to occur together.
6. $A \cup B = S$ and $\overline{A \cap B} = \phi$, means that B is the complementary event of A. B can be denoted as $\overline{A}$, and $\overline{A} = S - A$.

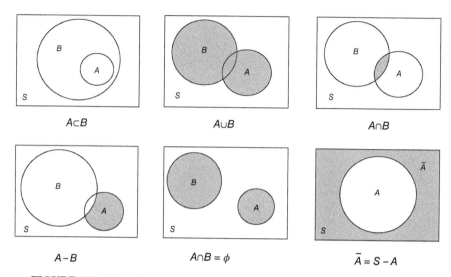

FIGURE A.1 Venn diagrams – relationships between events for a sample space S.

Figure A.1 illustrates the above relationships between events in a sample space S. The outer rectangle represents the sample space S, while events A and B are visualised as circles. The shadowed area is the result of the operations applied to the events. For example, the shadowed area illustrated in the first row of the third figure is the result of the intersection operation $(A \cap B)$.

The union ($\cup$) and the intersection ($\cap$) operations have the following algebraic properties. They are commutative, meaning that the sets can be written in any order:

$$A \cup B = B \cup A \tag{A.2a}$$

$$A \cap B = B \cap A \tag{A.2b}$$

They are associative – that is, multiple operations can be performed in any order:

$$A \cup (B \cup C) = (A \cup B) \cup C \tag{A.3a}$$

$$A \cap (B \cap C) = (A \cap B) \cap C \tag{A.3b}$$

They are distributive:

$$A \cup (B \cap C) = (A \cup B) \cap (A \cup C) \tag{A.4a}$$

$$A \cap (B \cup C) = (A \cap B) \cup (A \cap C) \tag{A.4b}$$

The above algebraic properties lead to De Morgan's laws, shown in Eq. (A.5):

$$\overline{A \cup B} = \overline{A} \cap \overline{B} \tag{A.5a}$$

$$\overline{A \cap B} = \overline{A} \cup \overline{B} \tag{A.5b}$$

Example A.1.3. *In Example A.1.1, the following operations can be performed on events $A_{2,1}$ and $A_{2,2}$:*

$$A_{2,1} \cup A_{2,2} = \{HH, HT\}, \text{ in fact } A_{2,2} \subset A_{2,1},$$
$$A_{2,1} \cap A_{2,2} = \{HH\},$$
$$A_{2,1} - A_{2,2} = \{HT\}, \text{ and}$$
$$\overline{A \cup B} = \overline{A} \cap \overline{B} = \{TT, TH\} \cap \{HT, TT, TH\} = \{TT, TH\}.$$

A.1.2 Frequency and Probability

An event may or may not occur in an experiment. We are usually interested in the likelihood that a specific event occurs in an experiment. For example, we would like to know the possibility of water exceeding a certain level when deciding the height of a dam during the designing phase. In this case, a quantitative method needs to be employed to express the likelihood of the occurrences of this event. To understand how to do this, we start by introducing the concept of frequency.

Definition A.1.4. *An experiment is run n times under the same conditions. Assume that, in these n runs an event A occurs n_A times. Then, n_A is called the **frequency** (or **absolute frequency**) of event A. The ratio $\frac{n_A}{n}$ is called the **relative frequency** of event A and is denoted by $f_n(A)$.*

It becomes clear from the above discussion that relative frequency has the following properties:

1. $0 \leq f_n(A) \leq 1$.
2. $f_n(S) = 1$.
3. If $\{A_1, A_2, ..., A_n\}$ are mutually exclusive to each other, then $f_n(A_1 \cup A_2 \cup ... \cup A_n\} = f_n(A_1) + f_n(A_2) + ... + f_n(A_n)$.

Given that relative frequency is the ratio between the number of runs in which an event occurs and the total number of runs, we can infer that, if an event has larger relative frequency in an experiment, that means it has more chances of occurring during the experiment, and vice versa. Thus, the relative frequency can be used to quantify the probability of an event. To clarify how this can be done, let us first see how probability is defined:

Definition A.1.5. *A **probability** (P(A)) is the quantitative description of the chance that a specific event (A) may occur in an experiment (E).*

The question is whether the relative frequency of a particular event can be the probability of the event in an experiment. Let us first proceed with a simple experiment. In this experiment, we toss a coin five times and record the number of heads (H) occurrences. We can repeat this process 50 times, 100 times, 200 times, and more. If we calculate the relative frequency of event H occurrences for different numbers of

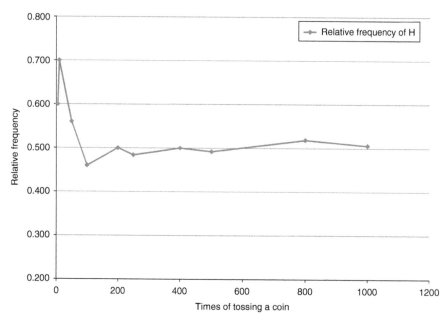

FIGURE A.2   The relative frequency of event H ($f_n(H)$) when tossing a coin different numbers of times.

experiment runs, we can display the results in a graphical manner, as in Figure A.2. We see from the figure that $f_n(H)$ always fluctuates around the value of 0.5, and moves closer to 0.5 as the number of coin tosses increases.

In fact, such types of experiments have been performed by many researchers in the past, and Table A.1 lists the results of some of these experiments.

Given that the sample space of tossing a coin contains only two elements, $\{H, T\}$, both H and T have a 50/50 chance of occurrence in an experiment. Obviously, the theoretical probability of event H is 0.5 in the coin-tossing experiment. However, as the results in Table A.1 suggest, $f_n(H)$ is closer to 0.5 and becomes more stable as n increases. Another example is found in the frequency of the alphabet letters in

TABLE A.1   Coin-tossing Experiments in History (Rows Are Ordered by the Second Column – the Number of Experiments, n

Tosser	n	n_H	$f_n(H)$
De Morgan	2 048	1 061	0.5181
Count Buffon	4 040	2 048	0.5069
John Kerrich	10 000	5 067	0.5067
Karl Pearson	12 000	6 019	0.5016
Karl Pearson	24 000	12 012	0.5005

English [115], where the frequency of letters appearing in words becomes more stable when more words are counted.

From the above examples, we can conclude that the relative frequency of an event $(f_n(A))$ becomes more stable with the number of experiments (under the same conditions), and will settle to a certain value when $n \to \infty$. Therefore, the probability of an event can be represented using the relative frequency. The relative frequency is also called empirical probability because it is derived directly from experimental results.

However, in real life, it is impossible to perform an infinite number of experiments and then calculate the relative frequency of a specific event to obtain the corresponding probability. Instead, inspired by the stability aspect and using the properties of relative frequency, we can induce the mathematical definition of probability to undertake further theoretical analysis.

Given a random experiment, E, and its sample space, S, every event A in E is associated with a real number $P(A)$, which is the probability of event A. $P(\cdot)$ has the following properties:

1. $P(A) \geq 0$, and $P(\phi) = 0$
2. $P(S) = 1$
3. if $\{A_1, A_2, ..., A_n\}$ are mutually exclusive to each other, then
   $P(A_1 \cup A_2 \cup ... \cup A_n\} = P(A_1) + P(A_2) + ... + P(A_n)$
4. if $A \subset B$, then
   $P(B - A) = P(B) - P(A)$
   $P(B) > P(A)$
5. $P(A) \leq 1$
6. $P(\overline{A}) = 1 - P(A)$
7. given any two events A and B, $P(A \cup B) = P(A) + P(B) - P(A \cap B)$.

Assuming that a sample space S contains a finite number of simple events $(e_1, e_2, ..., e_n)$, and each simple event has equal chance of occurring in an experiment, then:

$$P(\{e_1\}) = P(\{e_2\}) = ... = P(\{e_n\}) \tag{A.6}$$

Further, simple events of the sample space are mutually exclusive to each other; hence:

$$1 = P(S) = P(\{e_1\} \cup \{e_2\} \cup ... \cup \{e_n\} = P(\{e_1\}) + P(\{e_2\}) + ... + P(\{e_n\}) \tag{A.7}$$

The probability of a simple event e_i can be derived from Eqs. (A.6) and (A.7) as follows:

$$P(e_i) = \frac{1}{n} \quad i = 1, 2, ..., n \tag{A.8}$$

If an event A contains k simple events $(A = \{e_{A,1}\} \cup \{e_{A,2}\} \cup ... \cup \{e_{A,k}\}$, then the probability of event A is calculated as below:

$$P(A) = \sum_{j=1}^{k} P(\{e_{A,j}\}) = \frac{k}{n}. \tag{A.9}$$

As the equation shows, the probability of event A is the ratio between the number of simple events contained by A and the total number of simple events in the sample space.

Example A.1.4. *If an experiment consists of tossing a coin three times, let us assume that event A is 'H occurs only once', and B is 'H occurs at least once'. What are P(A) and P(B)? The following steps demonstrate how to calculate the required probabilities:*

1. The sample space of this experiment is:
   $S = \{HHH, HHT, HTH, THH, HTT, THT, TTH, TTT\}$,
   and
   $A = \{HTT, THT, TTH\}$.
2. $P(A) = \frac{3}{8}$.
3. Since $\bar{B} = \{TTT\}$, $P(B) = 1 - P(\bar{B}) = 1 - \frac{1}{8} = \frac{7}{8}$

A.1.3 Conditional Probability

In many cases, the occurrence of an event (A) is affected by another event B. In this case, the probability of event A occurring is called **conditional probability**. The formal definition is given below.

Definition A.1.6. *A conditional probability is the probability of an event A only on the condition that another event B has occurred before A. This is denoted as P(A|B).*

Let us consider an example first.

Example A.1.5. *Assuming that an experiment consists of tossing a coin three times, let event A be the same side (either H or T) occurring twice, and event B be H occurring only once. What is the probability of A occurring if B has occurred?*
Given that $S = \{HH, HT, TH, TT\}$, $A = \{HH, TT\}$, and $B = \{HH, HT, TH\}$, TT of A cannot occur because B (at least one H in two tosses) has occurred before. Given that three elements in B and only one element (HH) belong to A, $P(A|B) = \frac{1}{3}$.
Here, $P(A) \neq \frac{2}{4} \neq P(A|B)$ because there is a condition restricting the occurrence of event B. the following equation can be used to calculate $P(A|B)$:

$$P(A|B) = \frac{P(A \cap B)}{P(B)}. \tag{A.10}$$

The above equations can be easily explained using a Venn diagram. In this example,
$P(A \cap B) = \frac{1}{4}$ *and* $P(B) = \frac{3}{4}$, *therefore,* $P(A|B) = \frac{1/4}{3/4} = \frac{1}{3}$.

From Eq. (A.10), the multiplication rule can be derived as:

$$P(A \cap B) = P(A|B)P(B). \tag{A.11}$$

A.1.4 Law of Total Probability and Bayes' Theorem

Here, we introduce two important equations for calculating probabilities. First, the
law of total probability can be written using set theory, as follows:

$$P(A) = P(A \cap B) + P(A \cap \overline{B}) \tag{A.12}$$

Blended with Eq. (A.11), the above equation can also be written as:

$$P(A) = P(A|B)P(B) + P(A|\overline{B})P(\overline{B}). \tag{A.13}$$

Both the above equations are useful when $P(A)$ is difficult to obtain directly, but $P(B)$
and $P(A|B)$ are known or can be easily calculated. The above equation can be written
in different manners using partitions of a sample space. The definition of a partition
of a sample space is given as below.

Definition A.1.7. *Given a sample space S of experiment E,* $B_1, B_2, ..., B_n$ *are events
of E, if*

1. $B_i \cap B_j = \phi$, $i \neq j$, *and* $i, j = 1, 2, ..., n$
2. $B_1 \cup B_2 \cup ... \cup B_n = S$

then, $B_1, B_2, ..., B_n$ *are the partitions of sample space S.*
*Therefore, a **partition** of a sample space S is a collection of subsets* $B_i \subset S$, *so that
every element* $e \in S$ *occurs in exactly one of the* B_i.

Partitions can be expressed in a graphical manner, as in Figure A.3. Therefore, the
law of total probability can also be written as follows:

$$P(A) = P(A|B_1)P(B_1) + P(A|B_2)P(B_2) + ... + P(A|B_n)P(B_n) \tag{A.14}$$

where, $B_1, B_2, ..., B_n$ are the partitions of sample space S.
Bayes' theorem is another important theorem for conditional and joint probabilities. Its mathematical formulation is described as follows:

$$P(B_i|A) = \frac{P(A|B_i)P(B_i)}{\sum_{j=0}^{n} P(A|B_j)P(B_j)} \tag{A.15}$$

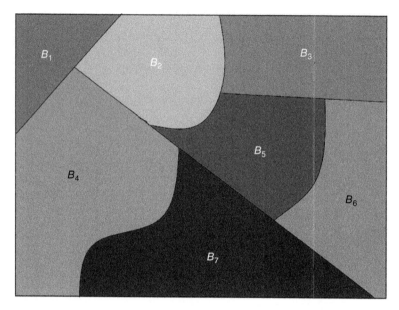

FIGURE A.3   Partitions $B_1, B_2, ..., B_7$ in a sample space S.

where, A is an event in sample space S of an experiment E; $B_1, B_2, ..., B_n$ are partitions of S; and $P(A) > 0$, $P(B_i) > 0$, $i = 1, 2, ..., n$. If we use the total probability equation (Eq. (A.12)) and assume that n is 2, so that B_1 is B and B_2 is $\overline{B}$, then, Bayes' theorem can be expressed in a simpler manner, as follows:

$$P(B|A) = \frac{P(A|B)P(B)}{P(A|B)P(B) + P(A|\overline{B})P(\overline{B})}. \tag{A.16}$$

Equations (A.12) and (A.16) are commonly used in real problems.

Example A.1.6. *An electrical part is supplied by three suppliers, and the historical records are summarised in the following table.*

Supplier	% of supply	Faulty rate
1	15%	0.02
2	80%	0.01
3	5%	0.03

For a random sample, what is the probability of finding it faulty? If a random sample is faulty, what are the probabilities for this faulty part to come from Supplier 1, 2, and 3, respectively?

To solve the problems, let A be an event in which a random sample is faulty, and $B_i (i = 1, 2, 3)$ be an event in which a random sample is from a supplier i. Obviously,

B_1, B_2, B_3 *are partitions of sample space S, and* $P(B_1) = 0.15$, $P(B_2) = 0.8$, $P(B_3) =$ *0.05. Correspondingly,* $P(A|B_1) = 0.02$, $P(A|B_2) = 0.01$, *and* $P(A|B_3) = 0.03$. *Based on the law of total probability:*

$$P(A) = P(A|B_1)P(B_1) + P(A|B_2)P(B_2) + P(A|B_3)P(B_3) = 0.0125$$

Based on Bayes' theorem:

$$P(B_1|A) = \frac{P(A|B_1)P(B_1)}{P(A)} = 0.24$$

$$P(B_2|A) = \frac{P(A|B_2)P(B_2)}{P(A)} = 0.64$$

$$P(B_3|A) = \frac{P(A|B_3)P(B_3)}{P(A)} = 0.12$$

Thus, the probability of finding a random sample faulty is 0.0125 and the probability that a random faulty part is supplied by Supplier 2 is the highest.

A.1.5 Independent Events

In some cases, an event occurs independently of other events. For example, in an experiment of tossing two coins (*a* and *b*), event *A* is that coin *a* shows *H* side, and event *B* is that coin *b* shows *H* side. Obviously the occurrence of each of these two events does not affect the probability of the other; therefore, these two events are independent events.

Definition A.1.8. *Two events A and B are independent if:*

$$P(A \cap B) = P(A)P(B) \tag{A.17}$$

If *A* and *B* are independent, we can express this fact using conditional probabilities (Eq. (A.10)), as follows:

$$P(B|A) = P(B) \tag{A.18}$$

Equation (A.17) can also be extended to three independent events, *A*, *B*, and *C*, as follows:

$$P(A \cap B \cap C) = P(A)P(B)P(C). \tag{A.19}$$

Example A.1.7. *In an experiment of rolling two dice, what is the probability of rolling a six with both dice? Let A be the event of rolling a six with the first die, and B be the event of rolling a six with the second die. Then:*

$$P(A) = \frac{1}{6}, \quad and \ p(B) = \frac{1}{6}$$

$$P(A \cap B) = P(A)P(B) = \frac{1}{6} \times \frac{1}{6} = \frac{1}{36}$$

Thus, the probability of rolling a six with both dice is $\frac{1}{36}$.

A.1.6 Random Variables and Distributions

In many cases, especially in modelling and simulation contexts, we are interested in the overall features related to the random experiment results, rather than the results themselves. For example, in an experiment of tossing a coin three times, we are interested in the number of H or T occurrences. For example, we may be concerned about the cases in which the total number of H occurrences is two, but not about how it occurred – that is, 'HHT', 'HTH', and 'THH' are all treated as the same case. If a variable X is used to record the number of H occurrences for this experiment, we could assign a real number (X) to each sample point (e) in the sample space (S), as shown in Table A.1.

As shown in the table, X is a variable and its value depends on the sample points; therefore, we can say X is a random variable. A formal definition of a random variable is given below.

Definition A.1.9. *Given a sample space $S = \{e\}$, a **random variable** $X = X(e)$ is a function that assigns a real number to each sample point in S.*

The value of a random variable depends on the experiment results, and the occurrences of the experiment results are associated with some probabilities; therefore, the values of random variables also depend on some probabilities.

Example A.1.8. *For the experiment of tossing a coin three times, let $X = 2$. Then, the corresponding collection of sample points $A = \{HHT, HTH, THH\}$ is the event associated with variable X, so we can determine the probability of $X = 2$ as:*

$$P(X = 2) = P(A) = \frac{3}{8}$$

Similarly, the probability of $X \leq 2$ is:

$$P(X \leq 2) = P(\{HHT, THT, TTH, TTT\}) = \frac{4}{8}.$$

Further, we note that the values of random variables are decided by the results of random experiments, where these results are unknown before the experiments occur. Thus, random variables are fundamentally different from deterministic ones. Random variables enable us to study and investigate random experimental results mathematically for many random phenomena.

In the above example, the random variable X is a **discrete random variable** that can only take a countable number of values – that is, X only takes $0, 1, 2, 3$. Therefore, a random variable that takes only a finite number of values $(x_1, x_2, x_3, ..., x_n)$ is discrete. Understanding the statistical regularities of a discrete random variable X only requires knowing all possible values for X and the associated probabilities for each value.

Definition A.1.10. *Given a discrete random variable X and all its possible values* $x_k (k = 1, 2, ...)$, *the probability of an event* $\{X = x_k\}$ *is:*

$$P(X = x_k) = p_k, \quad k = 1, 2, ... \tag{A.20}$$

and we must have:

$$P(X = x_k) \geq 0 \tag{A.21a}$$

$$\sum_{k}^{\infty} P(X = x_k) = 1 \tag{A.21b}$$

$P(X = x_k)$ *is called the* **probability mass function** *for the discrete random variable X, since it can compute all probability statements for X.*

The probability mass function defines a discrete probability distribution for a discrete random variable.

Another important function is introduced in the last question ($P(X \leq 2)$) of Example A.1.8, which is the **distribution function** or **cumulative distribution function** (CDF).

Definition A.1.11. *Given a random variable X and any real number x, the function:*

$$F(x) = P(X \leq x)$$

is the distribution function of X, where $P(X \leq x)$ *indicates the probability of the event* $\{X \leq x\}$.

Hence, the value of $F(x)$ is the probability of $X \in (-\infty, x]$. The distribution function has the following properties:

1. $F(x)$ is non-decreasing – for example, for any x_1, x_2 ($x_1 < x_2$), $F(x_1) \leq F(x_2)$. Therefore:

$$P(\{x_1 < X \leq x_2\}) = P(\{X \leq x_2\}) - P(\{X \leq x_1\}) = F(x_2) - F(x_1) \geq 0 \tag{A.22}$$

2. $0 \leq F(x) \leq 1$ for any x, and:

$$F(-\infty) = \lim_{x \to -\infty} F(x) = 0$$

$$F(\infty) = \lim_{x \to \infty} F(x) = 1.$$

Example A.1.9. *The probabilities associated with the number of H occurrences in an experiment of tossing a coin three times can be calculated according to Table A.2.*

TABLE A.2   Number of *H* Occurrences in an Experiment of Tossing a Coin Three Times

Sample point(*e*)	HHH	HHT	HTH	THH	HTT	THT	TTH	TTT
X	3	2	2	2	1	1	1	0

TABLE A.3   Probabilities Associated with the Number of H Occurrences in an Experiment of Tossing a Coin Three Times

Number of *H* occurrences (X)	0	1	2	3
Probability of $X = x_k$ (p_k)	1/8	3/8	3/8	1/8

Based on the results shown in the second row of Table A.3, we display the corresponding probability mass function in Figure A.4. We note that only four variables have associated probabilities greater than 0. Thus:

$$F(x) = \begin{cases} 0 & x < 0 \\ P(X = 0) = \frac{1}{8} & 0 \leq x < 1 \\ P(X = 0) + P(X = 1) = \frac{4}{8} & 1 \leq x < 2 \\ P(X = 0) + P(X = 1) + P(X = 2) = \frac{7}{8} & 2 \leq x < 3 \\ 1 & x \geq 3 \end{cases}$$

$F(X)$ is visualised as a stepped curve in Figure A.5. It jumps when $x = 0, 1, 2, 3$, and the increment values are 1/8, 3/8, 3/8, and 1/8, for each jump, respectively.

From the above example, the equation to calculate $F(x)$ from the probability of discrete random variable X can be derived as below:

$$F(x) = P(\{X \leq x\}) = \sum_{x_k \leq x} P(\{X = x_k\}). \tag{A.23}$$

In many real problems, a random variable X is a **continuous random variable** that can take an uncountable/infinite number of different values (real numbers), such as the average daily temperature of a city in the example experiment E_5, or the time intervals between two bus departures in E_6.

Definition A.1.12. *For a distribution function $F(x)$ of a random variable X, if there is a non-negative function $f(x)$ such that for any real number x:*

$$F(x) = \int_{-\infty}^{x} f(t)\, dt \tag{A.24}$$

*X is said to be a **continuous random variable**. $f(x)$ is called the **PDF** of X.*

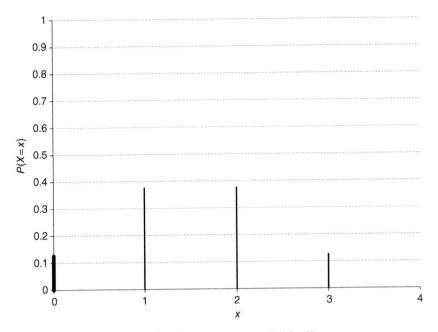

FIGURE A.4   Probability mass function of X for H occurrences.

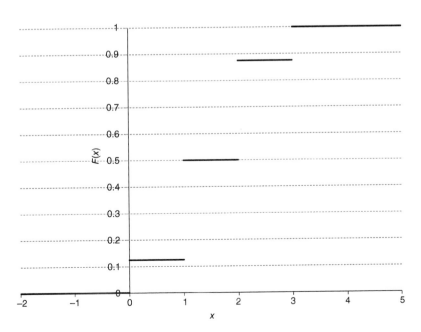

FIGURE A.5   CDF of X for H occurrences.

The PDF $f(x)$ has the following properties:

1. $f(x) \geq 0$
2. $\int_{-\infty}^{\infty} f(x)\, dt = 1$
3. For any real numbers, x_1, x_2, $(x_1 \leq x_2)$:

$$P(x_1 < X \leq x_2) = F(x_2) - F(x_1) = \int_{x_1}^{x_2} f(x)\, dx$$

4. $F'(x) = f(x)$, if $f(x)$ is derivable at x.

For a discrete random variable X, each value of x is associated with an actual probability p_k, as illustrated in the above example. In fact, the probability that a continuous random variable X has the value x (that is, $X = x$) is zero. According to the fourth property listed above, we can obtain:

$$f(x) = \lim_{\Delta x \to 0^+} \frac{F(x + \Delta x) - F(x)}{\Delta x}$$

$$= \lim_{\Delta x \to 0^+} \frac{P(\{x < X \leq x + \Delta x\})}{\Delta x}. \qquad (A.25)$$

Therefore, an approximation of the probability that the continuous random variable X falls in the interval $(x, x + \Delta x]$ can be obtained when Δx is small enough:

$$P(x < X \leq x + \Delta x) \approx f(x)\, \Delta x. \qquad (A.26)$$

Given that we know that the probability of a random variable taking a single value is 0 (i.e. $P(X = a) = 0$), it does not matter if the endpoints of an interval are included or excluded when calculating the probability of X falling in the interval:

$$P(a < X \leq b) = P(a \leq X \leq b) = P(a < X < b). \qquad (A.27)$$

Example A.1.10. *Assume that the PDF of a continuous variable X is:*

$$f(x) = \begin{cases} \frac{x}{6} & 0 \leq x < 3 \\ 2 - \frac{x}{2} & 3 \leq x < 4 \\ 0 & \text{otherwise} \end{cases}$$

Then, the CDF can be derived as below:

$$F(x) = \begin{cases} 0 & x < 0 \\ \int_0^x \frac{x}{6} dx & 0 \leq x < 3 \\ \int_0^3 \frac{x}{6} dx + \int_3^x (2 - \frac{x}{2})\, dx & 3 \leq x < 4 \\ 1 & x \geq 4 \end{cases}$$

and becomes:

$$F(x) = \begin{cases} 0 & x < 0 \\ \frac{x^2}{12} & 0 \le x < 3 \\ -3 + 2x - \frac{x^2}{4} & 3 \le x < 4 \\ 1 & x \ge 4 \end{cases}$$

For example, $P(\{1 \le X \le 3.5\}) = F(3.5) - F(1) = \frac{41}{48}$ is the probability that X falls in the interval of $[1, 3.5]$. The shadowed area under the PDF in Figure A.6 is the probability that X is in the interval of $[1, 3.5]$. Further, Figure A.7 illustrates the CDF of X for the given example.

A.1.7 Two-Dimensional Random Variables

In simulation or other real problems, we usually have to deal with more than one random variable. For example, to study the throughput of a bus terminal, we are interested in the time of buses arriving $(A_1, A_2, ..., A_n)$ at and departing $(D_1, D_2, ..., D_m)$ from the terminal.

Definition A.1.13. *Let the two-dimensional random variable (X, Y) be any pair of real number values (x, y); then, the distribution function of (X, Y) is:*

$$F(x, y) = P(X \le x,) \cap P(Y \le y) = P(X \le x, Y \le y)$$

*The distribution function of (X, Y) is also called the **joint probability density function** of random variables X and Y.*

Let us assume that a two-dimensional random variable (X, Y) marks the position of a random point on a plane. The value of $F(x, y)$ is the point falling within the shadow area shown in Figure A.8. (Note: there are no left and bottom edges on the shadow area.)

Based on Figure A.9, it is easy to calculate the probability of (X, Y) using the rectangle area $[x_1 < X \le x_2, y_1 < Y \le y_2]$, as follows:

$$P(x_1 < X \le x_2, y_1 < Y \le y_2) = F(x_2, y_2) - F(x_2, y_1) + F(x_1, y_1) - F(x_1, y_2).$$

For two discrete random variables X and Y, let:

$$P(X = x_i, Y = y_j) = p_{ij}, \quad i, j = 1, 2, 3, ...$$

Then,

$$p_{ij} \ge 0, \quad \text{and} \quad \sum_{i=1}^{\infty} \sum_{j=1}^{\infty} p_{ij} = 1$$

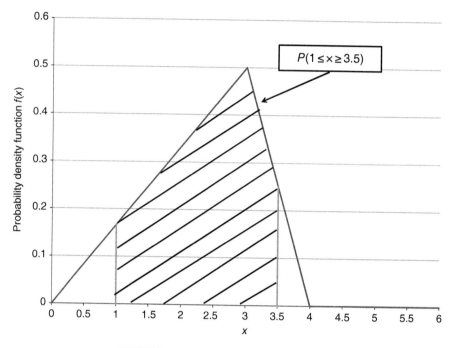

FIGURE A.6 PDF of X for H occurrences.

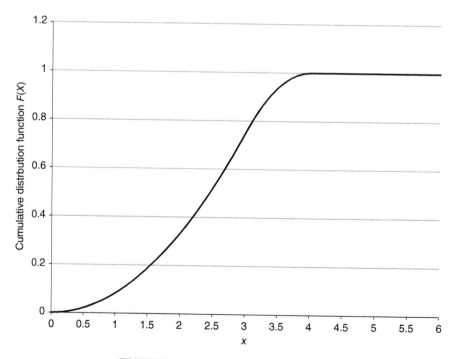

FIGURE A.7 CDF of X for H occurrences.

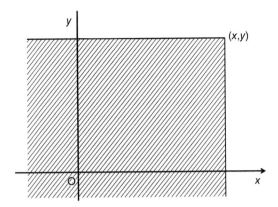

FIGURE A.8   Joint probability of $(X \le x, Y \le y)$.

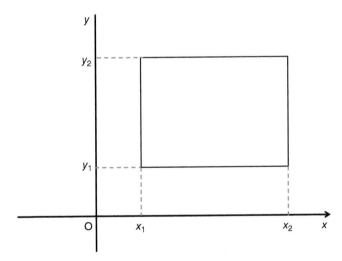

FIGURE A.9   Probability of $(x_1 < X \le x_2, y_1 < y \le y_2)$.

where $P(x, y)$ is called the **joint probability mass function** of (X, Y), (x_i, y_j), representing all possible values for (X, Y), and p_{ij} is the associated probability. Based on the above equations:

$$P(X = x_i) = \sum_{j=1}^{\infty} p_{ij} \quad i = 1, 2, 3, \ldots$$

and

$$P(Y = y_j) = \sum_{i=1}^{\infty} p_{ij} \quad j = 1, 2, 3, \ldots$$

are the **marginal probability mass functions** of X and Y, respectively.

If there is a non-negative PDF, $f(x, y)$, of the continuous random variable (X, Y), the joint probability density function of (X, Y) is:

$$F(x, y) = \int_{-\infty}^{y} \int_{-\infty}^{x} f(u, v) du dv$$

and the marginal PDFs of X and Y are:

$$f_X(x) = \int_{-\infty}^{\infty} f(x, y) dy$$

and:

$$f_Y(y) = \int_{-\infty}^{\infty} f(x, y) dx$$

Similar to the independent event probability, X and Y are independent when they satisfy:

$$P(X \leq x, Y \leq y) = P(X \leq x)P(Y \leq y)$$

or in another form:

$$F(x, y) = F_X(x)F_Y(y). \tag{A.28}$$

The fact that X and Y means that the value of one random variable does not tell us anything about the distribution of the other random variable. We say that X and Y are dependent when they are not independent.

Example A.1.11. *Assume that the PDF of the two-dimensional random variable (X, Y) is as follows:*

$$f(x, y) = \begin{cases} 2e^{-(2x+y)} & x > 0, y > 0 \\ 0 & \text{otherwise} \end{cases}$$

Then, the joint probability density function of (X, Y) is:

$$\begin{aligned} F(x, y) &= \int_{-\infty}^{y} \int_{-\infty}^{x} f(x, y) dx dy \\ &= \begin{cases} \int_{0}^{y} \int_{0}^{x} 2e^{-(2x+y)} dx dy & x > 0, y > 0 \\ 0 & \text{otherwise} \end{cases} \\ &= \begin{cases} (1 - e^{-2x})(1 - e^{-y}) & x > 0, y > 0 \\ 0 & \text{otherwise} \end{cases} \end{aligned}$$

The marginal PDFs of X and Y are:

$$f_X(x) = \begin{cases} 2e^{-2x} & x > 0 \\ 0 & \text{otherwise} \end{cases}$$

and

$$f_Y(y) = \begin{cases} 2e^{-y} & y > 0 \\ 0 & \text{otherwise} \end{cases}$$

Given that $f(x,y) = f_X(x)f_Y(y)$, X and Y are independent.

Example A.1.12. *Given a sample space $N = 1, 2, 3, 4, 5, 6, 7, 8, 9, 10$, $D = D(N)$ the number of the positive integers by which N is divisible, and $F = F(N)$ is the number of prime numbers (1 is not a prime number) by which N is divisible. The sample space and values of D and F are listed in the table below.*

Sample point	1	2	3	4	5	6	7	8	9	10
D	1	2	2	3	2	4	2	4	3	4
F	0	1	1	1	1	2	1	1	1	2

The possible values for D are $1, 2, 3, 4$, while F has only three possible values: $0, 1, 2$. Let (D, F) map to the value (i, j), where $i = 1, 2, 3, 4$ and $j = 0, 1, 2$. Then, the probability distribution of (D, F) can be derived as follows:

F \ D	1	2	3	4	$P(F = j)$
0	1/10	0	0	0	1/10
1	0	4/10	2/10	1/10	7/10
2	0	0	0	2/10	2/10
$P(D = i)$	1/10	4/10	2/10	3/10	

As seen in the above table, $P(D = 1, F = 0) = 1/10 \neq (1/10)^2 = P(D = 1)$ $P(F = 0)$. Therefore, D and F are not independent.

A.2 USEFUL DISTRIBUTIONS

In the previous section, we briefly reviewed the fundamental elements of probability theory and introduced basic concepts. In this section, we will present a number of distributions that are commonly used in simulation for modelling various random phenomena.

A.2.1 Uniform Distribution

Uniform distribution is used to quantify a continuous variable that takes random values between a and b, with constant probability. A Uniform distribution for X in the interval of $[a, b]$ is denoted as $X \sim U(a, b)$. Uniform distribution has the following characteristics:

1. a and b are real numbers: a is the location parameter, while $b - a$ is a scale parameter.
2. the PDF of $U(a, b)$ is:

$$f(x) = \begin{cases} \frac{1}{b-a} & a \leq x \leq b \\ 0 & \text{otherwise} \end{cases}$$

3. the distribution function of $U(a, b)$ is:

$$F(x) = \begin{cases} 0 & a < 0 \\ \frac{x-a}{b-a} & a \leq x \leq b \\ 1 & x < b \end{cases}$$

4. $X \in [a, b]$
5. the mean value is $\frac{a+b}{2}$
6. the variance is $\frac{(b-a)^2}{12}$.

$U(0, 1)$ distribution is essential for generating random values for other distributions. This aspect is described in detail in Appendix B. Figures A.10 and A.11 illustrate some examples of PDF and CDF for uniform distributions in different intervals.

A.2.2 Exponential Distribution

Exponential distribution is typically used to model the time intervals of events that occur at a constant rate, such as the lifespan of an electrical part or the time interval of customers arriving to a server (queueing theory).

The characteristics of exponential distribution are summarised as follows:

1. the PDF is

$$f(x) = \begin{cases} \frac{1}{\theta}e^{-x/\theta} & x \geq 0 \\ 0 & \text{otherwise} \end{cases}$$

2. the distribution function is

$$F(x) = \begin{cases} 1 - e^{-x/\theta} & x \geq 0 \\ 0 & \text{otherwise} \end{cases}$$

3. an exponential distribution for continuous random variable X is usually abbreviated as $X \sim expo(\theta)$
4. θ is the scale parameter, $\theta \geq 0$

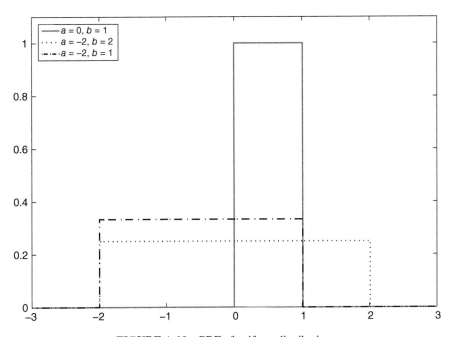

FIGURE A.10   PDF of uniform distributions.

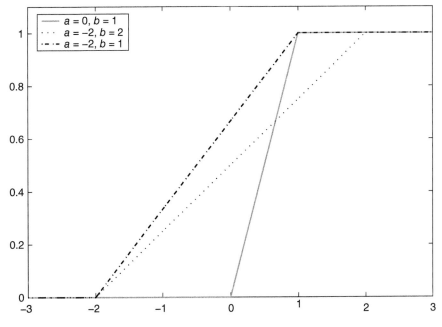

FIGURE A.11   CDF of uniform distributions.

5. e is a mathematical constant that is the base of the natural logarithm, also known as Euler's number
6. $X \in [0, \infty)$
7. the mean value is θ
8. the variance is θ^2.

Figures A.12 and A.13 plot some examples of PDF and CDF for exponential distributions with different θ values.

An exponentially distributed random variable t obeys a relation that is called 'memorylessness':

$$P(X > s + t | X > s) = P(X > t) \quad s, t > 0$$

For example, assume that X is the lifespan of an electrical part. If this part has been used for s hours, then the probability distribution of the remaining life time t of this part is the same as the original unconditioned distribution.

A.2.3 Gamma Distribution

Gamma distribution is useful for representing the time to complete a task, such as the customer service time of a bank teller or a car service time. The mathematical characteristics of a gamma distribution, $gamma(\alpha, \beta)$, are presented as follows:

1. the PDF is

$$f(x) = \begin{cases} \frac{1}{\beta^\alpha \Gamma(\alpha)} x^{\alpha-1} e^{-x/\beta} & x > 0 \\ 0 & \text{otherwise} \end{cases}$$

$\Gamma(\alpha)$ is the gamma function, and is expressed as:

$$\Gamma(\alpha) = \int_0^\infty t^{z-1} e^{-t} dt$$

2. if α is a positive integer, the distribution function is:

$$F(x) \begin{cases} 1 - e^{-x/\beta} \sum_{i=0}^{\alpha-1} \frac{(x/\beta)^i}{i!} & x > 0 \\ 0 & \text{otherwise} \end{cases}$$

if α is not an integer, there is no closed form for the distribution function
3. α is the shape parameter and β is the scale parameter; both α and β are greater than zero
4. $X \in [0, \infty)$
5. the mean value is $\alpha\beta$
6. the variance is $\alpha\beta^2$.

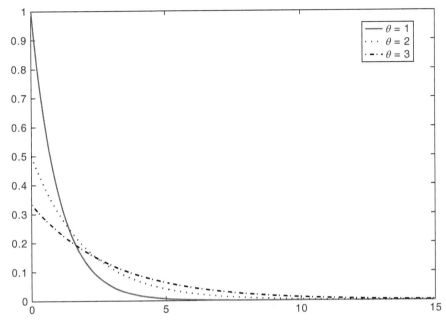

FIGURE A.12   PDF of exponential distributions.

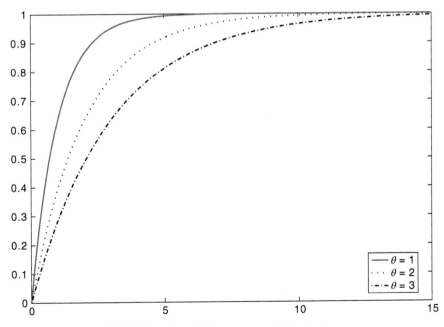

FIGURE A.13   CDF of exponential distributions.

Examples of PDF and CDF for gamma distributions with different α and β values are plotted in Figures A.14 and A.15. Exponential distribution, expo(β), is a special case of gamma distribution in which $\alpha = 1$ (i.e. *gamma*$(1, \beta)$). Through comparing the shape of expo(1) in Figures A.12 and A.13 with the shape of *gamma*$(1, 1)$, we can see that they are identical.

A.2.4 Weibull Distribution

Weibull distribution is another special case of gamma distribution; therefore, it can also be used to model the time to complete a task. At times, it can be used as a rough model in some cases where the absence of data occurs. Weibull distribution has the following characteristics:

1. the PDF is:

$$f(x) = \begin{cases} \frac{\beta}{\eta}(\frac{x}{\eta})^{\beta-1}e^{-(x/\eta)^{\beta}} & x > 0 \\ 0 & \text{otherwise} \end{cases}$$

2. the distribution function is:

$$F(x) = \begin{cases} 1 - e^{-(x/\beta)^{\eta}} & x > 0 \\ 0 & \text{otherwise} \end{cases}$$

3. η is the shape parameter and β is the scale parameter; both η and β are greater than zero
4. $X \in [0, \infty)$
5. the mean value is $\eta\Gamma(\frac{1}{\beta} + 1)$
6. the variance is $\eta^2\{\Gamma(\frac{2}{\beta} + 1) - [\Gamma(\frac{1}{\beta} + 1)]^2\}$.

As mentioned above, Weibull distribution, *Weibull*$(1, \beta)$ is similar to gamma distribution, *gamma*$(1, \beta)$; hence, it is also equivalent to an exponential distribution, expo(β). In other words, exponential distribution is a special case of Weibull distribution, in which $\beta = 1$; this is shown in Figures A.16 and A.17.

A.2.5 Normal Distribution

Normal (or Gaussian) distribution describes the probability of a continuous random variable falling in a range limited by two real numbers. There are many examples of random real-world phenomena that obey normal distribution, such as sea levels, the heights of male adults in a certain region and the voltages of power lines. Therefore, normal distribution is an important distribution in statistics for numerous natural and social studies. It is also commonly used in simulation for modelling the errors or variances of some real observations. The characteristics of Normal distribution are presented below.

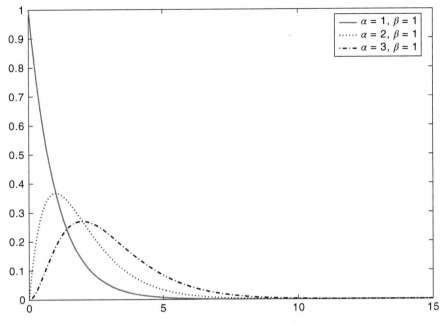

FIGURE A.14   PDF of gamma distributions.

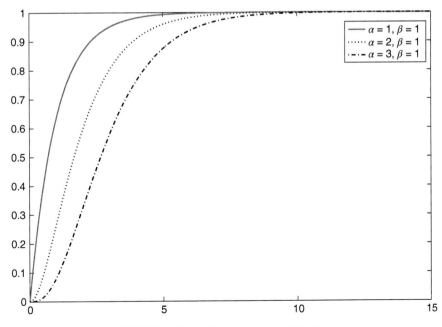

FIGURE A.15   CDF of gamma distributions.

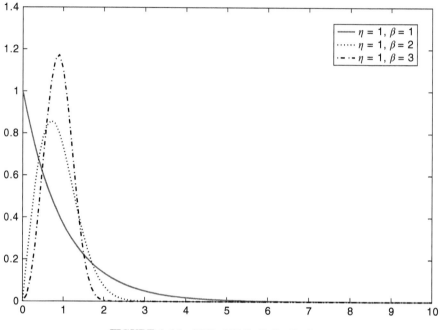

FIGURE A.16   PDF of Weibull distributions.

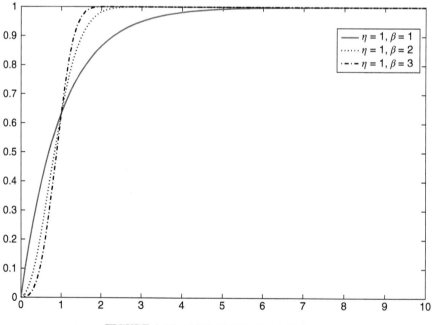

FIGURE A.17   CDF of Weibull distributions.

1. the PDF is:

$$f(x) = \frac{1}{\sqrt{2\pi}\sigma} e^{-\frac{(x-\mu)^2}{2\sigma^2}}, \quad -\infty < x < \infty$$

2. the distribution function is:

$$F(x) = \frac{1}{\sqrt{2\pi}\sigma} \int_{-\infty}^{x} e^{\frac{(t-u)^2}{2\sigma^2}} \, dt$$

where $t = (x - u)/\sigma$ ithe changing variable of the density function of a normal distribution; therefore, $dt = dx/\sigma$

3. a normal distribution for a continuous random variable X is denoted as $X \sim N(\mu, \sigma^2)$

4. μ is the location parameter, with $\mu \in (-\infty, \infty)$

5. σ is the scale parameter, with $\sigma > 0$

6. the mean value is μ, and the variance is σ^2.

A particular and widely used case of normal distribution is the standard normal distribution, in which $\mu = 0$ and $\sigma^2 = 1$ (i.e. $N(0, 1)$). Accordingly, the density function (denoted $\phi(x)$) and the distribution function (denoted $\Phi(x)$) become:

$$\phi(x) = \frac{1}{\sqrt{2\pi}} e^{-\frac{x^2}{2}}$$

$$\Phi(x) = \frac{1}{\sqrt{2\pi}} \int_{-\infty}^{x} e^{-t/2} \, dt.$$

The standard normal distribution is visualised as the solid lines Figures A.18 and A.19.

A.2.6 Lognormal Distribution

Lognormal distribution is another distribution that can be used to model the time to perform a task. Lognormal distribution is denoted as $LN(\mu, \sigma^2)$ and has the following characteristics:

1. the PDF is:

$$f(x) = \begin{cases} \dfrac{1}{\sqrt{2\pi}\sigma x} e^{-\frac{(\ln x - \mu)^2}{2\sigma^2}} & x > 0 \\ 0 & \text{otherwise} \end{cases}$$

2. there is no closed form for the distribution function of Lognormal

3. σ is the shape parameter and e^μ is the scale parameter; both σ and e^μ are greater than zero

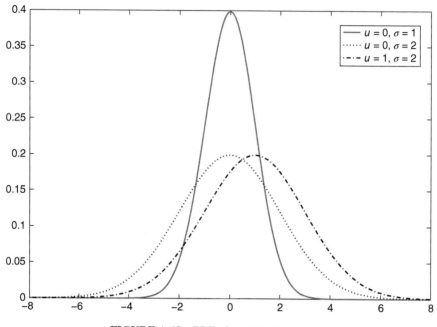

FIGURE A.18 PDF of normal distributions.

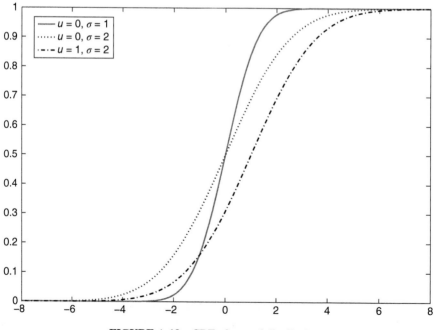

FIGURE A.19 CDF of normal distributions

4. $X \in [0, \infty)$
5. the mean value is $e^{\mu + \frac{\sigma^2}{2}}$
6. the variance is $e^{2\mu + \sigma^2}(e^{\sigma^2} - 1)$.

The density shape of lognormal is similar to *gamma*(α, β) and *Weibull*(η, β) when α and η are equal to 1. However, there is a large 'spike' in its probability density function when x is approaching 0, as shown in Figure A.20; and the corresponding CDF of lognormal distributions are illustrated in Figure A.21.

Thus far, we have discussed some common continuous distributions. Many other distributions for continuous random variables can be found in statistics textbooks, such as beta, Pearson type V, and log-logistic. These distributions are less popular in modelling and simulation; however, they can be used for similar purposes as the more popular distributions. For example, Pearson type V and log-logistic can also be used to model the time to perform a task.

In the following, we introduce some of the most common discrete distributions.

A.2.7 Bernoulli Distribution

Bernoulli distribution describes the random occurrence of events with two possible outcomes. A Bernoulli distribution, *Bernoulli*(p) has the following characteristics:

1. the probability mass function is:

$$P(x) = p^x (1-p)^{1-x} \quad x = 0, 1 \quad 0 < p < 1$$

Therefore, $P(0) = 1 - p$ and $P(1) = p$. In all cases other than $X = 0$ or $X = 1$, the probability is zero.

2. the distribution function is:

$$F(x) = \begin{cases} 0 & x < 0 \\ 1 - p & 0 \le x < 1 \\ 1 & x \ge 1 \end{cases}$$

3. the mean value is p
4. the variance is $p(1 - p)$.

Figures A.22 and A.23 illustrate the Bernoulli distribution, *Bernoulli*(p).

When an experiment has only two possible outcomes, the experiment is called a Bernoulli trial. For example, we can use *Bernoulli*(0.5) to model the outcomes from the experiment of tossing a coin, where 0 represents T, and 1 represents H. It is obvious that both sides have equal chances of appearing. When tossing the coin many times, this becomes a Bernoulli process involving a finite or infinite sequence of independent Bernoulli variables. Bernoulli distribution can be used to generate other discrete random variables, such as the binomial distributed variables presented in the next section.

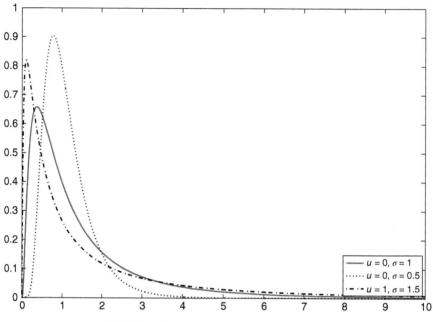

FIGURE A.20   PDF of lognormal distributions.

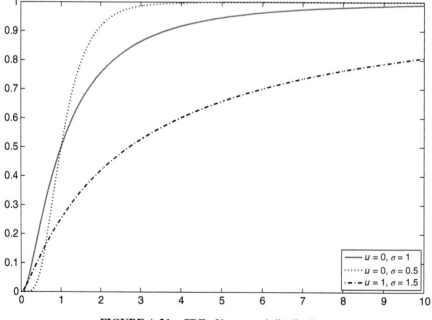

FIGURE A.21   CDF of lognormal distributions.

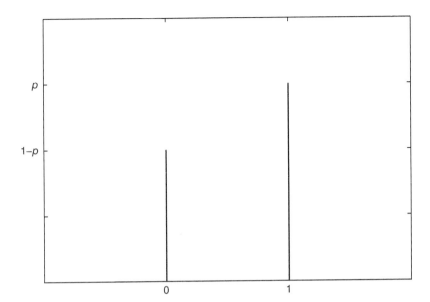

FIGURE A.22   Probability mass function of Bernoulli distribution.

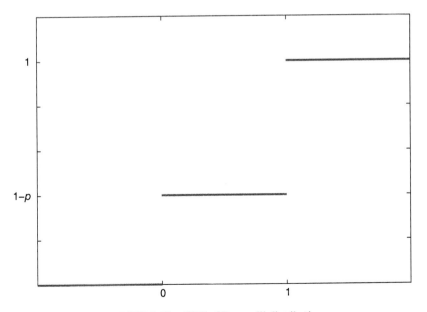

FIGURE A.23   CDF of Bernoulli distribution.

A.2.8 Binomial Distribution

Binomial distribution, denoted as $bin(n, p)$, is the distribution of the number of successful outcomes in n independent Bernoulli trials, where each trial has the same probability of success p. For example, we can use binomial distributions to represent the number of defective electrical parts in a batch of n, or to represent the demands for an inventory.

The characteristics of binomial distribution are listed below:

1. the probability mass function is:

$$P(x) = \binom{n}{x} p^x (1-p)^{n=x} \quad x = 0, 1, 3, ..., n \quad 0 < p < 1$$

where $\binom{n}{x}$ is the binomial coefficient:

$$\binom{n}{x} = \frac{n!}{x!(n-x)!}$$

This is why a random variable x obeying the above mass function is called binomial distribution.

2. the distribution function is:

$$F(x) = \begin{cases} 0 & x < 0 \\ \sum_{i=0}^{\lfloor x \rfloor} \binom{n}{i} p^i (1-p)^{n-i} & 0 \leq x \leq n \\ 1 & x > n \end{cases}$$

3. the mean value is np
4. the variance is $np(1-p)$.

When $n = 1$, it means that only one Bernoulli trial occurs; therefore, $bin(1, p)$ is identical to $Bernoulli(p)$. The probability mass functions of binomial distributions with various n and p values are visualised in Figures A.24–A.27.

A.2.9 Geometric Distribution

Geometric distribution is a discrete probability distribution that describes the probability distribution of the number of failures before the first success occurs in a sequence of independent Bernoulli trials, or vice versa. The mathematical characteristics of a geometric distribution, $geom(p)$, are as follows:

1. the probability mass function is:

$$P(x) = p(1-p)^{x-1}, \quad x = 0, 1, 2, ...$$

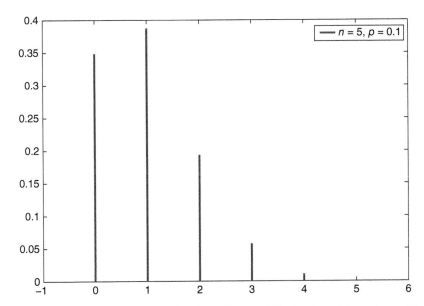

FIGURE A.24   Probability mass function of binomial distribution with $n = 5, p = 0.1$.

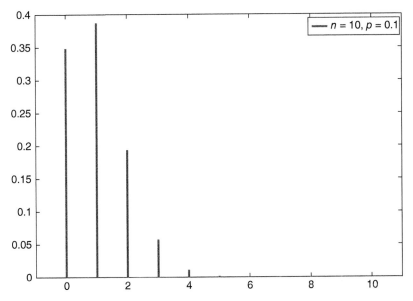

FIGURE A.25   Probability mass function of binomial distribution with $n = 10, p = 0.1$.

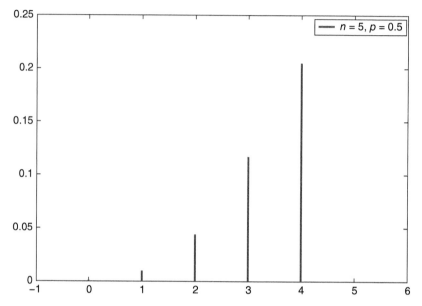

FIGURE A.26   Probability mass function of binomial distribution with $n = 5, p = 0.5$.

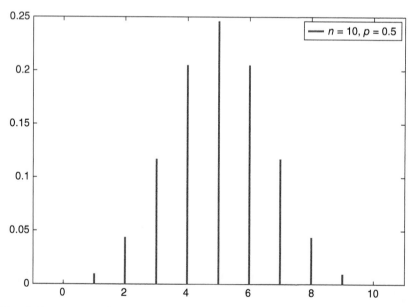

FIGURE A.27   Probability mass function of binomial distribution with $n = 10, p = 0.5$.

2. the distribution function is:

$$F(x) = \begin{cases} 1 - (1-p)^{\lfloor x \rfloor + 1} & x = 0, 1, 2, ... \\ 0 & \text{otherwise} \end{cases}$$

3. $p \in (0, 1)$
4. the range of X is $\{0, 1, 2, 3, ...\}$
5. the mean value is $\frac{1-p}{p}$
6. the variance is $\frac{1-p}{p^2}$.

Some examples of geometric distributions with different values of p are plotted in Figures A.28–A.31.

As the definition states, geometric distribution can be used to model the number of items inspected before encountering the first success or failure. It can also represent the number of items demanded from an inventory.

A.2.10 Poisson Distribution

Poisson distribution is an important distribution that describes the number of events that occur in a given period when the events occur at a constant rate. Poisson distribution can be used in numerous applications, such as the number of lost letters in a day for a region or the number of patients arriving at a clinic within an hour. The characteristics of Poisson distribution, *Possion*(λ), are listed below:

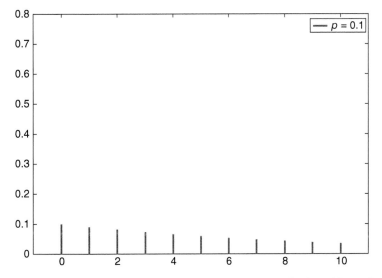

FIGURE A.28 Probability mass function of geometric distribution with $p = 0.1$.

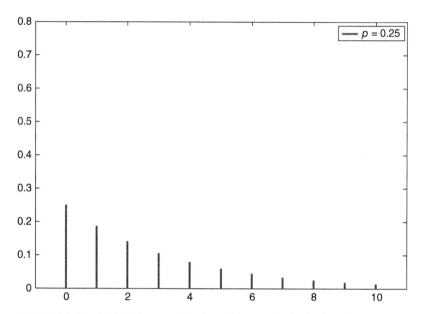

FIGURE A.29   Probability mass function of geometric distribution with $p = 0.25$.

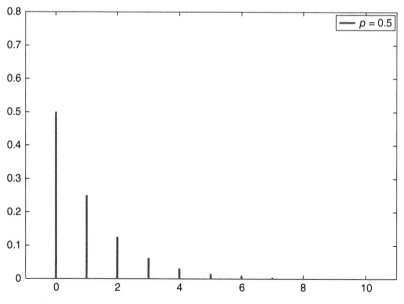

FIGURE A.30   Probability mass function of geometric distribution with $p = 0.5$.

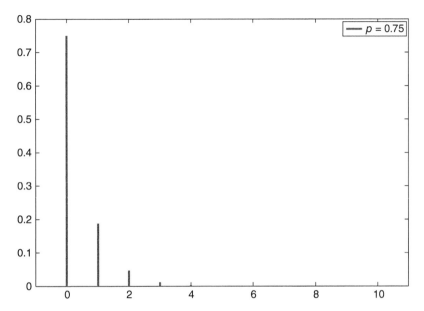

FIGURE A.31 Probability mass function of geometric distribution with $p = 0.75$.

1. the probability mass function is:

$$P(x) = \frac{\lambda^x e^{-\lambda}}{x!}, \quad x = 0, 1, 2, 3, \ldots$$

2. the distribution function is:

$$F(x) = \begin{cases} 0 & x < 0 \\ e^{-\lambda} \sum_{k=0}^{x} \frac{\lambda^k}{k!} & x = 0, 1, 2.3, \ldots \end{cases}$$

3. $\lambda > 0$
4. the range of X is $\{0, 1, 2, 3, \ldots\}$
5. the mean value is λ
6. the variance is λ.

Some examples of Poisson distributions with different values of λ are shown in Figures A.32–A.35. Poisson distributions can be found in many modelling and simulation applications, especially in the modelling and simulation of queueing systems.

The discrete probability distributions presented above are those with highest relevance to modelling and simulation. Many other discrete distributions exist, such as negative binomial distribution and hyper-geometric distribution, which are less used in the context of modelling and simulation, yet still useful in various other contexts. Hence, interested readers are encouraged to further consult the relevant statistical textbooks.

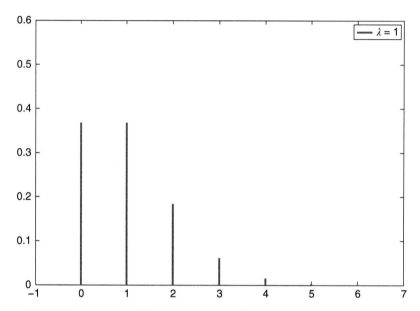

FIGURE A.32 Probability mass function of Poisson distribution with $\lambda = 1$.

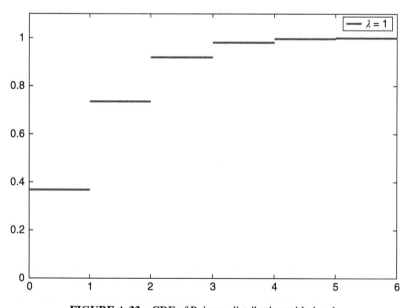

FIGURE A.33 CDF of Poisson distribution with $\lambda = 1$.

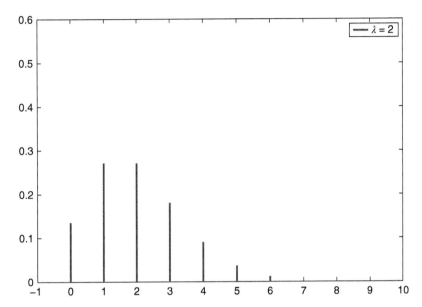

FIGURE A.34   Probability mass function of Poisson distribution with $\lambda = 2$.

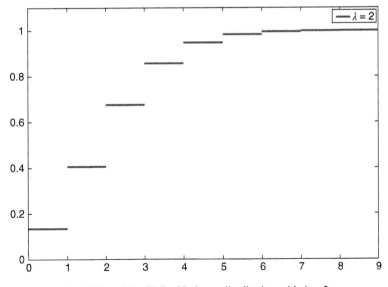

FIGURE A.35   CDF of Poisson distribution with $\lambda = 2$.

A.3 MATHEMATICAL CHARACTERISTICS OF RANDOM VARIABLES

In many studies, we may be interested in some characteristics of random variables, instead of their probability distribution. For example, we may be interested in the daily average number of cars manufactured by an automotive factory and the variance in daily production, or we may wish to know the average number of customers arriving at a bank in an hour and the differences between different hours of the business day. In the above examples, the values in which we are interested are not sufficient to fully describe the statistical distribution of the variables, yet do reveal some important characteristics of the variables that are relevant to us. In this section, we introduce those mathematical characteristics of random variables that are most commonly applied in various real-world situations (such as mean and variance).

Before proceeding to the description of these characteristics, let us first consider an example. Assume that a soldier is practising shooting at target. The shape of the target used in the training session is illustrated in Figure A.36. The amount of points earned by the soldier is based on the area hit:

1. three points are given for hitting the area inside the red circle (event e_3)
2. two points are given for hitting the area outside the red, but inside the blue circle (event e_2)
3. one point is given for hitting the area outside the blue circle, but inside the black circle (event e_1)
4. zero points are given for hitting the area outside the black circle (e_0).

We assume that, after N shots, the soldier receives 0 points for a_0 times, 1 point for a_1 times, 2 points for a_2 times, and 3 points for a_3 times, where

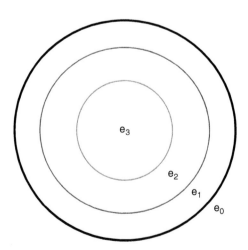

FIGURE A.36   A target used in a shooting training session.

$a_0 + a_1 + a_2 + a_3 = N$. Therefore, the total score is $a_0 \times 0 + a_1 \times 1 + a_2 \times 2 + a_3 \times 3$. Then, the average score for one shot is:

$$\frac{a_0 \times 0 + a_1 \times 1 + a_2 \times 2 + a_3 \times 3}{N} = \sum_{k=0}^{3} k \frac{a_k}{N}$$

where $\frac{a_k}{N}$ is the frequency of event $X = k$. When N is extremely large, the arithmetic average value calculated from the observation of the random variables, as above, is close to $\sum_{k=0}^{3} p_k$, where P_k is the probability that event $X = k$ occurs. $\sum_{k=0}^{3} k p_k$ is called the **expected value** or **mean**, and is usually denoted by $E(X)$ or $\mu(X)$. The mean can be defined as follows:

$$E(X) = \begin{cases} \sum_{k=1}^{\infty} x_k p_k & k = 1, 2, \dots \text{ and if } X \text{ is discrete} \\ \int_{-\infty}^{\infty} x f(x) \, dx & \text{if } x \text{ is continous} \end{cases} \tag{A.29}$$

The above equation includes two cases covering discrete and continuous random variables, respectively. $f(x)$ is the PDF for the continuous random variable X. The expected value has some important properties, listed below:

1. $E(CX) = CE(X)$, where C is a constant.
2. $E(X + Y) = E(X) + E(Y)$, where X and Y are random variables. Similarly, $E\left(\sum_{i}^{n} X_i\right) = \sum_{i}^{n} E(X_i)$.
3. $E(XY) = E(X)E(Y)$, where X and Y are independent random variables.

Example A.3.1. *We now assume that soldier A and soldier B perform the shooting training session described previously. The scores earned by the two soldiers are denoted by X_A and X_B, and the corresponding PDF are listed in Table A.4.*
The expected value for soldier A is:

$$E(X_A) = 0 \times 0.1 + 1 \times 0.2 + 2 \times 0.3 + 3 \times 0.4 = 2$$

while the expected value for soldier B is:

$$E(X_B) = 0 \times 0.1 + 1 \times 0.4 + 2 \times 0.3 + 3 \times 0.2 = 1.6$$

Obviously, soldier A is better than solider B in this training session.

TABLE A.4   The Probabilities of Scores for Soldiers A and B

X_A	0	1	2	3	X_B	0	1	2	3
p_k	0.1	0.2	0.3	0.4	p_k	0.1	0.4	0.3	0.2

Example A.3.2. *Now, let us consider the same conditions as in the previous example, but we assume that the radius of the target is 3, and the reward method changes to another method based on the distance between the centre of the target and the hit points (D), as follows:*

1. *if $D \leq 1$, the reward is three points*
2. *if $1 < D \leq 2$, the reward is two points*
3. *if $2 < D \leq 3$, the reward is one point*
4. *if $D > 3$, the reward is zero.*

The distances D between the target centre and the hit points follow some exponential distributions, as observed from the historical results for soldiers A and B, with $\theta_A = 2$ and $\theta_B = 5$ being the parameters for the exponential distributions for soldiers A and B, respectively. The probability $(P_A(D))$ of a hit point in each interval for soldier A can be calculated as:

$$P_B(D \leq 1) = \int_0^1 \frac{1}{2} e^{-d/2} \, \mathrm{d}d = 1 - e^{-1/2} = 0.3935$$

$$P_B(1 < D \leq 2) = \int_1^2 \frac{1}{2} e^{-d/2} \, \mathrm{d}d = e^{-1/2} - e^{-2/2} = 0.2387$$

$$P_B(2 < D \leq 3) = \int_2^3 \frac{1}{2} e^{-d/2} \, \mathrm{d}d = e^{-2/2} - e^{-3/2} = 0.1447$$

$$P_B(D > 3) = \int_3^\infty \frac{1}{2} e^{-d/2} \, \mathrm{d}d = e^{-3/2} = 0.2231$$

Similarly, the probability $(P_B(D))$ can be calculated as:

$$P_B(D \leq 1) = \int_0^1 \frac{1}{5} e^{-d/5} \, \mathrm{d}d = 1 - e^{-1/5} = 0.1813$$

$$P_B(1 < D \leq 2) = \int_1^2 \frac{1}{5} e^{-d/5} \, \mathrm{d}d = e^{-1/5} - e^{-2/5} = 0.1484$$

$$P_B(2 < D \leq 3) = \int_2^3 \frac{1}{5} e^{-d/5} \, \mathrm{d}d = e^{-2/5} - e^{-3/5} = 0.1215$$

$$P_B(D > 3) = \int_3^\infty \frac{1}{5} e^{-d/5} \, \mathrm{d}d = e^{-3/5} = 0.5488$$

Therefore, the probability distribution of the reward points for soldiers A and B can be derived as follows:

TABLE A.5   The Probabilities of Scores for Soldiers A and B by Distances Obeying Exponential Distribution

X_A	0	1	2	3	X_B	0	1	2	3
p_k	0.2231	0.1447	0.2387	0.3935	p_k	0.5488	0.1215	0.1484	0.1813

According to Table A.5, the expected reward points for soldier A can be calculated as:

$$E(X_A) = 0 \times 0.2231 + 1 \times 0.1447 + 2 \times 0.2387 + 3 \times 0.3935 = 1.8$$

In the same way, $E(X_B) = 0.96$.

Median is a numerical value that separates the higher half of the dataset from the lower half. It can be formally defined as a value m satisfying the following equation:

$$P(X \geq m) = P(X \leq m) = \frac{1}{2}. \tag{A.30}$$

Median is a better measure than mean in some cases, such as when there are only a few extremely large or extremely small samples in a given dataset. The median may reflect the central tendency better than the mean.

Apart from the mean and median, in many situations, we are also interested in another measure: the **mode**. Mode, usually denoted by m, is the most frequent value appearing in a random variable. For a discrete random variable X, the mode is the value x that maximises the probability mass function, while, for a continuous random variable X, is the value x maximising the PDF. In some cases, the mode may take more than one value. Mean, median, and mode are all measures of central tendency. Figures A.37 and A.38 illustrate two examples of the mean, median, and mode in gamma and lognormal distributions.

There are also situations in which we would like to see the variance of the values of a random variable to investigate the differences between these values. For example, the lifetime of electrical parts in a batch may vary from item to item. In one batch of electrical parts, half of the items are good quality and can be used for more than 1300 hours, and the other half only last for around 700 hours. To determine the quality of this batch, we need to compare the lifetime of each item against the expected lifetime value. If the difference between them is small enough, we can say that the quality of this batch is good. To measure this difference, **variance** (usually denoted $Var(X)$) is used, as follows:

$$Var(X) = E\{[X - E(X)]^2\}$$
$$= E(X^2) - E(X)^2 \tag{A.31}$$

where $E(X)$ is the mean or expected value of the given random variable X. Variance $Var(X)$ has the following properties:

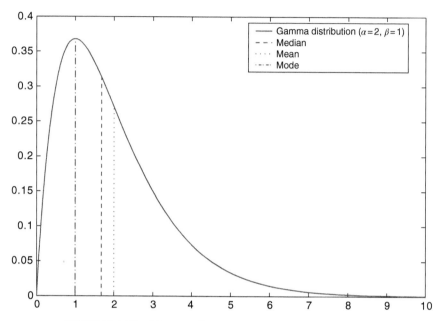

FIGURE A.37   Mean, median, and mode of gamma distribution.

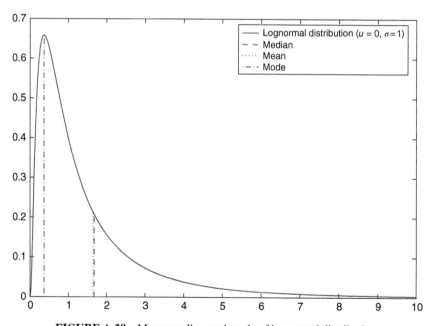

FIGURE A.38   Mean, median, and mode of lognormal distribution.

1. $Var(X) \geq 0$.
2. $Var(C) = 0$, if C is a constant.
3. $Var(CX) = C^2 Var(X)$, where C is a constant.
4. Given two random variables X and Y, then:

$$Var(X + Y) = Var(X) + Var(Y) - 2E\{[X - E(X)][Y - E(Y)]\}$$

If X and Y are mutually independent, then:

$$Var(X + Y) = Var(X) + Var(Y)$$

Therefore, for multiple independent random variables X_i,

$$Var\left(\sum_{i=1}^{n} X_i\right) = \sum_{i=1}^{n} Var(X_i).$$

The standard deviation of the random variable X is the square root of the variance, and is defined by:

$$\sigma(X) = \sqrt{Var(X)} \tag{A.32}$$

From the fourth property presented above, we see that $E\{[X - E(X)][Y - E(Y)]\} = 0$ only when the two random variables, X and Y, are independent. This means that a dependence exists between X and Y, if $E\{[X - E(X)][Y - E(Y)]\} \neq 0$. Therefore, we can say that $E\{[X - E(X)][Y - E(Y)]\}$ gives us a measure of the dependence between two random variables. **covariance** (denoted $Cov(X, Y)$) is the mathematical characteristic that measures the linear dependence between random variables, and can be expressed as follows, based on the fourth property of the variance:

$$Cov(X, Y) = E\{[X - E(X)][Y - E(Y)]\}$$
$$= E(XY) - E(X)E(Y) \tag{A.33}$$

The sign of the covariance decides the dependence between variables:

- if $Cov(X, Y) = 0$, X, and Y are uncorrelated
- if $Cov(X, Y) > 0$, X, and Y are positively correlated
- if $Cov(X, Y) < 0$, X, and Y are negatively correlated.

In simulation or other real problems, using the covariance to interpret the dependence between variables may be difficult because it is not dimensionless. For example, if the unit of measure for temperature variables is degrees Celsius, the resultant covariance will be measured in squared degrees Celsius. Therefore, we define the **correlation** ($\rho_{X,Y}$) as the primary measure of the linear dependence between random variable X and Y, as follows:

$$\rho_{XY} = \frac{Cov(XY)}{\sqrt{Var(X)Var(Y)}}. \tag{A.34}$$

Correlation is a dimensionless quantity that has the same sign as the covariance $Cov(X, Y)$. Correlation has the following properties:

1. $|\rho(XY)| \leq 1$
2. $|\rho(XY)| = 1$, if and only if two constants a and b exist, so that:

$$P(Y = a + bX) = 1.$$

According to the above properties, X and Y are highly correlated when $|\rho(XY)|$ is close to 1. However, when two variables are uncorrelated, this does not necessarily mean they are independent, given that the correlation is linear only.

Example A.3.3. *Assume that two variables X and Y have their probability distribution $P(X, Y)$ as in the table below.*

Y \ X	-2	-1	1	2	$P(Y = i)$
1	0	1/4	1/4	0	1/2
4	1/4	0	0	1/4	1/2
$P(X = i)$	1/4	1/4	1/4	1/4	1

$E(X) = 0$, $E(Y) = 5/2$ *and* $E(XY) = 0$, *therefore,* $\rho(XY) = 0$ *based on Eqs. (A.33) and (A.34). Thus, X and Y are not correlated. However, X and Y are not independent according to Eq. (A.28) – that is, $P(X = -2, Y = 1) = 0 \neq \frac{1}{8} = P(X = -2)P(Y = 1)$. In fact, a dependence exists, but the relationship between them is non-linear: $Y = X^2$.*

A.4 CONCLUSION

In this appendix, we have discussed the fundamental aspects of probability and statistics, covering many aspects, including sample space, event, probability distributions, random variables, and mathematical characteristics. All of these aspects provide the theoretical basis for how to sample the input data to a simulation, how to manipulate a simulator to cover all possible cases and how to analyse the output data for validation, which are critical to modelling and simulation.

Sampling and Random Numbers

Given that randomness in simulation cannot be avoided, a good random number generator is essential for successful investigation of any real system. In this chapter, we discuss in detail random number generators that produce random numbers that obey uniform distribution. The generators we describe mainly focus on linear methods and some extensions of them. We then discuss the relevant methods for testing the strength of random number generators, both through empirical and theoretical testing. Finally, we introduce random variates generators for the most common probability distributions.

B.1 INTRODUCTION

Randomness exists to various extents in virtually any real system or process, and consequently cannot be avoided in simulations, since simulations try to imitate those real systems and processes. We already presented many examples throughout this book to show how simulation of any real system/process requires certain methods to generate random numbers that reflect the randomness existing in those systems/processes. Thus, in this chapter, we describe several linear random number generators (RNGs) that have been extensively used by both researchers and practitioners over the years. Although many off-the-shelf simulation software packages provide built-in RNGs, such as the Wichmann-Hill generator [399], it is still necessary for us to know how these generators work because we would like to understand the effects of their flaws or biases on the simulation. For example, McCullough and Heiser pointed out the shortcomings of the RNG implemented in Excel [278].

In light of the above paragraph, it is clear that it is necessary to have a good understanding of the methods that generate random values efficiently and conveniently to execute simulation models. From a formal perspective, generating random numbers refers to generating random variates from the uniform distribution in the interval $[0, 1]$, denoted by $U(0, 1)$. The random variates produced from $U(0, 1)$ are called random numbers. These random numbers can be used in other methods to generate other

Simulation and Computational Red Teaming for Problem Solving, First Edition.
Jiangjun Tang, George Leu, and Hussein A. Abbass.
© 2020 by The Institute of Electrical and Electronics Engineers, Inc. Published 2020 by John Wiley & Sons, Inc.

random variates that obey other probability distributions, such as gamma distributions and normal distributions. Further, we need to ensure that the resultant random numbers satisfy the minimal randomness conditions established by the probability theory – that is, ideally, we would like to obtain independent and identically distributed uniform variables. To ensure the randomness of the generated numbers, we actually need to test the RNGs using specific methods for random strength testing. However, before we proceed to the discussion of RNGs and their quality, some definitions must first be introduced.

Definition B.1.1. *Independent and identically distributed (IID) random variables: Given a set of variables, $\{x_1, x_2, ..., x_n\}$, each of these variables (x_i) has the same probability distribution and all of them are mutually independent.*

An example of IID random variables can be found in the very simple case of tossing a coin multiple times. The result of tossing the coin is either heads (H) or tails (T), and the results are independent. However, the probability distribution of attaining H or T is exactly the same because the same coin is tossed.

The purpose of a RNG is to produce IID random numbers obeying $U(0, 1)$. In the early days, random numbers were generated manually, by tossing a coin, rolling a die, or drawing from cards. Later, various electrical or electronic devices were used to produce random numbers, such as the Electronic Random Number Indicator Equipment (ERNIE) [379]. In this appendix, we focus on the random numbers generated by digital computers, since the main objective here is to use random numbers in computer simulations. Although some hardware generators, such as ERNIE, can be used as inputs to computers, they come with inherent disadvantages when used in a simulation – for example, the sequence of random numbers is not repeatable; thus, hardware generators cannot be used in some cases where we need to investigate a problem several times with the same settings. In addition, a large amount of memory may be required to store and handle on a computer the random numbers generated by hardware devices such as ERNIE. In conclusion, software generators designed based on some mathematical/statistical approaches are of more interest for modelling and simulation practitioners.

The **middle-square** method [390] proposed by John von Neumann is one of the earliest arithmetic methods to generate random numbers. The steps are listed below:

1. Let $i = 0$ and Z_i be a four-digit positive integer.
2. Square Z_i to obtain an integer up to eight digits. If the number of digits is less than eight, append zeros to the left.
3. Take the middle four digits as the next four-digit number, Z_{i+1}.
4. Insert a decimal point at the left of Z_{i+1} to make it a $U(0, 1)$ random number, U_{i+1}.
5. Increase i by one, so $i = i + 1$.
6. Repeat the process from Steps 2 to 5.

TABLE B.1   Results from Middle-square Method with Initial $Z_0 = 3404$

i	Z_i	U_i	Z_i^2
0	3404		11 587 216
1	5872	0.5872	34 480 384
2	4803	0.4803	23 068 809
3	0688	0.0688	00 473 344
4	4733	0.4733	22 401 289
5	4012	0.4012	16 096 144
6	0961	0.0961	00 923 521
⋮	⋮	⋮	⋮

The above method can be implemented in Excel. An example of the results generated by middle-square with the initial $Z_0 = 3404$ is listed in Table B.1. In practice, we can specify the number of digits for the initial number, as well as the number of middle digits to be extracted. For example, we may initialise Z_0 as a six-digit positive integer, and then pick up the middle two digits from Z_0^2. In this case, the random numbers only have two decimals. Z_0 is the seed for the RNG because the sequence of the following random numbers is determined by it.

As the table shows, the middle-square method seems to be able to produce good random numbers. However, it suffers from several drawbacks. One problem is that it has strong tendency to degenerate fairly rapidly to zero – for example, it stays at zero forever since $i = 3$ when $Z_0 = 1001$. Another problem is that the numbers generated by this method show some patterns. For the example of $Z_0 = 3404$, the four numbers $\{0.61, 0.21, 0.41, 0.81\}$ appear repeatedly since $i = 65$. Thus, the middle-square method is not really 'random' because the sequence of the numbers repeats after a relatively low number of iterations once Z_0 is decided. For this reason, the middle-square method is rarely used in practice. Actually, the second problem we mentioned exists in all arithmetic generators, and leads to an argument about the true nature of random numbers. The random numbers generated using arithmetic generators are called pseudo-random numbers because they are not really random in nature, but somewhat deterministic. Consequently, the corresponding arithmetic generators are also called pseudo-RNGs. However, while they are not ideal, designing 'good' arithmetic RNGs is still attractive to researchers because of the ease of implementation of arithmetic operation in computers. In summary, a 'good' arithmetic RNG should have several properties, as follows:

- The random numbers generated by a generator should have good statistical properties, which means that the random numbers exhibit the properties of *IID* $U(0, 1)$.
- The generator should be efficient in terms of computational cost and storage cost.

- The stream of random numbers can be reproduced. In some cases, we could evaluate a problem by simulating it many times with the same sequence of random numbers (i.e. identical randomness).
- The generator should be portable such that it can be used in different computer systems.

In the next sections, we discuss in detail some of the most relevant (pseudo-)RNGs.

B.2   RANDOM NUMBER GENERATOR

B.2.1   Linear Congruential Generator

Linear congruential generators (LCGs) are the most popular RNGs. The concept of LCG was first introduced by Lehmer [244]. In this generator, a sequence of integers $Z_1, Z_2, ...$ is produced using the following formula:

$$Z_i = (aZ_{i-1}) \bmod m \qquad (B.1)$$

where a is the multiplier, c is the increment, m is the modulus, and Z_0 is the seed. All four parameters are non-negative integers. Thus, Z_1 is the remainder of the division of $aZ_0 + c$ by m. Similarly, Z_i is the remainder of aZ_{i-1} divided by m. To obtain a random number U_i (for $i = 1, 2, ...$) obeying $U(0, 1)$, let $U_i = Z_i / m$ because of $0 \leq Z_i \leq m - 1$. There are some additional conditions applied to the four non-negative parameters to obtain the expected U_i; these are: $0 < m$, $a < m$, $c < m$ and $Z_0 < m$. Algorithm 7 illustrates how LCG works.

Algorithm 7 Linear Congruential Generator

Require: $0 < m$, $a < m$, $c < m$, and $Z_0 < m$
  1: $i = 1$
  2: **while** TRUE **do**
  3:      $Zi = (aZ_{i-1}) \bmod m$
  4:      $Ui = \frac{Z_i}{m}$
  5:      $i + +$
  6: **end while**

As with all other arithmetic RNGs, LCG is not truly random. Given that Z_i is defined by an equation (Eq. (B.1)), any Z_i can be calculated immediately without recursive computation once all parameters are decided:

$$Z_i = \left[a^i Z_0 + \frac{c(a^i - 1)}{a - 1} \right] \bmod m. \qquad (B.2)$$

Arguably, we can still generate U_i's that appear to be IID $U(0, 1)$ by carefully choosing a, c, m, and Z_0. However, the U_i's can take on only the rational values $0, 1/m, 2/m, ..., (m-1)/m$, as shown in Algorithm 7. There is no possibility for LCGs to generate other values situated between these rational values. For example, if $1.5/m$ is possible from a mathematical and statistical perspective, it cannot be generated using LCGs. This is a second important drawback of LCGs, in addition to the pseudo-randomness. For this reason, m is usually set as a very large value, when using LCGs so that U_i can fall on points that are dense in the interval $[0, 1]$.

Example B.2.1. *Assume that an LCG has the following parameter settings:*

- $a = 5$
- $c = 5$
- $m = 8$
- $Z_0 = 7$.

In this example, m is a small number and is only for illustrating the LCG algorithms. In reality, no LCGs take such a small value for m. Using Eq. (B.1), the sequence of values for Z_i can be determined once the parameters are decided. The resultant random numbers, according to Algorithm 7, are shown in Table B.2.

There is an obvious pattern in the random numbers shown in the table, in which a finite sequence of values repeats endlessly. The cyclic behaviour is inevitable and this cycle is called the **period** of a generator. From Eq. (B.1), it is clear that Z_i depends on only the previous integer Z_{i-1}; thus, the period of LCGs is dependent on m because $0 \leq Z_i \leq m$. In the above example, the period is 8. If we consider $m = 17$, then the period becomes 16. When the period of an LCG is exactly m, we say that the LCG has **full period**.

Given that large-scale simulations usually require a large amount of random numbers, it is essential to make an LCG have a very long period. However, when a

TABLE B.2   Random Numbers Generated by LCG with the Parameters $a = 9, c = 5, m = 8$, and $Z_0 = 7$

i	Z_i	U_i	i	Z_i	U_i	i	Z_i	U_i
0	7	—						
1	4	0	9	4	0	17	4	0
2	1	0.625	10	1	0.625	18	1	0.625
3	6	0.75	11	6	0.75	19	6	0.75
4	3	0.375	12	3	0.375	20	3	0.375
5	0	0.5	13	0	0.5	21	0	0.5
6	5	0.125	14	5	0.125	22	5	0.125
7	2	0.25	15	2	0.25	23	2	0.25
8	7	0.875	16	7	0.875	24	7	0.875

generator is full period, any choice of the initial Z_0 (from $\{0, 1, ..., m-1\}$) can produce the entire cycle (all numbers in the set) in some order, and can contribute to the
uniformity of U_i because every integer between 0 and $m-1$ occurs exactly once in a
cycle. This immediately leads to the question of how to choose m, a, and c so that the
corresponding LCG has a full period. As shown by Hull and Dobell [192], an LCG
has a full period if and only if it satisfies the following requirements:

1. The only positive integer that exactly divides both m and c is 1.
2. If q is a prime number that divides m, then q divides $a-1$.
3. If 4 divides m, then 4 divides $a-1$.

Let us now revisit the parameters in the previous example. We see that they meet
all three conditions as follows:

1. Only 1 can divide both $m=8$ and $c=1$.
2. $q=2$ is a prime number that divides $m=8$ and $a-1=4$.
3. 4 divides both m and $a-1$.

This is why the LCG in the example, with $a=9, c=5, m=8$, and $Z_0=7$, has a full
period of 8.

LCGs can be split in two categories, which have significantly different behaviours:
LCGs with $c>0$ (called **mixed LCGs**) and LCGs with $c=0$ (called **multiplicative
LCGs**).

From Condition 1, we see that we may obtain a full-period LCG when $c>0$.
Given that computers work in a binary manner, a good choice of m is that $m=2^b$,
to avoid explicit division for efficiency purposes. For example, m could be 2^{31} for a
32-bit computer system. According to the conditions (listed above) for obtaining a
full period, c must be odd and $a-1$ is divisible by 4 with the choice $m=2^b$.

When $c=0$, it is impossible to attain a full-period LCG according to Condition 1.
However, it is possible to obtain multiplicative LCGs with period of $m-1$ by carefully choosing m and a. If one selects the modulus m as 2^b for a multiplicative LCG,
its period is at most 2^{b-2}, where only one-fourth of the integers from 0 to $m-1$ can
be obtained as the values of Z_i [218]. Obviously, there are some gaps in that range.
A well-known example of this type of multiplicative generator is RANDU, which
has been widely used since the 1970s. In RANDU, $m=2^{31}, a=2^{16}+3=65\,539$,
and $c=0$. However, RANDU has poor statistical properties that will be discussed in
Section B.3.

Given that it is not easy to set other parameters for multiplicative LCGs when
choosing $m=2^b$, Hutchinson proposed a way to set m as a prime number that is less
than 2^b [193]. For example, $2^{31}-1=2\,147\,483\,647$ is the largest prime number that
is less than 2^{31}. Based on this idea (m is a prime number), a should be a prime element of modulo m so that the a^l-1 can be divisible by m when $l=m-1$, which
is the smallest integer. In this way, each integer in $1, 2, ..., m-1$ can be obtained
exactly once in each cycle. These methods are called prime modulus multiplicative

LCGs (PMMLCGs). Selecting a good m and a is still an open question in PMML-CGs, investigated by many researchers [140, 141, 252, 316]. In the literature, two particular values for a, $a_1 = 7^5 = 16\,807$, and $a_2 = 630\,360\,016$ with the modulus $m = 2^{31} - 1$ are widely used with PMMLCGs. For example, PMMLCGs with $m = 2^{31} - 1$, and $a = 630\,360\,016$ is acceptable in practice for many applications that do not require a large number of random numbers, even though, from a theoretical perspective, researchers have suggested not using PMMLCGs with these parameter settings because of poor statistical properties and short periods [156, 242].

Many alternative forms of LCG have been developed to obtain longer periods and better statistical properties. In the next three sections, we briefly discuss some popular alternatives to LCGs.

B.2.2   More General Congruential Generators

We will first consider the generalisation of LCGs. Let us assume a special case of LCG defined by the following formula:

$$Z_i = g(Z_{i-1}, Z_{i-2}, ...) \quad \text{mod} \ m \tag{B.3}$$

where g is a fixed deterministic function of previous Zs. Comparing the above equation with Eq. (B.1), we can see they are fairly similar, if we consider $g(Z_{i-1}, Z_{i-2}, ...) = aZ_i - 1 + c$. Thus, in this example we still have an LCG, just in a more general form. Thus, in this example, we still have an LCG, just in a more general form. Thus, we can imagine plenty of these generalisations, depending on the problem of interest. However, in the following subsections, we only introduce the most relevant generalisations, which have gained popularity over time. Extensive reviews of the other generators can be found in the books written by Knuth [218] and L'Ecuyer [241].

B.2.2.1 *Quadratic Congruential Generators*   The function g of the **quadratic congruential generator** is defined as the sum of the previous integer square and the integer itself, weighted by some coefficients. The complete equation for generating integer sequences is defined by:

$$Z_i = (a'Z_{i-1}^2 + aZ_{i-1} + c) \quad \text{mod} \ m. \tag{B.4}$$

One special case of a quadratic congruential generator that is of special interest to researchers is the one defined by $a' = a = 1$ and $c = 0$. Although it is closely related to the middle-square generator, it has better statistical properties. The period of quadratic congruential generators is at most m because Z_i depends only on Z_{i-1} and $0 \leq Z_i \leq m - 1$.

B.2.2.2 *Multiple Recursive Generators* As the name suggests, **multiple recursive generators (MRGs)** use a number of previous integers to construct the function g, as in the following equation:

$$Z_i = (a_1 Z_{i-1} + a_2 Z_{i-2} + \ldots + a_q Z_{i-q}) \quad \text{mod} \quad m \tag{B.5}$$

where $a_1, a_2, \ldots, a_q$ are constants. The period can reach $m^q - 1$ if the parameters are carefully chosen [218]. This is also one of the MCGs that, according to the literature, perform well in a wide range of applications.

B.2.3 Composite Generators

Another way to obtain numbers with a higher level of randomness is to combine more generators in various manners. The resultant complex generators are called **composite generators**.

One of the early composite generators, proposed by MacLaren and Marsaglia [261], used a construction with two LCGs, in which the output of the first LCG was simply shuffled by the second one. Algorithm 8 describes this generator.

Algorithm 8 Composite Generator 1

1: Let LCG_1 be the first LCG and LCG_2 be the second LCG
2: Use LCG_1 to generate k random numbers: $v = (v_1, v_2, \ldots, v_k)$, where $v\ U\,(0, 1)$
   {Refer to Algorithm 7}
3: **while** TRUE **do**
4:    Generate a random number I on integers 1, 2, $\ldots, k$ by LCG_2
5:    Obtain the random number $U = v_I$
6:    Generate a random number u by LCG_1
7:    Replace the v_I in v with u
8: **end while**

Shuffling easily breaks up any correlation and also extends the period significantly, as reported in the literature [299]. The above generator also shows that we can obtain random numbers with good statistical properties even if the two individual LCGs are not very good [40].

Another option based on shuffling concept, which is random in nature, is to perform fixed permutation, which actually implements a deterministic shuffling. This method has a certain disadvantage in terms of the level of randomness of the generated numbers, but in exchange allows traceability and repeatability when these are needed in a simulation. Besides, the loss of randomness is not very significant; the literature reports that permutation shuffling can still generate random numbers with good characteristics [28]. Another aspect that needs to be noted here is that it is impossible to reach an arbitrary point of a shuffled generator's output sequence without producing all the intermediate points (e.g., the LCG described Eq. (B.2)).

An easy way to combine two different LCGs is also proposed by L'Ecuyer [237] as follows:

$$Z_i = (Z_{1,i} - Z_{2,i}) \quad \text{mod} \quad m \tag{B.6}$$

where Z_1 and Z_2 are integers generated from two different LCGs with different moduli, and the corresponding random number is obtained by $U = Z_i/m$. This generator can be easily extended to use more than two LCGs. The advantages of this generator include a long period, good statistical performance and efficiency in generating random numbers.

Composite generators could also use specific combinations of MRGs [238]. Assume J different MRGs defined by Eq. (B.5). We can obtain a sequence composed of J random numbers $Z_{1i}, Z_{2i}, ..., Z_{Ji}$ generated simultaneously from MRGs. Then, we take the first modulo m_1 of the first MRG as the modulus m and calculate the integer numbers as below:

$$Z_i = (\delta_1 Z_{1,i} + \delta_2 Z_{2,i} + ... + \delta_1 Z_{J,i}) \quad \text{mod} \quad m \tag{B.7}$$

where δ_j's are specified constants. After extensive experimental investigation, L'Ecuyer suggested the following specific settings for δ_j's and m to obtain a simple implementation (only two MRGs) with a long period and good statistical characteristics:

$$Z_{1,i} = (1\ 403\ 580 Z_{1,i-2} - 810\ 728 Z_{1,i-3}) \quad \text{mod} \ (2^{32} - 209) \tag{B.8a}$$

$$Z_{2,i} = (527\ 612 Z_{2,i-2} - 1\ 370\ 589 Z_{2,i-3}) \quad \text{mod} \ (2^{32} - 22\ 853) \tag{B.8b}$$

$$Z_i = (Z_{1,i} - Z_{2,i}) \quad \text{mod} \ (2^{32} - 209) \tag{B.8c}$$

$$U_i n = \frac{Z_i}{(2^{32} - 209)}. \tag{B.8d}$$

The above settings are able to provide a period of around 2^{191} and good statistical properties.

Wichmann and Hill proposed another popular composite generator, which uses three individual generators [399]. The basic idea of this generator is presented below:

- Sum three random numbers $(U_{1,i}, U_{2,i}, U_{3,i})$ on [0, 1] produced by three separate generators,
- Take the fractional part of the sum as a random number U_i on [0, 1].

The Wichmann-Hill generator is well known as a generator with a long period, portability, speed, and usability on common computers [280], and is implemented in Microsoft Excel 2010. However, we note here that this algorithm has some numerical difficulties in some computer architectures.

B.2.4 Feedback Shift Register Generators

Inspired by the work of Tausworthe [375], some interesting generators based on cryptographic methods have been developed to produce random numbers. These operate directly on bits at machine code or communication channel levels.

A sequence of bits, $b_1, b_2, ...,$ is defined by the recurrence

$$b_i = (c_1 b_{i-1} + c_2 b_{i-2} + ... + c_q b_{i-q}) \mod 2 \tag{B.9}$$

where $c_1, c_2, ..., c_q$ are constants with values 0 or 1, and $c_q = 1$. For computational simplicity, in most Tausworthe generators, only two c_j coefficients have the value 1. Therefore, the above equations can be represented simply as:

$$b_i = (b_{i-r} + b_{i-q}) \mod 2 \tag{B.10}$$

where integers r and q satisfy $0 < r < q$. Given that the modulo 2 operation in Eq. (B.10) is equivalent to the exclusive-or instruction on bits, this equation is equivalent to the one below:

$$b_i = b_{i-r} \bigoplus b_{i-q}. \tag{B.11}$$

The values of b_i are the result of the exclusive-or operation on b_{i-1} and b_{i-q}. If $b_{i-1} \equiv b_{i-q}$, then $b_i = 0$; otherwise, $b_i = 1$.

For this generator, we still need to specify a seed, as with the other generators, which is a sequence of length q: $b_1, b_2, ..., b_q$. Starting from this, a binary integer Z with l-tuple consecutive bits in base 2 (usually $l \le q$) can be constructed as follows:

$$Z_i = b_{(i-1)l+1} b_{(i-1)l+2} ... b_{(i-1)l+q} \quad i = 2, 3, ...$$

As shown above, the integer numbers can be easily obtained; for example, $Z_1 = b_1 b_2 ... b_q$. In fact, In fact, the recurrence for Z_i's is the same as the recurrence of the bits in Eq. (B.9), and therefore:

$$Z_i = Z_{i-r} \bigoplus Z_{i-q}. \tag{B.12}$$

The exclusive-or operations on binary integers Z are performed bitwise, with the underlying trinomial over the finite field expressed as in Eq. (B.12):

$$f(x) = x^q + x^{q-r} + 1. \tag{B.13}$$

Consequently, a random number can be produced by the equation as below.

$$U_i = \frac{Z_i}{2^l}. \tag{B.14}$$

The maximum period of the b recurrence is $2^q - 1$ because the sequence of q bits can take 2^q possible combinations. If l is relatively prime to $2^q - 1$, then the period of Z can be $2^q - 1$. Algorithm 9 summarises computationally how random numbers can be obtained using the above method.

Algorithm 9 Tauswortheg Generator

1: Let q be the length for the initial bit string
2: Let l be the length of the bits that construct a integer in base 2
3: Initialise an integer r, and $0 < r < q$
4: Specify a string B with q bits, $B = b_1, b_2, \ldots, b_q$, {the seed}
5: $i \Leftarrow q + 1$
6: $j \Leftarrow 1$ {the start position of bits for constructing an integer}
7: **while TRUE do**
8:    $b_i = b_{i-r} \oplus b_{i-q}$
9:    Append b_i at the end of B
10:   **if** $i \geq j + l$ **then**
11:      Construct an integer Z by bits $b_j, b_{j+1}, \ldots, b_{j+l}$ from B
12:      Obtain a random number $U = \frac{Z}{2^l}$
13:      $j \Leftarrow j + l$
14:   **end if**
15:   $i \Leftarrow i + 1$
16: **end while**

Example B.2.2. *Let* $r = 3$ *and* $q = 5$, *and the initial bit sequence* $b_i = 1$ ($i = 1, 2, \ldots, 5$). *Therefore, the trinomial becomes as below:*

$$x^5 + x^2 + 1$$

Applying Eq. (B.11) on bits b_i ($i \geq 6$), *we can attain the following sequence, as shown in the first row of Table B.3. The period for this sequence is* $31 = 2^5 - 1$.

If $l = 5$, *then* l *is also relative prime to* $2^5 - 1 = 31$, *and the period for the integers* Z_j *is also 31. Some first integers can be obtained as listed in the second row of Table B.3. Correspondingly, the random numbers on* $U(0, 1)$ *are generated by dividing* Z_j *by* $2^l = 32$, *as shown in the last row in the table.*

Given that the recurrence defined in Eq. (B.9) can be implemented on binary computers at hardware level (through a switching circuit), the Tausworthe generator is

TABLE B.3 A Sequence $\{b\}_1^{31}$ for $x^5 + x^2 + 1$, Using Tausworthe Generator

b_i	1 1 1 1 1	0 0 0 1 1	0 1 1 1 0	1 0 1 0 0	0 0 1 0 0	1 0 1 1 0	0
Z_j	31	3	14	20	4	22	
U_j	0.96875	0.09375	0.4375	0.625	0.128	0.6875	

TABLE B.4 Binary Integers Generated by GFSR for the Polynomial $x^5 + x^2 + 1$ with $l = 5$ and Delay $d = 6$

Z_1	1	0	1	0	0	Z_{11}	0	0	1	1	1	Z_{21}	0	0	1	0	1
Z_2	1	0	1	0	1	Z_{12}	1	1	0	0	1	Z_{22}	0	1	1	1	0
Z_3	1	1	0	0	0	Z_{13}	1	0	0	0	0	Z_{23}	1	1	1	1	1
Z_4	1	1	1	0	1	Z_{14}	1	0	1	1	0	Z_{24}	0	0	1	0	0
Z_5	1	0	0	1	1	Z_{15}	0	0	0	1	0	Z_{25}	0	0	0	1	1
Z_6	0	1	1	0	0	Z_{16}	1	0	1	1	1	Z_{26}	1	1	0	1	0
Z_7	0	1	0	0	0	Z_{17}	0	1	1	1	1	Z_{27}	0	1	0	1	0
Z_8	0	1	0	1	1	Z_{18}	1	0	0	1	0	Z_{28}	1	1	1	0	0
Z_9	1	0	0	0	1	Z_{19}	0	0	0	0	1	Z_{29}	1	1	1	1	0
Z_{10}	1	1	0	1	1	Z_{20}	0	1	1	0	1	Z_{30}	0	1	0	0	1
												Z_{31}	0	0	1	1	0

also called a **linear feedback shift register (LFSR)**. In the hardware implementation, Tausworthe/LFSR is an efficient generator, even though some studies in the literature have found that the resultant random numbers have poor statistical characteristics [273, 378]. However, this drawback can always be mitigated by combining multiple LFSR generators, as discussed in [240].

A variation of the LFSR generators, called a **generalized feedback shift register (GFSR) generator**, was introduced by Lewis and Payne [253]. To obtain integers Z_i constructed by l-tuple bits (produced by Eq. (B.11)), the leftmost binary position of the integers (the first column) must be filled first. Then, the next binary position of the integers (the second column) is filled using the same bit sequence, but with a delay d. Eq. (B.12) still holds in this situation.

Example B.2.3. *Following Example B.2.2, a GFSR with delay of 6 can generate the random numbers as shown in Table B.4.*

An extension of GFSR, **twisted GFSR (TGFSR)**, was proposed by Matsumoto and Kurita [272]. In this generator, the recurrence is replaced by:

$$Z_i = Z_{i-r} \bigoplus AY_{i-q} \qquad (B.15)$$

where Z are $l \times 1$ vector and A is an $l \times l$ matrix. Both the vector and the matrix contain zeros or ones. The twisted generators present excellent statistical properties. For the interested reader, more details can be found in the original paper.

B.3 TESTING RANDOM NUMBER GENERATORS

Thus far, we have introduced several RNGs. As discussed in Section B.1, a 'good' generator ideally produces random numbers on IDD $U(0, 1)$. To assess how 'good' a generator is, we introduce some testing methods in this section, both empirical and theoretical.

B.3.1 Empirical Tests

Empirical tests are methods that perform direct statistical examination on the random numbers U_i's produced by a generator, to see how close the random numbers are to IDD $U(0, 1)$. Several statistical tests can be used here. The first is a special case of the chi-square test with all parameters known, which checks if the random numbers appear to be uniformly distributed between 0 and 1. First, [0, 1] is divided into k ($k \geq$ 100) subintervals of equal length, and $U_1, U_2, ..., U_n$ aare generated. Then, Eq. (B.16) is used:

$$\chi^2 = \frac{k}{n} \sum_{j=1}^{k} \left(f_j - \frac{n}{k} \right)^2 \tag{B.16}$$

where f_j is the number of U_i's that are in the jth subinterval, for $j = 1, 2, ..., k$. χ^2 has an approximate chi-square distribution with $k - 1$ **degrees of freedom (df)** under the null hypothesis that U_i's are IDD $U(0, 1)$ when n is large. Therefore, this hypothesis can be rejected at the level α if $\chi^2 > \chi^2_{k-1,1-\alpha}$. The upper $1 - \alpha$, $\chi^2_{k-1,1-\alpha}$, is the critical point for chi-square distribution with $k - 1$ df. This point can be approximated by:

$$\chi^2_{k-1,1-\alpha} \approx (k - 1) \left[1 - \frac{2}{9(k - 1)} + z_{1-\alpha} \sqrt{\frac{2}{9(k - 1)}} \right] \tag{B.17}$$

where $z_{1-\alpha}$ is the upper $1 - \alpha$ critical value of the normal distribution $N(0, 1)$, which can be found in the critical value table of normal distribution.

Example B.3.1. *In this example, we apply a chi-square test on a RANDU LCG with* $m = 2^{31}$ *and* $a = 65\ 539$. *We take* $k = 2^{12} = 4096$, *so that the most significant 12 bits of* U_i *are examined for uniformity, and* $n = 2^{15} = 32\ 768$. *If the seed* $Z_0 = 1$, *we an obtain the* f_j's *and then the* $\chi^2 = 3950.6$. *Based on Eq. (B.17),* $\chi_{4095,0.95} = 4245$. *Therefore, the null hypothesis of uniformity is not rejected at level* $\alpha = 0.05$. *Thus, it seems that RANDU has good performance on uniformity; however, it has a number of issues that will be addressed later in the appendix.*

Serial test is an empirical test that generalises the chi-square test to higher dimensions. Given U_i's are IDD $U(0, 1)$ random numbers, the following non-overlapping d-tuples should be IDD random vectors distributed uniformly on the d-dimensional unit hypercube $[0, 1]^d$.

$$\mathbf{U_j} = (U_{(j-1)d+1}, U_{(j-1)d+1}, ..., U_{(j-1)d+d})$$

Then, we can divide the interval [0, 1] into k subintervals of equal size and generate n $\mathbf{U_j}$'s (totally nd U_i's). $f_{j_1,j_2...j_d}$ are the number of $\mathbf{U_j}$'s having the first component in the first subinterval j_1, second component in the second subinterval j_2 and so on, until the last component in the last subinterval j_d. Similar to the one-dimension test, we calculate the following:

$$\chi^2(d) = \frac{k^d}{n} \sum_{j_1=1}^{k} \sum_{j_2=1}^{k} \cdots \sum_{j_d=1}^{k} \left(f_{j_1j_2...j_d} - \frac{n}{k^d} \right)^2. \tag{B.18}$$

$\chi^2(d)$ will be approximately a chi-square distribution with $k-1$ df. Then, the same hypothesis test as for the one-dimension chi-square test can be performed.

The serial test indirectly checks if individual U_i's are independent because the distribution of the d-vectors $\mathbf{U_j}$ deviates from d-dimensional uniformity when the individual U_i's are correlated. For the interested reader, a more comprehensive discussion on chi-square and serial tests can be found in [242].

Another more direct empirical test of U_i's independence is the **run (or run-up) test**, which is focused on examining **run up** sub-sequences of U_j. A run-up sub-sequence is an unbroken sub-sequence of maximal length within which the U_i's increase monotonically. For example, given a sequence $U_1, U_2, ..., U_{12}$ as $\{0.63, 0.23, 0.42, 0.53, 0.87, 0.12, 0.15, 0.20, 0.5, 0.1, 0.96, 0.18\}$, we obtain the following runs:

1. run up 1: $\{0.63\}$, length is 1
2. run up 2: $\{0.23, 0.42, 0.53, 0.87\}$, length is 4
3. run up 3: $\{0.12, 0.15, 0.20, 0.5\}$, length is 4
4. run up 4: $\{0.1, 0.96\}$, length is 2
5. run up 5: $\{0.18\}$, length is 1.

We then define:

$$r_i = \begin{cases} \text{number of runs of length} i & i = 1, 2, 3 \\ \text{number of runs of length} \geq 6 & i \geq 6 \end{cases}$$

Therefore, we further obtain $r_1 = 2$, $r_2 = 1$, and $r_3 = 0$, $r_4 = 2$, $r_5 = 0$, and $r_6 = 0$ for the above 12 U_i's, and the test statistics are defined as:

$$R = \frac{1}{n} \sum_{i=1}^{6} \sum_{j=1}^{6} a_{ij}(r_i - nb_i)(r_j - nb_j) \tag{B.19}$$

where both a_{ij} and b_i are coefficients. a_{ij} is the i, j element in a matrix that equals to:

$$a_{ij} = \begin{bmatrix} 4529.4 & 9044.9 & 13\,568 & 18\,091 & 22\,615 & 27\,892 \\ 9044.9 & 18\,097 & 27\,139 & 36\,187 & 45\,234 & 55\,789 \\ 13\,568 & 27\,139 & 40\,721 & 54\,281 & 67\,852 & 83\,685 \\ 18\,091 & 36\,187 & 54\,281 & 72\,414 & 90\,470 & 111\,580 \\ 22\,615 & 45\,234 & 67\,852 & 90\,470 & 113\,262 & 139\,476 \\ 27\,892 & 55\,789 & 83\,685 & 111\,580 & 139\,476 & 172\,860 \end{bmatrix}$$

and b_i equals to:

$$(b_1, b_2, b_3, b_4, b_5, b_6) = \left(\frac{1}{6}, \frac{5}{24}, \frac{11}{120}, \frac{19}{720}, \frac{29}{5040}, \frac{1}{840}\right)$$

The values are calculated using a set of formulas listed in Knuth's book [218], which also presents some alternatives to these coefficients. R has an approximate chi-square distribution with 6 df. U_i's are IDD variables if the null hypotheses are not rejected. In fact, the run test only checks the independence, not the uniformity.

B.3.2 Theoretical Tests

Theoretical tests for RNGs do not require generation of U_i's bbefore the actual test is performed. They indicate the performance of a generator by examining its structures and constants in some mathematical ways. Therefore, theoretical tests are usually sophisticated and complex. For this reason, in this section, we only briefly introduce some of the most important tests; however, interested readers can find more details in [138, 218, 239].

Theoretical tests examine the whole cycle of a generator, so they are global. In contrast, empirical tests only examine a segment of the whole cycle; therefore, they are local. It is difficult to know which is better, and this remains an open question in the literature. In general, if a generator is good from a global perspective, this does not necessarily mean that it is also good locally, and vice versa.

Sometimes, we can compute the mean, variance, and correlations of a 'sample' over an entire cycle directly from the constants defined in a generator. For a full-period LCG, the average of the U_i's over a whole cycle is $\frac{1}{2} - \frac{1}{2m}$. When m is an extremely large value, such as $m = 2^{31} - 1$, the average is close to $\frac{1}{2}$ — that is, the expected average value of $U(0, 1)$. The variance can also be computed for a full-period LCG, as $\frac{1}{12} - \frac{1}{12m^2}$. Similarly, this variance is close to the variance $\frac{1}{12}$ of $U(0, 1)$ when m is large. Kennedy and Gentle presented many of these results in their book [212].

Another popular theoretical test is the spectral test, based on the lattice structure formed by random numbers. This was first observed by Marsaglia [267], who noted that 'random numbers fall mainly in the planes'. Let us assume that $U_1, U_2, ...$ is a sequence of random numbers generated by an LCG. Then, all the overlapping d-tuples $(U_1, U_2, ...U_d)$, $(U_2, U_3, ...U_{d+1})$, $...$, fall on a relatively small number of $(d-1)$-dimensional hyperplanes passing through a d-dimensional unit hypercube $[0, 1]^d$. In other words, these d-tuples are arranged in a 'lattice' fashion. For example, U_i, U_{i+1} are all possible pairs of a full-period multiplication LCG, $Z_1 = 12Z_{i-1} \bmod 101$. As shown in Figure B.1, it seems that these pairs are not 'random' because a certain pattern can be observed in the figure. All pairs fill up the unit square quite well. It also seems that they are not well distributed because many spaces exist between points. The reason for this is that m is relatively small in this LCG. If we consider a second LCG, with the same seed, but $a = 2$ and $m = 101$, we see in Figure B.2 that only three parallel lines appear in the space, which is even worse than the previous LCG. Although both examples are not practical in simulation applications, they illustrate that lattice structures can determine whether a generator works well or not.

Figure B.3 illustrates that the triples from RANDU all fall in 15 parallel planes, which demonstrates that RANDU performs badly as well. By observing the lattice

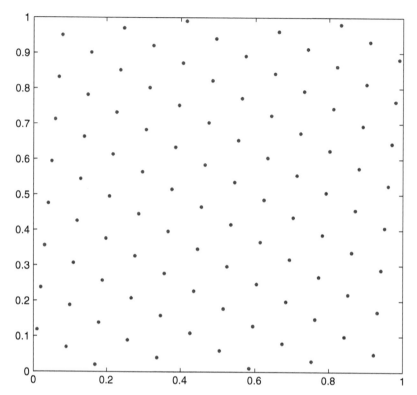

FIGURE B.1 Two-dimensional (U_i, U_{i+1}) lattice structure for full period LCGs: $Z_1 = 12Z_{i-1} \bmod 101$.

structure, we can test a generator visually; however, to obtain a better insight, we still need to generate these random variables. In addition, it is difficult to visualise the high-dimensional data, especially when d > 3, to examine the lattice structure.

Instead of observation, we can select a hyperplane whose adjacent hyperplanes are farthest apart, and then calculate the distance δ_d. If this distance is small, we could say that the corresponding generator can fill up the d-dimensional unit hypercube $[0, 1]^d$ uniformly. This is called a **spectral test** and it involves complex calculations; therefore, we only present it briefly here. The interested reader can find the details Knuth's book [218]. The fundamental idea of this test is to find the value of:

$$v_d = \min \sqrt{Z_1^2 + Z_2^2 + ... + Z_d^2} \tag{B.20}$$

subject to:

$$Z_1 + aZ_2 + ...a^{d-1}Z_d \equiv 0 \quad \bmod m \tag{B.21}$$

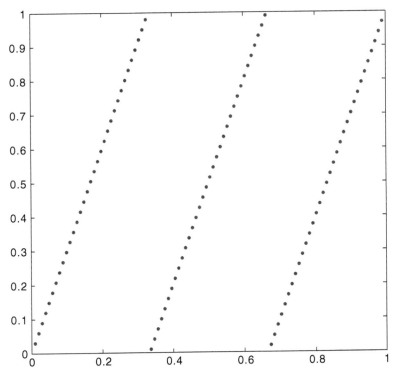

FIGURE B.2   Two-dimensional (U_i, U_{i+1}) lattice structure for full period LCGs ($Z_1 = 3Z_{i-1}$ mod 101).

where v_d is the inverse of δ_d. Therefore, a good LCG should have a higher v_d. In theory, $v_d = p^{\frac{1}{d}}$, where p is the period length of a generator. RANDU has $v_3 = 10.86$, which is much less than the theoretical value 812.75 (the maximum period for RANDU is 2^{29}), and the distance $\delta_d = \frac{1}{10.86} = 0.09$. Thus, RANDU is not a good generator according to the spectral test.

B.4   APPROACHES TO GENERATING RANDOM VARIATES

In the previous sections, we discussed some number generators for IID uniform distributed random numbers, including LCGs [244], composite generators [237, 399], and feedback shift register generators (FSRGs) [375]. However, many systems require random variates from different probability distributions, such as the Gaussian (or normal) distribution. For example, if we consider Monte Carlo simulation, we know that it employs random numbers that are not only limited to uniform distribution to solve various real-world problems; thus, generating these random numbers is essential to it. In the following, we introduce the generators that produce random variates from a certain probability distribution, and we discuss in detail two

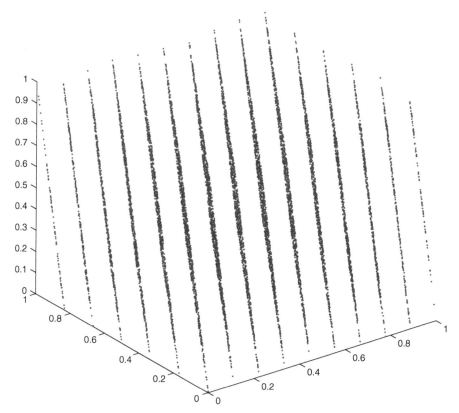

FIGURE B.3 Three-dimensional (U_i, U_{i+1}, U_{i+2}) lattice structure for 10 000 triples from RANDU ($m = 2^{31}$ and $a = 65\ 539$).

of the most common approaches for obtaining such generators: the inverse-transform method and the acceptance-rejection method.

B.4.1 Inverse-Transform Method

A continuous random variable X has a CDF, F, that is continuous and monotonic increasing when $0 < F(x) < 1$. Let F^{-1} denote the inverse function of F and U be a uniform random number on $U(0, 1)$ ($U \sim U(0, 1)$); then,

$$P(X \leq x) = P(F^{-1} \leq x) = P(U \leq F(x)) = F(x). \tag{B.22}$$

This equation leads to the first approach to generating random variates called the 'inverse-transform method'. The algorithm of this method is detailed as below:

1. Generate $U \sim U(0, 1)$.
2. Return $X = F^{-1}(U)$.

This method can also be used for a discrete random variable X. The distribution function of a discrete variable is:

$$F(x) = P(X \leq x) = \sum_{x_i \leq x} p(x_i) \tag{B.23}$$

where $p(x_i)$ is the probability mass function. Therefore, we can use the following algorithm to obtain a discrete variate:

1. Generate $U \sim U(0, 1)$.
2. Return x_I, where I is the smallest positive integer such that $U \leq F(x_I)$.

The inverse-transform method requires a formula of F^{-1} in closed form for the desired distribution. A disadvantage of this aspect is that it is not always possible to obtain the simple closed-form inverse function for some distributions, such as Gaussian (normal) distribution. In such cases, some numerical methods have been proposed to approximate F^{-1} [212]. In addition, the inverse-transform method may not be an efficient way to generate random variates for some distributions. Beside these disadvantages, the inverse-transform method is an intuitive approach that also has a contribution to variance-reduction (not discussed in this book).

B.4.2 Acceptance-Rejection Method

As discussed above, we must use other approaches when a closed form of the inverse function of some distribution is not available. The acceptance-rejection method is one efficient way to obtain random variates for such distributions. The basic idea of this approach is to find an alternative distribution with an 'easier' PDF, $g(x)$, that is close to the original density function, $f(x)$. Then, another method can be applied (e.g., the inverse-transform method) to generate random variates from $g(x)$. We assume that the ratio $f(x)/g(x)$ is bounded by a constant $C \geq 1$. Then, a variable X is drawn from $g(x)$ and acceptance of rejection on X is made by satisfying $U \leq \frac{f(x)}{Cg(x)}$ or not. The algorithm of this approach is depicted in Algorithm 10.

Algorithm 10 Acceptance-Rejection Method

1: Generate $X \sim g$, that X is from PDF g
2: Generate $U \sim U(0, 1)$, independently of X
3: **loop**
4:   **if** $U \leq \frac{f(X)}{Cg(X)}$ **then**
5:     **return** X
6:   **else**
7:     Reject X
8:   **end if**
9: **end loop**

The variable X from PDF g is independent of U. The probability of accepting a drawn sample is $1/C$, which defines the efficiency of this method. Therefore, it is preferable to find a g that makes C close to 1 for rejecting fewer samples. The proof for this method is detailed in Kalos and Whitlock's book [207].

Example B.4.1. *A Beta distribution, Beta(5, 3), has the PDF:*

$$f(x) = \begin{cases} 105x^4(1-x)^2 & 0 \le x \le 1 \\ 0 & \text{otherwise} \end{cases}$$

It is not an easy task to use the inverse-transform or other numerical methods to solve the above Beta distribution because its distribution function involves a complex polynomial construct. Thus, the acceptance-rejection method can be used to generate the variables.

Let $g(x) = 1$ and $x \in (0, 1)$, then $f(x)/g(x) = f(x)$. Given that C is the bounding constant of the ratio, we can set C to be the maximum value of $f(x)$, which can be obtained by standard differential calculus at the point where $\frac{df}{dx} = 0$. For the above Beta(5, 3), the maximum value of $f(x)$ is 2.3045 exactly when $x = \frac{2}{3}$. Now we generate two uniformly distributed random numbers, X and U, respectively, and check if:

$$U \le \frac{105X^4(1-X)^2}{2.3045}.$$

If so, we return X; otherwise, we reject it and repeat the process described at Steps 1 and 2. Figure B.4 shows the results from the acceptance-rejection method for Beta(5, 3) with the accepted sample of 50 X's.

The black crosses along $Cg(x)$ show all X's, and the green crosses at the bottom are the accepted samples. The top crosses are uniformly distributed in the interval $(0, 1)$, while the density of the bottom crosses is higher when the value of the density function $f(x)$ is higher. As illustrated in the figure, the green dots that are under the curve of the density function are the pairs of X, UC while all the rejected pairs are outside the curve.

The efficiency of the acceptance-rejection method can be improved in various ways [10, 90, 346], all with the same approach: they identify a good approximation $g(x)$ for the density function $f(x)$ of a given distribution, and then find the smallest C, so that $f(x) \le Cg(x)$ for all x.

B.5 GENERATING RANDOM VARIATES

There are numerous practical ways to generate random variables from a given distribution. In the following, we briefly introduce the most common methods.

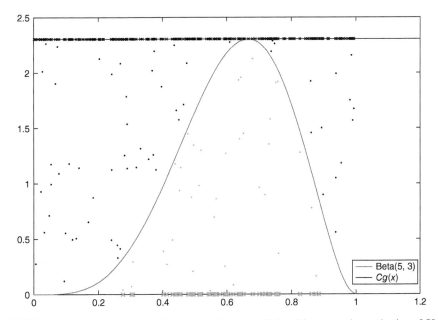

FIGURE B.4 Acceptance-rejection method for beta $(5, 3)$ with accepted sample size of 50.

B.5.1 Uniform Distribution

The inverse function of the distribution function of a $U(a, b)$ is:

$$x = F^{-1}(u) = a + (b - a)u \tag{B.24}$$

Therefore, the algorithm for generating a uniform random variable in (a, b) is:

1. Generate $U \sim U(0, 1)$.
2. Return $X = a + (b - a)U$.

B.5.2 Exponential Distribution

The distribution function of an exponential distribution, $\exp(\theta)$, with the mean $\theta > 0$ can be inverted as below:

$$x = F^{-1}(u) = -\theta \ln u \tag{B.25}$$

This leads to the following steps for generating an exponential variable:

1. Generate $U \sim U(0, 1)$.
2. Return $X = \theta \ln U$.

B.5.3 Weibull Distribution

The inverse function of a Weibull distribution function is:

$$x = F^{-1}(u) = \beta[-\ln(1-u)]^{\frac{1}{\eta}} \tag{B.26}$$

Hence, the method to generate a Weibull distributed random variable is:

1. Generate $U \sim U(0, 1)$.
2. Return $X = \beta[-\ln(1-u)]^{1/\eta}$.

B.5.4 Gamma Distribution

It is more complicated to generate gamma random variates than to generate variates from the previous three distributions. Given $X \sim gamma(\alpha, 1)$, any $X' \sim gamma(\alpha, \beta)$ for $\beta > 0$, we can obtain $X' = \beta X$. Therefore, the algorithm for obtaining gamma random variates focuses on only one side of α interval, either $0 < \alpha < 1$ or $\alpha > 1$. For the case of $0 < \alpha < 1$, the GS algorithm developed by Ahrens and Dieter [10] is widely used. This is essentially an acceptance-rejection method in which the alternative density function is described as follows:

$$g(x) = \begin{cases} 0 & x \leq 0 \\ \dfrac{\alpha x^{\alpha-1}}{b} & 0 < x < 1 \\ \dfrac{\alpha e^{-x}}{b} & x > 1 \end{cases} \tag{B.27}$$

where $b = \frac{e+\alpha}{e} > 1$. In this case, the constant C is:

$$C = \frac{b}{\alpha\Gamma(\alpha)}$$

The distribution function of $g(x)$ can be derived as below:

$$G(x) = \int_0^x g(x)dx = \begin{cases} \dfrac{x^\alpha}{b} & 0 < x < 1 \\ 1 - \dfrac{\alpha e^{-x}}{b} & x > 1 \end{cases} \tag{B.28}$$

The above equation can be inverted as follows:

$$G^{-1}(u) = \begin{cases} (bu)^{1/\alpha} & u \leq \dfrac{1}{b} \\ -\ln \dfrac{b(1-u)}{\alpha} & \text{otherwise} \end{cases} \tag{B.29}$$

Then the steps described in Algorithm 11 are followed to generate the random variates $X \sim gamma(\alpha, 1)$ for $0 < \alpha < 1$.

Algorithm 11 GS Algorithm for Gamma(α, 1) for $0 < \alpha < 1$

Require: $b = \frac{e+\alpha}{e}$
1: **loop**
2:   Generate $U_1 \sim U(0, 1)$
3:   Generate $U_2 \sim U(0, 1)$
4:   $P = bU_1$
5:   **if** $p > 1$ **then**
6:     $Y = -\ln\left(\frac{b-p}{\alpha}\right)$
7:     **if** $U_2 \leq Y^{\alpha-1}$ **then**
8:       **return** $X = Y$
9:     **end if**
10:   **else**
11:     $Y = p^{1/\alpha}$
12:     **if** $U_2 \leq e^{-Y}$ **then**
13:       **return** $X = Y$
14:     **end if**
15:   **end if**
16: **end loop**

For the cases where $\alpha > 1$, a modified acceptance-rejection method called GB algorithm [91] is usually employed. The alternative density function is defined as:

$$g(x) = \begin{cases} \frac{\lambda\mu x^{\lambda-1}}{(\mu+x^\lambda)^2} & x \geq 0 \\ 0 & \text{otherwise} \end{cases} \tag{B.30}$$

where $\lambda = \sqrt{2\alpha - 1}$, $\mu = \alpha^\lambda$, thus:

$$C = \frac{4\alpha^\alpha e^{-\alpha}}{\lambda\Gamma(\alpha)}$$

The distribution function to the density function $g(x)$ is:

$$G(x) = \begin{cases} \frac{x^\lambda}{\mu+x^\lambda} & x \geq 0 \\ 0 & \text{otherwise} \end{cases} \tag{B.31}$$

Then, the inverted function of $G(x)$ is:

$$G^{-1}(u) = \left(\frac{\mu u}{1-u}\right)^{1/\lambda} \quad 0 < u < 1 \tag{B.32}$$

Following Cheng's recommendations [89], we present the details in Algorithm 12, which adds a pre-test for acceptance to improve efficiency.

Algorithm 12 GB Algorithm for Gamma(α, 1) for $\alpha > 1$

Require: $a = 1/\sqrt{2\alpha - 1}$
Require: $b = \alpha - \ln 4$
Require: $q = \alpha + 1/\alpha$
Require: $\theta = 4.5$
Require: $d = 1 + \ln \theta$
1: **loop**
2:   Generate $U1$ and $U2$ as IID $U(0, 1)$
3:   $V = \alpha \ln(U1/(1 - U1))$
4:   $Y = \alpha e^V$
5:   $Z = U_1^2 U_2$
6:   $W = b + qV - Y$
7:   **if** $W + d - \theta Z \geq 0$ **then**
8:     **return** $X = Y$ {Pretest to avoid logarithm}
9:   **else**
10:    **if** $W \geq \ln Z$ **then**
11:      **return** $X = Y$
12:    **end if**
13: **end if**
14: **end loop**

B.5.5 Normal Distribution

The Box–Muller method [51] for generating a random variable from a standard normal (Gaussian) distribution is one of the most popular methods that has been widely used in practice over the years. The method includes two steps:

1. Generate $U_1, U_2 \sim U(0, 1)$, U_1 and U_2 are IID.
2. Generate two independent standard normal variables, X and Y, by:

$$X = \sqrt{-2 \ln U_1} \cos(2\pi U_2), \quad and$$
$$Y = \sqrt{-2 \ln U_1} \sin(2\pi U_2) \tag{B.33}$$

X and Y are IDD N(0, 1) random variates. A normal distribution, $X'N(\mu, \sigma)$, can be obtained via a standard normal distribution, $X N(0, 1)$, by

$$X' = \mu + \sigma X.$$

Thus, we can obtain random variables for any other normal distribution by obtaining the variables from the standard normal distribution. An improved method, called the polar method, was proposed by Marsaglia and Bray [268] to eliminate the trigonometric calculation in the Box and Muller method. The polar method generates $N(0, 1)$ random variables in pairs, as described in Algorithm 13.

Algorithm 13 Polar Method for $N(0, 1)$

1: **repeat**
2:   Generate U_1 and U_2 as IID $U(0, 1)$
3:     $V_1 = 2U_1 - 1$
4:     $V_2 = 2U_2 - 1$
5:     $S = V_1^2 + V_2^2$
6: **until** $0 < S \leq 1$
7: $Y = \sqrt{(-2 \ln S/S)}$
8: $X_1 = Y V_1$
9: $X_2 = Y V_2$

B.5.6   Lognormal Distribution

Given a normal random variable $Y \sim N(\mu, \sigma^2)$, $e^Y \sim LN(\mu, \sigma^2)$, we can apply the following steps to obtain the lognormal variates:

1. Generate $Y \sim N(\mu, \sigma^2)$ by the method discussed in the last section.
2. Return $X = e^Y$.

B.5.7   Beta Distribution

We have previously discussed the acceptance-rejection method to obtain $X \sim beta(\alpha_1, \alpha_2)$. However, there is another convenient method to achieve this. Let $Y_1 \sim gamma(\alpha_1, 1)$ and $Y_2 \sim gamma(\alpha_2, 1)$ for any $\alpha_1 > 0$ and $\alpha_2 > 0$. Then, $Y_1/(Y_1 + Y_2) \sim beta(\alpha_1, \alpha_2)$. Thus, the following method can generate beta variates:

1. Generate $Y_1 \sim gamma(\alpha_1, 1)$.
2. Generate $Y_2 \sim gamma(\alpha_2, 1)$ independent of Y_1.
3. Return $X = Y_1/(Y_1 + Y_2)$.

Y_1 and Y_2 can use the methods discussed in Section B.5.4.

B.5.8   Bernoulli Distribution

Given the distribution function of Bernoulli distribution as below:

$$F(x) = \begin{cases} 0 & x < 0 \\ 1 - p & 0 \leq x < 1 \\ 1 & x \geq 1 \end{cases}$$

We use a method similar to inverse-transform method to obtain the Bernoulli variates:

1. Generate $U \sim U(0, 1)$.
2. If $U \leq p$, return $X = 1$. Otherwise, return $X = 0$.

B.5.9 Discrete Uniform Distribution

Similar to the approach for Bernoulli, the following steps generate a discrete uniform random variate $X \sim DU(a, b)$:

1. Generate $U \sim U(0, 1)$.
2. Return $X = a + \lfloor (b - a + 1)U \rfloor$.

Clearly, $(b - a + 1)$ can be treated as a constant and be calculated in advance.

B.5.10 Binomial Distribution

Given that $bin(1, p)$ is as same as $Bernoulli(p)$, $Binomial(t, p)$ is the sum of t IID $Bernoulli(p)$. This leads to the following convolution method:

1. Generate $b_1, b_2, b_3, ..., b_t$ as IID Bernoulli random variates.
2. Return $X = \sum_{i=1}^{t} b_i$.

We note that it is also possible to use the inverse-transform method to generate binomial random variates.

B.5.11 Geometric Distribution

The inverse-transform method can be also used to generate geometric distributed random variates. The inverted function of the geometric distribution function is:

$$F^{-1}(u) = \frac{\ln u}{\ln(1 - p)}. \tag{B.34}$$

Thus, the steps are:

1. Generate $U \sim U(0, 1)$.
2. Return $X = \frac{\ln u}{\ln(1-p)}$.

If p is small, then $\ln(1 - p)$ is close to zero, thereby leading to potential round-off errors on a computer. Therefore, special consideration of this issue should be involved in implementation.

B.5.12 Poisson Distribution

Poisson distribution is closely related to exponential distribution. It is easy to prove that if $Y \sim Exp(\lambda)$, then X, as defined in the following equation, is a Poisson distribution:

$$X = \max \left\{ n : \sum_{j=1}^{n} Y_j \leq 1 \right\} \sim Poi(\lambda)$$

We use $U \sim U(0, 1)$ to rewrite the above equation and obtain:

$$X = \max \left\{ n : \sum_{j=1}^{n} -\ln U_j \leq \lambda \right\}$$

$$= \max \left\{ n : \ln \left(\prod_{j=1}^{n} U_j \right) \geq -\lambda \right\} \qquad (B.35)$$

$$= \max \left\{ n : \prod_{j=1}^{n} U_j \geq e^{-\lambda} \right\}$$

Then, the following algorithm can be used to generate Poisson distributed random variates.

Algorithm 14 Poisson Random Variates Generator

1: $n = 0$
2: $a = 1$
3: **repeat**
4:    $n = n + 1$
5:    Generate $U_n \sim U(0, 1)$
6:    $a = aU_n$
7: **until** $a < e^{\lambda}$
8: **return** $X = n - 1$

It is obvious that the efficiency of Algorithm 14 decreases when λ increases. Hence, some other methods – such as the inverse-transform method with efficient search (described in [27]) – could be better options when λ is larger.

B.6 MONTE CARLO METHOD

Monte Carlo simulation (or method) is a computational algorithm based on probability and statistic theories, and employs random numbers to solve certain stochastic or deterministic problems. The algorithm is widely used to solve problems in various domains, such as mathematics, computational physics, macroeconomics, computational finance, engineering, biology, and medicine. In this section, we discuss in detail the methods for performing a Monte Carlo simulation based on random number and variate generators. We also describe a number of relevant applications using Monte Carlo simulation, such as integration and optimisation.

    The initial idea of this method can be traced back to Buffon's needle problem [97], which estimates the value of π by the number of intersections between a number of needles dropped randomly on the floor and a number of equally distanced parallel lines. Since the development of this method, many other researchers have used similar approaches for different problems, such as approximating solutions for differential equations. The modern Monte Carol simulation was introduced by Stanislaw Ulam in the 1940s and formalised by John von Neumann [281] when they both worked on the Manhattan Project for the development of atomic weapons. Von Neumann encoded this method into the Electronic Numerical Integrator and Computer (ENIAC) and created the middle-square method to obtain a large amount of random numbers. This method was used to facilitate simulations for the Manhattan Project. The method was named 'Monte Carlo' by Nicholas Metropolis to emphasise its resemblance with the city of Monaco and its famous casinos (both the method and gambling involve randomness). Monte Carlo simulation became popular and was adopted in physics, economics, operation research and many other fields. With the unprecedented advances in computing technology during the last decades, performing Monte Carlo simulations became much easier because of the increase of computational power, which allows large amounts of evaluations in a short timeframe for both random number generating and numerical evaluation.

There are numerous ways to perform a Monte Carlo simulation; however, they all follow a core pattern, as follows:

1. Generate random numbers from a probability distribution as inputs over a predefined domain.
2. Perform deterministic computation on the inputs and aggregate the results.

Example B.6.1. *To estimate the area of an irregular polygon that resides in a 1×1 square, we can follow the above steps to perform a Monte Carlo simulation. First, we can generate N random points ((x, y), $0 \le x \le 1$ and $0 \le y \le 1$) uniformly falling within this 1×1 square, with N being a large number, and count the number of points (n) that are inside the irregular polygon or on its edges. Then, the ratio of the points inside the polygon to the total number of points (n/N) can be seen as an approximation for the polygon area.*

As seen in the above example, Monte Carlo simulation requires a method to generate a large number of random points in a defined domain, which are random numbers: $x \sim U(0, 1)$ and $y \sim U(0, 1)$. Therefore, an approach that can generate random variates from a given distribution is necessary to perform a Monte Carlo simulation. Various uniform RNGs have been discussed previously. In addition, we need to define a function to structure the problem or system from which we can obtain the results using the respective random variates. For this example, the function is defined as a mechanism to count the number of points falling into the irregular polygon. Finally, these results can be aggregated and abstracted to produce an approximated solution to the problem. If N is large enough to cover all the area of the square, n/N can be seen as the polygon area because the total area of the square is 1. In fact, the ratio n/N is the frequency of points falling inside the polygon and can be taken as the probability of the event according to the law of large numbers. According to the law of large numbers, the average of the results obtained from a large number of trials of a random process should be close to the expected value, and tends to become closer as more trials are undertaken. Based on this theorem, the probability of an event is the frequency of this event occurring in an experiment in which the number of trials is large. Thus, with the support of probability and statistical theories, Monte Carlo simulation can be used for complex problems in many real-world situations.

In the rest of the section, we present several applications of Monte Carlo simulation that are relevant for computer-based simulation from both theoretical and practical perspectives.

B.6.1 Applications of Monte Carlo Simulation

B.6.1.1 Buffon's Needle Problem   Buffon's needle problem was posed by French naturalist Buffon in the 1770s and is one of the oldest problems that was solved by geometrical probability. It is also a classic example to demonstrate how Monte Carlo simulation works. Assume we have a number of parallel lines on the floor, and the distance between every pair of parallel lines is the same. We then drop many needles on the floor and try to determine the probability of the needles intersecting the parallel lines. Interestingly, the probability of intersection is directly related to the value of π.

Example B.6.2. *Let us consider the simplest case in which only two parallel lines are drawn on the floor and the distance between them is 2a. We then consider the length of a needle as 2l, and assume $a > l > 0$ to avoid situations where a needle intersects two lines simultaneously. Let M be the centre point of a needle, d be the distance between M and the closet parallel line to the needle, and ω $(0 \leq \omega \leq \pi)$ be the intersection angle between intersected parallel line and needle. Clearly, the necessary and sufficient condition for a needle to intersect this parallel line is that $0 \leq d \leq l \sin \omega$, as depicted in Figure B.5.*

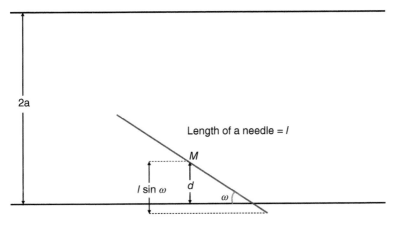

FIGURE B.5   Situation of a needle intersected with a line.

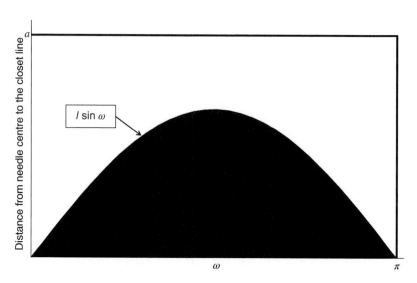

FIGURE B.6   The probability of intersections.

The shadowed area in Figure B.6 plots all possible d's along ordinates that are on or under the curve of $l\sin()$, which means that $d \leq l\sin\alpha$ and, consequently, the needles with these d's intersect a parallel line. Therefore, the probability of a needle intersecting a line is the ratio between the area under the curve and the entire rectangle enclosed by blue lines.

$$
\begin{aligned}
P\{y \leq l\sin\omega\} &= \frac{\int_0^\pi l\sin\omega \, d\omega}{\pi a} \\
&= \frac{-l\cos\pi - l\cos 0}{\pi a} \\
&= \frac{2l}{\pi a}
\end{aligned}
\tag{B.36}
$$

Thus, we can obtain the value π by:

$$
\pi = \frac{2l}{pa}
\tag{B.37}
$$

Now we drop N needles on the floor. When N is large enough, we can consider the frequency of needles intersecting lines as a probability. If we observe that n needles intersect lines, then the probability can be estimated as $p \approx \frac{n}{N}$. Thus the value of pi can be approximated:

$$
\pi \approx \frac{2lN}{na}.
\tag{B.38}
$$

Further, we implement Buffon's needle problem in NetLogo, as shown in Figure B.7. There are six vertical parallel lines on a 50×50 floor. The distance

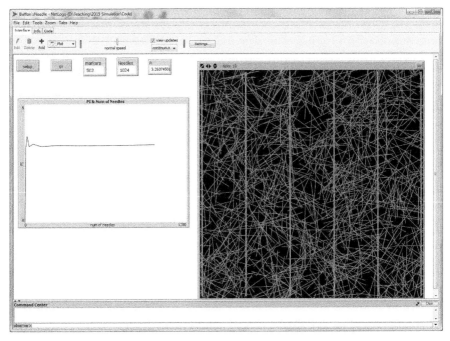

FIGURE B.7   Situation of a needle intersecting a line.

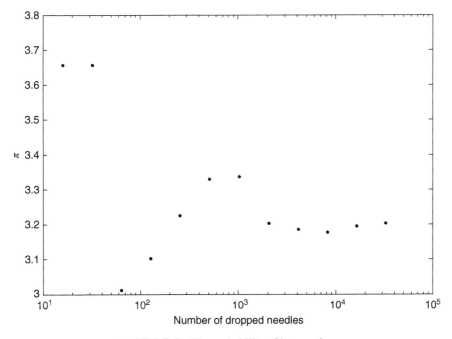

FIGURE B.8   The probability of intersection.

between each pair of lines is 10, and the length of a needle is 8. During the simulation, the position and direction of each dropped needle are randomly initialised. Once an intersection between a needle and a line occurs, the number n of intersections is updated. Then, the value of π is estimated based on Eq. (B.38). Figure B.8 shows the estimated π value versus the number of needles dropped in the simulation. As the number of dropped needles increases, the estimation is closer to the desired value of π.

For the above example of Buffon's needle problem, instead of dropping needles on the floor, we can use sampled random points and check whether they are inside the shadowed area shown in Figure B.6. Then the value of π can be estimated by the frequency of points falling inside. The simulation steps are illustrated in Algorithm 15.

Algorithm 15 Buffon's Needle Problem by Monte Carol Simulation

---

Require: a, l, and N
1: $n = 0$
2: **for** i=1 to N **do**
3:     Generate $\omega \sim U(0, \pi)$
4:     Generate $y \sim U(0, a)$
5:     **if** $y \leq l \sin \omega$ **then**
6:         $n = n + 1$
7:     **end if**
8: **end for**
9: **return** $\pi = \frac{2lN}{na}$

Algorithm 15 pprovides similar results to the simulation implemented in NetLogo, as shown in Figure B.9. This method is also called 'hit-and-miss'.

B.6.1.2 *Integration by Monte Carlo Simulation* The previous example implies that we can use Monte Carlo simulation for solving integrals. While single integrals can be easily and accurately solved by various numeric methods, multidimensional definite integrals require more computation and generally involve more approximations. Thus, Monte Carlo simulation becomes a pertinent way to efficiently solve the latter. In the following, we describe a Monte Carlo approach to solving single integrals, and then generalise the approach to the case of multiple integrals.

Given the following integral:

$$I = \int_a^b f(x)\, dx.$$

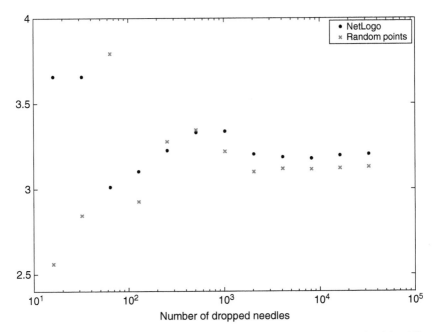

FIGURE B.9   The estimated π values by NetLogo and random points (Algorithm 15).

If $f(x)$ is the PDF of a continuous random variable ζ, and $f(x)$ satisfies the following conditions:

$$f(x) \geq 0 \quad \text{and} \quad \int_{-\infty}^{+\infty} f(x)\, dx = 1$$

then I is obviously a probability integral, and its value equals to the probability of $P(a \leq \zeta \leq b)$. To approximate this probability for the given $f(x)$ using Monte Carlo simulation, the following steps are applied:

1. Generate random variates x_i, $i = 1, 2, ..., N$ that obey the distribution with density function $f(x)$.
2. Count the times n that x falls into the range $[a, b]$ ($a \leq x \leq b$).
3. Approximate the probability (or the integral) by

$$I \approx \frac{n}{N}.$$

In many cases, $f(x)$ may not be a PDF, requiring us to transform it into some probability distribution and then apply the above Monte Carlo simulation to estimate the integral. However, this can involve some complicated transformations and calculations. For these cases, we can always use the method described in Algorithm 15.

Alternatively, let Y be the random variable $(b-a)f(X)$, and X be a continuous uniformly distributed variable on $[a,b]$. Then, the expected value of Y is:

$$E(Y) = E((b-a)f(X))$$
$$= (b-a)E(f(X))$$
$$= (b-a)\int_a^b f(x)U_X(x)\,dx$$
$$= (b-a)\frac{\int_a^b f(x)\,dx}{b-1}$$
$$= I$$

where $U_X(x) = \frac{1}{b-1}$ is the PDF of a $U(a,b)$. Given that X has a uniform density function $U_X(x)$, the expected value of a measurable function $f(X)$ of it, is the inner product of $U(x)$ and $f(x)$. Therefore, the problem of evaluating the integral I can be reduced to evaluating the expected value $E(Y)$, which can be achieved by estimating the mean of samples. This approach is often called the 'crude Monte Carlo' method.

$$I = E(Y) \cong \overline{Y}(n) \approx \frac{\sum_{i=1}^N Y_i}{N} = \frac{(b-a)}{N}\sum_{i=1}^N f(X_i) \tag{B.39}$$

Example B.6.3. *Let us now evaluate the following integral using Monte Carlo simulation:*

$$I = \int_0^\pi e^x \sin x \, dx$$

Table B.5 shows the results from Monte Carlo simulation for different values of N. Although the results show some errors, Monte Carlo simulation provides a fast and easy way to evaluate integrals.

It is easy to generalise the Monte Carlo simulation to multiple integrals. For example, a double integral can be evaluated as below:

$$I = \iint_D f(x,y)\,dxdy \cong \frac{|D|}{N}\sum_{i=1}^N f(x,y)$$

TABLE B.5   Results by Monte Carlo Simulation for $I = \int_0^\pi e^x \sin x \, dx = 12.0703$ with Various Values of N

N	10	100	1 000	10 000	100 000
$\overline{(Y)}$	10.9272	11.3158	12.2723	12.0648	12.0619
Error	−1.1430	−0.7545	0.2020	−0.0055	−0.0084

where D is the region of integration in the 2-D plane and $|D|$ is the area of this region D. Similarly, we can evaluate a triple integral by:

$$I = \iint_{\Omega} f(x, y) \, \mathrm{d}x\mathrm{d}y\mathrm{d}z \cong \frac{|\Omega|}{N} \sum_{i=1}^{N} f(x, y, z)$$

where Ω is the space of the integration in the 3-D space and $|\Omega|$ is the volume of the space D.

B.6.1.3 Optimisation using Monte Carlo Simulation

Example B.6.4. *A shop sells cakes at the price of three dollars each, with a production cost for a cake of two dollars. This cake shop bakes n of these cakes in the morning every day. The number of customers visiting the shop is a Poisson distributed random variable, and the average number of visiting customers is 15. Suppose that every customer buys only one of these cakes, and any unsold cakes cannot be sold the next day and must be discarded after the shop closes. How does the shop owner decide the number of cakes to be baked in the morning every day to maximise the profit?*

In this example, Monte Carlo simulation can be easily applied to investigate the number of cakes to achieve the maximum profit. First, the number of daily customers k follows Poisson distribution:

$$P(k) = \frac{m^k e^m}{k!}.$$

Thus, we can use Algorithm 14 presented in Section B.5.12 to generate k_i, $i = 1, 2, ..., N$. Further, the daily profit for one day with k customers can be formulated as:

$$a(c, s) = \begin{cases} ks - na & k < n \\ ns - na & k \geq n \end{cases}$$

where, c and s are the cost and price for a cake, respectively, and n is the number of cakes baked daily. The average daily profit can be easily expressed as:

$$\bar{a} = \frac{\sum_{i=1}^{N} a(c, s)}{N}.$$

Now, we can run this simulation with different values of n to discover the number of baked cakes that maximises the profit. The results are listed in Table B.6 and suggest that the maximum profit ($10.87) can be achieved by baking 13 cakes a day.

TABLE B.6   Daily Profits of a Cake Shop with Various Numbers of Cakes Baked, Based on an Average Customer Number per Day of 15

Number of cakes	10	11	12	**13**	14	15	16	17	18	19	20
Profit by Monte Carlo	9.76	9.98	10.5	**10.87**	10.13	9.78	8.38	8.36	8.52	4.87	4.73
Profit by calculation		9.59	10.23	10.68	**10.88**	10.79	10.39	9.69	8.69	7.45	5.99	4.36

To verify the above results, we can also solve the problem using an analytical approach, as below:

$$A(n) = \sum_{k=0}^{\infty} a(n,k)P(k)$$

$$= \sum_{k=0}^{n-1}(ks - nc)P(k) + \sum_{k=n}^{\infty}(ns - nc)P(k)$$

Given $\sum_{k=0}^{\infty} P(k) = 1$, we can obtain the following equation:

$$A(n) = \sum_{k=0}^{n-1}(k - n)sP(k) + n(s - c)$$

The results from this approach are presented in the third row of Table B.6 and the maximum profit is $10.88 when 13 cakes are baked. Clearly, both methods provide the same suggestion – that baking 13 cakes per day can generate the maximum profit, although the actual profit from the Monte Carlo simulation ($10.87) is slightly different from the one indicated by the analytical solution ($10.88).

B.7   CONCLUSION

In this appendix, we have introduced LCGs, as well as some types of feedback shift register generators. Some of these arithmetic generators are widely used in many applications, including simulation. However, empirical and theoretical random number testing methods are required to examine the quality of the outputs from a generator in terms of statistical properties, as discussed in Section B.3. Otherwise, the results from a simulation with a 'bad' RNG may not be valid. We also demonstrated that, in addition to the statistical properties, a 'good' generator needs to be efficient, portable, and repeatable, so that it can be used in situations requiring large amounts of random numbers and/or simulation runs in different computer architectures. Thus, developing a RNG is an important step in the whole simulation process. In addition, because random processes in the real world can follow a variety of distributions, it is important to build a 'good' RNG for the distribution required by the actual application.

We demonstrated in this appendix that uniformly distributed random numbers are essential to obtain random variates of many other distributions.

We then discussed the fundamental aspects of Monte Carlo simulation, and provided a number of relevant examples in which we showed how both mathematical and real problems can be solved in a simple manner using Monte Carlo simulation. Overall, the appendix demonstrated that Monte Carlo simulation can be a simple and efficient method that is usable in many application fields.

■ BIBLIOGRAPHY

1. H. A. Abbass. Real-time computational red teaming of human cognition using encephalographic (EEG) data. In *The 18th Asia Pacific Symposium on Intelligent and Evolutionary Systems*, Singapore, 10–12 November 2014.

2. H. A. Abbass. Analytics of risk and challenge. In *Computational Red Teaming*, pages 47–104. Springer International Publishing, 2015.

3. H. A. Abbass. Big-data-to-decisions red teaming systems. In *Computational Red Teaming*, pages 105–158. Springer International Publishing, 2015.

4. H. A. Abbass. *Computational Red Teaming*. Springer International Publishing, 2015.

5. H. A. Abbass, A. Bender, S. Gaidow, and P. Whitbread. Computational red teaming: Past, present and future. *IEEE Computational Intelligence Magazine*, 6(1):30–42, 2011.

6. H. A. Abbass, J. Tang, R. Amin, M. Ellejmi, and S. Kirby. The computational air traffic control brain: Computational red teaming and big data for real-time seamless brain-traffic integration. *Journal of Air Traffic Control*, 56(2):10–17, 2014.

7. H. A. Abbass, J. Tang, R. Amin, M. Ellejmi, and S. Kirby. Augmented cognition using real-time eeg-based adaptive strategies for air traffic control. In *Proceedings of the Human Factors and Ergonomics Society Annual Meeting*, volume 58, pages 230–234, 2014. SAGE Publications.

8. A. A. Afifi and S. P. Azen. *Statistical Analysis: A Computer Oriented Approach*. Academic Press, New York, 1972.

9. F. f. I. P. Agents. Fipa contract net interaction protocol, 03.12.2002, 2002.

10. J. H. Ahrens and U. Dieter. Computer methods for sampling from gamma, beta, poisson and bionomial distributions. *Computing*, 12(3):223–246, 1974.

11. S. Alam, H. Abbass, and M. Barlow. Atoms: Air traffic operations and management simulator. *IEEE Transactions on Intelligent Transportation Systems*, 9(2):209–225, June 2008.

12. S. Alam, W. Zhao, J. Tang, C. Lokan, M. Ellejmi, S. Kirby, and H. Abbass. Discovering delay patterns in arrival traffic with dynamic continuous descent approaches using co-evolutionary red teaming. *Air Traffic Control Quarterly*, 20(1):47, 2012.

13. K. A. Albashiri, F. Coenen, and P. Leng. Emads: An extendible multi-agent data miner. *Knowledge-Based Systems*, 22(7):523–528, 2009. Artificial Intelligence 2008 AI-2008 the twenty-eighth (SGAI) International Conference on Artificial Intelligence.

Simulation and Computational Red Teaming for Problem Solving, First Edition.
Jiangjun Tang, George Leu, and Hussein A. Abbass.
© 2020 by The Institute of Electrical and Electronics Engineers, Inc. Published 2020 by John Wiley & Sons, Inc.

14. R. Alcala, Y. Nojima, F. Herrera, and H. Ishibuchi. Multiobjective genetic fuzzy rule selection of single granularity-based fuzzy classification rules and its interaction with the lateral tuning of membership functions. *Soft Computing*, 15(12):2303–2318, 2011.

15. J. Allik and R. R. McCrae. Towards a geography of personality traits: Patterns of profiles across 36 cultures. *Journal of Cross-Cultural Psychology*, 35:13–28, 2004.

16. R. Amin, J. Tang, M. Ellejmi, S. Kirby, and H. A. Abbass. Computational red teaming for correction of traffic events in real time human performance studies. In *Proceedings of 10th USA/Europe Air Traffic Management Research and Development Seminar*, Chicago, IL, 10–13 June 2013.

17. J. R. Anderson. Acquisition of cognitive skill. *Psychological Review*, 89(4):369–406, July 1982.

18. J. R. Anderson. A spreading activation theory of memory. *Journal of Verbal Learning and Verbal Behavior*, 22(3):261–295, 1983.

19. J. R. Anderson. Act: A simple theory of complex cognition. *American Psychologist*, 51:355–365, 1996.

20. J. R. Anderson. *Cognitive Psychology and Its Implications*. WH Freeman/Times Books/ Henry Holt & Co., 1990.

21. Y. Ang, H. A. Abbass, and R. Sarker. Characterizing warfare in red teaming. *IEEE Transactions on Systems, Man, and Cybernetics, Part B: Cybernetics*, 36(2):268–285, 2006.

22. AnyLogic. http://www.anylogic.com/, 2014. [Online; accessed 14 November 2014].

23. G. Aoude, V. Desaraju, L. Stephens, and J. How. Driver behavior classification at intersections and validation on large naturalistic data set. *IEEE Transactions on Intelligent Transportation Systems*, 13(2):724–736, 2012.

24. M. A. Arbib. *Brains, Machines, and Mathematics*. Springer Science & Business Media, 2012.

25. U. Arend. *Analyzing Complex Tasks with an Extended GOMS Model*, pages 115–133. Elsevier, B.V. North-Holland, 1991.

26. H. Aslaksen. The mathematics of sudoku, 2014. http://en.wikipedia.org/wiki/Sudoku [Online; accessed 22 August 2019].

27. A. C. Atkinson. The computer generation of poisson random variables. *Journal of the Royal Statistical Society. Series C (Applied Statistics)*, 28(1):29–35, 1979.

28. A. C. Atkinson. Tests of pseudo-random numbers. *Applied Statistics*, 29:164–171, 1980.

29. N. Aussenac-Gilles and N. Matta. Making a method of problem solving explicit with MACAO. *International Journal of Human-Computer Studies*, 40(2):193–219, 1994.

30. Y. Baek, B. Kim, S. Yun, and D. Cheong. Effects of two types of sudoku puzzles on students' logical thinking. In T. Connelly and M. Stansfield, editors, *The Second European Conference on Games Based Learning*, pages 19–24. Academic Publishing Limited, 2008.

31. W. S. Bainbridge. The scientific research potential of virtual worlds. *Science*, 317(5837):472–476, 2007.

32. J. Balter, A. Labarre-Vila, D. Ziebelin, and C. Garbay. A knowledge-driven agent-centred framework for data mining in EMG. *Comptes Rendus Biologies*, 325(4):375–382, 2002.

33. A. Bandura. Social cognitive theory: An agentic perspective. *Annual Review of Psychology*, 52(1):1–26, 2001.

34. S. Bandyopadhyay, U. Maulik, and A. Mukhopadhyay. Multiobjective genetic clustering for pixel classification in remote sensing imagery. *IEEE Transactions on Geoscience and Remote Sensing*, 45(5):1506–1511, May 2007.

35. J. Banks. *Handbook of Simulation*. Wiley Online Library, 1998.

36. J. Barceló, J. Ferrer, D. García, R. Grau, M. Forian, I. Chabini, and E. Le Saux. Microscopic traffic simulation for ATT systems analysis. A parallel computing version. *Contribution to the 25th Aniversary of CRT*, 35, 1998.

37. A. Barnes and P. Thagard. Emotional decisions. In *Proceedings of the Eighteenth Annual Conference of the Cognitive Science Society*, pages 426–429, Erlbaum, 12–15 July 1996.

38. B. Bauer and J. Odell. UML 2.0 and agents: How to build agent-based systems with the new uml standard. *Engineering Applications of Artificial Intelligence*, 18(2):141–157, 2005.

39. S. L. Baughcum, T. G. Tritz, S. C. Henderson, and D. C. Pickett. Scheduled civil aircraft emission inventories for 1992: Database development and analysis, NASA contractor report 4700. Technical report, NASA, April 1996.

40. C. Bays and S. Durham. Improving a poor random number generator. *ACM Transactions on Mathematical Software (TOMS)*, 2(1):59–64, 1976.

41. D. Beach and R. B. Pedersen. *Process-Tracing Methods: Foundations and Guidelines*. University of Michigan Press, Ann Arbor, 2013.

42. E. Begoli and J. Horey. Design principles for effective knowledge discovery from big data. In *2012 Joint Working IEEE/IFIP Conference on Software Architecture (WICSA) and European Conference on Software Architecture (ECSA)*, pages 215–218, Helsinki, Finland, 20–24 August 2012.

43. Y. Benjamini and M. Leshno. Statistical methods for data mining. In O. Maimon and L. Rokach, editors, *Data Mining and Knowledge Discovery Handbook*, pages 523–540. Springer US, 2010.

44. P. Berggren and D. Nilsson. A study of sudoku solving algorithms. Master's thesis, Royal Institute of Technology, Stockholm, 2012.

45. B. Bettonvil and J. P. Kleijnen. Searching for important factors in simulation models with many factors: Sequential bifurcation. *European Journal of Operational Research*, 96(1):180–194, 1997.

46. M. Bishop. About penetration testing. *IEEE Security & Privacy*, 5(6):84–87, 2007.

47. E. Bonabeau. Agent-based modeling: Methods and techniques for simulating human systems. *Proceedings of the National Academy of Sciences of the United States of America*, 99(Suppl 3):7280–7287, 2002.

48. J. H. Boose. A survey of knowledge acquisition techniques and tools. *Knowledge Acquisition*, 1(1):3–37, 1989.

49. M. M. Botvinick, Y. Niv, and A. C. Barto. Hierarchically organized behavior and its neural foundations: A reinforcement learning perspective. *Cognition*, 113(3):262–280, 2009.

50. G. E. Box and J. S. Hunter. The 2 k-p fractional factorial designs. *Technometrics*, 3(3):311–351, 1961.

51. G. E. Box and M. E. Muller. A note on the generation of random normal deviates. *The Annals of Mathematical Statistics*, 29:610–611, 1958.

52. G. E. Box and K. Wilson. On the experimental attainment of optimum conditions. *Journal of the Royal Statistical Society. Series B (Methodological)*, 13(1):1–45, 1951.

53. M. Brackstone and M. McDonald. Car-following: A historical review. *Transportation Research Part F: Traffic Psychology and Behaviour*, 2(4):181–196, 1999.

54. J. M. Bradshaw and J. H. Boose. Decision analysis techniques for knowledge acquisition: Combining information and preferences using aquinas and axotl. *International Journal of Man-Machine Studies*, 32(2):121–186, 1990.

55. J. M. Bradshaw, K. M. Ford, J. R. Adams-Webber, and J. H. Boose. Beyond the repertory grid: New approaches to constructivist knowledge acquisition tool development. *International Journal of Intelligent Systems*, 8(2):287–333, 1993.

56. M. Bratman. *Intention, Plans, and Practical Reason*, volume 10. Harvard University Press, Cambridge, MA, 1987.

57. R. Brette and W. Gerstner. Adaptive exponential integrate-and-fire model as an effective description of neuronal activity. *Journal of Neurophysiology*, 94(5):3637–3642, 2005.

58. R. A. Brooks. Intelligence without representation. *Artificial Intelligence*, 47:139–159, 1991.

59. A. Burkitt. A review of the integrate-and-fire neuron model: I. homogeneous synaptic input. *Biological Cybernetics*, 95(1):1–19, 2006.

60. A. Burkitt. A review of the integrate-and-fire neuron model: Ii. inhomogeneous synaptic input and network properties. *Biological Cybernetics*, 95(2):97–112, 2006.

61. A. W. Burks. *Essays on Cellular Automata*. University of Illinois Press, 1970.

62. M. D. Byrne and J. R. Anderson. Enhancing act-r's perceptual-motor abilites. In *the 19th Annual Conference of the Cognitive Science Society*, page 880. Erlbaum, Mahwah, NJ, 1997.

63. S. Wells and R. RAAD. Performance measures for road networks: a survey of Canadian use. In *Proceedings of the 23rd PIARC World Road Congress*, Paris, 17–21 September 2007.

64. J. Cano, F. Herrera, and M. Lozano. Using evolutionary algorithms as instance selection for data reduction in kdd: An experimental study. *IEEE Transactions on Evolutionary Computation*, 7(6):561–575, Dec 2003.

65. L. Cao, V. Gorodetsky, and P. Mitkas. Agent mining: The synergy of agents and data mining. *IEEE Intelligent Systems*, 24(3):64–72, May 2009.

66. L. Cao, C. Luo, and C. Zhang. Agent-mining interaction: An emerging area. In V. Gorodetsky, C. Zhang, V. Skormin, and L. Cao, editors, *Autonomous Intelligent Systems: Multi-Agents and Data Mining, volume 4476 of Lecture Notes in Computer Science*, pages 60–73. Springer, Berlin Heidelberg, 2007.

67. L. Cao, G. Weiss, and P. Yu. A brief introduction to agent mining. *Autonomous Agents and Multi-Agent Systems*, 25(3):419–424, 2012.

68. S. K. Card, T. P. Moran, and A. L. Newell. *The Psychology of the Human-Computer Interface*. Lawrence Erlbaum Associates, Hillsdale, NJ, 1983.

69. S. K. Card, T. P. Moran, and A. L. Newell. *The Model Human Processor: An Engineering Model of Human Performance*, volume 2. Wiley, New York, 1986.

70. G. A. Carpenter and S. Grossberg. *Adaptive Resonance Theory*, pages 87–90. MIT Press, Cambridge, MA, 2 edition, 2003.

71. G. A. Carpenter and S. Grossberg. *Adaptive Resonance Theory*. Springer US, 2009.

72. G. A. Carpenter, S. Martens, and O. J. Ogas. Self-organizing information fusion and hierarchical knowledge discovery: A new framework using artmap neural networks. *Neural Networks*, 18(3):287–295, 2005.

73. J. Carroll and J. R. Olson. Mental models in human-computer interaction. In M. Helander, editor, *Handbook of Human-Computer Interaction* Elsevier, Pages 45–65. Amsterdam, 1988.

74. I. Carson and S. John. Introduction to modeling and simulation. In *Proceedings of the 36th Conference on Winter Simulation*, pages 9–16. Winter Simulation Conference, Savannah, GA, 7–10 December 2004.

75. C. G. Cassandras and S. Lafortune. *Introduction to Discrete Event Systems*. Springer Science & Business Media, 2008.

76. A. R. R. Casti, A. Omurtag, A. Sornborger, E. Kaplan, B. Knight, J. Victor, and L. Sirovich. A population study of integrate-and-fire-or-burst neurons. *Neural Computation*, 14(5):957–986, 2002.

77. J. L. Casti. *Would-Be Worlds: How Simulation Is Changing the Frontiers of Science*. Wiley, New York, 1997.

78. E. E. Center. User manual for the base of aircraft data (bada), revision 3.6. *EEC note*, (10/04), 2004.

79. S. B. Chadwick, R. M. Krieg, and C. E. Granade. Ease and toil: Analyzing sudoku. *UMAP Journal*, 29(3):363, 2007.

80. H.-S. Chang and J. M. Gibson. The odd-even effect in sudoku puzzles: Effects of working memory, aging, and experience. *The American Journal of Psychology*, 124(3):313–324, 2011.

81. C. Chao, G. Salvendy, and N. J. Lightner. Development of a methodology for optimizing elicited knowledge. *Behaviour & Information Technology*, 18(6):413–430, 1999.

82. M. Chattopadhyay, P. K. Dan, and S. Mazumdar. Comparison of visualization of optimal clustering using self-organizing map and growing hierarchical self-organizing map in cellular manufacturing system. *Applied Soft Computing*, 22:528–543, 2014.

83. M. Chau, D. Zeng, H. Chen, M. Huang, and D. Hendriawan. Design and evaluation of a multi-agent collaborative web mining system. *Decision Support Systems*, 35(1):167–183, 2003. Web Retrieval and Mining.

84. A. Chemchem and H. Drias. From data mining to knowledge mining: Application to intelligent agents. *Expert Systems with Applications*, 42(3):1436–1445, 2015.

85. H. Chen, R. H. Chiang, and V. C. Storey. Business intelligence and analytics: From big data to big impact. *MIS Quarterly*, 36(4):1165–1188, 2012.

86. M. Chen, Q. Zhu, and Z. Chen. An integrated interactive environment for knowledge discovery from heterogeneous data resources. *Information and Software Technology*, 43(8):487–496, 2001.

87. C.-B. Cheng, C.-C. H. Chan, and K.-C. Lin. Intelligent agents for e-marketplace: Negotiation with issue trade-offs by fuzzy inference systems. *Decision Support Systems*, 42(2):626–638, 2006.

88. H. Cheng, N. Zheng, X. Zhang, J. Qin, and H. Van de Wetering. Interactive road situation analysis for driver assistance and safety warning systems: Framework and algorithms. *IEEE Transactions on Intelligent Transportation Systems*, 8(1):157–167, 2007.

89. R. C. H. Cheng. The generation of gamma variables with non-integral shape parameter. *Journal of the Royal Statistical Society. Series C (Applied Statistics)*, 26(1):71–75, 1977.

90. R. C. H. Cheng. Generating beta variates with nonintegral shape parameters. *Communications of the ACM*, 21(4):317–322, 1978.

91. R. C. H. Cheng and G. M. Feast. Some simple gamma variate generators. *Journal of the Royal Statistical Society. Series C (Applied Statistics)*, 28(3):290–295, 1979.

92. C. S. Choo, C. L. Chua, and S.-H. V. Tay. Automated red teaming: A proposed framework for military application, In *Proceedings of the 9th Annual Conference on Genetic and Evolutionary Computation*, pages 1936–1942. London, 7–11 July 2007. ACM.

93. C. S. Choo, E. C. Ng, D. Ang, and C. L. Chua. Data farming in singapore: A brief history, In *Proceedings of the 40th Conference on Winter Simulation*, pages 1448–1455. Winter Simulation Conference, Miami, FL, 7–10 December 2008.

94. R. E. Clark, D. Feldon, J. J. G. Van Merrienboer, K. Yates, and S. Early. *Cognitive Task Analysis*. Lawrence Erlbaum Associates, Mahwah, NJ, 3 edition, 2008.

95. CogAff. The cognition and affect project, 2013. www.cs.bham.ac.uk/research/projects/cogaff/, [Online; accessed 15 August 2019].

96. M. Brennan. Defence simulation strategy and roadmap. In *SimTecT 2011*, Melbourne, Australia, 31 May–2 June 2011.

97. G. L. L. comte de Buffon. *Essai d'arithmétique morale*, 1777.

98. N. J. Cooke. Varieties of knowledge elicitation techniques. *International Journal of Human-Computer Studies*, 41(6):801–849, 1994.

99. A. C. Coolen, R. Kuhn, and P. Sollich. *Theory of Neural Information Processing Systems*. Oxford University Press, 2005.

100. D. Corapi, A. Russo, and E. Lupu. Inductive logic programming in answer set programming. In S. H. Muggleton, A. Tamaddoni-Nezhad, and F. A. Lisi, editors, *Inductive Logic Programming*, volume 7207 of *Lecture Notes in Computer Science*, pages 91–97. Springer, Berlin Heidelberg, 2012.

101. T. H. Cormen. *Introduction to Algorithms*. MIT Press, 2009.

102. B. Crandall, G. Klein, and R. R. Hoffman. *Working Minds: A Practitioner's Guide to Cognitive Task Analysis*. MIT Press, Cambridge, MA, 2006.

103. J. F. Crook. A pencil-and-paper algorithm for solving sudoku puzzles. *Notices of the AMS*, 56(4):460–468, 2009.

104. J. Cullen and A. Bryman. The knowledge acquisition bottleneck: Time for reassessment? *Expert Systems*, 5(3):216–225, 1988.

105. J. S. Dahmann, R. M. Fujimoto, and R. M. Weatherly. The department of defense high level architecture. In *Proceedings of the 29th Conference on Winter Simulation*, WSC'97, pages 142–149, Washington, DC, 7–10 December 1997. IEEE Computer Society.

106. A. R. Damasio. *Descartes' Error: Emotion, Reason, and the Human Brain*. Putnam, New York, 1994.

107. A. R. Damasio, D. Tranel, and H. C. Damasio. *Somatic Markers and the Guidance of Behaviour, pages 122–135*. Blackwell Publishers, 1998.

108. F. David and C. M. David. Adapting cognitive walkthrough to support game based learning design. *International Journal of Game-Based Learning (IJGBL)*, 4(3):23–34, 2014.

109. T. Davis. The math of sudoku, 2008.

110. D. L. DeAngelis and L. J. Gross. *Individual-Based Models and Approaches in Ecology: Populations, Communities and Ecosystems*. Chapman & Hall, 1992.

111. K. Deb and R. B. Agrawal. Simulated binary crossover for continuous search space. *Complex Systems*, 9(2):115–148, 1995.

112. J. Decraene, M. Y. H. Low, and P. Hingston. Evolving tactical plans for strategy games using automated red teaming, In *Proceedings of the 4th Annual International Conference on Computer Games, Multimedia & Allied Technology (CGAT 2011)*, Penang, Malaysia, 25–26 April 2011.

113. S. Dehuri, S. Patnaik, A. Ghosh, and R. Mall. Application of elitist multi-objective genetic algorithm for classification rule generation. *Applied Soft Computing*, 8(1):477–487, 2008.

114. DESMO-J. http://desmoj.sourceforge.net/home.html/, 2014. [Online; accessed 14 November 2014].

115. O. Dictionary. What is the frequency of the letters of the alphabet in english? http://www .oxforddictionaries.com/words/what-is-the-frequency-of-the-letters-of-the-alphabet-in-english, 2014. [Online; accessed 5 January 2015].

116. J. Diederich, I. Ruhmann, and M. May. Kriton: A knowledge-acquisition tool for expert systems. *International Journal of Man-Machine Studies*, 26(1):29–40, 1987.

117. S. Donikian. Hpts: A behaviour modelling language for autonomous agents. In *Proceedings of the Fifth International Conference on Autonomous Agents*, AGENTS'01, pages 401–408, New York, 28 May–1 June 2001. ACM.

118. C. dos Santos and A. Bazzan. Integrating knowledge through cooperative negotiation – A case study in bioinformatics. In V. Gorodetsky, J. Liu, and V. Skormin, editors, *Autonomous Intelligent Systems: Agents and Data Mining*, volume 3505 of *Lecture Notes in Computer Science*, pages 277–288. Springer, Berlin Heidelberg, 2005.

119. G. Dozier, D. Brown, J. Hurley, and K. Cain. Vulnerability analysis of ais-based intrusion detection systems via genetic and particle swarm red teams. In *Congress on Evolutionary Computation, 2004. CEC2004*, volume 1, pages 111–116, 2004.

120. N. R. Draper and H. Smith. *Applied Regression Analysis*. Wiley, 3 edition, 2014.

121. C. G. Drury. Methods for direct observation of performance. In J. R. Wilson and E. N. Corlett, editors, *Evaluation of Human Work: A Practical Ergonomics Methodology*, pages 35–57. Taylor & Francis, London, 1990.

122. I. N. Durbach and T. J. Stewart. Modeling uncertainty in multi-criteria decision analysis. *European Journal of Operational Research*, 223(1):1–14, 2012.

123. S. M. Eack. Cognitive remediation: A new generation of psychosocial interventions for people with schizophrenia. *Social Work*, 57(3):235–246, 2012.

124. A. E. Eiben and J. E. Smith. *Introduction to Evolutionary Computing*. Natural Computing Series. Springer, 2 edition, 2015.

125. J. Elkerton and S. L. Palmiter. Designing help using a goms model: An information retrieval evaluation. *Human Factors: The Journal of the Human Factors and Ergonomics Society*, 33(2):185–204, 1991.

126. C. Emmanouilidis, C. Batsalas, and N. Papamarkos. Development and evaluation of text localization techniques based on structural texture features and neural classifiers. In *10th International Conference on Document Analysis and Recognition, 2009. ICDAR'09*, pages 1270–1274, 26–29 July 2009.

127. J. M. Epstein. *Generative Social Science: Studies in Agent-Based Computational Modeling*. Princeton University Press, 2006.

128. R. M. Ercsey and Z. Toroczkai. The chaos within sudoku. *Scientific Reports*, 2, 2012. doi: 10.1038/srep00725.

129. G. B. Ermentrout and N. Kopell. Parabolic bursting in an excitable system coupled with a slow oscillation. *SIAM Journal on Applied Mathematics*, 46(2):233–253, 1986.

130. L. Eshelman, D. Ehret, J. McDermott, and M. Tan. Mole: A tenacious knowledge-acquisition tool. *International Journal of Man-Machine Studies*, 26(1): 41–54, 1987.

131. J. Fan, A. Kalyanpur, D. C. Gondek, and D. A. Ferrucci. *IBM Journal of Research and Development*, 56(3/4), 2012.

132. Z. Fanchao, J. Decraene, M. Y. H. Low, W. Cai, P. Hingston, and S. Zhou. High-dimensional objective-based data farming. In *2011 IEEE Symposium on Computational Intelligence for Security and Defense Applications (CISDA)*, pages 80–87, Paris, France, 11–15 April 2011.

133. Z. Fanchao, J. Decraene, M. Y. H. Low, S. Zhou, and C. Wentong. Evolving optimal and diversified military operational plans for computational red teaming. *IEEE Systems Journal*, 6(3):499–509, 2012.

134. J. Ferber. *Multi-Agent Systems: An Introduction to Distributed Artificial Intelligence, volume 1*. Addison-Wesley, Reading, 1999.

135. H. K. Fernlund, A. J. Gonzalez, M. Georgiopoulos, and R. F. DeMara. Learning tactical human behavior through observation of human performance. *IEEE Transactions on Systems, Man, and Cybernetics, Part B: Cybernetics*, 36(1):128–140, Feb 2006.

136. K. Fischer, J. P. Muller, and M. Pischel. Unifying control in a layered agent architecture. *IJCAI95, Agent Theory, Architecture and Language Workshop*, Montreal, Quebec, Canada, 20–25 August 1995.

137. R. A. Fisher. The arrangement of field experiments. In S. Kotz and N. L. Johnson, editors, *Breakthroughs in Statistics*, pages 82–91. Springer, 1992.

138. G. S. Fishman. *Monte Carlo*. Springer-Verlag, New York, 1996.

139. G. S. Fishman. *Discrete-Event Simulation: Modeling, Programming, and Analysis*. Springer Science & Business Media, 2013.

140. G. S. Fishman and L. R. Moore, III. A statistical evaluation of multiplicative congruential random number generators with modulus 2^{31}-1. *Journal of the American Statistical Association*, 77(377):129–136, 1982.

141. G. S. Fishman and L. R. Moore, III. An exhaustive analysis of multiplicative congruential random number generators with modulus 2^{31}-1. *SIAM Journal on Scientific and Statistical Computing*, 7(1):24–45, 1986.

142. D. B. Fogel. An introduction to simulated evolutionary optimization. *IEEE Transactions on Neural Networks*, 5(1):3–14, Jan 1994.

143. D. B. Fogel. *Evolutionary Computation: The Fossil Record*. Wiley-IEEE Press, 1998.

144. L. J. Fogel, A. J. Owens, and M. J. Walsh. Artificial intelligence through a simulation of evolution. In A. Callahan, M. Maxfield, and L. J. Fogel, editors, *Biophysics and Cybernetic Systems: Proceedings of the 2nd Cybernetic Sciences Symposium*, pages 131–155, Washington, DC, 1965. Spartan.

145. K. M. Ford, J. M. Bradshaw, J. R. Adams-Webber, and N. M. Agnew. Knowledge acquisition as a constructive modeling activity. *International Journal of Intelligent Systems*, 8(1):9–32, 1993.

146. T. Fotherby. Visual traffic simulation. Thesis, Imperial College, June 2002.

147. N. Fourcaud-Trocme, D. Hansel, C. van Vreeswijk, and N. Brunel. How spike genera-tion mechanisms determine the neuronal response to fluctuating inputs. *The Journal of Neuroscience*, 23(37):11628–11640, 2003.

148. M. C. Fox, K. A. Ericsson, and R. Best. Do procedures for verbal reporting of thinking have to be reactive? *A meta-analysis and recommendations for best reporting methods. Psychological Bulletin*, 137(2):316–344, 2011.

149. A. S. Fraser. Simulation of genetic systems by automatic digital computers. i. introduc-tion. *Australian Journal of Biological Sciences*, 10:848–491, 1957.

150. R. M. Fujimoto. Parallel and distributed simulation. In *Proceedings of the 31st Conference on Winter Simulation: Simulation – A bridge to the Future-Volume 1*, pages 122–131, Phoenix, AZ, 5–8 December 1999. ACM.

151. F. Gabbiani and S. J. Cox. Reduced single neuron models. In F. Gabbiani and S. J. Cox, editors, *Mathematics for Neuroscientists*, pages 143–154. Academic Press, London, 2010.

152. B. Gaines and M. Shaw. Integrated knowledge acquisition architectures. *Journal of Intelligent Information Systems*, 1(1):9–34, 1992.

153. M. Gardner. Mathematical games: The fantastic combinations of john conway's new solitaire game? *Scientific American*, 223(4):120–123, 1970.

154. D. C. Gazis, R. Herman, and R. W. Rothery. Nonlinear follow-the-leader models of traffic flow. *Operations Research*, 9(4):545–567, 1961.

155. J. Geiwitz, R. L. Klatsky, and M. B. P. *Knowledge Acquisition for Expert Systems: Conceptual and Empirical Comparisons.* Anacapa Sciences, Santa Barbara, CA, 1988.

156. J. E. Gentle. *Random Number Generation and Monte Carlo Methods.* Springer Science & Business Media, 2003.

157. W. Gerstner. A framework for spiking neuron models – The spike response model. In F. Moss and S. Gielen, editors, *Handbook of Biological Physics*, volume 4, pages 469–516. Elsevier, 2001.

158. W. Gerstner and R. Naud. How good are neuron models? *Science*, 326(5951):379–380, 2009.

159. A. Gill. *Introduction to the Theory of Finite-State Machines*, volume 16. McGraw-Hill New York, 1962.

160. D. E. Goldberg and K. Deb. A comparative analysis of selection schemes used in genetic algorithms. *Foundations of Genetic Algorithms*, 1:69–93, 1991.

161. L. R. Goldberg. An alternative "description of personality": The big-five factor structure. *Journal of Personality and Social Psychology*, 59(6):1216–1229, 1990.

162. S. E. Gordon, K. A. Schmierer, and R. T. Gill. Conceptual graph analysis: Knowledge acquisition for instructional systems design. *Human Factors*, 35:459–481, 1993.

163. M. Govaerts, M. Van de Wiel, L. Schuwirth, C. Van der Vleuten, and A. Muijtjens. Workplace-based assessment: Raters' performance theories and constructs. *Advances in Health Sciences Education*, 18(3):375–396, 2013.

164. J. W. Grabbe. Sudoku and working memory performance for older adults. *Activities, Adaptation & Aging*, 35(3):241–254, 2011.

165. W. D. Gray. Cognitive architectures: Choreographing the dance of mental operations with the task environment. *Human Factors: The Journal of the Human Factors and Ergonomics Society*, 50(3):497–505, 2008.

166. W. D. Gray, B. E. John, and M. E. Atwood. Project ernestine: Validating a goms analysis for predicting and explaining real-world task performance. *Human-Computer Interaction*, 8(3):237–309, 1993.

167. V. Grimm. Ten years of individual-based modelling in ecology: What have we learned and what could we learn in the future? *Ecological Modelling*, 115(2):129–148, 1999.

168. V. Grimm, U. Berger, F. Bastiansen, S., et al. A standard protocol for describing individual-based and agent-based models. *Ecological Modelling*, 198(1):115–126, 2006.

169. S. Grimnes and O. G. Martinsen. Excitable tissue and bioelectric signals. In S. Grimnes and O. G. Martinsen, editors, *Bioimpedance and Bioelectricity Basics*, pages 119–139. Academic Press, Oxford, 3rd edition, 2015.

170. D. Gross. *Fundamentals of Queueing Theory*. Wiley, 2008.

171. T. R. Gruber. Automated knowledge acquisition for strategic knowledge. *Machine Learning*, 4(3–4):293–336, 1989.

172. J. A. Guhde. An evaluation tool to measure interdisciplinary critical incident verbal reports. *Nursing Education Perspectives*, 35(3):180–184, 2014.

173. T. Guyet, C. Garbay, and M. Dojat. Knowledge construction from time series data using a collaborative exploration system. *Journal of Biomedical Informatics*, 40(6):672–687, 2007. Intelligent Data Analysis in Biomedicine.

174. D. Z. Hambrick, T. A. Salthouse, and E. J. Meinz. Predictors of crossword puzzle proficiency and moderators of age–cognition relations. *Journal of Experimental Psychology: General*, 128(2):131–164, June 1999.

175. R. Harré and P. F. Secord. *The Explanation of Social Behaviour*. Rowman & Littlefield, Lanham, MD, 1972.

176. B. S. Hasler, P. Tuchman, and D. Friedman. Virtual research assistants: Replacing human interviewers by automated avatars in virtual worlds. *Computers in Human Behavior*, 29(4):1608–1616, 2013.

177. S. S. Haykin, S. S. Haykin, S. S. Haykin, and S. S. Haykin. *Neural Networks and Learning Machines*, volume 3. Pearson Education, Upper Saddle River, 2009.

178. H. J. M. Hermans. The dialogical self as a society of mind: Introduction. *Theory and Psychology*, 12(2):147–160, 2002.

179. P. Hingston, M. Preuss, and D. Spierling. Redtnet: A network model for strategy games. In *2010 IEEE Congress on Evolutionary Computation (CEC)*, pages 1–9, Barcelona, Spain, 18–23 July 2010.

180. R. R. Hoffman. The problem of extracting the knowledge of experts from the perspective of experimental-psychology. *Ai Magazine*, 8(2):53–67, 1987.

181. R. R. Hoffman and L. Militello. *Perspectives on Cognitive Task Analysis: Historical Origins and Modern Communities of Practice*. CRC Press/Taylor & Francis, Boca Raton, FL, 2008.

182. R. R. Hoffman, N. R. Shadbolt, A. Burton, and G. Klein. Eliciting knowledge from experts: A methodological analysis. *Organizational Behavior and Human Decision Processes*, 62(2):129–158, 1995.

183. J. H. Holland. Genetic algorithms and the optimal allocation of trials. *SIAM Journal of Computing*, 2:88–105, 1973.

184. J. H. Holland. *Adaptation in Natural and Artificial Systems: An Introductory Analysis with Applications to Biology, Control, and Artificial Intelligence*. University of Michigan Press, 1975.

185. J. H. Holland and J. H. Miller. Artificial adaptive agents in economic theory. *The American Economic Review*, 81:365–370, 1991.

186. P. W. Holland. Statistics and causal inference. *Journal of the American Statistical Association*, 81(396):945–960, 1986.

187. J. E. Hopcroft. *Introduction to Automata Theory, Languages, and Computation*. Pearson Education India, 1979.

188. J. J. Hopfield. Neural networks and physical systems with emergent collective computational abilities. *Proceedings of the National Academy of Sciences*, 79(8):2554–2558, 1982.

189. J. J. Hopfield. Searching for memories, sudoku, implicit check bits, and the iterative use of not-always-correct rapid neural computation. *Neural Computation*, 20(5):1119–1164, 2008.

190. R. J. Howlett and L. C. Jain. *Radial Basis Function Networks 2: New Advances in Design*, volume 67 of *Studies in Fuzziness and Soft Computing*. Springer-Verlag, Berlin Heidelberg, 2001.

191. I. B. Huang, J. Keisler, and I. Linkov. Multi-criteria decision analysis in environmental sciences: Ten years of applications and trends. *Science of The Total Environment*, 409(19):3578–3594, 2011.

192. T. E. Hull and A. R. Dobell. Random number generators. *SIAM Review*, 4(3):230–254, 1962.

193. D. W. Hutchinson. A new uniform pseudorandom number generator. *Communications of the ACM*, 9(6):432–433, 1966.

194. IEEE standard for floating-point arithmetic. *IEEE Std 754-2008*, pages 1–70, Aug 2008.

195. F. F. Ingrand, M. P. Georgeff, and A. S. Rao. An architecture for real-time reasoning and system control. *IEEE Expert*, 7(6):34–44, 1992.

196. H. Ishibuchi and Y. Nojima. Comparison between fuzzy and interval partitions in evolutionary multiobjective design of rule-based classification systems. In *The 14th IEEE International Conference on Fuzzy Systems, 2005. FUZZ'05*, pages 430–435, Reno, NV, 25 May 2005.

197. E. M. Izhikevich. Resonate-and-fire neurons. *Neural Networks*, 14(6–7):883–894, 2001.

198. E. M. Izhikevich. Simple model of spiking neurons. *IEEE Transactions on Neural Networks*, 14(6):1569–1572, Nov 2003.

199. V. Jagannathan and A. S. Elmaghraby. Medkat: multiple expert delphi-based knowledge acquisition tool. In *Proceedings of the ACM NE Regional Conference*, pages 103–110, Framingham, MA, 28–30 October 1985.

200. I. Jagielska, C. Matthews, and T. Whitfort. An investigation into the application of neural networks, fuzzy logic, genetic algorithms, and rough sets to automated knowledge acquisition for classification problems. *Neurocomputing*, 24(1–3):37–54, 1999.

201. N. R. Jennings. On agent-based software engineering. *Artificial intelligence*, 117(2):277–296, 2000.

202. R. Jolivet, T. J. Lewis, and W. Gerstner. Generalized integrate-and-fire models of neuronal activity approximate spike trains of a detailed model to a high degree of accuracy. *Journal of Neurophysiology*, 92(2):959–976, 2004.

203. D. H. Jonassen, K. Beissner, and M. Yacci. *Structural Knowledge: Techniques for Representing, Conveying, and Acquiring Structural Knowledge*. Routledge, 2013.

204. S.-k. Jun, M. S. Narayanan, P. Agarwal, A. Eddib, P. Singhal, S. Garimella, and V. Krovi. Robotic minimally invasive surgical skill assessment based on automated video-analysis motion studies. In *2012 4th IEEE RAS EMBS International Conference on Biomedical Robotics and Biomechatronics (BioRob)*, pages 25–31, Rome, Italy, 24–27 June 2012.

205. M. Kadhim, M. Alam, and H. Kaur. A multi-intelligent agent for knowledge discovery in database (miakdd): Cooperative approach with domain expert for rules extraction. In *D.-S. Huang, K.-H. Jo, and L. Wang, editors, Intelligent Computing Methodologies, volume 8589 of Lecture Notes in Computer Science, pages 602–614. Springer International Publishing*, 2014.

206. G. Kahn, S. Nowlan, and J. McDermott. More: An intelligent knowledge acquisition tool. In *Proceedings of the Ninth International Conference on Artificial Intelligence*, pages 581–584, Los Angelos, CA, 18–23 August 1985.

207. M. H. Kalos and P. A. Whitlock. *Monte Carlo Methods*. Wiley, 2008.

208. M. Kantardzic. *Data Mining: Concepts, Models, Methods, and Algorithms*. Wiley, New Jersey, 2 edition, 2011.

209. T. Kanungo, D. Mount, N. Netanyahu, C. Piatko, R. Silverman, and A. Wu. An efficient k-means clustering algorithm: Analysis and implementation. *IEEE Transactions on Pattern Analysis and Machine Intelligence*, 24(7):881–892, July 2002.

210. R. M. Karp. Reducibility among combinatorial problems. In R. E. Miller and J. W. Thatcher, editors, *Symposium on the Complexity of Computer Computations*, pages 85–103. Plenum, New York, 1972.

211. R. L. Keeney. Foundations for group decision analysis. *Decision Analysis*, 10(2):103–120, 2013.

212. W. J. Kennedy and J. E. Gentle. *Statistical Computing*. Routledge, New York, 1980.

213. A. Kesting, M. Treiber, and D. Helbing. General lane-changing model mobil for car-following models. *Transportation Research Record: Journal of the Transportation Research Board*, 1999(-1):86–94, 2007.

214. D. E. Kieras. Towards a practical GOMS model methodology for user interface design. In M. Helander, editor, *Handbook of Human-Computer Interaction*, pages 135–157. Amsterdam: Elsevier, 1988.

215. I. S. Kim. Human reliability analysis in the man-machine interface design review. *Annals of Nuclear Energy*, 28(11):1069–1081, 2001.

216. K. Kim, R. B. McKay, and B.-R. Moon. Multiobjective evolutionary algorithms for dynamic social network clustering. In *Proceedings of the 12th Annual Conference on Genetic and Evolutionary Computation*, GECCO '10, pages 1179–1186, New York, 7–11 July 2010. ACM.

217. G. Klein. Using cognitive task analysis to build a cognitive model. *Proceedings of the Human Factors and Ergonomics Society Annual Meeting*, 44(6):596–599, 2000.

218. D. E. Knuth. *The Art of Programming, vol. 2, Semi-Numerical Algorithms*. Pearson Education, 1998.

219. J. Kober and J. Peters. Reinforcement learning in robotics: A survey. In M. Wiering and M. van Otterlo, editors, *Reinforcement Learning, volume 12 of Adaptation, Learning, and Optimization*, pages 579–610. Springer, Berlin Heidelberg, 2012.

220. M. Köhler, D. Moldt, and H. Rölke. Modelling the structure and behaviour of petri net agents. In J.-M. Colom, and M. Koutny, editors, *Applications and Theory of Petri Nets 2001*, pages 224–241. Springer, 2001.

221. T. Kohonen. Self-organized formation of topologically correct feature maps. *Biological Cybernetics*, 43(1):59–69, 1982.

222. J. R. Koza. *Genetic Programming*. MIT Press, Cambridge, MA, 1992.

223. J. R. Koza. *Genetic Programming II*. MIT Press, Cambridge, MA, 1994.

224. J. R. Koza, M. A. Keane, and M. J. Streeter. Evolving inventions. *Scientific American*, 288(2):52–59, 2003.

225. R. Kuo, J. Liao, and C. Tu. Integration of ART2 neural network and genetic k-means algorithm for analyzing web browsing paths in electronic commerce. *Decision Support Systems*, 40(2):355–374, 2005.

226. L. A. Kurgan and P. Musilek. A survey of knowledge discovery and data mining process models. *The Knowledge Engineering Review*, 21(1):1–24, 2006.

227. E. Kuriscak, P. Marsalek, J. Stroffek, and P. G. Toth. Biological context of hebb learning in artificial neural networks, a review. *Neurocomputing*, 152:27–35, 2015.

228. A. W. Kushniruk, H. Monkman, D. Tuden, P. Bellwood, and E. M. Borycki. Integrating heuristic evaluation with cognitive walkthrough: Development of a hybrid usability inspection method. *Studies in Health Technology and Informatics*, 208:221–225, 2015.

229. J. E. Laird. The soar cognitive architecture. *AISB Quarterly*, 134:1–4, 2012.

230. J. E. Laird, A. Newell, and P. S. Rosenbloom. Soar: An architecture for general intelligence. *Artificial Intelligence*, 33(1):1–64, 1987.

231. F. W. Lanchester. Mathematics in warfare. *The World of Mathematics*, 4:2138–2157, 1956.

232. C. G. Langton. *Artificial Life*. Addison-Wesley Publishing Company, Redwood City, CA, 1989.

233. E. V. Larson, R. E. Darilek, D. Gibran, B. Nichiporuk, A. Richardson, L. H. Schwartz, and C. Q. Thurston. Foundations of effective influence operations: A framework for enhancing army capabilities. Technical report, DTIC Document, 2009.

234. A. Law. *Simulation Modeling and Analysis*. McGraw-Hill series in industrial engineering and management science. McGraw-Hill Education, 2014.

235. R. Y. Lau, Y. Li, D. Song, and R. C. W. Kwok. Knowledge discovery for adaptive negotiation agents in e-marketplaces. *Decision Support Systems*, 45(2):310–323, 2008. I.T. and Value Creation.

236. N. Lechevin, C. A. Rabbath, and M. Lauzon. A decision policy for the routing and munitions management of multiformations of unmanned combat vehicles in adversarial urban environments. *IEEE Transactions on Control Systems Technology*, 17(3):505–519, 2009.

237. P. L'Ecuyer. Efficient and portable combined random number generators. *Communications of the ACM*, 31(6):742–751, 1988.

238. P. L'Ecuyer. Combined multiple recursive random number generators. *Operations Research*, 44(5):816–822, 1996.

239. P. L'Ecuyer. Random number generation. In J. Banks, editors, *Handbook of Simulation*, Springer Handbooks of Computational Statistics. Wiley Online Library, 1998.

240. P. L'Ecuyer. Tables of maximally equidistributed combined lfsr generators. *Mathematics of Computation of the American Mathematical Society*, 68(225):261–269, 1999.

241. P. L'Ecuyer. Random number generation. In J. E. Gentle, W. K. Hrdle, and Y. Mori, editors, *Handbook of Computational Statistics*, Springer Handbooks of Computational Statistics, pages 35–71. Springer, Berlin Heidelberg, 2012.

242. P. L'Ecuyer, R. Simard, E. J. Chen, and W. D. Kelton. An object-oriented random-number package with many long streams and substreams. *Operations Research*, 50(6):1073–1075, 2002.

243. D. Lee, H. Seo, and M. W. Jung. Neural basis of reinforcement learning and decision making. *Annual Review of Neuroscience*, 35:287–308, 2012.

244. D. H. Lehmer. Mathematical methods in large-scale computing units. In *Proceedings of the 2nd Symposium on Large-Scale Digital Calculating Machinery*, pages 141–146, Cambridge, MA, 1951. Harvard University Press.

245. J. Lemke. *Analyzing Verbal Data: Principles, Methods, and Problems, volume 24 of Springer International Handbooks of Education, book section 94*, pages 1471–1484. Springer Netherlands, 2012.

246. J. W. Lepingwell. The laws of combat? lanchester reexamined. *International Security*, 12(1):89–134, 1987.

247. G. Leu and H. Abbass. Computational red teaming in a sudoku solving context: Neural network based skill representation and acquisition. In K. Lavangnananda, S. Phon-Amnuaisuk, W. Engchuan, and J. H. Chan, editors, *Intelligent and Evolutionary Systems*, pages 319–332. Springer, 2016.

248. G. Leu and H. Abbass. A multi-disciplinary review of knowledge acquisition methods: From human to autonomous eliciting agents. *Knowledge-Based Systems*, 105:1–22, 2016.

249. G. Leu, H. Abbass, and N. Curtis. Resilience of ground transportation networks: A case study on melbourne. In *Australasian Transport Research Forum (ATRF), 33rd*, 2010, Canberra, ACT, Australia, 2010.

250. G. Leu, N. J. Curtis, and H. A. Abbass. Society of mind cognitive agent architecture applied to drivers adapting in a traffic context. *Adaptive Behavior*, 22(2):123–145, 2014.

251. G. Leu, J. Tang, and H. Abbass. On the role of working memory in trading-off skills and situation awareness in sudoku. In C. Loo, K. Yap, K. Wong, A. Beng Jin, and K. Huang, editors, *Neural Information Processing, volume 8836 of Lecture Notes in Computer Science*, pages 571–578. Springer International Publishing, 2014.

252. P. A. W. Lewis, A. S. Goodman, and J. M. Miller. A pseudo-random number generator for the system/360. *IBM Systems Journal*, 8(2):136–146, 1969.

253. T. G. Lewis and W. H. Payne. Generalized feedback shift register pseudorandom number algorithm. *Journal of the ACM (JACM)*, 20(3):456–468, 1973.

254. Y. Liu, R. Feyen, and O. Tsimhoni. Queueing network-model human processor (qn-mhp): A computational architecture for multitask performance in human-machine systems. *ACM Transactions on Computer-Human Interaction*, 13(1):37–70, March 2006.

255. A. Lotem and J. Y. Halpern. Coevolution of learning and data-acquisition mechanisms: A model for cognitive evolution. *Philosophical Transactions of the Royal Society of London B: Biological Sciences*, 367(1603):2686–2694, 2012.

256. N. Y. Louis Lee, G. P. Goodwin, and P. N. Johnson-Laird. The psychological puzzle of sudoku. *Thinking and Reasoning*, 14(4):342–364, 2008.

257. P. H. Lysaker and J. T. Lysaker. Narrative structure in psychosis: Schizophrenia and disruptions in the dialogical self. *Theory and Psychology*, 12:207–220, 2002.

258. C. M. Macal and M. J. North. Tutorial on agent-based modeling and simulation. In *Proceedings of the 37th Conference on Winter Simulation*, WSC'05, pages 2–15. Winter Simulation Conference, Orlando, FL, 4–7 December 2005.

259. C. M. Macal and M. J. North. Agent-based modeling and simulation. In *Winter Simulation Conference*, pages 86–98. Winter Simulation Conference, 2009.

260. C. M. Macal, M. J. North, and D. A. Samuelson. Agent-based simulation. In S. I. Gass and M. C. Fu, editors, *Encyclopedia of Operations Research and Management Science*, pages 8–16. Springer, 2013.

261. M. D. MacLaren and G. Marsaglia. Uniform random number generators. *Journal of the ACM (JACM)*, 12(1):83–89, 1965.

262. P. Maes. The agent network architecture (ana). *SIGART Bulletin*, 2(4):115–120, 1991.

263. T. Mahatody, M. Sagar, and C. Kolski. State of the art on the cognitive walkthrough method, its variants and evolutions. *International Journal of Human-Computer Interaction*, 2(8):741–785, 2010.

264. S. M. Manson. Bounded rationality in agent-based models: Experiments with evolutionary programs. *International Journal of Geographical Information Science*, 20(9):991–1012, 2006.

265. T. Mantere and J. Koljonen. Solving, rating and generating sudoku puzzles with ga. In *IEEE Congress on Evolutionary Computation*, pages 1382–1389. IEEE, 2007.

266. S. Marcus and J. McDermott. Salt: A knowledge acquisition language for propose-and-revise systems. *Artificial Intelligence*, 39(1):1–37, 1989.

267. G. Marsaglia. Random numbers fall mainly in the planes. *Proceedings of the National Academy of Sciences of the United States of America*, 61(1):25, 1968.

268. G. Marsaglia and T. A. Bray. A convenient method for generating normal variables. *SIAM Review*, 6(3):260–264, 1964.

269. S. Marsland. *Machine Learning: An Algorithmic Perspective*. Macine Learning & Pattern Recognition. CRC Press, Boca Raton, FL, 2 edition, 2014.

270. D. Martin, E. Cross, and M. Alexander. Cracking the sudoku: A deterministic approach. *UMAP Journal*, 29:381–394, 2008.

271. A. J. Masalonis, M. B. Callaham, and C. R. Wanke. Dynamic density and complexity metrics for realtime traffic flow management. In *Proceedings of the 5th USA/Europe Air Traffic Management R & D Seminar*, Budapest, Hungary 23–27 June 2003.

272. M. Matsumoto and Y. Kurita. Twisted gfsr generators ii. *ACM Transactions on Modeling and Computer Simulation (TOMACS)*, 4(3):254–266, 1994.

273. M. Matsumoto and Y. Kurita. Strong deviations from randomness in m-sequences based on trinomials. *ACM Transactions on Modeling and Computer Simulation (TOMACS)*, 6(2):99–106, 1996.

274. B. P. McCloskey, J. Geiwitz, and J. Kornell. Empirical comparisons of knowledge acquisition techniques. *Proceedings of the Human Factors and Ergonomics Society Annual Meeting*, 35(5):268–272, 1991.

275. R. R. McCrae. *NEO-PI-R Data from 36 Cultures: Further Intercultural Comparisons*, pages 105–126. Kluwer Academic/Plenum, New York, 2002.

276. R. R. McCrae and A. Terracciano. Universal features of personality traits from the observer's perspective: Data from 50 cultures. *Journal of Personality and Social Psychology*, 88(3):547–561, 2005.

277. W. McCulloch and W. Pitts. A logical calculus of the ideas immanent in nervous activity. *The Bulletin of Mathematical Biophysics*, 5(4):115–133, 1943.

278. B. D. McCullough and D. A. Heiser. On the accuracy of statistical procedures in microsoft excel 2007. *Computational Statistics & Data Analysis*, 52(10):4570–4578, 2008.

279. T. M. McKenna, J. L. Davis, and S. F. Zornetzer. *Single Neuron Computation*. Academic Press, 1992.

280. A. I. McLeod. Remark as r58: A remark on algorithm as 183. An efficient and portable pseudo-random number generator. *Applied Statistics*, 31(2):198–200, 1985.

281. N. Metropolis. The beginning of the monte carlo method. *Los Alamos Science*, 15(584):125–130, 1987.

282. M. A. Meyer. How to apply the anthropological technique of participant observation to knowledge acquisition for expert systems. *IEEE Transactions on Systems, Man and Cybernetics*, 22(5):983–991, Sep 1992.

283. S. Mihalas and E. Niebur. A generalized linear integrate-and-fire neural model produces diverse spiking behaviors. *Neural Computation*, 21(3):704–718, 2008.

284. A. Milani and V. Poggioni. Planning in reactive environments. *Computational Intelligence*, 23(4):439–463, 2007.

285. L. G. Militello and R. R. Hoffman. The forgotten history of cognitive task analysis. *Proceedings of the Human Factors and Ergonomics Society Annual Meeting*, 52(4):383–387, 2008.

286. B. L. Miller and D. E. Goldberg. Genetic algorithms, tournament selection, and the effects of noise. *Complex Systems*, 9(3):193–212, 1995.

287. M. Minsky. *The Society of Mind*. Simon and Schuster, New York, 1985.

288. M. Minsky. Society of mind: A response to four reviews. *Artificial Intelligence*, 48(3):371–396, 1991.

289. T. M. Mitchell. *Machine Learning. McGraw Hill*, Burr Ridge, IL, page 45, 1997.

290. R. M. Miura. Analysis of excitable cell models. *Journal of Computational and Applied Mathematics*, 144(1–2):29–47, 2002. Selected papers of the International symposium on Applied Mathematics, August 2000, Dalian, China.

291. M. Mohri, A. Rostamizadeh, and A. Talwalkar. *Foundations of Machine Learning*. MIT Press, 2012.

292. D. C. Montgomery. *Design and Analysis of Experiments*. Wiley, 2008.

293. M. Moradi, A. Aghaie, and M. Hosseini. Knowledge-collector agents: Applying intelligent agents in marketing decisions with knowledge management approach. *Knowledge-Based Systems*, 52:181–193, 2013.

294. W. M. Mount, D. C. Tucek, and H. A. Abbass. A psychophysiological analysis of weak annoyances in human computer interfaces. In T. Huang, Z. Zeng, C. Li, and C. Leung, editors, *Neural Information Processing*, volume 7663 of *Lecture Notes in Computer Science*, pages 202–209. Springer, Berlin Heidelberg, 2012.

295. W. M. Mount, D. C. Tucek, and H. A. Abbass. Psychophysiological evaluation of task complexity and cognitive performance in a human computer interface experiment. In T. Huang, Z. Zeng, C. Li, and C. Leung, editors, *Neural Information Processing*, volume

7663 of *Lecture Notes in Computer Science*, pages 600–607. Springer, Berlin Heidelberg, 2012.

296. A. Mukhopadhyay and U. Maulik. A multiobjective approach to MR brain image segmentation. *Applied Soft Computing*, 11(1):872–880, 2011.

297. A. Mukhopadhyay, U. Maulik, S. Bandyopadhyay, and C. Coello. Survey of multiobjective evolutionary algorithms for data mining: Part ii. *IEEE Transactions on Evolutionary Computation*, 18(1):20–35, Feb 2014.

298. A. Mukhopadhyay, U. Maulik, S. Bandyopadhyay, and C. Coello. A survey of multiobjective evolutionary algorithms for data mining: Part i. *IEEE Transactions on Evolutionary Computation*, 18(1):4–19, Feb 2014.

299. R. E. Nance and C. Overstreet Jr. Some experimental observations on the behavior of composite random number generators. *Operations Research*, 26(5):915–935, 1978.

300. I. M. Neale. First generation expert systems: A review of knowledge acquisition methodologies. *The Knowledge Engineering Review*, 3:105–145, 1988.

301. R. E. Neapolitan. *Probabilistic Reasoning in Expert Systems: Theory and Algorithms*. CreateSpace Independent Publishing Platform, USA, 2012.

302. A. Newell. *Unified Theories of Cognition*. Harvard University Press, Cambridge, MA, 1990.

303. E. W. T. Ngai, L. Xiu, and D. C. K. Chau. Application of data mining techniques in customer relationship management: A literature review and classification. *Expert Systems with Applications*, 36(2, Part 2):2592–2602, 2009.

304. H. Nguyen, T.-D. Luu, O. Poch, and J. D. Thompson. Knowledge discovery in variant databases using inductive logic programming. *Bioinformatics and Biology Insights*, 7:119–131, 2013.

305. C. Nombela, P. J. Bustillo, P. Castell, V. Medina, and M.-T. Herrero. Cognitive rehabilitation in parkinson's disease: Evidences from neuroimaging. *Frontiers in Neurology*, 2:82, 2011.

306. P. Norvig. Solving every sudoku puzzle, 2014. https://norvig.com/sudoku.html [Online; accessed 22 August 2019].

307. J. J. Nutaro. *Discrete-Time Systems*, pages 32–99. Wiley, 2010.

308. L. Nyberg, J. Eriksson, A. Larsson, and P. Marklund. Learning by doing versus learning by thinking: an fmri study of motor and mental training. *Neuropsychologia*, 44(5):711–717, 2006.

309. N. M. Oliver, B. Rosario, and A. P. Pentland. A bayesian computer vision system for modeling human interactions. *IEEE Transactions on Pattern Analysis and Machine Intelligence*, 22(8):831–843, 2000.

310. OneSAF. 2015. https://www.peostri.army.mil/onesaf [Online; accessed 22 August 2019].

311. M. Oprea. An adaptive negotiation model for agent-based electronic commerce. *Studies in Informatics and Control*, 11(3):271–279, 2002.

312. G. Orru, W. Pettersson-Yeo, A. F. Marquand, G. Sartori, and A. Mechelli. Using support vector machine to identify imaging biomarkers of neurological and psychiatric disease: A critical review. *Neuroscience & Biobehavioral Reviews*, 36(4):1140–1152, 2012.

313. L. A. Overbey, G. McKoy, J. Gordon, and S. McKitrick. Automated sensing and social network analysis in virtual worlds. In *2010 IEEE International Conference on Intelligence and Security Informatics (ISI)*, pages 179–184, May 2010.

314. J. A. Pacurib, G. M. M. Seno, and J. P. T. Yusiong. Solving sudoku puzzles using improved artificial bee colony algorithm. In *Fourth International Conference on Innovative Computing, Information and Control*, pages 885–888. IEEE, 2009.

315. H. Paugam-Moisy and S. Bohte. Computing with spiking neuron networks. In G. Rozenberg, T. Back, and J. N. Kok, editors, *Handbook of Natural Computing*, pages 335–376. Springer, Berlin Heidelberg, 2012.

316. W. Payne, J. R. Rabung, and T. Bogyo. Coding the lehmer pseudo-random number generator. *Communications of the ACM*, 12(2):85–86, 1969.

317. M. Perez and T. Marwala. Stochastic optimization approaches for solving sudoku. *e-print arXiv:0805.0697*, May 2008.

318. E. Petraki and H. Abbass. On trust and influence: A computational red teaming game theoretic perspective. In *2014 Seventh IEEE Symposium on Computational Intelligence for Security and Defense Applications (CISDA)*, pages 1–7. IEEE, December 2014.

319. O. Petrovic and A. Brand. *Serious Games on the Move*. Springer, 2009.

320. J. Pitts. *Master Sudoku*. Teach yourself. McGraw-Hill Companies, Inc., 2010.

321. Powersim. http://www.powersim.com/, 2014. [Online; accessed 14 October 2014].

322. W. H. Press. *Numerical Recipes 3rd Edition: The Art of Scientific Computing*. Cambridge University Press, 2007.

323. A. A. B. Pritsker. *Introduction to Stimulation and Slam II*. Wiley, New York, 1986.

324. J. R. Quinlan. Simplifying decision trees. *International Journal of Man-Machine Studies*, 27(3):221–234, 1987.

325. M. Raberto, S. Cincotti, S. M. Focardi, and M. Marchesi. Agent-based simulation of a financial market. *Physica A: Statistical Mechanics and its Applications*, 299(1):319–327, 2001.

326. C. G. Ralha and C. V. S. Silva. A multi-agent data mining system for cartel detection in brazilian government procurement. *Expert Systems with Applications*, 39(14):11642–11656, 2012.

327. A. Ralston and P. Rabinowitz. *A First Course in Numerical Analysis*. Courier Corporation, 2012.

328. A. S. Rao and M. P. Georgeff. Bdi-agents: From theory to practice. In *The First International Conference on Multiagent Systems (ICMAS'95)*, 1995.

329. S. Rastegari, P. Hingston, L. Chiou-Peng, and M. Brand. Testing a distributed denial of service defence mechanism using red teaming. In *2013 IEEE Symposium on Computational Intelligence for Security and Defense Applications (CISDA)*, pages 23–29, 2013.

330. P. Rebentrost, M. Mohseni, and S. Lloyd. Quantum support vector machine for big data classification. *Physical Review Letters*, 113:130503, Sep 2014.

331. I. Rechenberg. *Evolutionsstrategie–Optimierung Technisher Systeme nach Prinzipien der Biologischen Evolution*. Frommann-Holzboog, 1973.

332. C. Reed and G. Rowe. Araucaria: Software for argument analysis, diagramming and representation. *International Journal on Artificial Intelligence Tools*, 13(4):961–979, 2004.

333. Repast. http://repast.sourceforge.net/docs.php, 2015. [Online; accessed 26 May 2015].

334. C. W. Reynolds. Flocks, herds and schools: A distributed behavioral model. In *ACM SIGGRAPH Computer Graphics*, volume 21, pages 25–34. ACM, 1987.

335. C. W. Reynolds. Boids, 2006. https://www.red3d.com/cwr/boids/ [Online; accessed 25 May 2014].

336. L. Rokach. *Data Mining with Decision Trees: Theory and Applications*. Machine Perception and Artificial Intelligence. World scientific, 2007.

337. F. Rosenblatt. The perceptron: A probabilistic model for information storage and organization in the brain. *Psychological Review*, 65(6):386–408, 1958.

338. E. M. Roth, J. O'Hara, A. Bisantz, M. R. Endsley, R. Hoffman, G. Klein, L. Militello, and J. D. Pfautz. Discussion panel: How to recognize a "good" cognitive task analysis? *Proceedings of the Human Factors and Ergonomics Society Annual Meeting*, 58(1):320–324, 2014.

339. E. M. Roth, D. D. Woods, and H. E. Pople. Cognitive simulation as a tool for cognitive task analysis. *Ergonomics*, 35(10):1163–1198, 1992.

340. S. Russell and P. Norvig. *Artificial Intelligence: A Modern Approach*. Prentice Hall, New York, 1995.

341. V. Rybakov. Logic of knowledge and discovery via interacting agents – Decision algorithm for true and satisfiable statements. *Information Sciences*, 179(11):1608–1614, 2009. Including Special Issue on Chance Discovery Discovery of Significant Events for Decision.

342. K. Salmon, M.-E. Pipe, A. Malloy, and K. Mackay. Do non-verbal aids increase the effectiveness of best practice verbal interview techniques? an experimental study. *Applied Cognitive Psychology*, 26(3):370–380, 2012.

343. D. D. Salvucci. Modeling driver behavior in a cognitive architecture. *Human Factors: The Journal of the Human Factors and Ergonomics Society*, 48(2):362–380, 2006.

344. D. D. Salvucci. Integration and reuse in cognitive skill acquisition. *Cognitive Science*, 37(5):829–860, 2013.

345. M. Scheutz and B. Logan. Affective vs. deliberative agent control. In *AISB'01 Symposium on Emotion, Cognition and Affective Computing*, pages 1–10, 2001.

346. B. W. Schmeiser and M. A. Shalaby. Acceptance/rejection methods for beta variate generation. *Journal of the American Statistical Association*, 75(371):673–678, 1980.

347. J. Schmidhuber. Deep learning in neural networks: An overview. *Neural Networks*, 61:85–117, 2015.

348. J. W. Schmidt and R. E. Taylor. *Simulation and Analysis of Industrial Systems*. RD Irwin, 1970.

349. D. P. Schmitt, J. Allik, R. McCrae, and V. Benet-Martínez. The geographic distribution of big five personality traits: Patterns and profiles of human self-description across 56 nations. *Journal of Cross-Cultural Psychology*, 38(2):173–212, 2007.

350. W. Schneider and A. D. Fisk. Attention theory and mechanisms for skilled performance. In R. A. Magill, editor, *Memory and Control of Action, volume 12 of Advances in Psychology*, pages 119–143. North-Holland, 1983.

351. J. M. Schraagen, S. F. Chipman, and V. L. Shalin. *Cognitive Task Analysis*. Lawrence Erlbaum Associates, Mahwah, NJ, 2000.

352. T. J. Schriber, D. T. Brunner, and J. S. Smith. Inside discrete-event simulation software: How it works and why it matters. In *Simulation Conference (WSC), 2013 Winter*, pages 424–438. IEEE, 2013.

353. L. F. Schroeder and A. L. C. Bazzan. A multi-agent system to facilitate knowledge discovery: An application to bioinformatics. In *Workshop on Bioinformatics and Multi-Agent Systems*, pages 44–50, 2002.

354. H. P. Schwefel. *Evolution and Optimum Seeking.* Wiley, New York, 1995.

355. J. Secretan, M. Georgiopoulos, A. Koufakou, and K. Cardona. Aphid: An architecture for private, high-performance integrated data mining. *Future Generation Computer Systems*, 26(7):891–904, 2010.

356. L. Servi and S. B. Elson. A mathematical approach to gauging influence by identifying shifts in the emotions of social media users. *IEEE Transactions on Computational Social Systems*, 1(4):180–190, 2014.

357. E. Shmueli, V. K. Singh, B. Lepri, and A. Pentland. Sensing, understanding, and shaping social behavior. *IEEE Transactions on Computational Social Systems*, 1(1):22–34, 2014.

358. H. A. Simon. A behavioral model of rational choice. *The Quarterly Journal of Economics*, 69(1):99–118, 1955.

359. H. Simonis. Sudoku as a constraint problem. In *CP Workshop on Modeling and Reformulating Constraint Satisfaction Problems*, volume 12, pages 13–27. Citeseer, 2005.

360. A. Sloman. *The cognition and affect projetc: Architectures, architecture-schemas, and the new science of mind.* Technical report, School of Computer Science, University of Birmingham, 2008.

361. G. D. Smith, C. L. Cox, S. M. Sherman, and J. Rinzel. Fourier analysis of sinusoidally driven thalamocortical relay neurons and a minimal integrate-and-fire-or-burst model. *Journal of Neurophysiology*, 83(1):588–610, 2000.

362. J. F. Sowa. Conceptual analysis as a basis for knowledge acquisition. In R. R. Hoffman, editor, *The Psychology of Expertise*, pages 80–96. Psychology Press, New York, 2014.

363. N. A. Stanton, S. P. M., G. H. Walker, L. A. Rafferty, C. Baber, and D. P. Jenkins. *Human Factors Methods: A Practical Guide for Engineering and Design.* Ashgate Publishing, Ltd., 2 edition, 2013.

364. R. B. Stein. A theoretical analysis of neuronal variability. *Biophysical Journal*, 5(2):173–194, 1965.

365. J. D. Sterman. *Business Dynamics: Systems Thinking and Modeling for a Complex World*, volume 19. Irwin/McGraw-Hill, Boston, MA, 2000.

366. C. F. Stevens and A. M. Zador. Novel integrate-and-fire-like model of repetitive firing in cortical neurons. In *The 5th Joint Symposium on Neural Computation*, La Jolla, CA, 1998.

367. F. Stulp and O. Sigaud. Many regression algorithms, one unified model: A review. *Neural Networks*, 69:60–79, 2015.

368. R. Sun. A tutorial on clarion 5.0. Technical report, Cognitive Science Department Rensselaer Polytechnic Institute, 2002.

369. R. Sun. *The CLARION Cognitive Architecture: Extending Cognitive Modeling to Social Simulation.* Cambridge University Press, New York, 2006.

370. M. Sung, M. Gleicher, and S. Chenney. Scalable behaviors for crowd simulation. In M. P. Cani and M. Slater, editors, *Computer Graphics Forum*, volume 23, pages 519–528. Wiley Online Library, 2004.

371. J. M. Swaminathan, S. F. Smith, and N. M. Sadeh. Modeling supply chain dynamics: A multiagent approach. *Decision Sciences*, 29(3):607–632, 1998.

372. H. Takagi. Statitical tests, 2013. Kyushu University. http://www.design.kyushu-u.ac .jp/~takagi/TAKAGI/downloadable/StatisticalTests_en.ppsx [Online: accessed on 22 August 2019]

373. Y. Takayuki and S. Takahiro. Complexity and completeness of finding another solution and its application to puzzles. *IEICE Transactions on Fundamentals of Electronics, Communications and Computer Sciences*, 86(5):1052–1060, 2003.

374. J. Tang, E. Petraki, and H. Abbass. Shaping influence and influencing shaping: A computational red teaming trust-based swarm intelligence model. In *International Conference in Swarm Intelligence*, pages 14–23. Springer, 2016.

375. R. C. Tausworthe. Random numbers generated by linear recurrence modulo two. *Mathematics of Computation*, 19(90):201–209, 1965.

376. J. G. Taylor. *Lanchester Models of Warfare*, volume 2. Ketron, Inc., 1983.

377. L. Tesfatsion. Agent-based computational economics: Growing economies from the bottom up. *Artificial Life*, 8(1):55–82, 2002.

378. S. Tezuka. *Uniform Random Numbers: Theory and Practice*, volume 315. Springer, 1995.

379. W. Thomson. Ernie–a mathematical and statistical analysis. *Journal of the Royal Statistical Society. Series A (General)*, 122(3):301–333, 1959.

380. C. Tofel-Grehl and D. F. Feldon. Cognitive task analysis-based training: A meta-analysis of studies. *Journal of Cognitive Engineering and Decision Making*, 7(3):293–304, 2013.

381. D. C. Tucek, W. M. Mount, and H. A. Abbass. Neural and speech indicators of cognitive load for sudoku game interfaces. In T. Huang, Z. Zeng, C. Li, and C. Leung, editors, *Neural Information Processing*, volume 7663 of *Lecture Notes in Computer Science*, pages 210–217. Springer, Berlin Heidelberg, 2012.

382. A. M. Turing. On computable numbers, with an application to the entscheidungsproblem. *Journal of Math*, 58(345–363):5, 1936.

383. A. M. Turing. Intelligent machinery, a heretical theory. *The Turing Test: Verbal Behavior as the Hallmark of Intelligence*, 4(3):105, 1948.

384. A. M. Turing. *Computing Machinery and Intelligence*, pages 23–65. Springer Netherlands, Dordrecht, 2009.

385. C. W. Ueberhuber. *Numerical Computation 1: Methods, Software, and Analysis.*, volume 16. Springer Science & Business Media, 1997.

386. E. G. Ulrich. Event manipulation for discrete simulations requiring large numbers of events. *Communications of the ACM*, 21(9):777–785, Sep 1978.

387. S. B. Van Hemel, J. MacMillan, G. L. Zacharias, et al. *Behavioral Modeling and Simulation:: From Individuals to Societies*. National Academies Press, 2008.

388. I. Vatolkin. Exploration of two-objective scenarios on supervised evolutionary feature selection: A survey and a case study (application to music categorisation). In A. Gaspar-Cunha, C. Henggeler Antunes, and C. C. Coello, editors, *Evolutionary Multi-Criterion Optimization, volume 9019 of Lecture Notes in Computer Science*, pages 529–543. Springer International Publishing, 2015.

389. E. Vidal, F. Thollard, C. De La Higuera, F. Casacuberta, and R. C. Carrasco. Probabilistic finite-state machines-part i. *IEEE Transactions on Pattern Analysis and Machine Intelligence*, 27(7):1013–1025, 2005.

390. J. Von Neumann. Various techniques used in connection with random digits. *National Bureau of Standards Applied Mathematics Series*, 12:36–38, 1951.

391. VPPIA. Victoria's project prioritisation submission to infrastructure australia 2008. Report, Department of Transport, State Government of Victoria, Australia, 2008.

392. R. Wang. Simulating working memory guiding visual attention for capturing target by computational cognitive model. In J. Zhang, editor, *Applied Informatics and Communication*, volume 226 of *Communications in Computer and Information Science*, pages 352–359. Springer, Berlin Heidelberg, 2011.

393. R. Wang and N. Zhong. Effect of advanced cognitive processing to brain activation pattern and cognitive system simulation. *Application Research of Computers*, 9:21, 2011.

394. S. L. Wang, K. Shafi, C. Lokan, and H. A. Abbass. An agent-based model to simulate and analyse behaviour under noisy and deceptive information. *Adaptive Behavior*, 21(2):96–117, 2013.

395. S. Ward. 6.004 computation structures, 2009. (Accessed 11 May 2015). License: Creative Commons BY-NC-SA.

396. J. Watson, H. A. Abbass, C. Lokan, and P. Lindsay. Software engineering for artificial life, complex systems, and agent-based distillation. In *Proceedings of the 7th Asia-Pacific Conference on Complex Systems*, Cairns, Australia, 6–10 December 2004.

397. T. Weber. A sat-based sudoku solver. In *The 12th International Conference on Logic for Programming Artificial Intelligence and Reasoning*, pages 11–15, 2005.

398. J. Wei and G. Salvendy. The cognitive task analysis methods for job and task design: Review and reappraisal. *Behaviour & Information Technology*, 23(4):273–299, 2004.

399. B. A. Wichmann and I. D. Hill. Algorithm as 183: An efficient and portable pseudo-random number generator. *Applied Statistics*, pages 188–190, 1982.

400. B. Widrow and M. Lehr. 30 years of adaptive neural networks: Perceptron, madaline, and backpropagation. *Proceedings of the IEEE*, 78(9):1415–1442, Sep 1990.

401. U. Wilensky. Flocking. Center for Connected Learning and Computer-Based Modeling, Northwestern University, Evanston, IL. http://ccl.northwestern.edu/netlogo/models/Flocking, 1999. [Online; accessed 25 May 2014].

402. U. Wilensky. Netlogo. Center for Connected Learning and Computer-Based Modeling, Northwestern University, Evanston, IL. https://ccl.northwestern.edu/netlogo/, 1999. [Online; accessed 14 November 2014].

403. U. Wilensky. Wolf sheep predation model. Center for Connected Learning and Computer-Based Modeling, Northwestern University, Evanston, IL. http://ccl.northwestern.edu/netlogo/models/WolfSheepPredation, 1999. [Online; accessed 25 May 2014].

404. B. Woodward. Knowledge acquisition at the front end: defining the domain. *Knowledge Acquisition*, 2(1):73–94, 1990.

405. A. Yang, H. Abbass, and R. Sarker. Wisdom-ii: A network centric model for warfare. In R. Khosla, R. Howlett, and L. Jain, editors, *Knowledge-Based Intelligent Information and Engineering Systems, volume 3683 of Lecture Notes in Computer Science*, pages 813–819. Springer, Berlin Heidelberg, 2005.

406. K. A. Yates. Towards a taxonomy of cognitive task analysis moethods: A search for cognition and task analysis interactions. Thesis, 2007.

407. K. A. Yates and D. F. Feldon. Advancing the practice of cognitive task analysis: A call for taxonomic research. *Theoretical Issues in Ergonomics Science*, 12(6):472–495, 2011.

408. N. Yee and J. N. Bailenson. A method for longitudinal behavioral data collection in second life. *Presence: Teleoperators and Virtual Environments*, 17(6):594–596, 2008.

409. T.-W. Yue and Z.-C. Lee. *Sudoku Solver by Q'tron Neural Networks*, volume 4113 of Lecture Notes in Computer Science, book section 115, pages 943–952. Springer, Berlin Heidelberg, 2006.

410. W. Zhao, S. Alam, and H. A. Abbass. Evaluating ground-air network vulnerability in an integrated terminal maneuvering area using co-evolutionary computational red teaming. *Transportation Research Part C: Emerging Technologies*, 29(4):32–54, 2013.

411. A. Zhou, B.-Y. Qu, H. Li, S.-Z. Zhao, P. N. Suganthan, and Q. Zhang. Multiobjective evolutionary algorithms: A survey of the state of the art. *Swarm and Evolutionary Computation*, 1(1):32–49, 2011.

412. D. Zhou, W. Rao, and F. Lv. A multi-agent distributed data mining model based on algorithm analysis and task prediction. In *2nd International Conference on Information Engineering and Computer Science*, pages 1–4, Dec 2010.

abstraction, 6, 13, 19, 20, 28–30, 39, 73–76, 78, 80, 82, 84, 86, 88, 90, 92, 94, 96, 98, 127, 239, 271, 305, 306
activity scanning, 57, 58, 60, 61, 64
adaptation, 222, 234, 257, 271
agent, 58, 62, 63, 67, 68, 72, 79, 81, 99, 179–187, 190–195, 203–205, 208, 209, 211–217, 242, 244–246, 256–260, 264, 273, 275, 284, 301–312, 314, 316, 318, 322, 326, 330, 331, 334–337, 340–348
   heterarchy, 306, 307
agent-based modelling, 179, 185, 263
agent-based simulation, 11, 23, 62, 63, 67, 179–194
agent-oriented worldview, 58, 62–64
air traffic, 263–270, 272
   controller, 263
   simulation, 263, 265, 267, 269
air traffic operations and management simulator (ATOMS), 13, 263–267, 270, 272
analytic representation, 85
artificial intelligence, 3, 81
artificial neural networks, 213, 219, 221, 232, 235, 237, 239
assumption, 7–9, 12, 17–19, 28–30, 34, 38, 39, 74, 85, 86, 97, 101, 102, 110, 111, 149, 153, 180, 182, 210, 211, 258, 281, 298, 300, 304, 306, 311, 350
autonomous machine agents, 199

battlefield management simulation, 256, 257, 259
behaviour, 5–8, 11–14, 17–20, 23, 28, 32, 36, 46, 62, 64, 73–77, 79, 81, 84, 86–90, 94, 95, 97–99, 101, 110, 113, 118–120, 123, 124, 147, 150–153, 170, 172, 179–187,

189, 192–195, 199–201, 203, 205, 206, 210–212, 214, 219–224, 232, 239, 240, 242, 244, 249, 255–257, 261, 264, 281, 296, 298, 300–304, 311, 313, 314, 316, 317, 320, 322, 326, 328, 330, 331, 333–335, 343, 345–348, 401
blue agent, 243, 244, 273, 275, 334–337, 340–347

challenge, 30, 163, 216, 240, 242, 245, 248, 249, 273–275
   loop, 242
cognitive agent, 211, 302–307
cognitive state, 270
cognitive task analysis, 199, 201, 274, 275
computational intelligence, 212, 219, 220, 222, 224–226, 228, 230, 232, 234–236, 238–241, 255, 288
computational red teaming, 1, 3, 4, 6, 8, 9, 11, 27, 57, 73, 101, 123, 143, 157, 179, 197, 199, 216, 219, 241–250, 253, 255, 256, 258, 260, 263, 264, 266, 268, 270, 272–274, 276, 278, 280, 282, 284, 286, 288, 290, 292, 294, 296, 298, 300–302, 304, 306, 308, 310, 312, 314, 316, 318, 320, 322, 324, 326, 328, 330, 333, 334, 336, 340, 342, 344, 346, 348, 349, 397
conditional probabilities, 356, 359
conflict resolution, 57, 58, 60, 62, 64, 66, 68, 70, 72, 264
constraints, 7, 17, 28, 67, 68, 72, 75, 205, 247, 249, 273, 276–278, 282, 283, 287, 334, 335
continuous simulation, 159, 164, 172, 177
continuous system, 157–159, 161–164, 167, 175–177
cumulative distribution function, 48, 361, 366

Simulation and Computational Red Teaming for Problem Solving, First Edition.
Jiangjun Tang, George Leu, and Hussein A. Abbass.
© 2020 by The Institute of Electrical and Electronics Engineers, Inc. Published 2020 by John Wiley & Sons, Inc.

decentralised control, 256
decision making, 4, 5, 81, 200, 210, 241–244,
    258, 261, 300, 302–307
decision tree, 81, 82, 203, 204, 212, 215
deep neural network, 276, 284, 286, 288, 289
discrete–continuous simulation, 157, 174,
    175, 177
discrete event simulation, 11, 21, 58, 123, 124,
    126–130, 132–142, 149
discrete event system, 123–126, 139, 141, 142,
    145, 155
discrete time simulation, 143–146, 148–150,
    152, 154
discrete time system, 143–148, 154
distribution function, 48, 116, 132, 134, 315,
    361, 362, 365, 366, 368, 370, 372, 374,
    377, 379, 382, 385, 387, 415–419,
    421, 422
domain propagation skills, 278–280, 284, 286,
    288, 293
driver agent, 301, 302, 306, 308, 309, 311,
    314–316, 318, 319, 326, 330, 331
driver behaviour, 301, 302, 328

effect, 5, 7, 14, 17, 102, 103, 105–111, 113,
    114, 133, 145, 175, 200, 221, 234, 245,
    246, 259, 270, 306, 322, 326, 333–336,
    338–348
environment, 6, 14–17, 24, 27–29, 33, 36, 79,
    89, 146, 147, 179–183, 185, 186, 190,
    199, 210, 211, 220–223, 232, 239, 243,
    244, 246, 256–258, 263, 264, 266, 268,
    271, 272, 301–303, 309–313, 315, 317,
    319, 321, 323, 328, 331, 333, 334, 343
Euler's method, 22, 39, 159, 164–170,
    172, 177
event, 11, 21, 23, 24, 30, 31, 57–62, 64–72, 81,
    86–88, 94, 116, 117, 120, 123–142, 145,
    149–151, 155, 157, 174–176, 184, 189,
    190, 192, 194, 195, 207, 242, 250, 304,
    305, 307, 349, 351, 353–361, 368, 370,
    379, 385, 390, 391, 396, 424, 425
    priority, 67–69, 71
    scheduling, 57–59, 61, 62, 64, 65, 185
evolutionary algorithm, 223, 225
evolutionary computation, 86, 212, 213, 223,
    225, 227, 231

factor screening, 102, 103, 105, 109, 111,
    113, 117
fidelity, 19, 20, 74
finite-state machine, 86, 87, 89, 91, 93, 95, 97
flocking, 185, 187, 188, 195
flow, 76, 79, 268

flowchart, 79, 80, 104, 131, 137, 138
formal representation, 76, 77, 79, 81–83, 85,
    199

hierarchical structure, 256, 257
human activity system, 200, 201,
    212, 215, 243
human-in-the-loop, 263, 270, 271
hypothesis, 33, 101, 110, 111, 118, 133, 319,
    409–411
    test, 110, 118, 133, 410

independent event, 359, 368
influence, 222, 316, 334
informal representation, 75
input sampling, 116
interaction space, 181, 183–187, 192, 194

knowledge acquisition, 5, 199–202, 205, 206,
    208–210, 212, 214–217
knowledge discovery, 199, 201, 202,
    212–214

logical representation, 74, 82

machine learning, 82, 86, 212–214, 219, 223,
    235, 255, 287, 288
mining agent, 213, 214
modelling, 3, 4, 6–9, 11–24, 27–35, 37–39, 41,
    43, 46, 51, 55, 57, 58, 61, 64, 69, 70,
    72–75, 78–82, 85–90, 94–95, 97, 99,
    101–105, 108–111, 113–120, 125–130,
    133, 134, 141–147, 149–155, 159–161,
    163, 172–175, 177, 179–185, 187–191,
    194, 195, 199, 202–205, 208–211, 214,
    215, 219–222, 232, 234, 235, 239–243,
    245, 251, 255–257, 260–261, 263, 264,
    267, 271, 274–276, 280, 283, 284, 286,
    290, 296, 298, 300–303, 305, 306, 311,
    314, 333–335, 337, 340, 341, 343, 344,
    347, 349, 360, 369, 370, 374, 377, 379,
    385, 387, 396, 398
Monte Carlo, 21, 413, 423–425, 427–433
    simulations, 424, 428
multi-agent system, 179

natural system, 179, 200, 201
neighbour, 181, 183, 186, 187, 313, 314, 316,
    334–337, 340, 343
non-linear interaction, 256, 333
numerical solution technique, 164, 165, 167,
    169, 171

objective, 6, 8, 18, 20, 21, 27–30, 36, 40, 67, 72, 74, 86, 99, 101, 102, 115, 118, 120, 125, 127, 139, 141, 143, 147, 149, 219, 220, 223, 225–227, 239, 241, 242, 245, 247–250, 256, 270, 274, 350, 398
output analysis, 101, 117–120

parallel and distributed simulation, 23
predator-prey, 158, 187, 195
priority queue, 57, 68, 69, 71, 72, 102
probability, 30, 32, 38, 46, 48, 49, 79, 102, 110, 117, 130, 131, 133, 134, 225, 228–231, 258, 315, 328, 329, 336, 340, 349–370, 372, 374, 376, 378–394, 396–398, 413, 415, 423–429
problem solving, 1, 3–9, 11, 12, 27, 34, 57, 73, 101, 123, 143, 157, 179, 199, 210, 211, 219, 224, 241, 255, 263, 273, 301, 333, 349, 397
process interaction, 57, 58, 60–62, 64, 214

queue, 57–61, 68, 69, 71, 72, 102, 118, 125–129, 132, 133, 136–141
queueing system, 21, 30, 58, 118, 123–127, 129, 132, 136, 137, 139, 141, 142, 387

random event, 81, 349, 351
random variable, 21, 110, 116, 117, 134, 139, 360–362, 364, 365, 368, 370, 372, 374, 377, 379, 382, 390, 391, 393, 395, 396, 398, 412, 414–418, 420, 421, 429–431
random variates, 133–136, 141, 142, 397, 398, 413–424, 429, 433
red agent, 242, 246, 273, 334–348
red teaming, 1, 3, 4, 6, 8, 9, 11, 27, 57, 73, 101, 123, 143, 157, 179, 197, 199, 216, 219, 241–250, 253, 255, 256, 258, 260, 263, 264, 266, 268, 270, 272–274, 276, 278, 280, 282, 284, 286, 288, 290, 292, 294, 296, 298, 300–302, 304, 306, 308, 310, 312, 314, 316, 318, 320, 322, 324, 326, 328, 330, 333, 334, 336, 340, 342, 344, 346, 348, 349, 397
relationship, 4, 7, 12, 13, 17–20, 33, 35, 36, 38, 41, 73, 77, 85, 113, 130, 131, 142, 144–146, 160, 174, 176, 179, 202, 203, 207, 208, 211, 234, 236, 251, 259, 333, 352, 396
report generator, 130, 131, 139
representation, 5–7, 13, 17, 18, 21, 29, 30, 34, 40, 43, 44, 73–86, 88, 90, 92, 94, 96, 98, 99, 105, 115, 150, 152, 161, 182, 183, 185, 199, 200, 202, 204, 207, 208, 210, 211, 215, 226, 227, 231, 234, 236, 242,

273, 274, 282, 303, 304, 308, 311, 312, 322, 326
resolution, 19, 20, 28, 29, 37, 39, 57, 58, 60, 62, 64, 66–68, 70, 72–74, 86, 89, 90, 127, 210, 264, 271, 306
response, 22, 89, 101–116, 119, 120, 151, 152, 205, 207, 232, 234, 236, 304, 305, 344
surface, 101, 113, 115, 116, 120
risk, 4, 5, 12, 17, 30, 240–242, 244, 245
road traffic system, 12, 301, 302
routine, 59, 60, 129–131, 133, 136–139
rule-based representation, 76, 81
Runge–Kutta method, 157, 159, 167, 169, 170, 172, 177

sample, 19, 28, 32, 33, 51, 116, 132, 133, 148, 149, 288, 289, 291, 293, 349–352, 354–360, 362, 369, 393, 396, 411, 415–417, 430
path, 148, 149
space, 349–352, 354–360, 369, 396
sampling mechanism, 28, 32
scanning skill, 277, 283–286, 288–290, 294, 296
self-organise, 179, 235, 257
self-verification, 241, 242, 245, 251
semi-formal representation, 76, 77, 79, 81
shaping, 5, 221, 222, 333–335, 340, 342–345, 347, 348
simulation, 1, 3, 4, 6–9, 11–25, 27–55, 57–76, 78, 79, 81, 84–86, 98, 99, 101–105, 113, 115–121, 123, 124, 126–154, 157–167, 169–172, 174–177, 179–195, 197, 199, 210, 211, 219–222, 232, 239–242, 245, 251, 253, 255–261, 263–265, 267, 269–274, 293–295, 297, 299, 301–303, 308, 312, 313, 316, 318, 319, 326, 328, 333, 341–344, 346, 347, 349, 350, 352, 354, 356, 358, 360, 362, 364–366, 368–370, 372, 374, 376, 378–380, 382, 384, 386–388, 390, 392, 394–398, 401, 404, 411, 413, 423–425, 427–433
software, 31, 58, 61, 72, 79, 135, 185, 397
simulator, 8, 13, 17, 19, 20, 28, 30–35, 39, 41, 43–46, 51, 53, 55, 66, 67, 73, 74, 95, 97, 98, 127, 129–133, 136, 139, 141, 142, 157, 159–161, 163, 164, 177, 190, 192, 219–222, 258, 263, 272, 312, 313, 396
simultaneous events, 57, 64–67, 72
skill-based computational solver, 282, 283, 285, 287, 289, 291

skills, 5, 24, 37, 39, 200, 202, 208, 210–211,
243, 246, 249, 258, 273–294, 296–300,
302, 305, 308
acquisition, 211, 243, 273–275, 284,
287–290, 300
assessment, 273
representation, 273, 274
society of mind, 211, 301, 302, 306–309,
311–313, 315, 317, 319,
321, 323
socio-technical system, 241, 243, 273, 333
stakeholder, 4–6, 15, 28
state, 5, 14, 17, 21–23, 40, 43, 44, 52, 57, 58,
60, 62, 63, 77–79, 85–88, 90–99, 118,
123, 124, 126, 127, 129–132, 136, 138,
140, 141, 143–151, 153, 155, 157–160,
163, 164, 174–176, 181, 182, 184–187,
192, 207, 234, 244, 257, 270, 277, 301,
303, 304, 306–312, 385
transition diagrams, 77–79
state-update, 184
statistical analysis, 117, 212, 213
statistical event, 351
statistical variable, 129–132, 139, 141
statistics, 30, 111, 129, 237, 298, 300,
349–368, 370, 372, 374, 376, 378–380,
382, 384, 386, 388, 390, 392, 394,
396, 410
stock, 14, 124, 143, 145, 158, 172, 173,
177, 187
Sudoku, 273–285, 287–293, 296, 298–300,
302
system, 3–6, 8, 11–23, 27–37, 39, 40, 42, 46,
55, 57–65, 67, 68, 72–77, 79–82, 84–88,
99, 101, 102, 105, 116, 118, 120,
123–133, 136–139, 141–151, 154, 155,

157–164, 167, 172–177, 179–181, 183–187,
197, 199–201, 207, 210, 212–215,
219–222, 232, 234, 239–243, 245, 246,
248, 255–258, 260, 263, 266–268, 270–
273, 275, 301–305, 312–314, 325, 328,
330, 331, 333–336, 340, 342, 344, 346,
348, 349, 387, 397, 400, 402, 413, 424
dynamics, 62, 148, 157, 172–174,
177, 179

task load, 267, 268, 270
task probing, 243, 273
technical systems, 200, 201, 241, 243, 273,
333
three-phase worldview, 58, 61–64
time-advancing mechanism, 31, 60, 61,
127–129, 141, 142, 145, 163, 181, 184,
194
traffic performance, 315
trajectory optimisation, 263, 267, 270
trajectory optimisation and prediction of live
air traffic (TOP-LAT), 263, 267, 269,
270, 272
transition, 77–79, 86–88, 90–94, 96, 99, 123,
124, 126, 146, 150, 151
trust, 256, 333–337, 339–348
trusted autonomous systems, 333, 334, 336,
340, 342, 344, 346, 348

verification and validation, 7–9, 34, 35, 101,
116, 245
vulnerabilities, 8, 240, 243, 245, 246, 302

WISDOM, 255–261
workload, 268, 270
worldview, 57–64, 66, 68, 70, 72

IEEE Press Series on
COMPUTATIONAL INTELLIGENCE

Series Editor, **David B. Fogel**

The IEEE Press Series on Computational Intelligence includes books on neural, fuzzy, and evolutionary computation, and related technologies, of interest to the engineering and scientific communities. Computational intelligence focuses on emulating aspects of biological systems to construct software and/or hardware that learns and adapts. Such systems include neural networks, our use of language to convey complex ideas, and the evolutionary process of variation and selection. The series highlights the most-recent and groundbreaking research and development in these areas, as well as the important hybridization of concepts and applications across these areas. The audiences for books in the series include undergraduate and graduate students, practitioners, and researchers in computational intelligence.

Computational Intelligence: The Experts Speak. Edited by David B. Fogel and
   Charles J. Robinson. 2003. 978-0-471-27454-4
Handbook of Learning and Appropriate Dynamic Programming. Edited by Jennie
   Si, Andrew G. Barto, Warren B. Powell, and Donald Wunsch II. 2004.
   978-0471-66054-X
Computationally Intelligent Hybrid Systems. Edited by Seppo J. Ovaska. 2005.
   978-0471-47668-4
Evolutionary Computation: Toward a New Philosophy of Machine Intelligence,
   Third Edition. David B. Fogel. 2006. 978-0471-66951-7
Emergent Information Technologies and Enabling Policies for Counter-Terrorism.
   Edited by Robert L. Popp and John Yen. 2006. 978-0471-77615-4
*Introduction to Evolvable Hardware: A Practical Guide for Designing
   Self-Adaptive Systems.* Garrison W. Greenwood and Andrew M. Tyrrell. 2007.
   978-0471-71977-9
Computational Intelligence in Bioinformatics. Edited by Gary B. Fogel, David W.
   Corne, and Yi Pan. 2008. 978-0470-10526-9
Computational Intelligence and Feature Selection: Rough and Fuzzy Approaches.
   Richard Jensen and Qiang Shen. 2008. 978-0470-22975-0 *Clustering.* Rui Xu
   and Donald C. Wunsch II. 2009. 978-0470-27680-8
Biometrics: Theory, Methods, and Applications. Edited by: N.V. Boulgouris,
   Konstantinos N. Plataniotis, and Evangelia Micheli-Tzanakou. 2009.
   978-0470-24782-2
Evolving Intelligent Systems: Methodology and Applications. Edited by Plamen
   Angelov, Dimitar P. Filev, and Nikola Kasabov. 2010. 978-0470-28719-4
Perceptual Computing: Aiding People in Making Subjective Judgments. Jerry
   Mendel and Dongrui Lui. 2010. 978-0470-47876-9

Reinforcement Learning and Approximate Dynamic Programming for Feedback Control. Edited by Frank L. Lewis and Derong Liu. 2012. 978-1-118-10420-0

Complex-Valued Neural Networks: Advances and Applications. Edited by Akira Hirose. 2013. 978-1-118-34460-6

Unsupervised Learning: A Dynamic Approach. Matthew Kyan, Paisarn Muneesawang, Kambiz Jarrah, and Ling Guan. 2014. 978-0470-27833-8

Introduction to Type-2 Fuzzy Logic Control: Theory and Applications. Jerry M. Mendel, Hani Hagras, Woei-Wan Tan, William W. Melek, and Hao Ying. 2014. 978-1118-278291

Fundamentals of Computational Intelligence: Neural Networks, Fuzzy Systems, and Evolutionary Computation. James M. Keller, Derong Liu, and David B. Fogel. 2015. 978-1119-214342

Simulation and Computational Red Teaming for Problem Solving. Jiangjun Tang, George Leu, and Hussein A. Abbass. 2020. 978-1-119-52717-6